SPORTS LEGENDS OF CLEVELAND

*The Story of the Greatest Athletes and Teams of Cleveland's
Senate Athletic League*

Timothy L. Hudak

Sports Legends of Cleveland: A Century of Excellence (1904-2024)
Copyright © 2025 Sports Legends of Cleveland

All Rights Reserved.
Published 2025.

No part of this publication may be reproduced, distributed, or transmitted in any form or by any means, including photocopying, recording, or other electronic or mechanical methods, without the prior written permission of the publisher, except in the case of brief quotations embodied in critical reviews and specific other noncommercial uses permitted by copyright law. For permission requests, write to the publisher, addressed "Attention: Permissions Coordinator," at the address below.

First published by Nicole Antoinette Publishing
ISBN 9781939761996
Printed in the United States of America.
This book is printed on acid-free paper.

Nicole Antoinette Publishing
8 Westfield Place
Athens, OH 45701
info@nicoleantoinette.net
nicoleantoinette.net

Sports Heritage Specialty Publications
4814 Broadview Rd.
Cleveland, Ohio 44109
216-741-6532
tlhudak@roadrunner.com

Ordering Information:
Quantity sales. Special discounts are available for corporations, associations, and others who purchase bulk. For details, contact the publisher at the address above.

Orders by U.S. trade bookstores and wholesalers.
Please contact Ingram Content Group LLC:
Tel: (615) 793-5000
Email: customerservice@ingramcontent.com or
ipage.ingrambook.com

SPORTS LEGENDS OF CLEVELAND
A CENTURY *of* EXCELLENCE
1904 – 2024

Acknowledgments
This book would not have been possible without the dedication, passion, and stories of the countless coaches and athletes who brought these pages to life.

CONTENTS

FOREWORD	i
PREFACE	iii
PROLOGUE	v
INTRODUCTION	ix
PART I - ELITE ATHLETES	
Chapter 1 - Olympians	1
Chapter 2 - Hall of Fame	15
Chapter 3 - Special Awards & Accomplishments	27
PART II - GONE BUT NOT FORGOTTEN	
Chapter 4 - Central High School	35
Chapter 5 - East High School	43
Chapter 6 - Lincoln High School	53
Chapter 7 - South High School	61
Chapter 8 - West High School	73
Chapter 9 - West Tech High School	83
HISTORIC PHOTO GALLERY	95
PART III - CARRYING ON THE TRADITION OF EXCELLENCE	
Chapter 10 - Collinwood High School	127
Chapter 11 - East Tech High School	143
Chapter 12 - Glenville High School	169
Chapter 13 - John Adams High School	189
Chapter 14 - John Hay High School	203
Chapter 15 - John F. Kennedy High School	209
Chapter 16 - John Marshall High School	217
Chapter 17 - James Ford Rhodes High School	231
Chapter 18 - Lincoln-West High School	243
EPILOGUE	247
APPENDIX	
Appendix I - Olympians	263
Appendix II - College and Professional Halls of Fame	265
Appendix III - Greater Cleveland Sports Hall of Fame	267
Appendix IV - College All-America	269
Appendix V - All-Ohio	273
Appendix VI - High School All-America	363
Appendix VII - Professional Athletes	365
Appendix VIII - Team State Champions and Runner-Up	369
Appendix IX - Title IX Senate League Athletes	371
Appendix X - Sports Legends of Cleveland	375
Appendix XI - Sports Legends of Cleveland Hall of Fame	417

FOREWORD

by
Dan Coughlin

This will get personal, so if you can't warm up to it, skip ahead to Chapter One. Otherwise, come aboard and share the memories.

In 1964, I was fresh out of the Army and had just signed on at *The Plain Dealer*, becoming the last reporter hired by Gordon Cobbledick before he retired as sports editor. Within a year, Hal Lebovitz moved up to sports editor, and everyone fastened his seat belt. Ed Chay, who had covered the high school beat for the previous 10 years, moved to the college sports beat, focusing primarily on Ohio State. Hal pointed a bony finger at me and said, "You're our new scholastic writer."

That was quite a responsibility because Cleveland is a high school town. High school sports sell papers, a significant consideration at *The Plain Dealer*, the second-largest paper in Ohio, behind the *Cleveland Press*. We were going after the Press, and we were going to ride the high school beat to get there. The fastest horse in the race was the Cleveland Senate.

I jumped on that saddle.

My first basketball season featured some of the best players in Cleveland public school history—Phil Argento of West High, Billy Hann of Rhodes, and John Petch of Lincoln, who would eventually transfer to West High.

Bob (Railbird) Roberts, the acclaimed racetrack handicapper, and writer, was an Eastlake North High School student and recalled reading about Argento, Hann, and Petch in *The Plain Dealer* and the *Press*.

"Those guys were like mythical gods to us," said Roberts. "We had to see them in real life. Three of us made the trip. One of the guys was able to use his parents' car. We drove from Lake County to West High, somewhere on the west side of Cleveland. It was snowing. That didn't bother us. It was winter. That was when winters were winter. The gym was packed. Maybe 700 people, half of them kids, and they were sick. Despite the hacking and coughing, they raised a steady roar. We'll never forget it. It was not the night that Argento scored 66 against South High, but he didn't disappoint us. He scored his 30. Billy Hann scored 21 and had 15 assists. They lived up to their press clippings."

Cleveland schools were covered like the NBA. No—they were covered better than the NBA because Cleveland did not have an NBA franchise. We had a Cleveland Pipers team in the National Industrial Basketball League. They were pros, but the Cleveland high schools got more publicity.

Publicity was why the Great moved from Parma to Cleveland in the 1940s. Horvath was an outstanding running back at Parma Schaaf High School when it was a small country school. Playing in Parma in the early 1940s was slightly above the witness protection program. Horvath and his family harbored loftier aspirations. In the summer before Les' senior football season, the Horvaths moved into a rented apartment on the Cleveland side of Brookpark Road to allow the boy to transfer to Rhodes.

It was there that the spotlight of three Cleveland daily newspapers illuminated him. Les received a scholarship to Ohio State and won the Heisman Trophy.

The Charity Game at Cleveland remains unique in Cleveland's academic history, and it is covered extensively in the following pages. It was a fundraiser for impoverished families during the bleakest days of the Depression in the 1930s. *The Plain Dealer* wasn't merely connected to the Charity Game; *The Plain Dealer* invented it and promoted it. Initially, it was an invitational, like the early college bowl games. Very shortly, it morphed into the Cleveland Senate Championship Game.

By 1966, when I was involved in *The Plain Dealer*'s rankings of high school football teams, our ratings were subliminally influenced by their effects on the Charity Game promotion. I ranked Benedictine number one, which was convenient because Benedictine was headed to the Charity Game against lightly-ranked South High. I think Benedictine was number one, and they proved it in the Charity Game with a convincing victory over South High. However, some complained that Shaw High School had defeated Benedictine in a pre-season scrimmage; maybe Shaw could be considered number one.

However, it was easy to assuage my conscience because Shaw, while undefeated, was not a Cleveland school. Shaw was from East Cleveland and a member of the Lake Erie League.

However, the following year, 1967, I thought we could appease our friends at Shaw by making the East Cleveland school number one in *The Plain Dealer* pre-season rankings. This was all before the playoff system determined state championships on the field of play. I got no argument from Dick Zunt or Chuck Webster, the other members of our committee.

All that changed, however, when Collinwood shocked Shaw, 12-2, in a monsoon at Shaw in its opening game of the 1967 season.

"That makes Collinwood number one," I said to Dick Zunt. "What?" said Dick.

"Shaw was number one in our pre-season rankings. Collinwood beat them. They should be number one," I said.

"The game was a fluke. Collinwood isn't that good," Zunt insisted.

He had a point. The mud at Shaw was ankle-deep. Everything that happened in that game was an accident. Nevertheless, we had made Shaw number one. Now, we could make Collinwood number one. Such power!

"Let them enjoy their day," I said. "They won't be there long. Benedictine will beat them. So will Cathedral Latin. They'll lose a couple of other games."

So, Collinwood became number one in *The Plain Dealer*'s Top 25. Some people thought we had lost our minds. But something was going on. Collinwood won nine straight games on fumbles, interceptions, and punting. Look at the scores:

Collinwood 12, Shaw 2
Collinwood 18, Euclid 14
Collinwood 14, John F. Kennedy 8
Collinwood 14, John Hay 6
Collinwood 12, Benedictine 9
Collinwood 24, John Adams 6
Collinwood 28, East High 12
Collinwood 12, Glenville 10
Collinwood 6, Cathedral Latin 0

The Collinwood neighborhood was in a frenzy. Collinwood lost the Charity Game to St. Ignatius, 21-0, but that did not dissipate the excitement. *The Plain Dealer* ran a favorite coach contest, which Collinwood Coach Joe Trivisonno won. The prize was a trip to the Rose Bowl for Joe and his wife, Sally. *However*, the *Plain Dealer*'s travel agent absconded with the money, and there were no game tickets for Joe and Sally, so they went to Pasadena to watch the Rose Bowl game on television. They had no complaints. *The Plain Dealer* gave them a second summer trip to New York City.

The Favorite Coach campaign increased *The Plain Dealer*'s circulation so dramatically that it passed the Press. Collinwood became number one, and so did *The Plain Dealer*.

For me, high school sports have been a life-changing experience.

PREFACE

by
Coach Tyrone Owens
(cousin of Jesse Owens)

Sports Legends of Cleveland would not have been possible without the courageously brilliant Nicole Antoinette Smith. I have known Nicole since she was a tenth-grade student at James Ford Rhodes High School in Cleveland, Ohio. She joined my track team as a skinny six-foot-one freshman. I immediately noticed her very high level of maturity and that she was determined to be successful at whatever she attempted. It was with her many personal strengths and talents that I was able to mold her into an outstanding athlete and college scholarship recipient.

While being inducted into the Rhodes High School Hall of Fame, Nicole questioned why many student-athletes, including herself, didn't know their school history. At that point, she enlisted my help to form the Sports Legends of Cleveland. Initially, we started formally recognizing the Cleveland Public School student-athletes from the past.

Nicole is an out-of-the-box thinker with incredible vision and extraordinary leadership skills. The contents and format of this book were a product of her endurance and ability to lead a group to the completion of what was thought by others to be an insurmountable task. Nicole eventually began to elicit other people's participation and help with her vision. She nurtured her group and her dream, forming solid alliances. Other people started to see her dream as well. This book was researched and completed solely with the money the Sports Legends of Cleveland raised from galas, donations, and the sale of memorabilia. All this was accomplished because one woman had a vision and a dream and wanted Cleveland's children to have a legacy.

It took six years to write, research, and complete this book. I want to acknowledge the other people besides myself who helped Nicole accomplish her goal. Thank you to John Ramicone from South High School (1962), Al Drews from West High School (1959), Michael Cunningham from John Marshall (1981), Michael Bailey, former teacher and coach at West Tech High School, and special thanks to Tim L. Hudak, the author.

The Senate Athletic League is one of the oldest leagues in Ohio, if not the nation. It was established in 1904 and, to date, is still operating. The purpose of this book is to fill in critical missing pieces, especially involving the Cleveland Public Schools as it relates to the Senate Athletic League. Many of Cleveland Public Schools' great athletes and outstanding accomplishments have been lost, misplaced, or trashed. Many fine athletes are no longer remembered for their extraordinary feats and sacrifices. This book serves as a stepping stone into the journey to the past and the Cleveland Public School student athletes' invaluable contributions to that glorious history.

PROLOGUE

by
Nicole Antoinette Smith
(Founder of the Sports Legends of Cleveland)

This book, this project, is a testament to the enduring spirit of Cleveland athletes. It's a recovery mission, a rescue operation for a history that nearly slipped our fingers. When we embarked on this journey in 2018, we had 300 names, a fraction of the true story. Today, that number has swelled to over 4,000, a testament to the power of community and shared memory. We've faced hurdles, from incomplete records to misspellings and omissions. Many names have yet to be added, and we continue to rely on alums, families, coaches, and community members to fill these gaps. This is not a project that can succeed without collective effort. The stories we uncover are about wins and losses, resilience, pride, and overcoming the odds—especially in a city like Cleveland, where inner-city youth often face immense challenges. This history project honors the athletes and the spirit of perseverance that runs deep in the city.

Cleveland's sports history is rich, but much of it risks being lost due to school closings, lack of records, and missed opportunities to document these stories. This project is a living testament to those legends who competed, triumphed, and shaped the city's sports identity. The Senate Athletic League's history has been fragmented due to school closings and other challenges. We rely on Alumni Associations, Athletic Directors, Coaches, individual athletes, and their families to provide the necessary information. For instance, I added my uncle, London Baker, to the East High list because he played in the State Championship game for East High's boys basketball team. This personal connection underscores the importance of community involvement in our project.

But the journey is far from over. The Sports Legends of Cleveland History Project is more than just a book; it's a living archive, a bridge connecting generations of athletes who have competed under the Senate League banner since 1904. It's about reclaiming a narrative fragmented by school closures and the passage of time. It's about correcting misspelled names and honoring those overlooked, ensuring that every athlete, coach, and administrator receives the recognition they deserve.

This is a story of resilience, celebrating those who defied the odds. Growing up in an inner city often means facing challenges that can seem impossible. Yet, champions emerge from these very streets. The athletes in this book embody what photographer David Liam Kyle so aptly captured in his collection *SHEAR STRENGTH CLEVELAND*™. They are a testament to the unwavering spirit forged in the heart of our city.

My journey from a directionless teenager to a Division I college athlete underscores the transformative power of sports. It's a power that can change lives, instill belief, and open doors of opportunity. My high school track coach, Mr. Tyrone Owens, instilled in me the belief that I could achieve anything. He saw potential where I saw limitations, and his unwavering support changed the trajectory of my life.

This project is driven by a desire to provide that same spark of hope and opportunity for future generations. By revitalizing middle school and high school sports programs within the Cleveland Metropolitan School District, we aim to create a sustainable model for athletic success that empowers student-athletes to compete at the highest levels.

Cleveland has produced legends long before our organization existed, and through the Sports Legends of Cleveland initiative, we are reconnecting the past with the present to inspire future generations. Whether through our ongoing research, the Hall of Fame inductions, or our work with the Cleveland Metropolitan School District (CMSD), we aim to preserve this extraordinary legacy for years.

With this prologue, we invite you to become part of the journey, ensuring that the entire history of Cleveland's sports legends—names both known and forgotten—is documented, celebrated, and remembered. We owe it to the athletes, coaches, and administrators who shaped this league to finish this historic work.

Our mission is clear: to document and celebrate the achievements of those who have competed under the Senate Athletic League banner. To qualify as a Sports Legend, individuals must have been high school athletes, coaches, staff, athletic directors, or administrators from the Cleveland Metropolitan School District (CMSD) and meet specific criteria, such as being city, district, regional, or state champions or runners-up, or having competed at the collegiate, professional, or international levels.

The odds of success are often stacked against graduates from inner-city public schools, yet our sports legends have defied these odds. As a Cleveland public high school graduate, I understand the challenges and limited opportunities many students face. My journey from confusion and lack of direction to earning a Division I basketball scholarship at Ohio University was made possible by the encouragement and belief of my high school track coach, Mr. Tyrone Owens. His faith in me changed the trajectory of my life, and I am committed to providing similar opportunities for future generations.

The Sports Legends of Cleveland History Project is a labor of love, a collaborative effort fueled by passion and purpose; it is a movement to honor our past and inspire our future. We invite you to join us in this endeavor, ensuring that Cleveland's sports legends' legacy endures for generations. Together, we can celebrate the achievements of those who have made our city proud and pave the way for new legends to emerge.

We owe it to ourselves, our city and the Senate League's legacy to tell this story and ensure that these legends are not just born but bred, Cleveland-bred. Your support and involvement are integral to this project, and we couldn't do it without you.

Legends are not just born—they are **BORN – BRED – CLEVELAND BRED**™.

SPORTS LEGENDS OF CLEVELAND

BORN
BRED
CLEVELAND
BRED

INTRODUCTION

There had been no organization of Cleveland's interscholastic athletic competition; no real need existed until 1890 when the schools started playing interscholastic football. Until then, the schools had been playing under a loose set of rules, but nothing was in place to enforce or discipline those who failed to abide by them. However, the Cleveland School Athletic Association, which was formed to organize interscholastic football, and the similarly named associations that followed, did little more than schedule games.

Then, in the winter of 1904, the leaders of the Cleveland schools finally did something to regulate athletics in the city's schools. A Senate of the Cleveland public high schools, composed of the principals and key administrators from Central, East, South, West, and Lincoln high schools, developed a constitution to govern athletics for grammar and high schools in the city. This constitution, finalized on Nov. 10, 1904, "fairly revolutionizes school athletics in the city... As a result of the new constitution, the men who participate in interscholastic contests will be governed by regulations that are even more rigid than those of the Big Six [Ohio's premier collegiate league at the time] or any of the eastern college leagues. It will place the Cleveland schools from the standpoint of pure athletics on a par with those of any city of the country." (PD)

Please note that this refers to "the men who participate in interscholastic contests" since girls did not participate in such activities at this time, partly because it was not considered ladylike or even safe for them to do so. Organizing high school athletics for Cleveland's girls was still about 20 years away.

The new city league was called the Public Schools Athletic League of Cleveland, and its objective was "to regulate the athletic relations of the schools of the league, promote healthful rivalry, and stimulate the spirit of true sportsmanship." The league governing body would be a Senate composed of a supervisor of physical training, plus two faculty members from each member school, to be chosen by that school's principal. Among its many new duties, the Senate would have the power to act on questions of player eligibility.

Regarding that eligibility, the Senate's rules and regulations were indeed rigid. A student had to attend his school for an entire year before he could represent it in athletics; at this time, many students did not participate in school regularly due to the need for them to work to help support their families. Regarding grades, a student (the actual wording was "high school boy") had to not only carry a passing grade in three significant subjects during the current school year but also have passing grades in three significant subjects during the previous school year. No student who had reached the age of 20 could participate in interscholastic athletics; this was later amended so that a student who turned 20 during a semester could play through that semester. (As mentioned above, kids often dropped out of high school for a year or two to help support their families. Hence, this rule.)

Each athlete was required to have the written permission of his parent or guardian, countersigned by his principal. He also had to have written proof that he had passed a physical exam.

As far as the teams themselves were concerned, the new Senate constitution formalized the scheduling process and eliminated games against non-high school opponents, such as YMCA teams, college teams, and teams representing athletic clubs. The constitution also called for a yearly championship to be held for each of the various sports.

The new Senate constitution and its bylaws went into effect on Dec. 1, 1904, except for the rule requiring one year's attendance, enacted in 1905.

As might be expected, not everyone was pleased with the new situation. Some of the rules adopted by the league "did not appeal to the athletes" (PD) at East High School, and the result was that East did not join the other four Cleveland high schools in the new organization. Although the differences between East High and the other schools were discussed repeatedly at Senate meets to resolve them and thus get East High into the fold, it would be 1908 before East High School finally joined the Senate league. However, the league added a new school in 1905, the "suburbanites" from Glenville High School.

Thus was born what has been known down through the years as the "Senate Athletic League," or simply "The Senate."

Except for adding newly built city high schools, very few changes were made to the membership of the Senate Athletic League during the more than two dozen years since its formation in 1904. By 1931, the league consisted of nine Cleveland high schools: East Tech, East High, West High, West Tech, Glenville, Central, John Adams, Lincoln, and South. In Nov. 1931, an article appeared in the Cleveland Press, one of the city's afternoon newspapers, stating that "the Senate in 1933 will probably be a 12-school circuit with two divisions." That expansion did not occur, but Collinwood High School joined the Senate League in 1932.

However, in October 1936, the often-rumored expansion did take place. Coming as something of a surprise, the expansion was heralded by The Plain Dealer as "the most far-reaching realignment in the history of Greater Cleveland scholastic athletics." The Senate League would take on no less than six new schools in 1937, bringing its total to 16. The teams would be divided into an East Side League and a West Side League of eight. The two main reasons given for the Senate's expansion, according to The Plain Dealer, were "that it would improve competition and reduce travel expenses." (PD) Hoped for, but not explicitly stated, was that the increased competition and rivalry for the two divisional championships would increase attendance at games and thus increase school revenues. As The Plain Dealer noted at the time: "The ultimate goal is to make athletics 'pay their way.'"

Not only did this move make the Cleveland Senate the largest interscholastic league in Ohio, but the overall quality of the teams entering the Senate would ensure the continued high caliber of play for which the league was known around the state. All four of Cleveland's Catholic high schools joined the Senate due to this expansion. Cathedral Latin was a perennial city power and had already appeared in three football Charity Games without a defeat. Holy Name had been fielding excellent teams for several seasons and played in the 1935 Charity Game. Saint Ignatius, a city power in the mid-1920s, had not been very competitive for the last half-dozen years, while Benedictine, which had been open barely 10 years, was still trying to make a name for itself.

The other two schools joining the Senate came from the Greater Cleveland Conference. John Marshall and Rhodes High School would add much to their new league. Both were West Side schools—Marshall in the West Park area and Rhodes from Old Brooklyn—and the two schools consistently fielded good teams, including former conference football champions.

After this expansion was announced, a seventh school joined the league at the beginning of the 1937 school year. John Hay High School, located on East 107th Street, decided to leave the Greater Cleveland Conference and join the Senate. Like Marshall and Rhodes, Hay was also a former G.C.C. champion.

The Senate League now included every high school (except all-girl schools) that fielded sports teams within Cleveland's boundaries. The league's two divisions were aligned: the East Side League would include Cathedral Latin, Central, Collinwood, East High, East Tech, Glenville, John Adams, Benedictine, and John Hay. The West

Side League comprised Holy Name, James Ford Rhodes, John Marshall, Lincoln, Saint Ignatius, South, West High, and West Tech. (The East Side League and West Side League names were shortened to the less cumbersome East Senate and West Senate.)

One immediate effect of this vast expansion and division of the Senate League was that the format of Cleveland's annual city football championship Charity Game was revamped. Instead of selecting the two top teams from throughout Cuyahoga County, the winners of the race in each of the Senate's two divisions would now play off for the Cleveland championship in the Charity Game. This change dramatically and immediately affected the attendance, and thus the money raised, by this annual championship game.

The Senate League membership remained almost unchanged for the next 30 years. By the first decade of the 21st century, however, changes on and off the playing field would cause the Senate League to lose members. Competition issues would cause four teams to leave the league (Cathedral Latin, 1967; Benedictine, 1971; Holy Name, 1974; and Saint Ignatius, 1978). The city's population loss over the years would require consolidation and closing. Central High merged with East Tech in 1952, West and Lincoln High Schools merged into Lincoln-West in 1970, West Tech closed in 1995, and South and East high schools followed in 2010. The current Senate League membership includes Collinwood, East Tech, Glenville, John Adams, John Hay, John F. Kennedy, John Marshall, Lincoln-West, Martin Luther King, Max Hayes, and James Ford Rhodes.

PART I

Elite Athletes

CHAPTER 1

Olympians

> **OLYMPIC MEDAL WINNERS**
>
> *To be known as an Olympic champion is the highest accolade any athlete can aspire to. Cleveland's Senate Athletic League has been most fortunate to have had some genuinely outstanding alumni who have won Olympic glory. Here, listed in alphabetical order, are the stories of the great and near-great Olympians from the Senate Athletic League.*

Dave Albritton
East Tech – Track

Who could have guessed back in 1913 that two boys, born five months and 6½ miles apart in rural Alabama, would grow up to have such parallel lives in Cleveland, Ohio? One of those boys was Jesse Owens; the other was David Albritton. Jesse Owens' story is told later in this chapter; here is David Albritton's story.

David Albritton was born in Danville, Alabama, on April 13, 1913. During the 1920s, when he was still a little boy, Albritton's family moved to Cleveland. Dave would attend East Tech High School, where he excelled in basketball as a center and football at the end. However, he was especially good at track and field. He ran the hurdles and on relay teams, but his specialty was the high jump. In his senior year at East Tech, Albritton won the state championship in the high jump while also running relays and hurdles on the school's track team. He was also a two-time Golden Gloves boxing champion while in high school.

Upon graduating from East Tech in 1934, Albritton enrolled at The Ohio State University (OSU), where he continued his track career. His 1934 East Tech classmate, Jesse Owens, also went to Ohio State that year. As a sophomore at OSU in 1936, David won the NCAA high jump championship as one of the first high jumpers to use the straddle technique to clear the bar.

Also in 1936, Albritton attended the United States Olympic team tryouts. During those tryouts, Albritton and Cornelius Johnson tied the world high jump record of 6' 9¾", becoming one of the first African Americans to hold the record. Both men were named to the Olympic team. On Aug. 2, 1936, at the Olympics in

Berlin, Germany, Albritton finished second in the high jump, winning the silver medal, while his teammate Cornelius Johnson won the gold.

After the Olympics, Albritton returned to Ohio State, graduating in 1938. In 1937 and 1938, he won the NCAA high jump championship again, giving him three consecutive high jump titles. Following his collegiate career, David continued competing in the high jump in AAU track competitions every year from 1936-1951, except for 1941-1943, when he was serving in the U.S. Army during World War II. In those AAU championships, he won or tied for first place five times, finished in second place once, and got third (or tied) four times.

During the 1940s, Albritton was an industrial arts teacher and track coach at Dayton's Dunbar High School. His boys track team won state championships in 1948, 1963, and 1964. From 1954 to 1957, David worked for the U.S. Department of State, setting up athletic programs overseas, mainly in Middle Eastern countries. In 1960, he was elected to the Ohio House of Representatives, where he eventually served six terms; he became the first African-American in Ohio history to head a House committee.

In 1974, David Albritton was named "Outstanding High Jumper from 1930 to the Present" by the Inter-Collegiate Conference Athletic Association. David Albritton has been named to several halls of fame, including the Greater Cleveland Sports Hall of Fame, the Ohio State Athletics Hall of Fame, and the National Track and Field Hall of Fame. He is also the first Alabama native ever to win an Olympic medal.

Carmen Barth (Carmine R. DiBartholomeo)
Collinwood - Boxing

Carmen Barth, born Carmine R. DiBartholomeo, was born on Sept. 13, 1912, in Cleveland's Collinwood neighborhood, where he grew up. In 1931, he won Cleveland's amateur boxing championship in the 160-pound weight class. In 1932, Barth qualified for the U.S. Olympic team for the Summer Olympics in Los Angeles. Fighting in the middleweight division, Barth defeated Amado Azar of Argentina to win the Olympic gold medal.

Following the Olympics, Barth went on to fight professionally from 1932 to 1941, finishing with a record of 48-15-4.

Nate Brooks
John Adams – Boxing

Nathan E. "Nate" Brooks was born on Aug. 8, 1933, and attended John Adams High School. He became involved in amateur boxing and was quite successful, most notably winning the Cleveland Golden Gloves tournament three times and the Chicago Golden Gloves tournament in his weight class in 1950 and 1951. Brooks earned a spot as a flyweight (112 pounds) boxer on the USA Olympic team for the 1952 Summer Olympics in Helsinki, Finland. He advanced through four preliminary bouts before winning a 3-0 decision over Edgar Basel of West Germany for the gold medal.

Following the Olympics, Brooks boxed professionally from 1953-1958, winning 10 of his first 11 bouts. He was the 1954 North American Bantamweight Champion. Following his boxing career, Brooks was a survey engineer for the Ohio Department of Transportation for 32 years.

Nate Brooks is an inductee into the Greater Cleveland Sports Hall of Fame.

Dartanyon Crockett
Lincoln-West – Judo

Dartanyon Crockett was born in Cleveland in 1991. He is legally blind, having been born with Liber's Hereditary Optic Neuropathy. This degenerative disease limits vision to the point where one can only make out faces within a few feet. He took up wrestling at Lincoln-West and soon became one of the city's best, finishing his senior year with a 26-3 record.

In 2010, at the insistence of the USA Judo coaches, Dartanyon switched from wrestling to judo. His rise in the sport was quite meteoric, and just two years later, he won a bronze medal at the 2012 London Paralympic Games. In 2014, in Brazil, he won the gold medal in the 90 kg category at the World Championships, qualifying him for the 2016 Paralympic Games in Rio de Janeiro. At those 2016 games, he repeated as the bronze medalist.

Among the other highlights of his career are winning a gold medal at the 2012 Pajulahti Games in Finland, winning five consecutive Senior National Paralympic Championships (2010-2014), and being a five-time gold medalist (2010, 2011, 2012, 2014, 2015) in the USA Judo National Championships for the Blind and

Visually Impaired.

Harrison Dillard
East Tech – Track

Harrison Dillard was born in Cleveland on July 8, 1923. He grew up on the city's eastside and attended Kennard Junior High before moving to East Tech. When Jesse Owens returned from the 1936 Summer Olympics in Berlin, Dillard was on hand for the parade honoring Owens and was inspired by Owens to take up the track.

Dillard ran track in various events in junior high and during his years at East Tech and was one of the better athletes on the team. Following graduation, he enrolled at Baldwin Wallace College (now University) in 1941, where he continued his track career. Dillard's college education and his track career were interrupted by World War II. In 1943, Dillard was drafted into the U.S. Army and served as a sharpshooter in Italy with the 92nd Division, the famed all-Black Buffalo Soldiers.

Following the end of the war, Dillard (nicknamed "Bones") returned to Baldwin Wallace in 1946 to complete his degree (Class of 1949) and continue with his track career—and it was at this time that his track career took off. 1946, he won the NCAA and AAU championships in the 100-meter and 200-meter hurdles, tying the world record in both events. Dillard came back to win those same championships in 1947.

At the U.S. trials for that summer's Olympics in 1948, the unimaginable happened: Harrison failed to qualify for the 100m hurdles, ending a string of 82 consecutive wins. However, he did qualify for the 100m dash, finishing third at the trials.

At the Olympic Games held in London that year, Harrison Dillard stunned the world by winning the 100m race in the first Olympic photo finish, setting a world record in the process. "When he walked into the Olympic dining room for supper that night, the assembled athletes gave him a standing ovation." (Bob Dolgan)

Dillard was also on the American 4x100 relay team that won the Olympic gold medal that year.

Following the 1948 Olympics, Dillard continued his track career, eventually winning the AAU indoor 60-high hurdles every year from 1947 through 1953 and again in 1955. When it came time for the 1952 Olympic Games in Helsinki, Finland, Dillard was again ready. He qualified for the U.S. team and won the gold medal in his premier event, the 100m hurdles. In 1948, he was again a gold-medal-winning member of the 4x100 relay team.

Harrison Dillard is still the only male athlete ever to win the 100m race and the 100m hurdles at the Olympics.

1956, Harrison Dillard won the AAU James E. Sullivan Award as the nation's best amateur athlete. In addition to his four Olympic gold medals, he has held or tied five world records during his track career. Harrison Dillard has been inducted into no less than 14 world and American halls of fame. He is considered the finest male student-athlete ever to attend Baldwin-Wallace University. He is one of the all-time greatest sprinters and hurdlers in U. S. Olympic history.

Thomas Jefferson
John Marshall – Track

Thomas Jefferson was born on June 8, 1962, and was a member of the John Marshall Class of 1980. While at John Marshall, he participated in cross-country, basketball, and track. He was a good but not spectacular runner; in his senior year, for example, Jefferson did not qualify for the state meet. Nonetheless, Jefferson continued running track after entering Kent State University and kept improving, eventually earning All-American honors in the 100m dash.

In 1984, Jefferson stunned the track world when he finished third in the 200m at the U.S. Olympic trials and thus earned a spot on the team competing at that year's Los Angeles Summer Olympics. At those Olympics, Jefferson, running in the 200m, finished first in his two preliminary heats and second in the semifinals. In the finals, he finished third with a personal best time of 20.26, earning a bronze medal. With Americans Carl Lewis finishing first and Kirk Baptiste finishing second, the USA won the sweep of that event. Later, Jefferson was a bronze medal-winning 4x100 relay team member.

Thomas Jefferson was ranked third in the world in the 200m in 1984 and was ranked in the U.S. top 10 four times between 1984 and 1991.

Louis Laurie
East Tech – Boxing

Louis Laurie was born in Cleveland on Nov. 19, 1917, and graduated from East Tech High School. At East Tech, he took up boxing and acrobatics, in which Laurie was twice Cleveland's champion.

Upon graduating from East Tech, Laurie worked as a service station attendant while pursuing an amateur boxing career. Despite having just 22 amateur bouts, his talent was recognized, and he was named to the U.S. Olympic team for the 1936 Berlin Summer Olympics. At 18 years old, Laurie was the youngest boxer on the team. He won four of his five bouts at the Olympics, earning a bronze medal.

Because his boxing style was so impressive, Laurie was asked to stay in Germany after the Olympics to give boxing demonstrations. After a two-month exhibition tour around Germany, Lou was presented with the Val Barker trophy for being the most scientific boxer in all classes that year.

Returning to the United States, Lou turned professional and had a record of 5-8-1 before retiring from the ring in 1941. He briefly resumed boxing while serving in the U. S. Army in Europe during World War II.

Louis Laurie was inducted into the Greater Cleveland Sports Hall of Fame in 1984, and in 1988, the Ohio State Former Boxers and Associates gave him a similar honor.

Madeline Manning-Jackson
John Hay – Track

Born on Jan. 11, 1948, Manning-Jackson was a sickly child until almost the age of 14. Having overcome her childhood illnesses, she participated in track, basketball, and volleyball at John Hay High School, often staying late to practice independently after the regular practice sessions. Upon graduation from John Hay, Manning-Jackson attended and graduated from Tennessee State University, where she ran track as a member of the Tigerbelles, the women's track team.

In 1967, Manning-Jackson won gold in the 800m at the Pan American Games in Winnipeg, Canada, and at the Summer Universiade in Tokyo.

Manning-Jackson was a member of four consecutive U.S. Olympic track teams. At the 1968 Mexico City Olympics, she won a gold medal in the 800m. In winning that event, she set a record time of 2:00.90, becoming the first Black woman in the world ever to win. She is still the only American woman to win gold in an Olympic 800m race.

At the 1972 Munich Summer Olympics, Manning-Jackson won a silver medal as a U.S. 4x400m relay team member. She participated in but did not medal at the 1976 Montreal Summer Olympics. In 1980, in preparation for that year's Summer Olympics in Moscow, Manning-Jackson won the U.S.A. Olympic trials in the 800m with a time of 1:58.3, the second-best time of her career. Although named to the U.S. Olympic team in 1980, Manning-Jackson and all other members of the U.S.A. The Olympic squad could not participate in the games when the United States boycotted them.

Between 1967 and 1981, Madeline Manning-Jackson won 10 national titles, both indoors and outdoors, set several American records, and ran on four consecutive U.S. Olympic teams. 1984, she was inducted into the National Track and Field Hall of Fame.

Manning-Jackson is the founder and president of the United States Council for Sports Chaplaincy and has continued her participation with the U.S. Olympic team as a chaplain at the 1988 Seoul, 1992 Barcelona, 1996 Atlanta, 2000 Sydney, 2004 Athens, and 2008 Beijing Olympic Games. She is also an author, speaker, and contemporary gospel recording artist who was inducted into the Oklahoma Jazz Hall of Fame in 2005.

Jesse Owens
East Tech – Track

What Babe Ruth was to baseball and Jim Brown was to football, Jesse Owens was to track—and then some.

James Cleveland Owens was the youngest of 10 children (three girls and seven boys) born to Henry Cleveland Owens (a sharecropper) and Mary Emma Fitzgerald in Oakville, Ala., on Sept. 12, 1913. When Owens was 9 years old, the family moved to Cleveland, Ohio, in search of better opportunities. At that time, James was known as J.C. to his family, but his Cleveland teachers mistook it for "Jesse," that name stayed with him.

Jesse first became interested in track at Fairmount Junior High School. Following junior high, Owens went to East Tech High School, where he continued to excel at track. He first came to national attention when participating in the 1933 National High School Championships in Chicago. At that event, he equaled the world record of 9.4 seconds in the 100-yard dash and long-jumped 24' 9½". In 2020, MaxPreps retroactively named Jesse Owens the best high school athlete in the country for 1933.

After graduation from East Tech, Jesse Owens continued his education and track career at The Ohio State University. At OSU, Owens was known as the "Buckeye Bullet" for his outstanding speed. Under the coaching of Larry Snyder, Owens won a record eight individual NCAA championships, four each in 1935 and 1936. This record of four individual gold medals in a single NCAA championship has never been equaled – and Jesse Owens did it twice.

The highlight of Owens' college career, and undoubtedly his entire track career, came on May 25, 1935, during the Big Ten meet at Ferry Field in Ann Arbor, Michigan. On that day, Jesse Owens set three world records and tied a fourth—all within just 45 minutes. He equaled the world record for the 100-yard dash at 9.4 seconds. Just 10 minutes later, Jesse set the world record in the long jump with a leap of 26'8¼", lasting 25 years. Next, and only nine minutes later, came Owens' new world record in the 220-yard dash of 20.3 seconds. Finally, after a break of 26 minutes, he conquered the 220-yard low hurdles in a time of 22.6 seconds, becoming the first person ever to break 23 seconds in that event.

Owens' incredible accomplishment in Ann Arbor that day has no parallel, not just in track and field but in any other sport. His astonishing feat at the Big Ten meet has never been equaled, and he has been hailed as "the greatest 45 minutes ever in the sport."

In 2005, University of Central Florida professor of sports history Richard C. Crepeau named Owens' achievement on that single day the most impressive athletic achievement of the last 150 years, going back to 1850.

Jesse Owens is best known by the general public for his outstanding accomplishments at the 1936 Summer Olympics in Berlin, Germany. German Chancellor Adolph Hitler was using these games to both show the world a resurgent Nazi Germany and to promote Hitler's doctrine of Aryan supremacy. He and other government officials hoped that German athletes would dominate the games. However, Chancellor Hitler did not count on Jesse Owens.

Owens competed in the first two qualifying rounds for the 100m race on Aug. 2. In his first qualifying run, Owens equaled both the Olympic and world records and broke both in the second race. However, the new records were not recognized because that run was ruled wind assisted. The next day, in the 100m finals, Owens won with a time of 10.3 seconds. On Aug. 4, Jesse won the long jump with a leap of 26' 5" (8.06 m)—3¼ inches short of his world record. On Aug. 5, he won the 200m dash with a time of 20.7 seconds. On Aug. 9, Owens won his fourth gold medal as a member of the U. S. team that won the 4×100m relay.

Jesse Owens was the most successful athlete at the Berlin Olympics. His record-breaking performance of four gold medals was not equaled until Carl Lewis won gold medals in the same four events at the 1984 Summer Olympics in Los Angeles. As a Black man, Jesse was credited with single-handedly crushing Hitler's myth of Aryan supremacy. However, although Hitler did not congratulate him for his wins, he "wasn't invited to the White House to shake hands with the President, either."

After the games, the entire U.S. Olympic team was invited to compete in Sweden. Owens, however, decided to capitalize on his success by returning to the United States to take up some of the more lucrative endorsement offers that his success had made available to him. U.S. athletic officials were furious and withdrew his amateur status, effectively ending Jesse's track career at 22.

Owens' dominant week in Berlin in 1936 is part of American athletic lore. If someone in the United States knows only one thing about athletics, it is probably what Jesse Owens accomplished at those Olympics. Jesse Owens was recognized during his lifetime as being "perhaps the greatest and most famous athlete in track and field history." Today, you can probably amend that by dropping off track and field and saying, "in history," period.

Over the years, Owens has received many honors. USA Track and Field created the Jesse Owens Award, which is given annually to the country's top track-and-field athlete. In 1999, ESPN rated him the sixth greatest North American athlete of the 20th century and the highest-ranked track-and-field athlete. That same year, the BBC ranked Jesse Owens among the world's top six Sports Personalities of the 20th Century.

Stella Walsh
South High – Track

Stella Walsh was born Stanislawa Walasiewicz on April 3, 1911, in Wierzchownin, Poland. The family moved to Cleveland in 1913, settling in the Slavic Village neighborhood, and she attended both South and Notre Dame high schools. During high school, Walsh became an outstanding athlete and played on numerous teams, including the boys baseball team. She amassed an impressive collection of ribbons, trophies, and medals while participating in high school track meets.

Stella Walsh (her Americanized name) first rose to prominence in the summer of 1926. Just a 15-year-old student at South High, she won the 50-yard dash for girls at a meet staged by a Cleveland newspaper, astonishing track fans by equaling the women's American outdoor record of six seconds flat. Gaining prominence with each event she entered, Stella moved to New York City in 1929 to continue her training. That year, she represented the Polish Falcons at the World Pan-Slovanic Track and Field Championships in Poznan, Poland. At that meet, Walsh captured the all-around scoring title in the women's division by winning the 60m, 100m, and 200m dashes and placing third in the high jump.

That same year, Walsh anchored a New York City relay team at a meet in Newark, N.J., setting a new world mark of 1:57.6 for the 880-yard relay. In the summer of 1930, she ran the 100-yard dash in 10.8 seconds—the first time a woman had ever broken 11 seconds in that event.

Walsh continued participating in track meets in Poland and the United States, winning numerous gold medals in the running events and the long jump. In 1930, her time of 6.0 seconds broke the world indoor record for the 50-yard dash at the Millrose Games in New York City. In those days, there were also separate Olympics for women, held over a cycle of years, unlike the regular games. At the 1930 Women's Olympics in Prague, Walsh won gold in the 60m, 100m, and 200m races. In 1934, she again won gold in the 60m race at the London Women's Olympics.

In the years leading up to the 1932 Summer Olympics, she won American national championships in the 100-yard dash (1930), 220-yard dash (1930, 1931), and long jump (1930).

Still not a United States citizen (she would finally gain U.S. citizenship in 1947), Walsh ran in the 1932 Los Angeles Olympics for Poland, winning the gold medal in the 100m dash, one of only two medals Poland won that summer. Following the Olympics, she moved to Warsaw to attend college, but six months after her move, she sprained an ankle and returned to Cleveland to rehab.

In the spring of 1933, Stella Walsh participated in the Championships of Warsaw, where she won an incredible nine gold medals, including the 80m hurdles, the 4×200m relay, and the long jump. On Sept. 17 of that same year, Walsh broke two world records at a meet in Poznan, Poland: 7.4 seconds in the 60m dash and 11.8 seconds in the 100m.

Between 1933 and 1935, Walsh won numerous medals, including at the European Athletic Championships and the Women's World Games. She broke records in the 100m dash, hurdles, broad jump, and shot-put events. Newspapers admiringly called her "The Queen of Sprint" and "The Cleveland Flyer."

Stella Walsh again ran for Poland at the 1936 Berlin Summer Olympics, finishing second in the 100m dash, missing out on the gold medal by just 0.02 seconds.

After the Berlin Olympics, Walsh announced her retirement, but she never really stopped competing. 1937, she tied the 100m dash mark at the Berlin Olympics. Between the years 1938 and 1951, Walsh won numerous American national championships, including the 100m (1943, 1944, and 1948), the 200m (1939, 1940, and 1942 through 1948), the discus (1941, 1942), and the long jump (1938 through 46, 1948, and 1951). In 1954, at 43, Walsh won her fifth consecutive U.S. pentathlon championship. Still competing into her fifties, in 1967 Stella Walsh won a 60-yard dash in 7.7 seconds, less than a half-second slower than her world record time of 7.3 seconds set 33 years earlier in 1934. She even took part in pitching exhibitions and played basketball.

To fulfill her dream of representing the United States in the Olympics, Walsh tried out for the U.S. Olympic team in 1956 and 1960 but did not make the team either year. Through her 50s and 60s, Stella Walsh organized athletic competitions and scholarships for Polish American athletes while coaching young sprinters.

The people in Stella's Cleveland community were aware of the rumors about her gender, but Stella was accepted for who she was; no one questioned her about her masculine appearance. She was a cherished hometown celebrity. In 1970, Cleveland Mayor Ralph Locher proclaimed April 13 as Stella Walsh Day.

Stella Walsh set over 100 national and world track records, including 51 Polish, 18 world, and eight European records. Although races measured in yards are rare now, Stella's European record for the 100-yard dash remained unbeaten as of 2006.

In 1951, Walsh was named the most incredible woman athlete of the first half of the 20th century. In 1974, she was inducted into the National Polish-American Sports Hall of Fame, and the following year, she was inducted into the U.S. Track and Field Hall of Fame.

Cleveland sports columnist Dan Coughlin, a longtime friend, wrote that Stella Walsh was always a world-class athlete, first and foremost. "She trained relentlessly. She was always an Olympian..."

George G. "Jackie" Wilson
East Tech – Boxing

At the 1936 Summer Olympics in Berlin, "Jackie" Wilson lost in the bantamweight boxing finals to Italian Ulderico Sergo and was awarded the silver medal. Later that year, Wilson defeated Sergo in an amateur about and avenged his earlier loss. Wilson then left the amateur ranks after having amassed an outstanding record of 50 wins and just one loss; his titles included Golden Gloves championships in New York, Chicago, and Cleveland and the 1936 AAU flyweight crown.

As a professional from 1936 to 1949, Jackie Wilson attained moderate success. He took on most of the great fighters of his day, Sugar Ray Robinson and Jake LaMotta among them—but he never fought for a championship. He was ranked as the #2 welterweight in the world in 1941. Jackie retired from boxing in 1949 with a professional record of 69 wins, 19 losses, and five draws.

OLYMPIANS

To be known as an Olympic champion is a title very few earn. Others earn the title of "Olympic Athlete," who put in all the effort and work yet do not become champions, as recognized by a medal. The Senate League proudly recognizes these Olympic athletes for their outstanding achievements.

Vivian Brown (Brown-Reed)
East Tech – Track

Vivian Brown-Reed was born in Detroit in 1948, and her family moved to Cleveland when she was very young. After graduating from East Tech in 1960, Brown-Reed went on a scholarship to Tennessee State University in Nashville, earning a bachelor's degree in health, physical education, and recreation in 1965. As a member of the U.S. team at the 1963 Pan American games, she won a gold medal in the 200m dash and the 4x400m relay. Brown-Reed was also a member of the U.S. team at the 1964 Tokyo Summer Olympics but was eliminated in the semifinals of the 200m dash. Following the Olympics, she taught physical education, was a basketball and track coach, and worked as a drug prevention counselor for the Cleveland public schools. Before retiring in 1993, Brown-Reed coached several John Adams High School championship track and basketball teams. She was inducted into the Greater Cleveland Sports Hall of Fame in 1976, the East Technical High School Hall of Fame in 1978, and the Ohio Association of Track and Cross Country Hall of Fame in 1983.

Paul Fina
East Tech – Gymnastics

Paul Fina, of Czechoslovakian descent, was born in Cleveland on May 18, 1916. He attended East Tech High School as a star gymnast under coach G. P. Thompson, one of the state's great early gymnastics coaches. During high school, Fina was a three-time state champion in the flying rings, 1935-37, and a two-time winner on the horizontal bar, 1936-37. In 1936, he was the All-Around state high school gymnastics champion.

Upon graduation from East Tech, Fina followed another East Tech gymnast, Joe Giallombardo, to the University of Illinois. In 1940, Paul was the NCAA All-Around champion, an honor he shared that season with Giallombardo, making for a genuinely unique All-Ohio, All-East Tech, NCAA championship. Fina also won the All-Around championship in 1941. He graduated from the U. of Illinois with a degree in education.

Due to a knee injury, Fina could not serve in the military during World War II; he instead supported the country's war effort by working for the Western Electric Company.

Paul Fina was one of the country's best gymnasts during the 1940s. He was a University of Illinois gymnastics team member and won four consecutive NCAA championships from 1939-1942. Unable to show the world his talents because the 1940 and 1944 Olympic Games were canceled due to the Second World War, Fina demonstrated his outstanding ability at various NCAA and AAU events, where he won numerous individual championships and medals during the war years.

Despite missing out on the 1940 and 1944 Olympics due to the war, Paul Fina's outstanding ability did not go unrecognized. The National Collegiate Gymnastics Alumni Association Magazine, with the help of several legendary U.S. gymnasts, picked those who would have made the U. S. Olympic gymnastics teams in 1940 and 1944 had the Olympics been held. Paul Fina was named an Honorary Olympic Team Member for both U. S. Olympic teams.

Paul Fina stayed active in gymnastics well into adulthood, competing into the 1980s. He medaled over 100 times from 1936 to 1950 and was selected as a U.S. International Gymnastic Team member in 1947. He was also involved as an official, chairman of the 1959 Pan American Games, on the Gymnastics Olympic Committee in both 1968 and 1972, and organizer of the U.S. Gymnastics Federation.

East Tech's Paul Fina is one of the nation's all-time great gymnasts and is enshrined in several halls of fame, including the U.S. Gymnastic Hall of Fame and the Greater Cleveland Sports Hall of Fame.

Terrell Gausha
Glenville - Boxing

A 2005 Glenville grad, Terrell Gausha has been boxing since 10. He won the USA National Title in 2009. On Feb. 26, 2012, he entered the USA Championship tournament in Colorado Springs, Colorado, as an unseeded at-large entry. In winning six fights in seven days, he upset the field. In that tournament, Gausha defeated the National Golden Gloves Champion, the #1 and #2 nationally ranked boxers, and the previous champion captured the USA National Championship.

On May 9, 2012, he won a quarterfinal match of the Americas Olympic Qualification Tournament in Rio De Janeiro, Brazil, guaranteeing himself a berth on Team USA for the 2012 London Olympics. Four days later, Gausha won the gold medal in the qualifying tournament. He won his first Olympic bout, defeating Armenian boxer Andranik Hakobyan with a sensational knockout. However, after a controversial decision, India's Vijender Singh eliminated him from the Olympics in his next bout.

Following the Olympics, Gausha turned professional. Fighting as a super welterweight from 2012-2019, Terrell compiled a record of 21-1-1, winning his first 20 consecutive bouts.

Ted Kara
East Tech – Boxing

Theodore Ernst Kara was born on April 2, 1916, and graduated from East Tech. In 1936, Ted was a member of the U. S. Olympic team at the Berlin Summer Olympics, where he was the captain of the U.S. boxing team. Kara did not medal at the 1936 Olympics.

He later attended the University of Idaho, where he became the first athlete in NCAA history to win three national championships, taking boxing titles in 1939 (127 pounds), 1940 (120 pounds), and 1941 (120 pounds). With Kara leading the way, the Idaho boxing team won the Pacific Coast Conference championship in 1940 and back-to-back NCAA titles in 1940 and 1941. In 1941, with his brother Frank winning the 127-pound championship for Idaho, the Kara brothers became the first in NCAA history to win national titles in the same tournament.

Kara was later inducted into the University of Idaho Hall of Fame. The university's website notes, "According to the *Moscow Idahonian*, Ted Kara was 'the outstanding college fighter ever toss leather on the West Coast.' There won't be much argument to that statement."

During the Second World War, Ted Kara joined the Army Air Corps and served as a radioman. He was declared dead after the plane in which he was a crew member went missing over the Pacific Ocean. Ted Kara's official death date is Feb. 14, 1944.

Frances Kaszubski (Sobczak)
South – Track

Frances Theresa Kaszubski (May 15, 1916 - April 11, 2010) was an American-born athlete of Polish descent. She was better known as a track and field star, specializing in discus and shot put, but she always considered basketball her best sport.

Kaszubski graduated from South High in 1934, two years after her friend and neighbor, fellow Olympic star athlete Stella Walsh. Kaszubski was the AAU national shot-put champion six times from 1943-1951. She was the AAU national discus champion seven times during that same period, including five from 1947-1951. Kaszubski qualified for the 1948 Summer Olympics in London in discus and shot put. In the discus, she finished 11th place but did not make it out of the qualifying round for the shot put.

Her distinguished athletic career earned Kaszubski the manager's position for the U.S. women's Olympic team for the 1960 Rome Olympics. Frances Kaszubski was also the director of the Cleveland City Recreation Department from 1956-1978.

Kaszubski has been enshrined in several halls of fame, including the Helms Athletic Foundation Women's Hall of Fame and the Greater Cleveland Sports Hall of Fame, to which she was inducted three times.

Morelle McCane
Glenville – Boxing

A 2013 graduate of Glenville High School, McCane is the first woman boxer from Cleveland to ever qualify for the Olympics, doing so for the 2024 Paris Summer Olympics. In addition to being a four-time national Golden Gloves champion (the only person ever to do so), Morelle won championships at the 2020 and 2021 USA Boxing Elite Nationals and the 2022 USA Boxing International Invitational Championships. More recently, McCane won a 2023 Gee Bee International Tournament championship and earned silver medals at the 2023 Czech Republic Grand Prix and the 2023 Pan American Games. She qualified for the Olympic Games in Paris 2024 by securing a silver medal at the Pan American Games in Santiago 2023.

Eleanor Montgomery
John Adams – Track

Eleanor Montgomery, a native Clevelander, was born on Nov. 13, 1946. While she earned fame as a high jumper, Eleanor won her first national title in the long jump at 14. Eleanor competed in the long jump, and the pentathlon throughout her career, but the high jump was her specialty.

Montgomery is still a John Adams High School student and has participated in international events. At the 1963 Pan American Games, she won the gold medal in the high jump, setting a meet record. She participated in the high jump at the Tokyo Olympics in 1964 but failed to medal, finishing eighth.

Following high school graduation, Montgomery attended Tennessee State University, where she was a member of the famous Tigerbelles track team. It was at TSU that she won the bulk of her medals. Later, she represented the Cleveland Recreation Department at national and international track meets.

From 1963 to 1967, plus 1969, Montgomery won six AAU outdoor high jump championships and added seven more titles while participating in indoor events. 1967, she returned to the Pan Am Games, again winning gold in the high jump. Montgomery repeated as a member of Team USA for the 1968 Mexico City Olympics, but she again failed to medal. In July 1969, at the U.S. National Championships in Dayton, Ohio, Eleanor Montgomery set her best in the high jump, 1.80m, a new American record.

During her career, Montgomery won 13 national championships and several international titles.

She later worked for the Cleveland Municipal School District, supervising its attendance office. She stayed connected to sports, particularly track, by helping the Interchurch Youth Activities Program with its annual track meets and serving as an official for high school track and cross-country meets. Montgomery also served as the executive director of the NFL Players Association Youth Camp and has worked with the Special Olympics.

Montgomery was inducted into the Greater Cleveland Sports Hall of Fame in 1976. On her 67th birthday in 2013, Eleanor Montgomery was inducted into the U.S. Track and Field Hall of Fame

Toccara Montgomery
East Tech – Wrestling

Toccara Montgomery was born in 1982 on Cleveland's east side and began her wrestling career at East Tech High School. She was one of the first members of the school's wrestling team and one of the first girls to compete in the male-dominated sport at the high school level. In early 1999, she won a silver medal at the girls national championship in Michigan. With the help of her coach, Kip Flanik, Montgomery went on to win her first national open title in 2000 as a senior at East Tech. After graduating in 2001, she was named the FILA International Female Wrestler of the Year, the first woman from the United States to win that honor. She was also called "Women's Wrestler of the Year" by USA Wrestling that same year.

Montgomery continued her education at the University of the Cumberlands, where she earned a degree in elementary education in 2006. Continuing her college wrestling career, she had a perfect 29-0 record in dual matches and won the 2004 Women's Collegiate National Championship. In her years at the University, Montgomery helped develop the program into one of the best in the nation, ranked first or second every year from 2004 through 2009. She won the first two college national championships ever held for women, in addition to more than 40 top finishes and other awards during her college days.

Montgomery's accomplishments on the international scene are also impressive. She was a gold medal winner at the Pan American Games in 2002 and 2003 and a silver medalist at the World Championships in 2001 and 2003. In 2004, Montgomery was a member of the first women's wrestling team to represent the United States at the Summer Olympics in Athens (Greece), finishing a very creditable seventh.

Montgomery was a member of the U.S. national team from 2001 to 2006 and won four U.S. junior and senior national championships between 2001 and 2004.

Toccara Montgomery was the head coach of the women's wrestling program at Lindenwood University from 2010 to 2019. She is now retired from wrestling and pursuing a career in elementary education.

Cynthia Bernice Robinson-Holland (Bernice Holland)
John Adams - Track

Born on Feb. 28, 1927, Bernice Robinson-Holland ran for the Washington Park Track Club and won three national titles: the AAU Outdoor 80m hurdles in 1948 and 1949 and the AAU Indoor 50-yard hurdles in 1949.

At the 1948 Olympic Trials, Robinson-Holland won the high hurdles. (This event also doubled as the AAU Meet.) She also ran in the 80m hurdles at the 1948 Olympics in London but did not medal.

Later in life, living in Cleveland, Robinson-Holland coached track at John Adams High School. She also expanded her track activities to include shot put, discus, and javelin, setting records in all three events at the Masters Pan American Games in the early 1980s.

Robinson-Holland continued to compete in Masters Track & Field events into the 21st century.

OLYMPIC TRIAL ATHLETES

Many outstanding athletes make it to the Olympic trials but miss making the final cut for the team, sometimes by mere fractions of a second or an inch or two. Nonetheless, they are genuinely outstanding athletes.

Ron Addison
Rhodes - Track

1972, as a Rhodes senior, Ron Addison won the OHSAA cross-country and mile state championships and was named to the U.S. National Junior Team.

Addison continued his career at the University of Tennessee. There, he was a member of the Volunteers' NCAA championship cross-country team. He was named the Southeastern Conference Track and Field Championships MVP and a three-time SEC individual champion.

1974 Addison finished second to teammate Doug Brown in the steeplechase at the NCAA championships. That helped Tennessee wins the national championship, and the Volunteers were also the first team representing a Southern school to win the NCAA track championship since 1933.

Following college, Addison earned a bronze medal in the 3000m steeplechase at the 1977 World University Games, and he won that event at the 1977 Pacific Conference Games. At one time during his career, Ron Addison held the second fastest time ever run by an American in the 3,000m steeplechase. In 1976, 1980, and 1984, he participated in the Olympic trials for Team USA. His best finish came in 1980 when he finished in fourth place and missed making the team by two-tenths of a second.

Stanley Albright
Glenville - Track

Stanley Albright was a 1965 OHSAA state championship track team member from Glenville. That year, he won the high jump competition and finished second in the long jump. 1966, at the USA Outdoor Track and Field Championships, Albright finished third in the high jump. In

1972, as a member of the Cleveland Striders, he was invited to the USA Olympic trials, but he failed to qualify for the team in the high jump..

Aki Bradley
East Tech - Track

In 1989, Aki Bradley earned All-Ohio status at the State Meet in the 100m and 200m races, repeated that in 1990, and added All-Ohio status in 1990 as a member of East Tech's 4x100m relay team.

Following graduation, Bradley attended Mississippi State University. While there, Bradley was the 1994 Southeastern Conference champion in the 200m dash, was three times named an All-American, and was later inducted into the MSU Hall of Fame. In 1992 and 1996, Aki Bradley participated in the Olympic trials for Team USA.

Quincy Downing Jr.
Glenville - Track

As a junior in 2010 at the OHSAA Division I State Meet, Downing was a member of Glenville's state champion 4x200m relay team and the school's second-place 4x400m relay and third-place 4x100m relay teams. The following year, as a senior, Downing won a state championship in the 400m race and was a championship 4x400m relay team member. Also, during his high school career, he was a four-time OHSAA champion, a five-time OHSAA district champion, and a member of three indoor state championship relay teams.

After graduating from Glenville, Downing continued his education and track career at Louisiana State University, where he was twice NCAA champion, a nine-time All-American, a five-time All-SEC selection, and a 2012 World Junior Gold Medalist (4x400m relay). In 2016, Quincy Downing competed in the Olympic trials for Team USA.

LeShaunte Edwards
Rhodes - Track

In 1997, LeShaunte won the 200m at the OHSAA Division I state championships to close out his high school track career on a very high note.

Continuing his education and athletic pursuits at the University of Akron, Edwards would have a stellar intercollegiate track career, becoming the greatest sprinter in the school's history. As an Akron Zip, LeShaunte won 10 Mid-American Conference championships, was named the MVP of the MAC championship meet three times, and became the first male student-athlete at the University of Akron to earn NCAA All-American honors three times. He earned the James Horrigan Award as the Akron "Male Athlete of The Year" thrice.

Edwards holds seven University of Akron records, including those in the 100 meters (10.23) and 200 meters (20.34) outdoors and the 60 meters (6.67) and 200 meters (20.92) indoors. He has been inducted into the University of Akron's Sports Hall of Fame.

In 2004, Edwards participated in the Olympic trials for Team USA.

Dorian Green
John Marshall - Track

In 1992, Dorian Green closed out an incredible season by winning the state championship in the 400m; he was undefeated in that event the entire season. That same year, he also finished third in the 200m state finals. In 1993, Green finished second in the 400m at the state meet.

Continuing his education and track career at the University of Illinois, Green finished second in the 400m at the Big Ten Indoor Championships in 1994, returning to win that event the following year. In 1996, he was named MVP of the Big Ten Indoor Championships when he won the 200m and 400m and was a member of the winning 4x400m relay team.

1996, Green was invited to the Olympic qualifying meet for Team USA in the 400m, but he did not qualify for the team.

Darian coached high school sprinters after college and continued his running career. His best track success came in the 2009 USA Masters when he finished second in the 400m and third in the 200m. At the 2013 Masters, Dorian came in second as a member of the 4x100m relay team.

Willie Hibbler
East Tech - Track

At the 1992 OHSAA state track meet, Willie Hibler won the 100m and 300m hurdle races. Upon graduating from East Tech, Hibler continued his education and track career at the University of Nebraska. Hibler was a three-time All-American (Indoor) in the 110m hurdles. In 1996, he participated in the Olympic trials for Team USA in the 110m hurdles but missed qualifying for the team when he finished fourth.

Mahagony Jones
Rhodes - Track

In 2009, as a senior at Rhodes, Mahagony Jones was a three-time winner at the OHSAA Indoor State championships, winning the 60m, 200m, and 400m races at the OHSAA outdoor state championships that year; she again landed on the podium three times with a second-place finish in the 100m and a pair of third-place finishes in the 200m and 400m races. She also took top honors in the 100m and 400m races at the Midwest Meet of Champions against Michigan, Indiana, and Ohio competitions.

Continuing her education and

running career at Penn State, Jones won the 60m, 200m, and 4x400m races at the 2013 Sykes & Sabock Challenge Cup, after which she was named the "Athlete of the Meet."

In 2014, Jones finished first or second in every event she competed in during the regular season. Highlights of that season included running on the 4x200m relay team that set the collegiate record with a time of 1:35.65 at the Penn State Indoor Relays, being named Mid-Atlantic Women's Track Athlete of the Year (Indoor) and being named First Team All-America for both the indoor and outdoor seasons.

In 2015, Jones was a member of the women's team that set the indoor world record in the distance medley relay (1200m, 400m, 800m, 1600m) with a time of 10:42.57.

During her college career, Jones was a five-time indoor and outdoor All-American and a two-time Big Ten champion.

In 2016, Mahagony competed in the U.S. Olympic trials in the 200m but did not qualify for the team.

Markeya Jones
South High – Track

In 1988, Markeya Jones helped South High to a fifth-place finish at the OHSAA girls state track meet by finishing first in the 200m, second in the 100m, and fifth-place member of the 4x100m relay team. In 1991, she set the Kansas State University school record at 200m and was a member of the Big Eight Champion mile relay team that set a record that year. 1996, Jones participated in the Olympic trials for that year's games in Atlanta.

Harold Madox
John Adams – Track

During his senior year at John Adams in 1984, Madox won both the 400m and 200m races in the Senate League championships, as well as in the state district and regional competition. In addition, he was on the winning 1600m relay team at all three events; in the State Meet that year, Madox won the 400m race and was a member of the championship 1600m relay team, which set a then-state record time of 3:13.57. He also won the 400m race at the AAU Junior Olympic national competition and the Midwest Meet of Champions.

Continuing his education and track career at Odessa Junior College, Madox was a nine-time national champion in both indoor and outdoor events. In 1986, he set the national junior college record in the 400m with a time of 44.89, which was the sixth fastest time in the world at that time.

In 1988, Madox attended the U. S. Olympic trials but did not qualify for the team.

Dr. Estus Newberry
East Tech – Track

From Dr. Newberry's Cleveland Sports Hall of Fame plaque:

"A graduate of East Technical High School, he went on to NAIA All-American honors (1955-56) and (1956-57) in college in the high hurdles and long jump. He qualified for the U.S. Olympic trials in 1956 as a hurdler. A consistent competitor, his participation always showed excellence, which marked his distinguished career."

Estus Newberry was a sports star at East Tech in the early 1950s. He played football and basketball, ran track, and even played badminton. 1953, he was captain of the school's basketball and track teams.

After graduating from East Tech, he moved on to Baldwin-Wallace College, where he continued his track career at the collegiate level. He held the Baldwin-Wallace long jump record at 24'2½". In 1956, he won NAIA All-America honors in three events and participated in the 1956 Olympic trials for Team USA. He participated on the All-American Team in the long jump and was voted the Outstanding Track Athlete and the Outstanding Ohio AAU Athlete.

As a high school track coach, Coach Newberry's teams won 33 individual and 18 championship titles. He was selected as the Outstanding Track and Field Coach in Cleveland four times.

In addition to being inducted into the Cleveland Sports Hall of Fame, Newberry has also been inducted into the East Tech and Baldwin-Wallace Athletic Halls of Fame.

Robert Ware
Glenville

Robert Ware, often referred to as "Bullet" Bob Ware, is considered by many to be the greatest sprinter ever to attend Glenville High School. Ware won multiple state meet titles in the 100 and 200yd dashes and was a member of several winning relay teams. Ware was a member of the Glenville track teams that won consecutive Division I state championships in 1966, 1967, and 1968, setting meet records as a member of the winning 880-yard relay teams.

Ware continued his education and track career at Cuyahoga Community College and Western Kentucky University. In 1972, Robert was invited to the Olympic trials for Team USA, running in the 100m dash. Also in 1972, while running with the Philadelphia Pioneer Track Club, "Bullet" Bob ran the fastest time in the world as a 400 m relay team member.

In 2002, Robert "Bullet Bob" Ware was inducted into the Ohio Association of Track & Cross-Country Coaches Hall of Fame.

CHAPTER 2

Hall of Fame

Short of winning an Olympic gold medal, being named to the national Hall of Fame of an athlete's sport is the highest honor one can achieve. For some sports, such as football and baseball, where there is no Olympic competition, being named to your sport's Hall of Fame is the ultimate honor. Hall of Fame induction identifies the athlete as having made an outstanding contribution to the history of that sport, as reflected by their accomplishments throughout their careers.

Cleveland's Senate Athletic League has produced several outstanding athletes who have been inducted into their sport's college and professional Hall of Fame throughout the League's long and distinguished history. What follows is a brief description of the outstanding athletic careers of these nationally recognized athletes.

(See Appendix II for a listing of those athletes whose accomplishments have earned them induction into other halls of fame, such as the Greater Cleveland Sports Hall of Fame and the Ohio Association of Track and Cross-Country Coaches Hall of Fame.)

Collegiate and Professional Hall of Fame Inductees

BASEBALL HALL OF FAME

Gordon Cobbledick

Gordon Cobbledick was a 1918 graduate of East Tech, where he was an All-Scholastic halfback on the Scarabs football team his senior year. The Scarabs won the Senate championship all three years (1915, 1916, 1917) that "Cobby" (a nickname that stuck with him) was on the team. They were also co-city champions with University School in 1917. (No city champion was named in either 1915 or 1916.)

Upon graduating from East Tech, Cobbledick enlisted in the Marines, where his proficiency as a sharpshooter earned him the designation of a shooting instructor. Upon his discharge in 1919, Cobby enrolled at the Case School of Applied Science (now Case Western Reserve University), where he studied mining engineering and played football.

Cobby did not find engineering to his liking, and on Jan. 3, 1923, a chance meeting at *The Plain Dealer* office of sportswriter Henry Edwards led to Cobbledick signing on as a reporter for the newspaper. The rest, as the saying goes, is history. The following is how Cobbledick's journalism career is described by the Great Cleveland Sports Hall of Fame, into which he was inducted in 2007: "Gordon Cobbledick was the sports editor of *The Plain Dealer* from 1946 until his retirement in 1964. Before that, he had covered the Cleveland Indians for 25 years. ... He would turn into a war correspondent, writing from the Pacific Theatre during World War II, then returning to become PD sports editor soon after. During his long career, he served a term as president of the Baseball Writers' Association of America. In 1977, nine years after his death, he would become the first Ohio writer to be inducted into the Writers Wing of the Baseball Hall of Fame in Cooperstown. Another posthumous honor would come his way in 1982 when he was inducted into the Journalism Hall of Fame.

Edward Delahanty

A graduate of Central High School, Edward Delahanty was referred to as "Big Ed" by sports reporters and "Del" by teammates and fans. His achievements during his 15-year baseball career are among the most extraordinary of any player. And some of those accomplishments have remained unequaled to this day. While not much is written about his fielding ability, Delahanty's achievements were almost legendary when he stepped into the batter's box. He was the National League batting champion in 1899, led the league in home runs in 1893 and 1896, and led the senior circuit in RBIs in 1893, 1896, and 1899. With a lifetime batting average of .346 (fifth best all-time), Delahanty was the first player to hit 400 or better in three seasons; the only player to match that accomplishment was the legendary Ty Cobb.

On July 13, 1896, Delahanty hit four home runs in the same game; three years later, he hit four doubles in the same game. He is still the only player in Major League Baseball history to achieve that unique feat.

Ed Delahanty died in 1903, apparently falling from a train into the Niagara River while traveling between Buffalo and Niagara Falls (the actual cause of his fall has never been determined). He is buried in Cleveland's Calvary Cemetery. 1945, he was inducted into the Major League Baseball Hall of Fame.

Hal Lebovitz

Hal Lebovitz was a graduate of Glenville High School in 1934. He attended Western Reserve University, graduating with a degree in chemistry, but first and foremost, he always wanted to be a journalist.

He got his first job covering high school sports for the *Cleveland News* in 1942 and soon covered both the Cleveland Browns and the Cleveland Indians. When the *Cleveland News* folded in 1960, Lebovitz was hired by *The Plain Dealer* and became the paper's sports editor in 1964, holding that position until 1982.

His writing appeared regularly in *The News-Herald* and *The Morning Journal* (Lorain, Ohio) until he died in 2005 at 89. He was famous for his in-depth knowledge of the rules of all sports, which was on display in his popular newspaper column, "Ask Hal the Referee," which ran in both *The Plain Dealer* and the *National Sporting News*. His writing earned him many awards, and he was featured 17 times in the annual *Best Sports Stories* and selected for numerous other anthologies.

A lover of almost every sport, Lebovitz coached baseball, basketball, and football and officiated all three sports, including time spent as a referee traveling with the Harlem Globetrotters.

In 1999, Hal Lebovitz was enshrined in the writers' recognition area of the Baseball Hall of Fame. He is also in the Greater Cleveland Sports Hall of Fame and ten other halls of fame.

NAISMITH BASKETBALL HALL OF FAME

William T. (Wee Willie) Smith
(The following information about William T. Smith is from The Encyclopedia of Cleveland History and the Greater Cleveland Sports Hall of Fame.)

William T. Smith was an outstanding professional basketball player in the 1930s and a National Basketball Hall of Fame member. He was born in Montgomery, Ala., but his family moved to Cleveland when he was young. He learned to play basketball at Cleveland's Hiram House. Big for his age, Smith played on adult amateur teams at night while attending East Tech.

While playing for the Slaughter Bros. company team in 1931, one of the city's better amateur teams, Smith caught the eye of Robert Douglas, owner of the New York Renaissance, a successful all-Black professional team; the 6'5" "Wee Willie" Smith joined the team in 1932. The "Rens" took on all comers, playing one-night stands, and from 1932-36, Smith and his six teammates were considered the best team in the world. Smith was a starter on the Rens' 1932-1933 team, which set a professional record of 88 consecutive wins. As a result of that incredible accomplishment, the entire Rens team was inducted into the Naismith Memorial Basketball Hall of Fame in 1963.

Willie Smith was picked as the top Rens' 1937-1938 team player and played on the first World Professional Championship team in 1939. Smith played for the Rens from 1932 until 1942, during which time the team had an outstanding record of 473-49, a winning percentage of .906.

In addition to being in the Naismith Basketball Hall of Fame, Willie Smith was elected to the Harlem Hall of Fame and the Greater Cleveland Sports Hall of Fame in 1977.

PROFESSIONAL AND COLLEGE FOOTBALL HALLS OF FAME

Robert Stanford Brown

Robert Stanford Brown, better known as Bob Brown, was born in Cleveland on Dec. 8, 1941. Brown played football at East Tech, starring for the Scarabs on the offensive line. Although the major colleges did not widely recruit him, Brown received a football scholarship to the University of Nebraska upon graduation.

He was listed as a third-team offensive lineman at Nebraska, but only until Bob Devaney, a future college hall of fame selection, was named the Cornhuskers' head coach for the 1962 season. Devaney made Brown a starting offensive guard that season, and the young man rewarded that decision by earning All-Conference recognition. In 1963, Brown's senior year at Nebraska, his stellar play at guard continued, and he was chosen as a consensus All-American and named the national "Lineman of the Year" in college football. A two-way player, Brown also starred as a linebacker for the Cornhuskers, earning the nickname "Boomer" for his tremendous hits on opposing players. Coach Devaney would later say of Bob Brown that he was "the best two-way player I ever coached." Brown's number "64" has been permanently retired by the University of Nebraska, one of only two to receive that distinguished honor.

Bob Brown graduated from Nebraska with his class in 1964. Many articles about him mention this because, unfortunately, many people seem to think that it is unusual for a college athlete actually to graduate, much less graduate on time – and Bob Brown did both.

In the 1964 NFL draft, Bob Brown was the second overall pick, going to the Philadelphia Eagles. The Eagles soon realized they had made an excellent selection as Brown was named the NFL "Rookie of the Year" after the 1964 season. He played for the Eagles through the 1968 campaign, was traded to the Los Angeles Rams (1969 and 1970), and finally to the Oakland Raiders (1971-1973).

In his 10-year professional career, one no doubt cut short by knee injuries, Bob Brown was named All-Pro each of his first nine seasons, five times as a First-Team selection and four times as Second-Team. He also played in the Pro Bowl six times. Among his numerous honors was being named the NFL/NFC "Lineman of the Year" three consecutive times, 1968-1970, and to the NFL 1960s All-Decade team.

Not surprisingly, Bob Brown is enshrined in the College and Professional Football Halls of Fame and named to the Philadelphia Eagles Hall of Fame.

Benjamin "Benny" Friedman

There was a relatively small running back on the East Tech scrub football team at the end of the 1920 season. When it came time to start practicing for the 1921 campaign, East Tech Coach Sam Willaman told that young lad that he would be too light for the East Tech varsity and that if he wanted to play football, he should transfer to Glenville, his neighborhood school. The young running back did just that. His name was Benny Friedman (1905-1982). In the second game of the 1922 season, his senior year, Friedman and his Glenville teammates destroyed East Tech, the team that had dominated Cleveland high school football during the previous seven seasons, by a score of 31-0. Friedman led the assault by scoring four touchdowns. Glenville would be the 1922 Senate League champions and share the city title with Lakewood High School and University School.

After graduating from Glenville, Friedman entered the University of Michigan. In 1924, sophomore Benny Friedman was named a starting halfback for the second game of the season, and he would be a starter for the remainder of that season. He was then named the starting quarterback in both 1925 and 1926. Against Indiana in only his second game at quarterback in 1925, Friedman accounted for 50 of his team's 63 points by scoring a touchdown, throwing for five more TDs, and kicking two field goals and eight extra points. With Benny Friedman throwing the ball and end Bennie Oosterbaan catching it (known as "The Benny to Bennie Show"), they became "one of the greatest passing combinations in college football history" at a time when passing was still in its infancy. During the 1926 season, Benny Friedman did it all: the team's passing, kicking, and place-kicking; returned punts, caught a few passes, and played in both the offensive and defensive backfields.

Under Friedman's leadership, the Wolverines were a combined 14-2-0 and the Big Ten champions each season in 1925 and 1926. Unsurprisingly, he was named to the First-Team All-America team both years.

After his college playing days were over, Benny Friedman went on to play in the National Football League for eight years, but his first four years were the years of his most tremendous success. From 1927 through 1930, Benny Friedman led the NFL in passing, setting records for passing yards and touchdowns that few had ever thought possible. In 1928, Friedman led the NFL in rushing and passing touchdowns, becoming the only player in NFL history ever to accomplish that feat. George Halas, one of the founders of the NFL and head coach of the Chicago Bears for 46 years, said of Friedman, "Benny revolutionized football."

When his playing days were over, Friedman spent 18 years as a college administrator and football coach, compiling a record of 65-66-5.

During World War II, Friedman answered his country's call by joining the U.S. Navy. His duties included being an assistant football coach at the Great Lakes Naval Training Station (Chicago) and as the deck officer aboard the aircraft carrier USS Shangri-La.

Friedman was undoubtedly the greatest quarterback of his day. In 2005, in its College Football Encyclopedia, ESPN released a retroactive list of Heisman Trophy winners covering 1905-1934. In 1926, they determined that Benny Friedman would have won if a Heisman Trophy had been awarded that season. More than a few people still consider Benny Friedman to be the best player that football has ever seen. He is enshrined in numerous halls of fame, including the National Collegiate Football Hall of Fame and the Pro Football Hall of Fame.

John Charles Hicks, Jr.

John Charles Hicks Jr. was born in Cleveland and attended John Hay High School. At John Hay, he was an outstanding football player who starred on offense and defense, mainly at guard. In a 2013 poll taken by The Cleveland Plain Dealer to determine the top 50 Cleveland high school football players of the previous 50 years (1963-2013), John Hicks was ranked sixth overall, and both the highest-ranked Senate player and the highest-ranked offensive lineman.

Upon graduating, Hicks continued his education at The Ohio State University. He did not play on the varsity as a freshman in 1969 (first-year students were ineligible), but he did play the next four years, 1970-1973, gaining an extra year of eligibility due to an injury in 1971 that cut short his playing time.

In 1972, Hicks was named All-Big Ten and also to the All-America First Team. In 1973, John was again named All-Big Ten and All-America First Team, this time as a unanimous choice. In addition, he won the Outland Trophy as the best interior lineman in the country and the Lombardi Trophy as the nation's best offensive lineman. In the balloting for the Heisman Trophy that year, John Hicks finished second – a distinction unheard of for a lineman, and he was the last lineman to finish that high in the balloting for the nation's best collegiate football player.

Following the 1973 season, John's head coach, Woody Hayes, in an interview with the New York Times, said, "John Hicks has never had a bad game. He's the best football player on our team and the best interior lineman I have ever seen."

Of his 1973 college teammate, two-time Heisman Trophy winner Archie Griffin told The Columbus Dispatch in 2001, "I just had so much confidence running behind him because I knew that what was supposed to be there was going to be there."

In the three years that John started on the Ohio State offensive line, the Buckeyes posted a record of 28-3-1 and won the Big Ten championship each year. Ohio State also went to the

Rose Bowl each of those three years, and John Hicks became the first player ever to start in three different Rose Bowl games. How important was John Hicks to the success of the Ohio State football team? After he was injured in 1971, the Buckeyes won only one game over the balance of the season.

Moving on to the NFL after college, John was the third player picked in the 1974 draft, going to the New York Giants. That season, he was named as the NFC Rookie of the Year. Unfortunately, John Hicks played only three more years in the NFL, his career cut short by injuries.

After he retired from football, Hicks was a tireless fundraiser for John Hay High School.

John Hicks is enshrined in the College Football Hall of Fame, as well as the Rose Bowl Hall of Fame.

Leslie "Les" Horvath

Leslie Horvath was born in South Bend, Indiana. Shortly thereafter, the Horvath family moved to Ohio, settling in the Parma area. When he was of high school age, Les Horvath naturally attended his local school, Parma High. At Parma, Les Horvath emerged as a natural athlete, competing in football, basketball, and track. He was outstanding in all three, especially football, despite being relatively small at about 5' 10" and 170 pounds.

Horvath had a keen competitive edge and always played to win. As the story goes, during the 1937-38 basketball season, Horvath became disenchanted with his teammates, feeling that they were not interested in playing to win. Therefore, he transferred to nearby James F. Rhodes High School in Cleveland for his senior year; to make this happen, the whole family also moved to Cleveland.

Rhodes had an excellent football team at the time. When Horvath transferred, he became the Rams' quarterback and helped extend the team's winning streak to 25 games since 1936. However, the Rams lost their West Senate finale to West Tech.

After graduating from Rhodes, Horvath enrolled at The Ohio State University, where he played football for three seasons, 1940-1942 (first-year students were not allowed to play on the varsity then). He was the right halfback on the 1942 Buckeyes team coached by the soon-to-be-legendary Paul Brown. With Horvath leading the way, the Buckeyes finished that season with a record of 9-1-0 and won Ohio State's first national championship.

With his three years of college football eligibility used up, Les Horvath entered the Ohio State dental school upon graduation and figured that his football playing days were over. However, due to the shortage of college-aged players caused by the workforce demands of World War II, football players were given an extra year of eligibility. Wishing to concentrate on his dental studies, Horvath initially did not want to resume playing. But OSU head coach Carroll Widdoes talked Les into taking to the gridiron again. The result was the most incredible year of Horvath's football playing days.

Behind the leadership of Les Horvath, the 1944 Buckeyes went 9-0-0, their first undefeated season in 28 years. That leadership included calling all of the plays on the field, earning Les the nickname of the "playing coach." That season, the Buckeyes finished second in the nation to West Point. In leading the Buckeyes to victory, Horvath rushed for 905 yards (a Big Ten record) and passed for another 345 yards; his rushing total was second in the nation, his total yardage third. His overall performance that season showed why Les Horvath was considered America's most versatile football player. He could do it all — kick, block, tackle, pass, and run — and do it better than just about anyone else.

Based on this exceptional performance, Les Horvath was named the Most Valuable Player in the Big Ten Conference, a unanimous All-America selection, the Sporting News "Player of the Year," and the first Ohio State Buckeye ever to win the Heisman Trophy. Horvath winning the Heisman was all the more impressive considering that he sat out the entire previous season — the only player to ever win the Heisman Trophy after not playing the last season and only one of two graduate students to ever win the Heisman.

After completing his dental studies in 1945, Les Horvath entered the U.S. Navy and was stationed in Hawaii. While there, he practiced dentistry daily and helped coach a service football team in the evening; his team won the service championship that year. Upon leaving the Navy in 1947, Les Horvath played three years of professional football in 1949 as a member of the All-American Football Conference champion Cleveland Browns. When his playing days were over, Horvath moved to Los Angeles, where he continued practicing dentistry and coaching little league football. Of his involvement with minor league football, his wife noted, "Not many people know that he loved coaching kids. That is one thing he loved to do. He took much pride in coaching and inspired those young kids."

As a football player, Les Horvath has been described as "a disciplined team player who met each challenge with determination, stamina and drive. He was an outstanding breakaway runner and a good passer and blocker." Jack Graf, a teammate of Horvath's in 1941, said, "The only bad thing about Les is that he wasn't huge, but he was swift and aggressive and was the key to our whole season. Les used his brains to make up for his lack of size."

Bill Willis, another Ohio State and Cleveland Brown teammate of Horvath's and himself enshrined in both the College and Pro Football Halls of Fame said about Les Horvath: "He had an outstanding personality. To me, he was an All-American both on and off the field. He was the best player of our day. He could never bull you over, so he had to dance around you. There weren't many people who were able to catch him. There are two people responsible for the boost in national recognition we (OSU) received during that time: Les Horvath and Paul Brown. Before those two individuals, Ohio State was not recognized nationally as it is today. Those two were why Ohio State won its first national title in 1942..."

Les Horvath is enshrined in the College Football Hall of Fame at Ohio State University. Ohio State has retired his jersey number, 22, one of only seven numbers that will ever be so honored.

Gomer Thomas Jones

Gomer Thomas Jones was born in Cleveland and entered his neighborhood high school, South High, as a freshman in 1928. In 1929, 1930, and 1931, Jones was the leading member of the school's football team, earning All-Scholastic recognition all three seasons. He played on offense (center) and defense (linebacker), as was the norm back then, starting at center in 1930 and 1931. Gomer was named the Flyers' team captain for the 1931 season based on his outstanding ability and team leadership. Not only was Jones an exceptional football player, but he was also a three-year starter on the South High basketball team.

Upon graduating from South High, Jones continued his education at The Ohio State University, majoring in industrial art and biology. During the 1932 football season, he played on the first-year team, but Gomer Jones was a fixture on the Buckeyes varsity squad after that first year. He anchored the offensive line for three years as the starting center and, on defense, starred as a linebacker. As a result of his outstanding play, after the 1934 season, Jones was named his team's Most Valuable Player.

The 1935 campaign would be even more significant for Gomer Jones and the Buckeyes. Named the team captain, Jones' hard-nosed play at center and linebacker would lead his team to a 7-1-0 season, the only loss being a tough 18-13 decision at the hands of Notre Dame. However, the Buckeyes were a perfect 5-0-0 in Western Conference (Big Ten) play, winning their first conference championship in 15 years. Gomer Jones was again named the Buckeyes MVP, but this time added First Team All-Conference and Consensus All-America to his postseason awards. Jones was one of the first Ohio State Buckeyes to play in the East-West Game, being named the captain of the East squad.

Upon graduation, Gomer was chosen in the first round of the 1936 NFL draft by the Chicago Cardinals, the 15th player selected overall. However, Jones turned down the chance to play with the more established Cardinals to take a position with his hometown Cleveland Rams, a team just starting in the newly formed American Football League. In recognition of Gomer's decision to play for the Cleveland Rams, the opening day of the 1936 AFL season in Cleveland was declared "Gomer Jones Day," Cleveland Mayor Harold H. Burton threw out the first ball to Gomer. Gomer's professional football career would last just one year; he was suspended for the 1937 season due to a contract dispute and never returned to the professional game.

Although Gomer's professional football career was now over, he was not finished with football — far from it. Turning to coaching, Jones took an assistant coach position at Ohio State from 1936-1940. He then moved on to an assistant coaching position at John Carroll University in 1941. In 1943, Gomer left his duties at John Carroll and entered military service with the U.S. Navy, during which he spent three years as the line coach at St. Mary's Pre-Flight Training Center in Moraga, California. In 1946, Jones was an assistant coach at the University of Nebraska.

However, Gomer Jones' most lasting coaching success came at his next stop along the coaching trail. In 1947, Jones joined the staff of legendary head coach Bud Wilkinson at the University of Oklahoma, where he spent 17 years, 1946-1963, as the Sooners' line coach. The lines that Gomer coached became the backbone of one of college football's greatest dynasties.

During those years, the Sooners compiled a record of 145-29-4 and were named national champion five times. And they accomplished all of this behind the lines that Gomer Jones developed and coached, which featured no less than 16 All-America selections and were known far and wide as the best in college football.

Despite many lucrative offers from other schools to become a head coach, Gomer Jones remained at Oklahoma. In 1963, Bud Wilkinson resigned as the head football coach and athletic director to make a run for the U.S. Senate. Gomer Jones replaced Wilkinson in both positions. After compiling a record of 9-11-1 during the 1964 and 1965 seasons, Jones stepped down as the football coach, but he remained at Oklahoma as the athletic director until he died in 1971.

The following from former Oklahoma high school Coach Ray Goldsby gives an idea of the type of person Gomer Jones was: "... I took a class, 'Theory of Football,' when I was in college, and Gomer taught the class. I have always believed that if you were a good coach, you had to be a good teacher. I know in reality that that is not true in many instances. In this case, though, it was true. Gomer was an excellent teacher, and what he taught us was very applicable, especially to me later in my coaching career. Also, during this time, he never discussed his background. He knew the class was not about him, and he did an outstanding job teaching us the nuts and bolts of the fundamentals of football."

Following his untimely death in 1971, Gomer Jones was inducted into the College Football Hall of Fame and the Ohio State Athletic Hall of Fame.

James Richard Martin

James Richard Martin was born in Cleveland and attended East Tech High School, where he was on both the football (center) and the swim teams for three years, captaining both teams his senior year.

Upon graduating from East Tech in 1942, with World War II raging, Jim immediately entered the U. S. Marine Corps; he would perform distinguished service for the balance of the war for 30 months. One of his most crucial and dangerous assignments occurred in July 1944 when he was a member of the Marine's Fifth Amphibious Reconnaissance Battalion. For this particularly hazardous assignment, Jim was part of a three-person crew, wearing only swim trunks, swim fins, and face masks, that snuck ashore on the island of Tinian in a rubber raft to scout the terrain and pick a safe landing spot for the Marines' upcoming invasion. It was perilous missions like this that earned Jim Martin a Bronze Star and also helped to earn him the nickname "Jungle Jim."

Following the war, Jim entered Notre Dame University as a 22-year-old freshman in the fall of 1946. At that time, Notre Dame was coached by the legendary Frank Leahy, who had met and recruited Martin when both men were serving in the Pacific Theatre. To say Jim Martin's years with the Fighting Irish were unprecedented would be a bit of an understatement. With college football still under some wartime rules, Jim could play on the varsity all four years. He started at the end of his first three seasons, and when Notre Dame needed a tackle in his senior year, Jim voluntarily switched positions. Jim also played on both offense and defense his entire Notre Dame career. During his senior season in 1949, Jim was the team's co-captain, the first Clevelander to captain the Fighting Irish since Stan Cofall (also an East Tech grad) in 1916. During Jim Martin's four years on the Notre Dame football team, the Fighting Irish did not lose a single game, posting a 36-0-2 record, were the national champions in 1946, 1947, and 1949, and finished second in the national poll in 1948. In 1949, Jim was named First Team All-America by the Associated Press, the International News Service, and the Newspaper Enterprise Association.

Jim Martin did not limit his athletic achievements at Notre Dame to the gridiron. He also participated in intramural sports, most notably swimming and boxing, winning the school's heavyweight boxing championship. In 1950, Jim Martin received the coveted George Gipp Award as an outstanding school athlete.

Upon graduation, Jim Martin was drafted by the Cleveland Browns in the second round of the NFL draft, the third player ever drafted by the Browns in the NFL. Jim Martin played defensive end for the Browns that season as they posted a 10-2 record and won the NFL championship in their first year in the league. In the divisional championship game that season against the New York Giants, Martin sacked Giants quarterback Charlie Conerly in the end zone for a safety with less than a minute left in the game to help secure the Browns' crucial 8-3 victory.

However, after the season, Martin was traded to the Detroit Lions, for whom he would play the next 11 years. Ironically, with Jim Martin on the Lions, the Detroiters would beat the Browns in the 1952 and 1953 NFL championship games and again in 1957. Later in his career, Martin switched to linebacker and did the kickoffs and place-kicking for the Lions. In 1960, he was the first player ever to kick two field goals of more than 50 yards in the same game, and in 1961, Jim's 15 field goals made him the Lions' all-time leading field goal kicker. Martin's 70 points scored (15 field goals and 25 extra points) also led the Lions in scoring that season. Jim Martin was named to the 1961 Pro Bowl.

Martin left the Lions after the 1961 season to become an assistant coach for the Denver Broncos. Still, he returned to the playing field the following year with the Baltimore Colts, earning the league's "Comeback Player of the Year" award. Martin retired from playing after the 1964 season, spending the next 11 years coaching at the high school, college, and professional levels.

Later in life, Jim Martin worked as a court officer in Michigan. He was inducted into the Greater Cleveland Sports Hall of Fame in 1976 and the College Football Hall of Fame in 1995.

August Michael "Mike" Michalske

August Michael "Mike" Michalske was born in Cleveland and attended West Tech High School, Class of 1920, where he starred in three sports, including football and track.

He graduated from Penn State University, starring in football and track in 1923, 1924, and 1925. On the football team, Mike was used primarily as a guard before being moved to fullback by head coach Hugo Bezdek during the 1925 season. That move paid immediate dividends when, in his first game at fullback, Michalske scored both Penn State touchdowns in a 13-6 win over Michigan State. Mike was a true "60-minute man" who seldom left the field, playing offense and defense. By the end of the 1925 campaign, Mike was rated as "one of the greatest defensive fullbacks of the season" and was named All-American.

After college, Mike began an exceptional career in professional football. In 1926, he signed with the New York Yankees of the original American Football League and then moved with the Yankees to the National Football League the following season. While playing with the Yankees, Mike was named First Team All-Pro in 1927 and 1928.

The Yankees folded after the 1928 season, but Mike Michalske was far from finished as an outstanding professional football player. Already rated as "the best guard in the National Football League," Mike had little difficulty signing a contract with the Green Bay Packers in 1929. In that campaign, the Packers went 12-0-1 and won their first NFL championship; they would then win the NFL title each of the next two years. In those three seasons, Mike was named First Team All-Pro, earning the nickname "Iron Mike" by playing offense and defense, seldom leaving the field of play. (He was considered a defensive specialist.)

During the 1931 season, Mike made the outstanding play of his career when he intercepted a pass against the Chicago Bears and returned it 80 yards for a touchdown. This gave the Packers their only points in a key 6-2 victory en route to the NFL championship.

Mike Michalske was again named First Team All-Pro in 1934 and 1935. After retiring after the 1935 season, Mike came back to play for the Packers in 1937 but played only six games before injuring his back, which resulted in his permanent retirement.

Michalske started his coaching career as an assistant coach at Ashland College while playing with the New York Yankees in 1928 and 1929. He then resumed coaching in 1936, a career at the college and professional levels that lasted until 1956. Most of his time was as an assistant coach, but from 1942 to 1946, he was the head coach at Iowa State, compiling a record of 18-18-1 during those mainly war years.

In the earliest years of the National Football League, Mike Michalske was one of its greatest players. He was named to the league's All-Decade team for the 1920s and was considered one of the greatest players during the first 30 years of the NFL. Mike's speed and agility allowed him to pull and lead plays when playing on offense. On defense, Mike was known as a "deadly tackler," and his speed allowed him to "run plays down before they developed … he was so quick he could tail a guard from the opposite side and tackle the ball carrier before he reached the line of scrimmage."

Hall of Fame quarterback Benny Friedman (a Glenville grad) said this of Michalske more than a decade after Mike had retired: "I would put him down in my book as the best guard, bar none, I ever saw."

The Packers teammate and fellow Hall of Famer Johnny Blood told Mike Michalske: "He was as great as any football player Green Bay ever had. He had swift reflexes. He would start moving before his opponent. That was his chief asset, besides his tremendous fighting spirit."

Among his many honors, Mike Michalske is enshrined in the Pro Football Hall of Fame, the Green Bay Packers Hall of Fame, and the Wisconsin Athletic Hall of Fame.

William Earl Sprackling

Ironically, William Earl "Bill" Sprackling was born on Sept. 26, 1890, just about one month before the first high school football game in Cleveland history was played. However, when he was finally old enough to play high school and college football, Bill Sprackling was the best of his day and one of the city's all-time greats.

Sprackling attended East High School, where he was the quarterback in 1906 and 1907 on one of the best early Cleveland area high school teams. Despite tipping the scales at a mere 124 pounds, small for a football player even back then, Sprackling led the team to a 7-0-0 record and the Cleveland city championship in 1906.

Sprackling's big season, however, came in 1907. Once again, he led East High to the city championship with a perfect 7-0-0 record as the team outscored the opposition by a whopping 270-5. That season, Bill Sprackling also came in for some well-deserved personal recognition. At a time when only 11 players were named to the local All-Scholastic First Team, the highest honor that a local player could receive at that time, Sprackling was not only named the All-Scholastic First Team quarterback. Still, he was honored to be named the team's captain. In describing his abilities, The Plain Dealer noted that Sprackling was fast and an excellent passer who used "rare judgment" when leading his team. When playing on defense, Sprackling was known as a sure tackler. (Players typically played both ways in those days.)

After graduating from East High, Sprackling continued his education at the Ivy League's Brown University. He played on the varsity football team in 1909, 1910, and 1911 and was named an All-America selection yearly. Sprackling's best season at Brown came in 1910. A unanimous First Team All-America selection that season, he was rated as not only the best quarterback in the country but also the best football player — and this was compared with such great players of that season, such as the legendary Jim Thorpe. Ivy League historian George Trevor called Sprackling an "eye-dazzler in the open field, a flashy punt-handler and bulls-eye passer. In addition, he could drop-kick field goals from nearly mid-field under pressure. As a quarterback, he was a marvel at unerringly calling plays, picking out soft spots in an opponent's defense."

During his career at Brown, Bill Sprackling set records for the most field goals kicked in a game, a season, and a job. His record for kickoff return yardage in a game, 147 yards, still stands today, more than 110 years after he set it. Perhaps Sprackling's most famous play came in 1909 during Brown's 21-8 upset win over Jim Thorpe and his Carlisle Indians; in that game, Sprackling ran back a kickoff 110 yards for a spectacular touchdown.

On Nov. 5, 1910, Brown was playing at Yale. The Bears had never defeated Yale, the best team of that era, in 18 previous encounters. Almost single-handedly, Bill Sprackling brought Brown's run of futility to an end. In that game, Sprackling kicked three field goals, completed five of six passes for 180 yards, made one touchdown, carried the ball nine times for 36 yards, and returned 13 punts for 150 yards and five kickoffs for 90 yards. In winning 21-0, the Brown football team amassed 608 yards — with Bill Sprackling alone accounting for an incredible 456 yards.

The great Walter Camp wrote about Sprackling's incredible performance against Yale: "Rarely has a quarterback on an American college 11 come out of a big contest with so fine a record. Sprackling, by his unexcelled play in every department, demonstrated more clearly than ever that he is the best quarterback in the country."

In 2005, ESPN published its "College Football Encyclopedia." One feature of the book was that ESPN reviewed the records of all the top players for each season from 1905 to 1934, the 30 years before the Heisman Trophy was first awarded in 1935. In 1910, they decided that Bill Sprackling would have won if the Heisman Trophy had been awarded that year. Sports Illustrated made a similar list in 2008, and again, Bill Sprackling was chosen as the 1910 Heisman winner.

After graduating from Brown, Bill Sprackling worked as an assistant coach at the school, a position he held when Brown University played in the 1916 Rose Bowl game in Pasadena, California. One of the stars of that Brown football team was running back Fritz Pollard, one of the great early African American college football players. When the Pasadena Hotel, where the team was staying, refused to allow Pollard to remain with the rest, Bill Sprackling demanded to see the hotel manager. According to an account published in

Sports Illustrated: "When the clerk refused (to give Pollard a room), Sprackling pounded on the desk bell and shouted, 'If there isn't a room for Fritz Pollard, none of us wants one.' The manager appeared, and Pollard got a room."

Bill Sprackling went on to have a very successful business career, eventually becoming the President and CEO of the Anaconda Wire and Cable Company.

Sprackling is enshrined in the Brown University Hall of Fame and the College Football Hall of Fame.

GYMNASTICS

Joe Giallombardo
Cleveland's Greatest Gymnast

Joe Giallombardo was born in Cleveland in 1917, the youngest of seven children. He took up gymnastics at East Tech under the direction of G. P. Thompson, the best gymnastics coach in Ohio then and one of the all-time greats. Giallombardo was the first person in Ohio to win the same event at the state gymnastics tournament three consecutive years, taking first place in tumbling in 1933-34-35. He also took first place in the long horse in 1934 and second in both the long horse and the parallel bars in 1935.

Following graduation from East Tech, Giallombardo continued his education and gymnastics career at the University of Illinois. At Illinois, Joe Giallombardo had one of the most excellent collegiate gymnastics careers ever. His most notable achievements include winning seven gold medals from 1938 to 1940, a record that still stands (though tied once), and winning the first three NCAA All-Around championships in 1938, 1939, and 1940.

Giallombardo would have been a star of the 1940 and 1944 Olympic Games, but those games were canceled due to World War II. During the war, he served his country as a training officer in the Navy. Following his military service, Giallombardo had an outstanding career as a high school gymnastics coach in Illinois. He is the only high school gymnastics coach to be honored twice by the College Coaches Association.

Joe Giallombardo received virtually every award available in gymnastics. Still, he is incredibly proud of the A.R. Rizzuto Award given to outstanding American athletes of Italian descent in any sport. Coach Giallombardo has been inducted into the U.S. Gymnastics Hall of Fame, the Illinois High School Gymnastics Coaches Hall of Fame, and the Greater Cleveland Sports Hall of Fame. He received a special Olympic judge's diploma at the 20th World Games in Dallas, Texas.

The ultimate gymnastics award, the Helms Hall of Fame Award, was presented to Giallombardo in 1966.

NATIONAL TRACK AND FIELD HALL OF FAME

Former Senate League athletes have been inducted into the National Track and Field Hall of Fame. Their biographies are extensively covered in the previous chapter—Olympians.

David Albritton – East Tech

Harrison Dillard – East Tech

Madeline Manning Mims – John Hay High School

Eleanor Montgomery – John Adams High School

Jesse Owens – East Tech

Stella Walsh – South High School

NATIONAL WRESTLING HALL OF FAME

Richard "Dick" Bonacci

A graduate of West High in 1952, Dick Bonnacci was only the second three-time state wrestling champion (1949, 1950, 1951) and undefeated all three seasons. At the University of Toledo, he was a three-time MAC champion (1953-1954-1955). After graduating from UT, Bonnacci started the wrestling program at Fenn College, later renamed Cleveland State University (CSU). In his 36 years as the CSU coach, his teams won 296 dual matches and had 31 winning seasons, including 17 consecutive ones from 1965 to 1981. His coaching at CSU produced eight All-Americans and sent wrestlers to 34 consecutive national championships.

Dick Bonnacci has been inducted into seven halls of fame, including the Greater Cleveland Sports Hall of Fame, the Ohio Wrestling Hall of Fame, and the National Wrestling Hall of Fame.

Pat Galbincea
Best Wrestling Writer Ever

Not every person who is outstanding in athletics does so on the field of play. One such legend is Pat Galbincea, acclaimed as the country's most excellent-ever high school wrestling writer. Galbincea graduated from John Marshall High School in 1965 and Cleveland State University in 1970. He began his long and distinguished reporting career with The Plain Dealer in 1969 while attending Cleveland State. While at The Plain Dealer, he covered many sports during his long and illustrious career, but his passion was wrestling in high school and college. Galbincea retired from The Plain Dealer in 2013 after a stellar career of 45 years.

His love of wrestling came out in his writing, which won him many awards and the respect and admiration of his peers. It all culminated in 2017 when Galbincea was inducted into the Ohio chapter of the National Wrestling Hall of Fame, the highest award for that sport. He was inducted into the Ohio Prep Sportswriters Association Hall of Fame in 2020 and twice won national wrestling writing awards.

Gary Abbott of USA Wrestling in Colorado Springs said of Galbincea: "He was an icon. He set a high standard for others to follow. ... He made a difference to people."

Bob Preusse, the high school editor of Amateur Wrestling News, a national publication, noted that Pat Galbincea is "... synonymous with the golden era of Cleveland wrestling. He was something. He got his referee's license but not to referee. He did it to help him better understand the sport and to be a better reporter. That's who he was."

Tim Rogers, a high school classmate of Galbincea's at John Marshall and a fellow reporter on The Plain Dealer's sports desk noted that "Galbincea's knowledge and dedication were incomparable."

As Tim Warsinskey, another Plain Dealer colleague, noted, "It was an honor to work with him. He made us all better."

Gene Gibbons

A member of the West High School Class of 1947, Gibbons was a three-time Ohio state wrestling runner-up. Moving on to Michigan State after graduation, Gibbons was named an All-American in 1950 and 1951. In 1951, he was both a Big Ten and NCAA champion. As an amateur wrestler, Gibbons was a national AAU Junior champion in 1948 and a five-time Lake Erie AAU champion.

Gene Gibbons went on to coach at John Marshall for 24 years, producing 13 individual state champions and leading the Lawyers to the 1961 state team championship. In 1969, Gibbons was named the Amateur News Coach of the Year.

In 1970, Gibbons was honored as a charter member of the Ohio Wrestling Hall of Fame. In 1976, he became a member of the inaugural class of the Greater Cleveland Sports Hall of Fame, and in 2012, Gibbons was inducted into the National Wrestling Hall of Fame.

Vincent R. Matteucci

Vince Matteucci was a native Clevelander and a graduate of West High School in 1952. A West High Wrestling team member during its heyday in the early 1950s, Vince was on the famous West High state championship team of 1951 that included six individual state champions. One is Matteucci, a record that has never been equaled or surpassed.

Often referred to as the Godfather of Ohio Wrestling, Vince Matteucci was involved in Ohio wrestling for over 60 years as an official and a rules interpreter. He was a prime mover in helping to establish the Ohio Wrestling Officials Association (OWOA). There is even an annual award given by the OWOA called the Vince Matteucci Person of the Year Award.

Matteucci has been inducted into every wrestling and wrestling official hall of fame, including the National Wrestling Hall of Fame and the Ohio Wrestling Hall of Fame. He has also received the Western Reserve Wrestling Officials Association Legend Award for his contributions to the sport.

CHAPTER 3

Special Awards & Accomplishments

> *Teams and athletes may not necessarily win a championship, yet their overall performance may be such that they earn special recognition. They may also have a truly unique accomplishment that has never been done before and that is possibly never to be repeated. This may be for a single season, a career, etc. Some exceptional Senate League athletes have merited awards of this type, and they are further recognized here.*

SENATE LEAGUE FIRSTS

A league as old as Cleveland's Senate League has had a few "firsts" over the years. Here are some of them:

- The first high school football game in Cleveland history, Oct. 20, 1890, in which Central High School, the oldest high school in the city (and the biggest west of the Appalachian Mountains), lost to University School, the newest high school in the city, barely a month old, by a score of 20-0.
- The first Ohio high school football state champion – Central High in 1895.
- The first basketball game in Cleveland between two high schools was played in 1898. Central defeated South High, 15-8.
- Charles "Doc" Freeman became Cleveland's first high school basketball coach when he coached the Central High team during the 1904-05 season. That team was one of the greatest basketball teams in Cleveland High School history, posting a record of 19-1 (that lone loss was by one point) and winning both the Cleveland and state championships.

- John Hay High School won the first state wrestling tournament in 1938. The John Hay wrestling team won the first four consecutive tournaments and five of the first six.
- In 1951, West High was not only the first Cleveland area wrestling team to be named National Champion but remains the only wrestling team in Ohio history with six individual champions in the same state tournament.

A UNIQUE OLYMPIC RECORD

In 1936, five East Tech High School graduates accomplished something that has never been equaled or surpassed. All five were on the U. S. Olympic team that went to Berlin for the Summer Olympics that year. As far as can be determined, no other high school in the United States has ever sent that many athletes to a single Olympic Games, summer or winter. Between them, these outstanding athletes won four gold medals, two silver medals, and one bronze medal.

The five athletes are as follows:

Jesse Owens – *Track – 4 Gold Medals 100m, 200m, long jump, 4x100 relay*

David Albritton – *Track – Silver Medal high jump*

Ted Kara – *Boxing – Boxing Team Captain*

George G. "Jackie" Wilson – *Boxing – Silver Medal, Bantamweight*

Louis Laurie – *Boxing – Bronze Medal, Flyweight*

In addition to these five athletes, a sixth Senate League alum participated in the 1936 Olympic Games. Stella Walsh, a South High graduate, was also a contestant at the 1936 games, running track for her native Poland. That made six Senate League alumni participate in the same Olympics, no doubt another first.

GLENVILLE FOOTBALL HONORS

All-Time Best Unit. The years 1998-2022 have produced some of the most significant accomplishments in the history of Senate League football. This is especially true of the Glenville team coached by Ted Ginn, a time called the golden era of Glenville High School football. Two aspects of those teams have been singled out for special recognition at the all-time national level.

The first of these honors goes to the defensive backfield unit that took the field for the Tarblooders in 2002. In 2019, the high school sports website MaxPreps came up with its choices for the most outstanding offensive and defensive position units of all time in high school football. As MaxPreps readily admits, the options for those all-time units were the most challenging problems to solve, but, as they also admitted, "MaxPreps is going to give it a shot." When MaxPreps issued its choices in September of 2019, part of its criteria was as follows: "After extensive research of the Pro-Football-Reference high school database for NFL players, here are the top positional groups to play at the prep level. We tried to look for players who competed on highly successful teams and performed well at the high school level and above."

When the selection process came to defense—and defensive backs in particular—the unit that was selected as the all-time best in the history of high school football was the one that played for Glenville High School during the 2002 season. The three defensive backs noted were Donte Whitner, Dareus Hiley, and Ted Ginn Jr. This is what the MaxPreps write-up about that unit and those players had to say:

"Defensive Backs - Glenville (Cleveland, Ohio) – 2002: "Always one of the most competitive programs in Northern Ohio, Glenville fielded a tremendous defensive backfield in the early 2000s. Donte Whitner was one of the top recruits in the state in 2002, and he earned special mention all-state as a senior before heading to Ohio State. Dareus Hiley was considered a spectacular all-around athlete and earned special mention all-state before accepting a scholarship with the Buckeyes. Ted Ginn Jr. was a junior on the team and one of the fastest players in the country. He went on to earn USA Today Defensive Player of the Year honors as a senior in 2003. Ginn Jr. played at Ohio State but was used more as a receiver. Whitner was All-Big 10 in college and was a two-time Pro Bowl selection in the NFL. Hiley ran into academic problems in college and never played for the Buckeyes. Ginn Jr. was a three-time All-American at Ohio State, is in his 13th season in the NFL, and ranks among the all-time leaders in career return touchdowns."

GREATEST HIGH SCHOOL ATHLETES

In 2019, in May of that year, MaxPreps chose the 50 most outstanding high school athletes. Some of the criteria for selection into this group are as follows:

"While many excellent high school lists focus on performance at the college and professional level and also include athletes who played just one sport, this list tries to focus on all-around athletes who participate and excel in two or more sports. So some of the greatest high school athletes you won't see on this list include basketball-only greats like Oscar Robertson and Lew Alcindor or football-only greats like Peyton Manning or Dick Butkus. Instead, you will find names like Dwight Eddleman, Stan Rome, and Basil Shabazz — outstanding all-around high school athletes who saw some time at the professional level but were genuinely fantastic at the high school level.

"This is not to say that professional and college performance is not considered. Excellence at those levels helps give context and confirm greatness at the high school level. However, a lack of excellent credentials at the college or professional level doesn't preclude the great all-around high school athletes from making this list. No athletes who have graduated in the past three years (2016-2018) were considered for the list."

A list of this sort, even with as many as 50 players, is exclusive. Only two Ohioans made the list. Coming in at #26 is LeBron James from Akron's St. Vincent-St. Mary High School. The other is from the Senate League: Ted Ginn Jr., Glenville Class of 2004, who was chosen at #36 on this list. The following is what MaxPreps had to say about Ginn:

"Ted Ginn Jr., Glenville (Cleveland), 2004: The USA Today Defensive Player of the Year as a senior at Glenville, Ginn was also one of the fastest players in the nation. He excelled in track and field, especially the 110-meter hurdles, where he had the best times in the nation as a junior and senior. A three-time football All-American in college at Ohio State, Ginn has played 12 seasons in the NFL."

In June of 2020, MaxPreps also named Ted Ginn Jr. as the top male high school athlete in the country for 2004, noting that Ted was "a star in football and track and field, Ginn was USA Today's Defensive Player of the Year in football, and he recorded some of the fastest hurdle and sprint times in the nation in track."

HEISMAN TROPHY WINNER

Troy Smith, Glenville Class of 2002, was named the winner of the Heisman Memorial Trophy on Dec. 9, 2006. In winning the 2006 Heisman Trophy, Smith took 91.6% of the first-place votes, a record that would stand for 13 years. His margin of victory, 1,662 votes, was the second largest in the award's history. Troy Smith joined Les Horvath (1944), Vic Janowicz (1950), Howard "Hopalong" Cassady (1955), Archie Griffin (1974 and 1975), and Eddie George (1995) as Ohio State's only Heisman winners. Troy is the second Senate League player to win the Heisman, Les Horvath (Rhodes) being the first.

The year 2006 was a banner year for Troy Smith. The Heisman Trophy was just the biggest and most prestigious of the many awards that came his way that year: consensus All-America, Sporting News college football "Player of the Year," Fiesta Bowl MVP, Walter Camp collegiate "Player of the Year," Davey O'Brien Award (best quarterback in the NCAA), Ohio State MVP, Associated Press Player of the Year, and Chicago Tribune Silver Football - Big Ten Most Valuable Player.

In 2014, Troy Smith's number at Ohio State, 10, was retired, one of eight numbers so honored.

NATIONALLY RENOWNED SWIMMERS

East High's swim team was formed in 1913. Although the team lasted barely a dozen years, it had some local success in winning several Senate and Cleveland championships from 1919 to 1924. However, in 1922 and 1923, the team achieved its most tremendous success with several national championships and setting at least one national record.

Following the 1922 Cleveland interscholastic swim championship, which East High won for the third consecutive season, the boys from East High still had one more meet in which they would compete. After a rally at the school, five 1922 East High swim team members, along with Coach Harold Ulen and the team manager, boarded a train for Chicago to participate in the National Interscholastic Swim Championships sponsored by the Illinois Athletic Club. The five boys were Rudolph Cooks, Arthur Matsu, Donald Hester, Ted Abrams, and Town. They would be competing against 14 other teams, many of which came with upwards of two dozen boys.

What the East High team lacked in numbers, it made up for in skill. Arthur Matsu won the national championship in the diving competition, with teammate Town finishing second. Ted Abrams took home the national championship in his specialty, the plunge, covering the 60-yard course in 26.20 seconds (Abrams tied the world record in the preliminary round but fell a little short of that time in winning the finals). Don Hester brought home a second-place finish in the 220-yard freestyle.

When the final points were totaled, East High had finished a very commendable third and returned to Cleveland with two national championship swimmers. By today's standards, Matsu, Town, Abrams, and Hester would all be recognized as high school All-Americans.

The 1922 swim season marked the high point of East

High swimming, but there was still some glory to be had. In 1923, Melvin Mott brought some individual glory to East High when he set a National Record in the 100-yard backstroke with a time of 1:10.40.

Although Ted Abrams had graduated in 1923, he was not finished in the pool. In 1924, Abrams set the world record in his specialty with a plunge of 84'6". He held that world record for only a brief two years, but his distance is still the fourth best in the world and remains the best by an American.

RUNNING AWAY WITH THE CHAMPIONSHIPS

In the 115 years (1908-2023) of the OHSAA boys state track meet, Cleveland's Senate Athletic League teams have finished first 42 times and as runner-ups another 18 times. This gives the Senate a first- or second-place team finish in over half of all state track meets. There were also three times when Senate schools finished in both first and second place: 1943 – East Tech first and John Marshall second; 1973 – Glenville first and Collinwood second; 1991 – John Marshall first and John Adams second.

Unsurprisingly, a few Senate League schools have won more state track championships than others. Glenville leads the state with 18 track titles, all coming since 1959; East Tech has won 13 state championships before 1955. East Tech, with seven runner-up finishes, has a combined 20 first or second finishes, but Glenville's four runner-up placings give the Tarblooders a state high of 22 first or second finishes. Both totals are the best in Ohio, regardless of division.

HALL OF FAME TRIFECTA

To have one alumnus from a high school inducted into a national sports hall of fame is quite an honor for that school, but what if your school had athletes in three different halls of fame?

East Tech grad Ike Smith has discovered a unique accomplishment by graduates of his alma mater. As best as can be determined, East Tech is one of only three high schools in the country with graduates in three different sports halls of fame. Jesse Owens and Harrison Dillard are enshrined in the National Track & Field Hall of Fame, while Bob Brown is enshrined in the Pro Football Hall of Fame, and Willie Smith is in the Naismith Basketball Hall of Fame as a member of the 1932-33 New York Rens basketball team.

East Tech is the only school in the country with graduates in those three halls of fame. Galileo HS in San Francisco has grads in the basketball, baseball, and football halls of fame. In contrast, Mc Clymonds HS in Oakland, California, has alums in the basketball, baseball, and track halls of fame.

EAST TECH – HIGH SCHOOL NATIONAL TRACK CHAMPIONS – 1933

By early June 1933, the East Tech High School track team was riding high. The team, coached by Ed Weil, had won three consecutive Cleveland city track championships and the last two OHSAA state track titles. But team members still had one more mountain to climb. In June 1933, the East Tech track team was entered in the National Scholastic Track Championships, held in Chicago on June 16-17.7

Only four members of the team were entered. Senior sprinter Jesse Owens and high jumper David Albritton were obvious choices. The other two team members going to Chicago were members of the relay teams: sprinters Jerome Williams and Alfred Storey.

Despite having only four team members at the national championships, along with Coach Weil and Charlie Riley from Fairmount Junior High (in essence, Jesse Owens' coach), the team was entered in eight different events. Owens was entered in the 100yd. and 220yd. dashes and the broad jump. David Albritton was entered in the high jump and both the low and high hurdle competitions. Williams, "probably the best shot putter in Ohio" (PD), entered that event. Storey was entered in the 100yd. and 220yd. dashes with Jesse Owens.

For the eighth event, all four boys made up the 880yd. relay team (4x220yd.). However, this was not East Tech's regular relay team. While Owens, Williams, and Storey usually ran that race, the regular fourth man, Tiff, was left back in Cleveland as a cost-saving move. In explaining this move, *The Plain Dealer* noted, "In dropping Tiff from the relay ... the Carpenters will lose no strength for although Albritton has never run 220 yards in a major meet, he can give even Owens an interesting fight in practice."

The six members of the East Tech contingent left Cleveland by car early on Thursday, June 15. The preliminary events would be held on the afternoon of the 16th, with the semifinals and finals on Saturday afternoon, June

17. Once the six East Techers reached Chicago, one small problem came up. Jesse Owens was quickly the most well-known of the high schoolers at this event. Still, the national collegiate championships were also being held that weekend, and college recruiters almost immediately besieged Owens. He found it nearly impossible to get himself off the track. The distractions became so great that Coach Weil finally moved Owens out of the hotel where the team was staying and into the local YMCA under an assumed name – problem solved.

The headline on The Plain Dealer sports page on Sunday, June 18, 1933, read as follows:

**"Owens Shatters 3 World Scholastic Marks
Blazes 100 in 9.4 as East Tech wins U.S. Title."**

Competing against boys from about 100 schools, the Scarabs scored 54 points, easily outdistancing second-place Wichita North (KS) High School and its 35 points and third-place Fort Collins (CO) High School and its 32-1/11 points. This is how the Scarabs did it.

In the preliminary of the 100yd. dash, Jesse Owens tied the world high school record of 9.6 seconds; it was the third time that year that he had matched that record. In the finals, Owens got off to a somewhat slow start because he was not used to running from starting blocks; he usually dug a small hole in the track to place his foot. He was just in fourth place at the halfway point of the race, but he flew over the final 50 yards and won by 2 yards – and was pulling away from the rest of the runners as he crossed the finish line.

Owens' 9.4 seconds was a new high school world record and tied the then-world record. As The Plain Dealer noted, it was the fastest 100-yard dash ever run by a boy still in high school.

Just "a few minutes later" (PD), Owens was running in the finals of the 220. In this race, he got out in front early and stayed there. His winning time, 20.7, was four-tenths of a second better than the world prep record and only one-tenth of a second off the world record.

In the broad jump, Owens had already won the event with a leap of 24 feet 7/8 inches, but he still had three jumps remaining. On one of those jumps, he covered 24'9-5/8", a whopping 7 inches farther than the current high school record. (At the Senate meet two weeks earlier, Jesse had jumped 24'11¼", but that was considered an unofficial record.)

The East Tech team very nearly won the 880yd. relay race, but a few minor problems cost them precious tenths of a second. Jerome Williams was the leadoff runner; he false started and was set back 1 yard for the restart. Dave Albritton was running second, and Alfred Storey was third for East Tech, but both runners "were partly blocked" (PD) as they made their way around the track. Jesse Owens was the team's anchorman. He "took the baton 12 yards behind the Wichita (Kansas) anchorman and was fast making up ground when he was forced to break stride around the last turn." (PD)

These little incidents cost the Scarabs a gold medal in the race, but they did finish second in the preliminary running of the 880yd. Relay, the East Tech team finished at 1:30.5, breaking the then-world scholastic record by two-tenths of a second.

David Albritton added to his team's point total by finishing second in the 120-yard high hurdles, then winning the high jump with a leap of 6'2".

It was a total East Tech team effort to win the Scholastic National Championship, but Jesse Owens was quickly the star of the meet. The 30 points scored by Jesse Owens Except were more than any of the other 84 teams that had scored points, except for the second-and third-place teams. The Plain Dealer's account of the Meet noted that Jesse Owens' performance was "the greatest display of individual brilliance in the 29-year history of the national interscholastic track and field championships."

A FAMILY AFFAIR

More than 100 years ago, writer E. D. Soden described the Delahanty brothers of Cleveland as the "greatest baseball family in the history of the game," and they still might be. In part, this is because the brothers, five of them—all of whom grew up in Cleveland and most of whom attended and/or graduated from Central High School—comprise the most extensive set of brothers ever to play major league baseball. There would have been six Delahanty boys in the majors, but the youngest brother, Will, gave up that dream after eight years of knocking around the minor leagues.

The oldest brother, Ed, was quickly the most famous and the best of this significant league quintet. Born on Oct. 30, 1867, Ed, of all of the Delahanty brothers, is the only one known for sure to have graduated from Central High. Ed, who was primarily a left fielder but played infield occasionally, started his major league career in 1888 with the Philadelphia Quakers, then moved to the Cleveland Infants in 1890. In 1891, Ed began a 10-year stint playing for the Philadelphia Phillies before joining the Washington Senators for his final two years in baseball.

Referred to as "Big Ed" by sports reporters and "Del"

by teammates and fans, Ed Delahanty's achievements in baseball are among the most extraordinary of any player, and some of them have remained unequaled to this day. While not much is ever written about his fielding ability, Ed's achievements were almost legendary when he stepped into the batter's box. He was the National League batting champion in 1899, led the league in home runs in 1893 and 1896, and led the senior circuit in RBIs in 1893, 1896, and 1899. With a lifetime batting average of .346 (fifth best, all-time), Ed was the first player ever to hit 400 or better in three different seasons; the only other player to match that accomplishment is the legendary Ty Cob

On July 13, 1896, Ed hit four home runs in the same game; three years later, he hit four doubles in the same game. He is still the only player in Major League Baseball history to achieve that unique feat.

Ed Delahanty died in 1903, apparently falling from a train into the Niagara River while traveling between Buffalo, New York, and Niagara Falls (the actual cause of his fall has never been determined); he is buried at Cleveland's Calvary Cemetery. He was inducted into the Major League Baseball Hall of Fame in 1945.

Tom, an infielder, was the next Delahanty brother to make it to the major leagues. In his brief career in the big leagues, Tom Delahanty played in just 19 games from 1894-1897, including a short time with the Cleveland Spiders. His lifetime batting average was just .239.

After Ed, Jim Delahanty was the most successful of the five brothers in the major leagues. In a career that spanned 13 seasons from 1901-1915, Jim played infield for eight teams, primarily at second base. He is the only Delahanty brother to ever play in the World Series, hitting .346 (lifetime .283) for the Detroit Tigers in the 1909 Series. Jim had the dubious distinction of getting hit by a pitch 92 times during his career.

Frank Delahanty, another outfielder by profession, played in the American League from 1905-1908 and then in the Federal League in 1914 and 1915. This included one season with the hometown Cleveland Naps (named after star player Napoleon Lajoie), in which he played in just 15 games with a "lusty" .173 batting average. Frank is the only Delahanty brother who did not go to Central High. His parents, devout Catholics, sent him to Saint Ignatius High School.

The last of the Delahanty brothers to play major league baseball was Joe, who played three seasons (1906-1908) with the St. Louis Cardinals.

LIKE FATHER, LIKE SON

In 2023, Ted Ginn Sr. was a member of the first class of the National High School Football Hall of Fame in Canton at the Pro Football Hall of Fame. A 1973 graduate of Glenville High School, Coach Ginn's career had a humble beginning as a Glenville security guard and volunteer assistant football coach, progressing to a paid assistant after 10 years.

In 1997, he was named the team's head coach, and things have never been the same for the Tarblooders. Under Coach Ginn's leadership and mentoring, over the last 26 seasons, the Tarblooders have had only one losing season, have lost only one Senate League football game, and have qualified for the state football playoffs 20 times. And as a little—make that a lot—of icing on the Glenville cake, Coach Ginn has led the football team to two consecutive Division IV state football championships in 2022 and 2023. Those are the only state football championships a Senate League school won during the playoff era.

Ted Ginn Sr. is also the track coach at Glenville, and he has led the Tarblooders thin clads to the last eight of their state high 18 championships.

Not to be outdone, just one year after his father, Ted Ginn Jr., was inducted into the 2024 National High School Football Hall of Fame class. Ted Jr's athletic career started at Glenville in the early 2000s, playing football and running track – and excelling at both the state and national level. After graduation, he continued his career at The Ohio State University. After graduating from OSU, Ted enjoyed a very successful 14-year career in the NFL. Since retiring from professional football, Ted has returned to Cleveland, where he works with his father, mentoring the Ginn Elite youth teams.

Ted Ginn Sr. and Ted Ginn Jr. – the only father-son duo in the National High School Football Hall of Fame.

PART II

Gone But Not Forgotten

CHAPTER 4

> ## CENTRAL HIGH SCHOOL
>
> *Established in 1847 on East 55th Street, Central High School was the first public high school— the first school to provide secondary education at public expense— in the country west of the Allegheny Mountains. By the early 1890s, it was also the most significant public high school in the United States, with an enrollment of more than 1,500 students. Over its first 100 years, the school changed location thrice, settling at its final residence on East 40th Street in 1940. In 1952, Central High and East Tech merged at the East Tech location and retained the East Tech name; the old Central High School became Central Junior High.*

BASKETBALL

The earliest known basketball games between two high schools in Cleveland occurred in 1898, and Central High was involved in both games. In the first of these, played on Jan. 19, 1898, Central defeated South High by a score of 15-8. About three weeks later, Central and West High met on the court, with Central again coming away the winner, 14-5.

The area's next several years of high school basketball were quite haphazard. However, the 1902-1903 season would emerge as the first season in which Central High shined on the basketball court. Except for an early season defeat, 35-23, at the hands of the Western Reserve University team, Central went through its schedule unscathed.

On Jan. 2, 1903, the team defeated Canton High School (later to be Canton McKinley), 24-12. This would prove to be one of the season's most important games. With the loss to Central, the only blemish on its record, Canton wanted a rematch since it was claiming the state championship. Central refused, the manager of the team writing the following to The Plain Dealer on March 13: "The Central high basketball team beat the Canton team on the latter's home floor.

Central has not been beaten [by a high school team] this year and, if victorious at Port Clinton on March 21, will have a clear title to the state championship. Why would Central give Canton another game when she has nothing to gain and everything to lose?"

On March 21, playing at Port Clinton High School, the Central boys trailed 6-2 at the half. They battled back during the second half, took the lead with just 30 seconds left to play, and held on for a 15-13 win. This victory solidified Central's claim to the state high school basketball championship. The Plain Dealer noted: "As a result [of this win], the Forest City team is not now hampered in the chase for the state championship."

Although it ended the season as the recognized state champion, the Central High team, a member of the YMCA league, did not win its league title. The team chose to "not enter the championship series, studies and other work interfering." (PD)

In 1904, there was the "scholastic championship series," a series of 10 games between the city's high schools to determine the Cleveland champion. Once again, Central fielded a competitive team, but key losses to East and West High Schools eliminated them from the championship picture.

The 1904-05 season would again find the Central basketball team in top form. The Central Cagers cruised through the season from the opening tipoff on Dec. 21, 1904, in a game against the Central Alumni (won by the varsity squad 25-20). By Feb. 8, 1905, the team was 11-0 and won its games by an average of 18 points. On Feb. 10, the team ran up against a tough bunch from Mansfield High School and suffered a loss by the slimmest of margins, 27-26 – it would prove to be the only blemish on Central's record that season.

Two weeks later, "in the greatest game ever played in the Central High gymnasium, West High, the aspirants for the interscholastic championship, went down to defeat" by a score of 22-19. This victory clinched Central High the Cleveland interscholastic championship, but they still had three challenging games against top out-of-town rivals. The day after that big win over West High, Central had a rematch with Mansfield High. This time, Central emerged victorious, 22-13 – both teams now have just one loss each. Central defeated Canton High on March 3 by a score of 25-19.

With that victory, Central's interscholastic season had ended, and they had won the Ohio high school championship – or so they thought. The very same day that Central defeated Canton, they received a letter from Fremont High School, a team that was also claiming the state championship. The Fremont team was challenging Central to a game to decide the state title, but they did so in a very unflattering way, saying that if Central did not accept the challenge, they were "cowards and babies." B. Pasini, the captain of the Central team, responded with a letter to the sports editor of The Plain Dealer, stating that Central "does not bar any interscholastic team in the country" and said that "if they are game, then play us."

A game with Fremont was quickly arranged for March 8 at Central High. As The Plain Dealer noted the following day, "Central High wound up its scholastic season last night in a blaze of glory by winning the state championship, defeating Fremont High, the only logical factor left, at Central gymnasium by the decisive score of 29-16."

On March 11, Central's season ended with a 28-17 win over the Hirams of Hiram House, the "junior champions of Ohio."

In one of the finest seasons ever played by a Cleveland area school, the 1905 city and state champions representing Central High School finished with a record of 19-1, outscoring their opponents 636-347.

It would be another 10 seasons before Central High again perched itself atop the Senate and Cleveland basketball rankings. Led by head coach Chauncey B. (C.B.) Lewis would dominate the area's scholastic basketball scene for three years running.

The 1914-1915 Senate basketball race was a tight one. On Feb. 27, East High handed Central a 14-12 defeat "in one of the fastest and roughest contests ever seen in interscholastic games." (PD) Both teams were now tied in the Senate standings with 6-1 records. On March 5, Central closed its season with an 18-5 win over West Tech. East played South High (3-4) the next day, needing a victory to share the Senate and city titles with Central. Instead, South pulled off a big upset by handing East a 14-13 defeat, handing the Senate and Cleveland championships to Central High.

The team representing Central during the 1915-16 season was not supposed to be that good, but by season's end, it was recognized as one of the best high school basketball teams Cleveland had ever seen. Captain Al Goldhamer led the team as forward, and Frank Civiletto at guard. These two players were one-two, respectively, on the city's list of top scorers that season. The other three starters were Abe Greenspun (F), Fred Schoff (C), and Alex Michalsky (G).

By mid-February, the Central team was 7-0 and outscored the opposition by an average of 37-10. In a big midseason showdown, Central defeated East Tech 38-5. Central went on to finish the season undefeated at 11-0. An article in The Plain Dealer on April 1, 1916, noted that the Central High basketball team, besides being the Senate League champion, was also the Cleveland and Midwest champion. How good was this Central High basketball team? In an unprecedented move, all three Cleveland newspapers named the entire Central High starting quintet - Goldhamer, Civiletto, Greenspun, Schoff, and Michalsky – to the city's All-Scholastic First Team.

It was more of the same for the Central High School basketball team in the 1916-1917 season. Another undefeated campaign and, according to the prestigious Spalding's Official Basketball Guide, a second consecutive Cleveland championship. On March 16, Central squared off against Pittsburgh's city champion, Schenley High School (18-2). The Clevelanders kept their record clean with another big win against another Midwest opponent — and again gained the Midwest championship. That year, Central again dominated Cleveland's All-Scholastic team, with Abe Greenspun, Frank Civiletto, and Fred Schoff (his third time) being named to the First Team.

Frank Civiletto deserves special mention, as he might have been the most outstanding athlete ever to represent Central High School. He played football (four times All-Scholastic), basketball (two times All-Scholastic), tennis, and ran track — and excelled in each sport. On the basketball team, he led the city in scoring three times. In 1917, Civiletto set local records in the shot put and discus. He coached and played on the school's tennis team that same year. On Jan. 21, 1918, The Plain Dealer said of him, "...one of the gamest and greatest athletes developed by the Cleveland high schools."

Civiletto continued his education at Springfield (Mass.) College, where he was a small college All-America selection and football team captain in 1922. After graduating from Springfield, Frank returned to Cleveland, where he coached football, basketball, bowling, track, and tennis at Central High from 1923 to 1941. He led the Central football team to the city's first Charity Game in 1931. From 1941 to 1962, he coached at Glenville.

Frank Civiletto is enshrined in the Central-East Tech Hall of Fame, the Greater Cleveland Sports Hall of Fame, and the Springfield College Athletic Hall of Fame.

The late 1920s saw Central again at the top of the Senate basketball standings. In 1926, Central defeated East High, 21-13, in the season finale for both teams — clinching the Senate championship for the red and blue. In 1927, now coached by former player Frank Civiletto, Central again took Senate League honors with a record of 6-1. In 1935, Central won its last Senate League basketball championship, going undefeated in league play with a record of 9-0. Central never again won an overall Senate League championship. Still, in 1949, 1950, and 1952, the team finished first in the East Senate but lost each season to the West Senate titleholder in the Cleveland City championship game.

FOOTBALL

Football started in Cleveland's high schools in 1890 with the formation of the Cleveland School Athletic Association. There were four original members of the Association: Central High School, University School (which had just opened in June of that year), and the Case Institute and Adelbert College first-year teams.

Each game between the Association's four teams was called a "championship game" or a "game of the championship series," the championship being that of the City of Cleveland. The first of these games occurred on Oct. 25, 1890, at 2:30 p.m., between University School and Central High, and was the first interscholastic football game ever played in Cleveland. Although the University School had only existed for four months, its team achieved a 20-0 victory.

The Central High team was not very good in 1891 or 1892, but from 1893 to 1897, Central High would rule Cleveland's interscholastic football scene. 1893, only two Association games took place, with Central High emerging victorious in both and thus winning the city championship. Central also won the Cleveland city championship the following season, with the team's great halfback, "Bud" Dautel, scoring the game's only touchdown in the rivalry game with University School on a fumble recovery.

Although Central lost the city championship to University School in 1895, the High team (as they were often referred) did manage to come away with another, even more significant, honor. The Central High team was declared the champion of the state of Ohio – the first high school football team ever to be awarded that honor. By the day's standard, a distinction was made between the University School, a "prep" school, and Central, a "high" school. University School was considered the "prep" champion of northern Ohio, while Central High was the "high school" champion of the State of Ohio.

In 1896 and 1897, Central and University School met in their traditional season-ending game at League Park before large crowds. As had been the case over the last several seasons, this game would decide Cleveland's championship. The Central High boys won the title both years, giving them four Cleveland championships in the previous five seasons. Ironically, the one year that they were not Cleveland champions, 1895, they had been declared state champions.

Central High would not rise to the top of the Cleveland high school football scene again until 1900, one of the best seasons that the High team (as they were often called) had ever enjoyed. Not only did they again win the city championship, but playing a varied schedule of teams from around the northern half of Ohio, Central had compiled a record of 3-1-1, its only loss coming against the team from Masten Park High School in Buffalo, New York.

That 1900 season was the first time since high school football began in Cleveland that Central did not play University School. Central arranged a game with Columbus North High School to replace this traditional match-up. Since North was considered the champion of southern Ohio, this game had "state championship" written all over it. The game was played at Case Institute's Adelbert Field on Saturday, Nov. 17, a terrible day with a cold drizzle and the occasional snowflake falling and with the field "covered inches with slush and water." (PD) The Central team pushed across a touchdown in the first half, with the goal kick giving the Clevelanders a 6-0 lead that held up for the rest of the game.

Having beaten the southern Ohio champions, the people at Central High believed they were now the state champions. It would not be that easy. Several other teams also claimed that title, including Oberlin High School (no losses and only a tie with Central to mar its record) and Youngstown Rayen High School (4-1-1). Eventually, it was decided that all three teams would share the Ohio high school football championship for 1900, giving Central High its second state championship.

The Public Schools Athletic League, commonly known as the Senate Athletic League or simply the Senate, was formed in 1905, of which Central High was a charter member along with West, South, and Lincoln high schools. The first Senate League football championship battle that year came down to the season's final game on Nov. 25. Central entered the game with a record of 4-3-2, while Lincoln was 5-2-1, but both teams were undefeated in league play. Central scored an early touchdown to take a 6-0 lead at the half, then added two more touchdowns in the second half to come away with an 18-4 victory and the first Senate football championship.

The 1906 Senate race was very close – and had an astonishing finish. In the final and deciding game of the season, Lincoln and West High both entered with 2-1-0 league marks. Central High had already finished its season with a 3-1-0 Senate record. The winner of the

Lincoln-West clash would thus end up tied with Central for the league title. So what happened? Lincoln and West played to a 6-6 tie, leaving Central to take home its second Senate crown!

The 1907 Senate championship would come down to the games played between West, Central, and Lakewood (having joined the Senate that year but only remaining a league member for that one year). Lakewood, in an upset, defeated Central 7-0. West High remained undefeated by handing the "suburbanites" from Lakewood their only league loss, 5-0. However, Central, on a 90-yard touchdown pass play and a touchdown from a blocked punt, gave West High its only league loss, 10-0. All three teams ended with identical 4-1-0 league records. Since there were no Senate provisions for tiebreakers, Central, Lakewood, and West shared the league title for 1907.

Central High went winless in 1908, but the High team returned in 1909 with a truly incredible season.

The 1909 season's first week would produce one of the year's key games. In a match-up usually reserved for the season finale, Central High and University School tangled on Saturday, Oct. 2. Playing under new head coach Merril Barden, Central surprised most everyone by taking a 6-0 lead at the half on two field goals. Adding a touchdown on a 40-yard return of a fumble recovery, Central came away with a big 11-0 win over the Preps, a loss that would prove very costly for University School.

Central's big win was followed by Senate League victories over Lincoln, 32-0; West High, 9-0; South, 36-0; Tech, 13-0; and Glenville, 11-0. Closing its Senate schedule on Saturday, Nov. 13, Central's Joe Blue booted a 47-yard dropkick field goal, providing the only points in Central's 3-0 victory over East High.

Central's thrilling victory earned the team its fourth Senate championship in the league's first five seasons. Having won the Senate title, Central High was trying to duplicate East's effort of 1908 by also copping the Cleveland championship. Standing in Central's way was the team from Shaw High School. The whole season, and the 1909 city championship, came down to literally the last few seconds of this most crucial game.

The contest had been "one of the best that had ever been played on a local gridiron between two preparatory schools. From start to finish, the game was a battle royal..." (PD), but with time running out, the score was as it had been before the opening kickoff, 0-0. With three ticks left on the clock, Central lined up in field goal formation with their fullback, Burton Coates, preparing to try the drop kick from Shaw's 30-yard line.

Central had already missed on no fewer than five previous field goal attempts. Goodman, the Central quarterback, saw that all the Shaw defenders were massed on the line of scrimmage to block Coates' kick again.

Goodman quickly ran back and whispered something into Coates' ear. When the ball was snapped, "the Shaw players charged fast and jumped in front of Coates to intercept the anticipated kick..." (PD). Instead of a kick, Coates let loose with a pass downfield to Goodman, who caught the ball and made for the end zone. The only Shaw defender who did not rush the kicker hit Goodman at the 5-yard line. Goodman went down, but he rolled over the goal line before the other Shaw players could stop him. Although Coach Canfield of Shaw protested the touchdown, the referee allowed it to stand since Goodman was not in anyone's grasp — no knee on the ground rule back then.

Central had done it! A 5-0 victory! A perfect 8-0-0 season. Unscored upon. Senate Champions! Cleveland's Champions! It's not a bad start for Central's first-year head coach, Merril Barden.

As in 1909, the 1910 Senate League championship would again be a two-team race between Central High and East High. Central and East went through the season's first five games, all against Senate foes, unscathed. Tied atop the Senate League, Central and East were also in the thick of it for the Cleveland championship.

On Friday, November 11, Central and East met at Shaw Field to decide on the Senate championship. "The temperature was not many degrees short of the freezing point. An almost steady north wind of considerable velocity swept across the field" (PD). Shaw Field was covered with 6 inches of snow, but the contest went on as scheduled. In a game where East appeared to have the better, the only points scored came late in the fourth quarter. East, punting from its end zone, had the kick blocked and recovered by Central in the end zone for a touchdown. The kick for goal was good, giving Central High a 6-0 win and its second straight Senate League championship. However, a 23-14 loss to University School the following week would cost Central the city championship, which went to the Preps.

After the 1910 season, Central was well represented on the local postseason "all-star" football teams. Six of the boys made The Plain Dealer's All-Senate team, four of whom also made the paper's All-Scholastic squad; three also made the All-Scholastic team put out by the Cleveland Leader.

It would be a few more years before Central again contended for the Senate championship. The race for that title in 1914 was one of the closest and most competitive the Senate League had yet seen. Central and East High, along with an upstart West High team, would battle for the league championship during the latter half of the season.

Heading into the final weeks of league play, Central (4-0-1) and West High (3-1-0) both had a chance to finish atop the Senate. On Saturday, Nov. 7, Central's hopes of another league title suffered a considerable blow when East High "sprung one of the biggest surprises of the season by defeating Central's pre-supposed championship eleven by a score of 15-0." (PD) All West High had to do was beat East Tech and West Tech, and the Cowboys would capture their first Senate title. But it was time for another upset as the hard-charging East Techers (ending the season with three wins and a tie) knocked off West High by a 9-0 count. Although West High beat West Tech, Central High (6-1-1), with some help, had backed into the Senate crown for 1914, just edging out East High (5-1-2).

Central High's next and last great season of football came in 1931. In its second game of the season, the "unheralded 11" (PD) from Central High upset the defending state champions from Lorain High School, 12-7. Central and East Tech would end the season with one loss in one of the closest Senate football races in many years. However, Central would be named the Senate champion by playing only one tie game, while East Tech had played three draws.

In 1931 and until 1937, a Charity Game committee selected the two teams to play in the Charity Game for the Cleveland championship. That committee selected Central High as one of the two Charity Game participants in its Senate championship. The other team selected for that first Charity Game represented Cathedral Latin School.

Central High had some truly star players in 1931, and it all started with head coach Frank Civiletto. Civiletto, a future Central-East Tech Hall of Fame inductee, was an All-Senate/All-Scholastic football player at Central for four years (Class of 1919) and was known as a halfback "who fired passes with startling accuracy." (PD)

Perhaps the best player on the field for either team in that first Charity Game, Central's Tony Patti, could do it all. Playing at either halfback or quarterback and sometimes at the end, Patti was "one of the best passers and kickers ever to play in the district. His kicking and running leave little to be desired - and wait till you see him throw that apple." (PD) Patti would also later be inducted into the Central-East Tech Hall of Fame.

When he was not throwing the ball, Central quarterback Henry McGinnis was often on the receiving end of Tony Patti's aerials. However, the primary pass catcher for Coach Civiletto's team was Paul Rose. Although opposing defenses knew the ball usually came Rose's way, they could seldom stop him. Rose was the fourth member of that great team to be inducted into the Central-East Tech Hall of Fame.

Central's aerial attack was rated among the area's best. Plain Dealer sports reporter Alex Zirin said Central's opponent in the Charity Game, Cathedral Latin, would have its work cut out for it: "Patti to McGinnis – Patti to Rose – McGinnis to Patti – or McGinnis to Rose - Latin will have to stop that aerial offense, something every other team the Red and Blue has faced this year was not able to do."

Coach Civiletto also had a decent line anchored by tackles Bob Borcer, Sterling Saulsberry, and center/guard Coleman Lewis. However, Borcer and Lewis were injured, and it was uncertain whether either of these fine players would be available by game time. This fact pointed to one significant advantage that Cathedral Latin enjoyed—depth. The central team lived and died by its starters, using few substitutes.

The 19,304 fans who showed up at Cleveland's Municipal Stadium on Saturday, Nov. 28, 1931, saw a great game, much closer than the 18-0 final might indicate. Central was on the short end of that score, but as The Plain Dealer noted, Tony Patti and Paul Rose were the standouts for the Red and Blue.

The 1931 Charity Game would end Central High's last excellent football season.

In 1943, Russell Alexander took over as the football coach at Central High School, becoming the first African American head coach in Cleveland high school history.

TRACK

Central High School enjoyed its first success at the state track meet with a third-place finish in Class A in 1934. The team scored 18 points, just three points behind second-place Collinwood and 8-2/3 points behind state champion Toledo Scott. Leading the way for Central were the school's first two state champions. A young man whose last name was Caesar was the state champion in the 880-yard run, and the other champion was Buble, who won the high jump with a new state record of 6'4½".

It would be another four years, 1938, before Central again finished among the elite in the state Class A track meet, scoring 17 points for another third-place finish, just a half-point ahead of East Tech. That year, the Central team of S. Thompson, Shaw, Withers, and Smith won the mile relay with a time of 3:28.1, while Rufus Allison won the broad jump with a leap of 22'11¾".

Central had its most remarkable track and field success from 1947 through 1952, especially in 1947-1949 when Central-East Tech Hall of Fame inductee Russ Alexander, the first Black track coach in Cleveland history, coached the track team. In 1947, Central High won the state championship at the Class A track meet with a score of 23½ points. Leading the way for the Red and Blue was Wilkes, who won the 220-yard low hurdles. Central had two other first-place finishes, though they were a bit unusual. In the high jump, the winning jump was 5'11", a height that four contestants attained. Two of those winning jumpers were from Central High, Jarvis and Lauderdale.

In 1948, the team slipped to fourth place with a score of 12 points. Again, Jarvis won the high jump, this time with a leap of 5'11¾".

In 1949, Russ Alexander's Central track team scored its most points ever at the State Meet, winning in Class A with a total of 33 points and almost doubling second-place Columbus Central and its score of 17 points. Lenny Blair got Central off to a fast start when he brought home the state championship in the 100-yard dash with a time of 10 seconds flat; he also finished on the podium (third) in the 220-yard dash. The school's 880-yard relay team of Walter DeVaughn, Nate Moore, Ed Sweeney, and Lenny Blair took the state championship with a time of 1:30.6. Ken Mischal contributed to the Central point total with second-place finishes in both the 120-yard high hurdles and the 220-yard low hurdles. At the same time, Jarvis closed out his team's scoring with a second place in the high jump.

In 1950, Central finished tied for sixth place. Reggie Victor led the way, bringing home the state title in the 880-yard run.

1951 saw the Red and Blue again finish sixth in the state meet, led by Clarence Smith, who finished among the leaders in the 180-yard low (second) and the 120-yard high (third) hurdles. The 880-yard relay team also added to the Central point total.

1952 would be Central High School's last year, and the track team celebrated by finishing fifth at the state meet, one of only five teams to score in double figures that year. The 880-yard relay (third) and mile relay (fifth) teams landed on the podium, while Ray Clark finished second in the broad jump, and Bernard Brison finished third with a satisfactory performance in the 180-yard low hurdles.

CHAPTER 5

East High School

> *East High School, which opened on Nov. 26, 1900, was referred to as a "20th-century schoolhouse" at that time, but by 1905, the school's enrollment had jumped to 1,200 students. The East High students were known as "Easties," the school's athletic teams were called the Blue Bombers, and the school's colors were blue and gold. After 110 years of service to the Cleveland community, East High was closed on June 10, 2010, due to the Cleveland School System's Academic Transformation Plan.*

BASEBALL

According to a year-end review of sports in Cleveland by The Plain Dealer on Dec. 30, 1906, East High's baseball team was the "scholastic champions of northern Ohio, taking the title by their victory over University [School] of this city." East was also the city champion in 1908. As an article on March 7, 1909, Plain Dealer states, "At present, East holds the football, basketball, and baseball championships..."

1950 East won the East Senate title and defeated Saint Ignatius for the Cleveland championship trophy. Fred Konrad was the winning pitcher for East in that city championship game, ending the season with an excellent record of 9-1.

East was in the hunt for state honors in both 1951 and 1952. In 1951, they made it to the Class A state semifinals by defeating Saint Ignatius in the regional finals. In its state semifinal game, East dropped a 4-1 decision to Columbus Linden McKinley High School.

In 1952, it was more of the same. After defeating West High, 5-4 in 11 innings, to take the Cleveland championship, East again advanced to the Class A semifinals, but this time, it dropped a 7-1 decision to eventual state champion Cincinnati Elder—it was the Blue Bombers' only loss that season.

In 1953, East again gained the city title—its fourth in a row—with another win over West High, this time by a score of 10-6, but they could not duplicate their state tournament success of the previous two seasons.

BASKETBALL

East High played its first interscholastic basketball game in 1902. That year, the league consisted of seven teams: Lincoln, Glenville, Technical High School (later to be named East Technical), South High, East High, West High, and Central. This was a season of firsts: it was the first year that the new Technical High School fielded athletic teams, and it was the first year that East High played as part of the Senate League.

East indicated things to come when, on Jan. 8, 1909, the high schoolers dominated the team from Baldwin-Wallace College by scoring 33-2. Team captain Jimmy Prosser and center Roger Peckinpaugh (future major league baseball star and Cleveland Indians manager) combined for 29 points.

While West High had dominated Cleveland's high school basketball scene for most of the past half-dozen years, the focus would swing to the city's east side this season. That became quite evident when East and West highs squared off on Jan. 15 in their first game of the Senate season. As The Plain Dealer noted, West High was "outplayed in every point of the game," while "the boys from East High handled the ball cleanly and fast, and they displayed excellent teamwork." Led by Jimmy Prosser's 12 points, East easily defeated West, 26-8.

East High won its next four games during the following two weeks, defeating three Senate foes and Shaw High School. One of the key games of the 1909 Cleveland high school basketball season took place on Feb. 21 between East High and University School, the last two undefeated teams in Cleveland. With Jimmy Prosser again leading the team with a double-digit effort (10 points), East High doubled up the Preppers, 18-9. As The Plain Dealer noted about East High, "... this victory gives the unconquered five from East 82nd Street an unquestioned right to the championship," the championship being that of Cleveland.

East High's league mark stood at 8-0 On March 5, the last day of the Senate League season, the boys came up against a determined quintet from Central High. Central played the East High five "... off their feet" (PD) in the first half and went to the locker room with an 8-4 lead at the intermission. East was still trailing, 14-13, with just three seconds left on the game clock when Roger Peckinpaugh scored the basket, giving East a thrilling 15-14 victory.

That victory left East High with a perfect 9-0 Senate record and the Senate and Cleveland championships. About a week after the Central game, both Oberlin Academy (9-0) and Canton High School (16-1, later to be renamed McKinley) challenged East (17-2) to a game for the state championship, but neither game was played.

On March 7, The Plain Dealer came out with its 1909 All-Senate basketball team, and five East High players, virtually the entire starting lineup, were somewhere on that team. Making the First Team were captain and forward Jimmy Prosser and at-center Roger Peckinpaugh. Both guards on the Second Team were East High players, Muggleston and Flescher. Making the "sub" list was another East High guard, Brady. The article's writer also picked an All-Cleveland First Team, and Prosser and Peckinpaugh were on that squad.

East High had a strong team in 1920. It finished the season with a league record of 7-2 and tied with South High for the Senate championship.

Under the direction of head coach E. U. McDonald, East High had a powerful team in 1923. In the final league game of the season, East had to go to overtime but finally defeated West Tech, 16-14, to capture the Senate championship with a perfect 8-0 record. On Feb. 27, the team faced Lakewood High School in the game to decide Cleveland's city championship. It was a hard-fought contest, but when the final whistle sounded, East High was on the long end of a 28-23 score and had added the Cleveland championship to the Senate title in its trophy case.

East High won the Senate and Cleveland championships for the second consecutive season in 1924, defeating West Tech in the city title game. Moving on to the state playoffs, East defeated Holy Name in a regional semifinal game, then beat West Tech again, 20-16, in the regional finals. That win over West Tech sent East High to Columbus as one of 16 final teams in the Class A state tournament. In its opening game, East High defeated Bucyrus 32-17, behind 12 points by Al Olszewski.

Moving on to the quarterfinals, East lost a very close game to Springfield High School, 30-28. That defeat also ended East's three-year win streak, which was 38 in a row. East's Ed Carlson was named to the All-Tournament team and All-Ohio.

It would be precisely 40 years before East High again advanced deep into the state tournament. In 1964, under the direction of head coach Chuck Lyons, the Blue Bombers breezed through district play to reach the Kent regionals. The Blue Bombers defeated Akron North 67-57 in a regional semifinal game. That win sent East to the regional finals to face their archrival, East Tech.

In that game, East High raced out to a 19-8 lead after the first quarter, but in the second frame, East Tech came back and outscored the Bombers by 10 points, making it a one-point game, 27-26, at the half — East High clinging to the narrowest of leads. East High regrouped during the intermission and came out to dominate the second half, winning the game by a score of 67-57. Manny Leaks dominated the boards for East High with 20 rebounds. This win ended East Tech's six-year reign as regional champions and marked East High's third win over the Scarabs that season.

Dayton Belmont blew open a close game in the state finals, outscoring East by 17 points in the second quarter as they routed the Bombers 89-60. Manny Leaks was named to the All-Tournament First Team, while Ray Holliday and Mike Childress were named to the Second Team. Leaks was also named All-Ohio Honorable Mention. East finished the season with a record of 21-4.

East would win the city championship again in 1968 (final overall record of 18-1), 1982, and 1986, but they would not return to the state tournament in Columbus until 1985. That year, under head coach Tony Wilcox, a 69-57 win over Saint Ignatius in the Kent Region finals sent the Blue Bombers to Columbus and the state tournament. There, they played Cincinnati Purcell Marian in a semifinal game. After the first quarter, the Bombers trailed by a point, 13-12, but held a 24-21 lead at the intermission. The third quarter would prove decisive, and Purcell Marian outscored East High 18-8. When the buzzer ended the game, East High (18-8) was on the short end of a 59-50 final score. The Blue Bombers' Brian Parker was named All-Ohio Honorable Mention.

CROSS-COUNTRY

East High has only finished three times in the top 10 of the state meet. In 1939, led by Furpaks, the team came in 10th. In 1953, the team came in eighth, but none of the runners were among the top finishers. Three years later, in 1956, the Blue Bombers, led by Randell Jefferson, finished ninth.

FOOTBALL

Although its overall record was only 3-3-1 in 1901, East's mark against Cleveland area foes was 3-0-1. By the day's standard, that was good enough for the East High School football team to win the Cleveland championship in only its first year of competition.

The East High football team enjoyed modest success in 1902 and 1903, but the team surged to the front as Cleveland's 1904 interscholastic football season began. Its success would be one of the most impressive, not just in the early days of Cleveland high school football but in the entire history of the sport in Cleveland. From 1904 through 1908, the Blue and Gold would win 33 games while losing only twice, with no ties. In the process, East High set a mark of 27 consecutive games without a loss (carrying over into 1909) — one of the longest runs of success in Cleveland high school football history.

1904, after losing a practice game to Wooster University on Oct. 1, East breezed through its first three interscholastic games. The team's fourth game was against West High, which was also off to a good start. When West and East met at League Park on Oct. 29, 3,000 fans were on hand for this battle between possible city champions.

"The greatest football contest that ever took place between local high schools…." was how *The Plain Dealer* described the game. It probably still is one of the city's all-time best. As often happens when two seemingly evenly matched teams meet, the game turned on, as they liked to say back then, a "fluke." The game was a punting duel until late in the first half when the East offense could finally start moving the ball. With the ball at the West 22-yard line, Steverding, the East High left halfback, broke through a large hole in the line and into the West secondary. He advanced to "within six feet of the (goal) line" (PD) but then fumbled the ball. One of the West High defenders picked up the loose pigskin inside the one-yard line and tried to advance it, only to be swarmed under "the charging avalanche of East High players" (PD) and dropped in the end zone for safety. The resulting two points would be the only points scored in the game, giving East High a very tough and vital 2-0 victory.

After defeating Ravenna High School, East took on the team from Columbus' East High School. The Columbus team was undefeated and unscored upon, claiming to be central and southern Ohio champions. However, their state title hopes were dashed when Cleveland's East High handed them a 22-0 whitewash.

The final game of the 1904 season would match East with Central High, which would decide Cleveland's championship. This game was one of the most anticipated games ever played in the City of Cleveland, and "in the presence of about the largest crowd that ever witnessed a football game in Cleveland, nearly 6,000 persons"(PD), the game got underway at League Park. It was soon apparent that Central was outclassed entirely; it would not be until midway through the second half before Central could register its initial first down. East, on the other hand, pretty much did as it pleased en route to a compelling 38-5 victory, and with that win came Cleveland's football championship for 1904.

A new feature of Cleveland High School football occurred after the 1904 season — naming an All-Scholastic football team. The coaches selected the first team from East, Central, West, and Lincoln high schools. Coach Joe Fogg of East High, one of Cleveland's all-time great high school coaches, named his entire starting 11 to the All-Scholastic team, and at least one other coach initially agreed with him. However, when the team was finally announced, eight East High starters had made the All-Scholastic squad, along with two from Central and one from West High School.

The Public Schools Athletic League of Cleveland, i.e., the Senate Athletic League, was formed on Nov. 10, 1904, but not everyone was pleased with the new situation. Some of the rules adopted by the league "did not appeal to the athletes" (PD) at East High School, so East did not join the other four high schools (Central, South, West, and Lincoln) in the new organization. Although the differences between East High and the other schools were discussed repeatedly at Senate meets to get East High into the fold, it would not be until 1908 before East High School finally joined the Senate League.

East High finished the 1905 season with an excellent 6-2-0 record. However, from 1906 through 1908, the Blue and Gold team was the undisputed king of Cleveland high school football.

In 1906, East High's record stood at 5-0-0 when the team went up against University School on Saturday, Nov. 24. University School entered the game with a record of 6-1-1, and this season finale for both teams would decide the Cleveland championship.

East High trailed at the intermission by a score of 5-0 after the Preps had turned a misplayed punt reception by East into a touchdown. East High, however, struck for two touchdowns in the second half and kicked the goals after each of them to come away with an exhilarating 12-5 victory. East had avenged its 1905 loss to the Preps (its only loss to a local team since the end of 1903) and had won Cleveland's interscholastic football championship for 1906.

A significant change took place at East High School for the 1907 season. Joe Fogg, who had guided the Blue and Gold to an 18-2-0 record and two city championships from 1904 to 1906, decided to take over the head coaching job at Case Institute in Cleveland, at that time one of the most prestigious college coaching positions in the Midwest. Fogg was a graduate of the University of Wisconsin, where he was the starting quarterback for two years, and his record at Case was an excellent 26-8-4 and 4-0-0 against Ohio State; he is in the Case Western Reserve University Hall of Fame. During World War I, Fogg served with the 49th Iowa Volunteer Infantry. A part-owner of the Cleveland Rams of the NFL, Fogg was also the founder and first president of the Cleveland Touchdown Club. He was a partner from 1909-1946 in the law firm that he started.

Another capable football man, Robert Dawson, took over as head coach at East High. If any of Cleveland's scholastic football squads thought they would now have it a little easier against East High, they were in for a rude awakening. In 1907 and 1908, the Blue and Gold did not just beat their opponents… they destroyed them.

East opened the 1907 season with a 34-0 thrashing of Lincoln High, in which the East defense did not allow a single first down. They then went on to win their next five games by a combined 224-0. The final match on East's schedule was with University School. With a less-than-stellar record of 3-5-0, the Preps looked easy pickings for the East High bunch. However, five minutes into the game, the Preps scored a touchdown to take a 5-0 lead — the first points East had allowed all season. That lead held up until well into the second half when East, led by its great fullback Louis Ahlman, scored two touchdowns to pull out a thrilling 12-5 win.

The 1908 edition of the Spalding's Official Foot Ball Guide, looking back on the '07 season, had this to say about the East High team: "In this class [Ohio], although there were several crack teams, East High School, Cleveland, was easily the champion, being scored on but once and scoring a point a minute themselves. This team was one of the strongest high school teams ever seen in this part of the country and would have proven a worthy antagonist for the famous prep schools of the East."

With that endorsement, East High shares the 1907 Ohio high school championship with Fostoria High School.

East High won 14 consecutive games and its second consecutive Cleveland championship.

Unsurprisingly, East High dominated the 1907 All-Scholastic selections, with six players making the first team. The best of this group was the East High quarterback, Earl Sprackling. Sprackling was noted for being fast, an excellent passer, using "rare judgment" (PD) when leading his team, and being a sure tackler when playing defense. Sprackling's football success did not end at East High. Moving on to Brown University, the famed Walter Camp called him the best quarterback in the country in 1911. In 1909, 1910, and 1911, he was named to Camp's All-America team three times, the only Brown University player ever named All-America. Sprackling was named to the National Collegiate Football Hall of Fame in 1964.

East High became a member in 1908 after settling its differences with the Senate schools. It would now compete for both the Senate and the Cleveland football championships.

The first four games on the Blue and Gold's 1908 schedule were all against Senate foes. The East High 11 picked up right where it had left off the previous season by defeating Glenville, 33-0, Lincoln, 51-0, South High, 40-0, and West High, 19-0, giving East High 10 shutouts in its last 11 games.

East High's next game would prove to be one of the biggest that any Cleveland 11 had ever played up to that time and one of the all-time biggest in Cleveland high school football history. East's original schedule had the team traveling to Ann Arbor, Michigan, on Oct. 31 to play that city's high school. However, the Wednesday before the game, Ann Arbor suddenly canceled the match after it had arranged a game with a local high school. Scrambling to fill the now-open slot in their schedule, the East High people arranged a game with the two-time defending state champion team from Fostoria High School for Sunday, Nov. 1. The game would be played in Fostoria.

This would indeed be a big game. From 1905 through 1915, Fostoria would amass a record of 87-11-3, be declared state champions in seven of the eight years a champion was named, and in 1912, named national champions. In 1908, the Redmen were gunning for their third consecutive state title. They had not tasted defeat in their last 15 games and had shut out 19 of their previous 22 opponents, including all five teams that had already crossed their path in 1908. East High's 18-game winning streak would be tested in this contest.

A crowd of over 2,000 turned out at Fostoria Field for the game, "about one-fourth of the entire population of Fostoria being present." (PD) The only scoring of the first half came with about six minutes remaining when "Paddy" Ryan, East High's right halfback, drop-kicked a field goal to give his team a 4-0 lead. (Field goals were then worth four points.) Five minutes into the second half, Ryan duplicated his earlier effort with a 25-yard drop kick to put the Clevelanders ahead, 8-0. On East's next possession, Ryan culminated a long drive with a touchdown run around the left end; he then added the goal kick to account for all 14 of his team's points.

Fostoria finally scored on a 10-yard touchdown run with just three minutes left in the contest, bringing the final score to 14-5. It was an excellent win for East High that undoubtedly cost Fostoria High School a third straight state title.

Upon its return to Cleveland, East High had three more games to play, all of which it had to win if it wanted to defend its two Cleveland championships. After falling behind Shaw, 4-0, East scored a touchdown with 35 seconds remaining in the first half to take a 6-4 lead. A 28-yard East High field goal closed out the scoring as the Blue and Gold came away with a tough 10-4 win. East then handed a winless Central High team a 22-6 defeat, officially locking up the Senate League championship with a 5-0-0 record.

On Sunday, November 22, East High and University School had a traditional match-up. A pair of "Paddy" Ryan touchdowns led East High to an 11-6 victory. That victory left East with an unblemished record of 8-0-0. It was the Blue and Gold's third consecutive perfect season and ran its win streak to 22 in a row (it would eventually reach 27 the following year). East had also captured Cleveland's and the Senate's (their fourth in a row) interscholastic football championships - the first team to win both titles in the same season.

The 1909 edition of *Spalding's Official Football Guide* had this to say about the 1908 East High team: "Among scholastic circles, there was the usual amount of activity and interest. East High School of Cleveland had a powerful team and won the championship of All-Northern Ohio by their victory over Fostoria High School, champions of Northwestern Ohio." No team has been recognized as Ohio's high school champion for 1908, but a good case could be made for East High.

After losing out on the Senate and city championships in 1910, East High stormed back in 1911. In its first four games that season, all against Senate foes, the Blue and Gold emerged victorious by a combined 263-3 margin. The most impressive of these victories was a record 117-0 win over Commerce High in the second game of the season, which was mercifully halted with a few minutes left in the third quarter. East needed a fourth-quarter field goal in Week Five to eke out a 3-0 victory over a surprisingly tough Tech. Victories over Shaw, 8-5, and Central, 3-0, raised East's record to 7-0-0, the win over Central clinching the Senate championship. However, a last-game loss to University School, 21-0, cost East the city title.

In 1912, the Senate League comprised eight schools: East High, East Technical High, Central, Lincoln, South, Glenville, West High, and West Technical High. While the league that year was pretty competitive on the gridiron, East High would be retaking league honors. The Blue and Gold blasted its way through its first six games, outscoring the other schools by a 284-3 margin, including a 95-0 thrashing of South. East held off Central by a 7-6 score to win the Senate League championship again. But, for the third consecutive season, East lost out on city honors by losing to University School in the season finale, this time by a score of 40-6, which was the worst defeat in school history thus far.

For the 1913 Senate League race, it was business as usual as far as the leader went. With a league record 6-0-0, East had won its third straight Senate championship. Shaw High was initially declared the city champion, but the discovery of an ineligible player on the team caused Shaw to forfeit a couple of wins, one of which was over East High. East's 7-1-0 record (losing to University School, 14-7, in the last game of the season) was now the best in town. By today's standard, the city championship probably would have been given to East High, but in 1913, that was not done, and no team was named city champion.

That East High football team of 1913 was loaded with talent. The 1914 issue of *Spalding's Official Foot Ball Guide*, which reviewed the 1913 season, featured an article about the Senate League. As part of that article, an All-Senate team was chosen, and six of the 11 players selected for that team were from East High School: Craig (end), Henry (tackle), Siderman (guard), Bennett (guard), Hart (center), and Hanley (fullback)

It was not until 1919 that East High was again among the city's elite high school football teams. By Oct. 20, East High stood alone atop the Senate standings with a record of 3-0-0 (4-0-0). Although the newspapers were already anointing East High as both Senate and city champions, Central's stunning 10-7 upset on Nov. 15 dropped East High into a first-place Senate tie with East Tech. When the season ended the following week, East High and East Tech were co-champions of the Senate League. As for the 1919 Cleveland championship, East High, East Tech, and the University School were declared tri-champions.

While the East High football teams of 1921 and 1922 were average at best, they did feature one stellar player. Arthur Matsu was of Japanese and Scottish descent; his parents moved to Cleveland from Scotland when he was young. Matsu went out for football in 1921 as a junior, and even as an unknown, he was "attracting the coaches' attention... and [was] expected to [be a] star player." That year, he played end and did the team's punting while also filling in at quarterback when the starter was injured. Matsu's play earned him First Team All-Senate honors, and his teammates thought enough of him to elect him team captain for the 1922 season.

Matsu was the team's quarterback in 1922, and although he would be unable to finish the 1922 season, the year he was having almost certainly would have won him a spot on the city's All-Scholastic 11. Following graduation, Arthur Matsu played quarterback for four years at the College of William & Mary; in 1926, he was named the team's captain, the first Asian ever to captain a college football team. In leading his team to a record of 25-12-1 (.671), Matsu "was a sterling passer when such a thing still seemed a bit daring." He was a true triple-threat man who could score by running, passing, or kicking the ball; in 1925, he figured in every William & Mary scoring play. *The Richmond Times-Dispatch* later named Arthur Matsu as the team's best quarterback during the first half of the 20th century, while in 2010, The New York Sun rated him as the second-best quarterback in the school's history.

Following graduation, Matsu played a couple of years of professional football in the NFL with the Dayton Triangles. Not only was Matsu the first graduate of William & Mary to enter the professional ranks, but he was also the first Asian to play quarterback in the NFL. Following his short pro career, Matsu turned to coaching, spending 25 seasons as an assistant coach at Rutgers, where head coach Frank Burns said of him, "He was a master of offensive football, a true innovator."

Following its 1919 championship season, East High's next season of outstanding football success came in 1926. The Blue Bombers went through their league schedule undefeated, winning all six games. West Tech was also enjoying a perfect Senate campaign and, like East High, had only lost to Cathedral Latin in a nonleague match. Typically, East High and West Tech would have been named Senate co-champions. However, since the two teams had not yet played each other, the Senate authorities decided to settle the issue with a playoff game – the first in league history.

East running back Bob Colle scored a touchdown on a short plunge, with center John Follett adding the extra point to give East High a 7-0 lead. East maintained that lead until West Tech scored on a 40-yard touchdown pass late in the fourth quarter, but the East High defense blocked the extra point kick to preserve the lead and a 7-6 victory. East High had won its first Senate championship since 1919. (The city title that year went to Cathedral Latin.)

East High's football fans would have to wait 70 years for the Blue Bombers to win their next and last Senate League football championship in 1996. That season, the Blue Bombers won the North Senate title. They then had to play South Senate champion South High for the league championship. Played on a muddy and snow-covered Rhodes High Field, the East High defense dominated the championship game, with just enough Blue Bomber offense to pull out a 20-2 victory and give East High the 1996 Senate League championship.

SWIMMING

The East High swim team began in 1913. While the team's time was short-lived, the coming of the 1919 high school swimming season marked the beginning of the golden era of East High swimming. Although the boys were without a coach, that did not seem to hamper them. They won the Senate championship but lost the city championship to more substantial University School and Shaw teams.

The 1920 season saw the boys finally put it all together. They had some genuinely top-notch swimmers led by freshman Arthur Matsu (also the football team's star) and Taylor Nelson. Matsu's specialties were diving (fancy diving as it was then called) and the breaststroke, while Nelson excelled in sprints. The team won all its dual meets that year to bring home the Senate title. In its meet against University School, the Blue and Gold added excitement to its 43-25 win when Taylor Nelson trimmed one-fifth of a second off of the local record for the 25-yard dash. In the Cleveland Scholastic championship, the boys scored 30 points to claim their first city title.

Although still without a coach, the East High swim team had another successful season in 1921. Arthur Matsu added the relay team to his other events. Ted Abrams began his world and national record-setting career in the unique plunge event, and team captain Rudolph Cooks assisted the team with his backstroke. When one considers that the team started the season with just five swimmers, shortly adding two more, their success was truly remarkable.

In its third meet of the season, against Lakewood, the team smashed a couple of local interscholastic records. Matsu, Cooks, Donald Hester, and Frank Sherman lowered the 100yd. relay mark by a whopping four seconds to 51.60 seconds. Rudy Cooks added a second record to his resume when he lowered the 50-yard backstroke mark to 35.20 seconds. Later, against Pittsburgh Schenley High School, the team set two more marks: the 100-yard relay team dropped the record time to even 50.0 seconds, while Rudy Cooks set a record in the 100-yard swim at 1:04.25.

By the time the season ended, it was the best an East High team had ever experienced. They had won all of their dual meets and the Senate championship. At the Cleveland Interscholastic Championship meet, the Blue and Gold won six events and came in second five times—and in the process, they scored more points than all of the other teams combined.

In 1922, the team finally got what it lacked: a coach named Harold S. Ulen. Under Ulen's direction, the team won all its dual meets and fourth consecutive Senate championship. In the Cleveland Scholastic Championships, the team took home six first-place trophies and three for second place, winning its third straight city title.

Then, as mentioned in of this book, five members of the East High swim team and their coach were off to the National Interscholastic Swim Championships, where they won two individual national titles, added a pair of second-place finishes, and finished in a very commendable third place as a team.

Although Harold Ulen would again coach the team in 1923 (before moving on to a stellar coaching career at Syracuse University and then a 30-year stint at Harvard), the school's run of success was over. The boys would win only one dual meet in 1923. However, Melvin Mott brought some individual glory to East High when he set a national record in the 100-yard backstroke with a time of 1:10.40. Ted Abrams was the team captain that year, and he would win the plunge in every meet but one; the following year he set a World Record of 84'6" in the plunge, a mark that is currently the world's fourth all-time, but still the American record.

TENNIS

The state tennis tournament was still in its infancy when East High broke onto Ohio's big-time tennis scene. In 1928, under the tutelage of head coach J. E. Middagh, juniors Nate Ganger and Edward Funk advanced to the state finals of the Ohio High School doubles competition. The boys lost to the team from Struthers High School, thus earning runner-up status. However, this dynamic duo was far from finished.

In 1929, both boys again advanced to the state tournament. In singles competition, Nate Ganger took home the championship trophy by defeating Earl Bossong from Cincinnati Western Hills High School, 8-6, 6-1, 6-3.

Ganger was again in the doubles competition with Edward Funk. The boys advanced to the finals, where they played against a team from Lakewood High School. After dropping the first set 4-6, Ganger and Funk returned to win the following three sets, 6-2, 6-4, 6-2, to win the doubles state championship.

This was a historic pair of wins for the East High boys. The boys tennis tournament is one of Ohio's oldest high school state tournaments, beginning in 1920. In all that time, East High is the only school in the state to win the singles and doubles championships in the same year.

About 40 years later, the Blue Bombers had another stellar tennis player on their squad. His name was Greg Morton, and he qualified for the state singles tournament for three consecutive years – 1965, 1966, and 1967. Greg never advanced beyond the quarterfinals, but having made it to Columbus three straight years is quite an accomplishment.

TRACK

The OHSAA boys state track tournament began in 1908, but East High did not score its first points until 25 years later, in 1933. That year, one boy accounted for all of the team's scoring. His name was Politer, and he managed to finish among the leaders in the 100yd. and 220yd. dashes, as well as in the broad jump. This fine effort allowed East High to finish sixth in that year's state track tournament.

1937-1941 would find the East High thin clads with significant individual and team accomplishments at the state meet. In 1937, East finished eighth in the state tournament. The bulk of East High's points came when the 880yd relay team of Bibbs, Reitenbach, Rish, and Thomas took first place with a time of 1:31.0, the first state championship in track for the school. However, one boy who almost certainly was on that relay team was a sophomore named Rish. Running in his first state tournament, Rish reached the podium with a second-place finish in the 880yd run.

The 1938 state track tournament would find Rish and his teammates at it again, and this time, coached by George Arnold, they finished second in the meet – East High's highest placing ever in a state track meet. Leading the way was young Rish, who won the 880yd. run with a time of 1:59.6, and the 880yd relay team of Bibbs, Jackson, Thompson, and E. Thomas, which took home the first-place trophy for the second year in a row with a time of 1:30.5. Rish also scored points in the mile run, while Bibbs brought home points in the 100 yd—dash, E. Thomas scored in the 220 yd. dash and Thompson brought home points in the high jump.

The 1939 state track tournament was big for Senate schools, which finished in six of the top seven places, with East High coming in fourth. Again leading the way for the team was Rish, state champion in the 880yd. run with a new state meet record time of 1:58.5, and the mile run with a time of 4:28.

The 1939 state track tournament concluded Rish's remarkable career. He won five gold medals in three years, set one state meet record and earned All-Ohio recognition seven times.

In 1940, the team came in tied for seventh, led by a state championship from the mile relay team in a time of 3:29.8. The 1941 state meet would produce one of East High's last significant tournament placings, fifth place, for about 20 years. The Blue and Gold were again led by the mile relay team, which finished in second place.

The 1962 tournament saw East High again finish in the top 10 at #8, with Ed Shilling leading by winning the gold medal in the high jump with a leap of 6'3 ¼". In 1965, the team finished sixth place. Hurdler Don Foggio won the state championship in the 180yd. low hurdles in 1967 with a time of 19.0 seconds, carrying the Blue Bombers to a seventh-place finish.

Despite never again finishing in the top 10 of the state track meet, the Blue Bombers have produced two additional state champions. In 1972, Marvin Jones tied for first place in the 440yd. dash with a time of 48.5 seconds. In 1981, the school's 4x100m relay team took first place with a meet record time of 41.84 seconds; the members of that record-setting team were Keith Galloway, Ron Brown, Anthony Holmes, and Kenneth West.

CHAPTER 6

Lincoln High School

> *Lincoln High School, named in honor of President Abraham Lincoln, opened in 1901 at the corner of Scranton Road and Castle Avenue. It was the second high school on Cleveland's west side and was built to alleviate crowding at West High School.*
>
> *That first year, 474 pupils attended Lincoln High, but continued growth in the student population necessitated a new wing being built in 1922; by 1931, the school's enrollment had peaked at 4,020. Lincoln was known to have one of the most diverse student populations in the nation, at one time having students from 41 different countries speaking 25 different languages — a true melting pot of the country.*
>
> *With their student populations in decline during the 1960s, Lincoln and West High Schools were combined as Lincoln-West High School and relocated to a new building in 1970.*

BASEBALL

Lincoln made it to the state baseball playoffs twice in its history. In 1944, the Presidents lost in the first round, in what today would be known as the quarterfinals. However, two years later, they did much better. In 1946, under the first-year direction of head coach Howard Filiere, Lincoln's football and basketball coach in those days, the Lincoln Presidents again made it to the state tournament in Columbus. In their first-round game on the morning of May 24, the Presidents took the field against Ironton High School. Led by shortstop Milan Kubene, who had four hits and three RBIs, the Presidents handily defeated Ironton 10-0. Pitcher John Almasi went the first six innings for Lincoln, allowing just one hit and striking out 10.

That afternoon, Lincoln played a semifinal game against Columbus Linden McKinley. The Clevelanders jumped out to a 5-0 lead after two innings, but Linden McKinley came storming back with six runs in the top of the third to take a 6-5 lead. Lincoln failed to score in the bottom of the third and held Linden McKinley scoreless in the top of the fourth inning. In the bottom of the fourth, it was Lincoln's turn to explode as the Presidents plated six runs to take an 11-6 lead. Linden McKinley would not score again, while Lincoln added a couple of insurance runs in the bottom of the sixth inning. The Presidents' 13-6 victory sent them to the Class A state championship game, to be played the next day.

In the 1946 Class A state championship game, Lincoln took the field against Cincinnati Elder. The Presidents wasted little time getting on the scoreboard with a run in the top of the first. That would be the only run in the game until Lincoln plated two more in the fourth inning, then added two in the fifth and a final tally in the sixth. When the final out was registered, the Lincoln Presidents had a 6-0 win and the state Class A baseball championship.

John Almasi pitched in the previous day's games for Lincoln and put on a masterful performance in the title game. In pitching a complete game gem, Almasi allowed only four hits while striking out five, walking one, and allowing no runs. Shortstop Milan Kubene (double, triple, run) and second baseman Jim Canaris (two singles, two runs, two stolen bases) led the Lincoln offense.

BASKETBALL

Lincoln High first took to the basketball court during the 1902-03 season, but players had to wait almost 20 years before enjoying their first excellent team.

The Presidents had an excellent team during the 1920-21 season, defeating teams from around Northeastern Ohio, like Akron Central, Lorain, Bedford, and Mount Vernon high schools. The Presidents also won their first Senate League basketball championship that season, posting a perfect 9-0 league record. The team made it back-to-back league titles in 1922. In 1933, Lincoln had to play a stubborn Central team in the season finale. The Presidents led by only 15-12 at the half, but a strong second half, in which they outscored Central by 30-17, carried Lincoln to a 44-26 win and the Senate championship.

In both 1936 and 1937, Lincoln again won back-to-back Senate titles. In 1936, the Presidents dropped their season opener, then ran off nine wins to take the league crown. In 1937, the Presidents (10-1) tied both Holy Name (11-1) and South High (11-1) for the league championship.

Lincoln High played for the Cleveland High School basketball championship three times after the expansion and realignment of the Senate in the late 1930s. In 1945, as the West Senate champions, they dropped a heartbreaker, 34-32, to Cathedral Latin in the city title game. In 1948, they lost the city championship to Benedictine, 50-32. But in 1950, things would turn out a little bit differently.

On Feb. 21, 1950, Lincoln (9-3) faced off against East Senate champion Central High (10-1) in the Cleveland city championship game at the old Cleveland Arena before a packed house of 8,085. Lincoln was coached by Howard Filiere and led by co-captains Joe Futey and Ted Zelek. The Presidents took a 7-5 lead after the first quarter and led 15-11 at the half. They then pushed their lead to 24-17 after three quarters, but in the final frame, Central came charging back and managed to tie the game, 29-29. With 17 seconds remaining in the game, Lincoln's Ted Zelek (15 points for the game) missed a foul shot that would have given Lincoln the lead, and the game ended tied at 29-29. In the overtime period, Zelek canned a field goal around a pair of Central foul shots, leaving the game still tied after the three-minute overtime period, 31-31.

The second overtime session was to be played as "sudden death," the rule back then being that the first team to score two consecutive points in the OT period would be the winner. If neither team scored two straight points (either a field goal or two foul shots), the team in the lead would be the winner after three minutes. That second overtime period was scoreless until Lincoln's Joe Futey sank a foul shot with just 13 seconds remaining. Neither team scored during those final 13 seconds, leaving Lincoln the winner and new Cleveland champion by 32-31.

A couple of weeks later, Lincoln began play in the Class A district playoffs at Baldwin-Wallace Gym. Led by Ted Zelek's 21 points (one point shy of the tournament record) and Joe Futey's 19 markers, the Presidents defeated South High on March 3, 62-51. Five days later, the Presidents continued their playoff march with a 51-45 win over Lorain High in a district semifinal game. This win set up a showdown in the district finals with Saint Ignatius, who had defeated Lincoln earlier in the season.

In that district final, Lincoln took a 17-15 lead after the first quarter, but the Wildcats roared back to lead, 32-26, at the intermission. In the third quarter, the Presidents outscored the Wildcats, 16-9, to take a one-point lead, 42-41, into the final period. The fourth quarter went back and forth, and three minutes into the session, the Wildcats were back on top, 45-44. Over the game's last five minutes, the Presidents went on a tear on offense and defense, outscoring the Wildcats 13-4 to come away with a big 57-49 victory.

That win sent the Presidents to the Kent regionals as one of 16 remaining teams in the Class A state tournament. Lincoln's (13-5) opponent in its regional semifinal game on March 17 was Akron Garfield (12-6). It was a close game throughout; with just 15 seconds left to play, Lincoln center Del Zacharias tied the game at 46-46 with a field goal. Those 15 seconds would prove Lincoln's undoing as Garfield scored four points on a field goal and two foul shots to win the game, 50-46. Thus ended the best year in Lincoln High School basketball history.

Howard Filiere was one of Lincoln's all-time best coaches. Still, before beginning a 27-year coaching career with the Presidents, he was an outstanding athlete at Bowling Green State University from 1926-1929, winning 10 letters playing football, baseball, and basketball. He was an All-Northwestern Ohio Conference end on the football team for three years. On the basketball team, Howard was a starting guard for three years. As a sophomore, he was named captain of the baseball team, where he played third base and outfield when not toeing the rubber on the mound. Howard is the only BGSU athlete to win the school's Brown Award (most valuable player) in two different sports, taking baseball honors in 1928 and basketball in 1929. After graduating from BGSU in 1929, Filiere began his long, distinguished coaching career at Lincoln. Besides coaching, Howard Filiere also served as Lincoln's assistant principal and athletic director before becoming the principal at Thomas Jefferson Junior High.

CROSS-COUNTRY

The 1930s were Lincoln's best decade as far as the state cross-country meet was concerned. It was the only decade in which the team placed in the top 10—and it did so every year but one.

In 1930, the Presidents finished 11th, the highest finish of any Senate team. Lincoln did not participate in the state meet in 1931 (only six schools did), but the Presidents were back in the state meet in 1932. That year, coached by Don Emery, the Presidents finished with a score of 67, second only to the team from Lakewood High School and its total of 53 points. Matulus, White, and Westfall were leading the way for Lincoln.

In 1933, Coach Emery's boys finished with a score of 95 points, but it was again only good enough for second place, this time behind Akron East. The same three boys led the team across the finish line, this time with a slightly changed order of White, Westfall, and Matulus. In 1934, the team's total of 124 points put them in fifth place, but none of the boys were among the early finishers. A 106-point score in 1935 earned the boys a third-place finish, Bean and Scuba leading the way. In 1936, Peticwany and Kolzynski were Lincoln runners among the early finishers, allowing the Presidents to claim sixth-place honors.

Led by the fine running of Patlowany (fourth place), Kolzynski (14th), and Gubanich (16th), the Presidents very nearly won the state championship in 1937. With 81 points, the team's second-best score ever, the Presidents finished in a tie for third place, just one point out of second place and a mere eight out of first. Their score in 1938 was not nearly as good, 136, but it was good enough for another third-place finish; only Stasuk was among the early runners across the finish line.

Lincoln, led by Lytle and Langner, finished sixth in 1939, and the Presidents came seventh in 1940.

It had been a very successful decade for the Lincoln harriers, but the Presidents never competed in the state cross-country meet again.

FOOTBALL

The Lincoln High Red Raiders, as they were often called, had not enjoyed much success on the gridiron until 1936. Lincoln opened that season with five consecutive wins, two against Senate foes.

Lincoln then had a date to meet West Tech on Friday, Oct. 23, in a night game at Municipal Stadium. Many expected the game to decide on the Senate championship as both teams entered the game undefeated in league play. Before some 17,000 fans, West Tech scored a late fourth-quarter touchdown to pull out a 7-0 win. However, a couple of weeks later, it was discovered that West Tech had three ineligible players on the team; Tech was thus forced to forfeit the six games it had already won.

With its loss to West Tech now reversed, Lincoln High was back in first place in the Senate. The Red Raiders closed the season by defeating Collinwood, 20-6, playing the West High Cowboys to a 13-13 tie, and upending Glenville, 27-6. Their 5-0-1 Senate mark earned the Lincoln High football team its first Senate League championship. Lincoln's overall record of 8-0-1 was the best yet in school history and its first undefeated season. However, that outstanding record would not be good enough to get the Red Raiders selected to play in the Charity Game for the Cleveland championship; those two spots went to Cathedral Latin and Cleveland Heights High Schools, which played to a 0-0 tie.

Following that very successful 1936 campaign, it would be another five years before the Lincoln High football team was again among the area's elites. By then, the Senate had expanded to 17 teams, divided into West and East divisions.

Playing in the West Senate in 1941, Lincoln High School got off to a quick and impressive start by upsetting a formidable Toledo Scott aggregation, 7-0. The rest of the Presidents' (as they were now known) games would be just as close.

In their West Senate opener, the Presidents, behind two first-half touchdown receptions by fullback Stan Zylowski, defeated South 12 to 0 – twice, stopping South drives in the fourth quarter at the Lincoln 7-yard line by recovering fumbles. On Saturday, Oct. 4, Lincoln again used first-half scoring to defeat a stubborn West High team; Walt Poremba scored on a 70-yard interception return, and Len Romankowski on a 3-yard TD scamper gave Lincoln a 14-7 victory.

On Saturday, Oct. 11, Lincoln needed some fourth-quarter heroics to defeat an upset-minded Rhodes 11. In the fourth quarter, with the score tied 6-6, Lincoln end Andy Hotz caught a pass at the Rhodes 15-yard line but promptly fumbled it. Lincoln halfback Joe Karbo recovered the loose ball at the Rhodes 3-yard line. Stan Zylowski put the Presidents back into the lead with a 3-yard run on the very next play. A late touchdown by Lincoln off a pass interception completed the scoring and gave the Presidents a 19-6 victory.

Now 3-0-0 (4-0-0) in league play, Lincoln defeated East Tech in a non-league tussle 12-7. (Although East Tech was a Senate team, all games outside the West Senate were considered non-league games.) Tied atop the West Senate with both Holy Name and Saint Ignatius, Lincoln next had a key match-up with defending league champion West Tech (2-1-0) on Saturday, Oct. 25. Before more than 7,000 fans at Municipal Stadium and with his team trailing 6-0, Lincoln end Andy Hotz scored on a reverse around his left side with less than a minute to play. Team captain Walter Poremba's successful extra point kick provided the deciding point in Lincoln's 7-6 victory.

Now tied with only Holy Name for first place in the West Senate, that tie would be broken the following Saturday, Nov. 1, when the Presidents handed Holy Name a 13-0 defeat before 3,000 spectators at League Park.

The season's final weekend would find Coach Glen Fraser's Lincoln Presidents, 6-0-0, battling the Saint Ignatius Wildcats, 5-1-0, for the West Senate crown. The Wildcats needed to win, but a tie would do the trick for the Presidents. Almost 6,000 fans packed West Tech Field for the big showdown that would send one of these teams to the Charity Game for the first time. Lincoln jumped out to a 13-0 lead in the first quarter but led by only 13-6 at the half. The game's balance was a defensive struggle, except for one play. On the first play of the fourth quarter, Lincoln's Len Romankowski "blazed around left end" (PD) and outran the Saint Ignatius defenders 79 yards for a touchdown. After the ensuing kickoff, Saint Ignatius began play at its 6-yard line, but a bad snap on first down sent the ball out of the end zone for a safety.

There would be no more scoring.

Lincoln's 22-6 victory earned the Presidents their first West Senate title and their first trip to The Plain Dealer's Charity Game to play for the city championship. Their opponent would be the East Senate champions from Collinwood High School.

Lincoln High School, like Collinwood, was a genuinely blue-collar school. The school was located on Cleveland's near west side, in an area of factories and shops, and, as mentioned above, the area's population was very diverse as far as its nationality makeup was concerned. As with virtually every other high school in town, Coach Glen Fraser's team did not have a regular gridiron to practice. The boys practiced in a field under the Clark Avenue Bridge; Fraser's team cleared the field of rocks, tin cans, and broken glass and "cut what grass there was to give themselves a decent place to practice." (PD) Never before known as a good football team, under Fraser's tutelage, the Presidents learned to play good football. They had been one of the west side's better teams since 1936, and their best days were right around the corner.

The Presidents were led all season by a pair of sophomore running backs, Len Romankowski and Don Bania, two of the city's best despite their tender years. Some other sophomores, such as quarterback Larry Piorkowski and halfback Walt Simich, were not starters but still significantly contributed to the team's success. Yet another sophomore, Bill Ebel, established himself as one of the team's starting ends midway through the season. All of this young talent certainly boded well for future Lincoln teams.

The President's best upper-level students were center and team captain Walt Poremba. Poremba played almost every minute of every game and was a sure kicker from placement for extra points. Rounding out the rest of Coach Fraser's starting lineup were fullback Stan Zylowski, end Andy Hotz, guards Frank Makarek and Al Danelishen, and tackles Joe Messuri and Chet Budney.

The fans came out in droves for the 1941 Charity Game. On November 29, 1941, 46,686 fans packed Municipal Stadium, the third-highest total for a Charity Game.

Plain Dealer sports reporter Alex Zirin later described the game as "the all-time best thriller." Lincoln scored a touchdown on its first possession, then held onto its thin 6-0 lead as the teams left the field at the intermission.

The second half, especially the third quarter, was spectacular. Collinwood reached into its bag of tricks and opened the second half by recovering an onside kick but could not score. After Collinwood was forced to punt, it appeared they had the Presidents pinned deep in their end of the field at the 9-yard line. Three plays advanced the ball to the Lincoln 21-yard line. "Then came the play of the day. Romankowski broke wide to his right, cut inside and around his right tackle, and was off. He headed for the center of the field and was out in the open and loose. Cannovino, the fastest player on the Collinwood squad, made a desperate lunge for him on the Collinwood 20 and fell on his face as Len ran over (the goal line) untouched" (PD) for an exciting 79-yard TD run. The extra-point try failed, but Lincoln's lead now stood at 12-0.

Collinwood returned and scored a quick pair of touchdowns, leaving the score tied at 12 to 12 late in the fourth quarter. Neither team was able to score in the few short minutes that remained. This fascinating game ended in a 12-12 tie, leaving Lincoln and Collinwood as Cleveland's co-champions. Despite becoming the first West Senate team to be city champion, the Presidents had to share the honor with Collinwood.

The Lincoln Presidents were a very tough football team in 1941. They had come within one tie game of a perfect season and their first outright city championship. In 1942, they would again assert dominance and take that next big step.

Lincoln opened the 1942 season with a 6-0 victory over a very tough Toledo Scott High School, then won their next four games, including three in the West Senate. On Saturday, Oct. 31, Halloween, the Presidents traveled to Rhodes Field for a West Senate showdown with the undefeated Rhodes High Rams. Playing in inclement weather, the two teams battled fiercely before some 4,000 fans. It was a defensive struggle, the game being played between the 30-yard lines. When the final whistle ended the game, the score was still 0-0, and both teams were still tied at the top of the West Senate.

The following Saturday, Lincoln defeated West Tech, 19-0, which allowed the Presidents to take an ever-so-slight lead in the West Senate race because Rhodes had played West High to a 6-6 tie.

The following week, both teams triumphed with shutout victories. Still, on Friday, Nov. 20, Lincoln clinched its second consecutive West Senate title and second trip to The Plain Dealer's Charity Game by defeating John Marshall 31-7.

The 1942 Plain Dealer Charity Game would be a re-match of the 1941 city title game, with Collinwood returning to the battle on the lakefront by its East Senate playoff win over Cathedral Latin, 13-6. Since the 1941 Charity Game had ended in a 12-12 tie, a year's worth of excitement had been building in anticipation of the lakefront contest scheduled for Saturday, Nov. 28. Lincoln and Collinwood had fueled that excitement by completing their 1942 football campaigns undefeated. The Presidents had finished with a mark of 8-0-1, running their streak to 20 games without a defeat since 1940. The Railroaders matched the President's stride for stride, completing a challenging 1942 schedule a perfect 10-0-0 over the past three seasons, amassing a record of 26-2-1. You could not have picked two better teams to battle it out for city honors, and it would genuinely be a rematch as no fewer than 15 players, eight from Lincoln and seven from Collinwood, also played in the 1941 title game.

Lincoln had improved itself since 1941. Lincoln never missed a beat despite losing stars like center Walt Poremba (graduation) and halfback Len Romankowski (transfer to South High). The President's defense was virtually impenetrable, yielding a paltry total of 13 points the entire season on a couple of touchdowns. Coach Glen Fraser's explanation was "a higher degree of teamwork" (PD) by his players, especially the defensive line. The Lincoln offense was powered by a backfield easily, and it was one of the best in school history. Fullback Stan Zylowski was the fourth leading scorer in the Senate, putting up 63 points on 10 touchdowns and three points after touchdowns. Halfback Gene Slusarski "has more than taken up the slack caused when Len Romankowski transferred" (PD), his specialty end sweeps resulting in five touchdowns. Quarterback Lawrence Piorkowski and halfbacks Don Bania and William Hallal rounded out a backfield that specialized in the run. However, Zylowski, Slusarski, and Bania could pass the ball if called upon.

The Presidents were rated a slight

favorite "because of their tighter defensive record and superior backfield replacements" (PD).

Snow flurries and a temperature in the 20s greeted the 28,077 who made it to Municipal Stadium that Saturday afternoon. The favored Presidents lived up to their pre-game billing in the first half, not so much on offense as on defense. Collinwood could not move the ball against the rock-solid Lincoln defensive unit, but neither team scored in the first quarter.

The second quarter was played almost entirely at the Collinwood end of the field as Lincoln punts continually left the Railroaders deep inside their 10-yard line. Late in the half, Lincoln faced a fourth down at the Collinwood 8-yard line. Lincoln coach Glen Fraser sent in halfback Don Bania with the play. Bania took the snap from center, rolled to his left, and connected with end Bill Ebel in the end zone for an 8-yard touchdown pass. Gene Slusarski replaced Bania in the backfield and ran across with the extra point to give Lincoln a hard-fought 7-0 halftime lead.

It was all Lincoln in the second half. While the Presidents' defense continued to stifle the Railroaders, the Lincoln offense added 19 points as Lincoln won the game 26-0.

Lincoln had not just beaten Collinwood; they completely dominated the Railroaders with a record-setting performance. The Railroaders were held to only 22 net yards of total offense, which was an all-time low in the 39-year history of the Charity Game. The Railroaders completed only three of 18 pass attempts, netting just 11 yards. The Collinwood running game was just as futile; its 11 net yards rushing was also an all-time Charity Game low.

One of Lincoln's West Senate opponents published in its school paper that Lincoln was so brutal that the President's school paper had an obituary section. On this day, not many Collinwood supporters would disagree with that.

With two consecutive city titles, the Presidents of Lincoln High School were still the team to beat Cleveland in 1943. As luck would have it, Lincoln opened the 1943 season against Collinwood, the last team they had played in 1942. The game was marked by a Collinwood offense that could not hold onto the ball and a Railroader defense that could not stop Lincoln fullback Don Bania. Bania passed for one touchdown and scored two others as Lincoln came away with a 26-0 victory, the same score by which Lincoln had defeated Collinwood in the previous year's Charity Game.

If Lincoln's back-to-back shutouts of Collinwood did not show that they were still the team to beat in Cleveland, then their next few games did as the Presidents shut out John Marshall, 20-0, and Saint Ignatius, 26-0, and handed the South High Flyers a 32-6 thrashing, before defeating East High in a non-league contest, 26-0. The victories for the Presidents continued to pile up as West High's Cowboys fell in a muddy, fumble-filled game, 13-0, and the Rhodes Rams were also held scoreless, 21-0.

With their streak now at 27 in a row without a defeat, the Presidents next opponent was West Tech, which had won only once thus far. Perhaps the Presidents were looking past Tech to its showdown the following week with Holy Name, which was tied with Lincoln atop the West Senate standings. Lincoln led 15-0 after the first quarter but trailed 19-15 at the half. Don Bania then took control of the game for Lincoln in the third quarter, scoring one touchdown and tossing a 9-yard touchdown aerial to Paul Maximuk. Bania added his fourth touchdown in the fourth quarter on a short run to put Lincoln up by a commanding 34-19. West Tech added a touchdown late in the final period to make it a 34-26 game, but that was as close as Tech would get, and 34-26 would be the final score.

One of the biggest games in West Senate history would take place on Saturday, Nov. 13. The undefeated Lincoln Presidents, 6-0-0 (8-0-0), put their Charity Game hopes and their string of 28 consecutive games without a loss (the longest streak in the state at the time), on the line against the undefeated Green Wave of Holy Name High School, also 6-0-0 (8-0-0). Lincoln High attempted to set a record by attending the Charity Game for a third consecutive year. Initially scheduled for John Adams Field, the game was moved to Municipal Stadium, anticipating a large crowd.

The Plain Dealer reported, "It wasn't a good day for football." The day was cold — and even more freezing on the lakefront at Municipal Stadium — with a strong wind blowing from the west and snow falling continuously. Despite the forbidding weather conditions, Lincoln and Holy Name played an extremely close and exciting game that was scoreless through the first three quarters. The Namers badly outplayed Lincoln until a fourth-quarter turnover doomed the Green and White. With just a few minutes remaining, Holy Name fumbled the ball, and Lincoln's Harold Paul recovered the loose pigskin on the Holy Name's 26-yard line. Two runs and a completed pass put the ball on the 12. On the next play, Don Bania slipped out of the backfield and was all alone at the 6-yard line, where fullback Ray Koscianski's perfectly thrown aerial found him. Bania went into the end zone untouched. Halfback Paul Maximuk added the point by plunging over the center of the line.

With just a few minutes remaining in the game, Holy Name "came raging back." (PD) Holy Name's furious effort was stopped just short of the end zone when a fumble was recovered by the Lincoln defense at the 3-yard line "as the gun went off." (PD)

The lineup was now set: Lincoln vs. Cathedral Latin for Cleveland's scholastic football championship.

For the past three seasons, Coach Glen Fraser's Lincoln Presidents have been one of the premier high school football teams in the state of Ohio. Since 1941, they have compiled an impeccable record of 27 wins, two ties, and no losses, better than even the mighty Massillon Tigers, who were picked as state champs in 1941 and 1942. The Presidents' 29 consecutive games without a loss broke the old Cleveland record of 27 set by the East High teams of 1905-1909.

Senior halfback Don Bania led the way for Coach Fraser's 1943 Presidents. In the terminology of those wartime days, Bania was the primary weapon in Fraser's arsenal. Bania, the last of six brothers to wear the Red and White of Lincoln High School, had personally accounted for almost half of Lincoln's points by scoring a city-high of 16 touchdowns and five points after touchdown. Equally adept at gaining yardage by skirting the ends or going off tackle, Bania was also his team's leading passer, as evidenced by the five touchdown aerials he had completed during the season. Joining Bania in the Lincoln backfield was his best friend and fellow senior quarterback Larry Piorkowski. As the lead blocker out of the backfield, Piorkowski called the plays and helped clear the way for Bania's runs. Both boys had played in all 29 of Lincoln's games over the last three seasons.

Although Lincoln was a senior-laden team with eight upper-level students as starters, Coach Fraser avoided using younger players who could get the job done. Filling out his backfield were a couple of sophomores, Paul Maximuk and Ted Urbanowicz. Urbanowicz alternated at fullback with Ray Koscianski. Maximuk, however, at 190 pounds, was the President' power runner when they needed those tough yards up the middle. Paul was the second leading scorer on the team (5 touchdowns, four extra points) and did all of his team's punting.

A considerable part of Lincoln's success was the play of its line and defensive unit. The Presidents had shut out 19 of 29 opponents over the last three seasons and had yielded two or more touchdowns on only two occasions. Leading the line for the 1943 Presidents was junior guard Al Kowalczyk. At 210 pounds, the 5'10" Kowalczyk was not only the most prominent man on the team but also one of the quickest. Coach Glen Fraser considered him "one of the outstanding linemen in the city." Some three-year varsity veterans were bolstering the line with Kowalczyk: ends Harold Paul and Ted Babicz, tackle Walt Simich, guard Roman Majerczak, tackle Fred Hilow, and center Joe Utlak.

Although Lincoln was considered a heavy favorite in winning the 1943 Charity Game, they could not overcome Latin. Latin took a 12-0 lead at the half and led 18-12 with seven minutes left in the game, but the Presidents could not close the gap, and 18-12 would be the final score. After two seasons as city champions, the Presidents had to settle for runner-up and see their city-best undefeated streak stop at 29.

Since 1937, when Cleveland's Senate League expanded to 17 teams, the races for the championship of the League's two divisions have always been close. The competition is keen, and the results are doubtful until the season's last week or two. All of that would change in 1944, as Lincoln and Cathedral Latin would dominate the local gridiron scene and their respective divisions of the Senate.

Lincoln opened the 1944 season with a new coach, Howard Filiere. (Glen Fraser was now serving his country in the U.S. Navy.) Lincoln's first game saw the team on the road against the always-tough Magics of Barberton High School. The Magic took a 7-0 lead in the first quarter and made it hold up for the rest of the game. It was only Lincoln's second loss since the end of the 1940 season.

The following Saturday, the Presidents opened their West Senate schedule with a 12-0 win over the scrappy Green Wave of Holy Name. Following that tough victory, the Lincoln High 11 marched through the rest of its Senate schedule. First came a 25-0 win over John Marshall, then a 19-6 victory over Saint Ignatius — a victory that marked Lincoln's 25th consecutive West Senate win dating back to November of 1940. After a non-league win over East High, 23-0, the Presidents ended South High's hopes for a divisional title with a 24-0 victory, then upped its West Senate mark to 5-0-0 with a 30-14 blasting of West High. On Saturday, Nov. 4, the Presidents clinched the West Senate title and an unprecedented fourth consecutive trip to the Charity Game by defeating Rhodes High, 28-0. The Presidents closed the regular season the following weekend by barely getting by West Tech, 6-0.

The Presidents now had two weeks to prepare for the Charity Game on Nov. 25 and a second consecutive match-up with Cathedral Latin.

The 1944 Charity Game for Cleveland's high school football championship, with the state title most probably hanging in the balance, also pitted two of the state's best teams

59

against each other. Since 1941, Lincoln owned Ohio's best mark at 35-2-2, including 29 wins in a row in Cleveland. Latin (6-0-0, 9-0-0) was 29-8-0 during that same period and enjoyed a 13-game win streak and the #1 ranking in Ohio.

Lincoln's head coach, Howard Filiere, had his team playing at the top of its game. With a vast line led by guard Al Kowalczyk, the defense held opponents to only 28 points and helped its cause by intercepting an incredible 28 enemy aerials. The Presidents' single-wing offense was led by fullback Paul Maximuk, rated as "one of the greatest all-around athletes in Cleveland history" (PD), halfback Ray Koscianski, the team's passer, and quarterback Ted Urbanowicz.

With "perfect football weather" (PD) as an added incentive, a near-record 52,888 spectators showed up at Municipal Stadium on Saturday afternoon, Nov. 25, to take in the 1944 Charity Game. With the city's two best teams going at it for the second straight year, a great game was anticipated. Unfortunately for the Presidents, the game was one-sided, and Latin came away with a 33-0 victory.

The completion of the season came with the end of Paul Maximuk's Lincoln football career. One of Cleveland's all-around great athletes, Maximuk starred in football, baseball, basketball, track, and boxing, earning 15 letters in his four years at Lincoln.

Lincoln had gotten off to another great start in the West Senate in 1945 with a record of 2-0-1 (3-0-1) when they met Saint Ignatius at Municipal Stadium. Unfortunately for the Presidents, the Saint Ignatius defense prevailed as the Wildcats handed Lincoln its first West Senate loss in five years, 12-7. Ironically, Saint Ignatius had handed Lincoln that last defeat back on November 8, 1940, and by the same 12-7 score.

That loss to Saint Ignatius also halted Lincoln's West Senate streak at 32 league games without a loss. Between 1940 and 1945, it was the longest such streak in Senate history. The golden era of Lincoln High School football had ended, but how good were the Presidents? If another year is added to this total, from 1941-1946, the Lincoln Presidents were arguably the second-best team in Ohio with a record of 46-6-4, behind only Cathedral Latin's 48-8-2. By comparison, state powerhouse teams Massillon Washington was 46-6-8 and Canton McKinley was 46-8-8. However, Lincoln had the best winning percentage among these state powers at .857, ahead of Latin's .845, Massillon's .833, and Canton McKinley's .806.

GYMNASTICS

In the earliest days of Ohio high school gymnastics, a boys-only sport, Lincoln enjoyed modest success at the state tournament from 1929 to 1931. 1929, the Presidents finished fifth out of 11 teams, but no one earned All-Ohio recognition. The following year, the team was seventh out of 13 teams. Earning All-Ohio recognition was Dianiska, who finished second on the parallel bars. In 1931, the Presidents repeated their fifth-place finish, with Dianiska again scoring a second place on the parallel bars.

TRACK

Lincoln High had its only real success at the state track meet 1934. That year, Cleveland teams took seven of the first 11 places in the meet. The President finished in fourth place with a total of 15 points. Toledo Scott won the meet with 26 2/3 points.

Lincoln's success at the state meet can be credited to one boy, Harold Vacha. A senior speedster who consistently finished second to the legendary Jesse Owens the previous year, Vacha won the 100-yard dash in 10 seconds flat and returned to win the 220-yard dash in 22.2 seconds. Harold Vacha's first-place finishes were the only state track championships ever won by a Lincoln High student.

A young man named East, who tied for second place in the high jump, also contributed to the president's excellent finish in 1934.

The Presidents never again finished higher than 19th in the state meet, but they did have a handful of athletes earn All-Ohio honors:

1936 – Dochtor, shot put, 4th place;

1937 – Mile Relay Team, 4th place, Dochtor – shot put, 5th place;

1940 – Lunger, mile run, 5th place;

1943 – Dodzinski, broad jump, 3rd place;

1944 – Paul Maximuk, shot put, 3rd place;

1945 – Paul Maximuk, shot put, 2nd place.

CHAPTER 7

South High School

South High School opened in 1894 at 7415 Broadway Avenue in Cleveland's Slavic Village neighborhood, the city's third high school to be established. The school's teams were known as the Flyers, and the team colors were orange and black. In 1932, a new high school building was constructed at the intersection of East 74th Street and Canton Avenue. In 1968, the high school moved into a modern new facility at the Broadway address. Throughout its history, A. B. Hart and Myron T. Herrick junior high schools were the feeder schools for South High, which was closed by the Cleveland Board of Education in 2010.

BASEBALL

Under Coach Frank Dillon, South High had an excellent season in 1959. In the season opener, Frank Reyes had thrown a 1-0 no-hitter against Cleveland Heights, striking out 14. In that game, Reyes scored the game's only run by stealing home plate. Playing at Edgewater Park on May 1, the Flyers defeated West Tech 9-1, which advanced South to the district tournament. In winning the team's eighth game against just two defeats, Reyes tossed a three-hitter, striking out 16.

Exactly one week later, on May 8, South won its first Class AA district championship.

Frank Reyes was again on the mound against Burton High School at Gordon Park. Reyes struck out the first two batters, then gave up hits to the next two. After that, Reyes was perfect, retiring the last 19 batters, and the Flyers came away with a 9-0 victory.

The Flyers continued their tournament success on May 14. A six-run first inning carried South to a 9-3 victory over Akron Garfield in a regional semifinal game. Frank Reyes went the first four innings to pick up his sixth win. Two days later, the Flyers returned to the diamond for a regional championship game against Bedford High School. Reyes would be the team's hero on the mound and at the plate this time. With the score tied 4-4 in the fifth inning, Reyes hit a single that drove in the two runs, providing the margin of victory in the Flyers' 6-4 win.

The victory gave the Flyers their first regional championship, sending them to the Class AA state finals in Columbus. However, the Flyers' quest for a state championship ended in a state semifinal game, as they fell to Barberton High School in a 4-1 decision. The loss was Reyes' only loss of the season.

Although, in 1960, the Flyers did not advance out of district play, a graduating senior and team captain, Dennis Woods, continued his baseball career at Miami University in Oxford, Ohio. Upon graduating from college, Dennis began a successful twenty-year coaching career at Glenville High School (1964-1984) and continued coaching high school baseball for over twenty more years throughout Northeast Ohio. Dennis is the current 3rd winningest coach in Ohio. His coaching exploits have earned him induction into the Glenville High School Hall of Fame (1988), the South High Hall of Fame (1995), the Ohio High School Baseball Coaches Hall of Fame (2005), the Northeast Ohio Baseball Coaches Hall of Fame (2008), and induction into the Sports Legends of Cleveland (2024).

In 1961, the Flyers were back in thickness of the Class AA state championship race. Still coached by Frank Dillon, the South High Flyers were locked in a terrific pitchers' duel in a Class AA sectional championship game with the West Tech Warriors on Monday, May 1. With the game scoreless in the third inning, Flyers' pitcher Tom Fisher was hit by a pitch. Jim Ciricola laid down a bunt to move Fisher to second base. The ball dribbled toward third base; the West Tech third baseman fielded the ball cleanly, but his throw sailed past the first baseman, allowing Fisher to come around the bases and score. That would be the game's only run as both pitchers hurled one-hitters, with Fisher striking out 14.

The Flyers (6-5) steadily advanced through district play. On May 12, they took the field against St. John Cantius (5-2-2) for the district championship at Gordon Park. The Flyers exploded for six runs in the first inning; that would be all Tom Fisher would need. The Flyers' ace hurled another one-hit shutout, striking out 13, as the team advanced to regional play with a 6-0 victory.

Regional play for South High began on May 18 in a game against Akron Kenmore High School at Gordon Park. Tom Fisher did not have his best stuff that day, but he held on for 5 1/3 innings, striking out 10, as the Flyers outlasted Kenmore with a 10-7 victory. The next day, South returned to Gordon Park for the regional finals, this time facing Benedictine, with Fisher again on the mound. The Flyers were trailing, 3-2, when they came to bat in the fourth inning, exploding for seven runs en route to a 9-5 victory. Fisher pitched a complete game.

By winning their regional final game for the second time in three years, the Flyers were headed to Columbus to play in the State Baseball Tournament. The Flyers' semifinal game on May 26 was against Ohio baseball power Elder High School of Cincinnati; Elder had won the last three Class AAA state championships and seven of the previous 10. It was a very close game. Tom Fisher threw a three-hitter for South, striking out five while walking three. Elder scratched out a pair of runs, but Fisher's teammates backed him up with three runs as the Flyers ended Elder's run with a 3-2 triumph.

With the win, the Flyers (12-6) advanced to the Class AA state championship game the next day. Their opponent would be the Lima Senior High School Spartans, who were 15-1. The Flyers would face Lima's ace, Vance Shuman, who entered the game with a 10-0 record.

Tom Ksieyzk started on the mound for South in the state championship game. He pitched what The Plain Dealer described as a "shaky first" but escaped without allowing a run. With the score still 0-0, the Flyers came to bat in the third inning. The South High hitters tore into Vance Shuman's offerings, blasting five hits, working the Lima pitcher for a pair of walks, and taking advantage of a

Spartan's error to score six times.

That would prove to be all the support Tom Fisher, who entered the game in relief in the second inning, would need. Lima scored an unearned run in the fifth inning. Still, otherwise, Fisher held the Spartans scoreless over the game's last six innings as the Flyers came away with a 7-1 victory and won their only state baseball championship.

Tom Fisher, a 1961 All-Scholastic and All-Ohio selection, whose won-lost record in the playoffs was a perfect 7-0, ended the season with a sparkling record of 8-1 and an ERA below 1.00. After graduation, Fisher signed a major league contract with the Baltimore Orioles and remained in their organization for nine years.

Another teammate of Fisher was his catcher, Ken Pflug. Ken was named 1st Team All-City Cacher and 2nd Team All-State Catcher and was selected to play in the annual Coaches Association All-Star Game. In 1964 and 1965, Ken served as bullpen and batting practice catcher for the Cleveland Indians. He was inducted into the South High Hall of Fame in 1999.

Although South High did not participate in another state championship game, the team, under the leadership of head coach Angelo Rodriguez, won the city championship in 1965, 1966, and 1968. Players recognized as All-State as selected by the Ohio High School Baseball Coaches Association were Ralph Wisniewski, outfield, 1957, and John Katona, pitcher, 1968.

South's successes, although sporadic, earned the Flyers a City Championship in 1976. The Flyers Rich Harnoz was named to the All-State Team that year. 1978, they were Co-City Champions, Division Champions in 1979, and South Senate Baseball Champions in 1985. In 1986, South won its final baseball City Championship.

In 1996, it was the last Senate Championship. Coach Rodriguez finished his 22nd year of coaching and was named the South Senate Coach of the Year.

One of Coach Rodriguez's high school teammates was Art Massey. Massey was also a nine-letter winner at South High and an All-American soccer selection while at Ohio University. In 1969, Massey became the head baseball coach at Cuyahoga Heights HS. In his 28 years at Heights, his teams won over 400 games. In 1976, they were the state runner-up and appeared in three regional finals. In 1997, Massey was inducted into the Ohio High School Baseball Coaches Association and the South High Hall of Fame.

Another outstanding Flyers baseball player was Henry "Hank" Ruszkowski. Although Hank lettered in football and baseball, it was baseball where he attracted the attention of professional scouts. After leaving the South in 1944, he caught fourteen games of the Cleveland Indians before entering the army in 1945. Following the war, Ruszkowski served as the backup catcher for the Indians Jim Hegan and Al Lopez during the 1947 season. Hank was an original inductee into the South Hall of Fame in 1995.

South High's John Turk was also an all-around athlete, earning All-Scholastic honors in football, basketball, and baseball. In baseball, he excelled as an All-Ohio catcher. After graduating from South in 1949, he enrolled at Ohio University, where he lettered in both baseball and football during each of his three years of attendance. Following graduation from OU, Turk signed with the Philadelphia Phillies in 1953. His career batting average was .327. Before leaving pro baseball, he managed three minor league teams for the Phillies. Upon leaving professional baseball, he taught and coached at several high schools in Northeast Ohio, including Willoughby South High School. He was inducted into the South Hall of Fame in 1996.

In 2017, the 1961 State Championship baseball team was inducted into the South Hall of Fame. Earlier members of the team inducted into the Hall of Fame included coach Frank Dillon (1995), pitcher Tom Fisher (1996), catcher Ken Pflug, outfielder Mario Morino (1999), and outfielder Jim Ciricola (2017).

BASKETBALL

South High had not been a significant factor in Cleveland High School or Senate League basketball until the 1914 season. South's season opened on January 2, 1914, with a 19-14 loss to Loyola High School of the East Side. Despite that loss to perhaps the city's best team at the time, South went on to have a great Senate League campaign. The Orange and Black received a scare from Lincoln on Feb. 20 but pulled out a 17-16 victory to keep their record clean. South would finish its Senate schedule with a record of 7-1, winning its first league basketball championship.

The 1919-1920 Senate League basketball season was very competitive. Going into the season's final league games in mid-March, South High and East High were tied for first place with identical 6-2 records in the league. East was scheduled to play West High on March 12, while South was an overwhelming favorite to defeat West Commerce High School the following day. As luck would have it, South and East were defeated, leaving them tied for the league championship since there were no tie-breaking playoff games back then.

Although South High had won the 1928 Senate football championship, the Flyers were not picked to win the 1928-29 basketball title. A loss to Fremont High in a non-league game in January did little to boost the Flyers' confidence in their chances for league supremacy. However, everything seemed to fall into place when the Flyers began league play. There were one or two close games, but on March 15, the Flyers defeated Lincoln, securing a perfect 7-0 league mark and clinching the Senate championship, which gave them both of the league's football and basketball titles that year. Carl Brubaker coached both the football and basketball teams that year.

South was back in the Senate basketball title chase during the 1930-31 and 1931-32 seasons. In the 1930-31 season, South High got off to a slow start, dropping a game to a powerful Elyria High squad in December 1930. However, things improved considerably for the Flyers once the calendar turned to the New Year and the Senate season started. They ran off four consecutive league victories, including a thrilling 31-30 overtime win over Lincoln, before suffering a loss at the hands of Central High on Friday, February 13. The Flyers closed their league campaign with two more wins, including another overtime thriller, 29-27, over East High. With identical 6-1 Senate records, South and West Tech shared the Senate crown for the 1931 basketball season.

The 1931-32 season would produce more success for South. After splitting a pair of non-league games, the Flyers started their Senate schedule on Jan. 15 with a game against one of the league's preseason favorites, John Adams. After a slow start, South took the lead early in the second quarter and never looked back, coming away with a 33-26 win. Future Flyers Coach Gene Wolanski, playing center, scored a game-high 10 points.

The Flyers then continued their winning ways with a 31-20 victory over Lincoln and closed out January with a non-league win over Garfield Heights, coasting to a 38-13 win behind Wolanski's game-high 16 points. The Flyers went 4-0 in February, including three more wins in the Senate, which gave them sole possession of first place with a 5-0 league mark. In their final Senate game on March 11, the Flyers came from behind with a big second half to hand East High a 36-25 defeat and clinch sole possession of first place and the 1932 Senate title.

South High would again be in the thick of the Senate title race during the 1936-37 campaign. By mid-February, they were still undefeated with a 7-0 league record, 8-0 overall. Once again, the Flyers played on Feb. 13; it fell on a Saturday in 1937, but as far as the Flyers were concerned, it might as well have been a Friday. The opponent that day was another undefeated Senate team, Lincoln High, which would remain undefeated following its 33-27 win over South.

The Flyers rebounded from that defeat by winning their next three Senate games. On Monday, March 1, the Senate standings had Lincoln in the lead with a 9-0 record, followed by South (10-1) and Holy Name (9-1). West Tech pulled off the season's upset that Friday by defeating Lincoln, 34-32, while South defeated East High, 28-24. When the final standings were announced on March 13, a three-way tie for the league championship emerged: South and Holy Name, both with 11-1 league records, and Lincoln with a 10-1 record.

It would be another 10 years before the Flyers again contend for league honors. Playing former star but now head coach Gene Wolanski, South High got off to a great start in the 1946-47 season. The team was already 6-0 in all games when it played the John Marshall Lawyers on Jan. 17, 1947. It was a close game, so close that it would go into two overtime periods. South's Chuck Bokar canned a pair of free throws in the second OT period to give the Flyers a 44-42 victory.

Over the next month, the Flyers would continue to win. In late February, a 45-30 victory over Lincoln gave the Flyers a 6-0 record in the West Senate, bringing their overall record to 13-0. It clinched the West Senate championship for the South, although the Flyers still had one West Senate game to play. Despite losing that game to Saint Ignatius, 56-46, the West Senate title still belonged to the Flyers.

Two weeks later, on March 14, the Flyers took the court at the Cleveland Arena to play East High for the city title before more than 9,900 high school basketball fans. It was a hotly contested game, but South held the lead throughout, taking a 28-22 advantage into the fourth quarter. However, East High rallied in the final frame to take a late 32-31 lead. With just 10 seconds left on the game clock, the score was tied at 34-34.

The Plain Dealer's Harry Jones described the game's final 10 seconds: "With the clock, just 10 ticks from the finish ... South's Glen Trhlin took a pass at side court, dribbled to the foul circle and with a one-hand shot scored a field goal that broke a 34-34 deadlock and brought the first [city] title to South in 15 years."

Flyers' head coach Gene Wolanski had played on South High's last Cleveland basketball championship team in 1932, and now he had led his alma mater to the 1947 city title.

1954 South won the West Senate title but lost the city championship game to East Tech by a score of 66-49.

While the Flyers would have to wait 35 years for their next championship team, it would be only three years before one of their all-time great stars came upon the scene. During the 1956-57 season, Fred Sawyer, a member of the Class of 1957, had an outstanding campaign and was named All-State Honorable Mention. Continuing his education and basketball career at the University of Louisville, Fred earned All-America honors his senior year. His 1,040 rebounds are the fourth-highest total in Louisville history, and he is ranked #21 among Louisville's all-time Top 50 basketball players. Sawyer was inducted into the South Hall of Fame in 1999. Gene Wolanski was a member of the inaugural Hall of Fame induction class in 1995.

The Flyers' long wait for a Senate championship finally ended in 1974 when they won the league championship with an 85-73 victory over the John Hay. In the years preceding the tournament, two players received Statewide recognition. In 1974, Ralph Carnes was selected to the AP All-Ohio Special Mention team. In 1977, Len Burris was named to the 1999 All-Ohio First Team.

In 1998, the Flyers lost the Senate championship game to East Tech, 79- 75, but came back two years later to capture their final league basketball title in 2000 by defeating East Tech, 70-56. In 1999, Jonathan Burga was named to the All-Ohio first team due to his outstanding overall play.

The 1999-2000 squad was led by Chester "Chet" Mason, who was named Ohio's Mr. Basketball that year, an honor he shared with Tony Stockman of Medina High School. Mason averaged a triple-double for the season, averaging 25 points, 13 rebounds, and 11 assists per game. Chet was named to the All-MAC team in 2005 in Miami, Ohio. He then played nine years of professional basketball in Europe, where he was named the MVP of the Adriatic League for the 2009-2010 season. After his playing days, he transitioned into coaching in the Cleveland area and has served as the head coach at Brush High School since 2015.

BASKETBALL (GIRLS)

Although very competitive in the Senate, South's girls' basketball team won just two Senate Basketball Championships. Under the direction of Coach Chuck Jancura, the Lady Flyers won the South Senate Championship in 1984 and 1985. Unfortunately, in 1984, the team played a hard-fought game against East High, losing the City Championship game by a score of 52-47. In 1985, the team lost to Glenville in the Championship game by a score of 53-24. One of the bright spots of the season was the play of Brenda Simmons, who, as a junior and senior, led the Flyers' basketball teams in both the 1984 and 1985 Championship games.

FOOTBALL

South High School was one of the first schools to play interscholastic football in Cleveland, joining the Cleveland Scholastic Athletic Association in 1894. Unfortunately, the South would not enjoy much success on the gridiron until 1928, more than 30 years later.

In 1928, the Senate would crown a different school as its champion for the fourth consecutive season. The title race was a two-team race between East High and South. After opening its Senate schedule with a 0-0 tie with Glenville, East would post five straight league victories and end the season with an excellent 5-0-1 Senate mark. South opened its Senate schedule with five consecutive wins.

South needed only a victory over winless East Tech to clinch its first Senate League championship. Coach Carl Brubaker's squad ensured there would be no upset; scoring in every quarter, the Flyers rolled to a 32-0 victory. South's 6-0-0 mark just edged out East High for the Senate title.

It would be another five years before South reached the top of Cleveland high school football again. The Flyers, who lost all six league games in 1932, opened the 1933 season by losing to Akron South, 18-0. They would then win three consecutive close games: West Tech, 7-6; Holy Name, 6-0; and Lincoln, 14-12, setting the tone for the balance of their season.

In first place in the Senate with a 2-0-0 (3-1-0) mark, the Flyers tightened their grip on the league's top spot with identical 7-0 wins over Glenville and East Tech. In their final two league contests, the Flyers thumped West High, 32-0, then turned John Adams' mistakes into South High points for a 15-0 victory.

East High was undefeated in the Senate, but they finished the season with a tie on their record, 5-0-1. With a perfect 6-0-0 record, the Flyers were awarded the 1933 Senate League championship. South and East did not play against each other in 1933.

On December 2, 1933, South High would play the Shaker Heights Red Raiders—9-0-0—the only undefeated and untied team in the Cleveland area—in the Charity Game for the city championship.

The Flyers would be battling an old friend for the city title. Carl Brubaker, who led South to its last and only Senate championship in 1928, had been the football mentor at Shaker Heights since 1930. Brubaker's teams had lost only three games in his four seasons as the Red Raiders head coach; they had won three consecutive Eastern Conference titles and owned the second-longest undefeated streak in Cleveland High School football history at 26 games. Brubaker's "suburbanites" were the popular choice as the favorites to take the city championship based on their more explosive offense.

South, on the other hand, was known as an opportunistic team. The Flyers had only scored 88 points all season but took advantage of the other team's mistakes and then left the game in the hands of one of the city's best defenses. Flyer Coach John Shallcross knew that his team was the underdog against the best team they would face all year, but the Flyers were determined to prove the "experts" wrong.

Game day, Dec. 2, was unseasonably warm, with a high of 45 degrees predicted and a chance of rain later in the day. At 2:15, South High kicked off, and the game was underway. After an exchange of punts, South had the ball at its 30-yard line. On first down at his 40-yard line, fullback Stan Iwucz took the snap from center and headed into the middle of the line. Instead of crashing into the line, Iwucz pitched the ball back to quarterback Dominic DiSanto. DiSanto faded back and threw a pass to halfback Len Janiak, who had gotten behind the Shaker defensive backs. Janiak made the catch and raced the remaining 40 years for a Flyers TD. Following the touchdown, Janiak raced around the right end for the extra point. The game was barely underway, and South had a 7-0 lead.

The game's balance would be a titanic defensive struggle featuring no less than 21 punts. South did what it had done all season in making a single, but very exciting, touchdown hold-up for the entire game. In doing so, the Flyers claimed the 1933 Cleveland interscholastic football championship.

There were heroes aplenty for Coach Shallcross' champion Flyers. Center Leo Werstok, guard Mike Merrick, and end Nick Meczka led the assault in the trenches as they "seemed to be in on every line play." (PD) Fullback Stan Iwucz, "a pile-driving line plunger and an expert blocker" (News), halfbacks Len Janiak and Dan Mancini, and quarterback Dominic DiSanto led the assault from the backfield. It was a case of South's best defeating Shaker's best, as each team used only three substitutes during the game. Janiak was named the game's MVP.

Len Janiak graduated from South in 1934 and attended Ohio University, where he earned All-Conference and All-Ohio honors in football and is a member of the Ohio University Hall of Fame. After a brief career in professional football, he became one of Cleveland's most outstanding high school football coaches. He coached at St. Stan's from 1948-1968, complying with a record of 103-64-6. In 1959, he was named "Coach of the Year" by the Greater Cleveland Football Coaches Association. Janiak was a member of the first class of inductees into the South High Hall of Fame in 1995.

It would be another half-dozen years before the South High Flyers again challenged for a city championship. In 1939, after opening the season by splitting a pair of non-league games, the Flyers won three consecutive Senate contests despite scoring just 12 points in each game.

Next up was a meeting between West Tech and South High, the West Senate's only remaining undefeated teams, teams that featured great defenses but low-scoring offenses. The Flyers trailed 7-0 at halftime, but early in the third quarter, South defensive back Tom Wilson intercepted a West Tech pass on his 30-yard line and returned it for a 70-yard touchdown; guard Gene Ruszkowski tied the game with the place kick. South again fell behind, 14-7, but rallied late to tie the score at 14-14. Neither team could score again, and the game ended in a tie.

South and West Tech remained tied at the top of the West Senate with identical 3-0-1 records, with three games remaining in the West Senate. West Tech won two in those games but had to settle for a 0-0 tie with Holy Name.

The Flyers won their next two league games and only needed to win the season's final game to secure a West Senate championship. The Flyer's opponent in that last game was the Wildcats of Saint Ignatius, which had won just two West Senate games. The game would be almost the last play in a much-closer-than-expected contest. Trailing the upstart Wildcats 12-6, the Flyers were not about to give up. With the ball at the Wildcats' 45-yard line and the game clock quickly running down, halfback Clarence Jarosz's pass connected with halfback John Rubaszewski at the Wildcats 10-yard line, with Rubaszewski racing those last 10 yards into the end zone for the touchdown that tied the score. The South High fans were cheering wildly as tackle Gene Ruszkowski "calmly booted the winning point to end one of the wildest games seen here this season" (PD).

The 1939 Charity Game card was now set. South High (7-1-1) would represent the West Senate, while John Adams (8-0-0) would try to uphold the honor of the East Senate. Adams had already beaten South 12-6 back in September, and it was imperative for the Flyers to even the score as the two teams were not scheduled to play each other in 1940.

Coach Ed Unger of South High did not have many quality running backs, but he did have two who were more than capable: halfback Clarence Jarosz and fullback Mike Smilonich. Jarosz, "one of the most deceptive backs in the district" (PD), was a 160-pound speedster and the number-one threat out of the Flyer's backfield. When the Flyers needed a few big yards up the middle, they went to their fullback, Mike Smilonich. A two-year starter, Smilonich was also a threat to take the ball outside.

With its limited running capability, South went to the air much more often than did Adams. The Flyers' central passer was Clarence Jarosz, whose primary receivers were halfback John Rubaszewski and tackle/end Ervin Glinka.

South's line was composed of veteran players, all seven starters being seniors. The team captain led them, guard Al Stuble, one of Cleveland's finest. John Gross was at the other guard slot, like Stuble, an excellent pulling guard. Lou and Al Birel, along with Henry Posendek and center Paul Marick, added their experience to the Flyers' line.

Saturday, Nov. 25, was a typical early winter day in Cleveland; the temperature remained in the 30s all day, with clouds drifting by but no precipitation. Over 40,000 high school football fans would brave the cold on Cleveland's lakefront for the third consecutive year, piling into Municipal Stadium to watch the 10th edition of the Charity Game, which would decide the Cleveland scholastic football championship. Many in this highly bi-partisan crowd hoped to see South High achieve one of those rarities in sports — going from dead last (0-6-0) one year to champion the next.

Midway through the first quarter, John Adams secured one of the game's first breaks by intercepting a pass. Several plays later, the Rebels turned it into a touchdown and an early 6-0 lead. In the second quarter, it would be the Flyers' turn to score, recovering a fumble and turning that miscue into a game-tying touchdown five minutes before halftime.

Thus far, the game was running quite close to how the first meeting between these two teams had gone back in September, but all that would change shortly after the intermission. Early in the third quarter, both Clarence Jarosz and Merrill Fiori of the Flyers were knocked out of the game with injuries, and the loss of these two-star players crippled the Flyers. The second half was all John Adams, as the Rebels outscored South 25-0 over the game's last two quarters to come away with a 31-6 victory and the city title.

South High's next shot at a city championship came in 1948. Third-year head coach Gene Wolanski had 14 lettermen returning from a team that had won only three games the previous year. However, the Flyers faltered in their season opener, dropping a 14-12 decision to Shaker Heights.

The Flyers' Senate League play also got off to a shaky start, their season opener with Lincoln ending in a 13-13 tie. After that, however, and behind one of the best defenses in the area, the Flyers were soon unbeatable, closing out the season with seven consecutive victories, six of which were West Senate wins. The Flyers had won the West Senate title, earning a spot in the Charity Game. Meeting the South in the Charity Game for Cleveland's championship would be the Bengals of Benedictine High School, which had gone undefeated, 9-0-0, for their first East Senate title.

Coach Wolanski gave much credit for the team's strong finish to his defense, which had not allowed a point in the team's last six games. Two of the best members of the South defensive unit were guard John Turk (Second Team All-Ohio) and tackle Bob Molasky; Coach Wolanski referred to these two as his "iron men" because they played almost every minute of every game. Rounding out the defensive line were ends Dick Hlatky and John Pisczak, guard Tony Waskiewicz, center Andy "Apple" Turowski, and the big boy of the team, 6'4", 230-pound tackle Dick Craig. These same players also operated the offensive line, providing the blocking for a very good, well-rounded backfield.

Leading the Flyer offensive attack was quarterback John Golembieski, "a shrewd and coldly efficient performer who is generally regarded as one of the best scholastic field generals in the city" (PD). It was an opinion to which Coach Wolanski subscribed: "I let John run the show, and he does an excellent job of it." In addition to being an excellent passer, Golembieski also served as the team's punter and defensive back, rarely leaving the field.

Rounding out the Flyers' backfield were fullback Wally Polcyn, "a powerful runner with plenty of drive and determination" (PD); halfback Art Nemec, the fastest man out of the backfield; and halfback Frank Cytlak, the team's leading scorer with five touchdowns to his credit.

Nov. 27, 1948, which dawned cloudy and cool but with no precipitation, marked the first meeting between South and Benedictine on the gridiron. The 45,117 high school football fans who poured into Municipal Stadium that day witnessed one of the all-time great Charity Games – a classic. It was a titanic defensive struggle that remained scoreless until Benedictine scored the game's only point on a 22-yard pass with just 30 seconds left, giving the Bengals a 7-0 win. The tremendous effort put up by the Flyers did not go unnoticed. John Turk was named the game's Most Valuable Player, edging out teammate John Golembieski in the postgame voting.

Despite losing the Charity Game, the South High Flyers were ranked #18 in the final AP state poll.

The Flyers waited 17 years before they had another chance at a city championship. In 1965, South High opened the season with a pair of losses in independent games, then began West Senate play with a 0-0 tie against West Tech before running off consecutive wins over John Marshall (16-0), Holy Name (14-0), and Lincoln (34-6).

With three weeks left in league play, South and West Tech were tied atop the West Senate with identical records of 3-0-1. On Saturday, Oct. 30, Coach John Gentile's South High Flyers faced the second-place Saint Ignatius Wildcats at West Tech Field. The game was a scoreless struggle until, with just 59 seconds on the clock, fullback Dale Szweda "bulled into the end zone" (PD), and halfback Mickey Gallegos ran in the two-point conversion. When the final whistle sounded, the Flyers earned their first victory over the Wildcats in 17 years by a score of 8-0. In the process, the Flyers dethroned the four-time divisional and reigning city champions.

The following week, South kept its championship hopes alive with a blowout win over the West High Cowboys, 42-6. The Flyers then soundly defeated Rhodes, 34-0. That victory gave South High a West Senate record of 6-0-1, edging West Tech and its 5-0-2 mark for the divisional title.

South High was finally back in the Charity Game for the first time since 1948. Benedictine, ranked among the top 10 teams in the state, cruised to the East Senate title and would meet the Flyers for the Cleveland championship. Benedictine was the same team South had played for the city title in 1948.

Coach Augie Bossu's Bengals were a formidable opponent, but John Gentile's South High Flyers were no pushovers. South had gotten off to a slow start, dropping its two nonleague games early on, but after Coach Gentile made some changes to the team's training regimen, it was most apparent that a different Flyers team took the field for its West Senate schedule.

The South defense had been near perfect in going undefeated through its West Senate schedule. The first-string defense had been perfect, not allowing a single point to a divisional foe. Jack Cook, the most prominent man on the team at 215 pounds, led the defensive line, along with Jack Zusy, George Hrivnak, Jim Ciesla, and Frank Berzansky. Backing up this line were stalwarts Al Ramicone (All-Ohio Honorable Mention) and two-way star Mickey Gallegos, the team's two leading tacklers. Mike Pescaru, Mike Abella, and safeties Jerry Musi-El and Vic Papushak completed the defensive backfield.

The Flyers' offense had scored only 148 points in the defense-oriented West Senate, 47 points fewer than Benedictine halfback Larry Zelina's total, but they were still a unit to be feared. Leading the charge for the Flyers was All-Scholastic tailback Mickey Gallegos. Gallegos had been a two-year starter at offensive guard for South, but Coach Gentile needed a good running back, and he liked what he saw in Gallegos. Mickey responded by becoming the outstanding running back in the West Senate and leading the division with 64 points and 72 overall. When he was not running with the ball, Gallegos did an excellent job as a lead blocker for junior fullback Dale Szweda and as a pass blocker for sophomore quarterback Don Lamka. Gallegos also praised the entire team, noting that the two underclassmen, Szweda and Lamka, had excellent seasons for South in their first year as starters.

Thanksgiving morning, Nov. 25, was an excellent day for a football game on the lakefront. It was 45 degrees, the field was dry, and a crowd of 36,202, better than expected, was on hand. The game was scoreless through the first quarter and much of the second until Benedictine scored a pair of touchdowns during the final four minutes of the first half. The Bengals extended their lead to 29-0 in the second half before South scored to make the final 29-8.

As they did in 1965, the defending West Senate champion Flyers had a tough time getting started in 1966, opening the campaign by dropping nonleague games to Lorain, 31-6, and Shaker Heights, 36-30.

The loss to Shaker was tough for Coach John Gentile's Flyers, but like every dark cloud, this one showed a silver lining. South High had never been known as a "scoring machine," but the 1966 season would be different. The 1966 Flyers would score more points than any previous South High team, which, coupled with another solid defense, meant that the Flyers' fans would be enjoying another good West Senate season.

South, and its newfound offense, opened the defense of its West Senate title by winning its first three league games by a combined 104-0. As the midway point of the Senate season approached, South and Holy Name led the West Senate with identical records of 3-0-0. On Friday night, October 21, the two teams would square off before a jam-packed West Tech Field. Held to just seven plays on offense during the first half, the Flyers trailed the Green Wave 6-0 at the intermission. In the locker room during the intermission, South's John Gentile had some strong words for his team, which they took to heart. When the Flyers returned to the field for the second half, they played like a completely different team. In shutting down the Holy Name offense, the South defense intercepted a pair of passes and recovered a fumble. All three turnovers resulted in touchdowns as the Flyers came storming back for a 24-6 win.

The following weekend, South scored a pair of touchdowns in each of the first three quarters to down Lincoln's winless Presidents, 46-14.

On Friday night, Nov. 4, South and second-place Saint Ignatius squared off in the showdown of the West Senate season. Although a week remained in the Senate season, this game would likely decide the West Senate title. Scoring on a 64-yard run by quarterback Don Lamka just 32 seconds into the game, the Flyers raced to a 16-6 lead after one quarter and never looked back. When the final whistle sounded, the Flyers had handed the Wildcats their worst loss of the last 10 years, 42-6. Don Lamka combined for over 300 all-purpose yards, rushing for 148 and passing for 152 more, while the Flyers' defense intercepted four Saint Ignatius passes to keep the Wildcats from getting back into the game.

The following Friday night at West Tech Field, South defeated a stubborn West High team, 38-20. South High had now won 17 consecutive West Senate games. Still, more importantly, the Flyers had secured a second successive West Senate championship, giving them a chance to even the score with Benedictine's Bengals in the Charity Game.

The 1966 edition of the Flyers was perhaps the most incredible team the school had yet seen, featuring a balanced offensive attack that had produced 290 points. Leading that attack was junior Don Lamka, who was the Flyers' starting quarterback in his second season. A true team leader, Lamka was equally adept at passing the ball or running with it, even as a junior. Don had amassed more than 1,100 yards of total offense in 1966, with 556 yards through the air and 557 yards rushing, for a team-high 8-yards-per-carry average. He scored eight touchdowns, completed a pair of two-point conversions, and tossed three touchdown passes.

Don Lamka's primary receivers were flanker Vic Papushak and end Ed Grzybowski. These two tall targets combined for 494 reception yards, averaging better than 15 yards every time they caught the ball. Papushak was also the team leader in punt and kickoff returns, including one for a 90-yard TD, and had a couple of interceptions from his defensive halfback position. Grzybowski also starred on defense and seemed to specialize in blocking punts, getting through on at least four of them, including blocks in three consecutive games; Grzybowski also had at least one interception to his credit.

As a team, the Flyers had rushed for 1,776 yards, mainly due to the play of a pair of All-Scholastic running backs: 219-pound fullback Dale Szweda and 205-pound halfback Dave Chojnowski. Although Szweda usually gained the tough yardage up the middle while Chojnowski skirted the ends, it did not matter where they ran. Chojnowski was the team's top ground gainer, accumulating 575 yards and scoring 76 points, including 10 touchdowns. Szweda led the team in scoring with 78 points, including 12 touchdowns, and had rushed for 371 yards. Both players were two-way performers, Szweda starting at linebacker and Chojnowski at defensive halfback.

Unfortunately for the West Senate and South High fans, the 36th annual Charity Game, despite being an evenly contested game throughout the first three quarters, would once again belong to the East Senate champion Benedictine Bengals by a score of 32-6. At the end of the game, Benedictine halfback Larry Zelina, the game's MVP, approached South High Coach John Gentile and said, "Coach, South never quit hitting. They hit right till the end."

Coach Gentile could not have received a better compliment for his team's effort.

Quarterback Don Lamka earned All-Scholastic, All-Ohio, and All-American honors. Lamka attended Ohio State on a football scholarship and played from 1968 to 1971. He lettered in football and was a member of the 1968 National Championship team coached by Woody Hayes. Lamka was inducted into the inaugural class of the South Hall of Fame in 1995.

South High's last Senate championship season came in 1987 when the Flyers won the Senate League title with a 12-6 victory over the West Tech Warriors.

However, the Flyers did have one more good season. In 2007, they qualified for the OHSAA Division II Region 5 playoffs with a record of 8-2. The Flyers' opponent in the regional quarterfinal game was the team from Normandy High School. The Invaders had an excellent team that year, and their 38-6 win over South proved it. In recognition of the Flyers' fine season, head coach Jarvis Gibson was named the NE Ohio Lakes District Division II Coach of the Year that season.

The "Pig Iron Trophy" - One of the greatest traditions in the West Senate was the Pig Iron Trophy competition between neighborhood rivals South High and Holy Name High School. The trophy competition began in 1932 as a symbol of victory between the two high football teams. It was named the Pig Iron based upon both schools being located in the steel industry area of Cleveland's southeast side. A spirited neighborhood rivalry developed over the years, and the trophy became a cherished possession for the fans and students of the football team that won the annual game. This great rivalry ended in 1973 with the Flyer's victory and the last game ever against Holy Name.

TRACK (GIRLS)

TheThe South High girls track team, coached by Track Coach Thurman "Weed Hopper" Tyus, scored all its points in the state tournament from 1985 to 1991. In 1985, Ghana Kennedy gave the Flyers all their points with a third-place finish in the 200m dash.

Markeya Jones was a sophomore in 1986 and a member of the sixth-place 4x200m team, but she was just getting started on a career that would mark her as arguably the most outstanding track star the Lady Flyers would ever have. Other team members included Sherry Wilson, Konswella Wilkerson, and Traci Washington. In 1997, Markeya scored all her team's points the following year with a second-place finish in the 200m.

1988 would prove to be the best year at state for Markeya Jones and one of the best for the Lady Flyers. After finishing second in the 100m, Markeya went on to win the 200m race — the only state championship ever won by the Lady Flyers. She then joined Konswella Wilkerson,

Angie Johnson, and Elizabeth Beasley on the 4x100 relay team, which finished in fifth place. All of these points resulted in a fifth-place overall finish for the Flyers.

Taking advantage of a full scholarship, Markeya Jones then continued her education and track career at Kansas State University, where she would set the school record in the 200m with a time of 23.28. Markeya was inducted into the South Hall of Fame in 1986. In 2024, Markeya Jones Owens was inducted into the Cleveland Sports Legends Hall of Fame.

The Lady Flyers did not qualify for the 1989 state meet, but in 1990, they returned to the podium in Columbus. The 4x200m relay team of Aloha Spy, Angie Quinn, Kimberly Mund, and Nicole Freeman finished sixth, and the identical four girls repeated that finish in the 4x400m to get another podium place.

The relay teams would again be the strength of the Lady Flyers in 1991, propelling them to their best-ever finish at the state meet. Carmen Banks started the team when she was second in the 100m hurdles. Then, the relay teams went to work. In the 4x100, Carmen Banks teamed with Angie Quinn, Kimberly Mund, and Nicole Freeman to secure a fourth-place finish. In the 4x200, it was Carmen Banks, Angie Quinn, Kimberly Mund, and Aloha Spy who finished second. Finally, in the 4x400, those identical four girls would place fifth. Now, with a total of twenty-two points, the team earned. All those points totaled 22, making it suitable for an outstanding fourth-place finish.

Although South did not have an active women's track team until the late 1980s to early 1990s, two South High lady graduates were prominent in the Olympics and the AAU Games from the early 1930s through the 1940s.

Stella Walsh, a 1929 graduate who ran for Poland in 1932, won a Gold Medal in the 100-yard dash. In 1936, she won the Silver Medal, finishing 2nd in the same race. Stella won five AAU Pentathlon championships and numerous track and field events throughout her career. After she retired from active competition, she offered coaching instruction to youngsters at the South's recreation center, which now holds her name: The Stella Walsh Recreation Center. Walsh was inducted into the South Hall of Fame in 1995.

Francis Sobczak Kaszubski, a 1934 graduate, participated in the Olympics but was better known for success in the AAU Championships. Miss Kaszubski was the AAU national shot put champion six times from 1943 to 1951. She participated in the 1948 Olympics in London, finishing in 11th place. Her distinguished athletic career earned her the manager's position of the 1960 Rome U.S. Women's Olympic team. Miss Kaszubski served as the Director of the Cleveland City Recreation Department from 1956 through 1978.

TRACK

Although the boys' track team participated in Senate and City meets, only a few Flyers qualified for state meets. In 1978, Kevin Howard finished 5th in the discus throw. Not until the 1990's did South's men's team place again at the State Meet. Marcus Turman qualified for the 1995 State meet, finishing 5th in the 800m run. In 1996, Marcus placed 3rd at the state meet again in the 800m run. His teammate, Lee Parks, finished 6th in the 200m dash.

SOFTBALL (GIRLS)

From the 1970s to the mid-nineties, South's softball teams won several Senate and City Championships. Under Coach Ron Aukerman, the Lady Flyers won City Titles from 1976 to 1981. With Al Abel as the head coach in the nineties, the Flyers won the City Championship in 1994 and 1995.

One of the outstanding softball players was 1980 graduate Marlene Smejkal Jess. Marlene was the first women's nine-letter winner at South High. During her senior year, she was the MVP of the volleyball, basketball, and softball teams. Marlene was inducted into the South Hall of Fame in 1995. She was inducted into the Cleveland Sports Legends Hall of Fame in 2024.

Another outstanding all-around female athlete at South was Brenda Simmons, a member of the class of 1985. A nine-letter winner, Brenda led the Flyers' softball team to a City Championship in 1985. She earned All-Senate honors in volleyball, basketball, and softball during her junior and senior years. Brenda was inducted into the South Hall of Fame in 1996.

TENNIS (GIRLS)

South's girls' tennis team had its best season in 1991, finishing second in the State. Danita Jiminez was the team's Most Valuable Player (MVP).

WRESTLING

The eight-year period from 1956 to 1963 was the best for South High wrestling. In 1956, the Senate League was still a formidable presence in the state tournament, with four teams finishing in the top 10; that year, South tied with West High for 10th place. Leading the way for the Flyers was junior Bob Mantarro, who won the state championship at 165 pounds.

1957, the Flyers were even better, finishing in sixth place with 27 points. Bob Mantarro again led the way by capturing his second consecutive state championship at 165 pounds. (Senate alum and perhaps the most outstanding high school wrestling writer, Pat Galbincea, later named Bob one of Cleveland's all-time great grapplers.) Adding to the South High point total was senior Ted Arslanian, who finished second at 175 pounds.

In 1958, the Flyers slipped 10th in the state tournament, but they could still claim a state championship when senior Henry "Hank" Arslanian won at 175 pounds. In 1959, the Flyers tied Euclid for ninth place, thanks to a second-place finish at 127 pounds by seniors Michael Craycraft and Darrall Popovich, as well as a third-place finish in the heavyweight division.

After a couple of off years, the Flyers made a strong comeback in 1962. That year, South High achieved its best finish in the state wrestling tournament, placing third. Junior Jan Maynard led the way with a state championship at 103 pounds, and senior Jim Williams finishing second at 112 pounds.

In 1963, the Flyers were both Senate and Sectional Champions. At the State Tournament, the team finished in 10th place behind Jan Maynard's second consecutive State Championship, this time at 112 pounds. Pat Galbincea also has Jan Maynard ranked among Cleveland's all-time great high school wrestlers.

Although South never had another State Wrestling Champion, in 1968, Don Lamka finished fourth in the 175 lb. class. In 1973, the Flyers tied with John Marshall HS for 7th place at the State Tournament. John Czarniakowski finished second at 175 lbs. Teammate Michael Kotowski took fourth place in the Unlimited class.

CHAPTER 8

West High School

> *Known initially as Branch High School since it was a division, or branch, of Central High School on the west side of Cleveland, West High School/Branch High School originally opened its doors in 1852 on West 38th Street as Cleveland's second high school. With the growth of the west side population, West High also grew, and by 1902, it was relocated to Franklin Boulevard and West 68th Street. In 1970, the school merged with Lincoln High School to form Lincoln-West High School and relocated to a new building in 1973.*

BASEBALL

One of the best years for the West High baseball team came in 1949 when the Cowboys advanced to the city championship game. The West High yearbook describes that season and the championship game in this way: "Despite rain, hail, snow, mud, and a shortage of pitchers, the Cowboys baseball team of 1949 slugged its way through the Senate season and clobbered East Tech in the City playoff at Old League Park, 9-1."

West High advanced to the city championship game in 1952 and 1953 but lost both times to East High, 5-4 in 11 innings in 1952 and 10-6 in 1953.

Perhaps the best player in school history was Ken McBride, who played baseball from 1951 to 1953 and starred on the basketball court. McBride was a pitcher, the ace of the Cowboys staff. After graduation, McBride was signed by the Boston Red Sox. He finally made it to the big leagues in 1959 with the Chicago White Sox. During his career with the White Sox and the California Angels, Ken McBride had a 40-50 record with a 3.79 ERA. He was selected for the All-Star game three times; in his one All-Star game at-bat, he slugged an RBI single. An injury to his arm cut short McBride's career, retiring after the 1965 season.

BASKETBALL

Being one of Cleveland's first public high schools, it is unsurprising that West High also had one of the area's first high school basketball teams, playing as early as the late 1890s. The team's first real success came in 1904 and would continue for six years in what would become one of the greatest eras for any Cleveland high school basketball team. That year, West battled the other city high schools for Cleveland's championship in what was then called the interscholastic championship series. In one of the season's more memorable games, West pulled out a 30-27 win over Central High, featuring no fewer than 56 fouls. The championship series was decided when West played East High in early March; the score has been lost to history, but we know that West High emerged victorious to claim the city championship.

After losing the 1905 city title to Central, 1906 West High would finally achieve the success that had eluded it the previous season and start the team on a run unlike most before or since. The Plain Dealer recognized early how good a team West High had when it noted, "West should be able to give the best teams in the state a hard tussle for the championship honors, as they have the best material they have ever had for a basketball team."

By Jan. 31, 1906, West was still undefeated overall and was 3-0 in what was then called the High School League, where the city title would be determined. West would finally secure the city championship on Feb. 16 by defeating South High, 21-16; West came from behind to win the game by six points in the last three minutes.

Having won the league and Cleveland city championships, West High still had a few games remaining. On Feb. 17, the boys defeated Sandusky High 23-9, and on Feb. 22, they handed Canal Dover, one of the better teams back then, a 15-11 defeat. After that victory, The Plain Dealer said of West High, "By the result of this game, West has a clear title to the state high school championship."

As if to put an exclamation point on that statement, West crushed Lincoln West the next day, 36-10, raising its record to a perfect 12-0. On March 2, the Cleveland News named Coach Luther's West High basketball team the 1906 high school basketball state champion. And on Dec. 30, in The Plain Dealer's year-end review of area sports, the paper noted, "...West High took off the undisputed championship of the state for high schools."

West High opened the 1906-07 basketball season by easily defeating the team from Saint Ignatius College by scoring 48-9; Walter Bonfield, team captain (for the third consecutive year) and a star forward, led the way with 18 points. On Jan. 23, 1907, with its record still perfect at 4-0, West High took the court against Central High. After trailing most of the game, West rallied and tied the score, sending it into overtime. In those days, a team needed to lead by two points to win overtime. The overtime session had already gone eight minutes when, with the score tied 21-21, there was a jump ball under the Central basket. The West High center, McClay, out-leaped his counterpart and swatted the ball right into the basket, an incredible shot that gave West a stunning 23-21 win.

West went on to win its next three games before suffering a big upset defeat at the hands of South High, 19-18. The Plain Dealer noted that the defeat had halted West High after 36 consecutive wins.

West closed the season by starting a new win streak, winning its last four contests.

West won the 1907 Senate title by its 7-1 record, a game better than South, which had two league losses, but now the 1907 Cleveland high school championship was to be decided. There were no playoff games back then, so the final determination came down to this: West High had finished the season with a 12-1 record, and most of its wins were over Cleveland schools. University School, like West, had just one loss; however, the Preppers had not played any Cleveland schools. By the day's standard, Coach Luther's West High team, with its better record against Cleveland teams, was named the 1907 Cleveland champion.

Now coached by Hatch, the 1907-1908 season would be another great season for West High basketball. The team opened its season with four consecutive wins. On Jan. 31, West squared off against Central High in a game that The Plain Dealer noted: "...will practically determine the senate championship in basketball this season..." West took a 10-5 lead at the half and continued to pull away in the second half for a 26-14 win.

West went on to win its next four games, all over Senate foes, by an average score of 39-10, giving the team the 1908 Senate championship. When Central upset the previously undefeated East High (not a member of the Senate that year) at the end of February, it left West High as the only team "in this section of the state which has gone through the season undefeated." (PD) On March 6, The Plain Dealer noted that "West High now claims the state championship title and is prepared to defend it."

After defeating Glenville in their next game, West High took to the road to play the strong team from Canal Dover High School, a game played before a massive crowd of 1,500. As The Plain Dealer reported, "The interscholastic basketball championship of the state was won by Cleveland West High here tonight when the score of 30-9 defeated Dover High. The locals were outclassed, and at no time did they have any chance of winning."

On March 26, East High and Shaw challenged undefeated West to a game; East High already had two losses and Shaw one. The next day, West High's principal, Charles P. Lynch, turned down both challenges, stating, "We have absolutely nothing to gain by such a contest."

With the 1908 season completed, West High had come away undefeated and won the high school basketball championship trifecta: Senate, Cleveland, and Ohio championships. It marked the third consecutive season that West High had won both the Senate and Cleveland championships and the second time in three seasons that the team had been named Ohio champion. On Jan. 9, 1909, The Plain Dealer had this to say about West High's recent success on the basketball court, "West High has in the past few years set a record indeed to be envied, having won their way for the past six years to the very top of the ladder."

Unfortunately, the team would not reach the "top of the ladder" in 1909. However, three players did have noteworthy seasons—the Plain Dealer First Team All-Cleveland named guard Leo Hyland. In addition, Hyland was named First Team All-Senate, as was his teammate Southern, who played forward, while West High center Hopkins was named to the All-Senate Second Team.

In 1910, the Senate now included eight teams: West High, Lincoln, Central, Tech (soon known as East Tech), South, East High, Glenville, and Commercial High (also known as Commerce or West Commerce). In an article on Jan. 7, 1910, they noted that the basketball teams from Central and West "appear to be stronger than any other in the city..."

Under Coach Stroup's direction, West High won its first three games but lost a key Senate match-up on Jan. 28 to Central, 15-7, leaving West and Central tied atop the Senate with identical 3-1 records. Over the remainder of the Senate season, Central dropped a few games, while West won all three contests. With a record of 6-1, West High gained both the Senate and Cleveland championships. On the All-Scholastic team that year, West High team center Cyril Hellencamp and guard Weber were named to the First Team, while forward Hopkinson was named to the Second Team.

The 1910 season concluded West High's era of incredible success on the basketball court. This era saw the team win four Senate championships, four city titles, and twice being recognized as the state champion.

While it would be more than 40 years before West High won another Senate championship, the team did manage to make several appearances in the Wesleyan Tournament, hosted by Ohio Wesleyan University, in what was then the state high school basketball tournament (the OHSAA started its state basketball tournament in 1923). The Cowboys played in the Wesleyan Tournament four times, but despite a few wins, they never advanced to the semifinals.

West High won the West Senate championship in 1939 but lost the city title game by one point, 18-17, to Collinwood.

The 1951-1952 season would again see West High on top of the local basketball scene. The Cowboys opened the campaign with relatively easy wins over Glenville and Lakewood but stumbled against Central High, dropping a close 54-53 decision. The Cowboys then went on an 11-game winning streak that carried them to the West Senate championship and a trip to the city title game.

Their opponent in that game would be the team that had defeated them in December, the East Senate champions from undefeated, 12-0, Central High. The game was played at 9 p.m. on Friday, Feb. 22, at the Cleveland Arena before a near-record crowd of 9,648. West held a comfortable lead throughout the game, but with about a half-minute to go, that lead had been cut to just three points, 55-52. Just as the final buzzer sounded, Central's Curt Goldsby canned a field goal — and was fouled by West High's Frank Bova. Since time had expired, only Goldsby and the referees were on the court as Goldsby took the shot that could send the game into overtime. But Goldsby missed the foul shot, allowing the Cowboys to come away with their first Cleveland basketball championship since 1910. Junior Ken McBride led West High with 17 points and was named his team's MVP.

Buoyed by their city championship after a successful run in the Senate, the Cowboys moved on to the Class A regional tournament at Baldwin-Wallace College. Led by Ken McBride, who averaged about 20 points throughout the tournament, the Cowboys advanced to the regional final, taking the measure of Cleveland Heights, 54-47. That victory punched West High's ticket to Columbus and the Class A state tournament.

The Cowboys first opponent in Columbus was the team from Akron North. Although West High stayed close throughout the game, they could never quite get ahead and suffered a 51-46 loss. Fouls proved a big problem for West, as they were whistled for 27, with three players fouling out of the contest, including the team's leading scorer, Ken McBride.

That loss snapped the Cowboys 16-game win streak, as they finished with an excellent 18-2 record. Ken McBride was also named All-Ohio Honorable Mention the following season.

West High's only other championship came in 1955, when the Cowboys won the West Senate title again but lost the city title game to East Tech, 60-43.

While the Cowboys did not win another championship over their last 15 years, it did not prevent them from producing one of the most exciting basketball players in Cleveland's history. Phil Argento played for West High from 1962 to 1965. A guard, he averaged almost 30 points per game during his junior and senior years, being named All-Scholastic and All-Ohio Honorable Mention both seasons. In 1964, against South High, Argento set the Cleveland single-game scoring record with a 66-point performance.

Following graduation, Argento continued his education and basketball career at the University of Kentucky. As a freshman, he practically rewrote the first-year team's record book (first-year students could not play on a college varsity team back then). Argento was a three-year starter on the Kentucky varsity and captained the team his senior year. After college, he was drafted by the Los Angeles Lakers but decided to play for the National Amateur Basketball League, later becoming a high school coach.

Phil Argento has been inducted into the Greater Cleveland Sports Hall of Fame. In a Plain Dealer poll taken in 2015 to determine the greatest high school basketball stars of The Plain Dealer's seven-county area for the past 50+ years, Phil Argento received the most votes for the 1960s All-Decade team and the third most votes overall.

CROSS-COUNTRY

The Cowboys of West High School had a nice run of success at the state cross-country meet from 1941 to 1953. In 1941, the team finished eighth, with Dick Hall coming in 20th overall. There was no state meet in 1942 due to World War II. In 1944, the Cowboys, under the direction of head coach Harmon Wolfe, came in second with a score of 89 points, behind Cincinnati Western Hills and its score of 74 points. Leading the way for West High was Edwards, who finished seventh place, and Grevin, who came in 10th.

It would not be until 1947 that the Cowboys again scored high in the state tournament. That year, they finished third, but none of the team's runners finished in the top 20. Two years later, the Cowboys again came in among the state leaders with a sixth-place finish. Still, nobody finished in the top 20 (the OHSAA only listed the top 20 individual finishers).

Then came 1950, the best year ever for the West High cross-country team. Coached by Cy Waffen, the Cowboys finished with a score of 90 points — which was good enough to take home the first-place trophy. Leading the way was Robert Fenton, who finished second overall, while Dick Benz also helped pace the Cowboys with a seventh-place finish.

In 1952, the Cowboys finished in ninth place but had two runners in the top 20; Don Bennett finished 13th, while Dominic Constanzo came in 20th. In 1953, the West High runners had an excellent placing with a fourth-place finish. Robert Stossner was 10th in that race, while Dominic Constanzo duplicated his previous year's effort with a 20th-place finish.

FOOTBALL

West High, eventually to be nicknamed the Cowboys, fielded its first football team in 1890. Along with South High School, West joined the Cleveland School Athletic Association in 1894 and was a charter member of the Senate League when it was formed in 1904. Despite this early start in the sport, the Cowboys did not enjoy their first real success on the gridiron until 1927.

West High opened the 1927 season by defeating its neighbor, Saint Ignatius High School, 6-0. West then rattled off five consecutive league victories. South and Lincoln fell quickly, 27-6 and 38-0, respectively. A minor upset of Glenville, 18-0, made West High the "odds-on favorite of the early season to cop the Senate League title." (PD) The going got rougher against East Tech. However, powered by two long touchdown gallops by halfback Bud Mitchell and a couple of excellent goal-line stands, West High repulsed East Tech 18-6. Against East High, the west Siders made an early first-quarter touchdown stand-up and came away with a 6-0 victory.

Sitting alone atop the Senate League standings with a record of 5-0-0, West High took time from its league schedule to play the always challenging and nationally renowned Toledo Scott High School. Some 350 fans traveled from Cleveland to Toledo with the West High team. It was a good game, but a Scott touchdown in the second quarter proved the margin of victory as West High suffered its first loss of the season, 7-0.

On November 19, West High closed its Senate schedule by defeating Central High by scoring 25-6. With a league record 6-0-0, West High, coached by Walter Shupp, had finally won its first Senate championship.

The final regularly scheduled game of Cleveland's 1927 interscholastic football season, pitting West High (7-1-1) against Cathedral Latin (8-0-0), would also decide Cleveland's interscholastic championship.

The game occurred Saturday after Thanksgiving at Luna Stadium on the city's east side. Reportedly, 12,000 fans endured a steady drizzle that muddied the field but were rewarded with a great game. Latin's Marty Sammon scored a touchdown from 3 yards out in the first quarter to give Latin a 6-0 lead. Both teams' defenses then took over, with the West's defense coming up with several big plays to prevent any further scoring by Cathedral Latin. Unfortunately for West High, they were unable to push across any points. When the gun sounded, ending the game, West High was still on the short end of that 6-0 score.

West High would have to wait seven years before it had another shot at the Senate and Cleveland championships.

While South and Collinwood got most of the attention in 1934, another team quietly kept pace in the Senate race. In 1933, West High had won only one game the entire season. It was probably a bit of a surprise when the Cowboys came from behind in the final couple of minutes to defeat a strong Holy Name team by a score of 7-6 in West's 1934 season opener.

The following week, the Cowboys opened their Senate campaign with a 24-0 shutout of Glenville. A big 20-point first quarter would propel West High to a 33-12 victory over East Tech the following week. The Cowboys then received a severe jolt at the hands of East High on Saturday, Oct. 13, letting an early 7-0 lead slip away as East came from behind to win the game 12-9.

After its loss to East, West High rebounded with a 12-2 Senate victory over John Adams High School. That win was followed by a 25-0 nonleague triumph over west-side neighbor Saint Ignatius.

Heading into the season's final three weeks, West High, with one league loss, was the definite underdog among the Senate's top three teams. However, the Cowboys had won two consecutive league games since falling to East High and then increased that modest win streak to three straight with a 27-13 win over Lakewood in a nonleague contest on Nov. 3.

West High's last two games of the season were crucial Senate contests against Central High and West Tech. The game with Central was an especially tough one. With the game still scoreless in the third quarter, West marched 86 yards from its 5-yard line to the Central nine. There, the Cowboys were stopped on downs. On Central's first-down play, the whole West defense came storming through, with Spartico "Sparky" DiBiasio dropping the Central quarterback in the end zone for a safety. The Cowboys would make those two points hold up for the rest of the game as West High came away with a "must have" 2-0 victory with just one game to go.

On Nov. 17, the Cowboys needed a victory over West Tech to at least gain a share of the Senate crown with Collinwood, which had just suffered its only Senate loss. In the first quarter, West halfback George Weber scored a touchdown on a 2-yard plunge, with Elmer Gedeon hauling in a DiBiasio pass for the extra point. Bob Wiswosser returned a West Tech punt 47 yards in the second quarter for another touchdown. Neither team scored in the second half. West's 13-0 victory left the Cowboys tied with Collinwood for the Senate League championship.

Shaker Heights had already been selected as one of the teams to play in the Charity Game on Dec. 1. The decision for Shaker's opponent was close. Based on its overall record of 8-1-0 and its win over Holy Name, West High was selected as the Red Raiders' opponent — making the Cowboys the first team from the city's west side to ever play in the Charity Game for Cleveland's high school football championship; this was also the first east side versus west side championship game.

Shaker Heights, losers of only one game out of its last 35, would be putting a formidable team on the stadium's gridiron. The Red Raiders defense had been almost impenetrable during the season. Their first-team defense yielded only seven points, which were not scored until the final regular season game with Cleveland Heights.

Like all the other teams that had played West High, Shaker Heights would have a decided weight advantage on the line. However, the Cowboys were a team that Shaker Heights Coach Carl Brubaker knew his team could not take lightly. Although Cleveland's second-oldest public high school did not have as glorious a football history as the oldest, Central High, in the last few years, the Cowboys had made a name for themselves under Coach Walter Schupp. Schupp, a graduate of Miami (Ohio) University, where he was an All-Ohio tackle, had been the coach at West High for the past 11 seasons, and his teams were usually in the thick of it in the Senate race.

Trying to survive in the rough Senate League was always a tough assignment, but Schupp's Cowboys managed to survive and even dominate the Senate in 1934 with an all-senior starting 11. Tackle Ed O'Malley led the line, guard Joe Kemer, and center Adam Falzareno. These boys played on both sides of the ball, leading the defensive charge while opening the holes for the backfield on offense. And what a backfield it was. Halfback Bob Wiswosser was considered the swiftest running back in the city; if he ever broke free, there would be no catching him. Playing alongside Wiswosser were running backs George Weber, Ed Szal, and Carl Estenik, all of whom could punish an enemy defense.

Also in the backfield was quarterback Spartico "Sparky" DiBiasio. At 5'3" and barely 125 pounds, DiBiasio looked "as if he should be playing junior high soccer instead of mixing with those burly gridiron stars" (PD) in a league like Cleveland's Senate. He was mixing it up with the bigger boys, and DiBiasio had been doing it successfully for the past three seasons. Coach Schupp called DiBiasio the most intelligent quarterback in Cleveland, and few would argue the point. Sparky's favorite receiver was 6'4" end Elmer Gedeon. Together, these two made up perhaps the best pass-and-catch tandem in the city.

On game day, the temperature at Municipal Stadium hovered just above the freezing mark, and a strong wind was blowing from the west. When the pregame festivities were completed, the 25,235 paid customers (the second-highest Charity Game total thus far) sat back in their seats to witness the battle for Cleveland's scholastic championship.

The game was a tense defensive struggle, and, with one brief exception, neither team penetrated beyond its opponent's 30-yard line over the final three-quarters of the game. That came in the fourth quarter when West High recovered a Shaker Heights fumble on the Red Raiders 15-yard line. West High had its best scoring opportunity of the game, but on the next play, the Cowboys Bob Wiswosser fumbled the ball, and Shaker Heights recovered the loose pigskin to kill the threat.

Shaker Heights put on its most sustained drive in the game's final minutes, moving from its own 31 to the West High 25-yard line. However, the Red Raiders ran out of time, and the game ended in a 0-0 tie.

It was an unusual end to the season for West High. The Cowboys had finished the regular season as co-champions of the Senate League. Now, they had ended the year as the co-champions of Cleveland. Charity Game manager John A. Crawford must have had a hunch something like this would happen. At the last minute, he ordered a second championship trophy; it arrived the day before the game.

GYMNASTICS

Gymnastics was one of the earliest sports to have a state tournament, the first in 1926. At that time, this was a boys-only sport, and the girls did not get their tournament until almost 50 years later, in 1971.

That first state tournament had only five teams, three from Columbus, one from Cincinnati, and West High, competing in just six events. The West High team scored 349 points, suitable for a third-place finish. Earning All-Ohio recognition was Stropp, who finished third in the Indian clubs (club swinging) event, and Duke, who placed second on the flying rings.

The next time West was in the state tournament was in 1931 when the team finished 13th out of 13. Helfer earned All-Ohio recognition with a fourth-place finish in the Indians clubs. The only other time that the Cowboys made it to the state tournament was in 1934, but like Collinwood, East High, and John Adams, the team failed to score a point.

WRESTLING

Since the OHSAA wrestling tournament began in 1938, Northeast Ohio has been the home to more state champions than any other part of the state. 1938 to 1953 represent the golden era of Senate League participation and success in that tournament.

West High School enjoyed its golden era of state wrestling success from 1945 to 1951, seven years that produced some remarkable accomplishments and some of Ohio's most outstanding high school wrestlers.

While West High had one state champion in Harry Bostwick (113) in 1944, it all started for the Cowboys at the 1945 tournament. They finished that tournament in third place but with two individual champions, Harry Bostwick (113) and Frank Giammarino (121).

The following year, Coach Harold Kester's matmen finished second, just three points behind West Tech, which had won its third consecutive state title. This time, however, West High had three individual champions: Bill Buckingham (103), John Matteucci (114), and John Sanders (121).

In 1947, the Cowboys finally took home their first state title. Bill Buckingham (104) and John Matteucci (121) won individual championships for the second consecutive year, while Joe DiBello also took home a title at 113 pounds. Gene Gibbons finished second at 155 pounds, and in doing so, he set a unique record: At that time, Gene was the only wrestler to finish second in the same weight class for three consecutive years.

In 1948, West High slipped to fourth place. John Matteucci was the Cowboy's lone state champion that year. Still, he had accomplished something no other wrestler up to that time had done – his championship was the third consecutive individual title of his outstanding career, the first wrestler in state history to accomplish that feat.

In 1949, the Cowboys missed a state championship by one point, finishing second to Euclid Shore High School. However, they did take home three individual titles as Dick Bonacci (139), Ralph Giammarino (121), and Joe Cassarino (104) all won championship trophies.

In 1950, the Cowboys, who were undefeated as members of the Senate League, were the heavy favorites among the 19 schools participating in that year's state tournament. This time, the Cowboys did not disappoint, winning the state championship and tying the record for most team points with a total of 39. Winning state titles for West High were Dick Bonacci (155), Ralph Giammarino (121), and Fred Darienzo (134).

When the 1951 state tournament rolled around, the Cowboys were again the heavy favorites, and when they qualified seven boys for the finals, it appeared to be a done deal. (An eighth title hopeful, Ernest Rocco (104), had to withdraw due to an injury.)

When the wrestling began, Coach Harold Kester's boys again came through with flying colors as they dominated the field and won their second straight championship. The Cowboys "Italian Connection" of Fred Darienzo (134), Richard Bonacci (166 – his third straight individual title), Vince Matteucci (128), Emil Palmieri (139), and Pete Rossi (155) all took home firsts, as did Robert Pogue (121). The Cowboys again set a team record by scoring 50 points, more than triple the score of second-place Euclid, which had 16 points. The previous record of 39 points had been set by the Cowboys just the year before.

Six individual champions in one tournament — a feat that has never been equaled.

Adding more than a bit of icing to their cake, Coach Kester's team was named the national high school wrestling champion that year, the first Ohio team so honored, and one of just three Ohio schools to ever reach that lofty plateau.

After the 1951 season, West High never again finished higher than third in the state tournament. Despite the school now being closed, the Cowboys proud legacy of success remains, as they are still ranked 10th all-time in Ohio with 28 individual state champions. West High's mark of 22 individual champions over seven years (1945-1951) has seldom been equaled.

Nationally renowned Wrestling Hall of Fame high school wrestling writer Pat Galbincea (John Marshall, 1965) was asked in 2019 to name the best Senate League wrestlers ever. Eight of those wrestlers are West High grads:

John Matteucci - Ohio's first and three-time state champion, at 114 pounds in 1946, then won it again at 121 pounds in 1947 and 1948. He also coached Eastlake North to a state team title in 1975. After a stellar coaching career at Eastlake North High School, John was later inducted into the National Wrestling Hall of Fame, joining his brother, Vince.

Dick Bonacci - Three-time state champion, at 139 pounds in 1949, 155 pounds in 1950, and 166 pounds in 1951. He captained the 1951 team, which at one time was considered the most incredible team in Ohio high school wrestling history, with six individual state champs and one runner-up in the 10 weight classes. Dick finished his career at West High with a record of 60-0. He founded the successful Cleveland State University wrestling program with several top 10 nationally ranked teams.

Harry Bostwick - Two-time Ohio champion, in 1944 and 1945 at the same weight, 113 pounds.

Gene Gibbons - At one time, Ohio's only three-time state runner-up, all at the same weight, 155 pounds, from 1945 through 1947. In 1951, he became an NCAA champion at Michigan State and coached John Marshall to a state team championship in 1961.

Bill Buckingham - Two-time state champion in 1946 and 1947 at the same weight class, 103 pounds.

Ralph Giammarino - Two-time state champion, both years at 121 pounds. (1949-50).

Fred Darienzo - Two-time Ohio champion, at 134 pounds in 1950 and 1951.

Charles Ferrari - Two-time Ohio champion, at 104 pounds in 1955 and 120 pounds in 1957, after finishing second at 103 pounds in 1956.

Add to this list of wrestling greats the name of Harold Kester, one of the all-time great Ohio high school wrestling coaches. From 1939 to 1951, his teams at both John Hay and West High won seven state championships and finished as the runner-up three times. Coach Kester was inducted into the Ohio High School Wrestling Coaches Hall of Fame in 1971.

Although he did not make Pat Galbincea's list of great wrestlers, Vince Matteucci, one of the six state champions from 1951, has earned many honors. Among the most distinguished of these are selection to the National Wrestling Hall of Fame (in significant part because of his outstanding tenure as a wrestling official and service in promoting the sport), the Ohio Wrestling Hall of Fame, and the Legend Award from the Western Reserve Wrestling Coaches Association.

DISTINGUISHED ALUMNUS

Once in a great while, a school will have an alumnus whose accomplishments, both at the school and beyond, are such that he deserves special recognition. West High School has such a person in Elmer Gedeon.

Elmer John Gedeon, Class of 1935, is one of the most distinguished athletes ever to walk the halls of West High School. He competed successfully in football, basketball, track, and baseball. As one of Cleveland's premier prep pass receivers, Gedeon was a central cog in the West High team that played in the city championship Charity Game in 1934. The following spring, he set a state record of 15.0 seconds in the high hurdles. Elmer's athletic accomplishments earned him a full scholarship to the University of Michigan.

Elmer continued his athletic success at Michigan by earning letters in football, track, and baseball. He won the Big Ten high hurdles crown two years in a row, and in 1938, Gedeon tied Jesse Owens' indoor low hurdles world record, earning All-America status. In 1983, Elmer was inducted into the University of Michigan Hall of Honor; he is one of only six athletes inducted in two sports, getting the nod for his accomplishments in track and baseball.

Although he had Olympic-quality potential as a hurdler, upon graduating from Michigan in 1939, Elmer signed a professional baseball contract with the Washington Senators. In September of that same year, he was elevated from the minor leagues to the Major League club. He appeared in five games with the Senators that month as a centerfielder and had three hits in 15 at-bats; ironically, all those hits came against his hometown team, the Cleveland Indians. Elmer was back in the minor leagues the following season, being groomed to be the Senator's future centerfielder. Still, before he could again reach the major leagues, Elmer was drafted into the U.S. Army in 1941.

Elmer Gedeon served in the Army Air Corps, where he was trained to be a bomber pilot. While in training, Elmer was involved in a serious accident when his plane crashed into a swamp in North Carolina. Despite receiving three broken ribs, Elmer returned to the burning plane to save the life of another pilot who was unable to move, and in the process of this rescue, he received very severe burns. Elmer received the Soldier's Medal, the highest non-combat military honor, for his extraordinary bravery. In recognition of his heroism, and after spending 12 weeks in the hospital, Elmer Gedeon was honored with a parade in the streets of Cleveland before returning to active duty. In April of 1944, while on a bombing mission over France, Elmer's plane was shot down, and he was killed at the age of 27. In 1945, Gedeon's remains were transferred to Arlington National Cemetery.

Elmer Gedeon was the first of only two Major League Baseball players to perish while serving their country during World War II. Elmer John Gedeon was indeed a very special West High Cowboy.

CHAPTER 9

West Tech High School

On Feb. 15, 1912, before the building was even finished, West Tech opened its doors to its first students, just over 200 of them. With the enrollment continually growing, the building went through several expansions, the most significant being in 1922 and the one that gave West Tech its final form.

In the 83 years of its existence, West Tech graduated more than 40,000 students. The school offered many innovations, including the first driver's education and auto mechanics classes and the nation's first high school classes in aircraft radio operations, repair, and metallurgy. In the fall of 1931, West Tech was the largest high school in Ohio, with more than 4,000 students, eventually exceeding the 5,000-student mark in 1939. Until 1947, the school's sports teams were known as the Carpenters, after which the name was changed to the Warriors.

To quote a West Tech Alumni Association publication, "West Tech had survived five wars, the Great Depression, epidemics, energy crises, and even court-ordered busing. But it had met one final foe it could not overcome — the Cleveland School Board. Sadly, West Tech closed its doors forever as a high school in June 1995."

BASKETBALL

The Warriors of West Tech came close to winning their first Senate basketball championship during the 1922-23 season, but East High defeated them in overtime, 16-14, to take the Senate title. The following year, it was again West Tech battling East High for Senate, and possibly city, honors, but again East High prevailed by the same 16-14 score.

In 1925, West Tech was again battling for a Senate championship, and by mid-March, the Warriors and Glenville shared the lead with identical 6-1 league records. West Tech and Glenville won their final league games and were declared 1925 Senate co-champions.

West Tech would next find itself in the Senate championship race during the 1930-1931 campaign. On March 6, a 33-24 defeat of Central High clinched for the Warriors a first-place tie with South, both teams finishing their league schedules with identical 6-1 records.

In 1937, the Senate expanded and split into two divisions, East Senate and West Senate. Over the next nine seasons, West Tech will enjoy outstanding success on the basketball court as a member of the Senate's west side division. The Warriors would finish the 1937-1938 season atop the West Senate and meet East Tech in the Senate championship game. That game would go down to the wire and beyond, but West Tech was a point short at the end of overtime, losing to East Tech 44-43.

The 1939-1940 basketball season would see another close race for the West Senate title. That season ended with West Tech and South High tied for the divisional crown. In the following playoff game, Coach Hal Cihlar's Warriors turned the tables on the Flyers and came away with a 36-34 victory to capture the West Senate crown. The Warriors now face Collinwood's East Senate champions in the Senate championship game. West Tech led throughout the first three quarters but could not hold off Collinwood's fourth-quarter rally and lost the game 24-22. Walter Horndeski ended the season with 165 points, a new West Tech single-season high.

The 1942-1943 season would be the Warriors' best thus far. On Feb. 26, 1943, West Tech, with a record of 5-1, met undefeated South High, 6-0, in the final West Senate game. The Warriors jumped out to an early lead, and South could not close the gap. West Tech came away with a 37-28 win. This left both teams with 6-1 records, making a playoff game necessary to decide the West Senate champion. The playoff game was held on March 5 at the John Marshall gym. Once again, the Warriors jumped out to an early lead, 12-4, after the first quarter, a lead they maintained and extended over the game's balance to win the West Senate title with a 38-29 victory.

The Warriors now had one more game to play, the Senate championship at Public Hall on March 12 against the East Senate champion, Collinwood. Collinwood entered the title game undefeated in league play at 8-0, overall 9-4; West Tech was 7-1, 11-3. "Playing a cautious brand of basketball while Collinwood was taking many hurried and unsuccessful shots at the basket" (PD), West Tech was able to grab the lead and hold onto it throughout the game until late in the fourth quarter when the Railroaders went on top, 29-28. Collinwood then tried to freeze the ball for the final couple of minutes, but West Tech came up with a steal with about a minute remaining on the game clock. Warriors guard Francis Pieper then took a jump shot that found nothing but net to give the Warriors a 30-29 victory and the overall Senate championship.

Since the Senate League expansion, West Tech had won 26 of 31 games, and now the school had a league title to go with all of those wins.

The Warriors were back in the Senate race in 1946 with another squad that looked its best. On Feb. 21, the Warriors clinched the West Senate title with a 57-44 win over West High. In that game, Warriors star Warren Hamula set two school scoring records: the first was a single-game high of 34 points, and the second was a single-season high of 217 points (which would eventually hit 235 points by the end of the season).

West Tech's next game would be for the city championship at Public Hall on March 11 against East Senate champion Benedictine. This would be a game between a couple of Cleveland area basketball powerhouses. West Tech entered the game with a record of 13-1, its only loss by two points to Cleveland Heights, 54-52. And Benedictine was a perfect 14-0, averaging 63.6 points per game. So many people wanted to see this game that the tickets sold out the first day they were on sale, with more than 7,500 filling the seats on game night.

After falling behind early, a 14-2 run late in the first quarter gave the Warriors a 16-12 lead. They led by two at the half, but a big third quarter by the Bengals would carry Benedictine to a 49-44 win.

It would be another 15 years, the 1960-61 season, before the West Tech faithful would see their Warriors again battling for a city basketball title. By late January of 1961, the Warriors of head coach Larry Chernauskas were 9-0 in the West Senate, 11-0 overall, and ranked #15 in the latest AP state poll. The Warriors had five games left on their schedule, all against West Senate foes, and they had a 1½- game lead over second-place Saint Ignatius.

On Jan. 27, the Warriors battled Saint Ignatius in a key West Senate game. The Warriors held a slim 39-38 lead at the half, but a big third quarter carried them to a 69-56 victory, assuring West Tech of a divisional title. The Warriors made it official by sweeping their last four games and finishing with a 14-0 record in the West Senate, 16-0 overall. It was the first undefeated regular season in West Tech basketball history. In the final AP state poll, the Warriors were ranked #7, and John Udris was named Honorable Mention All-Ohio.

But the Warriors still had some basketball to play, starting with the city championship game on Feb. 21 at the Arena against East Tech. After trailing throughout the game, a massive rally by the Warriors gave them a 60-53 lead with 3:40 left in the game, but a 10-2 run by East Tech over the next two minutes put the Scarabs back on top by a point, 63-62, with 1:20 remaining. Each team added two points over the game's final minute, leaving West Tech on the short end of a 65-64 final.

On Feb. 26, 1961, head coach Larry Chernauskas was named the Coach of the Year by the Cuyahoga County Basketball Coaches Association.

The Warriors now moved on to the OHSAA Class AA state tournament. In a surprisingly close game in the Berea Sectional, John Udris scored a buzzer-beater from under the basket to defeat Berea High School, 43-41. In the Sectional championship game, West Tech easily defeated Max Hayes, 92-59, with John Udris being named the sectional tournament MVP. Moving on to district play, the Warriors defeated Oberlin, 70-53, but saw their tournament run end in the district final with a 56-47 loss at the hands of Elyria High School.

The Warriors would not play for the city title for another five years but would dominate West Senate basketball for four consecutive seasons.

In the early days of the 1965-1966 basketball season, with a 4-4 record, hardly anyone gave the West Tech Warriors much of a chance to win the West Senate championship. The Warriors then ran off five consecutive wins, heading into the last day of the regular season, tied with both West High and South High for first place, all three with 9-4 records. West Tech defeated West High on that last day, 58-53. The Warriors then got some help from Saint Ignatius as the Wildcats upset South in overtime, 75-72. With a record of 10-4 (11-5), the Warriors had won the West Senate championship.

The Warriors then played East Tech for the city championship. After trailing by six points at the half, West Tech pulled within two of the Scarabs midway through the third quarter. East Tech then went on a 28-12 run over the game's final 12 minutes to win the city championship, 69-51.

West Tech then moved on to the Berea Sectional of the Class AA state tournament. The Warriors won their fourth Sectional championship of the last six seasons with convincing wins over Olmsted Falls, Rocky River, and Fairview. However, West Tech's season ended in the Lorain District tournament at the hands of Elyria High, 64-47.

Despite closing out the 1966-67 West Senate season with a one-point, 79-78, loss to Lincoln, the Warriors still captured their second consecutive West Senate crown with a 12-2 record, 14-2 overall. Next up was East Tech in the city championship game. Wholly outplayed by the Scarabs, West Tech dropped an 80-54 decision.

The Warriors entered the fray as the number one seed in the Berea Sectional of the state basketball tournament. They struggled in their first game but managed to hold off a spunky Rocky River team and emerge with a 55-51 win. In a Sectional semifinal game, the Warriors faced Senate foe Rhodes, which had won only three times in 17 previous games. The Warriors again struggled, and this time, it cost them as Rhodes pulled off the stunner of the sectional tournament by downing West Tech 36-34. The Warriors ended their season with a 15-4 record.

Heading into the late stages of the 1967-1968 West Senate season, head coach Larry Chernauskas' West Tech team was in a real battle to win the divisional championship for a third consecutive season. In early December, the Warriors suffered a 63-60 loss against Rhodes. As the season progressed, that loss was the only smudge on the Warriors record, but it kept them in second place behind Rhodes' undefeated Rams. On Jan. 26, West Tech and Rhodes had their rematch at the West Tech gym, both teams entering the game with just one league loss. As expected, it was a real battle, but this time the Warriors prevailed, 51-48.

With one game remaining, West Tech had only to get by John Marshall to claim the West Senate title. The game was tied 13-13 after the first quarter and 25-25 at the intermission. West Tech claimed a one-point lead, 38-37, as the game headed into its final eight minutes. The Warriors did not crack and came away with a 48-46 victory; by doing so, they became the first West Senate team to win three consecutive divisional championships.

Moving on to the city championship game on Feb. 21 at the Arena, the Warriors will face the Blue Bombers of East High. East entered this game a perfect 14-0. West Tech got a good start and led 10-9 after the first quarter, but it mainly was East High. Over the last three quarters, the Blue Bombers outscored the Warriors by almost 20 points to come away with a 60-42 victory.

Once again, West Tech was the top seed at the Class AA Berea Sectional tournament in 1968. The Warriors defeated Brooklyn High School in a first-round game, but they were again upset in the Sectional final, dropping a close 49-48 decision to St. Edward High School.

The 1968-1969 West Senate basketball season was much more of a horse race than the last several. From mid-January to the end of the Senate season, the Warriors bounced from second to first to third. The divisional title was finally decided in the West Senate's final games. West Tech defeated South High, 75-53, while Max Hayes' 70-63 defeat of Rhodes prevented the Rams from finishing in a tie with West Tech for first place. For the fourth consecutive season, West Tech reigned as West Senate champions.

Next up was the city championship game, and this time the Warriors (10-3, 11-4) would be facing John Adams (13-1, 14-2). After a slow start, the Warriors took the lead at 4:25 in the first quarter and held it for almost the rest of the game. Late in the game, Thomas Wooten of John Adams scored a field goal and a foul shot, giving the Rebels a 67-65 lead — there were only seven seconds left in the game. That proved to be the final score. For the ninth time since 1931, the Warriors failed to close the season with a city title.

The Warriors were again the top seed at the Berea Sectional tournament, as they had been in the previous few seasons. They defeated North Royalton, 57-35, in a Sectional semifinal game, but dropped the Sectional final to Lakewood, 56-48, closing out their season with a 13-6 record.

It would be another 10 years before the Warriors again competed for a West Senate title, but this time, there would be no doubt who was the league champion.

On Jan. 19, 1979, the Warriors defeated Lincoln-West, 69-54, to lift their West Senate record to 10-0, 13-0 overall. Only one team was standing between the Warriors and the West Senate title. On Jan. 26, West Tech hosted Saint Ignatius, which had only one defeat, which had come at the hands of the Warriors the previous month. The Warriors took the suspense out of the rematch early, jumping out to a 21-6 lead after the first quarter and never looking back. West Tech's 66-49 win clinched the West Senate title.

Finishing the season a perfect 12-0, 15-0, the Warriors now had a date to play Glenville (10-1, 12-1) for the city championship. This was a very close game throughout. The score was tied at 59-59 when, with just seven seconds left to play, the Warriors' Don Grant sank the shot, giving West Tech a 61-59 win and their first city championship in 36 years.

Next was the Warriors' annual trip to the Class AAA Baldwin-Wallace Sectional tournament in Berea, where the 17-1 Warriors were the number-one seed. (On Feb. 16, the Warriors had lost a nonleague game to John Adams, 74-62.) West Tech opened its tournament play with a 59-41 win over previously undefeated Valley Forge and then took home the Sectional championship with a 78-54 victory over Rhodes. That win was the team's 19th of the year, tying the school record for most wins in a season. Moving on to the Baldwin-Wallace District tournament, the Warriors dropped a 65-57 decision at the hands of the Parma Redmen. One of West Tech's best seasons ever ended with a final record of 19-2.

Larry Chernauskas started coaching basketball at West Tech in 1956 and retired from that position in 1982, having won five West Senate championships. He then coached three area girls high school teams until 1997, finishing with an overall record of 508-280. Among other honors, Larry has been inducted into the Ohio High School Basketball Coaches Hall of Fame and the Greater Cleveland Sports Hall of Fame.

The 1987-1988 season would be the last time the Warriors of West Tech would contend for the Senate basketball crown, the league now divided into North and South divisions. The Warriors finished league play with a record of 8-2, 12-4, edging out Glenville, 7-3, for the North Senate title. Next up for the Warriors was a date with the John Adams Rebels (10-0, 13-3) for the overall Senate championship. West Tech led throughout the game until the Rebels tied the score early in the final frame. West Tech then went on a 10-0 run to take what appeared to be a commanding lead, 57-47. But back came the Rebels with a 7-0 run of their own to make it 57-54 with 1:21 to play. However, the Warriors never lost their composure, and the game ended with West Tech on the long end of a 59-56 final score.

In the semifinals of the Division I District tournament at Valley Forge High School, the Warriors defeated Parma 70-52. Two days later, they played Valley Forge in the district finals and saw their season end with a 77-57 defeat. With a record of 16-6, it was the Warriors best season in the last nine years.

CROSS-COUNTRY

In 1933, West Tech finished eighth in the state meet, with Kreuger finishing among the top 20 runners and thus earning All-Ohio recognition. The following season, the Warriors jumped to third place, with Kreuger again leading the team with an eighth-place finish.

It would be another 10 years before the Warriors again finished on the leaderboard, but that 1944 season would usher in an era of success for the West Tech harriers that would last for the next dozen years. That year, West Tech finished sixth in the state meet, led by a pair of All-Ohio runners: Sewell, the second runner to cross the finish line, and Dunn, who came in 11th.

1945 would provide West Tech

with its first indeed banner year for cross-country. On Oct. 20, the Warriors outdueled Rhodes to win the district championship by scoring 45-52. West Tech and Rhodes went head to head the following Saturday, but it was at the State Meet in Mansfield this time. With team captain Walter Calkowski leading the way with a fourth-place finish, the Warriors again defeated the Rams by scoring 82-97. By so doing, West Tech had won its first cross-country state championship – becoming the first Senate League school to do so.

West Tech would again be among the state's elite cross-country teams in 1946. Running for head coach Karl Bauer on Oct. 26, the Warriors repeated as the district champions. George Gross won the race, followed by John Minnich (2), Don Smith (7), and Bob Gedeon (10), giving the Warriors four boys among the first 10 finishers. On Nov. 3 at the State Meet, George Gross (3) and Bob Gedeon (10) were again among the first runners to cross the finish line. However, the Warriors could not defend their state title, finishing second with 90 points, behind first place Akron North and its 66 points.

In 1947, the Warriors did not place in the team competition, but George Gross (who had set a record time of 9:54.7 in winning the Senate meet) represented his school well and earned All-Ohio status by finishing second in the race.

West Tech would again find itself atop the cross-country leaderboard throughout 1948. On Oct. 20, the Warriors won the Senate championship with a great score of 31, besting Cathedral Latin and its 43 points. In the district meet, the Warriors beat out Cathedral Latin again, finishing with 57 points to Latin's 79. Coach Karl Bauer took his all-senior team to the State Meet in Mansfield. With Jim Bennett finishing 10th and John Prokop 16th, the Warriors scored 84, good enough to outdistance Cincinnati Central and Akron East, which tied for second place with a score of 108.

With all of those great senior runners from the 1948 team having graduated in 1949 and 1950, Coach Bauer was in something of a rebuilding process. It all paid off in 1951. On Oct. 20 that year, West Tech won the Senate cross-country championship at Ridgewood Country Club for the third time. The Warriors' George Leith finished first in the race, and in the process, he set a new course record of 9:52.0.

The following Saturday, the Warriors were back at Ridgewood for the district meet. Behind another record-setting district and course performance by Leith, this time finishing in 9:51.3, the Warriors easily bested second-place Lakewood, 41-85.

On Nov. 3, the Warriors participated in the State Meet, which was held this time (and ever since) on the golf course at Ohio State University. George Leith finished first at 10:36.0, and the Warriors' score of 73 gave West Tech its third cross-country state championship.

Over the next few years, the Warriors were somewhat quiet in cross-country, although Milo Divjak finished seventh in the 1952 State Meet, and Art Sales came ninth in 1955. Both earned All-Ohio recognition.

The 1956 season would start the Warriors on a three-year run of success. That year, they finished third in the State Meet, with Don Tuckosh in sixth place and Jim Planicka in 16th.

Now coached by Eugene Kolach, the 1957 team easily won the West District Meet at Ridgewood with a score of 32. On Nov. 2 at the State Meet, the Warriors finished as state champions with a score of 84, besting second-place Akron Buchtel by 30 points. Jim Planicka, team captain, earned All-Ohio by finishing in ninth place, as did Arnold Ebert by finishing 17th.

West Tech returned with a veteran team in 1958. Six boys – Arnold Ebert, Rich Rios, Angelo Ancorvia, Larry Reim, Theo Goins, and Joe Incorvia – ran on the 1957 state championship team. This team showed its veteran strength on Oct. 25 when it easily won the West District Meet with a remarkable score of 27, burying second-place Lakewood and 96 points. West Tech had four runners finish among the top eight in that race: Arnold Eber came in first, Rich Rios was third, Ken Gailey fourth, and Larry Ream eighth.

At the State Meet, the Warriors had four boys finish among the top 21, but they fell short of defending their title, falling to Akron North, 38-56. The runners who made it close in that meet for West Tech were Arnold Ebert, who finished third, Richard Rios eighth, Joe Basko in 17th, and Ken Gailey in 21st place.

With that race came the end of West Tech's golden era of cross-country racing.

FOOTBALL

In 1916, the Senate championship ended in a tie between East Tech and West Tech, finishing with identical league marks of 5-2-0. There being no provision for a tie-breaker, it marked the first time in Senate history that a team from the western side of the Cuyahoga River had ever won or shared the Senate championship. West Tech had risen to the top of the league standings in only its fifth season.

Late in the 1923 season, West Tech kept its title hopes alive by defeating both Glenville, 6-0 and South, 46-0, to end the season with a league mark 4-1-0. East Tech also finished with a record of 4-1-0, so the two teams again shared the league title.

West Tech would enjoy another good season in 1924; this time, the team had its sites aimed higher than the Senate championship.

Riding a stifling defense, West Tech shut out its first seven opponents that season, including all six Senate foes. The other major high school gridiron force in the Cleveland district that year was Lakewood High School, the area's only undefeated team, averaging 34 points per game. It just so happened that West Tech and Lakewood were already scheduled to play each other on the last day of the season, their traditional Thanksgiving morning encounter. Due to the large crowd expected for this game, the site was switched from West Tech's field to Dunn Field (home of the Cleveland Indians), and the date changed from Thanksgiving to the Saturday after, Nov. 29.

Nov. 29 dawned with a snowstorm, but that did not stop this critical game. The weather would be a factor throughout and only enhance the defensive duel. West Tech would score a touchdown on a returned fumble but miss the extra-point try. Lakewood scored on a safety, a touchdown, and an extra point, resulting in a 9-6 win for Lakewood and Cleveland's high school football championship. Lakewood scored the only touchdown the West Tech defense allowed during the season.

In 1925, West Tech would be in the thick of it for both the Senate League and Cleveland championships for the third consecutive season. As Yogi Berra so uniquely put it, it would be "déjà vu all over again" as West Tech, Lakewood, Cathedral Latin, and Saint Ignatius would again battle down to the season's final game to decide Cleveland's interscholastic football championship.

The final two weeks of the Senate season would prove decisive. With a league record 2-0-1, West Tech found itself in second place behind West High (3-0-0) and Central (3-0-0). Defeating West High first by 7-0 and then topping Central, 14-0, for the third consecutive season, West Tech finished atop the Senate, its league mark standing at 5-0-1.

With barely a week remaining in the season, West Tech, Lakewood, Cathedral Latin, and Saint Ignatius were virtually even as regarded as the Cleveland city championship. As luck and the schedule would have it, these teams would decide the issue themselves. On Saturday, Nov. 21, Saint Ignatius defeated Latin, 27-6, setting up the showdown of the 1925 football season between West Tech and Lakewood High School. Played on Thanksgiving morning, that game ended in a 7-7 tie. Unfortunately for West Tech, since Saint Ignatius was the only area team without a loss or a tie, they were declared Cleveland's 1925 scholastic champions. However, being named to the various All-Scholastic teams were West Tech end Jimmy Owens (First Team) and halfback Johnny Reynolds (Second Team).

Following those three consecutive years of success, West Tech's football fortunes declined over the next dozen years; the team's next era of greatness began with the 1937 campaign.

The 1937 football season was the first under the new Senate League format that featured the addition of a half-dozen teams and the division of the league into eastern and western divisions, more commonly referred to as the East Senate and the West Senate. Every high school within Cleveland's city limits was now in the Senate League. This season also saw a revised Charity Game format, in which the winners of each Senate division would now play for the city title.

The real showdown of the 1937 West Senate season took place the first weekend of November when Lincoln and West Tech met at Municipal Stadium. By the time the 8:15 p.m. kickoff rolled around on Friday night, Nov. 5, 23,080 fans had filed into Cleveland Stadium – the largest crowd up to that time ever to watch a regular season high school football game in the city! Three touchdowns by West Tech fullback Alex Belaka led West Tech to a compelling 26-7 victory over Lincoln. The Carpenters made their West Senate championship official by trouncing John Marshall the following week, 31-0.

The stage was now set for the first All-Senate Charity Game to decide Cleveland's scholastic football championship. The Carpenters from West Tech (5-0-1, 7-0-2) would square off against the Rebels of John Adams (6-0-0, 8-1-0). At this time, the West Senate was considered the stronger of the two divisions, making West Tech the pre-game favorite.

On game day, Nov. 27, 47,315 people bought tickets to Municipal Stadium to see the game for the city championship. With just five minutes in the game, West Tech had jumped out to a 6-0 lead – and made all of the pre-game prophets look good. But those would prove all the points the Carpenters would muster that day. John Adams tied the score in the second quarter, then added 14 points in the second half to come away with a stunning 20-6 upset victory.

Being named to Cleveland's 1937 All-Scholastic squad from West Tech were Emil "Al" Hust (First Team), Alex Belaka (First Team), Joe Caraboolad (Second Team), and Honorable Mention selections Bob Kitzerow, Paul Clarke, Dick Bonde, and O'Dea.

West Tech would return to the thick of the West Senate race in 1938. West Tech and Rhodes entered the season's final week tied above the West Senate standings with identical 5-0-0 West Senate marks. As fate would have it, they were scheduled to meet in the West Senate finale for both teams on Saturday, Nov. 12. Outside of the Charity Game itself, this would be the biggest game of Cleveland's 1938 scholastic football season, featuring two of the city's best high school football teams over the last several years. West Tech had only lost one of its previous 20 games. An impressive mark until compared to that of Rhodes; since 1936, the Rams had gone 25 games without a loss.

Despite the large crowd expected for this game, the principals of both schools agreed to play the game as scheduled at the relatively small Rhodes Field rather than move to a larger venue. A huge overflow crowd of approximately 10,000 was on hand that Saturday afternoon at Rhodes Field, and they saw a whale of a game. The only scoring in the first three-quarters of this defense-oriented game came in the second quarter when Al Hust gave Tech a 6-0 lead on a short TD blast. In the fourth quarter, the physical size of the West Tech team will prove decisive. Al Hust added his second touchdown of the game, while end Jim Salem scored a six-pointer. West Tech's 20-0 victory gave it the West Senate crown and the date to meet Cathedral Latin in the Charity Game at Municipal Stadium.

As The Plain Dealer put it, the 1938 Charity Game would be the team, Cathedral Latin, which had not been scored upon in three previous Charity Games, versus West Tech, a team that had not been scored upon the whole season. Tech ended the 1938 season with a record of 7-0-1, all of the games shutouts, 32 consecutive quarters without yielding a point.

Although both teams featured outstanding defenses, Coach Charley Blickle's West Tech Carpenters were a big team in 1938, with a line that averaged 185 pounds. In recognition of their excellent play on both sides of the ball, five West Tech linemen were named All-Scholastic. Bill Salem, the premier passes catcher in the city, led that list, who, on defense, turned many an end run to the inside where his teammates were waiting. Center Bobby Eckhardt was the most petite man on the Tech line at 173 pounds, but he was also the team's captain and a great leader. Guards Bill Ruhrkraut and Orris Hicks used their 190 pounds to stop many runners up the middle. Tackle George Krudy, who rounded out the list of West Tech All-Scholastic linemen, seldom let an opposing runner get through his side of the line; while on offense, he opened gaping holes for his running backs.

The Carpenter's backfield was also sizeable, tipping the scales at 175 pounds. It was led by fullback Al Hust and halfback Dick Bonde, two more All-Scholastic selections. Hust was huge for a running back, going 6'1" and 205 pounds. A three-year varsity member, he led all Tech ball carriers with 12 touchdowns and 73 points scored. Like most starting players of his day, Al Hust also played defense. No doubt contributing to his All-Scholastic selection, Hust incredibly scored four of his touchdowns on intercepted passes.

When opponents rushed up to stop Hust's plunges into the center of the line, it was time to give the ball to tailback Dick Bonde for an end run. A great open-field runner, Bonde was a true triple-threat man who could pass accurately and did much of West Tech's punting.

Excitement was running at an all-time high as the date for the Charity Game between two of Northeastern Ohio's best schoolboy 11's neared. Latin had won 16 games in a row, while West Tech had only lost one of its last 21 games. Ticket sales were brisk, and despite the cold weather and a few snowflakes, a record crowd of 54,164 turned out on Nov. 26 for the Charity Game. It was the largest crowd ever to witness a high school football game in Cleveland and the third-largest attendance for any football game in Cleveland up to that time.

The game got underway promptly at 2:15 p.m. The first quarter ended with the score still tied at 0-0. The second quarter saw both teams threaten to score, but both 11s came up empty. Midway through the third frame, Latin's Jim Fenton went 74 yards on a reverse to score the first touchdown the West Tech defense had allowed the entire season. It would also prove to be the only score of the game, a heartbreaker that West Tech dropped to Latin, 7-0.

West Tech had another undefeated season in 1939, but it would not be good enough to win the West Senate title. The Carpenters finished their West Senate schedule with a record of 5-0-2 (7-0-2), the ties coming in back-to-back games against South, 14-14, and Holy Name, 0-0. But the South High Flyers did them one better, ending with a West Senate record of 6-0-1, thus edging West Tech out for the divisional title and the trip to the Charity Game.

The expansion and division of the Senate League had come in 1937. By 1940, with a record of 16-0-4 in West Senate play, West Tech was the only team in either division that had not tasted defeat at the hands of an intra-divisional opponent. The Carpenters' only two losses since 1937 had come in The Plain Dealer's Charity Game.

The winning continued in 1940, for when the season ended, West Tech's West Senate record stood at 5-0-2, and Tech had won its third West Senate championship in the last four seasons. The Carpenters' next stop would be Municipal Stadium, where on Saturday, Nov. 23, they would take on the Cathedral Latin Lions in the Charity Game, a rematch of the 1938 city championship contenders.

West Tech had another star-studded lineup. Leading the list was three-year starting fullback Melvin Diehl. Diehl made the varsity in 1938 as a sophomore and started in that year's Charity Game against Latin. After fracturing an ankle halfway through the 1939 season, Melvin returned to lead the Carpenters in 1940. Diehl was a triple-threat back on offense whose "defensive work is of the highest order" (PD). Tech Coach Charley Blickle rated him as good as any running back the Carpenters had ever had.

Two other veterans of that 1938 team were also looking to even the score with Latin. Frank Takacs, the Carpenters' starting halfback and punter, and John Cubar, a three-year tackle, were sure that over-confidence would not be a problem this time, as it may have been in 1938. It would have been difficult to pick a favorite or an underdog in the 1940 Charity Game. West Tech and Cathedral Latin had been the most successful high school football teams in Greater Cleveland over the last half dozen years. In 1935, Coach Charley Blickle's West Tech 11 had compiled a record of 43-3-8 using "smashing line plays" (PD) and a rock-solid defense.

Game day, Saturday, Nov. 23, dawned cold and crisp, with the temperature in the 30s under cloudy skies, and by the 2:15 p.m. kick-off, 39,917 fans had filed into their seats. The first quarter and a half were played to a scoreless tie, but with about five minutes remaining in the second quarter, Latin struck to take a 6-0 lead. Trying to get on the scoreboard before halftime, West Tech went to the air — but the strategy backfired disastrously. With less than a minute left in the half, Latin's Jack Sague picked off a Frank Takacs aerial at the Latin 35-yard line. Behind a couple of excellent blocks, Sague raced down the field for a 65-yard touchdown. Quarterback Tom McFadden's extra point gave the Lions a 13-0 lead at the intermission.

After a scoreless third quarter, each team scored in the final frame. West Tech's lone touchdown came on a short plunge by fullback Mel Diehl with less than a minute remaining in the game. When the final whistle sounded, the Carpenters were on the short end of a 20-6 score. It was only West Tech's third loss of the last four seasons, and all had come in the Charity Game.

West Tech would have to wait 35 years before playing for a Senate championship again. In 1975, the Warriors defeated Saint Ignatius, 21-0, to win the West Senate title but lost to John F. Kennedy, 14-6, in the Senate championship game. In 1987 and 1988, West Tech again qualified for the Senate championship game, but each time lost close contests. In 1987, they dropped a 12-6 decision to South High, and in 1988, the Warriors lost to John Marshall by a single point, 7-6.

GYMNASTICS

West Tech enjoyed limited success in the earliest days of the boys gymnastics state championship. The Carpenters made their first big splash in 1935 when they finished fourth; Sterba won the first of only two state gymnastics championships West Tech would ever win, taking home the top prize on the horizontal bars. Adding to the team's point total was Stechmeyer, who finished third on the parallel bars and fifth on both the side horse and the long horse.

1937 West Tech finished third place at the state meet, its best finish ever. The team was led by Lakovsky, who finished third on the long horse and fourth on both the parallel and horizontal bars. Adding to the team's point total were Osenberger (second) and Bruckner (third) in the side horse competition, with Rosenberg also coming in fifth on the horizontal bars.

In the 1968 state gymnastic meet for boys, West Tech finished a lowly 19th place. The big story was not that the Carpenters finished 19th but how they did it — and it was all due to the efforts of one outstanding athlete. That athlete was Ray Gura, one of the best gymnasts in Cleveland history. Ray always finished high in every event and entered almost all of them, which was the case at the 1968 state meet. At that meet, Gura tied for the state championship on the long horse, finished second on both the side horse and the horizontal bars, third on both the parallel bars and the floor exercise, and fifth on the still rings. Combining all of Gura's points, they totaled 41.15, placing him second in the all-around competition, a mere 1.025 points from being the all-around champion.

As for West Tech's team, which had a total of 41.15, Ray Gura scored all of it. Ray Gura, West Tech's most honored All-Ohio athlete, was inducted into the Greater Cleveland Sports Hall of Fame in 1984.

SOCCER

The year 1973 was a singular year in the history of Cleveland Senate League athletics, for it was the year the league claimed its only state championship in soccer.

At the end of October of that year, the Warriors' head coach, Nick Maric, played in the Western Division of the high school soccer league and had a record of 5-0-1. This record was enough to tie Rocky River High School for the divisional championship.

Next up was the Ohio Soccer Coaches Invitational Tournament for the state championship played at Baldwin-Wallace's Finnie Stadium from Nov. 3-8. On the afternoon of Nov. 3, the Warriors played Centerville in a quarterfinal match, winning by a 2-1 score.

Four days later, West Tech and Hudson High School tangled in a semifinal match. It was a close contest, and as it headed into the final minutes, the score tied at 2-2. All-Ohio sophomore Mike Hubach scored one goal for the Warriors, and Chris Berwald scored the other. As the clock wound down and showed less than a minute to play, it looked as if this one was going into overtime, but such was not to be the case. With just 20 seconds remaining, Mike Hubach broke the deadlock with a perfectly placed penalty kick that gave West Tech a stunning 3-2 win.

The next day, the Warriors took the field for the state championship match. Their opponent was the team from Anderson High School in Cincinnati. More than 2,000 fans were on hand to witness a tremendous defensive thriller. The first half ended with neither team able to score. The same was true for the second half, with the score still 0-0 at the end of regulation time. The game now went into overtime. It remained 0-0 after one overtime session and remained 0-0 after the second OT.

The game rules changed a little, as it was now being played under "sudden death" rules – the first team to score would be the winner. Finally, in the game's 89th minute, West Tech sophomore Wolfgang Urban kicked the ball past the Anderson goalie for the game's only point. West Tech had won the 1973 Ohio high school soccer championship, 1-0.

Warriors' goalie Dan Obrenic had been "sparkling" in preventing even one Anderson kick from getting past him. Senior Pat Kelly, an All-Ohio selection, added tournament MVP to his list of honors.

SWIMMING

West Tech qualified for the state swim tournament once, in 1929, and had a respectable finish, tying for sixth place. Oddly enough, two swimmers earned All-Ohio recognition in the same event. In the 220-yard freestyle, Eckhart came in second, and Krohn came in third.

TENNIS

Only three West Tech tennis players have ever advanced to the state tournament. In 1933, the doubles team of Wightman and Marchard earned Honorable Mention recognition.

Almost 50 years passed before the next West Tech tennis player advanced to the state tournament. That player was Mike Massie, arguably the greatest tennis player ever out of a Senate school. Not only did Massie advance to the state tournament, but he was also the state singles champion in 1981 and 1982.

TRACK

From 1932 to 1957, under the direction of head coach Lloyd Griffith (who was instrumental in helping to start the famous West Tech Relays), the West Tech track team earned points at the state meet 15 times. During those years, Coach Griffith had 20 boys earn All-Ohio recognition in 25 events.

In 1932, a boy named Seitz single-handedly carried West Tech to a seventh-place finish at the state meet. Seitz's specialty was the hurdles; he finished second in the 120yd. high hurdles and won the state championship in the 220yd. low hurdles with a time of 26.3 seconds, earning all of West Tech's points that year. His state championship in the high hurdles was one of only two state championships ever won by a West Tech track star at the state meet.

The following year, Seitz again scored all of West Tech's points at the state meet, where he finished second in both hurdle events, leading West Tech to an eighth-place finish. With a state championship and three second-place finishes at the state meet to his credit, Seitz was not only West Tech's first state champion athlete but also the school's all-time All-Ohio athlete, having earned that honor four times.

The team's best showing at the state meet came in 1939 when West Tech finished third. Leading the way for West Tech that year was a young man named Bill Ruhrkraut, who won the state championship in the shot put with a toss of 51'1". Also finishing on the podium for the Carpenters was Grumney, who had a second-place finish in the high jump, and Henderson, who came in fifth in the mile run.

Grumney and Ruhrkraut also medaled the previous year at the 1938 state meet. Both boys came in second in their respective specialties: Ruhrkraut's shot put and Grumney's high jump.

Years later, two more boys would have outstanding track careers running for the West Tech Warriors. In 1974 and 1975, Jay Miranda was one of the best middle-distance runners in the state. At the 1974 State Meet, he finished second in the 880-yard run with a time of 1:52.9. The following year, Jay was the state champion in that same event at 1:54.2.

In 1989 and 1990, another boy had an outstanding career in not one but two events. Eric Brown ran the hurdles, no matter how high or long the distance was. In 1989, Eric finished fifth at the State Meet in the 110m high hurdles and fourth in the 300m intermediate hurdles. The following year, he ran in the same two events, finishing fourth in the 110m high hurdles and second in the 300m intermediate hurdles

WRESTLING

West Tech was a Cleveland and Ohio wrestling power from the mid-1930s through the mid-1950s. An article in the Feb. 18, 1937, edition of The Plain Dealer noted that the Warriors had clinched the West Senate championship with a 31-10 win over South High. The article also stated that the Warriors "had lost only two meets in five years" under Coach Lloyd Griffith's guidance.

Lloyd Griffith was a great early Ohio high school wrestling coach and a true pioneer of the sport at the high school level. He was born on Sept. 11, 1907, in Chaney, Oklahoma. The family moved to Redfield, Iowa, where Lloyd played football, basketball, and track at Redfield High School. Upon graduation, he furthered his education at the University of Iowa.

When Lloyd graduated from the university, he moved to Cleveland, spending his first year teaching and coaching at Collinwood. In 1932, he began a long and successful career at West Tech, becoming the school's athletic director in 1937. But, first and foremost, Lloyd Griffith was a coach. Griffith's success as the West Tech track coach has been mentioned above, but as a wrestling coach, he truly made his mark at both the local and state levels.

Sportswriter Dan Coughlin noted that the Senate pioneered wrestling in Ohio under Lloyd Griffith's leadership. In the 1930s and 1940s, Griffith's West Tech wrestling teams were the ones to beat. Under his direction, they won 143 dual meets while losing only 22 for a .868 winning percentage. From 1932-1936, West Tech won 34 consecutive dual meets and would later have another winning streak of over 30 wins. 1934-1946, West Tech held the Cleveland wrestling championship nine times. The school would win four state championships from 1944 to 1948 (more on below).

Along with several other big-name coaches, Lloyd Griffith helped to create and run the Greater Cleveland Wrestling Coaches and Officials Association (GCWCOA) in the mid-1940s.

This governing body of wrestling allowed coaches and officials to meet and discuss improvements to the sport. For more than 15 years, the Association conducted the state wrestling tournament.

In 1969, after serving West Tech for 38 years, Lloyd Griffith retired and moved to Florida. He was inducted into the Ohio High School Wrestling Coaches Association Hall of Fame in 1971. (Note: In a significant oversight by the Cleveland athletic community, Lloyd Griffith has not been inducted into the Greater Cleveland Sports Hall of Fame, although he is in several wrestling halls of fame.)

1938, Lloyd Griffith, Al Carroll (a John Marshall grad), and Harold Kester (a local high school wrestling coach) organized the first state wrestling tournament. Held at John Hay High School on Friday, March 18, that year, Senate champion West Tech was one of the favorites. John Hay was named the team champion in that first tournament, but no other team rankings were listed. However, West Tech did have a few boys who finished high in the various events.

Over the next five years, West Tech finished second and fifth in the state wrestling tournament each season. In 1939, the Carpenters tied for second place with four other teams. That year, they also had their first state champions, as Joe DiCesare, at 125 pounds, and Oris Hicks, heavyweight, took home the gold. George Span, at 145, finished third.

In 1940, West Tech finished fourth in the state tournament. Joe Ruggiero was the state champion at 145, while Joe DiCesare (130) and Joe Stelbasky (185) finished second. The year 1941 again saw West Tech come in fourth, led by Joe DiCesare's state championship at 130 — only the fourth wrestler in the tournament's young history to win multiple state titles. In 1942, the Carpenters slipped to fifth place in the state tournament. However, led by state championships by Joe Naso (113) and Skogan (104), West Tech finished second in the 1943 state tournament.

1944 would usher in the golden era of West Tech wrestling, a time when Lloyd Griffith's teams would dominate the state high school wrestling scene. That year, the Carpenters would finish first in the state meet with 39 points, well ahead of John Hay's 28 points. West Tech had three state champions that year: Henry

DiCesare (121), Joe Naso (128), and Gus Tober (155). Also contributing to the team's point total were second-place finishes by Tony Vransky (146) and Julius Parsnick (166).

West Tech again finished first in 1945 with 35 points, well ahead of second-place Western Reserve Academy and its score of 24. In 1944, West Tech had three more individual titlists and a pair of second-place finishers. Bill Williamson (103), Bill Bassett (128), and Don Tighe (134) won state championships. Julius Parsnick (165) and Joe Prchlik (heavyweight) came in as runners-up.

The year 1946 would give West Tech its third consecutive state championship, but it would take a total team effort for the Carpenters to edge out fellow Senate school, West High, 33 to 30. Both schools had three state champions, but West Tech picked up more points by having four boys finish in third place and one in fourth place, while the West High Cowboys were only able to add a second and a third-place finisher to their three state champions. Winning state championships for West Tech that year were Tom Dubin (128), Bob Jakupca (131), and Dick Prchlik (heavyweight).

Despite state championships by Tom Dubin (128) and Ray Martinez (139) and high placings by three other boys in 1947, West Tech saw its string of state championships snapped as the team only managed to finish in third place.

Rebounding in 1948, West Tech won its fourth state championship of the last five seasons, although this time, they would have to share top honors with archrival Lakewood High, both teams finishing the state tournament with 25 points. Once again, this was a total team effort for the Carpenters. While Bob Jakupca (131) was the only boy to win a state championship, Steiner (121), Massa (155), and Arthur Prchlik (166) all finished in second place, with Lazar (103) finishing third and Mio (146) coming in fourth.

Following this incredible success, West Tech slumped over the next three years, producing no individual state champions and a team finish never higher than fifth place. Things picked up again in 1952 and 1953 under head coach Robert Lazzaro. In 1952, the team finished in a tie with Bedford for second place with 19 points. John Sforzo led the team to a state championship at 139 pounds.

The following year, 1953, West Tech finished first with 29 points. Three state champions helped carry West Tech to the top that year: Tom Nevits (121), John Sforzo (139), and Lino Deanna (155).

The year 1954 would produce two more state champions for West Tech in Dick Mendicino (128) and Joe Harbuck (134), but the team's total of 22 points was only good enough for a third-place finish. The same holds in 1955 when state championships by Al Sforzo (139) and Joe Ornowski (121) led the team to its third-highest point total, 36, but that was only good enough for another third-place finish.

Hall of Fame high school wrestling writer Pat Galbincea rated four West Tech grapplers among the Cleveland area's all-time best:

Joe DiCesare - two-time state champion, at 125 pounds in 1939 and 130 pounds in 1941, with a second place at 130 pounds in 1940.

Joe Naso - two-time state champion, at 113 pounds in 1943 and 128 pounds in 1944. In 1944, he beat future state champ John Milkovich of Garfield Heights in the finals.

Tom Dubin - two-time state champion in 1946 and 1947 in the same weight class, 128 pounds.

John Sforzo - two-time state champion, 1952 and 1953, in the 139-pound weight class.

CENTRAL HIGH SCHOOL

Jimmy Bivins

Ed Delahanty

Old Central High School 1869

1921 Basketball Team

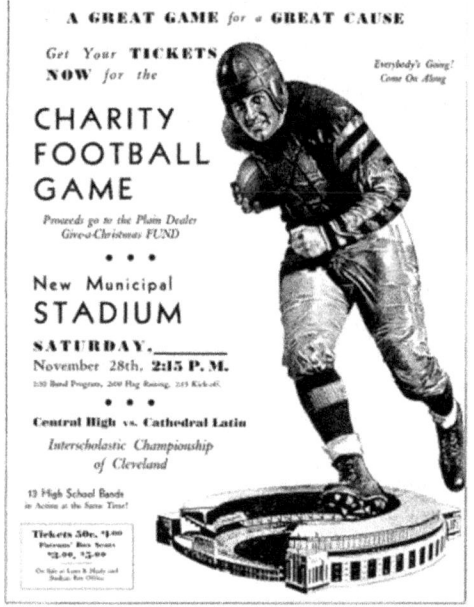

New Central High School 1939

1914 Class Logo

1921 Football Team

1921 Track captain Norman Minor

CENTRAL HIGH SCHOOL GREATER CLEVELAND SPORTS HALL OF FAME

Images provided by the Greater Cleveland Sports Hall of Fame

JIMMY BIVINS
Induction Year : 1978
Sport: Boxing

FRANK CIVILETTO
Induction Year : 1976
Sport: Footbnall

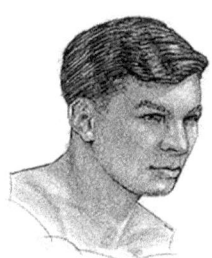

PHIL GOLDSTEIN
Induction Year : 1980
Sport: Boxing

LOUIS "BABE" PRESSLEY
Induction Year : 1976
Sport: Basketball

RALPH TYLER
Induction Year : 1984
Sport: Track & Field

COLLINWOOD RAILROADERS

*Charnee Lumbus, Track,
University of Michigan*

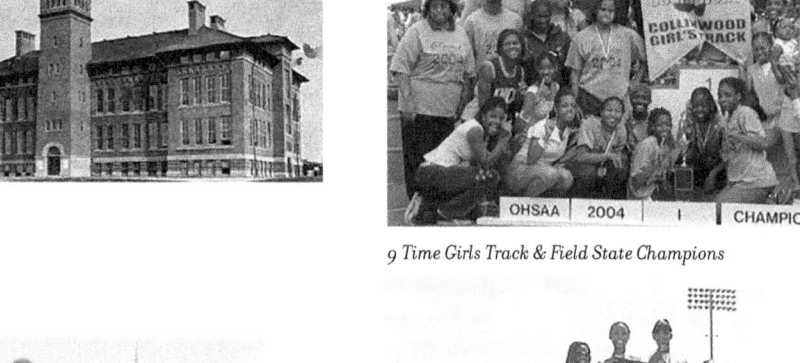

9 Time Girls Track & Field State Champions

*Carmen Barth
Champion Boxer*

*Latanya Johnson and John Kinton
Most Athletic Class of 1984*

*Joey Maxim
Champion Boxer*

COLLINWOOD HIGH SCHOOL GREATER CLEVELAND SPORTS HALL OF FAME

Images provided by the Greater Cleveland Sports Hall of Fame

TONY ADAMLE
Induction Year : 1976
Sport: Football

CARMEN BARTH
Induction Year : 1976
Sport: Boxing

JOEY MAXIM
Induction Year : 1976
Sport: Boxing

SAM PALUMBO
Induction Year : 2016
Sport: Football

Cecil Shorts, NFL

Charity Game: Collinwood 12 — Lincoln 12

LOU SLAPNIK
Induction Year : 2023
Sport: Track & Field

EAST HIGH BLUE BOMBERS

Boys Varsity Basketball team 1972-73

Back Row: Kiandra Ellis, Danielle Williams, Tonaisha Williams (Co-Captain), Aureldia Benjamin, Thea Orr, Coach Wallace. Front Row: Asia Smith, Jonay Young, Kalima McMillian (Co-Captain), Samantha Dickerson, Latasha Smith.

Girls Basketball Team 2006-07

1923 City Basketball Champions

Manny Leaks, Basketball, Kentucky Colonels

1923 Football Team

Bob Wren, Baseball Coach, Ohio University

EAST HIGH SCHOOL GREATER CLEVELAND SPORTS HALL OF FAME

Images provided by the Greater Cleveland Sports Hall of Fame

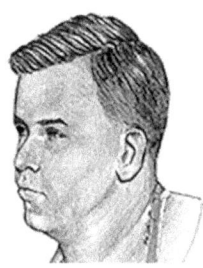

TED ABRAMS
Induction Year: 1976
Sport: Swimming & Diving

MANNY LEAKS
Induction Year: 2004
Sport: Basketball

JOHN OLSZEWSKI
Induction Year: 1976
Sport: Basketball

EAST TECH SCARABS

THE SCARABS

Jesse Owens, 1936 Berlin Olympics

Jesse Owens Memorial Track Stadium at Ohio State University

Jesse Owens, 1933, breaking the national high school record in the 100 yard dash

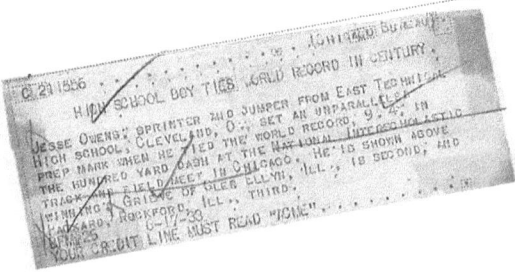

Harrison Dillard, 1948 London Olympics

Wanda Ford, Basketball, Drake

TOCCARA MONTGOMERY

Harrison Dillard, 1952 Helsinki Olympics Games

Harrison Dillard Statue, Baldwin Wallace College

Harrison Dillard, 1952 Wheaties Athlete of the Year

Barbara Turner, Basketball, UConn

Harrison Dillard

EAST TECH SCARABS

Jack Trice, Football, Iowa

2002 Division II State Tournament

Jack Trice Legacy

Mike St. Clair, NFL

Bob Brown, NFL

When East Tech was king of the hill in school basketball

EAST TECH HIGH SCHOOL GREATER CLEVELAND SPORTS HALL OF FAME

Images provided by the Greater Cleveland Sports Hall of Fame

JOE VOSMIK
Induction Year : 1976
Sport: Baseball

JESSE OWENS
Induction Year : 1976
Sport: Track & Field

JOHN BROSKI
Induction Year : 1986
Sport: Basketball

HARRISON DILLARD
Induction Year : 1976
Sport: Track & Field

JACK TRICE
Induction Year : 1976
Sport: Football

WILLIE SMITH
Induction Year : 1976
Sport: Basketball

ESTUS NEWBERRY
Induction Year : 1986
Sport: Track & Field

KEN GLENN
Induction Year : 1984
Sport: Basketball

VIVIAN BROWN REED
Induction Year : 1976
Sport: Track & Field

JOHN BEHM
Induction Year : 1976
Sport: Football

GUS KERN
Induction Year : 1978
Sport: Gymnastics

JIM STONE
Induction Year : 1986
Sport: Basketball

SHERLIE HERFORD RAINEY
Induction Year : 1992
Sport: Track & Field

ROGER PECKINPAUGH
Induction Year : 1984
Sport: Baseball

JIM MARTIN
Induction Year : 1976
Sport: Football

WALLY EDWARDS
Induction Year : 1978
Sport: Basketball

PETER AMICO
Induction Year : 1992
Sport: Basketball

TED THEODORE
Induction Year : 2007
Sport: Track & Field

BOB BROWN
Induction Year : 1976
Sport: Football

LOUIS FINA
Induction Year : 1984
Sport: Gymnastics

TED STEVENS
Induction Year : 1976
Sport: Swimming & Diving

GLENVILLE TARBLOODERS

2021 Ohio High School State Track Champion

2022 Ohio High School State Track Champion

Troy Smith, Football, Ohio State University, 2006 Heisman Trophy Winner

18 Time Track & Field State Champions
2 Time Football State Champions

GLENVILLE TARBLOODERS IN THE NFL PLAYERS

GLENVILLE HIGH SCHOOL GREATER CLEVELAND SPORTS HALL OF FAME

Images provided by the Greater Cleveland Sports Hall of Fame

Troy Smith

Ted Ginn Jr.

Shane Wynn

Cobe Bryant

Marshon Lattimore

Justin Hardee

Frank Clark

BENNY FRIEDMAN
Induction Year: 1976
Sport: Football

Jayrone Elliott

Willie Henry

Donte Whitner

Cardale Jones

HAL LEBOVITZ
Induction Year: 1999
Sport: Media

Christian Bryant

Jonathan Newsome

Benny Friedman

Pierre Woods

TED DINN, SR.
Induction Year: 2013
Sport: Footbnall

MERLE LEVIN
Induction Year: 2007
Sport: Media

JAMES FORD RHODES RAMS

Mahogany Jones

Dave Kyle, Basketball, Cleveland State University, All American

Coach Tyronne Owens

Les Horvath - Heisman Trophy Winner

Cynthia Anzalone

Steve Korinchak 1965 All Ohio Mile Record

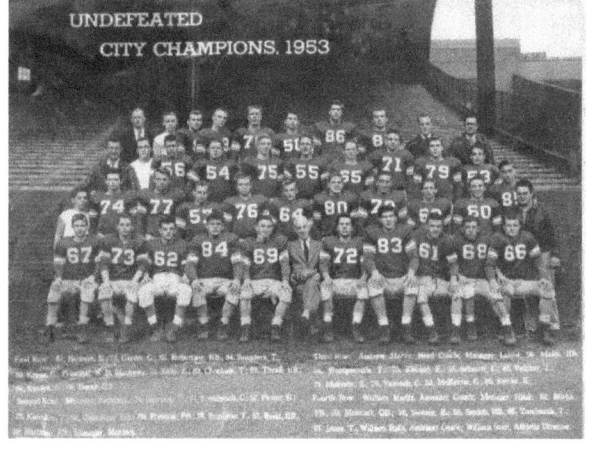

JAMES F. RHODES HIGH SCHOOL GREATER CLEVELAND SPORTS HALL OF FAME

Images provided by the Greater Cleveland Sports Hall of Fame

BOBBY BROWN
Induction Year: 2009
Sport: Basketball, Football

WILLIAM HANN
Induction Year: 1989
Sport: Basketball

Nicole Antoinette Smith, Basketball, Ohio University

LES HORVATH
Induction Year: 1978
Sport: Football

DON MCCAFFERTY
Induction Year: 1992
Sport: Football

Bill Putich, Football, University of Michigan, 1951 Rose Bowl

GEORGE SEEDHOUSE
Induction Year: 1976
Sport: Meritorious Service

Don McCafferty, Coach, Baltimore Coach

JOHN ADAMS REBELS

L: Jeff Mason R: Anthony Morgan

Coach Monica Gary

Coach Claude Holland

1969 John Adams Baseball Team, Captains John Hyde and Jerry Blanchard

1974 Indoor Track

JOHN ADAM HIGH SCHOOL GREATER CLEVELAND SPORTS HALL OF FAME

Images provided by the Greater Cleveland Sports Hall of Fame

Anthony Morgan, NFL

Tom Jackson, ESPN Football Analyst

Tom Jackson, NFL, All-Pro

1974 Varsity Football Team

Luke Owens, NFL

Harold Maddox

NAYE BROOKS
Induction Year : 1976
Sport: Boxing

LUKE OWENS
Induction Year : 1980
Sport: Football

WILLIAM "WILLIE" FLEISHAM
Induction Year : 1978
Sport: Basketball

EDDIE FINNAGAN
Induction Year : 1976
Sport: Track & Field

RAY MACK
Induction Year : 1986
Sport: Baseball

ELEANAOR MONTGOMERY
Induction Year : 1976
Sport: Track & Field

NICK MILETI
Induction Year : 2005
Sport: Basketball

BERNICE ROBINSON HOLLAND
Induction Year : 1976
Sport: Baseball, Football, Track & Field

JOHN F. KENNEDY EAGLES

Yesterday

Today

Coach Harold Kimball

Roye Kidd

JFK junior Marcus Wilkerson might turn his attention to just track when he gets to college. But for now, he can't imagine limiting himself to one sport.

"If you specialize, then go for it," Wilkerson said between events at a high school track meet last weekend. "But if you don't try other sports, you'll never know what you can do."

Wilkerson is a cornerback and wide receiver on the Cleveland school's football team, but at 5-9 and 160 pounds, he knows he would have to add weight to play that sport in college. He plays basketball in the winter.

In track, he is one of the region's top long jumpers, posting the 11th best jump in the nation during the indoor season at 23-3½. He also is a sprinter and valuable relay-team contributor. He plans to be a four-sport athlete his senior year, adding cross country to his fall schedule.

Wilkerson said he thinks each sport contributes to his track performance.

"Football helps my strength because I lift a lot of weights," Wilkerson said. "Basketball helps me with my jumping and my takeoff speed."

JFK track coach Harold Kimball said Wilkerson is a perfect team member — an honor student and leader who puts the team first.

"He had a chance to go to the [state indoor] meet as an individual," Kimball said. "But we had some injuries and he didn't want to go without the rest of the team. Most of today's kids would say, 'Just take me, coach.'"

2012 State Champion Antwoine Smith, 400-meter dash

Donnica Kibble, Indoor 55-yard dash Champion

Lawrence Boston, Basketball, University of Maryland

Lenin Eyes State Distance Double

CLEVELAND — The way Coach Harold Kimball of John F. Kennedy sees it, the time has come for someone to pull off an 800, 1,600 distance double in the Class AAA state meet June 5-6.

The last time anyone won the 800-1,600 was Reggie McAfee of Cincinnati Courter Tech in 1968. In those victories, McAfee set state meet records.

The last time anyone pulled off winning the mile and two-mile at the state in the "big class" was John Zishka of Lancaster in 1979.

Kimball would like to see his standout senior distance runner Lawrence Lenin II get the 800-1,600 double. Lenin has the leading mark in the state this season with 1:53.3 for the 800, and is fifth in the 1,600-meter run with 4:23.2.

"Lenin can do better. His goal is the state championship," said Kimball after Lenin won the Worthington Relays 800 in 1:53.3.

Lenin is taking a laid-back approach. He's not saying much, letting his performance on the track do the talking for him.

JFK has had a tradition of turing out outstanding half-milers, dating back to 1967 when James Epps won the state, followed by Kevin Black's victory in 1968.

Lenin has taken his success in stride. He plans to be ready when the state qualifying begins in two weeks. And he hopes the climax of his bid to be the best in the state will come at Columbus at the state meet finals.

Lawrence Lenin, Cleveland JFK - AAA 800 Leader

L: Coach Harold Kimball R: Lawrence Lenin

Cleveland JFK's Marcus Wilkerson, the defending state champion, reacts upon landing in the long jump. He was second.

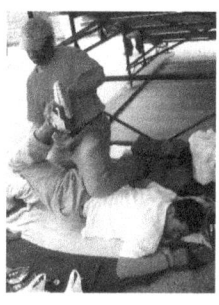

Coach Gary Caldwell

Walt Killian

JOHN HAY HORNETS

John Hicks, Football, Ohio State University All-American, Outland Trophy Winner

**JOHN HAY GIRLS BASKETBALL TEAMS
DAISY MAE LEAGUE WINNERS**

1966 Team

Tim McGhee, University of Tennessee All-American, NFL

1978 Team

1967 Team

1972 Team

1968 Team

Girls Track Team All American - 1988 & 1989

Olympic Champ Madeline Manning Mims

JOHN HAY HIGH SCHOOL GREATER CLEVELAND SPORTS HALL OF FAME

Images provided by the Greater Cleveland Sports Hall of Fame

MADELINE MANNING JACKSON
Induction Year : 1976
Sport: Track & Field

MARALYN WEST
Induction Year : 1978
Sport: Track & Field

HAROLD KESTER
Induction Year : 1976
Sport: Wrestling

JOHN HICKS
Induction Year : 1999
Sport: Football

TIM MCGEE
Induction Year : 2008
Sport: Football

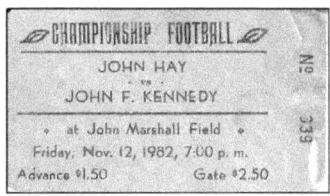

In 1978 Sam McClain, Rick Reynolds, Anthony Hancock, and Kevin Mondie were members of the 1978 Track Team, the team performed extremely well in the state finals winning the 880 relay and runner up to the Championship at The Ohio State University.

JOHN MARSHALL LAWYERS

Thomas Jefferson, 1984 Los Angeles Olympic, Bronze Medal

Thomas Stincic, Super Bowl Champion, Dallas Cowboys

Jonathan Burell

Thomas Jefferson, Olympic Medalist

Larry Coy

JOHN MARSHALL HIGH SCHOOL GREATER CLEVELAND SPORTS HALL OF FAME

Images provided by the Greater Cleveland Sports Hall of Fame

AL CARROLL
Induction Year: 2008
Sport: Wrestling

Vita Redding - All State

HOWARD FERGUSON
Induction Year: 2018
Sport: Wrestling

GENE GIBBONS
Induction Year: 1976
Sport: Wrestling

Jenetta Graham

115

LINCOLN HIGH SCHOOL PRESIDENTS

1969 Cheerleaders

Lincoln High School 1901-1970

Harold Vacha, 1934, Lincoln High School, State Champion - 100 yard dash and 220 yard dash

Marty Hunt, NBA, Boston Celtics

City Champion 1942

1955 Baseball Team

LINCOLN HIGH SCHOOL
GREATER CLEVELAND SPORTS
HALL OF FAME

Images provided by the Greater Cleveland Sports Hall of Fame

Around Lincoln HS 1965

IDA JEAN HOPKINS
Induction Year: 1976
Sport: Softball

1941 Senate Champions

Lou Groza, Greater Cleveland MVP Award Winner, 1968

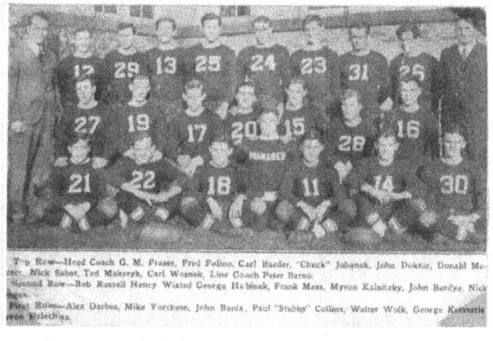

1936 Senate Football Champions

Willie Avery

Walt Yowarsky, General Manager, Dallas Cowboys, NFL, Super Bowl Champion

117

LINCOLN-WEST HIGH SCHOOL

Lincoln West Soccer

Dartanyon Crockett

Dave Ford, MLB, Baltimore Orioles

Lincoln West Basketball

Lincoln West Football

LINCOLN WEST HIGH SCHOOL
GREATER CLEVELAND SPORTS
HALL OF FAME

Images provided by the Greater Cleveland Sports Hall of Fame

SUE KOZIOL
Induction Year: 2004
Sport: Softball

SOUTH HIGH FLYERS

THE PIG IRON TROPHY

The Pig Iron Trophy originated in 1932 as a symbol of victory between the Holy Name and South High Football teams. It was named because both schools are located in the steel industry area on Cleveland's south east side.

For the uninformed, the Pig Iron is an alloy which melts at a lower temperature than steel, or wrought iron. The iron is so called because it was usually cast in stubby round ingots called pigs. A spirited neighborhood rivalry had developed over the years and the trophy had become a cherished possession to the fans of the winning school.

The Holy Name and South High School competition ended in 1973 with a South High Flyers Victory.

Jan Maynard, South High 1963, State Champion 103 lb. 1962, State Champion 112 lb. 1963, South High HOF, 1995, SLOC, 2019

Fred Sawyer, 1957 Un. of Louisville Basketball, 1958-61, Third Team All-American, Drafted by the Los Angeles Lakers, Played for Hawaii Cheifs, 1961-62

Markeya Jones Owens, 1988, Female Athlete of the Year, 1986-88, 1988 State Champion 200 meters All-American, Kansas State Track, South High HOF, 1996, SLOC, 2024

Dennis Woods, 1960 HS, 3 years Varsity Baseball, Miami of Ohio Baseball, 3rd Winning HS Baseball Coach in Ohio, OHSBCA Hall of Fame, South High HOF, 1995, SLOC 2024

South High's pride–the Senate Title Champions for eighth consecutive years relax before their latest victory. Our Lady Flyers softball team successfully defeated their rivals due to teamwork, determination, and love of the sport.

CLEVELAND SOUTH HIGH SCHOOL FOOT BALL TEAM

Girl's Basketball 1980

Pictured above is the 1961 South High School State Champion Baseball Team, who finished with a 14-7 record. Front row from left: Tony Quidatano, Mike Koppel, John Papushak, Manager Gary Brown, Jim Ciricola, John Zerucha and Bob Ferjo. Middle row from left: Dennis Canterbury, Dave Deptowicz, Mario Morino, Jeff Thomas, Tom Fisher, Jim Fay, Jim Gretta and Coach Frank Dillon. Third row from left: Ken Shields, Ken Pflug, Harry DiBuggio, Tom Ksienyk, Lou Drans, Joe Faircloth and Andy Fetchik.

Photo provided by Ken Pflug

1961 State High School Baseball Championship Team

19998 Boy's Basketball South Senate Champions

1963 Senate & Sectional Champions

Chet Mason, '2000, Ohio's Mr. Basketball Miami of Ohio, All-MAC CBA & European Basketball, South High HOF, 2015, SLOC, 2024

Don Lamka, 1963, HS All-Ohio & All-American, 3rd Place OHSAA Wrestling Championships, OSU Football, 1970 Rose Ball, South High HOF, 1995

Henry "Hank" Arslanian, 1958, State Wrestling Champion 175 lb.1958, Arslanian Brothers Carpeting Cleaning Co.

Marlene Smejkal Jess, 1980, 1st Women's Nine Letter Winner MVP (Volleyball, Basketball, Softball), South High HOF, 1995, SLOC, 2022

1965 Westr Senate Champions

SOUTH HIGH SCHOOL
GREATER CLEVELAND SPORTS
HALL OF FAME

Images provided by the Greater Cleveland Sports Hall of Fame

CHET ADAMS
South High '33
Collegiate & Professional Football

JOHN BROSKI
South High '49
State Champion Basketball Coach (East Tech HS)

GOMER JONES
South High '32
Collegiate Football

FRANCIS KASUBSKI
South High '34
AAU Basketballl

ANTHONY PIANOWSKI
South High '28
Football Official

STELLA WALSH
South High '29
Olympic Track Champion

WEST HIGH SCHOOL COWBOYS

Phil Argento, University of Kentucky

Baseball Team of '49 Captures City Title

In spite of rain, hail, snow, mud and a shortage of pitchers, the Cowboy baseball team of 1949 slugged its way through the Senate season and clobbered East Tech in the City playoff at Old League Park, 9-1.

The team, which will probably go down in history as West's greatest, is pictured left.

Back row (left to right): Coach Jim Torgler, Earl Sprague, Eddie Veltre, John Imperatore, Norm Colbert, Chris Nardi, Jerry Cicatko, Bill Pavlik, Leonard Warholic.

Middle row: Mascot Jimmy Torgler, Earl Hobson, John Morabito, Jim Fink, Dan DiVito, Tom Smith, Bill Mooney, Bill Warnkin.

Front row: Manager Bob Stilla, George Ittu, John Binder, Manager Ralph Izzo.

Al Drews, Baseball, Western Michigan

Dan Mason, Football, Purdue

Al Drews, National USHA Handball Champion

State Championships in 4 Sports Since 1949

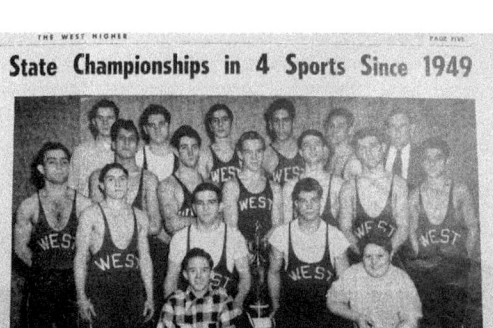

1951 Matmen Take State Crown for Third Time

Scoring 50 points on eight pins, six first places, a second, and a fourth, the 1951 Cowboy grapplers copped state honors for the second consecutive time and the third time since 1947.

State titlists Fritz Darienzo and Dick Bonacci successfully defended their crowns and were joined by Bob Pogue, Vince Matteucci, Emil Palmeri, and Pete Rossi as champs for '51 in their respective classes.

The 1951 campaigners are pictured at the right.

Back row (left to right): Manager Bill Warnkin, Charles Bilardo, Dan Vacca, Sandy Colosimo, Ron DePolo, and Coach Harold Kester. Middle row: Pete Rossi, Emil Palmeri, Fritz Darienzo, Jim Schiller, Bob Pogue, John Morabito, and Al Medaglia. Front row: Peppi Rocco, Manager Bob Stilla, Vince Matteucci, Dick Bonacci, and Manager Joe Searl.

Eugene "Sonny" Degyansky, Football, Baldwin Wallace Hall of Fame

Cagers Win 1952 City, District Championships

For the first time in Senate basketball history, the 1952 Cowboy cagers captured the City and the District crowns. The squad was undefeated in Senate play.

After winning the regional division title, the Cowboys, along with St. Ignatius, became the first in West Senate history to journey to the state tournament in Columbus.

Pictured at the right, the squad members were (standing, left to right): Assistant Coach Charley Blickle, Captain Pat Chambers, Marty Farkelman, Ken McBride, Bob Nesky, Jim Heins, Ed Dargaj, John Wise, Ed Naskoviak, Bob Koski, Frank Bova, and Coach Gene Degyanski.

In the front row are Manager Joe Chippi, Jim Keese, Ron Kaze, and Manager Ron Parsons.

WEST HIGH SCHOOL
GREATER CLEVELAND SPORTS
HALL OF FAME

Images provided by the Greater Cleveland Sports Hall of Fame

First Ohio 3-time State Wrestling Champion

Ken McBride

PHIL ARGENTO
Induction Year: 1996
Sport: Basketball

DICK BONACCI
Induction Year: 1978
Sport: Wrestling

PHIL BOVA
Induction Year: 2009
Sport: Basketball

ELMER GEDEON
Induction Year: 1976
Sport: Basketball, Football, Track & Field

Elmer Gedeon

Phil Bova, NCAA Basketball Official

GENE GIBBONS
Induction Year: 1976
Sport: Wrestling

HAROLD KESTER
Induction Year: 1979
Sport: Wrestling

1950 Harriers Cop Senate, District, State Titles

Compiling the best record in West High track history, the 1950 cross-country squad went through the season undefeated and untied. The high-riding harriers captured the Senate, the District, and the State championships, besides five dual and triangular meets.

The champs appear in the picture to the left.

In the top row, left to right, are Bob Clark, Larry Kornakovich, Carl Tremmel, Don Bennett, Steve Ibos, Dick Hart, and Coach Cy Waffen. Seated are Tom Schiller, Bill Clark, Dick Benz, and Bob Fenton.

The squad also boasted two individual champions. Bill Clark was the Senate champ, and Bob Fenton the District and State runner-up.

JIM THEILING
Induction Year: 2002
Sport: Football

KEN MCBRIDE
Induction Year: 2002
Sport: Baseball

WEST TECH HIGH SCHOOL WARRIORS

Larry Chernauskas

Mike Massie

1963 Varsity Football Squad

FIRST ROW, left to right: Bill Costello, manager; (30) Mike Gelsinger, (12) Howie Thompson, (10) John Parsons, (32) Gerry Lozan, (34) Rich Henz, Tom Koepke, manager.
SECOND ROW, left to right: (20) Dan Kuhn, (52) Bob Clark, (50) **Chuck Frimel**, (44) Nick Goranc, (42) Chuck Katona, (24) Jim Kortovich.

1963 Basketball Team

West Tech High School 1912 – 2012

John Henry H. Johnson – Capt, Sprinter & Hurdler

WEST TECH HIGH SCHOOL GREATER CLEVELAND SPORTS HALL OF FAME

Images provided by the Greater Cleveland Sports Hall of Fame

Michael Michalske

Jesus Jay Miranda, Notre Dame University, All-American

Arthur R. Prchlik

Mike Hubach, University of Kansas, NFL, New England Patriots

George Catavolos, Purdue University, 1967 Rose Bowl, NFL

Eric Brown

BARCLAY "BARKE" SANDER
Induction Year: 1978
Sport: Football

GEORGE KOZAK
Induction Year: 1976
Sport: Meritorious Service

JOHN SFORZO
Induction Year: 1984
Sport: Wrestling

Larry Chernauskas
Induction Year: 2012
Sport: Basketball

MARTY KAROW
Induction Year: 1976
Sport: Baseball, Football

RUSS SCHNEIDER
Induction Year: 2006
Sport: Media

STEVE RUDO, JR.
Induction Year: 1992
Sport: Wrestling

PART III

Carrying On
The Tradition *of* Excellence

CHAPTER 10

> ## COLLINWOOD HIGH SCHOOL
>
> *Located at East 152 Street and St. Clair Avenue, Collinwood High School is about seven miles northeast of Cleveland's Public Square. Until the 1940s, this was one of the most industrialized regions in the United States and worldwide. It was also the country's main railway center. The area was populated by Irish, Italian, and Slovenian families who earned their living in the area's factories and railyards. Opened in 1924, Collinwood High School had about 3,100 students at its height.*

BASEBALL

The 1938 season proved to be the best for Collinwood as far as the state tournament was concerned. The Railroaders made it to the Final Eight by advancing through district and sectional play. The Railroaders defeated Akron Kenmore in their quarterfinal game, 3-1. Now having advanced to the Final Four, the Railroaders saw their hopes of a state championship derailed with a 6-2 loss to Cincinnati.

BASKETBALL

The Railroaders had their first taste of success on the basketball court in 1928. In late February of that year, a 46-13 win over Lincoln left the Railroaders first in the Senate with a 4-0 league record. An article in The Plain Dealer heaped lavish praise on the team, noting that "Collinwood has one of the best cage combinations ever turned out here and is a potential national champion."

The national tournament would be held in Chicago in March 1928, and the Ohio high school championship winner would undoubtedly be invited to participate. However, there was one major obstacle in Collinwood's path. In 1927, the Cleveland high school principals voted to ban participation in basketball tournaments by the Cleveland high schools. Although the Railroaders were considered one of the best teams in the state, by not playing in the state tournament—and thus unable to capture the state championship—they would not be invited to play in the national tournament.

Nonetheless, the boys did not let that disappointment affect their play. They captured the Senate championship with a 7-0 record and finished the season undefeated in all games.

The Railroaders continued their winning ways into the next season. But all good things do come to an end, and on Feb. 1, 1929, they dropped a 30-19 decision to the Canton McKinley Bulldogs, ending their winning streak at 30.

Playing under first-year head coach Harry Newman, the Railroaders were back in the hunt for a Senate championship in 1930. In the season finale on March 14, the Railroaders defeated West Tech, 26-19, finishing 7-0 in Senate play and capturing their second league crown in the last three seasons. Overall, the Railroaders had a great season, losing only once in overtime to Akron North.

Leading the team on the court that season, as he also had for the previous two seasons, was guard Joe Oros. In his three years on the Railroaders team, Oros had started all 40 games, scoring 521 points for a 13 points per game average. While that may not sound like a lot by today's standards, back then, Oros' performance was good enough to make him Cleveland's top scorer for all three seasons. In 1934, Joe scored 29 points against Shaw and 25 points against East Tech — each game outscoring the opposing team by himself. Not bad for a 5'9" player.

The Railroaders' championship ambitions went unfulfilled for almost the rest of the decade but were revived in 1939. In their East Senate final, the Railroaders completed their march to the divisional title with a 28-22 win over East Tech, finishing with a 7-1 league mark.

Next up was the city championship game. The Railroaders' opponent would be the champions of the West Senate, West High. Collinwood was trailing 15-9 late in the third quarter when help came from a most unexpected source. Mike Gerl, who had been riding the bench and getting occasional playing time as a substitute, was sent into the game. Gerl made one long shot to cut the West lead to 15-11, and with about 30 seconds left in the third quarter, he canned another shot, this one from almost midcourt.

The fourth quarter opened with Collinwood cutting the West High lead to 15-13 on Mike Gerl's long-range shooting. Mike did it again three minutes into the final frame, canning another long-range shot that now tied the score at 15-15. Later in the final quarter, Collinwood team captain Jim Neff sank a two-pointer, then added a foul shot to give the Railroaders an 18-15 lead. The Cowboys scored with 40 seconds remaining in the game, but they could not get any closer. Collinwood held on to win the city championship game, 18-17.

The 1940 Senate basketball season, especially in the East Senate, would produce one of the league's closest races. Heading into the final weekend of play, Collinwood was tied with three other teams atop the East Senate standings, all with identical 5-2 records. When the weekend's games were completed, Collinwood and East Tech remained tied atop the East Senate standings with identical 6-2 records.

To determine which team would play in the city championship game, Collinwood and East Tech met in a playoff game on March 1 at Public Hall. East Tech had defeated the Railroaders two weeks previously, so this was a highly anticipated game. Collinwood jumped out to an early 7-0 lead, but East Tech stormed back early in the second quarter to take the lead, 8-7. After that, however, it was all Collinwood as the Railroaders rolled to a 40-28 victory.

That win sent Collinwood into the city championship game, played on March 15 at the Cleveland Arena. The opponent would be West Senate champions from West Tech. It was a very close game, one in which the Warriors held the advantage for most of the contest. Collinwood was able to chip away in the third quarter but still trailed by 18-17 as the game entered the final eight minutes.

In that fourth quarter, two boys would stand tall for the Railroaders. Mike Gerl, the previous year's hero off the bench but now the team's leading scorer, poured in five points, while substitute junior center Dick Cousins chipped in with two points. With the Collinwood defense holding West Tech to just four points in the final period, the Railroaders came away with a thrilling 24-22 victory and a city title.

Collinwood finished the season with an excellent 13-2 record, and Mike Gerl set a school single-season scoring record of 167 points.

It would be another 40 years, until 1980, before the Railroaders enjoyed another championship season while playing for head coach Ray Kennedy. In the last game of the Senate season, the Railroaders claimed the North Senate title outright with a hard-fought 63-57 win over Max Hayes.

On Feb. 22, the Railroaders (11-1, 12-3) took the court for the overall Senate championship against the undefeated champions of the South Senate, John Adams (10-0, 13-1). The Railroaders took a 16-11 lead after the first quarter and never relinquished it. When the final buzzer sounded, Collinwood had secured its first Senate championship in 40 years, 61-55. The Railroaders' Theodis Windham had a huge game, finishing with 23 points, 12 rebounds, eight assists, and three steals. David Griffin chipped in with 22 points and nine rebounds.

With their record now at 13-3, the Railroaders moved on to the OHSAA state tournament. In an Euclid Class AAA district game, Collinwood defeated Eastlake North but dropped a 59-49 decision to Ashtabula Edgewood 59-49. Collinwood's final record was 14-4.

The Railroaders would not win another divisional championship until 1990, then got crushed in the Senate championship game by John Marshall, 91-39. In 1995, the Railroaders would again make it to the Senate title game, playing Glenville, only to lose a heartbreaker, 78-77.

That '95 season only served as a warm-up for the 1996 campaign, one of the greatest in Collinwood history.

The 1996 Senate season would conclude with a championship tournament between the league's top four teams on Feb. 7 and 9. Collinwood entered this tournament 12-0 in league play, a sparkling 16-0 overall, and ranked #4 in Ohio's Division I. In one playoff game, the Railroaders defeated South High, 77-68, while Glenville disposed of East Tech, 83-74.

Two days later, Collinwood and Glenville met for the Senate championship. It was a close, challenging-fought game throughout, but with 20 seconds left in the fourth quarter, senior guard Louie Moore sank a field goal that gave the Railroaders a 55-54 lead. Melvin Scott intercepted a Glenville pass with just five seconds left to secure the Railroaders' 55-54 win and the Senate League championship. Louie Moore was named the Senate MVP.

The Railroaders had one final regular season game before moving on to the Division I state tournament. In that game, they defeated Bedford, 94-78, raising their record to 19-0. The Railroaders were ranked #2 in Division I in the final AP state poll.

Collinwood's winning ways continued through sectional and district play. In a district semifinal game, they defeated University School, 45-40; Mentor, 46-44; and Euclid, 57-54.

In the district championship game on March 9, the Railroaders met an old adversary, the Glenville Tarblooders. This was the fourth meeting that season between these two teams, and Collinwood had won each of the previous three games. However, this game did not go quite the way of the first three. Glenville sprinted to a 10-0 lead and never looked back, the Tarblooders emerging with a 63-42 win.

Collinwood head coach Ken Vana was named the 1996 Division I Coach of the Year, while senior forward Melvin Scott was named second-team All-Ohio.

It would be another eight years before the Railroaders made a big splash on the basketball court. In 2004, Collinwood lost to Rhodes, 59-55, in the Senate championship game. They then closed out the regular season with two big wins, squeaking by Villa Angela-St. Joe, 57-56, and Eastlake North, 51-48. Now, it was on to the tournament trail.

In a sectional semifinal, the Railroaders easily defeated Eastlake North for a 75-52 win. In the sectional final game, Collinwood would face Senate foe Glenville, the season's third meeting between the two teams. Collinwood had a 29-18 lead midway through the second quarter, but Glenville fought back, and the game was tied 39-39 entering the final eight minutes. The fourth quarter was tense, and the lead changed hands three times in the final 49 seconds alone. With mere seconds left on the clock and the Railroaders trailing 54-53, Collinwood's Jeremy Weaver grabbed an offensive rebound and put it back just as the buzzer sounded to give Collinwood a thrilling 55-54 victory.

Not only was Collinwood's 20th win of the season, but they had now advanced to the Division I Sweet 16 for the first time in team history, where they would face Bedford in a regional semifinal game. Collinwood had a 43-36 lead entering the fourth quarter. Bedford managed to cut that lead to three, but they could get no closer, and the Railroaders came away with a deceptively easy-looking 69-54 win.

Having advanced to the Great Eight, the Railroaders would face Canton McKinley, the state's all-time winningest basketball team, in the regional final. The Railroaders trailed 39-31 at the half but managed to trim that lead to just three points during the third quarter. The Bulldogs dominated play after that, however, and the Railroaders saw their dream of advancing to the Final Four halted with a 66-57 defeat. Collinwood's final record was a dazzling 21-4.

The 2005 season would be another great one for the Collinwood Railroaders. On Feb. 4, the Railroaders (13-3) played another Senate powerhouse, Glenville (13-2), for the league championship. The game was nip and tuck all the way. Trailing 52-49 with just seconds remaining in the fourth quarter, Collinwood guard Jonathan Moore "made an unlikely 3-point shot to send the game into overtime." (PD) With just seconds left in the overtime period, Collinwood had a 59-56 lead when a Glenville shot from 3-point land rimmed out. Glenville got the rebound and put it in to make the score 59-58 with just five seconds on the clock. Glenville's Ken McCarnell then stole the inbounds pass and appeared to make a 12-foot shot at the buzzer, but the officials waved it off. Collinwood's 59-58 win was its first Senate championship since 1996.

In the final regular season game, the Railroaders defeated Eastlake North to raise their record to 15-3 as they moved on to the state tournament.

Led by Jason Simon, who scored half of Collinwood's 42 points, the Railroaders won a sectional championship over Geneva, 42-32, on Feb. 25. The following week, they continued their playoff success by defeating Mentor, 89-72, behind senior Darnell Campbell's game-high 35 points. That win sent the Railroaders to the district finals against Glenville. There would be no last-second heroics for Collinwood against the Tarblooders this time as Glenville put the finishing touches on Collinwood's season with a 74-61 win. The Railroaders' final record of 17-4 marked another fine season.

BOXING

Arguably the greatest boxer ever to come out of Cleveland, Guiseppe Antonio Berardinelli, known by his boxing name as Joey Maxim, made boxing history in 1950 when he won the World Light Heavyweight title by knocking out heavily favored champion Freddie Mills in London, England. It was learned after the bout that Joey had three of Mills' teeth embedded in one of his gloves.

This championship was the highlight of Maxim's 18-year professional career from 1940 to 1958. During that span, his record was 82-29-4, and he fought 10 world champions, defeating legendary boxers such as Jersey Joe Walcott, Jimmy Bivins (a fellow Clevelander and Cleveland Sports Hall of Fame inductee), Sugar Ray Robinson, and Floyd Patterson.

Before his pro career, Joey fought over 200 amateur bouts, beginning at 13 when he entered the Cleveland Golden Gloves competition. Maxim became a Golden Gloves Award winner and a National AAU champion by 18. Still an amateur, Joey was a lock to be added to the 1940 USA Olympic team, but the 1940 Olympics were canceled because of the outbreak of World War II; he then turned professional. Maxim's professional career, however, was interrupted by the war, during which he served his country as a military policeman in the U.S. Army Air Corps from 1943-45. During the war, Joey fought in several exhibition matches.

The most famous fight of Maxim's career took place on the hot (104 degrees) and sultry night of June 25, 1952, at Yankee Stadium. On that date, Joey overcame the weather and his legendary Sugar Ray Robinson opponent to successfully defend and retain his light heavyweight title.

Joey was not known as a knockout puncher, but he was a master boxer who could elude and block punches and who was a very rapid puncher. He earned his name, Maxim, by being compared to a WWII rapid-fire Maxim machine gun. His Hollywood good looks were proof of his ability to avoid punches, and he was knocked out only once in his entire career!

In 1976, Maxim was inducted into the first class of the Greater Cleveland Sports Hall of Fame, and in 1994, he received boxing's highest honor by being inducted into the International Boxing Hall of Fame.

CROSS-COUNTRY

As a team, Collinwood's two best years at the state meet were in 1941 and 1952, when the Railroaders finished sixth each year.

Only four boys have earned All-Ohio status for Collinwood at the state meet. 1946, John Minnick finished sixth place, and Walter Draxler came eighth. Walter Drexler finished fourth the following year, and Frank Ulle finished 13th place. In 1948, Ulle moved up three spots to finish in 10th place. In 1952, Charles Hurd had the team's best placing when he finished in third place.

FOOTBALL

By the time the 1932 football season rolled around, Collinwood High School had been a member of the Senate League for just a few years. Although the school had a football team, it had not yet played as a conference member. In 1932, the Railroaders, named for the railyards that filled the area where the school was located, took the plunge.

After going through the entire 1931 season without a victory, Collinwood came roaring out of the gate in 1932. Five weeks into the schedule, not only was the Collinwood football team undefeated, including four consecutive Senate wins, but it was also unscored upon. Collinwood closed out its league season by quickly disposing of South High, 31-6, and West Tech, 20-6, to gain the Senate championship with a perfect 6-0-0 league record in its first season of Senate League play.

The Railroaders (7-0-0) still had one game remaining, a non-league contest against Shaw (6-1-1), a game which was, in essence, a playoff for an invitation to play for the city championship in the Charity Game. More than 7,500 spectators jammed into Shaw Stadium on Friday, Nov. 18, for the big game. Collinwood jumped out to a quick 12-0 lead in the first quarter, then added another tally in the third frame to come away with a 19-0 victory. That night, it was made official: Collinwood and Cathedral Latin formally accepted their invitations to play for the city championship at Municipal Stadium on Saturday, Nov. 25.

The 1932 Charity Game would feature "the two greatest backfield combinations produced by scholastic gridders here in recent years." (PD) Coach Paul Yost's Railroaders backfield was led by junior triple-threat quarterback Dick Nardi, who specialized in bursts off tackle, while his passes "traveled like bullets." (PD) He was also rated as one of the top punters in the state. Joining Nardi in the Collinwood backfield was a trio of outstanding running backs. Perhaps the quickest back in the city was halfback Dave Thoss, whose speed enabled him to quickly turn the corner on end runs for sizeable gains. Fullback Joe Whelan was primarily a blocking back and defensive halfback, but he could pick up key yardage for the Railroaders when needed. And halfback Milan Jenko filled out Coach Yost's backfield. Jenko had gotten off to a great start early in the season, but injuries had sidelined him over the latter part of the schedule. Now healthy, Jenko's return to the Collinwood backfield would bring it full strength.

With two relatively equal backfields going against each other, many felt the game would hinge on the line play, especially defense. Here, Collinwood was given a slight edge; its line was rated the strongest in Cleveland, and it was a bunch of smart ball players.

Saturday, Nov. 26, was a cold, blustery day in downtown Cleveland, especially if you happened to be on the lakefront in Municipal Stadium. As 25,274 chilled high school football fans looked on, Latin jumped out to a quick 13-0 lead in the first quarter — and those would prove to be the only points of the game as the Collinwood Railroaders dropped the 13-0 decision.

The Railroaders had another good Senate season in 1933, finishing 4-0-2, but that was only good enough for third place behind undefeated South (6-0-0) and once tied East (5-0-1).

The 1934 Senate season came down almost to the last game. With a 5-0-0 league mark and only one Senate game left on its schedule, Collinwood seemed assured of winning the league crown. But the Railroaders dropped their Senate finale to Central High, 24-13. Collinwood's Senate mark now stood at 5-1-0, earning the Railroaders a share of the Senate League championship with West High, which also finished 5-1-0. The Charity Game committee, however, chose West High's Cowboys to play in the city championship game based on its better overall record of 8-1-0.

In 1935, Collinwood opened its season with a non-league victory over Cleveland Heights, 14-6. Led by the running and passing of ace halfback Paul Lundblad, the Railroaders then rattled off four lopsided victories. With a league mark of 3-0-0, Collinwood was in a good position to defend its share of the league title. And it did, closing out its league slate with a tie and two wins, finishing atop the Senate at 5-0-1, the league's only undefeated team, and winning its third Senate championship in the last four seasons.

On Saturday evening, Nov. 23, after deliberating for three hours, the Charity Game selection committee chose Collinwood and Holy Name High Schools to play in the 1935 Charity Game.

"A heavy battering ram, reminiscent of old-time powerhouse elevens …will combat a lighter, more deceptive team of the modern school …" is how Plain Dealer sportswriter Alex Zirin described the Collinwood-Holy Name match-up. The Collinwood

Railroaders, champion of Ohio's largest scholastic league, played a game dependent primarily on power football. However, Coach Yost's team avoided using the forward pass or a "trick maneuver" when the situation warranted.

Leading the Collinwood attack was a senior halfback, Paul Lundblad, "a slippery, hip-shaking back" (PD) who was also a crack passer and punter — your basic triple-threat man. Lundblad had been the backbone of the Collinwood offense for the past three seasons, but he was not the only weapon coming out of the Railroader's backfield. Combining with Lundblad to score 30 touchdowns were halfback Ken Lucha, quarterback George McKinnon, and fullback Val Pernush. Not only were these boys great runners, but each of them was also a pinpoint passer — and their main target was end Frank Zakrajsek, nicknamed the "ironman" because he had played all but two quarters during the season. Helping Zakrajsek anchor the line on both sides was tackle Nick Cannarozzi and guard Vic Tomaro.

The temperature for the Charity Game at its 2:15 p.m. kickoff time was right around the freezing point, and the field was still blanketed with a light covering of snow. Late in the first quarter, Holy Name recovered a Collinwood fumble and turned it into six points, a lead the Green Wave held until halftime.

After the intermission, a fired-up Collinwood team charged onto the field. Starting the second half at its 16-yard line, the Green Wave could not gain a single yard on its first two plays, so they went back to punt on third down. A fierce charge by the Collinwood defense forced the punter to rush his kick, with the ball bouncing out of bounds at the Holy Name 30-yard line. Railroaders' fullback Dave Aaron closed out the short drive with a 5-yard touchdown run over right guard. Aaron then put his team into the lead, 7-6, with a pass to quarterback George McKinnon for the extra point. It was still a one-point game after three quarters, but a pair of fourth-quarter touchdowns by Collinwood gave the Railroaders a 21-6 win and its first Cleveland championship.

It would be six years before the Railroaders had another shot at a city title. Behind the running and passing of star fullback Tony Adamle, the play of halfback Pete Palumbo, and a rock-solid defense, Collinwood won its first six games of the 1941 campaign. On Saturday, Nov. 2, Collinwood defeated East Tech, 13-0. That victory, combined with John Adams' 13-0 upset of Cathedral Latin, put the Railroaders atop the East Senate. Collinwood clinched its first East Senate crown the following Saturday by defeating East High 33-0. The game marked the Railroaders' eighth consecutive shutout, leaving them with a perfect East Senate mark of 6-0-0.

The Railroaders still had one game before the Charity Game against undefeated Lakewood High (5-0-3). Scoring "one of the season's major scholastic surprises" (PD), the Lakewood Rangers humbled Collinwood 27-6. The Railroaders now had two weeks to regroup and prepare for the Charity Game and the Presidents of Lincoln High, the champions of the West Senate.

The Collinwood Railroaders of Coach Urban Vaccariello in 1941 were a big and fast team. With a line that averaged 194 pounds and a backfield that tipped the scales at 180 pounds (both very big by the standard of the day), it was not hard to see why they had been able to post eight successive shutouts during the season. Leading the Railroaders was their big fullback, Tony Adamle. Rated as the best running back in the school's history and one of the best in the state, Adamle was big like a fullback should be, with the added dimension of breakaway speed. He did it through the air with pinpoint passes when he was not beating you on the ground. His defensive work was also of the highest caliber.

Teaming up with Adamle in the Collinwood backfield was halfback Pete Palumbo, a three-year varsity player. Palumbo was the team's second-leading scorer behind Adamle and the Railroaders' on-field leader, calling the signals for the offense and defense. The team's other halfback was junior speedster Bill Hiller. Quarterbacking the Railroaders was the team's lone starting sophomore, Mike Cannovino, whose main contribution was as a blocking back. Anchoring Coach Vaccariello's big line were ends Roland Baeslach and Len Heiss, with tackle Nick Plescia, guard Lou Frederico, and center Bernie McGroarty.

Making it to The Plain Dealer's Charity Game had to be incredibly satisfying for Coach Vaccariello. A Collinwood alum from the school's first graduating class in 1928, Vaccariello had been a star center for the Railroaders. He then earned All-Ohio status as a tackle at Miami University, where he would lay down the blocks for a quarterback named Paul Brown. Coach "Vac" had been coaching football at his alma mater for 10 years, but only the last three as the mentor of the varsity. This was Vaccariello's first trip to the Charity Game with his alma mater, but the Railroaders were returning to the Municipal Stadium classic for the third time overall.

The fans came out in droves on Nov. 29, 1941, as 46,686, the third highest total thus far for a Charity Game, packed the stadium. Lincoln scored first in the opening quarter to take an early 6-0 lead. Holding the Railroaders at bay, the Presidents scored another touchdown in the third quarter to double their lead to 12-0.

The Railroaders may have been down, but they came right back and answered that Lincoln touchdown with one of their own but missed the extra point. The Railroaders then resorted to the onside kick – and recovered it as Len Heiss fell on the loose ball at the Lincoln 40-yard line. Collinwood steadily advanced to the 8-yard line by switching ball carriers on each play. On first and goal, Tony Adamle blasted over the left side, scoring the game-tying touchdown while dragging two Lincoln defenders into the end zone with him. The extra point try was again no good, leaving the score tied at 12 to 12.

And that was how the game ended: tied 12-12, with Lincoln and Collinwood becoming Cleveland's co-champions.

Collinwood continued winning by opening the 1942 season with six consecutive victories, three of which were Senate games. Collinwood now shared the East Senate lead with Cathedral Latin, each team with identical 3-0-0 Senate marks. They each had three league games yet to play, but since the two teams were not scheduled to play each other, an upset of one of them would be required to avoid an East Senate title tie. No upset presented itself, and Collinwood and Latin ended the season with identical 6-0-0 marks.

It was decided that the two Charity Game veterans (eight appearances in 11 years) would battle in a playoff game on Saturday, Nov. 21, at Municipal Stadium. The big playoff game got underway at 2:15 p.m. that Saturday afternoon. Late in the first quarter, Collinwood halfback Jack Caputo rifled a 10-yard touchdown pass to Jerry Jankovich, the extra point giving the Railroaders a 7-0 lead that held up for the balance of the first half.

Latin came out strong in the second half and scored a touchdown on its first possession of the third quarter but missed the extra point try, leaving the Railroaders with a slim 7-6 lead. Early in the fourth quarter, another Collinwood touchdown pushed the Railroaders' lead to 13-6. The Railroaders dominated the rest of the game, preventing Latin from adding more points to its total. Collinwood's 13-6 victory gave the Railroaders the East Senate crown and a return trip to the Charity Game to battle Lincoln High for Cleveland's high school football championship.

The 1942 Plain Dealer Charity Game would be a re-match of the 1941 city title game that had ended in a 12-12 tie. Lincoln (8-0-1) and Collinwood (10-0-0) had fueled that excitement by completing their 1942 football campaigns undefeated. You could not have picked two better teams to battle it out for city honors.

Although Lincoln was rated a slight favorite, Collinwood had arguably the more explosive offense. Leading the way was junior quarterback Mike Cannovino. A fast runner who occasionally enjoyed sweeping the ends, Cannovino was one of the state's leading scorers with 13 touchdowns. Mike was also the team's place-kicker, making good on 10 extra point attempts; he was also known to throw the ball occasionally.

Joining Cannovino in the Railroaders' backfield was sophomore fullback Norris Fair. A second-teamer at the season's start, Fair was made the starter when first-stringer Tom Hubbard was felled by illness. Fair's promotion by Coach Urban Vaccariello paid huge dividends as Norris scored four touchdowns down the stretch and was the Railroaders' leading ground gainer in the playoff game against Cathedral Latin.

Complementing the Collinwood running game was one of the best passing duos in the area. Halfback Jack Caputo to end Jerry Jankovich was usually suitable for big yardage. The two accounted for six touchdowns during the season, including both scores in the playoff game with Latin. Jankovich was also used to tripping up the opposing defense by carrying the ball on the end around play. Leading the Collinwood line on both offense and defense was 6-foot, 190-pound tackle Andy Post. It was feared that Post would miss the Charity Game due to three cracked ribs suffered against Latin, but heavy taping and a special brace allowed the youngster to compete in the big game.

Unfortunately for the Railroaders, this would not be their day. Neither team scored in the first quarter, while Lincoln took a 7-0 lead in the second. The Presidents built on their 7-0 halftime lead with a touchdown in the third quarter and two more in the final frame to come away with a 26-0 victory.

The 1951 Senate League football season was one of the most exciting and closely contested since the league's expansion almost 15 years earlier, and the Collinwood Railroaders were right in the thick of the action. The Railroaders were one of the most consistently successful teams in the East Senate, and in 1951, head coach Frank X. Lauterbur appeared to have another winner on his hands.

The Railroaders opened their season with a pair of big, non-conference wins, a 12-7 road win over Warren Harding, and a 12-0 victory over traditional rival Shaw High School. The Railroaders then played and won three consecutive East Senate games. In the third of these, a 46-26 win over East High, halfback Joe Trivisonno led the way for the Railroaders as he carried the ball 12 times for 251 yards and four touchdowns, adding a fifth score on a pass reception.

The Railroaders were now ranked fifth in the statewide AP poll.

Taking a break from Senate play, Collinwood defeated Lakewood High, 26-19. Resuming league play, the Railroaders did away with both John Adams, 13-0, and Central, 30-0.

On Saturday, Nov. 10, at John Adams Field, the Collinwood eleven had a real battle with Cathedral Latin. The handoff went to halfback Joe Trivisonno in the first quarter on second and 13 from their 36-yard line. Trivisonno burst through a massive hole at left tackle and raced 64 yards to the end zone. The extra point try was good. Those would prove to be the only points of the game, Collinwood keeping its record intact with a massive 7-0 victory.

The season was now completed, but the Railroaders were tied above the East Senate standings with Benedictine, both teams with 6-0-0 league marks. A playoff game was set for Saturday, Nov. 17.

However, a big, early-season snowstorm hit Cleveland early on the 17th. With at least 10 inches of snow covering the John Adams gridiron, the game was rescheduled for Monday, November 19, at West Tech Field. However, the predicted new snow failed to materialize, and some 3,000 fans showed up to watch the game in freezing temperatures and saw one of Cleveland's all-time best.

With Collinwood scoring 12 points in the first half and Benedictine 12 in the second half, the game ended in a 12-12 tie (no overtime periods back then). By prearrangement, the team that had gained the most net yardage would be declared the East Senate champion in the event of a tie. You could have heard a pin drop at West Tech Field as everyone waited for the two official scorers to total up the yardage for both teams. Finally, after what must have seemed forever, Lloyd Griffith, the West Tech athletic director, made the long-awaited announcement: "Ladies and gentlemen, the Senate eastern division champion and representative in Saturday's Charity Game is Collinwood. ..." (PD). By a margin of 162 yards to 128 yards, a difference of only 34 yards, the Railroaders had made it to their fifth Charity Game to take on West Senate champion Rhodes High.

The 1951 Plain Dealer Charity Game would see "two of the finest teams ever produced in the state" (PD) squaring off against each other. Collinwood had gone 12 straight games without a loss, while Rhodes was enjoying an 11-game win streak. Both teams were well placed in the state's high school football polls, with one poll ranking Collinwood at #7 and the Rams at #10.

Both Collinwood and Rhodes were loaded with all-scholastic caliber players. Collinwood was led on offense by junior halfback Joe Trivisonno and junior quarterback Dom Pannitto. Trivisonno, one of the city's leading runners, had already scored 14 touchdowns with his "bull-like rushes" (PD) and exceptional speed. Joe was the key to the Railroaders' running game, but he could also pass the ball if need be. He was the team's primary kicker and a starter on defense. Quarterback Dom Pannitto had accounted for 16 touchdowns, five rushing, and 11 with his "bullet passes" (PD). The diversified Railroaders' attack also featured running backs Dominic Grassie and Rich Fiorelli, an excellent place-kicker in Gene Dickard, and star end Al DeMell. The Railroader's defense, which yielded just 7.7 points per game with four shutouts, was led by end John McClurg, tackle Carmen Fatica and center Tom Chuidioni.

The Charity Game was played on Saturday, Nov. 24, a cold, damp day. It would not be Collinwood's day despite a pair of Joe Trivisonno touchdowns—one covering 76 yards, the longest run from scrimmage in the history of the Charity Game. When the final whistle sounded, Collinwood was on the short end of a 21-14 score. The Railroaders finished eighth in the final AP state poll that year.

It would be another 16 seasons before the Railroaders again played for the city championship. They opened the 1967 campaign with a massive upset of neighborhood rival Shaw at Shaw Stadium on Saturday afternoon, Sept. 9, a game "played under a thick blanket of rain" (PD). In less than four minutes, the Railroaders jumped to a 12-0 lead and then held on for a 12-2 victory.

After the Railroaders won another thriller over Euclid High School, 18-14, they would win their next six games, all East Senate contests. The divisional championship would be decided on Saturday night, Nov. 4, at John Adams Field, Collinwood's last game of the season. The Railroaders would take on the unanimous preseason favorite, Cathedral Latin Lions. With both teams entering the game undefeated in East Senate play, Collinwood at 6-0-0 and the Lions at 5-0-0, it would be winner-take-all.

The weather and field conditions were terrible for such an important game; snow fell throughout the game, and the mud was 6 inches deep in places. Nonetheless, the Railroaders took a 6-0 lead in the first quarter and made it hold up the entire game, coming away with a massive 6-0 win.

Collinwood finished the season a perfect 7-0-0 in the East Senate and 9-0-0 overall and will return to the Charity Game for the first time since 1951.

The Charity Game teams were now set. Collinwood (7-0-0, 9-0-0), ranked first in Cleveland by The Plain Dealer and sixth in the state by the Ohio Football News, would be trying to keep the city championship on the east side for a third straight year, while Saint Ignatius (7-0-0, 8-1-0) would be trying to bring the trophy back to the western banks of the Cuyahoga River.

Collinwood head coach Joe Trivisonno, in his fifth year at the helm of the Railroaders, was making history with his appearance in the Charity Game, becoming the first former Charity Game player (1951) to return as a coach.

Many observers felt this game would be a defensive struggle, and the Railroaders were well-equipped for that encounter. Although they had only one shutout to their credit, the Collinwood defense had allowed only 67 points. Two defensive ends led the defense, Gary Godina on the right and Bruce Kordic on the left. Godina, a solid 200-pounder, could "wipe out two or three blockers and smash the ball carrier" (PD). On the other side of the defensive line, Bruce Kordic was no pushover at 6'5" and 220 pounds. Together, these two were rated as "perhaps the two toughest defenders in the state" (PD).

In between the two ends were tackles Tom Wadsworth and Steve Giampapa, as well as middle guard Sid Jacobs, ably supported by linebackers Ken Parks and Jim Cellini and deep backs Tony Burdock, Rich Spisak, Dave Dawson, and Roger Hicks. These guys would have their hands while trying to stop a potent Saint Ignatius offense that had scored 273 points, including 70 in one game.

Collinwood's offense, although scoring only about half as many points as Saint Ignatius, was still solid. Its numbers were evenly split between running the ball and passing it. Quarterback Nick Lanese, a junior in his first season at the helm, was directing the attack. Lanese completed 58 percent of his passes, including 10 touchdowns. Lanese's job as a passer was made a little bit easier because of the "tall timber" he had as a receiver. Bruce Kordic and Tony Burdock combined to catch 58 passes for 874 yards and 10 touchdowns. When the Railroaders traveled by land, the primary ball carriers were halfbacks Rick Spisak and Dave Dawson.

The 1967 Charity Game, played on Nov. 23, went to the Wildcats, who won 21-0.

Collinwood's next shot at a Senate championship came in 1972. After losing its first three games, all non-league contests, the team regrouped under head coach Steve Graves and went through its East Senate schedule undefeated, 5-0-1. The Railroaders met West Senate champion Saint Ignatius at Finnie Stadium in Berea on Saturday, November 18, for the overall Senate championship.

Before some 4,500 fans, Collinwood took a 6-0 lead late in the first quarter on a 4-yard scamper by running back Tony Iliano. Saint Ignatius tied the score midway through the second quarter and then took the 14-6 lead with a touchdown with just 53 seconds left in the first half. However, Collinwood's Rick Citino returned the ensuing kickoff 88 yards to pull the Railroaders to within two points at 14-12. Collinwood went for the two-point conversion in an attempt to tie the score, but the ball was fumbled near the goal line and recovered by the Wildcats. There would be no scoring by either team in the second half, Collinwood dropping a heartbreaker, 14-12. Head coach Steve Graves was named the East Senate Coach of the Year.

Collinwood enjoyed a three-year run of Senate football glory from 1984-1986. By this time, the Senate had been divided into a North Division (Glenville, West Tech, Collinwood, John Hay, Lincoln-West, and East High) and a South Division (South High, John F. Kennedy, East Tech, John Marshall, John Adams, and Rhodes). In 1984, Collinwood tied with Glenville and John Hay for the North championship, and all had 4-1 league records. Collinwood was chosen to represent the division in the Senate championship game against

South Division champion John Adams. In that championship game, held on Nov. 9 at John Marshall Field, Collinwood lost by 18-12. Collinwood head coach Bob Fisher was named the 1984 Senate Coach of the Year.

Collinwood's 1985 season was divided into five-game halves, the first five games against non-league teams and the last five against North Senate foes. It was a rough start for the Railroaders as they dropped their first four contests, but they finally got on a winning track by defeating Dover High School, 19-0. The Railroaders scored 5-0 in their North Senate games, winning the North championship as their stifling defense limited their Senate foes to nine total points.

Next up for the Railroaders was the Senate League championship game, played on Friday, Nov. 8, at John Marshall Field. Their opponent would be the Eagles of John F. Kennedy High School, who had captured the South Division title. The defense was the strength of this Collinwood team, and it would be the difference in this game.

Late in the first quarter, Collinwood broke on top when halfback Darryl Wimberly returned a JFK punt 29 yards for a touchdown. Guard Willie Lee added the extra point to give the Railroaders a 7-0 lead at 3:22 of the first quarter. At 3:39 of the second quarter, the Eagles scored a touchdown on a 1-yard plunge; however, the pass for the two-point conversion was knocked down, leaving Collinwood with a 7-6 halftime advantage.

Collinwood's Steve Woods added to his team's lead with a 10-yard touchdown pass reception early in the fourth quarter, but the extra point try was no good. With 1:46 left in the game, Kennedy scored on an 8-yard pass play. Kennedy went for the lead with a two-point conversion, but the pass fell incomplete. The Collinwood offense then ran out the clock to preserve a close 13-12 win — and give the Railroaders their first outright Senate championship since 1935.

As in 1985, Collinwood's season was split 50-50 between non-league and league games. The Railroaders fared a little better in the non-league games than the previous season, winning two of the five. In North Senate play, the Railroaders won their first four games, setting up a showdown on Oct. 30 with West Tech, also 4-0, for the divisional championship.

West Tech jumped out to a quick 14-0 lead in the first quarter, and it looked as if Collinwood's reign as Senate champion would end. But then Railroaders' junior quarterback Bruce Davis went to work and almost single-handedly brought the Railroaders back. Davis completed nine of 15 passes for 237 yards, but that was just the sideshow. Davis scored three touchdowns and a pair of two-point conversions to account for all 22 of Collinwood's points. Also playing on defense, Davis came up with perhaps the key play of the game as he knocked down what appeared to be a sure West Tech TD pass in the fourth quarter to preserve the Railroaders' incredible 22-14 come-from-behind win.

That victory sent the Railroaders into the Senate championship game on Nov. 7 against the South Senate champion John Marshall Lawyers. With the Collinwood defense extending its shutout streak to seven consecutive quarters, the Railroaders won their second straight Senate League championship with a score of 23-0.

The Railroaders' 1990 season would be one of their most challenging ever, but it was also one of their most successful when all was said and done. Collinwood opened the season against a demanding non-league five-game schedule. After dropping a 31-19 decision to Massillon Jackson, they defeated Eastlake North when senior Sam Thomas intercepted a North pass in the end zone with 1:23 left in the game to preserve his team's 20-19 win. Collinwood held on for another one-point victory the following week, defeating Mansfield 7-6.

Off to their best start in years, the Railroaders had to play two of the toughest teams they had ever encountered, both nationally ranked. Against Brooke (W. Va.) High School, Collinwood dropped a 25-6 decision; Brooke would later finish at #23 in the country. The following week, the Railroaders had to face off against Saint Ignatius, the defending national champion. The boys played tough but returned on the short end of a 34-6 score.

It was now on to their North Senate schedule for the Railroaders. It was not easy at times, but the Railroaders rolled through their league schedule a perfect 5-0, outscoring the opposition 107-14.

Next up for Collinwood was the Senate championship game against a powerful John Marshall squad (5-0, 8-2). This would be another game where the Collinwood defense, dubbed "The Blue Steel Wall," would again be outstanding. John Marshall took a 3-0 lead in the first quarter, but it was all Collinwood after that. The Railroaders' defense held Marshall to just 63 total yards of offense. In contrast, the Collinwood offense would score single touchdowns in the final three quarters for a 20-3 victory, the Railroaders' third Senate championship in the last six seasons.

GYMNASTICS

Collinwood had one good year at the boys state gymnastics meet in 1931 when the Railroaders finished in third place. Leading the way for Collinwood was Frey, who won a state championship on the horizontal bars—the only gymnastics state championship ever won by a Collinwood student. Frey also finished fifth on the parallel bars. Also contributing to Collinwood's point total was Zorman, who placed fourth on the horizontal bars and fifth on the flying rings, and Mericle, who placed third with the Indian clubs and fourth on the flying rings.

TRACK

In 1929, Alex Zych finished fifth in the 220yd. low hurdles, and in the process, put himself into the Collinwood High School record book as the school's first All-Ohio athlete. Four years later, in 1933, the Railroaders had their first track and field state champion when a young man named Fair, who, unlike his name, was very good, won the 880yd. run at the state meet with a time of 2:01.5.

In 1934, under the direction of track coach Clarence Hudson, the railroaders piled up the points by scoring in six different events, with their overall point total of 21 good enough to claim second place. Charles Nance led the way by finishing among the leaders in two events, second in the 220yd. low hurdles and third in the 100yd. dash. Fair, who had won the 880yd. run the year before, finished fourth in the mile run this time. Ralph Ohlsen (220yd. dash) and Paul Lundblad (120yd. high hurdles) finished third in their respective races.

Coming home with a state championship was the Railroaders' 880yd. The relay team of Charles Nance, Dalton, Adolph Worthy, and Ralph Ohlsen had a time of 1:30.8 – just one-fifth of a second short of the state record. Nobody could have known it then, but the school's 880yd. The relay team would dominate that race for the next few years.

In 1935, the Railroaders again scored in several events at the state meet, scoring 16 points, which was good enough for a third-place finish. Once again, the school's 880yd. The relay team of Dalton, Charles Nance, Adolph Worthy, and Ralph Ohlsen, the same four runners who won this race in 1934, again took home the first-place medal with a time of 1:30.5. The individual hero for Collinwood was Adolph Worthy, who finished third in the 100-yards. dash and second in the 220yd. dash.

The 1936 state track meet saw the Railroaders finish in fourth place with 15 points. This time, the 880-yard relay team finished second to East Tech. Adolph Worthy finished second in the 100-yard dash, but in the 220-yard dash, he took home the first-place prize with a time of 21 seconds flat.

The Railroaders finished in third place in 1937. Dash man Carmony finished third in both the 100 yd. and 220yd. dashes, while hurdler Pierce finished second in both the 120 yards. high and the 220yd. low hurdles.

Sprinter Carmony was back at the state meet in 1938, finishing second in the 100yd. and 220yd. dashes to provide Collinwood with all of its points and an eighth-place finish.

For the fourth time in seven years, 1941, the Railroaders would again finish among the top four teams at the state meet, coming in at #3. They were once again led by the 880yd relay team, which brought home its third state championship in the last eight years with a time of 1:30.9. This year, the team was composed of Fred Nance, Sam Dawson, Wilbur Schweitzer, and Oliver Bailey. Bailey also contributed to his team's point total by finishing second in the 220-yard dash, while Schweitzer added team points with his fourth-place showing in the broad jump.

Over the next twenty years, the Railroaders earned only three points at the state meet, but that changed in 1962. Under the direction of head coach Charles Hofelich, the Railroaders earned 23 points to win a Class AA track state championship.

While Collinwood was listed as the team champion in 1962, this championship belongs to two outstanding athletes: Theo Morrow and Mike Cavotta. These two boys were the Railroaders' entire team that year, and they beat out a Dayton Dunbar team that competed with a contingent of 18 athletes for first place.

Morrow had a genuinely outstanding meet. Not only did he win the 100yd dash in 10.2 seconds "as a driving thunderstorm hit the stadium"

(Press) in Columbus, but he came in second in the 120yd high hurdles, second in the 180yd low hurdles, and third in the broad jump. His outstanding finish in those four events earned 17 points for the Railroaders and Theo Morrow the Most Valuable Athlete award at the state meet. Morrow was later selected to the High School All-America track team that year.

Earning the other six points for the Railroaders was Mike Cavotta, whose throw of 56' 5¼" was good enough to win the shot put competition. Mike was not simply a strongman athlete; he also excelled in the classroom and was a member of the National Honor Society. Mike continued as a shot putter at The Ohio State University (having earned a full scholarship) and well beyond. In 2015, 53 years after winning the state high school championship, Mike finished second in the National Senior Olympics.

It was not until 1973 that the Railroaders again finished high at the state meet, coming in second in Class AAA under the direction of head coach Don Vaccarello. In doing so, they scored their all-time high of 34 points. Leading the way was speedster Robert Hennings, who took home the first-place medal in both the 100-yard dash (9.7 sec.) and the 220-yard dash (21.6 sec.). Steve Graves scored the Railroaders' other points and finished second in the discus with a throw of 177' 1" and third in the shot put with a heave of 58' 11¼". Hennings was also named the winner of the prestigious Frank Castleman Award, which was named after the former Ohio State track coach.

In 1974, the Railroaders had another good time at the state meet, scoring 26 points and finishing in third place. As he did the year before, Robert Hennings again led the Railroaders; he scored all of the team's 26 points. This time, he finished second in both the 100-yard and 220-yard dashes. Hennings closed out his state meet career with a first-place finish in the 180-yard low hurdles, setting a new record of 18.9 seconds. In earning All-Ohio status five times at two state track meets, Robert Hennings became Collinwood's all-time top athlete.

The Railroaders would never again come close to winning another state track title, but they did produce two more state champions. In 1985, at the Class AAA state meet, Dennis Driggins won the discus competition with a throw of 168'10". Ten years later, while participating in the Division I state meet, Rah Sheen Clay won the state championship in the 400m dash with 48.13 seconds; he also finished fifth in the 200m dash.

TRACK (GIRLS)

While the state track meet for boys has been held since 1908, the girls had to wait until 1975 to compete for a state championship. In 1976, Debra Shealey, Blanche Jackson, Sandra Brown, and Julie Rufus took sixth place in the 4x440yd relay to score the first points for the Lady Railroaders at the state meet. In the process, they also became the first Lady Railroaders to earn All-Ohio status.

Over the next 15 years, there would be little success for Collinwood's track team at the state meet, except for 1984. That year, the girls capped off their best season thus far in a three-way tie for fourth place in Class AAA. Latanya Johnson led the way and won the 400m dash in 56.32, earning the Lady Railroaders' first state championship. Not to be outdone, Latanya joined Shawn Booker, Betty Brooks, and Angelique Strong on the state championship 4x400m relay team, which won the race in a state meet record time of 3:50.40.

Following 1984, the Collinwood girls had little success at the state meet over the next 10 years. However, in 1993, something changed the fortunes of the Collinwood girls track. Late that year, Lou Slapnik was hired to coach the Lady Railroaders. From 1994 through 2010, under Slapnik's guidance, the Lady Railroaders would become the most dominant Division I girls track team in Ohio, winning more state championships than all but two other schools in the entire state regardless of division.

In 1994, the Collinwood girls totaled 12 points by scoring in five different events, led by the school's state championship 4x100m relay team of Lakisha Zanders, Ernie Evans, Talisha Rogers, and Shonda Robinson.

The following year, 1995, the team did even better, finishing in a tie for fourth place. Sophomore Shonda Robinson led the team by scoring in three different events, including as a member of the state championship 4x100m relay team, including Lakisha Zanders, Dede Owens, and Talisha Rogers. This was the second year in a row that Collinwood had won the 4x100m, and that event would go on to become something of a team specialty; from 1994-2010, the Lady Railroaders would win the 4x100m relay eight times, with many other podium finishes. In 1995, Collinwood also brought home another individual state championship when Keomi Johnson won the long jump with a leap of 18'10½".

In 1996, the team continued its march toward a state championship by doubling its point output of the previous year, scoring 50 points for a third-place finish. Shonda Robinson again led the team by finishing on the podium in no less than four events, including the 100m (second), 200m (third), and 4x100m (second). Robinson was also a member of the team's state championship 4x400 relay team, which included Rhondalyn Crawford, Donita Scott, and Rashida Cameron.

Finally, in 1997, the Lady Railroaders achieved their goal of a state championship, and they did it with a meet performance that was one for the record books. The team finished with 56 points, 22 more than second-place Springfield South. As in the previous three state meets, the Lady Railroaders were led by Shonda Robinson, who that year put on a performance that has seldom been equaled. In leading Collinwood to the state championship, Robinson won four separate events: both the 100m (11.92) and 200m (24.28) dashes; she then joined Rhondalyn Crawford, Donita Scott, and Rashida Cameron on the winning 4x200m (1:38.34) and 4x400m (3:46.56) relay teams. Not only did these four girls win both events, but they also set the meet and state records for each, records that would last a dozen years.

One Collinwood freshman on that 1997 team would begin a run of success that has been seldom, if ever, equaled at the state meet. Even as a freshman, Christina Estrict was an incredible high jumper. At the 1997 state meet, she cleared the bar at 5'9", which equaled the meet best; however, because the other girl made the jump in fewer tries, Christina had to settle for second place. She would never again have to settle for second best.

The Lady Railroaders were good on the outdoor tracks in 1997 but could compete with the best indoors. In mid-March of that year, the team was invited to the National Scholastic Indoor Track Championships in Boston. The 4x400m team of Rhondalyn Crawford, Donita Scott, Shonda Robinson, and Rashida Cameron earned sixth-place medals with a time of 3:57.80, but their time was good enough to set a new Ohio girls indoor record for that event. The Collinwood team also did well in the 4x200m relay. With Crawford, Robinson, and Cameron now joined by Ocie Lassiter, the girls were clocked at 1:44.29, which earned them ninth place. And while this did not earn them a medal, that time was another Ohio indoor record by a girls team.

The 1997 state meet also ended the high school career of one of Collinwood's greatest athletes, Shonda Robinson. She had been on the Lady Railroaders track team since her first year in 1994. In four state meets, she reached the podium at least thrice yearly, with 14 All-Ohio performances that included seven state championships.

In 1998, the Lady Railroaders increased their point total to 58, good enough for a second consecutive state title, but one they had to share with Columbus Brookhaven, which also scored 58 points.

Leading the way for Collinwood were a senior and a couple of underclassmen. Senior Rhondalynn Crawford finished fourth in the 400m dash and was a member of the state championship 4x400m relay team, along with Donita Scott, Kandace Stone, and Kimberly Jordan. This marked the third consecutive year that Collinwood had won the 4x400m race; earlier in the year, these same four girls set a state record in this event with a time of 3:46.05. Freshman Kandace Stone made a big splash at her first state meet by winning both the 100m (14.11) and 300m hurdles (43.00), as well as being a member of both the third-place 4x100m and the state championship 4x400m relay teams. Not only did Christina Estrict win the state title in the high jump with another leap of 5'9", but she showed that she was a multi-talented athlete by finishing third in the 100m hurdles and as a member of the 4x100m relay team.

The 1999 Collinwood team again increased its point total by scoring 59 points at the state meet, which was enough for a third consecutive state championship. Once again, Kandace Stone and Christina Estrict led the Lady Railroaders to victory. Kandace finished second in the 100m hurdles and fourth in the 200m hurdles and was a member of the state championship 4x100m relay team, along with Kimberly Jordan, Christal Christian, and Christina Christian. Christina Estrict made the podium with an eighth-place finish in the 100m dash, finished fourth in the 100m hurdles, and was the state champion in both the high jump (5'8") and the long jump (19'½").

While the Lady Railroaders saw their point total fall to 47 at the 2000 state meet, it was still enough for them to win a fourth consecutive state championship. Kandace Stone again played a major role in the team's success. After finishing second in the 200m dash and the 100m hurdles, Kandace joined Christina Christian, Shamika Jones, and Christal Christian on two state championship relay teams, the 4x100m and the 4x200m.

Adding a little icing to the team's championship cake, Christina Estrict closed out her outstanding track career at Collinwood by not only winning her third consecutive state championship in the high jump (and the fourth year in a row in which she posted the best jump), but she did it with a state meet record leap of 6' even. That jump is still the second-best in the state meet history two decades later.

The competition at the 2001 state meet was again stiff, as the Lady Railroaders' score of 40 points, their lowest point total of the last five years, attested. However, those 40 points were enough to bring home yet another state title to Collinwood High School, though they had to share this with another Cleveland area school, Beaumont of Cleveland Heights. Those five consecutive championships comprise the most incredible state track championships ever run for a Division I girls team and the second-longest streak of success for any girls team in Ohio.

The Lady Railroaders scored all their points by winning state championships in four events, and Kandace Stone closed out her incredible high school track career by having a hand in all four gold medal finishes. Kandace won the 100m high and 300m low hurdles. She then joined Christina Christian, Mignon Banks, and Christal Christian on the state championship 4x100m and 4x200m relay teams. Like Shonda Robinson a few years earlier, Kandace Stone had won four gold medals in a single state meet. Like Robinson, Kandace finished her career with 14 All-Ohio performances and seven state championships.

After an absence of three years, the Lady Railroaders again finished atop the team standings at the 2004 state track meet, sharing the championship with Mason High School, each team scoring 54 points. Collinwood's success that year was due to the team's overwhelming dominance in the relay events. Charnee Lumbus, Jenice Williams, Shantell Lewis, and Courtney Jones finished first in the 4x100m. Christy Horn joined Williams, Lumbus, and Lewis on the state championship 4x200m team. Regina Adams, Brandy Taylor, Joi Smith, and Sabrina Parr brought gold medals in the 4x400m relay home. A third-place finish in the 4x800m, second- and third-place finishes in the 300m hurdles, and an eighth-place finish in the long jump rounded out the team's scoring.

Four girls who had started on the team as freshmen back in 2002 – Sabrina Parr, Joi Smith, Shantell Lewis, and Jenice Williams – finished their outstanding track careers at Collinwood in grand style by leading the team to a second consecutive championship as seniors in 2005 by scoring a then-school record 65 points, more than doubling second-place Lancaster High and its 31 points. The Lady Railroaders scored in 10 separate events, continuing their dominance in the relay races with a pair of wins, a second, and a third-place finish. The victories came in the 4x100m with Courtney Jones, Christy Horn, Jenice Williams, and Shantell Lewis racing around the track in 47.32, and in the 4x200m with Charnee Lumbus joining Williams, Horn and Lewis in covering the distance in 1:39.33.

Not only did Collinwood win the OHSAA state outdoor championship that year, but earlier in the spring, they also won the state indoor championships sponsored by the Ohio Association of Track and Cross Country Coaches (OATCCC).

The 2006 track season again saw the Lady Railroaders double up on state championships, winning both the OATCCC indoor title and the OHSAA outdoor championship; as best as can be determined, they are the only girls team ever to accomplish this feat. Leading the Lady Railroaders with three gold medals and one silver was Charnee Lumbus. Charnee won the 100m and the 300m hurdles and was a member of the winning 4x100m relay team, along with Courtney Jones, Laurin Slayton, and Christy Horn. She was also a member of the 4x400m relay team that finished second. Charnee Lumbus finished her outstanding track career at Collinwood with nine podium trips, including six first-place finishes.

Collinwood's run of outdoor state track championships stopped at three in a row in 2007, finishing second to Beaumont; however, the girls did win their third consecutive indoor championship that year. Collinwood came away with one OHSAA championship, not too surprisingly in a relay, as the team of Shannon Willis, Erin Busbee, Whitney Miller, and Christy Horn won the 4x200m race.

The team slipped to fifth place in the OHSAA state meet in 2008. Amber Smith scored big points for Collinwood with a state championship in the 300m hurdles, third place in the 100m hurdles, and participation in the 4x400m relay team that finished in fifth place.

2009, the Lady Railroaders won their fourth and final OATCCC indoor track championship. In the OHSAA state meet, they improved to third place without finishing first in any event.

The 2010 state meet was significant in Collinwood girls track history. First, the team was now competing in Division II. Second, the girls brought home their ninth state championship with an all-time Collinwood record of 77 points, needing everyone to hold off second-place Columbus Bishop Hartley, who scored 72 points.

Among the team's three state championships that year were two that set both a Division II state and meet record. The first came in the 4x200m relay, which the team of Brittini Brown, Amirah Harbour, Jasmine Lett, and Amber Smith ran in a record time of 1:39.76. Amber Smith set the second record in the 300m hurdles with a time of 42.83. Amber also finished second in the 100m hurdles and fifth in the long jump. Also having a big day was Erin Busbee, who won the long jump, finished second in the 100m dash, third in the 200m, and fourth in the high jump. Amber Smith and Erin Busbee had a hand in 69 of their team's 77 points. (Earlier in the season, Erin Busbee set a girls Ohio interscholastic record in the long jump at 19'11½", which still stands.)

It is no surprise that the extraordinary success of the Collinwood girls track team, which established the greatest era for any girls track team from the city of Cleveland and one of the most outstanding in all of Ohio, came to an end after the 2010 season when Lou Slapnik retired—as a coach, he was one of a kind.

Lou Slapnik grew up on St. Clair Ave. in Cleveland's Slovenian neighborhood and graduated from St. Joseph High School and Ashland College. After graduating from Ashland, Lou landed a job teaching physical education at Patrick Henry Junior High School. Although he knew nothing about coaching the sport, Slapnik took on the job of coaching the school's track team. Lou and his students proved to be quick studies, and the Patrick Henry team won eight consecutive middle school city championships from 1986-1993. Late in 1993, the job of coaching the Collinwood girls track team came open, and Lou took it.

All Patrick Henry track team girls followed Coach Slapnik to his new assignment – and the Collinwood girls track program was off and running. Years later, he told a reporter, "My goal at Collinwood was high right away - to compete for a state championship."

The Lady Railroaders did more than "compete for a state championship." Under Coach Slapnik's tutelage, they dominated track at city and state levels. In Lou's 17 years at Collinwood, the Lady Railroaders won the Jesse Owens City Championship yearly—a record that will probably never be broken.

At the state level, the accomplishments of the Lady Railroaders were almost as dominating. In each of the 17 years that Slapnik coached the team, the girls qualified for the state meet, where they never scored less than 10 points. The girls won the state championship on their fourth try and then kept winning. They would eventually total nine OHSAA track championships, including a Division I record five (second all-time in Ohio) and four OATCCC indoor championships (three in a row). In the process, they set six OHSAA state and/or meet records, all but two in relay events, two indoor state records, and also in relay events. In the OHSAA state meets, the girls took home an incredible 45 championship trophies, nine team championships, and another 36 event titles.

As one Collinwood parent said of Lou Slapnik: "He's a dedicated, tough, straightforward guy. All he wants to do is make them good athletes and people." Lou Slapnik was inducted into the Ohio Association of Track and Cross Country Coaches Hall of Fame in 2012 and into the Greater Cleveland Sports Hall of Fame in 2023.

WRESTLING

The Railroaders' only state championship in wrestling came in 1957, when Joe Putrizzi won the gold at 145 pounds. Steve Merencky finished fourth at 154 pounds that year, giving Collinwood its all-time best finish of 11th place.

One of Collinwood's all-time best wrestlers, Benny Bright, had back-to-back second-place finishes at the state meet in 1984 (126 pounds) and 1985 (132 pounds).

CHAPTER 11

East Tech High School

> *East Tech opened on Oct. 5, 1908, the first public trade school in Cleveland and only the fifth such school in the United States. The original building stood for 64 years until a new one was dedicated, and faculty, students, and administrators moved in on Oct. 11, 1972.*

BASKETBALL

Beginning with its first Senate and Cleveland championship in 1912, East Tech has produced a long and glorious history of basketball excellence that covers more than 100 years of interscholastic competition. The Scarabs own more Senate and city championships than any other Cleveland high school, including a record six consecutive of each (one of the best such championship runs in Ohio high school history). Statewide, East Tech is tied for second for the most consecutive state tournament appearances with six.

The following summary of the Scarabs' accomplishments scratches the surface of East Tech High School's excellent basketball story.

The Senate League basketball season of 1912 ran from Jan. 5 through Feb. 28. As East Tech was then known, Technical High was in only its fourth year of interscholastic athletics, but the boys had proven to be quick learners. Tech won its first five league games, setting up a mid-February showdown with Central High.

In a close game, Tech held on for a 19-14 win, then defeated South High, 22-11, to complete its undefeated league season with a record of 7-0.

For the 1913 season, the school, now known as East Technical after the addition of a new technical high school on the west side, won its first four Senate games by an average score of 20-13. East Tech continued its successful Senate campaign by sweeping the remaining four games on its league schedule to finish with another perfect Senate League record at 8-0 and a second consecutive Senate and Cleveland championship.

East Tech's next shot at the league title came in 1918, the Senate League schedule being played despite the World War and the early days of the Spanish Flu epidemic. The Senate championship that year would be one of the most hotly contested until then, but East Tech emerged as the Senate titleholder. Four East Tech players were named to the All-Senate team that season. Making the First Team were guards Mose Lefkowitz and William Edwards; getting named to the Second Team were guard Harry Neeley and forward Luge.

The 1919 season was another that would go right down to the final game. With four teams battling for the league's top spot, the Senate championship would be decided on March 21 when East Tech played West High. If East Tech wins the game, they are the Senate champions; however, if West High wins, the league race will end in a four-way tie between East Tech, West High, West Commerce, and South High. East Tech settled any doubt about the league champion by throttling West High, 31-14, to bring home a second consecutive Senate title.

East Tech also participated in the 1919 Ohio Wesleyan Tournament to determine the state high school champion. Eighty-four teams entered the tournament, divided into northern and southern sections, with East Tech playing in the north of the group. In early play, East Tech defeated Lima High School, 25-8, and Montpelier, 14-10. East Tech was now one of three remaining teams in the northern half and was next scheduled to play East Liverpool, with the Clevelanders squeezing out a 20-19 win. That victory sent East Tech to the tournament's Final Four.

In the Final Four, "25" would be the magic number. In one semifinal contest, Dayton Stivers defeated Marietta 25-15. In its game, East Tech efficiently handled Mansfield by the same 25-15 score; forward Harry Neely scored 15 of Tech's points.

It was now down to the last game, East Tech versus Dayton Stivers, for the tournament and state championships. A description of the game, as printed in The Plain Dealer, is as follows: "Stivers did not excel Cleveland East Tech in all-around play, for there was no question that East Tech was superior in passing, floor work and defensive play, but it was in basket shooting that the Dayton five excelled. This was the factor that decided the championship."

It was a close game and apparently a very physical one. With seven minutes remaining in the game, Dayton Stivers had a third-player foul out, leaving them with just four players on the court. Despite this workforce advantage, East Tech could not consistently find the basket. Although forward Harry Neely scored a game-high 16 points, it was not enough as Stivers held on for a 25-22 win—and their third consecutive tournament and state championship.

Coached by Sam Willaman, the team finished the season with a record of 16-2. Three East Tech players were named to the All-State team. Forward Harry Neely and guard Finn were named to the First Team, while forward Mose Lefkowitz was named to the All-State Second Team.

It would not be until the 1937-38 season that East Tech again found itself among the area's better basketball teams. That year, the first season in which the Senate League was divided into East and West divisions, the team was coached by Eric V. Calhoun, who was in the final year of a 14-year run as the school's basketball coach. On Feb. 5, East Tech defeated Collinwood, 39-22, for only the second time in the last nine seasons. That win also broke a first-place logjam, with East Tech taking over the eastern division's top spot with a 4-1 mark and finishing with an East Senate record of 7-1 and the divisional championship. Next up would be the city championship game against West Tech, which had won the western division title with a record of 7-0.

In that championship game, neither team could get much of a lead, but East Tech led 9-6 after the first quarter and 18-14 at the half. After the intermission, West Tech came storming back, outscoring the East Siders 15-8 to take a 29-26 lead into the final quarter. In a furious final period, the lead changed hands six times, and when the final buzzer sounded, the game was all even at 39-39.

The overtime session was just as furious, but East Tech's Frank "Dead-Eye" Dudek would be the difference.

Dudek scored a pair of field goals "from near midfloor" (PD), and he added a free throw that proved to be the difference as East Tech came away with a 44-43 win and the city title.

Fifteen years elapsed before East Tech would again reach the heights of Senate basketball, but then the Scarabs would dominate the Cleveland high school basketball scene for almost a quarter century while also making a name for themselves at the state level.

The 1952-53 school year would see the merging of East Tech and Central High into one school, East Tech. Joe Smith would be taking over as the head coach of the newly combined East Tech basketball team, who had enjoyed much success as the Central High mentor. Led by star player Steve Gwin, the Scarabs had little trouble dominating the East Senate and won the divisional title with a record of 8-0. Little known fact: All five East Tech starters that season had played for Central High the year before.

The Cleveland city championship game was played on Feb. 21 at the Cleveland Arena, with East Tech taking on West Senate champion Saint Ignatius. Following a slow start, the Scarabs took a 10-4 lead after the first quarter, expanding to 30-23 at the half. The second half was an evenly played affair, with East Tech maintaining its lead and emerging as the Cleveland champion with a 59-53 win.

East Tech, now 12-0 overall, moved on to the Class A Sectional Tournament at Euclid. The Scarabs easily defeated Benedictine, 48-27, and Cleveland Heights, 62-48, to advance to Euclid District play. It was more of the same in district play as the Scarabs humbled Mentor, 68-46, and Brush, 70-50, overcoming a five-point Brush lead late in the second quarter.

The Euclid District championship game would pose more of a challenge for the Scarabs. Playing the host team from Euclid High would be a closely fought contest, but East Tech held on for a 58-52 win. Center Steve Gwin and guard Percy Coleman were named to the All-District First Team.

With their record now a sparkling 18-0, the Scarabs had advanced to the Class A Kent Regional tournament for the first time in school history. Their opponent in a regional semifinal game would be Akron Garfield, also 18-0. As expected, this game was close throughout, but East Tech managed to grab a 46-41 lead after three quarters, then held off Garfield to come away with a 52-50 victory.

East Tech would be facing Saint Ignatius (18-2) in the regional finals, which they had defeated a few weeks earlier in the city championship game. After the first quarter, the Wildcats held a 13-12 lead, but as they had done against Akron Garfield, the Scarabs returned to take the lead at the intermission by 30-27. The Wildcats came out strong in the third quarter and regained the lead midway through that period, 34-30. The Wildcats would never be headed after that, holding on for a 55-49 victory.

East Tech ended the season with a stellar 19-1 record, with Steve Gwin making the All-Ohio Second Team.

The Scarabs opened the 1953-54 campaign with nine consecutive victories before dropping a decision to Akron North. The team lost star guard Percy Coleman to mid-year graduation and would lose Steve Gwin, "the backbone of the team" (PD), before the start of the state tournament. However, on Feb. 12, the Scarabs crushed Collinwood, 65-43, making their East Senate title official with a record of 7-0.

A record Arena crowd of 11,042 was on hand for the Cleveland city championship basketball game between East Tech and South High (11-1). The Scarabs, hoping to rebound from an upset loss, 61-54, to Painesville Harvey the previous Saturday, took a 6-4 lead midway through the first quarter and never gave it up en route to a 66-49 city championship game victory. Making this a double championship day, the East Tech Jayvee squad defeated Saint Ignatius, 53-44, to win the city Jayvee title.

Next up for the Scarabs was the Class A Sectional Tournament at Euclid High School. On March 8, East Tech defeated East High, 55-40. Two days later, the Scarabs faced one of the toughest teams they would see all season, Lutheran High, which carried a 17-game win streak into the contest. Lutheran led 14-12 after the first quarter, but East Tech rallied to take a 29-25 lead at the intermission. The third quarter ended in a 43-43 deadlock, but the Scarabs won the fourth quarter, and thus the game, by a final score of 56-53.

The next day, the Scarabs would meet East Senate foe Cathedral Latin in the Sectional finals. East Tech had defeated the Lions, who finished second in the division, during the regular season in a very close game, 71-66. This time, the game would be anything but close. The first quarter saw the Lions take a 16-13 lead, but in the second frame, it all fell apart for East Tech as Latin jumped to a 33-17 lead at the half on its way to a 70-49 win. East Tech finished the season with a 14-3 record.

John Broski was the new East Tech basketball coach for the 1954-55 season. This was Broski's first head coaching assignment; at 24 years old, he was one of the youngest head coaches in the state. For those who thought this young guy was not up to coaching an up-and-coming team like the East Tech Scarabs, Broski soon proved he knew his way around a basketball court. He had the

Scarabs in the win column from the first game, clinching their third consecutive East Senate crown with a 75-41 drubbing of Benedictine in mid-February.

The Scarabs had a nine-day wait until they played West High for the city championship. Still, the day after the Benedictine game, they had a regularly scheduled nonleague game with the Red Raiders (7-9) of Painesville Harvey. In a huge upset, Harvey stunned the Scarabs by a score of 56-52 — marking the second straight year that Painesville Harvey had upset East Tech.

On Feb. 21, East Tech and West High took the floor at the Arena to decide the city championship. Following a close first half, East Tech pulled away after the intermission and cruised to a 60-43 win and a third consecutive Cleveland championship.

Next up was the Class A Euclid Sectional tournament, which began on March 2. Tech's first opponent was the Mentor Cardinals. The Cardinals knew they could not run with the Scarabs, so they decided to slow things down and use a stalling tactic. It almost worked. The Scarabs only connected on seven field goals the entire game but won the game at the foul line, where they added 15 points. East Tech was thankful to walk away with a 29-27 win when the final buzzer sounded.

The following two games at Euclid were not as tricky for the Scarabs as they took the measure of Collinwood, 67-50, and put away Shaw, 61-51. With its record now at 16-3, the Scarabs had qualified for the Kent District tournament. East Tech's opponent at Kent was Berea High School (17-3). It was a challenging game throughout, but with the game tied at 69-69 midway through the fourth quarter, East Tech closed out the contest with a 9-4 run to win by a score of 78-73.

Having now won the Kent District, the Scarabs traveled back to Cleveland to play in the Cleveland Regional at the Arena. Their regional semifinal opponent was Glenville, which the Scarabs promptly disposed of by a score of 74-50. The Scarabs' opponent in the regional finals was Akron Central. The lead went back and forth in this game. Central regained the lead after three quarters, 46-39; this time, they stayed there, winning the game by 58-49.

East Tech finished a fantastic season with a record of 18-4, but it is still a little shy of its ultimate goal.

The East Tech Scarabs had just completed three of the finest seasons in Senate basketball history, posting an overall record of 50-7, losing just two of 31 league games. But they were just getting started. The 1955-56 high school basketball season would usher in an era of success for East Tech unequaled by any Senate or Cleveland area team, before or since, and by few throughout Ohio – or even the nation.

On Feb. 3, 1956, although the Scarabs still had two league games to play, their record of 12-0 in the East Senate was good enough to clinch the division title. On Feb. 8, the Scarabs received six first-place votes in the AP state poll and were ranked ninth. Over the next week, East Tech won its last two league games to make its East Senate championship official with a record of 14-0, 16-0 overall.

On Tuesday, Feb. 21, East Tech met West Senate champion Holy Name for the Cleveland city championship at the Arena. A sellout crowd 12,705 was on hand, with an additional 2,000 being turned away. Late in the first quarter, the Scarabs trailed 11-8 when they went on a 7-0 run to close the quarter with a 15-11 lead. East Tech never trailed after that, holding off the Green Wave for a 64-54 victory. With their overall record now a perfect 17-0, the Scarabs had moved to #6 in the AP poll.

East Tech had two reasons to celebrate when its Jayvee team defeated Saint Ignatius, 55-49, to win another junior varsity city championship.

It was state tournament time, with East Tech assigned to the Class A Sectional at Euclid High School. In a sectional semifinal against Euclid High, the Scarabs breezed to a 74-45 win. East Tech went up against Senate foe East High in the Sectional Final. This was a close game for three quarters, but East Tech opened the final frame with a 12-1 run that carried them to a 79-69 win and the sectional championship. With their record now at 19-0, the Scarabs were ranked #5 in the latest AP poll.

East Tech advanced to district play at the Cleveland Arena the following week. Playing a couple of West Senate teams, the Scarabs quickly advanced to regional play by defeating John Marshall, 74-63, then thumping Saint Ignatius, 64-36.

Entering the Berea Regional on March 16 with a record of 21-0, the Scarabs' regional semifinal opponent would be yet another West Senate team, West Tech (9-12), with the Scarabs coming away with a 60-50 win. The next day, East Tech met Columbus South (16-7) in the regional final. The Plain Dealer noted that East Tech was "never more superb." Led by forward Gene DeLoach and his 28 points and 11 rebounds, the Scarabs jumped out to an early 16-6 lead and cruised to a 79-55 victory.

With their record now at 23-0, East Tech Scarabs was off to Columbus and the state championship tournament for the first time. Their opponent in their semifinal game would be the five-time state championship team from Middletown High School (23-0), led by super-sophomore Jerry Lucas.

East Tech jumped out to a 24-18 lead after one quarter and still held a slim 39-38 advantage at the half. After that, Jerry Lucas scored 29 points in the second half on the way to a state tournament record of 53, leading Middletown to a 99-78 victory.

East Tech had ended its most excellent season with a 23-1 record, just one win short of its ultimate goal. Senior Gene DeLoach was named Second Team All-Ohio.

The 1956-57 basketball season would prove to be a letdown after the Scarabs' great run the previous season, but that would only make the succeeding years' success much more enjoyable.

East Tech finished second in the East Senate with a record of 7-4. In the city championship consolation game, the Scarabs defeated South High by a score of 72-57, raising the team's overall record to 12-5 as the state tournament began.

Once again advancing to regional play, East Tech would face an old adversary, the Lions of Cathedral Latin, in the regional final. The two teams had already met twice earlier in the season, Latin winning both times. As expected by the sellout crowd, this one was a real barnburner. Latin took a 17-14 lead after the first quarter, with East Tech returning to lead at the intermission, 30-28. The second half was a back-and-forth affair, but East Tech seemed to lose its shooting touch with four minutes to go in the game and Latin leading by a point. It was not by much, but it allowed Latin to pull away to a 69-65 victory.

East Tech finished the season with a 17-6 record.

Expectations were again high for the 1957-58 East Tech Scarabs, whom the junior tandem of Jim Stone and Ken Glenn would lead. By Jan. 31, 1958, those expectations appeared to be justified. With an overall record of 14-0, the Scarabs were called by The Plain Dealer "the district's top-ranked high school basketball team" and were currently second in the AP state poll behind #1 Middletown. (The ranking would remain like that through to the final survey at the end of the regular season.)

After capturing yet another East Senate title with a perfect 14-0 record, the Scarabs would meet Saint Ignatius (16-1) in the city championship game. With East Tech holding thin leads after each of the first three quarters, the final quarter proved decisive. The Scarabs outscored the Wildcats, 22-9, in that final frame to take home the Cleveland championship by a score of 75-59.

It was now on to the Class AA state tournament, first stop the Western Reserve Sectional. East Tech quickly dominated its Sectional opponents and did likewise in the Reserve District tournament. With its record now a perfect 22-0, East Tech had once again qualified for the Berea Regional tournament at Baldwin-Wallace College.

By the time the tournament reaches the regional level, only the best teams remain. However, this did not faze East Tech. In their regional semifinal game against Elyria High School (20-1), the Scarabs jumped to a 40-27 halftime lead and kept pouring it on until the final buzzer, winning by an 85-55 count. In the regional finals against Columbus East (18-6), the Scarabs again had a comfortable halftime lead of 40-29. East rallied in the third quarter and was closing the gap when the Scarabs themselves rallied, coming away with a 79-65 victory.

Having won the Berea Regional championship, East Tech qualified for the State Finals in Columbus for the second time in three years. Joining the Scarabs in the capital city were Columbus North, Zanesville, and two-time defending champion Middletown; all four teams entered the Final Four with identical 24-0 records.

The drawing paired East Tech with Zanesville to determine the semifinal matchups. It was a close game throughout. In the fourth quarter, Zanesville rallied to overcome the Scarabs' nine-point lead and took a 47-46 lead with just 2:35 left. East Tech closed the game with a 7-0 run, giving them a 53-47 victory.

In the other semifinal game, Columbus North edged out Middletown, 63-62, ending the Middies win streak at 76 games.

East Tech had now reached the Class AA finals, the only Cleveland area team to reach the state finals other than Lakewood High School, which did so in both 1925 and 1941. No Cleveland team had yet come away with a basketball state championship.

As expected, the championship game was a close nail-biter from the start. East Tech gained a 15-14 lead after one quarter and extended that lead to three points, 28-25, at the intermission — but this game was far from over. After the halftime break, Columbus North fired up and outscored the Scarabs 16-12 to take a 41-40 lead into the game's final eight minutes.

The fourth quarter was the lowest-scoring quarter of the game. With 1:15 left on the game clock, North had a two-point lead and the ball. The boys from Columbus then went into a stall to secure a victory. That tactic worked for a while, but East Tech got the ball with the clock running down to the last seconds. With just six seconds left in the game, Jim Stone took a shot "from near midcourt" (PD), which found nothing but net to tie the score at 48-48 as the final buzzer sounded.

In the three-minute overtime, neither team was able to score. This sent the game into a second overtime session, but, as was the rule back then, this second OT would be sudden death – the first team to score would be the winner.

Columbus North grabbed control of the ball as the second overtime began, but a bad pass was picked off by one of the Scarabs. After a pass from Ed Ferguson, Gerald Warren, the only senior on the team, took a jumper from 10 feet away and watched it go through the hoop just 34 seconds into the second overtime!

By a score of 50-48, East Tech had won the Class AA state basketball championship, bringing a state basketball championship back to Cleveland for the first time in the city's history while completing a perfect 26-0 season. Jim Stone and Ken Glenn were named to the All-Tournament team. Jim Stone was named to the All-Ohio Second Team, while Ken Glenn garnered an All-Ohio Honorable Mention.

With four starters returning from the previous year's state championship team, much was expected from the East Tech Scarabs of 1958-59. Those four players were Ken Glenn, LeMoyne Porter, Jim Stone, and Ed Ferguson – three of whom would end the season on the All-Ohio roster.

East Tech began the season right where the previous one had left off – winning. On Feb. 13, a 102-55 throttling of Collinwood made it official – the Scarabs had won another East Senate title.

Just before its win over Collinwood, the AP poll had named East Tech the #1 team in Ohio.

A week after being named #1, East Tech took the court against Saint Ignatius at the Arena for the city championship. Holding the Wildcats to a mere four points in the second quarter, East Tech jumped to a 38-14 lead at the half en route to a 79-56 win and their sixth city title in the last seven seasons. Those 79 points set a new team scoring record for the city championship game, while Ken Glenn's 27 points tied the individual scoring record.

Having completed the regular season at 17-0 (and #1 in the final AP poll), the Scarabs moved on to the tournament trail to defend their state title. They breezed through the Bedford Sectional, and the Bedford District tournament proved equally easy as the Scarabs crushed Saint Ignatius in the district final, 101-60. East Tech's 101 points was a new district tournament team scoring record.

Next up was the Berea Regional tournament, where East Tech's opponent would be the undefeated, 23-0, team from Elyria High School, the state's #3 Class AA team. The Pioneers went into a stall from the outset to slow down the Scarabs; that tactic kept the score down but did little else. East Tech led 14-12 after the first quarter and gradually expanded its early lead by a point or two, finishing with a 52-42 win.

The regional final proved to be even less of a problem for East Tech. Taking the court against Cleveland's St. Joseph High School (20-3), the Scarabs raced to a 46-23 halftime lead, with the final score a one-sided 89-51. Ken Glenn was named the regional MVP.

East Tech qualified for the Final Four in Columbus for the second consecutive season. 24-0, it was the only undefeated team left in the Class AA tournament. Joining East Tech for the last weekend of Ohio high school basketball were Salem (24-1), Middletown (21-4), and Toledo Scott (20-4). East Tech and Toledo Scott were placed in the same game in the draw for the semifinal matchups.

Once again, East Tech used the full-court press from the outset and proved most effective, leading East Tech to a resounding 83-47 semifinal win.

East Tech took the court against Salem in the state finals, which had defeated Middletown 68-65. This would be the second meeting that season between these two teams, with East Tech winning the first encounter by a score of 65-59.

The game started as many anticipated, with the first quarter ending in a 14-14 tie. But there, the drama would end. East Tech overwhelmed Salem in the second quarter, outscoring the Quakers 23-9 for a 37-23 halftime advantage. After three quarters, the lead remained by 14 points, 52-38, with East Tech pulling away in the fourth quarter to win by 20 points, 71-51.

East Tech won the Class AA state championship for the second consecutive season, extending its winning streak to 51. Ken Glenn was unanimously named the captain of the All-Tournament team, and Jim Stone was also named to the All-Tournament squad. Earning All-Ohio recognition were Ken Glenn, First Team; Jim Stone, Third Team; and Ed Ferguson, Honorable Mention. Head Coach John Broski was named the Ohio High School Basketball Coach of the Year.

The East Tech basketball team would undergo significant changes for the 1959-60 season. On the court, the team would lose all five starters from the previous year's championship squad to graduation: Ken Glenn, Jim Stone, Ed Ferguson, LeMoyne Porter, and Sam Franklin.

The Scarabs would also lose their leader of the last five seasons: head coach John Broski. At East Tech, Broski led the team to 109 wins and only 11 losses (and no losses in the last two seasons) for a winning percentage .908. His teams reached the Final Four three times and won two state championships. John Broski was inducted into the Ohio High School Basketball Coaches Hall of

Fame 1965.

Assistant Coach Joe Howell would move up to guide the Scarabs. He would have veteran 6'8" center senior Gene Lane to lead the team and see the emergence of one of the Scarabs' all-time greats, sophomore Wilson Graham.

The 1959-60 season started with one of the biggest upsets in Cleveland high school basketball history: Collinwood 49 - East Tech 40. The two-time defending Class AA state champions had seen their 51-game win streak come to a screeching halt.

The Scarabs may have gotten off to a slow start, but they were soon putting that one loss in the rear window. By Feb. 1, 1960, East Tech had improved to 12-1 and was ranked #2 in the AP state poll; the team was also in first place in the East Senate.

Three weeks later, having won the East Senate title, East Tech was at the Cleveland Arena to take on Saint Ignatius (16-1) in the annual city championship game. Behind Gene Lane's scoring and rebounding, the Scarabs finished the first half leading by 39-18 and coasted to a 69-54 victory.

On March 2, the Scarabs began play in the state tournament as the top seed at the Class AA Bedford sectional. They quickly disposed of Shaker Heights, 68-38, and three days later defeated Cathedral Latin, 69-60.

Moving on to the Berea district tournament, Tech defeated Brecksville (18-1) by a convincing 54-38. Two days later, the Scarabs played Saint Ignatius (19-3) for the district championship. Behind a big 21-point fourth quarter, the Scarabs moved on to the Kent regional with a 64-50 win.

The Kent regional semifinal game was played on March 17, and the Scarabs took on a surprising Niles Red Dragon (13-9) team. Behind Gene Lane's 18 points and 22 rebounds, East Tech cruised to a 66-50 win. Next up was Akron East (15-8) in the regional championship game, and once again, the Scarabs were led by the play of Gene Lane (24 rebounds, 26 points). When the final buzzer sounded, East Tech had outlasted Akron East 62-48, moving on to Columbus and the Class AA Final Four.

In its state semifinal game on March 25, East Tech (23-1) faced the undefeated team from Canton Timken High School (24-0). The drama in this game was over early, as the Scarabs raced out to a 25-10 lead after just the first quarter. The East Tech bench was cleared with a 20-point lead after three quarters. By a final score of 71-60, East Tech advanced to the Class AA state championship game for the third consecutive season.

Facing East Tech in the championship game was Dayton Roosevelt (26-0), making this a battle between the state's top two ranked teams. The game was tied 11- after the first quarter, but things were not looking suitable for the Scarabs. As The Plain Dealer would later note, East Tech "couldn't hit from the field and couldn't solve Roosevelt's man-for-man, all-court press." East Tech had built a 26-18 lead in the second quarter, but Roosevelt closed out the first half with a 14-0 run, taking a 32-26 lead — one they would never relinquish. When the final buzzer sounded, East Tech was on the short end of a 51-41 score, the team's second-lowest point total of the season.

Making the All-Ohio First Team was center Gene Lane, while sophomore guard Wilson Graham made All-Ohio Honorable Mention.

The 1960-1961 season would see a continuation of East Tech's outstanding run of basketball success. As the 1960 portion of its schedule ended, the Scarabs were already 7-1 but 7-0 in East Senate play. East Tech opened 1961 on Jan. 5 with another nonleague defeat, this time at the hands of Dayton Dunbar, 69-64.

After that game, the Scarabs returned to East Senate play, and the wins started to pile up again. Mid-January victories pushed the team's Senate mark to 10-0 (10-2). In the AP Class AA poll on Jan. 25, the Scarabs were ranked #4 in the state. Despite three more Senate victories, on Feb. 3, the Scarabs had slipped to #7, but four days later, they were at #5, with West Tech at #7.

East Tech closed its East Senate schedule at 14-0 with a record performance on Feb. 10 against Glenville. Tech won easily, 96-59, and set a school record by grabbing 62 rebounds.

The city championship game on Feb. 21 saw East Tech face undefeated West Senate champ West Tech (14-0, 16-0). On Feb. 15, the state AA poll had the West Tech Warriors at #4, edging out #5 East Tech by just three votes. Those who attended the championship game at the Cleveland Arena were anticipating a great showdown, and they were not disappointed.

It was a close game throughout the first three quarters, but East Tech stayed in front and led 51-47 after three quarters. This is where West Tech turned it on, and with 3:40 left in the game, the Warriors had charged back to take a sizeable 60-53 lead. Back came the Scarabs. With 1:20 to play, Wilson Graham's bucket put East Tech back in front, 63-62. Then, with 45 seconds remaining, Graham completed both ends of a one-and-one to push his team's lead to 65-62. West Tech cut the lead to 65-64 with about 30 seconds to play, but the Scarabs gained control of the ball with 17 seconds to go and ran out the clock.

East Tech's 65-64 was the team's fourth consecutive

city championship, eighth in the last nine years, and ninth overall. The Scarabs had yet to lose a Cleveland city championship basketball game.

Next was the state tournament; East Tech had been named the #1 seed at the Bedford sectional. The Scarabs easily won its two games to advance to the Bedford district tournament.

This was a much stricter tournament for East Tech. The Scarabs opened play against Parma High, which former East Tech mentor John Broski coached. It was a close game all the way, but with just four seconds on the game clock, Wilson Graham calmly added two free throws to clinch Tech's 66-62 win.

Two days later, the Bedford district final against Saint Ignatius ended as even more of a nail-biter, even though East Tech led most of the game. East Tech was up 66-57 after three quarters. They then went into a stall for the fourth quarter, nearly costing them the game. Wilson Graham accounted for all of East Tech's scoring in the final eight minutes on three foul shots. Saint Ignatius won the fourth quarter, 11-3, but they came up a point short as the Scarabs held on for a 69-68 victory.

Things got no more manageable for the Scarabs as they advanced to the Kent regional tournament. In a regional semifinal, the Scarabs (19-2) would face the Wildcats of Akron Central (19-3), the same team that defeated them in late December by two points. This was another thrilling high school tournament game that saw the lead bounce back and forth, with neither team able to pull away. With the score tied 51-51 and just three seconds left on the clock, East Tech sophomore Jim Robertson sank the foul shot, giving East Tech a thrilling 52-51 victory.

In the regional final, East Tech took the court against Cleveland's St. Joseph High School (23-0) three days later. The Scarabs led throughout the first three quarters, but the Vikings rallied to cut the lead to just two points, 39-37, as the game entered the final eight minutes. Jim Robertson again stepped up to pull this one out for his team when, with just 19 seconds remaining and the score tied at 47-47, the Scarabs' sophomore sank a pair of free throws. East Tech added another late point to make the final score 50-47.

The victory over St. Joe's sent the Scarabs to Columbus and the Class AA Final Four for the fourth consecutive season. Their opponent in one of the semifinal games would be the Hillclimbers of Urbana High School, who came to Columbus sporting a perfect 24-0 record.

It was a close game, but East Tech stayed in front at each quarter break. After three quarters, the Scarabs had a 44-42 lead and quickly pushed that to a 10-point bulge, 52-42. Then, the Hillclimbers made their final charge. The East Tech lead had fallen to 58-56 when the Scarabs went into a stall with 2:56 left on the game clock. That was too much time for Urbana to work with as they tied the score at 58-58, then took a 61-58 lead on three late free throws. Tech's Bob Rozier scored on a layup to make the score 61-60, but Urbana ran out the game's final nine seconds.

With a final record of 21-3, another great season of East Tech basketball had fallen just short of its goal. Junior Wilson Graham was named to the Class AA All-Ohio Third Team.

East Tech entered the 1961-62 season, losing only five games in the previous four while winning 95 and two state championships. More of the same was expected.

As the 1961 part of their schedule came to an end, the Scarabs were already 8-0 and had defeated both teams that had beaten them the previous year, Akron Central and Dayton Dunbar. They were also undefeated, 6-0, in East Senate play and entered 1962 ranked #1 in both the AP and UPI Class AA state polls.

The Scarabs' first game in 1962 came on Jan. 12. Showing no signs of their two-week layoff, they easily defeated Benedictine, 90-37. By Feb. 1, the Scarabs were 13-0 (15-0). Their fifth consecutive East Senate championship became official on Feb. 9 after defeating Benedictine 89-52.

Twelve days later, on Feb. 21, East Tech took the court at the Cleveland Arena against West Senate champion Saint Ignatius for the city championship. This would be the Scarabs most difficult city championship game thus far.

Saint Ignatius led throughout the game's first 24 minutes. As the game entered the fourth quarter, the Scarabs trailed 42-36. East Tech then rallied, and with 2:30 left in the game, Wilson Graham tied the score at 48-48 with a layup and a free throw. With 1:09 remaining, the Wildcats regained the lead, 50-48. A Bob Warmack foul shot made it a 50-49 game. The score stayed that way until, with just three seconds remaining, Warmack "...tipped in a shot. It came following a scramble under the basket and after the Scarabs missed two rebounding attempts." (PD)

Three seconds later, the buzzer sounded, ending the game, giving East Tech a 51-50 win in one of the most thrilling Cleveland championship games ever.

With the regular season completed, the Scarabs moved on to tournament play. Averaging 79 points per game while allowing just 46, East Tech was the top seed at the Class AA Bedford sectional.

The Scarabs opened tournament play on March 1 by

easily winning its sectional games by a combined 67 points. The following week, East Tech (18-0) moved on to the Bedford district tournament, coming away with two more wins to advance to the Kent regional tournament.

In their first game at Kent, the Scarabs faced East Senate rival Glenville (16-5). After a slow start, the Scarabs won 64-50 over the Tarbloaders.

In the regional final against Cuyahoga Falls, East Tech used a big second half to secure a win. Trailing 26-24 at the intermission, East Tech came out in the third quarter and grabbed control by outscoring Falls 23-10 in the third quarter en route to a 60-49 victory.

That victory in the Kent finals secured East Tech's fifth consecutive trip to the Final Four in Columbus. The upstart team from Lima Senior High met the undefeated Scarabs in a semifinal game. The Spartans had entered the playoffs with a modest record of 7-7, but here they were, one game away from a Class AA state championship with a record of 14-7.

While the closeness of this game may have surprised many, including the Scarabs themselves, nobody from Lima was. The game, tied eight times with no less than 17 lead changes, would go down as one of the tournament's all-time greats. The final few minutes saw the lead go back and forth, but the Scarabs could hold on for a 57-55 win.

That victory sent the undefeated Scarabs (24-0) into the state finals for the fourth time in the last five seasons. Another undefeated team, Hamilton Taft, would be facing them, which had won 26 consecutive games. It would be a battle of Ohio's #1 Class AA team in East Tech and the #2 team in Taft.

Not too unexpectedly, the two teams played the first quarter to a 12-12 tie. The game would be decided early in the second quarter when East Tech went scoreless for four and a half minutes, while Taft surged ahead to lead 27-20 at the half. In the fourth quarter, the Senators appeared to be running away with the game when they opened up a 17-point bulge. East Tech rallied, but they had too big a deficit to overcome. When the final buzzer sounded, East Tech was on the short end of a 59-52 score.

Finishing with a 24-1 record, the Scarabs had three players earn All-Ohio honors. Wilson Graham made the All-Ohio team for the third consecutive season, this time as a member of the First Team. Graham also gained national acclaim by being named to the Parade magazine High School All-America Basketball Third Team. James Robertson and Bob Warmack earned All-Ohio Honorable Mention status.

The 1962-63 basketball season was another outstanding campaign for the East Tech Scarabs, one in which they again went 24-1. Unfortunately, little remains to tell the story of that season because a strike by both Cleveland newspapers, The Plain Dealer and the Press, lasted the entire winter, from early November of 1962 until April 8, 1963. The only score that survives is Tech's trip to the Final Four in Columbus, where the Scarabs lost in the semifinals to Columbus East, 58-44.

Completing the 1962-63 basketball season saw the curtain come down on one of the greatest eras in Ohio high school basketball history. East Tech started making a name for itself in Cleveland by winning the 1953 city title and moved to a bigger stage with a state semifinal appearance in 1956. However, the six years from late 1958 to the end of the 1962-63 season made the team's reputation as an Ohio basketball power.

During those six seasons, East Tech compiled a record of 143-7, averaging just under 24 wins per season. The Scarabs' Senate record was an astounding 87-1, winning six consecutive Cleveland city championships. At the state level, the Scarabs reached the Final Four all six seasons, winning two state championships and twice finishing as runner-up. In all of Ohio, only the legendary teams from Middletown High School can surpass that record of achievement.

While that unprecedented run of success had come to an end, East Tech was not finished adding to its outstanding record.

It would be three years before the Scarabs would win another city championship, which they did by defeating West Tech, 69-51, in the 1966 Cleveland title game. However, the team's run in the state tournament abruptly stopped in its first game that season, a massive upset at the hands of the John F. Kennedy Eagles, 66-65, at the Bedford sectional. Nonetheless, Larry Mitchell was named All-Ohio Honorable Mention that season.

The 1966-67 edition of the East Tech Scarabs was coached by John Chavers and led on the court by Sam Thomas, Bill Lucas, and Myron "Timmy" Rogers. Tech lost Thomas to mid-year graduation in January 1967, but he still earned All-Ohio Honorable Mention recognition.

As of Jan. 6, the Scarabs were in a three-way tie for second place in the East Senate with a record of 5-2 (7-2). However, that record is a bit deceiving. The Scarabs were forced to forfeit victories in their first two games of the season after it was found that they had an overage player. Therefore, despite the two losses on their record, the Scarabs had yet to taste defeat on the court.

On Jan. 28, in his last game with East Tech, Sam Thomas "single-handedly sparked a rally" against East

High. In the critical fourth quarter, Thomas poured in 19 points (of his game-high 35) as the Scarabs overcame a 55-53 deficit to pull out an 81-78 win. That victory enabled Tech to move into first place in the East Senate. The Scarabs clinched the East Senate title in their final league game by defeating Glenville, 90-40. With a record of 12-2 (14-2), East Tech was now ranked fifth in the Ohio AP Class AA poll.

East Tech would play West Tech for the second consecutive season for the Cleveland championship. The Scarabs jumped out to a 23-8 lead after the first quarter and never looked back on their way to an 80-55 win.

Moving on to the Bedford sectional tournament, the folks at East Tech were painfully aware of their early exit from the previous year's postseason. However, lightning would not strike the team twice as the Scarabs easily disposed of all three opponents at Bedford. In doing so, the Scarabs set new scoring records for that tournament in single-game (105), two-game (202), and three-game (279). William Lucas' 38 points against Nordonia tied the sectional single-game scoring record.

Moving on to the Baldwin-Wallace district tournament, East Tech (18-2) met Bedford (18-3) in a semifinal game. The game was close, and one minute into the fourth quarter, Bedford had pulled to within two points of the Scarabs, 35-33, but over the last six minutes of the game, East Tech went on a 20-9 run to put this one away by a final of 55-42.

East Tech (19-2), coached by former Scarabs mentor John Broski, would play the undefeated Valley Forge Patriots (22-0) in the district final. It was the long-awaited showdown between the top two teams in the Greater Cleveland area. The Scarabs broke open a close game by starting the fourth quarter with an 18-2 run, winning by a score of 96-77.

That victory sent the Scarabs into the Sweet 16 and the Toledo-Bowling Green regional at the University of Toledo Field House. Their opponent in their regional semifinal game would be the Spartans of Lima Senior High School, 15-6. This would be a close, foul-filled game that saw East Tech stars William Lucas, Ray Reynolds, and Myron "Timmy" Rogers all foul out in the fourth quarter. Things were unsuitable for the Scarabs — but help arrived from a most unlikely source. Coming off the bench in the fourth quarter was little-used John Brister. All Brister did was score 14 points, including their final eight. Among that scoring binge was a perfect eight for eight in clutch free throws, including a crucial six for six in the game's final 32 seconds.

When the final buzzer sounded, the Scarabs ended with a 78-72 win, and John Brister was the hero of the hour.

East Tech had less than 24 hours to enjoy this big win; the next day, the team had to play Elyria High School in the regional finals. The Pioneers were something of a Cinderella team, having started tournament play with a losing record, but their successful postseason run had upped that mark to 15-9.

In a Plain Dealer article on the morning of the game, sportswriter Dan Coughlin called the Scarabs "the greatest show in schoolboy sports," the Scarabs showed why in this game. They never trailed throughout the game and had built up a 17-point lead early in the fourth quarter. Elyria made one last charge, but East Tech closed the game with a 14-6 run to win by a final score of 72-58.

That victory sent East Tech (22-2) to Columbus and the Class AA Final Four. In their semifinal game, the Scarabs would meet another Cinderella team, the Lancers of Cincinnati La Salle, 14-11. However, when teams reach the state Final Four, every game is challenging, which is no exception.

It seemed as if the Scarabs were playing from behind throughout this game. At the end of the first quarter, the score was deadlocked at 16-16, but East Tech trailed at both the half, 35-34, and after the third quarter, 48-45. Over halfway through the fourth quarter, East Tech's William Lucas poured in six quick points to propel the Scarabs to a 59-54 lead. After La Salle had pulled to within a point, Lucas again came through with another two-pointer to give East Tech a 63-60 lead at 1:15. The Lancers cut the lead to 63-62 with 25 seconds on the clock, but with just 20 seconds remaining the Scarabs lost the ball, and La Salle called a timeout.

After the Lancers inbounded the ball, they worked to set up for the game-winning shot. A quick pass found LaSalle's Chuck Kromer under the basket. As he went to put in a short layup, East Tech's Ray Reynolds "saved the day … as he leaped high to block Kromer's layup shot with seven seconds remaining." (PD) After Reynolds blocked the shot, he came down with the rebound. East Tech then called a timeout, after which they inbounded the ball and ran off the game's final two seconds.

What a game and victory: East Tech 63, LaSalle 62.

The next day, the Scarabs played in the Class AA state championship game for the fifth time in the last 10 seasons. The Scarabs, who finished the season ranked #5 in the final AP poll, faced #4 Columbus Linden McKinley, 21-2.

Of all the games to pick to have their worst outing of the season, East Tech could not have picked a worse time than the state championship game. Linden McKinley jumped out to an early lead and kept pouring it on. The Panthers took a 29-14 lead after the first quarter and were up 44-22 at the half. At one point in the first half, the Spartans went on a 19-2 run – and the East Tech points were scored on a goal-tending call!

The final score was Linden McKinley 88, East Tech 56. Tech finished with a record of 23-3.

It would not be until four years later, during the 1970-71 season, when the Scarabs would again play for a city title, much less go deep into the state tournament.

As January 1971 opened, the Scarabs were 7-0 in East Senate play but 0-2 in non-league play. That month proved suitable for the Scarabs as they cruised through their East Senate schedule. On Friday night, Jan. 29, led by Fred Beamon's game-high 28 points and 19 rebounds, East Tech pulled out a 65-60 win over East High that pushed its league record to 13-0 and clinched for the Scarabs the East Senate title. They closed their East Senate schedule the following week with a 71-61 win over Glenville.

On Feb. 12, the Scarabs took the Cuyahoga Community College Metro court against the undefeated, 16-0, Wildcats of Saint Ignatius in the annual city championship game. Both teams were ranked high in the latest AP Class AAA state poll, with East Tech at #13 and Saint Ignatius at #1.

The Wildcats jumped out to an early 6-0 lead, but the rest of the game belonged to the Scarabs, who came away with an 80-73 victory.

Since the championship series started in 1938, East Tech has played in 14 city championship basketball games, winning all 14 and defeating Saint Ignatius in seven.

It was time for the state tournament, with the Scarabs opening play in the sectional tournament at Cleveland's John F. Kennedy High School. East Tech cruised through its two games in the sectional tournament and did likewise in its two games at the JFK district tournament. Now playing in the Canton regional, the Scarabs continued to mow down their opponents, destroying Saint Ignatius, 96-54, and the Panthers of Euclid High, 81-60.

That victory over Euclid sent East Tech to the Class AAA Final Four in Columbus for the first time since 1967. Their semifinal game opponent was Dayton Dunbar (23-1). The Scarabs held a 19-10 lead after the first quarter and made it 21-10 early in the second period. Then, the Wolverines started their comeback, outscoring Tech 22-11 to take a 32-30 lead at the half. With 1:55 left in the game, the Scarabs trailed 73-61, but they then scored four quick baskets to close the gap to 73-69. Dunbar scored the last three points of the game to come away with a 76-69 win.

Fred Beamon was named to the All-Ohio First Team.

The 1971-72 East Tech basketball team was a high-caliber, senior-laden squad. Two seniors in the starting lineup were a pair of 6'6" tight ends from the Scarabs football team, Mike St. Clair and Nate Washington. Joining them were 6'4" James Abrams and 5'11" Lawrence Bolden (a junior), who would average about 21 points per game. Rounding out the starting five was senior 6'0" Van Glenn Neal.

The Scarabs started quickly, and on Dec. 11, 1971, had a record-setting day. On that day, in a game against John Hay, the Bookkeepers scored 71 points against the Scarabs. It was a good score, but that night, it was not even close to being enough points. East Tech almost doubled that John Hay score as they poured in 135 points. That is the record for most points in a game by any Cleveland high school basketball team during the regular season or the playoffs and the 12th-highest total in Ohio history.

On Jan. 4, 1972, the AP Class AAA poll had the Scarabs sitting at #7 with a record of 7-1 and undefeated thus far in Senate play. By Jan. 18, they were 10-0 (11-1), in first place in the East Senate by two games and ranked #3 in Class AAA. On Feb. 4, East Tech closed out a perfect East Senate season with an 89-74 win over East High.

Next up for Tech was the city championship game on Feb. 11. This season, they would be facing Holy Name (15-1), which had not played for the city title since 1956. The Scarabs jumped out to a 22-9 lead after one quarter and were never threatened. East Tech's 97-65 victory gave the Scarabs their 15th city title in 15 tries. Their 97 points are also the all-time high for a city or Senate championship game.

The postseason began for East Tech (17-1) on Feb. 25 in the Lincoln-West sectional, where they humbled Rhodes, 95-62, and Max Hayes, 89-57. Advancing to the Lincoln-West district tournament, it was more of the same. In the district semifinal, the Scarabs destroyed Valley Forge, 120-72, and three days later, they claimed the district title with a 76-42 victory over Brecksville High School.

Having advanced to the Class AAA Sweet 16, the Scarabs moved on to the Canton Field House for the regional tournament. They easily defeated a good Lorain Admiral King team, 81-54, but it was a sloppy game for both teams. In the regional final, East Tech took the court against Cleveland Heights. Led by Mike St. Clair's 25 points and 20 from Nate Washington, the Scarabs "Doomsday Offense" came away with a 90-72 victory. That win marked the 10th time in the last 17 seasons that East Tech would be advancing to the state tournament in Columbus.

On Friday, March 24, the Scarabs, 24-1, found themselves in a state semifinal game against the undefeated, 24-0, Bulldogs from Celina High School, AP's top-ranked team in Class AAA. Some 13,688 fans were on hand for this one. Celina took an early 9-5 lead and led 11-9 in the first quarter before East Tech started to pull away. Despite being hampered by committing a record-tying 27 fouls, the Scarabs led at each quarter break; sinking 23 of 29 foul shots also helped their cause. When the final buzzer sounded, East Tech was on the long end of an 87-80 score.

The next day, Saturday, March 25, the Scarabs took the court for the state championship against the Vikings of Cincinnati Princeton, 21-4. Princeton closed out the first quarter with a 20-16 lead. It would not be until 1:25 was left in the first half that James Abrams finally put East Tech into the lead, 32-30, with a shot from the corner. The Scarabs led 36-32 at the half and kept pulling away after that. With just over four minutes left in the fourth quarter, the Bulldogs mounted a comeback and outscored East Tech 18-5 down the stretch. However, it was not enough; when the clock hit 00:00, East Tech had won the game and the state championship, 78-67.

When the final balloting was in, James Abrams had been named All-Ohio Second Team and Lawrence Bolden All-Ohio Honorable Mention.

It would be more than 40 years before East Tech would again make the trip to Columbus in search of basketball glory, but the team had an incredible legacy to look back on. For the 20 seasons covering 1953-1972, the East Tech Scarabs had played in 11 Cleveland city championship games without a loss. They had reached the Final Four 10 times in the state tournament, including an incredible six from 1958-1963. They reached the state finals six times, with three state championships. In those 20 seasons, the Scarabs posted an astonishing record of 388-63, .864, and did not have one losing season. It is an accomplishment with few equals in the history of Ohio high school basketball and one that may never be equaled. It indeed was the golden era of East Tech boys basketball.

Although the Scarabs had to wait a while to get back to Columbus, they often were in the hunt for Cleveland's city championship. Following their victory in the 1972 city title game, the Scarabs were back in 1973 trying to make it a three-peat. However, East Tech failed to win the city title game for the first time, dropping a 73-68 decision to Saint Ignatius. In 1975, East Tech was again in the Cleveland championship game and defeated Lincoln-West 65-58. The Scarabs' next try for the city title came in 1984, but they lost to Glenville by 55-51, and they lost in the title game again in 1986, this time dropping a 70-64 decision to East High.

As the 20th century drew close, the championship game became known as the Senate Championship, and the Scarabs were regular participants. They won back-to-back titles in 1998 and 1999, then lost consecutive title games in 2000 and 2001.

Beginning in 2007 and continuing almost today, East Tech has consistently battled Glenville for the Senate championship. In 2007, East Tech defeated the Tarblooders, 74-65, for the title, but in 2009, it was Glenville's turn with an 86-79 win. After a four-year "layoff," these two teams played for the Senate championship every season from 2014 to 2018; East Tech won the first four of these games, while Glenville claimed the last one in 2018. The following year, East Tech again won the Senate championship, but this time, the team had to overtime to defeat Rhodes in an absolute thriller by scoring 67-63.

It had not been since 1972, a span of more than 40 years, that an East Tech boys basketball team had traveled to Columbus to play in the Final Four, but all that would change in the 2013-2014 season.

Playing for Coach Brett Moore, who is in his eighth year leading the Scarabs, East Tech opened the season with a five-game win streak before dropping two games at the end of December to nonleague opponents Delaware Hayes and Findlay.

After the holidays, East Tech played Solon on Saturday, Jan. 11. East Tech won easily by a final score of 96-40. This was also a historic game for one of the East Tech players. At 4:48 of the first quarter, Kyauta "KT" Taylor scored his 1,000th career point as an East Tech Scarab.

East Tech continued its winning ways against both Senate and non-league opponents. By early February, the Scarabs were undefeated in Senate play, 10-0, setting up a league championship encounter with Glenville, which East Tech won, 66-57.

A few days later, the Scarabs suffered their fourth season loss, falling 76-73 to Warrensville Heights – not how you want to prepare for the playoffs.

On March 5, Kyauta Taylor, who had already been named the Senate League's MVP, was named to the Northeast Lakes All-District Second Team; he was joined by teammate Johnell Free, who received Special Mention recognition.

In early March, the Scarabs breezed through district play, and on March 8, they took the court for the Euclid District championship against the Mentor Cardinals.

Mentor was the defending Division I state champion and the team that had knocked East Tech out of the tournament the previous season. But this was another season; the Scarabs won handily, 79-63, with senior guard KT Taylor leading the way with 30 points.

Moving on to Cleveland Regional play, the Scarabs (22-4) played Shaker Heights (20-5) in a regional semifinal. Anthony Carmon and his 25 points led East Tech to the regional final with a 70-54 victory.

In the regional final, the Scarabs would face Uniontown Lake (24-3), a team with one of its finest seasons. This was a close game all the way. East Tech had taken a 56-54 lead with 18 seconds to play, but Lake managed to tie the score at 56-56 with just four seconds remaining, sending the game into overtime. The overtime session was low-scoring. With the score deadlocked at 60-60 and just 3.1 seconds remaining on the game clock, East Tech's Markell Johnson took a shot from near the free-throw line, and the ball went in to give the Scarabs a thrilling 62-60 win. Johnson led the Scarabs with 27 points in that game.

That victory sent the Scarabs to Columbus and the Division I Final Four for the first time since their championship season in 1972. Their State semifinal opponent on March 21 was St. Edward High School, and this game was all St. Edward Eagles. The Eagles hit the Scarabs with a 17-0 run in the first quarter and never looked back; at one point, East Tech trailed by 61-28. The final score was 89-64, and the Scarabs finished the season with a 23-5 record.

BASKETBALL (GIRLS)

The Senate girls basketball championship games did not begin until 1978 (for the 1977-78 season). In 1982, East Tech came away with its first Senate championship with a 54-43 win over Glenville. On that 1981-1982 team was one of the Senate's all-time great basketball players: Wanda Ford. After being named All-Ohio Honorable Mention the previous season, Ward, with a 26.2-points-per-game scoring average, was named All-Ohio First Team after the 1981-1982 season.

The Golden Scarabs had to wait 13 years before they would again play for the Senate championship, but after that, they would be perennial challengers for Senate honors.

From 1996 to 2005, the Golden Scarabs played for the Senate championship every year but one. In 1996, East Tech lost the Senate title to Collinwood by a score of 91-54. The Scarabs "sat out" the 1997 championship game but were back, almost for good, in 1998. The five seasons from 1997-1998 through 2001-2002 are easily the golden era of East Tech girls basketball, led by head coach William Stovall. And, it should come as no surprise that for the last four seasons, leading the team on the court was perhaps the most incredible high school girls basketball player that the city of Cleveland has ever seen — Barbara Turner.

The 1997-1998 Golden Scarabs opened the season with just eight girls on the team, but they would be the right eight. After the first two weeks, the Golden Scarabs were 5-0, and by mid-January, they were 12-0, 8-0 in the Senate and the top-ranked girls team in the local Plain Dealer rankings.

In early February, in the Senate championship game against Glenville, the Golden Scarabs scored 68-25, giving them only their second Senate championship and their first since 1982. They were now in fifth place in the AP Ohio Division I girls poll

This championship was just one of many for East Tech in what could legitimately be called the "Year of the Golden Scarabs" in Senate League athletics. During the 1997-1998 school year, the Golden Scarabs won the Senate championship in boys and girls varsity basketball, varsity volleyball, and varsity football. Adding icing to its championship cake, East Tech returned with the Senate junior varsity championships in all four sports.

In the final AP state poll, the Golden Scarabs, still undefeated at 18-0, finished at #4 – the highest ranking ever by an East Tech girls basketball team.

It was now playoff time. On Feb. 26, East Tech defeated Brecksville-Broadview Heights, 64-48, in the Solon sectional final. Moving on to the Solon district, the girls overcame a 34-31 halftime deficit and outscored Warrensville Heights 43-19 over the last two quarters to come away with a 74-53 victory.

With their record now at 20-0, the Golden Scarabs took the court against Cleveland Heights (20-2) in the district championship game. East Tech grabbed a 17-12 lead after the first quarter and kept expanding. When the final buzzer sounded, the Golden Scarabs won the district championship with a score of 62-45 – the first district championship in team history.

Next up was the Canton regional, the farthest an East Tech girls basketball team had ever advanced in the state tournament. On March 10, the Golden Scarabs (21-0) took on the team representing Eastlake North (19-5). North jumped out to a 16-5 lead after the first quarter and, aided in significant part by poor shooting by the

Golden Scarabs, never looked back. The Golden Scarabs saw their season end with a 59-49 defeat – the team's only loss after 21 consecutive wins.

The Golden Scarabs' best season thus far brought some well-earned honors. Their 21 consecutive victories were a team record that still stands today. Head Coach William Stoval earned Ohio Division I Co-Coach of the Year honors, while junior guard Merelenea Dozier was named All-Ohio Second Team. Dozier, named All-Senate for the third year in a row, was picked by Reebok as one of the Top 50 juniors in the country and by Nike and Parade magazine among their top 100 juniors.

As the 1998-1999 girls basketball season was underway in December of 1998, East Tech head coach William Stovall told The Plain Dealer that in 6'1" freshman Barbara Turner, he had "one of the top freshmen in the nation."

From virtually the very first minute she stepped onto a basketball court for the East Tech Golden Scarabs, Barbara Turner's outstanding play proved her coach right. In the team's first three games that season—all of which it won—Turner scored 52 points, grabbed 49 rebounds, had 17 blocked shots, and grabbed 11 steals. Those may have been unusual numbers for most players, but for Barbara Turner, they were "another day at the office." By Dec. 23, with East Tech still undefeated, The Plain Dealer noted that Turner was averaging 18 points and 16 rebounds per game, to which the paper added that "last week" against Rhodes, Turner had scored 25 points and grabbed 19 rebounds, going 12 for 12 from the field and one for one from the free-throw line, and also had six blocked shots and nine steals – and she had played only 20 minutes! The newspaper noted that "in her last three games, Turner missed [only] four shots from the field."

It would be that way throughout Barbara Turner's four years at East Tech.

On Jan. 19, East Tech took the court against Cincinnati Princeton, the state's eighth-ranked team. The Princeton team had just too much height for the Scarabs to overcome as East Tech suffered its first loss by a score of 54-47. As for the Scarabs' height, Barbara Turner was the only player on the squad who stood better than 5'11"; she was 6'1".

By late January, Turner was still scoring at an 18ppg clip while also hauling 18 rebounds per contest.

On Feb. 12, East Tech (17-1) and Collinwood met in the Senate girls championship game. It was a close match for the first half; the second half was all East Tech, and the Scarabs came away with a second consecutive Senate championship, 95-56. Head coach William Stoval was named the Senate League Coach of the Year.

Tournament play for the Golden Scarabs began on March 4 with a Solon district semifinal win over Bedford Bearcats, followed by a 96-53 win in the district finals over t Brecksville-Broadview Heights.

For the second straight year, the Golden Scarabs had won a district title and moved on to regional play in Canton. This time, they would be facing undefeated Wooster High School, 23-0, the #3-ranked team in the state. Once again, the Scarabs would be victimized by poor shooting at the regional tournament. While Wooster filled the basket at 62%, the Scarabs struggled at 38%. That, and 20 turnovers, spelled defeat for East Tech; the final score was 76-60.

With a 17 points-per-game average, senior Merelenea Dozier was named Ohio's #1 shooting guard.

After advancing to the state regional tournament and winning at least 20 games in the previous two seasons, expectations were running high for the Golden Scarabs for the 1999-2000 season. By Jan. 5, 2000, the team was ranked #3 in the Top 25. On Jan. 12, the newspaper noted that "despite their success last year and this season…" a season in which they were still undefeated, the Scarabs placed a relatively low 10th in the Division I AP poll.

Three days later, East Tech pushed its record to 11-0 and 7-0 in the Senate with a compelling 76-40 win over Collinwood. Barbara Turner showed that her first year was no fluke as she poured in 32 points, grabbed 16 rebounds, and had six block shots. (Her whole season was going like this since she averaged 26 points and 19 rebounds per game.)

Now came one of the most challenging stretches any East Tech team ever had to play. From Jan. 15 to the 22, East Tech would play three of the toughest teams in the state. First up was the undefeated team from Shaw, ranked #5 in Division I; the East Tech girls won that game. Two days later, they had to play Dayton Chaminade-Julienne, another undefeated team and the top-ranked team in Division II; this time, the Scarabs did not do as well, suffering their first loss of the season, 60-43.

On Jan. 22 came the game that Cleveland area fans had been looking forward to all season: East Tech vs. Regina. The Scarabs entered the game at 12-1 and #2 in The Plain Dealer. Regina was 11-0, the #1 team in both The Plain Dealer and Ohio Division III, and ranked seventh in the country by USA Today. The game was tight and went back and forth throughout the first three quarters. Entering the fourth quarter, Regina held a 33-28 lead. With 4:13 left in the game, Regina was still in the lead, 41-37 – and that is when the Scarabs came alive. Over the last four minutes of the match, East Tech outscored Regina 19-8 and came away with an incredible 56-49 victory.

On Jan 26, Barbara Turner was named by Ohio Girls Basketball Magazine to its 6th Annual Dream Team.

On Feb. 9, East Tech and Collinwood met for the Senate championship, with the Golden Scarabs cruising to a 67-27 win. Barbara Turner was named the Senate's MVP.

Despite a stellar 19-1 record, East Tech was still ranked #10 in the AP Division I poll. The Scarabs were off for two weeks; their next scheduled game was Feb. 24 at the Solon sectional tournament.

East Tech cruised through sectional play, advancing to the Solon district tournament. For the third consecutive season, the Golden Scarabs defeated Cleveland Heights 68-35 and Brecksville-Broadview Heights 59-42, moving on to the Canton regional tournament as members of the Division I "Sweet 16."

On March 7, the Scarabs took the floor against Boardman in a regional semifinal game. When Boardman opened the third quarter with a 7-0 run to take a 30-19 lead, things were looking a bit bleak for East Tech. However, the Golden Scarabs pulled themselves together, and over the game's final 11 minutes, they outscored the Spartans 30-14 to pull out a 49-44 win. It was the first regional basketball victory for any Senate girls team.

Three days later, East Tech (24-1) faced Hudson (23-2) in the Canton regional final. As in the previous game against Boardman, the Golden Scarabs started slowly and trailed the entire first half. However, the Scarabs came out on fire in the third quarter and outscored Hudson 16-8 to take a 46-45 lead at 2:30 of the third quarter – and they would never trail again, pulling away for a 69-57 win.

A Senate team had advanced to the Final Four for the first time since the girls state basketball tournament had begun in 1976.

The state semifinal game between East Tech (25-1) and Mason (25-0) was a real thriller. Neither team could pull away, and the game was tied at intermission, 26-26. The Scarabs regained the lead after three quarters, 35-31. The fourth quarter was an absolute slugfest between these two teams, but Mason managed to hold a 44-42 lead when the final buzzer sounded.

With a final record of 25-2, the Lady Scarabs had come up just one game short of their ultimate goal despite winning more than any Cleveland girls basketball team had ever.

Barbara Turner earned more postseason honors. She was named the Division I Player of the Year and All-Ohio First Team, and those honors were a no-brainer with per-game stats like 24.6 points, 19.6 rebounds, 6.2 assists, and 4.3 steals.

Once again, when the 2000-2001 basketball season rolled around, the expectations at East Tech were high. Unfortunately, an early season loss brought everyone back to earth. The Golden Scarabs may have lost a game, but all they did was get back up and start winning again. The Scarabs had pushed their record to 11-1 by mid-January and then fell victim to Dayton's Chaminade-Julienne Catholic High School, which handed East Tech a 50-37 defeat at the All-Ohio Prep Girls Shootout. Despite that loss, the Golden Scarabs were ranked #2 in The Plain Dealer and #5 in the AP Division I poll.

On Jan. 21, the Golden Scarabs played another highly anticipated matchup with Regina. This time, the Golden Scarabs dominated the game from start to finish, and East Tech came away with a 50-37 win. That victory moved East Tech into first place in The Plain Dealer poll, where they would finish the season.

On Feb. 16, Barbara Turner was named to the Ohio Girls Basketball Magazine's Dream Team for the second consecutive season. Later that week, the Scarabs defeated John F. Kennedy 60-26 for the Senate championship.

The playoffs began for East Tech on Feb. 24, with the Scarabs defeating Garfield Heights for the Sectional title. They then moved on to the district tournament, where they again won the championship.

Having advanced to the regional semifinals for the fourth consecutive season, the Scarabs played a stubborn Hudson team but came away with a 66-56 win. Next up were the Spartans of Boardman High School in the regional final. Led by Barbara Turner's game-high 25 points, 15 rebounds, and three blocked shots, the Golden Scarabs defeated Boardman for the regional championship.

East Tech had advanced to the state Final Four for the second straight year. In their state semifinal game, the Scarabs, 23-2, would be taking on the #1 team in Division I: undefeated Beavercreek, 26-0. Once again, the Golden Scarabs could not score in a big playoff game. After the first quarter, they trailed 12-5, and it only got worse when Beavercreek opened the second frame on a 12-2 run. Trailing 24-7 late in the first half, the game was just about over. Beavercreek maintained that 17-point lead, coming away with a 48-31 victory.

The Golden Scarabs had had another great season, winning 23 times in 26 games, but for the second year in a row, they had come up one game short.

For the second year in a row, Barbara Turner was named the Division I "Player of the Year" and First Team All-Ohio. Her per-game numbers were mind-boggling, but nothing new for her: 20.3 points, 19.2 rebounds, 6.1 blocked shots, 6.8 assists, 5.2 steals, 78% from the free-throw line, and 47% from the three-point range.

The 2001-2002 season started with a change of venue for the East Tech girls basketball team. Based on the school's student population, the basketball team began playing in Division II, not Division I, as it had been until then.

When the season opened in December 2001, the Golden Scarabs were #2 in The Plain Dealer rankings. The Scarabs doubled on JFK in their first game, 63-32. Despite being only "75% healthy" because of a stress fracture of her right leg, Barbara Turner did not let this "inconvenience" slow her down as she scored 26 points, grabbed 14 rebounds, and had four steals and eight assists. She was started on another outstanding season. The following season, she would be playing for a national collegiate power, the University of Connecticut.

By mid-December, the Golden Scarabs were undefeated at 5-0 but still ranked #2 in The Plain Dealer poll behind Regina, which was #1 despite losing a game. In early January, East Tech again played in the Mason Holiday Classic, defeating Mount Notre Dame, 62-52, and Cincinnati Princeton, 66-55. Barbara Turner scored 46 points in the two games, grabbed 47 rebounds, and blocked 14 shots.

On Jan. 13, 2002, came the annual showdown between East Tech and Regina. The Royals won this meeting despite losing four games by scoring 51-47. It was East Tech's first loss after nine wins, but they were still ranked #2 in the first Division II state poll. A week later, the Scarabs were again playing in the All-Ohio Prep Shootout in Pickerington, defeating Reynoldsburg, 60-43, to gain their first victory in this tournament in the last four years.

The girls Senate championship featured the undefeated Golden Scarabs, 12-0 in league play, against the girls from John F. Kennedy. Great defense by East Tech and ice-cold shooting by the Kennedy team had East Tech leading 29-4 at the half. By a final score of 53-30, the Golden Scarabs had won their fifth consecutive Senate title.

On Feb. 15, 2002, The Plain Dealer had a story about how the Golden Scarabs were on the verge of becoming the best offensive and defensive team in school history. Thus far, they had averaged scoring 78.8 points per game, almost five points better than the current record of 74 set in the 1998-99 season, while the defense was allowing just 29.8 points per game, more than six points better than the current record of 36 set during that same 1998-1999 season.

When the final Division II poll came out, the Golden Scarabs were #2 behind #1 Dayton Chaminade-Julienne; they were #3 in the final Plain Dealer poll.

East Tech opened its playoff run with a 67-24 win over Orange High School in the sectional final at St. Joseph Academy. Moving on to the St. Joseph district tournament, the Scarabs easily disposed of Warrensville Heights, 80-39, in a semifinal game and took the measure of Bay High School (19-4), 59-29, in the finals to advance to the Barberton Regional tournament.

In the regional semifinal, East Tech (21-1) played Warren Howland (22-2). This was a much closer game than the Scarabs' previous playoff games, but behind Barbara Turner's 24 points, East Tech advanced to the regional finals with a 56-45 win. The regional final had East Tech pitted against Walsh Jesuit (22-2). The Golden Scarabs jumped out to a big early lead and never looked back, moving on to the Final Four for the third consecutive season with a 59-40 victory.

Joining the Golden Scarabs (23-1) in Columbus were Lima Bath (22-3), Kettering Alter (22-3), and Columbus Mifflin (19-6). Led by Barbara Turner's 25 points, the Scarabs handily defeated Lima Bath, 57-40, in a semifinal game. The girls would play for a state championship for the first time in school history.

In that state championship game, the Scarabs took the court against Columbus Mifflin (20-6). Perhaps showing nervousness but not taking anything away from the Mifflin girls, the Scarabs trailed at the end of the first quarter, 16-14. However, East Tech turned up its defense in the second period and held Mifflin to just four points, taking a 29-20 lead into the locker room at halftime. The game stayed tight, but the Scarabs' halftime margin held. When the final buzzer sounded, East Tech had come away with a 53-45 victory.

For the first, and so far the only time, a Senate girls basketball team had won a state championship. Not surprisingly, Barbara Turner led the way with a game-high 30 points. She also "chipped in" with nine rebounds, three blocked shots, and six assists. Barbara was also named the tournament's Outstanding Player.

With a record of 25-1, the Golden Scarabs tied their all-time win total and had their best season with a .962 winning percentage. East Tech finished the season at #18 in the USA Today final Super 25 rankings.

As she had done in her previous three seasons, Barbara Turner continued to collect the postseason accolades. For the third consecutive season, she was named Ohio's Player of the Year, this time in Division II, and the title of Ms. Ohio Basketball, the only Senate girl ever to achieve that honor. Her stats had been remarkably consistent throughout her four-year career, as attested to by her final numbers for 2001-02: 23.5 points, 17.4 rebounds, 10.4 assists, and 4.4 blocked shots. Adding one more honor to those already received, she was named a 2002 High School All-American.

Thus ended the golden era of the Golden Scarabs. While the East Tech girls have not again reached the heights at the state level they had attained from 1998-2003, there were still some Senate honors. The girls would continue to play for the Senate championship through the 2005 season, making it an incredible eight years in a row that they would vie for the league title. In 2003, they defeated John F. Kennedy 44-42 for the championship, their sixth in a row. In 2004, JFK finally had its day, with the Eagles ending with a 60-44 win. In 2005, the Golden Scarabs and the Eagles met for the Senate title for the fifth consecutive season, with East Tech coming away with a 57-47 win for the championship.

East Tech did not play again for the Senate title until 2013, but the Scarabs have played in every Senate championship game since then (2013-2019), winning four in a row from 2014 through 2017.

FOOTBALL

The first order of business for the 1909 school year was adding a new member to the Senate League. That school was the new Technical High School that had opened on Cleveland's East 55th Street the previous October. "Tech" fielded its first football eleven in 1909 and finished the season with a credible 3-2-1 record. In 1912, this school became known as East Tech when another technical high school was opened on Cleveland's west side. East Tech had its first real football success in 1915, beginning a run that would go almost unabated through the 1923 campaign.

After getting clubbed by Lakewood High in its 1915 season opener, East Tech bounced back with a big victory—its first over East High—in its first Senate League game. The Tech defense blocked an East High punt in the Blue and Gold's end zone, resulting in a safety and the only two points of the game.

East Tech was now atop the league standings, the only team without a defeat. After its narrow victory over East High, East Tech cruised past Lincoln, 28-0, Glenville, 33-6, and West High, 27-3. Against West Tech, East Tech rode a 40-yard field goal on its first offensive series to a 3-0 victory. The east-siders followed that close game with a 110-0 blowout of South High. Those 110 points are the most ever scored by one team in a Senate game.

The 1915 Senate title would come down to that East Tech-Central game played on Saturday, Nov. 20, at Shaw Field. Tech's Senate ledger was a perfect 6-0-0, while Central's stood at 4-1-1. An East Tech win or tie would give the Techsters their first Senate championship, while a loss would force them to share the title with East High, which finished the season at 6-1-0.

A cold, chilling rain made game conditions on Nov. 20 hardly ideal for a championship contest, but nearly 4,000 fans still showed up. The East Tech fans hardly noticed the weather as their team scored a touchdown in the second quarter and a 19-yard field goal in the final period to come away with a 9-0 victory and the school's first Senate League championship.

Used sparingly as a sub in this all-important game was halfback Gordon Cobbledick, who would go on to star for East Tech in 1916. (Yes, that is the same Gordon Cobbledick who became the great sportswriter and Sports Department editor for The Plain Dealer.)

At first glance, the 1915 championship of the city of Cleveland would appear to go to Shaw High School, which finished the season a perfect 8-0-0. However, since only two of its wins came against Cleveland area schools (Lakewood and University School), this was not considered enough to earn Shaw Cleveland's championship. No team was named Cleveland's titleholder for 1915, although East Tech (8-1-0) would certainly seem to have had a legitimate claim to that honor.

By early November of 1916, despite having played some very close league games, East Tech appeared well on its way to another league title with a Senate mark of 4-0-0 (6-0-0 overall). However, the season's last three weeks would destroy East Tech's championship hopes as they lost two of those games. These two late-season losses left East Tech with a 5-2-0 league mark. They were still in first place, but they would have to share league honors with that other technical school, West Tech, which also had a 5-2-0 record. Again, in 1916, no city champion was named for Cleveland.

For the third straight season, East Tech would be the toast of the Senate in 1917. Even though the east-side carpenters would march through their league schedule without yielding a point, the championship did not come as quickly as one might think. The season's big showdown came on Nov. 10, when the Senate's two undefeated teams, East Tech and Central High, did battle at Shaw Field. Both teams sported 4-0-0 league marks, with a loss to the University School as the only blemish on Central's overall record. A second-quarter fumble at its 10-yard line would prove Central's undoing. East Tech recovered the ball and promptly scored the game's only touchdown on a 10-yard pass.

East Tech's 7-0 victory over Central eliminated the last major obstacle in its march to the league crown. The Techsters made it official with convincing wins over East High, 20-0, and Lincoln High, 39-0, to close the season.

The 1917 city championship was a toss-up between East Tech and University School. East Tech had finished the season at 7-1-0. The U.S., fielding its best team since 1912, finished with an 8-1-1 mark, going 5-1-1 against Cleveland area teams. The Preppers' only loss came in a 10-0 upset by Shaw on the season's final day. When the final decision was made, East Tech and University School were granted championship recognition.

With more than half of all high school football games in the Cleveland area canceled in 1918 due to the Spanish Flu epidemic, no team was awarded the 1918 Senate championship, nor was a city champion named.

In 1919, after East High had given East Tech its only defeat, 14-6, Central stunned the local football world by handing East High a 10-7 defeat. The result was that East and East Tech were now tied for first place in the Senate race. When the season ended the following week, East Tech and East High were co-champions of the Senate League.

University School could have had the 1919 Cleveland city championship all to itself, but on the season's final day, the Preps suffered an upset loss at the hands of Shaw by a score of 7-6. East Tech, East High, and University School were declared Cleveland's tri-champions.

The most excellent season ever for East Tech football, one of the greatest for any Senate team, occurred in 1920. The Senate race that season was a two-team affair. East Tech and West Tech would go through their league schedules unscathed and meet on the final day of Cleveland area high school football to decide the issue. To say that East Tech went through its schedule "unscathed" is a bit of an understatement, as the 1920 East Tech eleven destroyed anything and anyone in its path.

By mid-November, East Tech was 8-0-0, averaging over 55 points per game – and had yet to be scored upon! Typical scores were 84-0 over Lincoln, 59-0 over Central, dropping Saint Ignatius 65-0, and utterly destroying Longwood High, 102-0. But, as would become all too familiar to Cleveland high school football fans over the coming years, these Clevelanders from East Tech were getting little respect around the state of Ohio. On Nov. 12, for instance, an article was printed in The Plain Dealer sports pages, datelined Mansfield, Ohio, about all of the undefeated teams remaining in the state. Even though Tech had gotten off to such a fantastic start and had won or shared the Senate and/or city championship every year since 1915, the team was not even mentioned.

Getting a lot of the ink in that article was Toledo's Scott High School, "one of the big contenders for (state) honors …" (PD). Scott High School was the defending state and national champion. It just so happened that East Tech was traveling to Toledo to play Scott High School the following week. In an interview a few days before that game, Scott Coach Doc Neill said, "Tech will discover that they play a different brand of football in the championship division from that staged in the common or garden variety class." (PD) It would not be the first time, nor the last, that a coach's words fired up the other team.

The 10,000 fans who witnessed the game in Toledo—better than 500 of them have made the trip from Cleveland—saw anything but "common or garden variety" football from East Tech. Near the end of the first quarter, the Scott team drove to the East Tech 20-yard line. On the next play, the ball was fumbled, with East Tech's "Swede" Carlson picking up the loose pigskin and racing for the opposite goal. "Aided by some fine interference" (PD), Carlson went all the way, 80 yards for the touchdown. Johnny Behm kicked the goal for a 7-0 East Tech lead.

Although most of the game was played on East Tech's end of the field, the Clevelanders halted Toledo's drives three times inside the East Tech 10-yard line, once at the 1-yard line. The score remained 7-0 until late in the fourth quarter when Scott could tie the game at 7-7.

With time running out, East Tech began its last drive. In the first play, the Clevelanders were penalized 15 yards, putting the ball back on their 5-yard line. A "Swede" Carlson pass completion regained those 15 yards. On the next play, the Tech quarterback Berkowitz threw another pass downfield. The ball bounced off both an East Tech player and a Scott player into the arms of Tech right-end Norton Behm. Behm had wide-open spaces in front of him as he raced the remaining 60 yards for the touchdown. Norton's brother, Johnny, kicked the goal for a 14-7 lead.

Scott's final drive got to the East Tech 10-yard line, where a pass into the end zone fell incomplete as time ran out.

East Tech was not only the first team to score on Toledo Scott in 1920, but Tech's 14-7 victory handed Scott, the defending state and national champion, its first defeat since 1917.

After one of the most significant victories ever registered by a Cleveland high school eleven, East Tech had to take on West Tech (5-0-0, 6-2-0) the following week in the game that would essentially decide both the Senate and city championships.

More than 10,000 fans poured into Dunn Field (the home of the Cleveland Indians) on Cleveland's east side on Saturday afternoon, Nov. 27. West Tech pulled out all the stops to gain the upset, except for one play they just might have succeeded. The west-siders opened the second half of a scoreless game with an onside kick, but it was recovered by an alert Norton Behm of East Tech at his 43-yard line. Halfback Johnny Behm took the handoff from quarterback Berkowitz, broke through the line and into the secondary, and was gone on a 57-yard touchdown gallop on the first play from scrimmage. Behm added the goal kick himself. Those were the game's only points as East Tech came away with a hard-fought 7-0 victory.

That victory gained the East Tech team the Senate and city championships and the honor of being named Ohio's scholastic champions for 1920. The team had finished a perfect 9-0-0 and had outscored its opponents by a whopping 462-7. However, East Tech still had one more game to play.

Everett High School of Everett, Washington, had already defeated the best teams in the west, and now they wanted to play the best eastern squad in a game for the national scholastic championship. Their choice was Cleveland's East Technical High School.

With a record of 8-0-0, the Everett High team was a powerful football machine that outscored its opponents 402-7 in 1920. Everett players had only suffered one loss in the previous eight seasons—and that one by a single point—and had been tied only twice. Everett High's 1920 schedule included two first-year college and high school teams from Oregon, California, and Utah.

The game with East Tech was popular and highly anticipated in Everett. Reserved seat tickets went on sale on Monday, Dec. 27, and sold out within three hours – all 20,000!

East Tech left Cleveland by train on Christmas Eve for the trip to the great Northwest and arrived in Seattle on Dec. 30. The game was played on New Year's Day, 1921. Everett High jumped to a 16-0 halftime lead on two touchdowns and a safety. East Tech managed a fourth-quarter score on a Berkowitz to Norman Behm 30-yard touchdown pass, but that was all the Clevelanders could muster as they fell 16-7.

East Tech finished the 1920 season as true champions. They were the Senate League champions, the Cleveland champions, the Ohio champions, and the national runner-up.

East Tech was still the team to beat in Cleveland in 1921. By the first week of November, East Tech was already 4-0-0. That week, the Scarabs had their rematch with Toledo Scott, the game being played in Cleveland at Dunn Field. The Plain Dealer described the two teams this way: "Tech and Scott are just about up to the class of the average college team, and both rank among the fastest and best-coached scholastic teams in the country."

With a buildup like that, it is little wonder that more than 13,000 people (about 1,000 of whom came from Toledo) showed up to see what was later called "the best high school game ever played in the city." (PD)

East Tech broke on top of the game's second play – and a trick play. After receiving the opening kickoff, East Tech lined up in punt formation at its 20-yard line. When the ball was snapped, the Toledoans charged "Swede" Carlson to block the kick. Carlson, however, faked the kick and threw a 20-yard pass to Norton Beam, who had lagged along the far sideline and was left uncovered. Behm caught the pass and raced 60 yards for the touchdown; it was the first touchdown Norton had scored since his game-winner against Toledo Scott the year before. In the second quarter, the Toledoans tied the game on a 65-yard touchdown pass play and the extra point kick.

The score remained 7-7 until the fourth quarter. A poor punt by Tech's "Swede" Carlson gave Toledo Scott the ball at the East Tech 20-yard line. Scott then attempted a field goal from the 28-yard line, but the onrushing Tech defenders blocked the dropkick. With players from both teams chasing after the loose ball, Norton Behm raced in, scooped it up, "and flashed off down the field with the Scott eleven in pursuit." (PD) Behm was almost caught at the Toledo 30-yard line, but he cut toward the corner of the end zone to put some added distance between himself and the Toledoans. At the goal line, he dived across for the touchdown. Behm's brother Johnny added the goal kick to give East Tech another thrilling 14-7 victory over Toledo Scott High School.

East Tech closed the season by defeating West High, 32-7, and Central High, 88-0. In the Central game, played on Nov. 18, 1921, Johnny Behm scored six touchdowns and booted home 10 extra points, giving him 46 points in that single game.

With a final record of 8-0-0, East Tech won the Senate title for the sixth time (no champion in 1918). They were Cleveland's champions for the fourth consecutive season, and this time, they did not have to share it with anyone. East Tech and Dayton Steele claimed to be Ohio's 1921 state scholastic football champions, but no state champion was ever declared for that year.

No fewer than six members of the East Tech team made the local 11-man All-Scholastic squad: Johnny Behm – QB, Norton Behm – E, Swede Carlson – FB, Jack Trice – T, Frato – G, and Hardy – C.

The 1921 season marked the final year for head coach Sam Willaman at East Tech. In his four seasons as East Tech's coach, Willaman, who would later be the head coach of the Ohio State Buckeyes, had amassed an excellent record of 29 wins and only four defeats, three Senate championships, three Cleveland championships, and a state title… His team had finished as the national high school football runner-up.

In 1923, East Tech and West Tech tied for the Senate championship with identical 4-1-0 records. In 1929, the silver anniversary season of the Senate League, East Tech, now coached by former East Tech quarterback Johnny Behm, would finish its league season a perfect 6-0-0 (8-1-0), good enough to earn the Senate League championship for the first time in six years.

The defending Senate champions from East Tech opened the 1930 season with four victories, three in the Senate League. On Saturday, Oct. 25, one of the biggest schoolboy matchups of the season would find East Tech traveling to Cleveland Heights Field to take on the Cleveland Heights Hilltoppers. Over 10,000 fans packed Heights Field and the surrounding rooftops for the big game. All the scoring came in the second quarter; each team scored a single touchdown and missed the try for the extra point. The game thus ended in a 6-6 tie.

East Tech's next game was against the always formidable Senate foe, East High, both 3-0-0 in league play. A third-quarter touchdown by East Tech, scored after a tremendous goal-line stand by East High, would prove to be all the points that Tech would need. East Tech's 6-0 victory moved it into a first-place tie with West High.

East Tech kept its record clean the following week by defeating John Adams 12-7.

On Saturday, Nov. 15, some 8,000 fans turned out at League Park to watch the big first-place Senate showdown between East Tech and West High, both teams 4-0-0 in league play. Taking the opening kickoff, Tech quickly drove 60 yards in six plays for an early 6-0 lead. Those would be the game's only points until the final quarter, when East Tech added 12 more on a pair of touchdowns for an 18-0 victory.

East Tech clinched its second straight Senate championship on Nov. 21 with a 9-6 win over Central High.

At 8-0-1, East Tech had the best record in town and had suffered defeat only once in its last 18 games. However, no record exists of any team awarded Cleveland's interscholastic football championship for 1930. Had the honor been bestowed that year, it would have gone to East Tech.

It would be another 19 years before East Tech battled for the Senate and city championships again. East Tech opened the 1949 season by tying West Tech, 12-12, followed by a 51-0 thumping of Cleveland Heights.

Opening East Senate play on Sept. 30, East Tech came from behind late in the fourth quarter to register a heart-stopping 13-12 win over John Adams. This was followed by a victory over Glenville, 41-6, a 19-19 tie with Cathedral Latin, and a 19-7 win over East High.

The first two weeks of November would close out East Senate play and determine whether East Tech (3-0-1), Central (4-0-0), or Collinwood (4-0-0) would play West Senate champ Saint Ignatius in the Charity Game. East Tech drew the most challenging assignments, playing Collinwood and Central.

On Saturday, Nov. 5, East Tech and Collinwood faced off. Coach Paul Anderson's Techsters were two-touchdown underdogs to the always-tough Railroaders. The Scarabs took a 19-7 lead after two quarters and held on for a 19-13 win.

The East Senate championship would now come down to the season finale that pitted East Tech against Central High on Friday, Nov. 11. In a very closely contested game, East Tech led by only 7-0 after three quarters. Central went to its passing game in the fourth quarter in a desperate attempt to score, but the Scarabs defenders intercepted five passes in that quarter alone, a total of eight. Those five interceptions resulted in three touchdowns and 20 points, giving East Tech a big 27-0 victory. It was the Scarabs first East Senate title, and their first trip to the Charity Game.

The lineup for the 1949 Charity Game was now set, with Saint Ignatius (7-0-0, 7-1-0) representing the West Senate and East Tech (5-0-1, 7-0-2) the East Senate. Playing in their first Charity Game, the Techsters would try to capture their first Cleveland championship in 28 years.

Quarterback Ed Bilinovich led coach Paul Anderson's Scarabs. Bilinovich was a great ball handler and a fast, shifty runner, but he lit up a game with his passing; thus far, in 1949, Bilinovich had already completed 14 touchdown aerials. Bilinovich's main target was end Chuck McMillan. The 6'2", 166-pound McMillan had an "amazing jumping ability and timing, making him the most feared receiver in the city" (PD). McMillan, who already had six touchdown receptions to his credit, was also an outstanding defensive player – he seldom left the field during a game.

Another of Bilinovich's favorite targets was end Steve Piskach. Piskach was a valuable man for Coach Anderson, often replacing Bilinovich in the backfield. And the Tech offense never missed a beat when that change was made. Ray Mickshaw, George Sentry, and Art Mallory were East Tech's main running backs, with "tremendous ground-gaining ability" (PD). The Tech line featured tackles Byron Hayes and Carl Ollich, Major Harris and Tony Mulec at the guards, with Cliff Prosek playing center.

The 1949 Charity Game was played on Saturday, Nov. 26, with just over 30,000 fans in attendance. Saint Ignatius took a 7-0 lead in the first quarter. The game stayed like that until the Wildcats added a second touchdown in the fourth quarter to push their lead to 13-0, which would be the final score in this defensive struggle.

Even though he was on the losing team and was limited to only two pass receptions for 14 yards, East Tech's Chuck McMillan was named the Most Valuable Player of the 1949 Charity Game for his outstanding play on both sides.

It would be another 45 years before East Tech again played for a Senate football championship. On Nov. 4, 1994, the Golden Scarabs (as they are now called) defeated John Marshall, 14-6, to gain their first South Senate division championship. The following week, East Tech squared off with Glenville for the overall Senate title, with Glenville coming away with a 20-16 win.

The following season, it would be more of the same. East Tech, with a South Senate record of 4-1, and Glenville, with a North Senate mark of 5-0, met at John Marshall Field on Nov. 9, 1995, to decide the overall Senate championship. As they had done the year before, the Tarblooders again won the league championship, this time by a score of 12-0.

The Golden Scarabs' last fling at Senate League supremacy came in 1997. On Oct. 31, they met South High in the game to decide the South Senate championship. It was a closely contested game that was not decided until the last seconds. With just 33 seconds remaining on the game clock, East Tech quarterback Michael Shropshire plowed through the line for a 4-yard touchdown, giving the Golden Scarabs a 32-24 victory.

The following week, on November 8, East Tech met Glenville at Rhodes Field to decide the overall Senate League champion. East Tech trailed 12-0 at the half and was still down by 12 points, 18-6, after three quarters. But things began to change as the Scarabs rallied in the fourth quarter for two touchdowns to take a 20-18 lead with about five minutes left to play. Glenville had the ball late in the game with one last chance for a score. They had crossed midfield when a pass was launched deep into East Tech territory, but Johnny-on-the-spot was East Tech defensive back John Freeman. Freeman intercepted the ball at his 15-yard line and returned it for an 85-yard touchdown that gave the Golden Scarabs a commanding 26-18 lead with only 33 seconds left.

The final score, 26-18, gave East Tech the Senate League championship. Head coach Gerry Steuber, who led the Golden Scarabs to a 6-0 Senate and 8-2 overall record, was named Ohio Division I Coach of the Year.

On Dec. 18, Cleveland Mayor Michael White presented a proclamation to the East Tech football team, honoring the team for its 26-18 victory over Glenville in the Senate championship game and Coach Gerry Steuber for being named 1997 Ohio Division I Co-Coach of the Year by the Associated Press.

GYMNASTICS

The first gymnastics state meet was held in 1926; at that time, it was for boys only, and the girls meet did not start until 1971. The boys tournament would last through 1937, then be halted until 1965, when it would continue until 1994. Senate schools dominated the competition from 1930 to 1937, especially the team from East Tech.

East Tech made its first mark at the state gymnastics meet in 1930 when the team finished third. A young man named Carter led the team by winning the championship in the tumbling event, while in other events, the team had one fourth-place finish and a pair of fifth places.

The following year, 1931, Tech would finish fourth on the efforts of a couple of boys. Lad Andahazy would earn All-Ohio honors in two events by placing second on the horizontal bars and fourth on the side horse. Carter, who won the state championship in tumbling the previous year, did it again in 1931.

In 1932, East Tech finished second at the state meet, but only two boys earned All-Ohio honors. Starting a three-year run of excellence at the state meet, Erker finished second on the horizontal bars, while Sadowsky came in third on the side horse.

After knocking on the door for several seasons, the Scarabs finally won the state championship in 1933, the first of five consecutive state titles that East Tech would bring back to Cleveland. As they had been for the last several years, the Scarabs were coached by G. P. Thompson. No fewer than five boys won individual state championships for East Tech that year. In his second year at the state meet, Erker captured the championship on the horizontal bars and won the state title on the flying rings. On the side horse, East Tech finished 1-2, with Kentor taking the state title and Goldstein coming in second. Joe Giallombardo, arguably the greatest gymnast to ever come out of Cleveland, participated at the state meet for the first time and made the most of the opportunity by taking the championship in tumbling. Lad Andahazy, who made the podium twice in 1931, did it again in 1933 by winning the parallel bars and finishing fourth in tumbling. Also scoring points for the Scarabs were Klosinski with a fourth with the Indian clubs and Gershon with a second on the parallel bars.

Led by Joe Giallombardo and Erker, the Scarabs won their second consecutive state championship in 1934 with 88 points, more than triple the 27 points scored by second-place finishers Columbus East and Columbus North. Erker won the horizontal bars for the second time and took third place on the flying rings. Joe Giallombardo won the tumbling event for the second time (Goldstein finishing second) and brought home the state championship on the long horse. Edwards (state champion) and Zupancic finished 1-2 on the parallel bars, Kiacz came in third on the horizontal bars, Stepnicka was third on the long horse, and Bogden placed second with the Indian clubs.

Eric Calhoun temporarily replaced G. P. Thompson as the Scarabs' coach in 1935, but that did not stop the team from winning its third consecutive state title, with West Tech finishing fourth and East High fifth. Joe Giallombardo led the way with his third straight tumbling championship while finishing second on both the parallel bars and the long horse (his teammate Walko placed third). Paul Fina won the state title on the flying rings and came in third on the horizontal bars. Also winning state championships were W. Cameron on the side horse (Metzdorf placing second) and Zupancic on the parallel bars.

G. P. Thompson was back as East Tech's coach in 1936, and the winning continued. At the state tournament, the Scarabs dominated the competition by scoring 53 points, more than the combined total for the other four teams in the meet. It also gave the Scarabs their fourth consecutive state championship. With Joe Giallombardo having graduated, Paul Fina led the team with state championships on both the horizontal bars (Neitzel came in second) and the flying rings (Hruska was second) and a third place on the long horse (Markowski placed second). W. Cameron could not repeat as champion on the side horse, finishing second to his teammate Yakovochuck. East Tech finished 1-2 in tumbling, with Musil taking the state championship and Faun coming in second. T. Cameron took the state title on the parallel bars and closed out the Scarabs' points.

Senate League schools dominated the 1937 state meet. East Tech won a fantastic fifth consecutive championship with 41 points, far outdistancing runner-up John Adams (18 points). West Tech was third, Glenville was sixth, and South High was seventh.

Again, Paul Fina led the way with state championships on the horizontal bars (Zollnick second) and the flying rings (Hruska second). East Tech's Tollis won the side horse, with Hruska placing fourth. Janu (second) and Tollis (fifth) scored points on the long horse, with Janu adding second place in tumbling and T. Cameron finishing second on the parallel bars.

1937 was the last year for boys gymnastics, and it would not reappear for another 28 years. Who knows how many state championships East Tech would have garnered had the state gymnastics meet continued?

SWIMMING

East Tech had a swim team as far back as 1913. That year, the team was led by Hollister Fergus, who acted as the team captain and coach and was one of the team's best swimmers; around school, Fergus was known as the "Human Fish." The boys won the Cleveland Interscholastic swim meet, taking a first in five of the six events; Hollister Fergus won four. Under Fergus' leadership, the team again took the Interscholastic Championship in 1914, his final year on the team. They also won the big East End Meet in 1914 and 1915.

Information about the team over the next 30 years is spotty; some years, they could not field a squad. Two East Tech swimmers of the late 1930s were referred to in the local papers as the East Tech "flashes," freestyler Hank Laub and diver Herb Fletcher. After graduating from East Tech, both boys swam for Fenn College (today's Cleveland State University). They were at Fenn until 1942 and then went off to serve their country in military service during World War II. After the war, both boys returned to finish their education at Fenn and resume their swimming careers, with Laub as the team captain and Fletcher as a champion diver.

The 1st Annual Greater Cleveland High School Swim Championships took place in 1940. Tech's Bill Olshasky finished first in the backstroke, while Joe Bunts and Ed Gillman did well in the freestyle competition. East Tech finished fourth.

The late 1940s would prove to be the golden era of East Tech swimming. Under the direction of Coach Paul Scherer, the Scarabs finished fourth at the state meet in 1946, their best finish yet.

The boys had come close and returned to the pool in 1947, determined to do better at the state meet. As The Plain Dealer noted in late February, East Tech "dominated the scholastic swimming scene in this part of the state all season [and] will be a heavy favorite to capture the Northeast Ohio district crown..." With two first-place finishes and placing in all eight events, Tech totaled 46 points to outpace second-place Lakewood and its 39 points.

At the 1947 state meet, the Scarabs scored 30 points to win their first state championship, just four ahead of runner-up Canton McKinley. East Tech finished the season undefeated, capturing the Cleveland district and state championships.

The Scarabs came back strong again for the 1948 swim season. At the preliminaries for the Cleveland Interscholastic Meet, three different East Tech swimmers qualified by setting city records: Yaro Macha broke the 200-yard freestyle record of 2:09.07 with a time of 2:07; Bob Foley swam a record time of 1:04.2 in the 100-yard backstroke; and Ted Stevens just managed to top the old mark of 56.7 seconds in the 100-yard freestyle with a time of 56.4.

On Jan. 24, 1948, East Tech and University School tied with four champions in the Interscholastic Finals. Still, East Tech totaled more points than the Preppers because they had more second-and third-place finishers, giving the Scarabs a 34-32 victory. It was also Tech's 21st consecutive swim win since 1946.

The Techers just kept winning. A month later, at the Northeastern Ohio district championship, East Tech easily outpointed second-place Lakewood, 43-27, with three first-place finishes, a pair of seconds, and a third.

The following week, led by Ted Stevens, the Scarabs won their second consecutive Ohio State swim championship with 31 points, nine better than second-place Lakewood. With a time of 2:02.7, Stevens broke the state and national interscholastic record of 2:03.1 in the 200-yard freestyle. Stevens was also a member of the winning 100-yard medley relay team, giving him a personal total of 9-1/3 points, second highest at the meet. Diver John Elkamek also took first place.

On Dec. 17, 1948, as the 1948-1949 swim season was underway, East Tech saw its winning streak end at 30 in a row with a 43-31 loss to Strong Vincent High School of Erie, Pa. However, that loss comes with something of an asterisk. Two boys on the team, Bob Paulin and Phil Portnick, were not permitted to participate because they were 19; Pennsylvania did not allow anyone over 18 to participate in high school athletics, while the age limit in Ohio was 20. Also, record-setting freestyle swimmer Ted Stevens was out due to a cold. As it was, East Tech still won three events, but that was not enough to win the meet.

The Scarabs went on to have another fine season in the pool, but at the state meet, they could not bring home a third consecutive title, finishing a very creditable sixth.

One of the last excellent Scarabs swimmers was Louis Connel. From 1952 to 1954, Connel swam at the state meet each season; his best finish was second place in the 100-yard backstroke in 1953. He earned All-Ohio honors at least three times, but probably as high as five since he most likely swam on two of East Tech's state podium relay teams.

TRACK

The Ohio high school state track championships for boys were first held in 1909, but East Tech did not appear until 1919. The team scored 18-1/3 points to finish third among a few entrants. While the team did not win individual championships, a young man named Fussner had a perfect day by finishing second in both the 120-yard high hurdles and the high jump and fourth in the 220-yard low hurdles.

The following year, under the direction of Coach Sam Willaman (who was also the East Tech football coach and who would later coach football at Ohio State), East Tech won the state championship with 18 points. The individual star of the team was "Swede" Carlson (also a star on the football team), who won the discus throw with a heave of 106'8" and the shot put with a toss of 40'7 ¾". Also bringing home a state title was the mile relay team, which set a state record with a time of 3:54.4.

At the 1921 state meet, the Scarabs scored two in a row by scoring 38½ points to outdistance second-place Lakewood and its 23 points easily. Coach Willaman's team only won three individual championships but scored points in nine different events to increase their points. The wins came in: the mile relay; the shot put, which Jack Trice won with a toss of 42'5¾"; and the broad jump, with Norton Behm dominating the event with a leap of 20'11½".

There were several multi-point performers that day. Jack Trice also earned some points with a second-place finish in the discus. "Swede" Carlson brought home a third in both the javelin and the discus, and Dan Willaman (the coach's brother) finished fourth in the javelin and second in the broad jump. Norton Behm added to his broad jump championship with a fourth-place finish in the high jump, while his brother, Johnny, took second place in the pole vault.

East Tech would have to wait 11 years for its next state track championship, but there were some high moments in between. In 1922, the team finished second to Lakewood High; Norton Behm took home a second consecutive broad jump championship, while his brother Johnny finished second in the 100-yard dash. 1923, the team finished sixth place, but Griswold tied for the state championship in the high jump with a leap of 5'10". In 1924, the team slipped to 11th place, with Dixon winning the 220-yard low hurdles in 22.1 seconds. In 1928, the team had its best showing in five years, finishing fourth thanks to Hanferd's state championship in the broad jump, an even 22'. In 1930, the team came in seventh, with Davis winning the shot put and setting a state record with a toss of 50'11¼".

The 1931 Ohio high school state track meet would see the dawn of two great eras of East Tech track excellence. The first would be the emergence of Jesse Owens onto the scene at the state level, where he would pretty much dominate the sport for the next three years.

The second significant era is what can only be called the golden era of East Tech track, a time of sports excellence unlike that of almost any other high school in Ohio. For the 13 years from 1932 to 1944, the Scarabs won nine state titles and finished second once.

In 1931, the Scarabs finished eighth, but it was notable as the first state championship in which Jesse Owens' name was on the East Tech roster. Owens made his debut at the state meet in a big way, winning the broad jump with a leap of 22'3-7/8".

The following year, 1932, with Ed Weil as the East Tech coach, the Scarabs won the state championship and did it convincingly by winning six events and setting four state records. Jesse Owens was on a state-champion relay team and won three individual state championships. His titles came in the 100-yard dash—a state record at 9.9 seconds—the broad jump, a state record at 22' 11¾", and the 220-yard dash, 22.6 seconds. He was also on the 880-yard relay team that won in a state record time of 1:30.8. Also setting a state record was David Albritton with a leap of 6'2½" in the high jump. The Scarabs other state championship was by Wrobbel in the shot put with a toss of 48'1¼".

Ed Weil's Scarabs again took top honors at the state meet in 1933, winning state championships in five events, all in state record time. Once again, Jesse Owens had a hand in four of those titles. Owens won the 100-yard dash in 9.6 seconds, the 220-yard dash in 20.8 seconds, and the broad jump with a leap of 24'3¾" – all new state records. (Owens' leap in the broad jump is still the seventh-best in state history.)

Once again, Jesse Owens was also on the 880-yard relay team, which set a state record with a time of 1:30.3. The fifth state record was set by David Albritton, who, for the second consecutive year, set a new record for the high jump at 6'3-8/10" (tying with another competitor).

With most of the stars of the 1933 team having graduated, the 1934 team finished eighth at the state meet but still managed to bring home one state championship. Marcus won the broad jump with a jump of 21'11 ¾".

With Ed Weil still the coach, the 1935 East Tech thin clads finished in a tie for second place with Sandusky High School, scoring 24 points. Most of the Scarabs' points came from Haven Robinson's speed, who won the 100-yard dash (10.1 seconds) and the 220-yard dash (22.2 seconds).

Charles Hofelich took over as the head track coach in 1936 and promptly led the team to a state championship. Leading the way for the Scarabs was sprinter Haven Robinson, who again won the 100-yard dash with a time of 10.1 seconds but finished second in the 220-yard dash. Daugherty, who came in second in the javelin throw, also contributed significant points.

The team finished fourth in 1937 and 1938. In both years, Leahy won the state championship in the mile run; his time in 1937 was 4:30.9, which he improved to 4:29.00 in 1938. Also winning a state championship in 1938 was Chester "Chet" Thomas, who took the 220yd. dash with a time of 21.6 seconds.

The 1939 state meet saw the Scarabs again reach the podium's top. Despite having four individual state champions on that team, Coach Ivan Greer's team had a real battle with Columbus North. The Scarabs' winning margin of one-sixth of a point is the smallest margin of victory in the history of the OHSAA state track meet: East Tech 35-1/6, Columbus North 35.

If it were not for sprinter Chet Thomas, the Scarabs would not have come anywhere near to winning the championship that year. He won the 100yd. dash in 10 seconds flat, and the 220yd. dash for the second year in a row, this time with a time of 21.8 seconds. Thomas was also on the state championship 880yd. relay team, along with Bill Clayton, Stanley Kuly, and Lloyd Crabbe, set a state record with a time of 1:29.4. Also earning big points for Tech was Harold Lane, who won the 220yd—low hurdles with a time of 24.0 seconds, while finishing fourth in the 120yd high hurdles.

The 1939 state meet was pretty much an All-Senate affair. Except for Columbus North, which placed second, Cleveland Senate teams filled every spot from first through seventh.

In 1940, Coach Ivan Greene got an inkling of how good a team he had when the Scarabs won the Mansfield Relays with a record-shattering total of 78 points. The boys proved him right at the state meet, and this time, there would be no doubt as to which team was the winner. East Tech, with 51 points, easily outdistanced second-place Columbus North and its 22½ points. Once again earning honors as the Scarabs' top point-getter was Chet Thomas; Thomas scored 17½ points, more than every other team's total except for the Scarabs and Columbus North. Chet Thomas won the 220-yard dash for the third consecutive year in 21.7 sec. Thomas also anchored the state championship 880yd for the second straight year. relay team behind Stan Kuly, Bill Clayton, and Harold Lane, a team that finished the race in 1:30.9.

Adding a third state title to his resume, Thomas won the broad jump with a leap of 23'10". He also came in second in the 100yd. dash. Rounding out East Tech's scoring was Harold Lane, who won both the 120-yard high hurdles and the 220-yard low hurdles. Harrison Dillard debuted his state meet in both hurdling events, coming in second in the high hurdles and third in the low.

Chester "Chet" Thomas was the backbone of the East Tech track team from 1938 to 1940. At the state meet, he won seven gold medals and a silver, one of the best performances in East Tech track history.

At the 1941 state meet, the Scarabs would only score 22 points, but it would be enough for another state championship, although it was one they had to share with the team from Cleveland Heights High School, which also scored 22 points. Leading the way for East Tech was the legendary Harrison Dillard, who won both the 120 high hurdles (15.0 sec.) and the 220 low hurdles (24.8 sec.). Also winning a state championship was George Clark, who won the broad jump with a leap of 22'9 ¾". For the third consecutive year, the 880yd. The relay team brought home points, this time with a second-place finish.

There is an old saying that winning can be habit forming, and it was becoming quite a habit for the East Tech Scarabs, who 1942 brought their fourth consecutive state championship back to East 55th Street in Cleveland. They did it by winning six events, including a 1-2 finish in the broad jump, to pile up 40 points and easily outdistance second-place Springfield and its 17 points. Jackson led the way for the Scarabs, who won the 120yd. high hurdles with a state record time of 14.6 seconds and the 220yd. low hurdles (25.0 sec.). Gassoway took home the gold medal in the 220yd. dash with a time of 22.3 sec. Few won the broad jump at 22' 4 3/8", while his teammate Boddie finished second. The Scarabs' 880yd. relay team (1:31.1) and mile relay team (3:28.6) also finished ahead of all the other teams.

The Scarabs continued winning at the state meet in 1943, scoring 33 points to outdistance John Marshal (22½ points), giving the Senate a 1-2 finish in Columbus. Once again, the Scarabs' relay teams were out front, with the mile relay team finishing first at 3:27.8 and the 880yd. relay team beating off the competition with a winning time of 1:29.2. The team's other first-place finish was provided by Boddie in the broad jump with a leap of 22'7". Carter added big points with a second-place finish in the 100-yard. dash.

For an unprecedented sixth consecutive year, Coach Ivan Greene's East Tech track masters won the state championship in 1944 with 41 points, easily defeating second-place Columbus East and its 26 points. Tech's six consecutive state titles are still the record for any boys team in the history of the state meet. The team's three state championships were won by Johnson, who won both the 220yd. low hurdles (24.6 sec.), the broad jump (22'6"), and Afzal in the 220yd. dash (21.7 sec.). Adding to the team's point total were second-place finishes by the mile relay team, Tolliver, in the 440yd. run, and White in the broad jump. Closing out the Tech scoring was a third-place finish in the 220yd—low hurdles by Jones.

It would be eight years before Coach Greene's Scarabs again claimed a state title, but they would come close—very close—a couple of times and win more individual glory along the way.

After finishing in seventh place in 1945, the Scarabs came in second in 1946, finishing just one point behind first-place Toledo DeVilbis High School. The team's 880yd. relay team brought home another state title (1:31.4), as did Ward in the high jump with a leap of 6'2-7/8". Despite finishing a distant eighth in 1947, East Tech again won a state championship in the broad jump when Scott jumped 22'7¼". There would be no glory in 1948 or 1949, but in 1950, the East Tech mile relay team of Bishop Harkness, Norman Jackson, Fred Jackson, and Emanuel Gleason won the gold medal with a time of 3:30 flat.

In 1951, in the second closest finish in state meet history, and despite scoring in eight different events, the Scarabs finished second to Cincinnati Central by a margin of just one-fifth of a point – 27-1/5 to 27.0. Leading the way for the Scarabs were the team's two state champions, the 880yd. relay team (1:30.9) and Hill, who won the shot put event with a heave of 52'8-5/8".

After a wait of eight years, the East Tech Scarabs were once again atop the state meet podium in 1952 with a point total of 30½, outdistancing Springfield High and its total of 19½ points. Leading the Scarabs to the winner's circle was Bill Whitman, who would return to Cleveland with no less than four gold medals. In the history of the state track meet, only 10 boys have ever won four events in a single meet. Bill Whitman is one, and East Tech's Jesse Owens is another. Owens is the only person to have accomplished that feat twice. For his efforts, Whitman took home an extra trophy for being the outstanding athlete at the state meet. Whitman won the 120yd. high hurdles with a time of 14.5 sec., followed by winning the 180yd. low hurdles with a state record time of 19.3 sec. He was also a member of the winning 880yd. relay team (1:31.4), and won the broad jump with a leap of 22'6½". The mile relay team added points with a second-place finish.

The team finished fourth in 1953, the 880yd. relay team taking the championship with a time of 1:32.4. No glory in 1954, but in 1955, the Scarabs would win their 13th state championship – at the time, that was more than twice as many state titles as any other school in Ohio. Once again, the team's relay teams would lead the way, the mile relay team of Fred Acoff, James Jackson, Robert Carter, and Charles Nance winning with a time of 3:25.8, while the 880yd. The relay team of Walter Killian, Don Jackson, Louis Laisure, and Joe Byrd won their event with a time of 1:31.0. Charles Nance and Joe Byrd would each win a second championship, Nance taking the 440 in 50 seconds flat, and Byrd winning the 120-yards. high hurdles with a time of 14.5 seconds. Byrd also finished second in the 180—yard—low hurdles.

While the Scarabs have yet to win another state championship, they have come close on three occasions. In 1959, they scored 25 points, only to finish second to state champion Glenville and its 29 points; the Scarabs' mile relay team of David Page, Willy Love, Eugene Hawkins, and Charles Cook brought home a gold medal with a time of 3:24.1.

In 1961, it was another second-place finish for East Tech, whose 24 points fell just three short of champion Dayton Roosevelt and its 27 points. The Scarabs won three events that year, with the mile relay team leading the way with a state record time of 3:21.7. The 880yd. The relay team also won its event with a time of 1:30.0. Sprinter Melvin Orr won the team's third gold medal with 21.4 in the 220yd. dash; Orr also finished second in the 100yd. dash.

In 1966, the Scarabs had another close finish, taking second place with 23 points to fall three points off the pace again, this time of state champion Glenville. Dwight Johnson won the 440yd. dash for East Tech with a time of 48.2 seconds. The team's mile relay also won another state title with a time of 3:22.7.

Since 1966, the Scarabs have never finished higher than ninth place at the state meet; however, they have had a few outstanding cindermen since then. In 1977, 1978, and 1979, Ray Marks was one of the better middle-distance runners in the Cleveland area. In 1977, Ray finished fourth in the 440yd. dash, and the following year, he improved to a third-place finish. 1979, at the state meet, he switched to the 880yd. run and came home with a state championship at 1:52.03; Ray's gold medal run was the last state championship an East Tech track athlete won.

The 1979 and 1980 track seasons saw the emergence of one of the best long-distance runners in East Tech history. In 1979, Ricky Pittman finished fifth in the mile run. In 1980, Pittman took third in the 1600m race and returned to finish second in the 3200m event.

From 1987 through 1990, Aki Bradley proved himself among the all-time East Tech sprinters by winning All-Ohio recognition no less than six times. In 1987, Bradley finished fourth in the 100m dash. He did not participate in the 1988 state meet, but in 1989, he was back in Columbus, finishing third in the 200m dash and fifth in the 100m race. In 1990, Aki closed out his high school track career by making the podium three times; he finished sixth in the 200m dash, took fifth in the 100m, and joined teammates Conner Torian, Craig Fields, and Eric Lee on the 4x100m relay team that finished in fourth place.

Ivan Greene and Estes Newberry, outstanding longtime track coaches at East Tech, are in the Greater Cleveland Sports Hall of Fame.

CHAPTER 12

Glenville High School

Glenville High School opened in 1892 on Parkwood Drive in the Village of Glenville. Because of its location, the school's early sports teams were often called the Parkwood Drivers. The student body increased so rapidly that the original building soon outgrew, and a new one was opened in 1904. In 1906, after the Village of Glenville was annexed by Cleveland, Glenville High School joined the Cleveland Metropolitan School District. The school's student population continued to grow, and despite several additions, it eventually became too small for its student population. A new Glenville High School was opened in 1966 at the current location on East 113th Street.

BASEBALL

Regarding baseball at Glenville High School, one season stands out above all the rest – 1973. And when it comes to Glenville baseball players, pitcher Terry Jones is the best.

For the 1973 scholastic baseball season, only four East Senate schools fielded baseball teams: Glenville, Collinwood, East Tech, and John F. Kennedy. According to The Plain Dealer's season preview of high school baseball, Collinwood had all its players returning from the previous season. However, as the newspaper noted: "According to one coach, 'Collinwood has everyone back, but Glenville has Terry Jones – and that makes everything even.'"

Jones was a great all-around athlete, having already been named All-Scholastic in football and basketball. If possible, he was even better when playing on a baseball diamond. One of the area's best high school pitchers, Jones would end his three-year career with a record of 25-8 and 30 complete games. His career ERA was around 0.87, with just under 300 strikeouts in 213 innings. With no designated hitter in those days, his three-year batting average of .396 had Terry batting in the #3 position. When he was not on the mound for the Tarblooders, Jones played some outfield.

Glenville, which had won the East Senate championship in 1972 under the direction of Coach Dennis Woods, got off to a slow start in 1973, losing its first two games to Shaw, 5-4, and Fairview, 2-1. However, the team soon turned itself around, and by the time the state tournament started in mid-May, the Tarblooders' record was a much more respectable 16-8, but they could not repeat as Senate champions. Terry Jones played a big part in Glenville's success on the ball diamond; his record by tournament time was already a very good 8-2, including a one-hitter in a 1-0 win over East Tech.

Jones' eighth victory was significant, coming on May 7 in a Class AAA tournament game against Parma. Behind Terry's 18 strikeouts, the Tarblooders pulled out a 2-1 victory to advance to AAA Cleveland District play at Brookside Park. The Tarblooders' opponent in a district semifinal game on May 15 was the Bengals of Benedictine High School, a team with the best record in the area at 17-1; just four days earlier, Benedictine had defeated Glenville in a regular season game, 7-2.

This time, however, there would be a different outcome.

Behind Terry Jones' one-hitter (a scratch infield single), the Tarblooders prevailed by a score of 5-1. Not only did he throw a gem from the mound, but Terry helped his team by accounting for all of its runs with his bat. Jones had three RBI and scored another run, with the fifth run scored on an error during one of his hits. In The Plain Dealer's story of the game, the writer noted that Jones was "the best all-around athlete the school has produced in 20 years…"

Two days later, Glenville played Cleveland Heights (11-11) in the District finals, and again, Terry Jones was at the center of the action. Aided by some sloppy play on the part of the Glenville defense, Cleveland Heights jumped out to a 3-0 lead after just two innings. Glenville responded with a run, but as the Tarblooders came to bat in the top of the seventh, they still trailed 3-1. The team was down to its last out when it managed to push across two runs to tie the score. They held Cleveland Heights without a run in the bottom of the inning, sending the game into extra innings. Glenville scored two more runs in the top of the eighth, with Terry Jones knocking in the fifth, which would be the deciding run. Heights scored one run in the bottom of the eighth before the side retired with the Tarblooders on top, 5-4. Terry Jones recorded 12 strikeouts in the game.

Moving down the tournament trail, the Tarblooders' next stop was the Euclid Regional tournament, where they would meet the Mentor Cardinals on May 25 in a regional semifinal game. All of the scoring in this one would take place in the fifth inning, and it would be the "Jones boys" in the center of the action, but none of them would be named Terry. Nate Jones started things with a single, moving to third on a one-out double by George Jones. Nate scored a run on a ground out, and George scored on a single by Lorenzo Hooks. That would be all of the scoring for the game, as Terry Jones pitched a shutout in Glenville's 2-0 win. (None of the "Jones boys" were related.)

The next day, the Tarblooders defeated Maple Heights in the regional finals, 6-3. Maple Heights' runs were unearned, and Terry Jones recorded 11 more strikeouts. A six-run fourth inning by Glenville had decided the issue.

That victory sent the Tarblooders to the AAA Final Four, where they would meet the team from Lancaster High School on Friday, June 1. Lancaster took a 1-0 lead in the first inning, but Glenville tied the score in the second on an RBI single by Norman Davis. Lancaster came right back in the bottom of the second to regain the lead, 2-1. The score remained like that through the third inning, but in the top of the fourth, Glenville scored a pair of runs on two bases-loaded walks to take a 3-2 lead. Terry Jones retired 12 of the final 13 Lancaster batters, including the last 10 in a row, to preserve the team's 3-2 win.

The next day, Glenville took the field against Cincinnati Elder (23-1) for the state championship. John Boykin was on the mound for Glenville since Jones had pitched a challenging game the day before, with Jones playing in the outfield. The game was scoreless through the first three innings when Terry Jones led off the fourth inning with a 375-foot home run to left-centerfield. However, the Tarblooders' celebration would be short-lived, as Elder came right back in the bottom of the inning to hit them with seven runs. Those were the only runs scored in the game, and Glenville saw its season end by that 7-1 score. The Tarblooders' final record was 22-13.

BASKETBALL

Glenville has not had much success along the state basketball tournament trail, never having advanced beyond regional play. However, in Senate and city play, the Tarblooders have enjoyed their share of success, especially in the 27 years from 1992 to 2018.

Glenville's first Senate basketball championship came in 1925 when the team tied West Tech for the Senate League title, both teams with 7-1 records. In 1941 and 1942, the Tarblooders represented the East Senate in the city championship game, but Glenville lost to West Senate champion John Marshall each time. Glenville would have to wait 37 years before it again had a chance to win city honors, but in another very close game, the Tarblooders fell to the West Senate leader, West Tech, by a score of 61-59.

Finally, in 1983, it all came together for the Tarblooders. That year, the team of head coach Ernie Fronczak was having one of its best seasons ever. On Feb. 2, the Tarblooders defeated Collinwood 66-63 to clinch the North Senate championship. Five days later, Glenville finished its league season with a perfect 11-0 record.

On Feb. 18, Glenville and South Senate champ John F. Kennedy squared off for the overall league title. It was a close game throughout, and with just 12 seconds remaining, the score was tied at 55-55 as the Tarblooders inbounded the ball. With just a few seconds remaining, a shot was taken but was missed. One Glenville rebound was put up and missed. Glenville senior guard Charles Jackson grabbed that rebound, and this time, his putback fell through the net as the game-ending buzzer sounded. By a score of 57-55, Glenville had won its first Senate basketball championship in 58 years. Even more significant, it was the school's first solo championship.

The Tarblooders had another outstanding season the following year, but an early league loss had kept them tied with East High for first place in the North Senate. As luck would have it, those two teams met in the league finale on Feb. 10, 1984, still tied with identical 10-1 records. East High jumped to an early lead, with the Tarblooders trailing at the half, 36-28. The second half was completely different as Glenville outscored East, 37-19, to come away with a 65-55 victory and the North Senate title.

A week later, on Feb. 17, Glenville and East Tech met for the overall Senate championship. This championship game was closely contested, just as the one had been in 1983, but the Tarblooders would again emerge victorious by a score of 55-51. This was a historic victory for the Tarblooders. It was East Tech's 18th trip to the Senate championship game, and in the previous 17 games, the Scarabs had never lost. Glenville was the first team to defeat East Tech in a Senate basketball championship game.

The Tarblooders would enjoy a nice tournament run that year, but in the district finals, their season ended with a 58-55 loss to Cleveland Heights. Glenville's final record that season was 20-3.

1985, Glenville made it a three-peat, winning the North Senate title and then defeating John Marshall 65-49 for the Senate League championship.

The 1991-92 season would begin a great run of Senate League success for the Tarblooders. In the 27 seasons ending in 2018, Glenville would reach the Senate League championship game 21 times, winning the championship in 10. For the three seasons from 1995 to 1997, the Tarblooders had a great rivalry with the Collinwood Railroaders. In the 1995 title game, Glenville pulled out a 78-77 win, while the Railroaders responded the next season with a one-point win of their own, 55-54. 1997, Glenville won the "rubber match," defeating Collinwood 73-59. From 2001 to 2003, the Tarblooders repeated their three-peat of almost 20 years earlier by defeating East Tech 80-65, then Rhodes 69-59, and finally Collinwood 66-63 to bring home three consecutive Senate League championships.

From 2005 to 2018, the Tarblooders reached the Senate League championship game every season but once, coming away with championships in 2006, 2009, 2013, and 2018.

BASKETBALL (GIRLS)

Gretchen Taylor coached the Glenville girls' basketball team for 23 years, compiling a record of 337-117. Her team qualified for the OHSAA girls' basketball tournament in the regional semi-finals in 1978 and 1979. She won two District Championships and eight city titles and coached three outstanding basketball players. The first player, Charlene Malone, was voted to the 1979 second-team All-Ohio. The next was Loraine Lofton, who earned second-team All-Ohio in 1984. The following year, 1985, the first team was All-Ohio. Sonja Swoope was the best player in Glenville history, who made the first-team All-Ohio and was voted Ohio co-player of the year in 1990.

FOOTBALL

In 1922, the big story in Cleveland high school football circles would be the emergence of Glenville High School, led by superstar quarterback Benny Friedman.

Glenville, a team without any previous success on the gridiron and thus one that nobody expected much of, opened the season on Sept. 30 with a somewhat surprising victory over influential Dayton Steele High School in a game played in Dayton. In a driving rain, Steele High took a 7-0 lead midway through the first period, which it carried to halftime. In the third quarter, Glenville returned a pair of Dayton fumbles 85 yards and 66 yards for touchdowns. Although the Steele offense "gained repeatedly in the overhead style, [they] lacked the necessary punch to place the ball behind the posts."(-Dayton Daily News) The Glenville defense played tough over the last two quarters to preserve the team's big 14-7 victory.

Glenville opened its Senate schedule with wins over South High, 13-0, and Lincoln, 31-0. After a week off, the "Parkwood drivers" (often called after the street on which the school was located) had their first big Senate test on Oct. 27 as they went up against East Tech. Tech had just been upset the week before by Lincoln High, but the carpenters were still considered the team to beat in Cleveland. This game, however, would highlight Benny Friedman's ability and the strength of the Glenville line.

In the first quarter, Glenville took a 12-0 lead on short touchdown runs by Friedman and fullback Paul Mattie. It would be in the second quarter "that the power of the Glenville attack was most forcibly demonstrated."(PD) Opening the quarter on its 1-yard line, the Red and Black marched the length of the field, using "straight football" on every play but one, that being a 15-yard pass completion thrown by Benny Friedman. Friedman closed out the drive with a short touchdown plunge. He added touchdown runs of 42 and 35 yards in the second half as Glenville humbled East Tech 31-0. As The Plain Dealer reported the next day: "They sang a requiem for East Tech's football supremacy yesterday afternoon at Shaw Field."

The following Saturday, Glenville would meet the last major obstacle to its first Senate championship – East High. East had opened the season with a 6-6 tie against Shaw before rattling off five consecutive shutouts, four against Senate foes. This would be a big game for both teams, especially for Glenville. Glenville had been meeting East High on the gridiron since 1908, and in those 15 contests, they had yet to taste victory. In fact, in all those games, Glenville had scored but one touchdown and only nine points – and none since 1911.

Over 15,000 spectators, the largest to ever witness a local football game, were on hand at Dunn Field on Nov. 3 for the big game. The first half had ended with the score 0-0, and the game was still scoreless as the fourth quarter opened, with Glenville having the ball at its 34-yard line. Behind the running of Benny Friedman and Paul Mattie, Glenville worked the ball down the field, and Friedman finally scored a touchdown on a 1-yard plunge. He also added the goal kick. A few minutes later, Friedman broke loose on a 40-yard touchdown run that sealed his team's 13-0 victory.

Glenville closed the season with wins over West High, 38-0, and Central, 53-7, to lock up the Senate championship. Lakewood High and the University School joined Glenville as the top contenders for the city title. Both schools were undefeated in the city, although Lakewood had dropped its season opener to Lorain High School. When Lakewood and the U.S. met on Nov. 18 to help settle the issue, they muddled it even more by playing to a 6-6 tie. Although a playoff between Glenville and Lakewood was supposedly arranged, the game never occurred. Ultimately, Glenville, Lakewood, and the University School were named tri-champions of Cleveland in 1922.

It would be more than 60 years before Glenville was again among the Senate League elite football teams – but then they would eventually become the Senate elite.

In 1983, the Tarblooders, led by North Senate MVP junior quarterback Dwayne Shields, went through their Senate schedule undefeated at 5-0 (8-2). Meeting them in the Senate championship game at John Marshall Field on Nov. 11 would be the South Senate champs from John Adams, who had finished with a 4-1 league mark.

The game was played under some of the worst conditions for a Senate title game, with snow, a 25 mph wind, and a muddy gridiron making for less-than-ideal conditions. The Tarblooders fell behind, 6-0, in the first quarter before both their offense and defense took over the game. The Glenville defense did not allow another point throughout the rest of the game. Meanwhile, Dwayne Shields led the offense to put up points. Shields scored two touchdowns and a pair of two-point conversions and threw a touchdown pass (he also had an interception while playing defense) as the Tarblooders came back to post a 28-6 win for their first Senate championship in 61 years.

The Tarblooders real success, however, would begin with the 1991 season. That year, Glenville reached the Senate title game only to lose to John Marshall, 26-20. The two teams would meet for a rematch on Nov. 13, 1992. John Marshall was the South Senate champ with a mark of 5-0, 7-3, and had won 19 consecutive Senate football games since the second game of the 1989 season. Glenville entered the game having posted a 4-1 Senate record, 6-4 overall.

On game day, the playing field was soaked from a week's worth of rain; the track ringing the field was still underwater. In the first quarter, John Marshall took a 6-0 lead, but at 9:52 of the second quarter, Glenville's Glen Elliot tied the game at 6-6 on a 1-yard run. The game stayed that way until almost midway through the third period. Then, Glenville recovered a bad snap on a Marshall punt at the John Marshall 8-yard line. Two plays later, Alfred Jemison put the Tarblooders into the lead with a 5-yard touchdown run, but that lead did not survive the quarter as Marshall came back to tie the score, 12-12, later in the period. Finally, at 7:52 of the fourth quarter, Glenville's Anthony Wallace raced 57 yards for the touchdown that would give the Tarblooders an 18-12 victory and the Senate championship.

After failing to qualify for the Senate championship game in 1993, the Tarblooders were back at it in 1994. That year, they would play East Tech for the Senate championship. In a game played at John Marshall Field, all but one of the game's touchdowns would be scored in a wild fourth quarter.

Neither team could put up any points during the entire first half. Finally, with just 2:20 left in the third quarter, Glenville broke the scoreless deadlock on a 14-yard touchdown pass from quarterback Derrick Davis (1994 North Senate MVP) to wide receiver Darren Spates. The Tarblooders added the two-point conversion on another Davis-to-Spates connection to take an 8-0 lead.

Then came the wild fourth quarter. East Tech struck first at 10:43 of the quarter with a touchdown and two-pointer to tie the game at 8-8. On its ensuing possession, Glenville took almost six minutes to march 75 yards, followed by running back Tim Overton going the final 2 yards to put Glenville back on top, 14-8 (the two-point attempt failing).

It took the Tarblooders only a minute and a half to add to their lead. Charles Johnson intercepted an East Tech pass and returned it 57 yards from his 30-yard line to the East Tech 13. Two plays later, Tim Overton ran 10 yards for another Glenville touchdown. The two-point try again failed, but with just 3:11 left on the game clock, Glenville had increased its lead to 20-8.

It took the Golden Scarabs only 13 seconds to respond, scoring a touchdown on a 79-yard run. East Tech added the two-point conversion to cut the Glenville lead to 20-16 with just 2:58 remaining.

Following East Tech's kickoff, the Tarblooders ran out the clock to preserve their 20-16 victory.

It would be more similar in 1995, but Glenville first had to stage a furious fourth-quarter rally to defeat John Marshall for the North Senate crown. That rally was spearheaded by quarterback Tavares Bolden, who scored the winning TD with just 1:28 left. In leading the Tarblooders to victory, Bolden had passed for three touchdowns and three two-point conversions as Glenville returned with a 36-28 win.

The following week, on Nov. 9, Glenville again met East Tech for the Senate championship. As had been the case in the previous season's championship game, this game was also scoreless at halftime. Glenville was on the receiving end of the second-half kickoff, and the Tarblooders promptly marched 78 yards for the game's first points, with Tim Overton scoring the touchdown for Glenville at 8:56 of the third quarter. The extra-point try failed, leaving Glenville with a 6-0 lead. Near the end of that same quarter, Overton, the North Senate's MVP that season, added to the Glenville lead with a 3-yard touchdown scamper that gave the Tarblooders a 12-0 lead at 1:15 of the third frame.

That would close out the scoring for the game as Glenville returned with its second consecutive Senate championship game victory.

Glenville was not in the Senate championship picture in 1996 but would return in 1997. 1997 would also be the last year for the Senate's North-South alignment. In 1998, the league would change to a one-division, 10-team league, with each team playing eight league football games. At the end of the season, the top two teams would play off for the league championship.

Also, in 1997, Ted Ginn took over as the Tarblooders' head coach, replacing James Hubbard, who had been the Glenville head coach since 1975.

It would take Glenville literally until the last play of the season, but on Oct. 31, the Tarblooders clinched the North Senate championship. Closing out an 80-yard drive that consumed the game's final 5:23, running back William "Butterball" Smith scored a touchdown on a 1-yard plunge with no time remaining on the game clock to give the Tarblooders a 28-23 victory.

With that win, Glenville qualified for the Senate championship game against South Senate champion East Tech, played on Nov. 8 at Rhodes Field. The title game would be wild, but East Tech's three touchdowns in the fourth quarter would be the difference as the Golden Scarabs came from behind to win their first Senate championship, 26-18.

Glenville opened the 1998 season with a loss to Mentor, but then the Tarblooders would cruise through their eight-game Senate schedule without a hitch. They finished the season with an 8-0 league record and played second-place John F. Kennedy for the Senate championship.

The 1998 Senate championship game was scoreless at the half. In the third quarter, the Tarblooders went on a 69-yard drive, closed out with a 1-yard touchdown run by running back Michael Wynn. Wynn's touchdown provided the game's only points, and Glenville came away with a 6-0 Senate championship game victory.

In winning all nine of its Senate games in 1998, Glenville had started a league-winning streak that no one could have foreseen, much less imagined. For the 22 seasons from 1998 through 2019, Glenville would not lose a single Senate League football game, a string of 162 consecutive league victories.

In 1999, the Glenville Tarblooders made Senate football history by becoming the first Cleveland public high school team to qualify for the OHSAA playoffs. Over the next twenty seasons, the Tarblooders qualified for the playoffs 17 times in three different divisions. Since we already know Glenville's regular season story, the rest of this report will deal with the Tarblooders' playoff record.

The Tarblooders finished the 1999 campaign with a record of 8-2. Since several of the Senate teams they defeated also had winning records, this allowed Glenville to accumulate the secondary computer points necessary for the team to qualify for the OHSAA playoffs.

In that first playoff game, the Tarblooders would take on Lakewood High School's Rangers (7-3). The Tarblooders came out on fire and, in the opening possession of the game, drove 65 yards in eight plays to take an early 8-0 lead. Glenville would add another touchdown later in the quarter and a third TD on the last play of the opening frame to lead 20-8 after the game's first 12 minutes. After that fast start, Glenville did not score in the second quarter but still held the lead, 20-14, at the intermission.

It would be a different game in the second half as the Lakewood defense took over. After the two teams traded touchdowns early in the third quarter, Lakewood took a 29-26 lead late in the period and never gave it up. Outscoring the Tarblooders 30-12 in the second half, the Lakewood Rangers came away with a 44-32 victory.

It was a disappointing end to the Tarblooders' first trip to the postseason, but they were just getting started.

Led by USA Today's Second Team High School All-America selection Pierre Woods, Glenville finished the 2000 regular season with a record of 9-1 and again qualified for the postseason. This time, they would face Shaker Heights High School, 10-0, in a Division I regional quarter-final game. Glenville took the early lead when tailback Shaun Williams scored on a 23-yard run just 29 seconds into the game. The extra point made it a 7-0 game, but Shaker Heights returned four minutes later to tie the score at 7-7. Before the first half was over, the Raiders added a second touchdown to lead 13-7 at the intermission.

On Shaker's first possession of the second half, Glenville's Shaun Williams intercepted a Raiders pass and returned it 43 yards for a Glenville touchdown, tying the score at

13-13. Shaker came right back to take a 20-13 lead before Dareus Hiley scored on a 1-yard run that cut the Shaker margin to just 20-19. Early in the fourth quarter, Shaker Heights added to its lead with a touchdown and extra point to go up 27-19, but Dareus Hiley again brought his team back, this time with a 5-yard touchdown run that made it a 27-25 game. The score stayed that way until, with just 35 seconds on the game clock, a pass from Hiley to Williams was suitable for a 12-yard touchdown. The two-point conversion made the score 33-27 – and that would be the final score.

For the second straight year, the Tarblooders made Senate League history. In 1999, they were the first team to qualify for the postseason, and now, in 2000, they were the first team to win a playoff game.

The Tarblooders' opponent in the regional semifinal game would be the undefeated, 11-0, Solon Comets. Glenville shocked the Comets when Dareus Hiley returned the opening kickoff 92 yards to give the Tarblooders a quick 6-0 lead. In the second quarter, Solon took advantage of a couple of Glenville turnovers to score a pair of touchdowns and take a 14-6 lead at the halftime break. Solon held onto its lead until early in the fourth quarter. With eight and a half minutes left in the game, Dareus Hiley scored on a 7-yard run and tossed a pass for the two-point conversion that tied the game at 14-14.

The game ended still tied at 14-14, sending it into overtime. Solon had the ball first in the extra session and scored a touchdown and the extra point to take a 21-14 lead. Glenville could not score on its possession and saw its season end by that 21-14 score.

In 2001, the Tarblooders finished the regular season with a 9-1 record and again qualified for the OHSAA playoffs. Their regional quarter-final game saw them in a playoff rematch with the Solon Comets. Unlike the previous year's playoff game between these two teams, this one was one-sided from the start. Solon took a 28-0 lead at the half and defeated Glenville 28-7.

Glenville did not qualify for the 2002 playoffs, but beginning with the 2003 season, they would be in the OHSAA postseason for eight consecutive years.

The Tarblooders finished the 2003 regular season with a 9-1 record to qualify for the Division I Region 1 playoffs. Their regional quarterfinal opponent was the Saint Ignatius Wildcats. This would mark the second time these two teams had ever met on the gridiron, the first time coming in 1924 when the Wildcats, then the Golden Tornadoes, had won 13-0.

Saint Ignatius took a 7-0 lead early in the second quarter, but Glenville came right back on a 20-yard touchdown pass from Ted Ginn Jr. to running back Ray Small to make it 7-6. In the third quarter, the Wildcats pushed their lead to 14-6 and then 17-6 early in the fourth period. Glenville was not done, however, and started its comeback on another Ginn touchdown aerial, covering 20 yards to wide receiver Lee Jordan. Ted Ginn then completed a pass to Ray Small for the two-point conversion, making it a 17-14 game.

A 46-yard touchdown pass from the Wildcats' Brian Hoyer to wide receiver Josiah Kedzior pushed the Wildcats lead back to 10 points at 24-14. But back came the Tarblooders. Ray Small returned the ensuing kickoff 60 yards, and a couple of plays later, a Ted Ginn pass again found Lee Jordan in the end zone for a 19-yard score. The extra point made it a 24-21 game with just under three minutes left. The Wildcats ran out the clock to end the Tarblooders' playoff run.

One of the most versatile athletes to ever play football in Northeastern Ohio, Ted Ginn Jr. ended his senior year by being named the Northeast Ohio Lakes District Co-Offensive Player of the Year. He was also named the All-Ohio Offensive Player of the Year, having accumulated more than 3,000 yards. Ginn's honors were not limited to Ohio or the offensive side of the ball, as that year, he was also named by USA Today as the national Defensive Player of the Year.

In 2004, Glenville again finished the regular season with a 9-1 record to qualify for OHSAA postseason play. The Tarblooders opened their playoffs with a regional quarterfinal game against Austintown Fitch on Nov. 6. After falling behind 21-8 in the second quarter, Glenville began its comeback. With just 26 seconds remaining in the first half, Ray Small returned a Fitch kickoff 96 yards for a touchdown that closed the gap to 21-14 at the half.

In the third quarter, Small again scored on a 28-yard pass from QB Arvell Nelson. Place-kicker Darren Gibbs then salvaged a botched extra point attempt by running the ball in for a two-pointer that gave Glenville a 22-21 lead. In the fourth quarter, fullback Curtis Smith put the game on ice with a 1-yard touchdown run with

1:40 left. Gibbs' extra point made it a 29-21 game. But it took an interception by Jacory Stone on the game's last play to ensure the score stayed at 29-21.

The following week, the Tarblooders advanced to a regional semifinal game against St. Edward High School. St. Ed's record was a deceiving 6-5 because the team had to forfeit four games due to an ineligible player. However, whether it was 6-5 or 10-1 this season, the Tarblooders would not be intimidated by the Eagles. The Tarblooders struck first in the opening quarter when defensive end Curtis Smith recovered an Eagles fumble in the end zone for a Glenville touchdown. Later in the same quarter, following Ray Small's second blocked field goal attempt, tailback Tim Conner scored on a 5-yard run to push the Glenville lead to 13-0.

St. Ed's scored the only points of the second quarter to make it a 13-7 game at the half. There would be no scoring in the third quarter. With the game still up for grabs, the Tarblooders scored three touchdowns late in the fourth quarter, two coming on interceptions by Freddie Lenix and linebacker Alex Williamston, to turn a close game into a rout and a 32-7 Glenville victory.

For the first time in school and Senate League history, the Tarblooders had advanced to the regional finals — and their "prize" for doing that was to play the Saint Ignatius Wildcats (10-2) before a standing-room-only crowd of some 11,000 fans at Lakewood Stadium. The first half was a classic defensive struggle in which neither offense scored. However, the Wildcats had taken a 7-0 lead when defensive end Jim Ramella recovered a Glenville fumble in the end zone for a Saint Ignatius touchdown.

Glenville finally got on the scoreboard at 2:27 of the third quarter when Tim Conner scored on a 9-yard run, cutting the Wildcats' lead to 7-6. Early in the fourth quarter, the Wildcats scored again to take a 14-6 lead. But back came the Tarblooders and Tim Conner, who closed out an 82-yard drive with a 1-yard touchdown run, which, with a two-point conversion, tied the game at 14-14 with 6:41 to play. On the Wildcats next possession the Tarblooders recovered an Ignatius fumble at the Glenville 49-yard line. They moved steadily toward the end zone, and with just over three minutes left to play, Tim Conner scored a touchdown on an 8-yard run. Another two-point conversion pushed the Glenville lead to 22-14 with just over three minutes left on the game clock. The Wildcats were driving for the game-tying points, but an interception by Ray Small sealed the victory for Glenville.

Not only had a league team won a regional championship for the first time in Senate League history, but now the Glenville Tarblooders had advanced to Ohio's high school football "final four," a state semifinal game.

This year, the Tarblooders would be playing one of the legendary teams of Ohio high school football, the Bulldogs of Canton McKinley High School, in a game to be played on Nov. 27 at Massillon's Paul Brown Tiger Stadium. The story of this game would be Glenville turnovers—four of which would result in two McKinley touchdowns. Despite these costly mistakes, it was still a very close game, and a 5-yard touchdown run by QB Arvell Nelson brought the Tarblooders to within three points of the Bulldogs, 20-17, with 9:05 to go. Late in the game, Glenville was driving for the go-ahead touchdown, but a McKinley interception in the end zone with less than a minute to play ended Glenville's chances.

Among the honors earned by Glenville (12-2) in 2004 was having Freddie Lenix named co-defensive Player of the Year for the Northeast Lakes District and head coach Ted Ginn Sr. named the District's Division I Coach of the Year.

Glenville was back in the OHSAA playoffs in 2005 after finishing the regular season a perfect 10-0. The Tarblooders were ranked first in The Plain Dealer's final local poll, third in the final AP Ohio Division I rankings, and in the top 10 of the Student Sports Fab 50 national rankings.

Glenville's opponent in the Region 1 quarterfinals on Nov. 5 was the Panthers of Euclid High School (7-3). Highlighted by Ray Small's 82-yard punt return for a touchdown, the Tarblooders scored three in the first quarter and never looked back. They led 26-0 at the half and added three more TDs in the second half en route to a 46-0 win.

Glenville will play in the regional semifinals on Nov. 12 as part of a semifinal doubleheader in Cleveland Browns Stadium. Their opponent in the nightcap will be undefeated Solon (11-0), with St. Edward High School meeting Brush in the first game.

Glenville led the Comets 14-7 at the intermission, but Solon returned to tie the score 14-14 at 4:51 of the third quarter. From then on, however, it would be all Glenville. A minute after the Solon touchdown, Glenville's Bruce Frieson scored on a 63-

yard touchdown pass play, and two minutes later, Frieson would punch in another touchdown, his fourth of the game, from a yard out. Glenville scored the only touchdown of the fourth quarter to advance to the regional finals with a 34-14 victory.

The Tarblooders' opponent in that regional final game would be St. Edward High School, which had defeated Brush High 49-0 in the other semifinal game. The game was played on Nov. 19 at Parma's Byers Field before some 12,000 fans. Glenville got on the scoreboard midway through the first quarter when Arvell Nelson and Bryant Milligan hooked up on a 32-yard touchdown pass play. St. Ed's would later score on a field goal, but Glenville held the lead, 7-3, at halftime.

The second half belonged to the Eagles on both offense and defense. St. Ed's scored single touchdowns in the third and fourth quarters and kept the Tarblooders off the scoreboard the entire second half. The 17-7 loss ended Glenville's playoff run and their season, which ended with a 12-1 record.

Postseason honors went to Glenville's senior defensive lineman Robert Rose, who was named Defensive Player of the Year on the All-District football team and the Cuyahoga County All-Star team, as well as being named First Team All-Ohio. Rose joined the All-Ohio First Team, which included offensive lineman, four-year starter Bryant Browning, and running back Bruce Frieson.

Glenville opened the 2006 season with a loss to Mentor by just two points but then went on to win its next nine games, finishing third in The Plain Dealer's local Top 25 and 10th in the AP Division I poll. Qualifying for the OHSAA playoffs for the fourth consecutive season, the Tarblooders traveled to Byers Field to take on the Saint Ignatius Wildcats (6-3) in a regional quarterfinal game.

In a game that would be heavy on defense, Glenville's touchdowns would outdo Saint Ignatius' field goals. At 7:50 of the second quarter, the Wildcats held a 6-0 lead on a pair of Nick Yako field goals, but then Glenville quarterback Jermale Hines went to work. Before the half was over, he got the Tarblooders back into the game with an 8-yard touchdown run, the extra point putting them into the lead 7-6. After holding the Wildcats to a three-and-out, the Tarblooders struck again, closing out an 84-yard drive with a 26-yard TD pass from Hines to Cordale Scott. The extra point try was blocked, but the Tarblooders had increased their lead to 13-6 at the half.

There was no scoring in the third quarter, and the Wildcats added a third Yako field goal to open the fourth quarter. Glenville came right back, answering that field goal with another Hines-to-Scott touchdown pass, covering 13 yards and giving Glenville a 19-9 lead at 10:02 of the fourth quarter. Nick Yako added his fourth field goal of the game about five minutes later, but the game was not decided until Glenville's LeBron Daniel intercepted a Saint Ignatius pass with just five seconds left on the game clock.

The Tarblooders' 19-12 win sent them to the regional semifinal game against the only team to have defeated them that season, the Cardinals of Mentor High School (10-1). In a game played at Cleveland Browns Stadium, the Tarblooders held a 13-7 lead late in the second quarter, but a 16-point Mentor scoring blitz in the last 3:14 of the half propelled the Cardinals to a 23-13 lead. Each team scored a touchdown in the second half, but turnovers hampered the Tarblooders' effort, and they lost the game 29-19.

QB/LB Jermale Hines was named All-Northeast Lakes District, while Bruce Davis was named All-Ohio and the Division I Co-Defensive Player of the Year.

Glenville finished the 2007 regular season with an 8-2 record and again qualified for the Division I playoffs. Their regional quarterfinal game had the Tarblooders traveling to Parma's Byers Field, where they would take on the Saint Ignatius Wildcats before some 11,000 fans. After a scoreless first quarter, the Tarblooders trailed 6-0 due to a 70-yard interception return of a Cardale Scott pass. However, Glenville returned to take a 13-6 lead on a short run by Shannon Frieson and an 89-yard touchdown return of an intercepted pass by Cordale Scott. The Wildcats scored the game, tying points just 40 seconds before the intermission.

A 1-yard touchdown run by quarterback Terrance Owens in the third quarter gave Glenville a short-lived advantage, the Wildcats coming back with a touchdown and a field goal to take a 23-20 lead after three quarters. At 4:13 of the fourth quarter, Glenville's Jermil Martin tackled Wildcats quarterback Mark Myers, forcing a fumble. The Tarblooders' Bobby Baker alertly scooped up the loose ball and returned it 66 yards for a Glenville touchdown. The extra-point try failed, but Glenville regained the lead, 26-23. The Tarblooders defense did the rest, stopping a couple of Wildcats drives, and the final stop came on an interception by Michael Edwards, with just 28 seconds left to play, which sealed their 26-23 win.

Moving on to the regional semifinal game, Glenville played Boardman (8-3). The Tarblooders led 7-3 at the half on a Shannon Frieson TD in a game heavy on defense. The Tarblooders were on the receiving end of the second-half kickoff. Freshman Shane Wynn, just called up to the varsity earlier that week, fielded the short kick at his 19-yard line and returned it for an 81-yard touchdown, giving his team a 14-3 lead. Boardman returned, marching to a first down at the Glenville 1-yard line. The Tarblooders defense dug in. Four plays later, Boardman had still not scored, and the ball returned to Glenville on downs. Glenville later added another touchdown for a 21-3 victory.

That victory propelled Glenville into the regional championship game at Lakewood Stadium against Mentor (10-2). This was an exciting game in which offense trumped defense, and the fourth quarter alone was worth the price of admission.

As the final 12 minutes got underway, Glenville trailed the Cardinals 31-21. However, a couple of Mentor turnovers, on a fumble and an interception, resulted in a pair of Shannon Frieson short-run touchdowns that gave Glenville a 34-31 lead. But the Cardinals, led by quarterback Bart Tanski, were not about to give up and scored a touchdown on their very next possession to take the lead, 38-34 again.

Back came Glenville. On the ensuing kickoff, Cordale Scott fielded the ball on his 1-yard line, got a few key blocks, and returned it for a 99-yard touchdown – his SECOND 99-yard kickoff return. Glenville went for a two-point conversion, but the pass fell incomplete.

The Tarblooders now led 40-38 with 4:04 left in the game – and those four minutes would prove to be more than enough for Mentor. With Tanski directing the attack, the Cardinals reached the Glenville 1-yard line. With just two seconds left, place-kicker Kevin Harper booted home the 17-yard field goal that gave the Cardinals a 41-40 victory.

It was a challenging game for the Tarblooders to lose, especially after Cordale Scott's dazzling kickoff returns and Shannon Frierson's great running that netted 171 yards and three touchdowns.

Glenville finished the 2008 regular season a perfect 10-0 and ranked #1 in The Plain Dealer's local poll and the Ohio AP Division I rankings. Reaching the playoffs for the sixth consecutive year, the Tarblooders were doing it with offense (35.5 points per game) and defense (giving up less than four points per game with six shutouts).

In a regional quarterfinal game, the Tarblooders would face Brecksville-Broadview Heights (7-3). This game followed the "script" of Glenville's previous 10 games, with the Bees held to just eight points while Glenville scored right at its seasonal average of 35 points. Easily the most spectacular play of the game came on the last play of the first half when Christian Bryant returned a blocked field goal try 96 yards for a Tarblooders touchdown. Bryant later added a touchdown on a 36-yard pass interception.

Following its 35-8 victory over Brecksville-Broadview Heights, Glenville next had to play the Wildcats of Saint Ignatius High School. This would be a game between two nationally ranked heavyweights, with Glenville ranked as high as #8 in the country and the Wildcats checking in at #17. This was the second season meeting between these two teams, Glenville having defeated the Wildcats, 20-17, back in Week 1 on a Marvel Brooks field goal on the game's last play.

This game would be a titanic defensive struggle from start to finish.

The game was still scoreless late in the second quarter when Glenville found itself with a first down at its 4-yard line. After three plays, they only advanced a yard, so the team punted on fourth and nine. The kick attempt was blocked, with the ball rolling out of the end zone for safety, giving Saint Ignatius a 2-0 lead at 4:33 of the second quarter. Following Glenville's free kick, the Wildcats marched down to the Tarblooders 4-yard line, where on the last play of the first half the Wildcats' Seamus Hennessey booted a 21-yard field goal to extend the Wildcats lead to 5-0.

The Tarblooders finally got on the scoreboard at 5:49 of the third quarter on a Terrance Owens-to-Mike Edwards 35-yard touchdown pass. The successful extra point gave Glenville a 7-5 lead. At 6:15 of the final quarter, the Wildcats' Seamus Hennessey put his team back into the lead 8-7 with a 37-yard field goal. At 1:06 of the fourth quarter, the Tarblooders faced a fourth and two and their 46-yard line. QB Terrance Owens dropped back to pass, but Wildcats' linebacker Scott McVey was all over him. Somehow, Owens could get the pass off – but it was intercepted. The Wildcats ran out the last minute of the game to end Glenville's season with an 8-7 defeat.

Glenville finished the 2009 season with a record of 9-1 and ranked sixth in the final AP Division I poll. The Tarblooders also again qualified for the OHSAA playoffs.

Glenville's first playoff game was a regional quarterfinal contest against North Royalton High School (9-1). The game started as a pretty even contest; North Royalton had even taken a 9-6 lead five minutes into the second quarter. However, the Tarblooders were just getting started. Two plays after North Royalton had taken that lead, Cardale Jones and Shane Wynn hooked up for a 48-yard touchdown pass. The start of a 35-point spurt by the Tarblooders carried them to a 41-16 triumph.

In the regional semifinals, the Tarblooders would face the top-ranked team in Ohio, the Wildcats of Saint Ignatius, before a standing-room-only crowd of more than 11,000 at Lakewood Stadium. The Wildcats were 11-0 and had handed Glenville its only defeat, 14-13, in the season's first game. This game would be decided by turnovers—a lot of them.

Early in the second quarter, the Tarblooders were up by an impressive 23-0. In their first six possessions, the Wildcats punted once and lost the ball on turnovers five times. But the Wildcats kept coming back, and late in the third quarter, they had trimmed Glenville's lead to 23-13 and had a third and goal at the Tarblooders 9-yard line. The Wildcats then went to the air, but Glenville's Latwan Anderson stepped in front of the receiver at the 1-yard line, made the interception, and returned it for a 99-yard Glenville touchdown. It was one of four interceptions that Anderson had in the game.

Glenville won the game, 30-13, and the team's defense's eight takeaways played a huge role in the victory.

That victory set up a regional final with undefeated Solon (12-0) on Saturday, Nov. 21. Glenville raced to a 28-7 lead by the intermission, led by Shane Wynn's three touchdown receptions. However, the game fell apart for Glenville in the second half. Glenville's errors and mistakes let the Comets back into the game. Solon outscored the Tarblooders 20-0 in the second half, but Glenville managed to hold on for a 28-27 victory.

Advancing to the Division I state semifinal game on Nov. 28, Glenville would be playing perhaps the most storied team in Ohio high school football, if not the country – the Tigers of Massillon Washington High School (10-3). The game was an absolute slugfest between two high school heavyweights, but Glenville held a 17-10 lead at the half. However, reminiscent of the previous week's game with Solon, Glenville's mistakes let the Tigers back into the game, Massillon scoring at 5:53 of the third quarter to tie the game at 17-17.

Early in the fourth quarter, Cardale Jones and Shane Wynn struck again, this time on a 71-yard pass-and-run touchdown play that put the Tarblooders back into the lead 24-17. A little bit later, with just over five minutes remaining on the game clock, Cardale Jones iced the game with a 26-yard touchdown scamper that gave the Tarblooders a 31-17 lead – which proved to be the final score.

Cardale Jones "played the best game of his career in this game." In leading Glenville to victory, he completed nine of 20 passes for 199 yards and two touchdowns and carried the ball 16 times for another 150 yards and a touchdown.

Glenville was now ranked #16 in the nation by USA Today.

That win over Massillon sent the Tarblooders to a place no Cleveland public school team had ever been—a state championship game. That game was played at Canton's Fawcett Stadium on Saturday, Dec. 5, against Hilliard Davidson High School (12-1), which had won the state championship in 2006.

This was a bruising defensive battle, but no more so than in the first half. After the game's first 24 minutes, the score was still as it had been just before the first kickoff: 0-0.

Hilliard Davidson was on the receiving end of the second-half kickoff. The Wildcats then proceeded to march right down the field, scoring a touchdown and adding the two-point conversion to take an 8-0 lead. Not to be outdone, the Tarblooders took the ensuing kickoff and marched right down the field. Cardale Jones closed out the drive with a 10-yard touchdown run, then tossed a pass to Shane Wynn for the two-pointer that tied the game at 8-8.

Later in the third quarter, the Glenville defense came up with a big play when Devonte Morgan recovered a Davidson fumble at the Wildcats' 20-yard line. Three plays later, Christian Bryant hauled in a Cardale Jones pass - but fumbled the ball at the 2-yard line. The Tarblooders Nicholas Davis picked up the loose ball and carried it into the end zone for a Glenville touchdown. Glenville added the PAT, and with 2:04 left in the third quarter, the Tarblooders had taken a 15-8 lead.

The score would remain that way until the last minute of the fourth quarter when Hilliard Davidson scored a touchdown. The Wildcats then scored another two-point conversion to take a 16-15 lead with just 1:04 left to play.

Glenville tried desperately to score again, but they did not have enough time. When the game ended, the Tarblooders saw their dream of a state championship fall short by just a single point, 16-15.

Glenville ended the 2010 season a perfect 10-0, ranked #1 in The Plain Dealer's local Top 25 and #5 in the AP Division I poll. The team would also get as high as #5 in the national election. Finishing second in the Division I, Region 1 computer rankings, their opponent in a regional quarterfinal game would be Warren Harding (8-2).

Glenville took an early lead against Harding when Shane Wynn scored on a 68-yard punt return less than two minutes into the game. The Tarblooders built that to a 27-6 advantage by halftime en route to a resounding 41-6 victory.

Advancing to the regional semifinals on Nov. 13, Glenville would take on St. Edward High School (11-0) at Byers Field. The Eagles had finished third in the AP Division I poll.

The first half was a tight game, heavy on defense. Each team scored a pair of touchdowns, but St. Ed's kicked the extra point after each score, while the Tarblooders converted a pair of two-pointers to take a 16-14 lead at the intermission.

The defense would rule the second half. Early in the third quarter, the Eagles took a 21-16 lead on an 85-yard interception return for a touchdown. Later in the same quarter, another Eagles interception (they would have four in the game) would lead to another St. Ed's TD. The Eagles closed out the game's scoring with a 96-yard drive in the fourth quarter, resulting in a fifth St. Ed touchdown.

The final score was 35-16, ending another fine season by the Tarblooders.

One of the state's most exciting players in 2010 was Glenville senior Shane Wynn. Besides being a great runner and pass receiver, Wynn was the state's premier kick returner. According to a story in The Plain Dealer, not only did he have "a knack for finding the wedge," but he also knew how to use it. Wynn averaged 36 yards on his punt returns, but his average on his kickoff returns was an even more incredible 63 yards. He also scored seven touchdowns on those returns.

After qualifying for the playoffs eight consecutive seasons, the Tarblooders missed out in 2011 and 2012. However, they were back in the postseason picture in 2013.

That 2013 season marked two significant milestones for Glenville football: One was the fact that the OHSAA's realignment put the team into Division II, playing out of the new Region 3; the other, and much more significant, milestone was the return of head coach Ted Ginn Sr. to the Glenville sideline. Coach Ginn had been battling pancreatic cancer for the past two years and had pretty much given up coaching to concentrate on regaining his health. By nothing short of a miracle, Coach Ginn overcame his cancer and returned to coach the Tarblooders in 2013 and beyond.

The Tarblooders finished the 2013 regular season with a record of 9-1 and were the top seed in Division II, Region 3. In their regional quarterfinal game, the Tarblooders drew Brush High School (7-3). Glenville scored a 35-0 victory and advanced to the regional semifinals.

Glenville's regional semifinal opponent was the Bearcats of Bedford High School (10-1). This was a real defensive struggle for the first three quarters. Bedford scored a touchdown on its opening possession, while the Tarblooders could not cross the Bearcats goal line until the first half's final seconds. The score was tied 6-6 at the intermission and remained that way after three quarters. In the fourth quarter, a pair of touchdown aerials by Glenville quarterback Quan Robinson Jr. broke the game open. The first went 16 yards to Marshon Lattimore, while the second covered 79 yards and was caught by Terrell Goss. Glenville added a third TD in the period to come away with a hard-fought 26-12 win.

Glenville's opponent in the regional finals was Madison High School, the Blue Streaks entering the game with a 10-2 record. This was all but over by the early seconds of the second quarter. Glenville scored early in the first quarter when linebacker Terrell Goss returned a blocked punt 36 yards for a touchdown. Later in the same quarter, quarterback Quan Robinson Jr. added a second

TD on a 57-yard run. On the first play of the second quarter, a 17-yard reception by Treyvon Story added a third Tarblooders touchdown. By the intermission, Glenville had expanded its lead to 27-0 en route to a 40-7 victory.

That win sent Glenville to a Division II state semifinal game against Highland High School on Nov. 29 at Parma's Byers Field. The story of this game would be about Marshon Lattimore's pass-catching, especially in the second half. Over the game's final two periods, Lattimore would have 141 yards in receptions and three touchdowns (Lattimore also had a touchdown reception in the first half), turning what had been a close game into one in which Glenville enjoyed a 28-point lead, 41-13, which would be the final score.

With that victory, the Tarblooders advanced to a state championship game for the first time since 2009. Their opponent in the Division II state championship game on Dec. 2 was listed as the Loveland Tigers (14-0), but Glenville's real opponent turned out to be the weather. It snowed throughout the game, and that snow played havoc with the Tarblooders. They committed seven turnovers in the game, five in just the first half – and Loveland turned every one of those first-half miscues into a touchdown and a 34-0 lead at the intermission. Glenville rebounded to win the second half, 23-7, but it was not enough as they dropped the game by a final score of 41-23.

There were a few postseason honors for Glenville players that year. Leading the list was Marshon Lattimore, who was named the Division II Defensive Player of the Year. Also making the Division II All-Ohio First Team was offensive lineman Marcelys Jones. Lattimore and Jones were also named U.S. Army All-Americans, as was WR Erick Smith.

Glenville posted a record of 8-2 in 2014 to again qualify for the postseason. However, their playoff run was decidedly short when they lost to Willoughby South in the regional quarterfinals by 34-12.

The Tarblooders fared much better in 2015. Finishing the regular season at 9-1, they qualified for the Division II playoffs and opened the postseason against Holland Springfield (9-1) High School. Running back Demerius Goodwin gave the Tarblooders an early 7-0 lead with a 56-yard touchdown run, but a pair of scoring passes had Springfield up 14-7 at the half. The game got exciting in the third quarter as the teams went back and forth, scoring touchdowns, but at the end of the quarter, Glenville still trailed 28-27.

Aaron Pope's interception of a Springfield pass as the fourth quarter got underway started the Tarblooders on their comeback. On the very next play Demerius Goodwin scored on a 6-yard run, and the two-point conversion gave Glenville its first lead of the game, 35-28. Over the remainder of the game, the Glenville defense held Springfield in check while the offense added three more touchdowns for a deceptively lopsided 56-28 win.

Moving on to the regional semifinals, their next opponent would be undefeated Midview (11-0). Glenville took an early first-quarter lead with a field goal, then added six more points that same quarter on a 59-yard pass from QB Marcus Drish to WR Ralph Davis. (It would prove to be Davis' only play on offense during the entire game.) The Glenville defense and a steady ball control offense preserved the lead and took the team to a 27-14 victory.

In the regional finals against Perrysburg (13-0), turnovers by the Tarblooders and extended touchdown plays by Perrysburg spelled doom for Glenville. The game was heavy on offense, with the two teams combining for just under 1,000 yards, but Glenville's five turnovers, two in the red zone, hampered the team's scoring efforts. Perrysburg used two miscues to take a 14-0 lead in the first quarter, stretching it to 21-0 in the second quarter before Glenville finally dented the scoreboard. But the Tarblooders had too much to overcome, especially with Perrysburg adding to its total throughout the game, and when the final whistle sounded, the Tarblooders were on the short end of a 50-19 score.

Over the next four seasons, Glenville qualified for the Division II and Division III playoffs every year (beginning in 2017). In 2018, however, they lost each season in the regional quarterfinal game.

From 1999 to 2019, the Glenville Tarblooders, coached by Ted Ginn, qualified for the OHSAA playoffs 18 times, compiling an overall playoff record of 21-18. They played in three different divisions and advanced to the state championship game twice.

During the 2020 pandemic, Senate League athletics was suspended, but the Tarblooders were back on the football field for the 2022 season, now playing in Division IV.

Opening the season with three non-league games, the Tarblooders defeated Akron St. Vincent-St. Mary, 25-0. They then held off Division I power Powell Olentangy Liberty 20-14 and local Division

II stalwart Avon High School 27-21. Next up was the Senate Athletic League schedule, which the Tarblooders breezed through by shutting out all six opponents and winning the Senate League championship for an unprecedented 25th consecutive year.

With the regular season over, Glenville advanced to the Division IV playoffs. In their first-round game, the Tarblooders disposed of Napoleon High School 46-8 and defeated Bellevue 43-6 and Elyria Catholic 54-7 to reach the regional finals. That regional final game against Van Wert High School was more challenging, but the Tarblooders remained undefeated with a 42-33 victory.

Having reached the Division IV Final Four, the Tarblooders' next opponent in a state semifinal game was Jefferson Area High School, which Glenville easily disposed of by a score of 52-7.

For the third time in school history, Ted Ginn's Glenville Tarblooders had advanced to the state championship game in Canton, Ohio. Their opponent would be the undefeated team from Cincinnati's Wyoming High School.

While the Glenville defense bottled up Wyoming star running back C.J. Hester, the game's real star would be Glenville running back D'Shawnte Jones. Jones rushed for 195 yards and three touchdowns, leading the Tarblooders to a 26-6 victory.

With its victory, Glenville became the first public school in Cleveland to win a state championship during the playoff era. The Tarblooders were also the first Cleveland Senate public school to be named state champion since East Tech did the trick in 1920.

The Tarblooders head coach Ted Ginn opened the 2023 season determined to defend their Division IV state championship. As had been the case, they began play with three challenging non-conference games. In their first game on Aug. 18, they took the field against Dinwiddie High School, one of Virginia's reigning state champions, in a game played at Massillon's Paul Brown Stadium. Giving notice as to what teams in Ohio could "look forward" to, the Tarblooders disposed of the Generals by a 36-13 score. It was more of the same the following week as the Tarblooders handed Olentangy Liberty, an Ohio Division I team, a 34-10 thumping. The Tarblooders luck ran out in Week 3 when they dropped a close 24-16 decision to Avon High School, one of the best Division II teams in the state.

After opening their Senate season by handing John Adams a 38-0 lacing, the Tarblooders headed south to Bradenton, Florida, for an encounter with national power IMG Academy. This game was broadcast on ESPN. Glenville played tough, but IMG was too powerful and defeated the Tarblooders by a 28-6 count.

Returning to Senate League play over the following two weeks, the team added victories over John Hay and Rhodes to raise its record to 5-2. On Oct. 6, Glenville again took the field against a Division II power, the Knights of Archbishop Hoban High School. It was another tough battle, but again, the D-II opponent won by a 28-16 score.

Glenville closed out the 2023 regular season with league wins over John F. Kennedy and John Marshall. With a final regular season record of 7-3, the team qualified for the Division IV playoffs as the number-two seed in Region 14.

The Tarblooders cruised through the playoffs, winning five consecutive games to again find themselves in Canton on Dec. 2 and playing in another Division IV state championship game. Their opponent was Kettering's Archbishop Alter High School (12-3). With the Tarblooders scoring touchdowns on each of their first six possessions, they dominated the Alter High School Knights, as the 38-3 final score showed. Leading the way for the Tarblooders was RB D'Shawntae Jones, who carried the ball 30 times for 161 yards and a touchdown. QB Ruel Tomlinson added to the offense both with his running and passing. Tomlinson carried the ball 10 times for 83 yards and a pair of touchdowns; when he went to the air, he completed 10 of 17 aerials for 207 yards and three TDs. Leading the Glenville receiving corps was Damarion Witten, who made five catches for 86 yards and two touchdowns.

Not to be outdone, the Glenville defense completely stymied the Alter offense, limiting the Knights to just 130 total yards. Jermaine Agee and Cincere Johnson led the defense with eight tackles each.

Following the 2023 season, eight Tarblooders were honored with All-Ohio recognition. D'Shawntae Jones, Damarion Witten, and Fred Johnson Jr. were named 1st Team All-Ohio Offense, while Jameil Hamm, Kareem Jennings, and Bryce West were called to the 1st Team All-Ohio Defense squad. Matthew Gary was named 2nd Team All-Ohio Offense, and Micquan Gravely earned 2nd Team All-Ohio Defense honors.

In addition to his All-Ohio recognition, D'Shawntae Jones was named the Division IV Player of the Year

TRACK

The boys OHSAA track and field championships were first run in 1908, but it would not be until 1926 that Glenville would begin to make its mark. That year, a young man by the name of Chuffin not only became the school's first points scorer at the state meet but also its first state champion when he won the mile run with a time of 4:44.7.

It would be nine years before the Tarblooders would have another state champion. In 1935, Wesley Allen won the high jump competition with a leap of an even 6 feet. Allen also finished second in the broad jump, scoring all 10 of his team's points to give Glenville a tie for sixth place. The following year, Allen also won the high jump (height not recorded), again scoring all of Glenville's points to give the team a tie for ninth place.

The 1941 state meet would produce Glenville's next state champion when Norman Sadofsky won the 220yd. dash with a time of 22.6 seconds. Sadofsky also finished second in the 100-yard—dash, accounting for his team's 10 points in its sixth-place finish. In 1945, Bill Wade won the state championship in the broad jump with a leap of 22'11¼". Wade also finished fifth in the 100-yard—dash, accounting for all his team's points and a tie for eighth place. In 1946, Bill Wade finished second in the broad jump.

Glenville would have to wait until 1955 for its next state champion. That year, Crawford White brought home the gold medal in the broad jump with a leap of 21'6".

In 1956, Glenville scored only three points at the state meet. In 1957, Frank Zubovich took over as the Tarblooders track coach — and things were about to change for the better dramatically. With only 20 boys going out for the track team that season, the Tarblooders produced one state champion, Walt Williams, in the broad jump with a leap of 22'1¾". The team's only other points came from Rod Crayton, who finished second in the high jump and fourth in the 120yd. High hurdles. The Tarblooders' 12 points were good enough for a fifth-place tie—Glenville's best finish to date at the state meet. The following year, 1958, the Tarblooders only scored eight points (no individual state champions), but they again finished in fourth place.

At the 1959 state track meet, Glenville would finally be standing atop the state meet podium. With 29 points, Coach Zubovich's team finally won its first state track championship, edging East Tech by just four points. Leading the way for the Tarblooders would be sprinter Nate Adams, who won both the 100-yard dash (9.9 sec.) and the 220-yard dash (21.7 sec.). Also coming in with a first-place finish was the 880-yard relay team of Al Woodall, Doug Williams, Vic Reed, and Nate Adams.

With a team-high of 31 points, Glenville won its second consecutive state championship at the 1960 state meet, outpointing Springfield and its 26 points. Once again, Nate Adams would lead the way by winning the 100-yard dash (9.6 sec.) and the 220-yard dash (21.0 sec.). Victor Reed finished third in the 100 and second in the 220. A pair of Glenville relay teams also won gold: the 880-yard team of Al Woodall, Frank Perez, Vic Reed, and Nate Adams with a time of 1:29.5 (the team had set a new state record of 1:28.8 during the preliminaries) and the mile relay team of Carl Jeter, Frank Perez, Frank Gordon, and Owen Patterson with a time of 3:25.1.

At both the 1961 and 1962 state meets, the Tarblooders would only score two points. At the 1963 state meet, Glenville rebounded and came within a point and a half of winning another Class AA state championship. Their point total of 28 was just that far off the pace set by Dayton Dunbar, which won the meet with a score of 29½ points. That Dunbar won the championship should not have surprised Clevelanders, as that team was coached by East Tech grad and Olympic champion David Albritton.

Leading the way for Glenville in 1963 were three gold medal performances. Bob Bailey, with a time of 9.9 seconds, finished in a three-way tie for first place in the 100-yard dash. With a time of 21.5 seconds, Bailey also took gold in the 220-yard dash; this time, there was no tie. The Tarblooders' third gold medal came in the 880-yard relay, with Warren Adam, Theron Sumpter, Louis Evans, and Bob Bailey setting a new state record of 1:28.5.

The 1964 state meet would be a rerun of the previous year's event, with Albritton's Dayton Dunbar team again edging out Glenville, this time by just a single point, 18 to 17. William Burt led the way for Glenville by taking gold in the 180-yard low hurdles and finishing in fourth place in the 120-yard high hurdles. (Burt had also scored points in both events the previous year.) Once again, the Tarblooders' 880-yard relay team of Henry Harris, Mike Alexander, Stan Robbins, and Stan Cay took gold, this time with a time of 1:30.0.

At the 1965 state track meet, Glenville would finally get the better of Dayton Dunbar, scoring 15 points to Dunbar's 13 to bring home the team's third state title. Frank Zubovich was still the head coach of the Tarblooders, but David Albritton was no longer at Dunbar. In this low-scoring meet, the Tarblooders won with just two gold medals. After finishing second the previous year, Ron Bolden finished in a tie for the long jump championship. Stanley Albright won the high jump with a state record leap of 6'6½" and finished second in the long jump.

Glenville made it two in a row with another state championship in 1966. It was another close finish, but the Tarblooders' 26 points was three more than East Tech. This time, Glenville used three state championship performances to propel it to the top of the podium. Dan Price won the 220-yard dash with a time of 21.6 seconds. Marvin Landingham won the 180-yard low hurdles in 19.7 and finished second in the 120-yard low hurdles. For the third time in the past four years, Glenville also won the 880-yard relay, and the team of Robert Ware, Willie Smith, Kervy Anderson, and Don Price finished with a state record time of 1:28.2.

Coach Frank Zubovich left Glenville after the 1966 season. In his 10 years as the Tarblooders' head track coach, he led the team to four state championships and two runner-up finishes. However, despite Zubovich's departure, the Tarblooders went right on winning.

At the 1967 Class AA state meet under the direction of head coach James Demo, Glenville again won the state title with a score of 26 points, five points better than runner-up Warren Harding. A pair of sprinters led the way for the Tarblooders. In the 100-yard dash, Robert Ware came in first with a time of 9.6 seconds, with Don Price right behind in second place. In the 220-yard dash, the two boys swapped their finishing positions, Price coming in first (21.3 seconds) and Ware a close second. Adding a third gold medal to that year's effort was the 880-yard relay team of James Biggom, William Clair, Robert Ware, and Don Price, which finished with another new state record time of 1:27.0.

For a fourth consecutive time, Glenville again brought the first-place trophy back to Cleveland in 1968, this time under the guidance of first-year head coach John Demo. The team only scored 17 points, but it was enough to edge out both Dayton Roth and Sandusky high schools, each finishing with 16 points. Bob Ware again led the Tarblooders, winning the 220-yard dash with 21.3 seconds and finishing second in the 100-yard dash. And, as it seemed to do almost every year of late, the Tarblooders' 880-yard relay team won for the seventh time in the last 10 years, the team of Ken Kuhn, James Biggom, Claude Reevers, and Robert Ware finishing with a time of 1:27.2. (The 1967 Glenville state champions track team may have been somewhat unique in that it was composed of only four boys: Ken Kuhn, James Biggom, Claude Reevers, and Robert Ware.)

In 1969, for the first time in 15 years, Glenville failed to score a single point at the state meet. However, under Coach Frank Perez, the Tarblooders rebounded in 1970 with yet another state championship. Their 37 points (the team's highest total yet) were enough to hold off second-place Dayton Dunbar and its 35 points (Dunbar again being coached by David Albritton). Gold medal efforts by Lewis DeFreeze in the 880-yard run (1:53.2) and Fred Lane in the 120-yard high hurdles (14.1) led the way, while both the 880-yard and mile relay teams finished in second place.

In 1971, the Tarblooders scored 26 points, and while that score was good enough to win the state championship in 1967, it was only good enough for a fourth-place finish this time. For the second year in a row, Lewis DeFreeze won the 880-yard run (1:53.0).

With 22 points in 1972, the Tarblooders finished in third place. As it had often done over the last decade, the 880-yard relay team brought home the team's only state championship with a time of 1:29.6. Manning that team was David White, Bobby Bridget, Floyd Ware, and Calvin Johnson.

With a new Glenville team record of 42 points, the Tarblooders of Coach Robert Taylor captured the Class AAA state championship in 1973. As it had been so frequently in the past, Glenville was paced by its 880-yard (1:27.6 – David White, Robert Martin, Floyd Ware, and Calvin Johnson) and mile (3:19.0 – David White, Kermit Woolfolk, Frank Lewis, and Charles Byrd) relay teams – both of which were state champions. Calvin Johnson and Floyd Ware also added greatly to the team total with points earned in the sprinting events. Both runners finished in a tie for third place in the 100-yard dash, while Johnson finished second and Ware took third in the 220-yard dash.

The following year, the Tarblooders saw their point total drop to 32, but it was still enough to win another state championship. Once again, the relay teams led the way with state championships. The 880-yard relay team of Derrick Harbour, Ron Page, David White, and Floyd Ware took the gold with a time of 1:28.3. In contrast, the mile relay team of Harbour, Page, White, and Frank Lewis won with a time of 3:17.6. Floyd Ware also added big points to the team total by finishing in a tie for second place in the 100-yard dash and a tie for fourth place in the 220.

Glenville's point total at the Class AAA state track meet again fell in 1975, but the 29 points they did score allowed Coach Robert Taylor's team to win a third consecutive state championship. However, the team would not have come close to a state championship were it not for the accomplishments of Derrick Harbour. Harbour won the state championship in the 220-yard dash with a time of 21.1 seconds. He then won the 440-yard dash in a record-setting time of 47.3 seconds. Harbour was also a member of Glenville's mile relay team, which finished in fourth place. Finally, Derrick Harbour finished second in the long jump – in essence, he accounted for all of Glenville's points.

From 1959 to 1975, Glenville had won 10 of 17 state championships, finishing in second place two other times. It was an incredible run of success, one of Ohio's all-time best, but the Tarblooders and their fans would have to wait almost 30 years for another state title. However, despite not winning a team championship, the Tarblooders were picking up a few individual state titles along the way. In 1977, the mile relay team of Thomas Grant, Robert Crawford, Donald Wright, and Calvin Thomas won at 3:18.4. Two years later, Leonard Scruggs took the gold in the 440 with a time of 49.5 seconds.

A long 15 years elapsed before Glenville had another individual state champion, but that year, 1994, the team would have two. Now racing in the newly named Division I, Omar Dhyll won the 400m race with a time of 48.12. Dhyll was also a member of the state championship 4x400m relay team, which included Jamain Owens, Eric Nix, and Christopher Chambers. Those two victories gave Glenville 20 points, good for fifth place, the team's best finish in 20 years.

It would be another eight years before the Tarblooders, now coached by Ted Ginn Sr., would again become a significant player at the state meet and begin another grand championship run. In 2002, Glenville scored 34 points at state, suitable for a third-place finish. Leading the way was a state championship performance by the 4x400m relay team of Freddie Lenix, Ted Ginn Jr., Dante Whitner, and Roland Sweet. Ginn Jr. also finished second in the 110m and the 300m intermediate hurdles and was joined by the other three boys on the second-place 4x100m relay team.

In 2003, the Tarblooders scored 56 points, winning the Division I state meet by easily outdistancing second-place Wadsworth and Huber Heights Wayne, which scored 28 points each. Ted Ginn Jr. was the team's star with first-place finishes in the 100m (13.84) and the 300m hurdles (36.73); Ginn also finished second in the 200m dash. Also bringing home state titles were a couple of the Tarblooders relay teams. The 4x100m team of Raheem Armstrong, Daven Jones, Stephon Fuqua, and Freddie Lenix won with a time of 41.20, while the 4x400m team of Antwaun Molden, Troy Cloud, Ted Ginn Jr., and Roland Sweet crossed the finish line in 3:14.57.

The 2004 Division I state track meet would be unique and memorable for the Glenville Tarblooders. Not only would the team post its highest point total ever, 80, but it would also have an all-time team high of five state champions. The relay teams would account for three of those first-place finishes. The 4x200m team of Freddie Lenix, Stephon Fuqua, Jamario O'Neal, and Andre Evans would race to the finish line in a state record time of 1:25.11. The 4x100m team of Lenix, Fuqua, Daven Jones, and Myron Howard won with a time of 41.59. The third relay victory came in the 4x400m event, with Lenix, Fuqua, Ted Ginn Jr., and Dante Cloud bringing home the gold in 3:15.04. The other two state championships belonged to Ted Ginn Jr., who won the 110m hurdles in a state record time of 13.40 and took the 200m sprint in 21.51, with Stephon Fuqua right behind in second place. (Note: In 2003 and 2004, Ted Ginn Jr. had the fastest times in Ohio and the U.S.A. in the 110m hurdles.)

At the 2005 state meet, the Tarblooders scored "only" 70 points in winning a third consecutive state championship, easily outdistancing second-place finisher Saint Ignatius and its 37 points. The team scored in 10 different events, winning four of them. Once again leading the way were the relay teams, three of which won state championships. Raymond Fisher, Derek Mcbryde, Freddie Lenix, and Andre Evans won the 4x200m race at 1:25.09, setting a new state record. The 4x100m team of Clenson Caffey, Daven Jones, Jamario O'Neal, and Derek Mcbryde also crossed the finish line ahead of everyone else with a time of 41.67. The third relay team to win its race was the 4x400m team of Eddie Mason, Freddie Lenix, Andre Evans, and Jamario O'Neal, with a time of 3:15.58. The only other state championship for Glenville that year was won by Curtis Smith in the shot put with a toss of 61' 9.5" – the first gold medal by a Glenville athlete in a non-racing event in 40 years.

Coach Ginn's Tarblooders made it four in a row in 2006 when they took the Division I state championship with 51 points, finishing four points ahead of runner-up Trotwood Madison. Once again, the relay teams led the way. For the fifth consecutive year, the 4x400m relay team was state champion with a time of 3:14.80. This year, it was manned by Eddie Mason, Kyle Jefferson, Xavier Clements, and Daven Jones. The 4x100m relay team of Clenson Caffey, Daven Jones, Otis Merrill, and De' Erick Barber came home with its fourth consecutive state title in a time of 41.98. Not to be left out, the 4x200m relay team won its third straight championship this year with a time of 1:25.78; the team consisted of Raymond Fisher, De' Erick Barber, Xavier Clements, and Kyle Jefferson.

For an incredible fifth consecutive year, in 2007, the Glenville Tarblooders won the state championship, this time with 66 points, easily outdistancing second-place Cleveland Heights and its 48 points. For a fifth consecutive year, the 4x100m relay team won gold with a time of 41.88; Tyshaun Peoples, Branden Goodall, Otis Merrill, and Xavier Clements were running on that team. The 4x200 relay team made it four in a row with a time of 1:25.59; racing across the finish line ahead of everyone else were Ernest Downing, Xavier Clements, Cordale Scott, and Kyle Jefferson. In the 110m hurdles, the Tarblooders finished 1-2, with Tyshaun Peoples gaining the gold with a time of 14.30 and Otis Merrill right behind him at 14.37. Kyle Jefferson also won gold in the 400m race with a time of 46.93.

It would be seven years before Glenville won another Division I state track championship, a record 16th. Still, the team did relatively well over those intervening years and won some individual state championships.

In 2008, the Tarblooders finished in fourth place, with long jumper Tyshaun Peoples winning the team's only gold medal with a jump of 23'1". The following year, Glenville missed a state championship by a mere three points, its 45 points good for only second place behind Gahanna Lincoln and its 48-point total. As they had many times recently, Glenville's relay teams led the way. The 4x800m team of Marcus Brooks, Lamar Thomas, Quincy Downing, and Marvel Brooks took first place with a time of 7:42.58, while the 4x200m team of Shane Wynn, Latwan Anderson, Marvel Brooks, and Marcus Brooks crossed the finish line in 1:26.38, suitable for another first-place finish.

In 2010, the Tarblooders finished in third place; again, the relay teams garnered big points. The 4x200m team of Justin Hardee, Quincy Downing, Shane Wynn, and Latwan Anderson won gold, while the 4x400m team came in second, and the 4x100m team finished third. In 2011, Glenville finished in fifth place, with all of the team's points coming in just two events. Quincy Downing won the 400m race with a time of 47.46, while the 4x400m team of Jacquez Riggs, Justin Hardee, Shane Wynn, and Quincy Downing also came in first with 3:14.87.

In 2014, with a point total of 40, the Glenville track team won its 16th state championship, with the vast majority of its points coming from three state championship performances. Davon Anderson won the 110m hurdles with a time of 13.64. The 4x100m relay team of Falonte Jackson, Darrien Hickman, Demarius Goodwin, and Davon Anderson finished first at 41.47. In contrast, the 4x400m team of Adam Lett, Falonte Jackson, Darrien Hickman, and Davon Anderson was also first across the finish line at 3:13.75.

In 2021, now participating in Division II, the Tarblooders were part of one of the closest team point total finishes in the history of the OHSAA state track meet. Unfortunately for Glenville, the team came up just a half-point short of the championship.

The team was led by two runners, Deasean Evans and Jeremiah Powell. The Tarblooders scored points in six different events, and one or both of these runners was in on every point, each boy earning All-Ohio honors four times. With Woodbridge High School leading the Tarblooders by 6.5 points, the meet championship came down to the final race, the 4x400m relay. The Glenville team of Deasean Evans, Jeremiah Powell, Malik Davis, and Eric Richards knew they had to win this race to win the championship. In a thrilling race, they did just that, winning points that gave Glenville a team score of 41. Woodbridge only had to finish fifth or better to win the meet, and they did just that. Woodbridge's fifth-place finish gave it a team total of 41.5, edging out Glenville by a mere one-half point.

The Tarblooders had to live with that heartbreaking loss for the next year until the 2022 state meet, but they were determined to write a new and better ending. Wearing shirts with the slogan "Unfinished Business" on them, they went to the Division II state meet with just one thought in mind - to win.

While the team only won one event, they scored well in seven events to pile up 45 points, good enough to hold off second place Keystone and its 35 points. Leading the way was the 4x200 relay team of Milique Herron, Jamari Townsend, Joe Larkins, and Bryce West, who won the race in a time of 42.16. The team added second-place finishes in the 300m hurdles and the 4x400m relay; third-place finishes in the high jump, 200m dash, and the 4x100m relay; and an eighth-place finish in the 100m dash to close out its scoring.

In 2023, after a couple of closely contested state meets, the Tarblooders left no doubt about who the Division II state champion was by scoring 60 points to finish well ahead of Woodridge High School and its 34 points. This championship was the school's 18th state record. Leading the way were a pair of state championship relay teams. The 4x400m team of Isaiah McCollum, Jamari Townsend, Jacob Rice, and Malik Davis won with a time of 3:18.37, while the 4x200m team of Micquan Gravely, Jamari Townsend, Milique Herron, and Bryce West took gold with a new state meet record time of 1:26.68. Bryce West also made the podium with a third-place finish in the 100m dash, as a member of the second-place 4x100m relay team, and with a third-place finish in the 200m dash.

While coverage and information are scarce, Glenville had a perfect run of success at the indoor track state championships from 2005 to 2010. The Tarblooders won state indoor titles in 2005, 2006, 2009, and 2010 and finished second in 2008.

TRACK (GIRLS)

The Glenville Tarblooders have produced several girl state champions. The first great track athlete was Kelli Turner, who won the OHSAA 1996 400-meter run. This was an unbelievable feat, as Kelli won this event as a ninth-grader. The other great track athlete was Raina Spencer, who won the 2007 OHSAA high jump championship with a leap of 5 feet 9 inches.

CHAPTER 13

John Adams High School

> *John Adams High School opened in 1923 at East 116th Street and Corlett Avenue. It was closed in 1995 to help cut the city's budget, but it was rebuilt and reopened in 2006.*

BASKETBALL

John Adams High School had been in the Senate League for about 10 years before its first perfect basketball season. The Rebels opened the 1933-1934 campaign with three nonleague victories; Ike Friedler led Adams by averaging about 15 points per game. In their first Senate game on Jan. 11, 1934, West High jumped ahead of the Rebels 17-13 following the first quarter, but after that, it was all Adams as the Rebels came away with a convincing 57-39 win.

By Feb. 2, the Rebels had pushed their record to 4-0 in league play and were the only undefeated Senate team. A week later, they lost 38-32 in the annual game with the John Adams alums, but that was an exhibition game and did not count in the standings. Feb. 16 was a big game for the Rebels, taking on the defending champion Lincoln Presidents. As expected, it was a close game, and Lincoln led at the intermission, 15-12. The halftime break proved what the Rebels needed; returning to the court for the second half, the Rebels outscored Lincoln 19-11 over the last two quarters to come away with a 31-26 victory.

Wins over West Tech, 43-33, and Glenville, 50-36, pushed the Adams record to 7-0, and it looked as if the Rebels had the league title well in hand. However, on March 9, East Tech pulled one of the season's biggest upsets and handed the Rebels their first league loss, 51-36. This dropped the Rebels into a first-place tie with Central, with both teams having 7-1 records.

Then things got interesting. The week following East Tech's win over Adams, the Scarabs were forced to forfeit a game because they had an ineligible player, their team captain having also played on an amateur team, which was against Senate rules. On March 16, the day after this ruling, Adams handed Central a 44-35 defeat. The following day, Cleveland Director of Physical Welfare Floyd Rowe reinstated the East Tech captain and East Tech's win over John Adams.

Because of the Adams win over Central, the reinstated East Tech victory made little difference in the final league standings, which were as follows: John Adams, 8-1; Collinwood and Central, both 7-2; and East Tech, 6-3. John Adams had finally won its first Senate League basketball championship.

Adams basketball fans would have to wait more than three decades before the Rebels again topped the league standings. However, during those lean years, the team produced some top-notch players. In 1962, George Phillips was named AP All-Ohio Honorable Mention, and in 1966, Garland Stallworth was rated among the state's best five players and named an AP All-Ohio First Team selection.

The 1968-1969 season, with Joe Ungvary as the Rebels head coach, would be one of the best in school history.

The season opened on Dec. 6, 1968, against Collinwood. Giving a glimpse of what their fans could expect over the season, the Rebels raced to a 68-19 lead at the half. Coach Ungvary cleared the bench in the third quarter as Adams mauled the Railroaders 108-49. By Christmas, the Rebels were 6-0 and had been held under 87 points only once when they defeated East High 69-61, behind George Gooden's 25 points.

Over Christmas break, the team played in the Farrell (Pa.) Tournament. In their first game, the Rebels played the host team from Farrell High School, the #1 ranked team in Pennsylvania. Adams held a 50-48 lead midway through the fourth quarter, but the Steelers put on a furious comeback and outscored Adams 20-13 over the game's balance for a 68-63 win. Two days later, the Rebels returned on a winning track by closing tournament play with a 56-50 victory over Hickory (Pa.) High School.

Returning to Senate play on Jan. 10, 1969, the Rebels received a real jolt with a 76-67 defeat at the hands of the East Tech Scarabs, who led from start to finish. The loss also dropped John Adams into a tie for first place in the East Senate with East High, both teams at 6-1. One week later, the Rebels took their frustrations on Collinwood, setting a school scoring record by drubbing the Railroaders 121-54. Their new winning streak reached four in a row the following week when the Rebels won a wild, high-scoring game with Benedictine, 101-90. That same day, East High lost to East Tech, leaving Adams alone atop the East Senate standings. Six days later, the Rebels solidified their first-place standing by defeating second-place East High, 80-69. John Adams also found itself atop the local Top 25 rankings, where they had been every week of the season except the previous one.

The Rebels closed their East Senate season with an absolute thriller against East Tech. The game went into overtime before Adams finally prevailed, avenging their earlier loss, 90-88, and giving the Rebels a 12-1 East Senate mark and the divisional championship. Adams now had to play West Senate champion West Tech (11-3, 12-4) to gain the overall Senate and city championship.

The big game was played on Valentine's Day, Friday, Feb. 14, 1969. It was an intense game, and although the lead went back and forth, it was one in which West Tech's Warriors seemed to have the upper hand most of the time. West Tech grabbed the lead with 4:25 to play, and with only two minutes remaining, the Rebels had fallen behind by nine points, 65-56. But then came the John Adams charge. After an 8-0 run had his team trailing by just a single point at 65-64, Thomas Wooten put in a shot for Adams and was fouled in the process. He calmly added the free throw, his three-point play giving Adams a 67-65 lead with just seven ticks left on the clock. The Adams defense prevented a West Tech score in those final, frantic seconds, giving the Rebels a heart-pounding 67-65 victory. It was the first time John Adams had won the Senate and Cleveland City basketball championship.

As Plain Dealer sportswriter Dick Zunt wrote the next day, "John Adams High last night found a way to win when there was none."

Coach Ungvary took his team on the Class AA Tournament Trail a week later. The first stop was Bedford High School for both sectional and district play. After disposing of Orange High (6-10) in a first-round sectional game, the Rebels crushed East Senate rival Cathedral Latin 120-55 in second-round action. They then defeated East Tech in the sectional's lower bracket final, raising their record to 18-2 and advancing to Bedford district play.

District semifinal play provided decidedly stiffer completion for Adams as the team went against Maple Heights and its 19-2 record. It was a close game, but the Rebels emerged with a 64-63 victory, their 12th in a row. Two days later, in the district final, the Rebels took the court against a surprising John F. Kennedy team. Despite a fourth-quarter charge by the Eagles, the Rebels came away with a 69-63 win. This was the team's 20th win of the season and advanced Adams to regional play – the Sweet 16!

On March 14, at the Bowling Green Regional, Adams (20-2) would face Lima Central Catholic (19-4). Adams built up a 15-point advantage at the halftime break, and things looked suitable for the Clevelanders. However, the Central Catholic Thunderbirds had regrouped during the break and came storming back in the second half. They might have completed their comeback had it not been for the Rebels' George Gooden. Gooden scored 33 points in the game, more than half of his team's total; more importantly, 22 came in the second half. When the final buzzer sounded, John Adams, thanks in no small part to Gooden's hot shooting in the second half, was clinging to a 62-58 lead. It was Adams' third trip to regional play in the last four years but only their first regional win.

In the regional final, Adams (21-2) would face Toledo Libby (22-1). Cold shooting by the Rebels doomed their effort from the very start. Libby jumped out to a 21-3 lead in the first quarter and cruised to a 72-51 win. John Adams' best basketball season ended with a 21-3 record. The Rebels' Cleophas McNeal was named AP All-Ohio Honorable Mention.

1977-1988 saw some of the most exciting John Adams basketball in the school's history. The Rebels played for the city championship seven times during those years and provided their fans with the excitement of watching the best John Adams team ever.

In the 1976-1977 season, under head coach Terry Lloyd, the Rebels were able to overcome a couple of league losses while getting some help from the rest of the league to edge out East Tech for the East Senate title; Adams finished with a 10-2 record while second-place East Tech was 9-3. In the city championship game, the Rebels took the court against the Wildcats of Saint Ignatius (16-1). It was a nip-and-tuck battle, but with just five seconds left on the game clock, the Wildcats' Oliver Luck sank a two-pointer to tie the score at 66-66 and send it into overtime. Luck then scored the first two points of the extra session, and the Wildcats went on to win 70-69. For Adams, Marvin Nelson would earn All-Ohio Honorable Mention recognition.

The 1977-78 season saw another tight East Senate race. After the final games had been played, both John Adams and JFK had finished with identical 9-3 league marks, setting up an East Senate championship playoff game. The two teams had split their two regular season contests. In this deciding game, Adams trailed until the final five minutes, then pulled ahead to win 68-63; Tony Grimes and Carl Jacobs each scored 20 points for the Rebels.

The Rebels again played Saint Ignatius (15-1) as they had done the previous season for the city title. This was a close, low-scoring game. Adams led twice by six points in the second quarter but could not shake the Wildcats. For the game, the Rebels outscored the Wildcats from the field, 44-34, but at the charity stripe, it was a different story. Adams made only three of seven foul shots, while the Wildcats canned 15 of 25, giving Saint Ignatius a 49-47 victory. When the postseason laurels were handed out, Carl Jacob was named All-Ohio Honorable Mention.

The 1979-1980 season saw the Senate divided into South and North divisions for the first time, with Adams playing in the South Senate under the direction of head coach John Soljanyk. On Feb. 15, the Rebels defeated John Marshall, 69-68, to complete a clean sweep of its South Senate schedule, taking the divisional title with a 10-0 record. They would now face off against North Senate champion Collinwood (10-1, 10-3) for the overall Senate championship. The Railroaders led the game to take the title, 61-56. The Rebels' Danny Miller was named All-Ohio Honorable Mention.

With the Rebels again coached by Terry Lloyd, who had returned after a two-year absence, the 1980-1981 season would be the greatest in John Adams' basketball history. Adding even more excitement to the season, the team was relatively short in stature but very quick afoot, earning themselves the nickname of the Runnin' Rebels for the way they raced up and down the court, daring the opposition to keep up.

The Rebels got off to a perfect start, playing a schedule almost evenly split between league and non-league teams. On Feb. 6, 1981, after a 110-51 thrashing of South High, the Rebels' league record was a perfect 9-0, 16-2 overall. A week later, the area's top-ranked Rebels took on #2 John Marshall; behind Clinton Smith's 30 points, the Rebels prevailed, 85-74. John Marshall had only lost two games thus far, and both were at the hands of the John Adams Rebels.

On Feb. 20, John Adams (17-2) met John Hay (15-2) in the Senate championship game. After a close first quarter, the game quickly went the Rebels' way. Behind 23 points and 14 rebounds by Greg Brown and 32 turnovers by Hay, the Rebels rolled to an 81-56 championship victory.

Entering the "second season" of OHSAA tournament play, the Rebels rolled through the Class AA sectional and district play right to the district final. Their opponent in the final would again be John Hay. While the game was a little closer than the Senate championship, the results were still the same: John Adams 88, John Hay 69. John Hay's story was much like that of John Marshall; Hay had only lost three games all season, and all three were to the Rebels.

Once again, the John Adams Rebels (22-2) made it to the Sweet 16 and advanced to the Kent Regional tournament. Their opponent would be the Vikings of St. Joseph High School (17-5). In a very close game, the Rebels led 15-12 after the first quarter and 28-24 at the half. However, the third quarter ended in a 34-34 tie, and when the buzzer ended the fourth quarter, the game was deadlocked at 48-all. The Rebels trailed 53-52 when Clinton Smith stepped to the free-throw line with just 29 seconds remaining. Smith made both shots to give the Rebels a thrilling 54-53 overtime win.

On March 21, the Rebels faced Lorain Southview (23-2) in the regional final. Southview had small leads at the end of the first quarter and the half. After the intermission, the Rebels came storming back, outscoring Southview 45-34 over the last two quarters to come away with a 76-66 victory. Leading the way for Adams was one of the shortest men on the court, 5'10" Robert Hall, who led all scorers with 23 points.

For the first time in school history, the John Adams Rebels, now 24-2, had advanced to the Final Four. Their State Semifinal opponent would be the Grizzlies of Wadsworth High School (21-5). As had been the case with the Rebels' last few tournament games, this one was another closely played affair. With just over four and a half minutes left in the game, the Rebels held a 54-49 lead, and then they went cold. The Rebels scored only three more points over the game's balance, missing their last four shots from the field and their previous attempt from the free-throw line.

When the final buzzer sounded, the Rebels found themselves on the short end of a 59-57 score. The top-ranked team in the Greater Cleveland area, and Ohio's ninth-ranked team, had come up just two games short of the ultimate prize, finishing with a 24-3 record. Greg Brown was named to the All-Ohio Second Team, while Robert Hall received All-Ohio Special Mention.

John Adams won the South Senate title in 1982, 1987, and 1989 but was defeated in the game for the Senate championship each time. In 1982, Clinton Smith was named All-Ohio First Team and had a stellar basketball career at Cleveland State University, where he earned All-America honors. In 1987, Leonard Cooper received an All-Ohio Special Mention, and in 1989, Troy Miller was named All-Ohio Honorable Mention.

Under the direction of head coach Terry Lloyd, the John Adams Rebels played Glenville for the Senate championship in 1994. Glenville took a 17-12 lead after the first quarter, but in the second frame, Adams went on a 20-8 run, giving the team a 32-25 lead at the intermission. Adams held a 47-43 advantage after three quarters, and the game remained close throughout the fourth period. Terry Smith, who would earn All-Ohio Special Mention, sank four free throws in the game's final 30 seconds to secure a 63-60 championship victory for the Rebels.

CROSS-COUNTRY

The OHSAA state championship boys cross-country race was first run in 1928. John Adams made its first mark in the race in 1940, finishing 13th, with Hunt the sixth-place finisher. It would be another 12 years before the Rebels again registered among the finalists, finishing 11th in 1952. This would begin a run of almost a dozen years, during which the John Adams team annually finished among the best in the state.

The 1953 Rebels finished a very strong fifth at the state meet, their best finish to date. Leonard Simms led the way by finishing fourth, also the best by an individual Rebels runner to date.

The following season, the Rebels, under the direction of Coach Mel Brodt, put it all together to win their first state cross-country championship; their 56 points bested second-place Columbus West by a whopping 88 points. Leonard Simms again led the team, this time with a ninth-place finish, but the team's subsequent three runners were all bunched together to give John Adams its winning margin. James Bahleda came in 14th, Sam Algeri crossed the finish line in 16th place, and Ed Simpson was behind him in 17th place.

In 1955, the Rebels finished a very fine third, with Ed Butler and Tyrone Smith leading the way with 14th- and 15th-place finishes, respectively. In 1956, the team slipped to ninth place, but Ed Butler led all of the runners across the finish line with a time of 10:10.5, while Tyrone Smith bettered his finish of the previous year by coming in 10th. The team failed to place in 1957, but in 1958, they were back among the best with a strong third-place finish led by Choice Phillips in 18th place.

The 1959 state meet was very close, but with a score of 123 points, Mel Brodt's Rebels runners beat out Parma by just two points to win their second state cross-country championship. Choice Phillips led all runners with a time of 9:52.0, while Darnell Mitchell finished sixth.

John Adams again failed to place in 1960, but in 1961, the team finished a strong seventh, pushing it up to fourth place in 1962. That year, Ron Farris came in 10th while George Leaks finished 15th.

The 1963 state met would see the John Adams Rebels take home the first-place trophy for the third time in the last 10 years, this time running under the direction of head coach G. Blount. Ben Brown, who would also be one of the state's top runners the following two seasons, led the Rebels with a fifth-place finish, while George Aloshen came in seventh. The following season, the Rebels slipped to sixth place, but Ben Brown again finished fifth. In 1965, the John Adams runners finished in ninth place, and Ben Brown closed out his career with a stellar third-place finish.

CROSS-COUNTRY (GIRLS)

Tangetta Miller succeeded in Cross Country (3.1 miles) because of her consistent hard work and dedication. She had numerous high-place finishes throughout her career, with her fastest time of 19:48.12. She racked up city meet champion and runner-up titles in the league in 1990 and 1991. Having excelled through the district and regional meets, Miller broke a barrier by being the first to compete in the State Cross Country Meet 1990 for John Adams High School. As of 2024, she is the only female for John Adams to have qualified for the State Cross Country Meet.

FOOTBALL

1937 was the first year of real greatness for the John Adams Rebels football team. After opening the season with a 31-13 loss to Toledo Scott, Adams won two consecutive East Senate games to open the East Senate part of its season. The Rebels made it three in a row on Oct. 8 by downing John Hay, 25-0, with brothers Nick and Angelo Barille each scoring a touchdown. Adams then won a non-league game against South High (South was in the West Senate), drubbing the Flyers by a 27-0 score. Returning to league play, the Rebels upped their East Senate mark to 5-0-0 by defeating East Tech, 13-4, and Glenville, 27-7. In a non-league thriller on Nov. 5 against Shaker Heights, Adams almost let the game slip away but held off a feverish Red Raider comeback in the final couple of minutes to emerge with a 13-7 win.

It was now Nov. 12, and time for a prominent East Senate showdown between John Adams (5-0-0) and East High (4-0-1), played at Municipal Stadium. The winner would move on to a Nov. 27 date at the stadium with West Tech in the Charity Game for the city championship. This game between the Rebels and the Bombers generated much excitement, as witnessed by the 21,046 spectators, one of the most significant area crowds ever for a regular season game, who filed into the stadium to watch the game.

John Adams jumped out to an early 19-0 halftime lead. The second half was scoreless. Coach George Kozak's Adams team emerged with a 19-0 victory and its first East Senate championship, the first championship of any type for the John Adams gridders.

The stage was now set for the first all-Senate Charity Game to decide the city's scholastic football championship. Representing the West Senate would be the Carpenters from West Tech (7-0-2), squaring off against the East Senate's John Adams (8-1-0) on Saturday, Nov. 27, at Cleveland's Municipal Stadium before a record crowd of 47,315.

Although the West Senate was considered the tougher of the two divisions, John Adams' accomplishment of an undefeated and untied trip through the East Senate could not be ignored. The Rebels' upset of the mighty Cathedral Latin Lions in September set the tone for the rest of their season. Head coach George Kozak had a team with experience that included 14 seniors, most of whom were starters. Perhaps not as large as their West Side opponents, the John Adams footballers nonetheless played every bit as hard. Typical were a pair of 175-pound tackles in Maurice Dworkin and Alex Woronkoff, rated the best in the city at their position by coach Kozak. These boys were expected to spend much time in the West Tech backfield. Adding to the Rebel line was end Joe Polgut, a fine pass receiver and one of the best defensive ends in the city, and guard Bob Kolesar.

Adams' all-senior backfield of quarterback Howard Mickovsky, halfbacks Gene Sliwinski and Bernie Kluga, and fullback Nick Barille was a "constant threat to break loose with dazzling runs."(PD) Using the famed Notre Dame system, coach Kozak's backfield excelled at the trickery and lightning execution that that system required. The key to it all was fullback Nick Barille. Tipping the scales at only 160 pounds, Nick was a "pile-driver" (PD) when running the ball and an excellent passer when called upon.

The Plain-Dealer reported that "47,315 persons, the greatest throng that ever witnessed a high school game in Cleveland," turned out on Nov. 27 for the 1937 Charity Game. After watching an outstanding pre-game show by the 25 marching bands, this record-breaking crowd sat back to enjoy an incredible game.

At 2:15 p.m., John Adams' Nick Barille got the game underway with a kick that Tech's Alex Belaka returned to his 47-yard line. West Tech, only able to advance the ball as far as midfield, was forced to punt. Also unable to move the ball, Adams was forced to punt from deep in its end of the field, with West Tech regaining possession with excellent field position at the John Adams 31-yard line. Tech turned that good field position into the game's first touchdown, but they did not make the extra point and were left with an early 6-0 lead just five minutes into the game.

After the ensuing kickoff, Adams could not make a first down and was again forced to punt. Tech's Paul O'Dea's 23-yard return of the punt gave the Carpenters excellent field position at their 48-yard line. West Tech marched down to the Adams 7-yard line, but there, the Adams defense held and forced Tech to give up the ball on downs on the last play of the first quarter.

So far, it had been all West Tech. John Adams pushed the ball out to its 27 as the second quarter got underway, but Nick Barille was smothered for a 16-yard loss while attempting to pass on third down. The teams exchanged possession of the ball a couple of times before a Nick Barille punt gave West Tech the ball at its 26-yard line. It was now late in the second quarter, but this was only the second play of the game to take place on West Tech soil. On first down, Dan Kincaid went over left guard for 9 yards, but he fumbled the ball, and Nick Barille recovered for John Adams at the Tech 35-yard line.

This was the break that the Rebels had been waiting for. Angelo Barille immediately went around the right end for 19 yards and a first down at the West Tech 16; it would prove to be the longest run of the day by either team. With their backs to their goal line, the big West Tech defense dug in, but the Adams offense was not to be denied. It took eight grueling plays, but with just seconds remaining in the half, Nick Barille smashed over the left guard for the game-tying touchdown. The hard-charging Carpenters blocked Barille's kick for the extra point.

The half ended after the ensuing kickoff. The score was tied 6-6, and, as predicted, West Tech had dominated the game. Adams' late rally, however, had signaled a change.

On the receiving end of the second-half kickoff, John Adams began to play at its 38-yard line. The Rebels advanced to the West Tech 43, from where a Nick Barille punt went out of bounds at the Tech 7. The fired-up Adams defense kept the Carpenters in check, forcing a West Tech punt. Gene Sliwinski's 12-yard punt return gave the Rebels excellent field position at the West Tech 33-yard line. Sliwinski picked up 1 yard on the first down. On second down, he dumped a short 1-yard pass to Nick Barille. Barille "shook himself loose from a tackler who seemed to have him and blazed over for the touchdown." (PD) Nick's perfect kick extended the Adams lead to 13-6.

A stunned West Tech was down but indeed not out. After being held on downs following the ensuing kickoff, the Carpenters received a huge break when a penalty against Adams during the punt gave Tech a first down at the John Adams 31-yard line. Tech made a first down at the 19. On third and six from the Adams 15, Dick Bonde went to the air in an attempt for the score, but Nick Barille picked off the pass at the one and returned it 34 yards down the sideline before being tackled.

On second and eighth from the 37-yard line, Nick Barille tossed a pass to halfback Ross Randazzo. Randazzo hauled in the ball, then "twisted and squirmed and shook off tackler after tackler to get to the West Tech 17."(PD) Randazzo's spectacular 46-yard pick-up came on the final play of the third quarter.

Angelo Barille opened the final period by picking up 3 yards for the Rebels. His brother Nick burst over right guard for 9 yards and a first and goal at the 5. After Ross Randazzo picked up three more yards, Nick Barille blasted into the end zone. Nick was sacked trying to pass for the extra point, but his team now enjoyed a commanding 19-6 advantage.

Most of the game was played at the West Tech end of the field. Late in the game, the Carpenters could advance to the Adams 22, but the Rebels' Bob Young ended that drive with an interception on the game's final play.

In what can only be called a stunning upset, the John Adams Rebels had defeated the mighty West Tech Carpenters to capture their first city football championship. Coach Kozak's team had played tough and hung in there when West Tech was on a roll in the first half, then completely shut down the Carpenters in the second half.

The best player on the field that day was John Adams halfback Nick Barille, who did it all on offense and defense. On offense, he led both teams with 17 carries. Although he netted only 26 yards rushing, Nick was able to punch over two touchdowns. He added a third touchdown on his only pass reception of the afternoon and kicked one extra point.

Nick only completed one pass in six attempts, but that 41-yarder set up the game's final touchdown. On defense, Barille's two interceptions and one fumble recovery were key to stopping West Tech's scoring drives. Had there been such an MVP award, Nick Barille would have been a unanimous choice.

In 1938, the John Adams Rebels were again in the thick of the East Senate race, but on Oct. 28, they were upset by East High, 12-0. That would be their only league loss, but it would be enough to cost them the East Senate title as the Rebels finished in second place.

In 1939, the Rebels hoped to regain the East Senate and city championships that had eluded them the year before. John Adams opened its season on Sept. 16 with an independent contest against Holy Name. The only points of the game came in the first quarter. Rebel halfback and sprint star Larry Evans showed how quick he was by sweeping around the right end and outracing the Green Wave secondary 85 yards for a touchdown. Adams halfback Angelo Consolo "hurdled over the center of the line for the extra point" (PD) to give John Adams a 7 to 0 victory. Adams snagged its second win the following week, a victory over South High.

Beginning its East Senate schedule on Monday, Oct. 2, John Adams defeated Glenville 28-6. Again, Larry Evans dialed long distance with a 54-yard touchdown scamper, while Angelo Consolo went 50 yards for another score. Consolo also had three extra-point conversions in the game. The Rebels made it two East Senate victories in one week by defeating East Tech 13-0 that Saturday. Fullback Steve Jadlowsky accounted for both John Adams touchdowns on short runs.

Two weeks later, John Adams maintained its thin lead over Cathedral Latin in the East Senate race by beating East High 13-2. The following week, each of the East Senate's three leading teams came through with easy victories. John Adams put away Benedictine by a 26-6 score, the Rebels' touchdowns coming from long distance on runs of 46, 50, 51, and 52 yards. Cathedral Latin defeated Central High 24-7, while Collinwood beat John Hay 25-6.

On Saturday, Nov. 4, John Adams and Collinwood squared off in a decisive game. Collinwood jumped to an 8-0 lead after one quarter on a touchdown and a safety, but after that, it was all John Adams. Touchdowns by Angelo Consolo and Steve Jadlowsky in the second quarter gave the Rebels a 12-8 halftime advantage, while a fourth-quarter touchdown by Consolo sealed the victory.

John Adams' 19-8 victory over Collinwood had just assured the Rebels of the East Senate crown. On Saturday, Nov. 11, the Rebels made it official by trouncing Central High, 36-0. Team captain and halfback Angelo Consolo led the attack by scoring four touchdowns as Coach George Kozak's Rebels became the first team in the 15-year history of John Adams High School to finish the season undefeated and untied with a record of 8-0-0.

The 1939 Charity Game card was now set. South High (7-1-1) would represent the West Senate, while John Adams (8-0-0) would try to uphold the honor of the East Senate. Both teams were gunning for a second Charity Game victory in as many tries, South having defeated Shaker Heights in 1933, while Adams had downed West Tech in 1937. This was also a big neighborhood rivalry, as both schools hailed from Cleveland's south side. Adams had already defeated South in a close game, 12-6, back in September, and it was imperative for the Flyers to even the score as the two teams were not scheduled to play each other in 1940.

With several good running backs, Adams relied almost exclusively on its ground game. The Rebels had two games in which they did not throw a single pass and two others where they went to the air twice. Fullback Steve Jadlowsky and halfbacks Angelo Consolo and Larry Evans led the attack for the Rebels. Jadlowsky, who could pound the ball up the middle, was the head coach George Kozak went to whenever he needed critical yardage. Angelo Consolo was "a low-charging, tricky type of runner" (PD) who knew how to elude would-be tacklers. Evans was the "speed merchant" (PD) out of the Rebel backfield, specializing in end sweeps and reverses. This high-stepping track star was hard to bring down and, once past the line of scrimmage, even more challenging to catch.

A good running game needs good blocking up front, and Adams had it, starting with its quarterback, Bob Koeth. Koeth was an accurate blocking back who never once carried the ball the entire season, but his blocks made it possible for the rest of the backfield to do their job. Leading the linemen were two of the best pulling guards in Cleveland, little Elmer Camaglia (5'2" and 147 pounds) and Johnny Scacutto. At the same time, tackle John Brograno was rated by coach Kozak as one of the best high school tackles he had ever seen.

The day of the Charity Game, Saturday, Nov. 25, was a typical early winter day in Cleveland. The temperature remained in the 30s all day, with clouds drifting by but no precipitation. The switch to the all-Senate make-up of the game had paid off in the attendance department as, for the third consecutive year, more than 40,000 high school football fans would brave the cold on Cleveland's lakefront and pile into Municipal Stadium there to see the 10th edition of Cleveland's Charity Game to decide both the Senate ("one of the largest and strongest scholastic leagues in the nation" (PD)) and Cleveland scholastic football championships. Many in this highly bi-partisan crowd hoped to see South High achieve one of those rarities in sports – going from dead last (0-6-0) one year to champion the next.

As usual, everything proceeded on schedule, and following the playing of the national anthem, the game got underway promptly at 2:15 p.m. Midway through the first quarter, John Adams got one of the first breaks of the game when the Rebels intercepted a South High pass. Moving into Flyers' territory, Adams advanced to the South High 33-yard line. Halfback Angelo Consolo then started on what appeared to be an end sweep, but he stopped suddenly and flipped a pass to halfback Larry Evans, standing alone at the 18-yard line. Evans gathered in the aerial and ran untouched into the end zone. The extra point try failed, but John Adams had taken an early 6-0 lead.

Another turnover, this time in the second quarter, would lead to the game's second touchdown. The Flyers recovered an Angelo Consolo fumble, one of five for Adams in the first half. The running and passing of Flyers' halfback Clarence Jarosz and the blocking of quarterback Merrill Fiori sparked the Flyers as they moved deep into the John Adams end of the field. On first and goal at the Rebels 3-3-yard line, the South drive appeared to stall as two straight running plays failed to gain ground. However, an off-side penalty against Adams put the ball less than a yard from the goal line, from where Clarence Jarosz went over right guard and into the end zone for the game-tying points with less than five minutes remaining in the half. The Flyers also failed to make the extra point, and the half ended in a 6-6 tie.

So far, the game has been running quite close to how the first meeting between these two teams went back in September. However, all of that would change shortly after the intermission.

After a nice return, John Adams received the second-half kickoff and began to play on its 35-yard line. The Rebels moved quickly down the field, and on the eighth play of the drive, Larry Evans "blasted around his left end for 22 yards and a touchdown." (PD)

The Flyers now trailed 12-6. They were down but still very much in the game. But then disaster struck. Shortly after Evans' touchdown, both Clarence Jarosz and Merrill Fiori of the Flyers were knocked out of the game with injuries. "Not only had the Flyers lost two of their outstanding players…, but they suffered a severe psychological blow." (PD)

The Flyers could hang on throughout the rest of the third quarter, keeping the score at 12-6, but the bigger Adams team was now beginning to wear them down. On the third play of the fourth quarter, Rebels junior halfback Bob Lazzaro gave Adams six more points on a touchdown run around his left end. South went to the air to score quickly, but Angelo Consolo picked off an Ed Olsheski pass at the Adams 40-yard line and returned it 29 yards to the South High 31-yard line. Four plays later, Angelo Consolo put the ball into the end zone with a 9-yard run. This time, the extra point try by John Biagiano was successful, and Adams' lead had ballooned to 25-6.

Both coaches started to empty their benches: Adams' Coach George Kozak because he had the big lead, and Flyers' Coach Ed Unger because his front-line players were getting worn out.

Late in the final quarter, Rebels second-string center Jicha intercepted another Ed Olsheski pass at midfield. When the John Adams drive stalled at the South 24-yard line, the Rebels returned to the air. This time, fullback Steve Jadlowsky "whipped one straight over the scrimmage line to (Bob) Lazzaro, who was grinning as he passed the last line." (PD)

The extra point try failed. Three plays later, the game was over, and John Adams had won the 1939 Charity Game, its 31-6 victory earning the Rebels their second city title in the last three years. South had given all it had, but the loss of both Clarence Jarosz and Merrill Fiori crippled the offense, while John Adams wore down the stellar Flyers' defense incredibly late in the game.

It would be almost 40 years before John Adams played for a Senate championship again. In 1977, representing the East Senate, the Rebels lost to West Senate champ Saint Ignatius, 27-0, in the Senate Championship game – but better days were just over the horizon.

Due to a labor dispute within the school district, there were no Senate championship games in 1978 or 1979. However, when championship play resumed in 1980, the John Adams Rebels were ready.

1980, the Rebels had a tough time in their non-Senate games, but they went through their current South Senate schedule without a stumble. They closed out league play on Oct. 30 by defeating John Marshall, 20-6. In that game, quarterback Lamont Walton completed 12 of 19 passes for

293 yards, three touchdowns, and a two-point conversion. Walton's primary receiver that day was Greg Jeffries, who hauled in a half-dozen passes for 208 yards and a pair of touchdowns. That victory, the Rebels' 16th consecutive South Senate win, sent John Adams to the Senate championship game, where they would face East High.

The Senate championship game was held on the afternoon of Nov. 7 at John Marshall Field. Adams took a quick 6-0 lead when running back Curtis Jackson scored on a 1-yard plunge just three minutes into the game. Adams had recovered an East High fumble at the East 30-yard line, then gave the ball to Jackson on seven consecutive plays, his last carry good for the score.

Despite that fast start, those would be the only points scored by either team in the first half. In the second half, the Adams defense continued to shut down and shut out East. Meanwhile, Lamont Walton put the game away with three touchdown passes, two of which were caught by Greg Jeffries, as John Adams went on to win the Senate title, 28-0.

The Rebels next won the South Senate championship in 1983, but in the Senate championship game that season, they lost to Glenville 28-6.

The following season, 1984, the John Adams Rebels were again in the thick of it for the South Senate title. On November 1, they defeated South High 27-6 at John Marshall Field to capture their second consecutive South Senate banner. In that game, South took a 6-0 lead with just 13 seconds left in the first quarter, but the Rebels tied the score in the second quarter by blocking a South punt and then returning the loose ball for a touchdown. The second half was all John Adams as the Rebels outscored the Flyers 16-0 to win the South Senate championship. Running back Darryl Mathews led the Rebels that day, carrying the ball 22 times for 182 yards, two touchdowns, and a two-point conversion.

The following week, the Rebels were back at John Marshall Field to face Collinwood in the Senate championship game. John Adams led at the intermission on a couple of touchdown passes from Rodney Best to Paul Thomas. Collinwood cut the Adams lead in half, 12-6, with a touchdown in the third quarter. The Rebels came right back and answered that score with one of their own on a 21-yard run by Darryl Mathews to take an 18-6 lead. Collinwood would score another touchdown to cut the lead to 18-12, but that would end the scoring as the Rebels returned with the Senate championship.

John Adams running back Darryl Mathews ended the season rushing for 1,001 yards and scoring 10 touchdowns.

In 1989, in head coach Gene Young's 19th season at the helm, the Rebels appeared to be headed for another South Senate title when they were upset by South High 26-14. When the season ended, South, John Marshall, and John Adams all had 4-1 league records. John Adams was selected to play in the Senate championship game by Senate rule because South and John Marshall had been to the game more recently than the Rebels.

The championship game was held on Nov. 3, and the Rebels' opponent would be Glenville's Tarblooders. After the first quarter, Glenville held an 8-0 lead, but that score was very deceiving. Over the next 2+ quarters, John Adams went on a 42-0 run to take an insurmountable 42-8 lead. Glenville came back with a couple of late touchdowns to make the score a bit more respectable, but when the final whistle was blown, John Adams had won the Senate championship by 42-20. Leading the way for the Rebels offense in this game was running back Pierre Sledge, who in 26 carries amassed 170 yards and three touchdowns. Quarterback Jonathan Allen chipped in by completing eight of 17 passes for 206 yards and two touchdowns while running for a third TD.

GYMNASTICS

John Adams enjoyed only success in boys gymnastics in 1937, when the team scored 18 points and finished second at the state meet behind champion East Tech. All the team's points came on three state championship performances, the only gymnastics state championships ever won by John Adams High School. Leading the way was Bailey, an outstanding gymnast who won state championships on both the long horse and the parallel bars. The team's other state championship was won by Adkins, who took home the top trophy in tumbling.

TRACK

Once the school opened in 1923, it took the John Adams Rebels six years to register points at the state track meet and capture the team's first individual state championship. In 1929, with a total of 8.1 points, the Rebels finished in ninth place. Leading the way was Jusak, who tied for first place in the high jump with a leap of 6'¼", followed by Prybe, who tied for third in the same event. Milligan finished third in the mile run.

It would be seven more years before the Rebels had another thinclad stand atop the podium. In 1936, Sam Goldman won the shot put with a toss of 49'9-1/8". Three other boys finished in the points to give Adams a sixth-place finish. Five years later, the Rebels had their third track state champion when Ben Payne won the 100yd dash in 1941 with a time of 10.1 seconds; Payne finished second the following year.

Ten years later, John Adams would begin a run of success that would see the team bring home a pair of state team championships in six years and many individual state titles. This success started in 1951 with a young man named Leon Pryor. Pryor set a state record of 19.6 seconds in winning the 180yd low hurdles; he then finished second in the 120yd high hurdles. Closing out a very successful state meet, Pryor joined teammates John Razdzierski, Frank Leath, and Burl Owens in winning the mile relay. The team totaled 17 points and finished in fourth place.

Burl Owens scored John Adams' only point at the 1952 state meet when he finished fifth in the 440-yard dash.

It would be quite a different story for Coach Mel Brodt's Rebels at the 1953 state meet. The team would score in seven different events, and they needed every point they earned. John Adams held off Springfield High by just one-half point, outscoring Springfield 27-26½ to win the team's first Class A state championship. Richard Danko and Luke Owens played a large part in the Rebels' victory. Danko won the 880-yard run with a time of 1:59.9 and finished third in the mile run. Luke Owens won the discus with a throw of 150'2½", then came back to finish second in the shot put. The team also scored big points in the 440-yard dash when Burl Owens finished second and Marshall Laney came in fourth. The mile relay team added a fourth-place finish to the winning point total.

In 1954, the Rebels finished in sixth place, but the mile relay team of Swann, Howell, Leonard Sims, and Marshall Laney won the gold medal with a time of 3:26.4.

The 1956 Class A state track meet was one of the closest ever. Coach Mel Brodt's team finished first with 19 points, but they had to share the title with the team from Akron North, which also scored 19 points. Right on the heels of these two teams was East Tech, with 17 points. E.N. Butler led the way for the Rebels, who won the mile run at 4:28.6. Tyrone Smith finished second in the 880yd run, and the 880yd relay team also came in second. Carl Sanford finished third in the 100-yard dash, while the Rebels' mile relay team came in fourth.

In 1959, the Rebels, now competing in Class AA, won their first individual state championship in three years when Choice Phillips won the mile run in 4:29.0. Right behind him in second place was teammate Darnell Mitchell. Mitchell also finished fourth in the 880-yard run, as these two boys accounted for all 12 of John Adams' points in a fourth-place finish.

In 1960, the Rebels scored 22 points to third place. This time, Darnell Mitchell won the mile run with a time of 4:25.1, and he finished second in the 880yd event. Charles Dawson brought another gold medal by winning the 120yd high hurdles in 14.7 seconds. He also finished fourth in the 180yd low hurdles to complete the team's point total.

The following 15 years were pretty lean for the John Adams track team, but they did manage to bring home a couple of state championships. In 1965, Harold Kimball won the 440-yard race with a time of 49.5 seconds. At the 1968 state meet, the John Adams mile relay team set a new record by winning the event at 3:18.2. Murcelle Leeth, Sidney Delooch, Larry Ramsey, and Bryan Jones ran on that record-setting team.

At the 1976 Class AAA state meet, the Rebels of Coach Dave Demming only scored in three events, but they made the most of it to win their third state championship, tying Alliance High School atop the scoreboard with 28 points. The Rebels two relay teams each finished first. The 880yd relay team of Anthony Thompson, Michael Murray, Gary Simpson, and Roy Hairston finished in a time of 1:28.5. The mile relay team of Murray, Hairston, Jeffrey Craft, and Stephen Davis raced around the track in a time of 3:17 flat. Closing out the team's scoring, Stephen Davis finished second in the 440-yard dash with a time of 47.5 seconds.

In 1979, the 440-yard relay team set a new state record by winning their event. Marty Freeman, Bryan Cleamons, Bryan McKinley, and Eric Anderson crossed the finish line in 42.9 seconds.

Under the direction of Coach Claude Holland, the Rebels won their fourth state championship in 1982 with a total of 32 points. (Coach Holland was a Rebels track alumnus, having run in the state meet for John Adams in 1973.) However, like their state title six years earlier, the Rebels had to share top honors with another school, this time Cleveland Heights. Kevin McKinley and Bill Jones were leading the way for the Rebels. McKinley won the 110m high hurdles with a time of 13.89 and finished second in the 300m low hurdles. McKinley and Jones were also on the state championship 800m relay team, and Bernard Strong and Henry McKnight won the race in a 3:19.03. Bill Jones added to his team total with a fourth-place finish in the 800m run.

After failing to score a single point in 1983, the Rebels came roaring back in 1984, scoring 26 points and finishing in fourth place. Harold Madox and Melran Leach led the way for John Adams. Madox won the 400m dash with a time of 47.35 seconds and finished fourth in the 200m. He and Melran Leach were also part of the 1600m relay team that took home the gold medal, along with Paul Thomas and Donald Taylor, in 3:13.57. Leach added to his team's point total with a fifth-place finish in the 100m dash.

After 1984, the school would earn just a few more gold medals and no state championships. In 1986, when the Rebels finished second, they did so by winning just one event. As they had done so often in the past, this came in a relay, the 4x400m to be exact. The winning time of 3:17.20 was made by Anthony Morgan, Ken Rucker, Shelby Redding, and Jeff Mason. Two of these runners, Ken Rucker and Shelby Redding, were part of the 3200m (4x800m) relay team that won the school's successive gold medal in 1988, the other half of that team being Kevin Chambers and Lorenzo Thomas.

The Rebels' last gold medals came in 1991 when John Adams ran in Division I. Unsurprisingly, three relay teams earned all of the Rebels points as they scored 28 and tied Cleveland Heights for second place. The team of Senghor Hobbs, Damione Williams, Joe Harman, and Antonio Cook won the 4x100m race with a time of 42.01 seconds. The Rebels also took home the gold in the 4x800m relay race, with Thurman Tyus, Wesley Edrington, Charles Weaver, and Donte Johnson crossing the finish line in a state meet record time of 7:44.29. Closing out the team's point total was the 4x400m relay team of Damione Williams, Frank Clark, Donte Johnson, and Clarence Howard, which finished in second place just a hair over a second behind Cleveland Heights.

TRACK (GIRLS)

The Ohio girls high school track and field state championships did not begin until 1975. During the first three years of the state tournament, John Adams did not qualify for the event. However, in 1978, the Lady Rebels burst onto the scene at the state tournament in a big way. The team's success, extending from 1978 until 1995, can be attributed to two factors: an outstanding head coach and several dozen outstanding athletes.

The coach of the John Adams girls track team was Monica Gary, a 1966 John Adams grad. Gary taught at John Adams from 1973 to 1995 and was the girls track coach from 1976 to 1995. During her 20 years of coaching at John Adams, Gary's teams won three state championships, finished as runner-up two other times, and produced numerous individual state champions who set many state meet records. She was named the Ohio Coach of the Year in Girls Track and Field in 1983 and served as the Ohio Head Coach at the Midwest Meet of Champions in 1986 and 1987. After leaving the Cleveland schools, Gary was an assistant track coach at Purdue University from 1999 until 2012.

At the 1978 state meet, the Lady Rebels scored 40 points to outdistance Euclid High School and its 33 points. Two outstanding relay teams led the way for the Rebels, both of which set state meet records in winning their event. The first meet record of 3:57.6 was set by the 4x440yd team of Querica Jackson, Twyla Scaly, Emma Edmonds, and Rochelle Nelson. The second meet record came in the 4x880yd medley relay with a time of 1:46.3, joining Sealy, Edmonds, and Nelson, along with Karen Kirtley, who were on that relay team. The team's other points came in the 440yd dash (second), the 4x110yd relay (fourth), and the 4x220yd relay (second).

With many identical girls still on the team, the Rebels returned in 1979 to win the state championship again, scoring the most points, 48, that any John Adams team would ever score at the state track tournament. As in the previous year, the relay teams would lead the way. The 4x880yd medley relay team of Deborah McMillon, Karen Kirtley, Emma Edmonds, and Rochelle Nelson would tie the school's meet record again, winning with a time of 1:46.3. The 4x440yd team of Nelson, Querica Jackson, Brenda Butts, and Peola Jefferson would win with a time of 4:00.6. Rochelle Nelson added a third gold medal to the team's total by winning the 440yd dash in 56.4 seconds. Adding to the team's point total was a third-place finish in the 220-yard dash, a second place in the 4x110-yard relay, and a fourth in the 4x220-yard relay.

Over the next 13 years, the Rebels enjoyed varying degrees of success, finishing as high as second in 1987 and 1992. Along the way, there are also outstanding examples of individual achievement. For instance, in her three years on the team, Marlene Flanagan would earn All-Ohio honors five times, topping her career in 1982 by winning the 100m low hurdles with a time of 14.61 seconds. From 1985 to 1987, Geneva Bivins never won a gold medal, but her steady performances earned her All-Ohio recognition no less than seven times.

In 1987, John Adams' team was the state meet runner-up, scoring

34 points. Cleo Anderson finished 2nd in the discus with a throw of 135 feet 3 ¼ inches. The 4x100m relay team of Benita Hobbs, Debra Malone, Sheila Smiley, and Bivins, along with the 4x400m relay team of Hobbs, Tonja Workman, Marie Lassiter, and Smiley, earned 2nd place finishes. Adding to the team's point total was Bivins, with 4th in the 100m and 3rd in the 200m.

In 1988, the Rebels finished in eighth place, but the team of Tonja Workman, Marie Lassiter, Tangetta Miller, and Debra Malone brought home the gold in the 4x400m relay at 3:52.89. Malone also scored points by finishing fourth in the 300m hurdles. The following year, in 1989, the 4x400m relay team repeated their state championship title, with Kelley Jones and Selena Murray joining Miller and Lassiter in the winner's circle. This same year, Tangetta Miller finished third in the 800m, and Marie Lassiter finished third in the 400m.

Despite 1991 being a rebuilding year for the Lady Rebels, Tangetta Miller and Kelley Jones ambitiously aimed to compete in the state meet final. With much hard work and double dedication, John Adams was able to have two athletes compete together in the 800m state meet finals. Miller returned to the podium by finishing second, while Jones finished fourth.

The years 1992 through 1994 came as they did at the end of the first era of John Adams. High School proved to be three of the most successful years for John Adams girls track, and this success was pretty much due to the accomplishments of one of the greatest track stars, girl or boy, in the history of Senate athletics.

The Rebels finished second place at the 1992 state track meet with 29 points. Had it not been for sophomore runner Carmen Banks, however, John Adams would have been shut out of any points as Banks scored all of her team's points. Carmen won the 200m dash with a time of 24.66. She then showed the state what it could expect over the next two tournaments in the hurdling events. She won the 100m high hurdles with a time of 14.16, then took home gold in the 300m low hurdles with 42.59 seconds.

At the 1993 state meet, Carmen Banks was again at the top of her game and contributed to all 22 points of her team, which was good enough for a fifth-place finish. While winning the 100m low hurdles (14.48) and the 300m high hurdles (43.83), Carmen took fifth place in the 200m dash and was on the 4x400m relay team that came in eighth.

In 1994, John Adams tied for the state championship with Magnificat High School, scoring 38 points. Once again, Carmen Banks led the way; this time, she outdid her previous performances. For the third consecutive year, Banks won both the 100m high hurdles (13.89) and the 300m low hurdles (41.80), but this time, she set a new meet record in both events; in fact, her time in the 300m high hurdles was the fastest in the nation that year. She also finished second in the 200m dash and was a member of the 4x200m relay team that finished in third place.

Carmen Banks earned All-Ohio status 11 times in three state tournaments, seven with state championship performances. That puts her in rare company with the legendary Jesse Owens, who earned All-Ohio 11 times. During her career at John Adams, Carmen set or tied 11 indoor and outdoor state records; her hurdling times are still among the state's all-time top 10. Upon graduation, she ran track at the University of Texas and was a longtime track coach at John Hay High School.

The 1995 track season would be the last for the Lady Rebels, with the school closing in 1996. Nonetheless, the girls went out with another top-10 finish in the state meet, scoring 18 points for a ninth-place finish. Leading the way was Candace Nicholson, a three-year veteran of the team who had already won All-Ohio recognition four times. Candace won the 800m race at 2:09.50, tying the state record. She added two more All-Ohio finishes (for a career total of seven) by running on the 4x200m and 4x400m relay teams, which finished in fourth place.

WRESTLING

The high point of John Adams High School wrestling came from 1940-1958. During those 19 seasons, the team consistently finished among the top five teams at the state tournament and produced 11 state champions.

The first Ohio high school wrestling tournament was held in 1938. John Adams did not participate that year or the next, but in 1940, the Rebels made their debut at the tournament in a big way. Steve Homolak finished second at 105, and Ignatius Jarzynski won the state championship at 122.

Team standings were not kept at those first few state tournaments, but team standings were kept beginning in 1941. Despite not having an individual state champion, the Rebels finished fourth in 1941 and 1942. The team scored no points in the next two tournaments, but in 1945, the Rebels again finished fourth, mainly due to Burman winning the state championship at 146. In 1946, the Rebels had their best finish to date when they came in third on the strength of second-place finishes by Dick Stack (128), Tom Grepher (166), and Ed Ferris (Heavyweight). The boys again finished fourth in 1947.

In 1948, the Rebels slipped to a tie for fifth place. Their success came from a pair of state championships won by Sciria at 113 and Fazio at 128.

The 1949 and 1950 state tournaments would be two of the best for the John Adams Rebels and feature the most outstanding wrestler in school history. 1949, the Rebels again tied for fifth place despite having four wrestlers earning points. Leading the way was Ed Casalicchio, who won the state championship at 128. The following year, 1950, the Rebels would have their best finish at the state tournament, scoring 18 points and finishing second place behind West High. Leading the way was Attillo Russo, who won the state championship at 104; he had finished third at that weight the year before.

He also brought home a state championship, and his second was Ed Casalicchio at 128, the only wrestler in John Adams history to win two state titles. Casalicchio earned All-America as a wrestler at Michigan State University in 1953, winning NCAA and AAU championships. Ed would later use his high school and college wrestling skills as a coach and referee. Ed Casalicchio is considered one of Cleveland's all-time great high school grapplers.

For the fourth consecutive year, the Rebels brought home an individual state championship in 1951, when Julius Competto won the state title at 113. Two years later, the team finished in third place, with one fourth-place finish, three second-place finishes, and a state championship at 134 by Angelo Incorvaia.

From 1954 through 1957, the Rebels did not have a state champion but finished among the state's top seven teams each year. The 1958 season would be the last year of any substance for John Adams wrestling. That year, the team scored its most points in the state tournament, 32, and finished fifth. Leading the way were two boys who had been Adams wrestling stalwarts for the past few seasons. Luke Grady was winning the state championship at 145, improving his second-place finish of the previous season. Thomas Kilroy also won a gold medal at 165, improving his fourth-place finish at the last year's state tournament.

In 1969, the John Adams grapplers won the East Senate championship and the first City Wrestling tournament, becoming the City Wrestling Champions.

CHAPTER 14

John Hay High School

John Hay High School opened on East 107th Street in September 1929. The school was then called a "commercial" school, offering business, commerce, and various office skills courses. For this reason, about 85% of the early students were girls; redesigning the school's curriculum attracted more boys in the 1950s and 1960s. Based on the courses taught at the school, the school's athletic teams were initially nicknamed the Bookkeepers but later changed to Hornets. The school closed for 2008 and part of 2009 to be remodeled, opening again in the fall of 2009. John Hay has had several students attend college on scholarships; some have played professional sports.

John Hay High School joined the Senate Athletic League during the 1937 expansion.

BASKETBALL

John Hay won the Senate boys basketball championship three times. In early February of 1987, under the guidance of head coach Chris Lett, the Hornets defeated West Tech 68-59, giving them a league record of 9-1, good enough to win sole possession of the North Senate championship for the first time in school history. One week later, on February 13 – Friday the 13th, the Hornets took the court against John Adams in the 50th Annual Senate Championship game. Shooting a sizzling 55% and leading throughout, the Hornets won their first Senate League championship by a score of 67-55. The team would go on to win the Cleveland South Class AAA sectional tournament with a 65-51 win over Shaker Heights High School, but their tournament run ended at the Maple Heights district with a 69-58 defeat at the hands of Cleveland Heights High School.

The Hornets' next chance at a Senate League championship came in 1993. They finished the league season tied with the John F. Kennedy Eagles with identical 10-1 records. In the four-team league tournament, both teams won their semifinal games. Meeting for the Senate City Series championship, the Hornets easily defeated the Eagles 69-46 to win their second championship while raising their overall record to 15-3.

Moving on to state tournament play, the Hornets won the South High sectional with a late come-from-behind win over Glenville, 72-71. In a South High district semifinal game, the team would struggle to get by John F. Kennedy. Taking advantage of numerous Kennedy fouls, the Hornets won this one at the foul stripe by converting 31 of 51 free throws. All-Ohio (Special Mention) sophomore Ruben Patterson connected on 23 of 35 foul shots and led all scorers with 36 points. The Hornets 'tournament run would end in the district finals with a loss to Cleveland Heights.

In 2011, the Hornets defeated Glenville 68-57 to win their third Senate League championship. Now playing in Division II, the team was made the #1 seed at the Kirtland sectional/district tournament. Raising their record to 13-8, the Hornets defeated Perry High School 55-53 in the sectional final. In the district final, the Hornets defeated Lake Catholic 72-45, raising their record to 15-8 and advancing to the Canton regional tournament for the first time in school history.

Meeting Struthers High School (21-2) in a regional semifinal game, the team of Coach Christopher Sanders moved to within three games of a state championship with a 74-60 win. In the regional title game, the Hornets would play a tournament veteran, St. Vincent-St. Mary of Akron High School (SVSM). It was a close game all the way, and entering the fourth quarter, the Hornets trailed by just a single point, 37-36. Then disaster struck as the Hornets missed their first six-quarter shots and committed two costly turnovers. Midway through the final quarter, SVSM had built its lead to 51-38. The Hornets fought back but had fallen too far behind; they lost by a final score of 59-53, finishing with a record of 16-8. Devon Carter was named the Division II Lakes District Player of the Year, finishing with a 20.1 points per game average.

BASKETBALL (GIRLS)

Coach Yvonne Renee Wright, head coach at John Hay, achieved a high success rate. At John Hay, Coach Wright led the Lady Hornets to two consecutive Senate Varsity Basketball Championships and one District Championship Basketball runner-up.

VOLLEYBALL

Coach Yvonne Renee Wright led the Lady Hornets to five Senate Varsity Volleyball Championships.

FOOTBALL

From the beginning, John Hay was a member of the Senate League, but it took quite a while before the Bookkeepers/Hornets had any success on the gridiron. However, success in the league finally came their way in 1982.

Despite losing their non-league games, the Hornets were undefeated in the North Senate that season. On Oct. 29, they defeated Collinwood 14-6 to secure at least a tie for the North Senate championship. Senior tailback Anthony Austin put the Hornets ahead with a 53-yard touchdown run on the game's second play. He later sealed the deal for Hay with a one-yard TD plunge in the third quarter. Austin totaled 125 yards in 15 carries during the game, along with his two touchdowns, which was good enough to earn him a spot on that week's Plain Dealer "Dream Team."

The following week against East High, Austin put his team into the lead with a 55-yard touchdown run in the first quarter. The Hornets added another touchdown in the second quarter for a 12-0 lead at halftime. That would be the final score, giving John Hay its first North Senate title.

On Nov. 12, John Hay and John F. Kennedy high schools met at John Marshall Field for the All-Senate championship. In a defense-oriented battle, the score was 0-0 at the half and still 0-0 after three quarters. At 7:36 of the fourth quarter, Kennedy was back in punt formation. With the snap of the ball, the John Hay defense came storming in, and the kick was blocked. Hornets' linebacker Averette Hagler picked up the loose ball and raced 42 yards untouched into the end zone for a John Hay touchdown. The extra point was missed.

Those would be the game's only points as John Hay won the Senate championship, 6-0 — the first championship of any kind in football for John Hay High School. Head coach William "Sonny" Harris was named the North Senate Coach of the Year. Anthony Austin, who ended the season with 1,014 yards rushing, 11 touchdowns, and a two-point conversion, was named the North Senate MVP and a Cleveland All-Scholastic.

Following the reopening of the school in 2009 after its remodel, John Hay resumed football under the direction of head coach Rodney Decipeda. In 2012, the Hornets went undefeated, 7-0, in Senate play and tied Glenville for the league championship (the two teams did not meet during the season). The team finished 1-2 in its non-league games for an overall record of 8-2. This record was good enough for the Hornets to finish fourth in the OHSAA Division III, Region 9, computer rankings and to qualify for the postseason state playoffs.

Several outstanding players would be leading the Hornets in their first playoff game. Running back Carlin Ray led the team with 877 yards rushing (a 12.2 yards per carry average), 17 touchdowns, and a team-high 32 pass receptions; he also excelled in the classroom with a 3.7 GPA. Sophomore quarterback Mylik Mitchell threw for 1,737 yards and 20 touchdowns, with only four interceptions. Fullback/middle linebacker Latif Hughes gained 849 yards. Senior defensive back Royce Griffin had 22.5 sacks - and a 4.5 GPA.

John Hay's opponent in its regional quarterfinal game was the team from Ravenna High School (6-4). Ravenna took a 7-0 lead in its first series of games. The Hornets later answered with a touchdown of their own but failed to make the extra point. Ravenna then pushed its lead to 13-6. Late in the third quarter, Hornets QB Mylik Mitchell completed a 31-yard pass to Deon Colvin that was good for a touchdown. John Hay then went for the lead with a two-point conversion try, but that effort was no good, leaving the Hornets down by just a single point, 13-12. Neither team scored over the game's final 14 minutes, and John Hay dropped a heartbreaker, 13-12.

In 2013, John Hay had another playoff-worthy season. The Hornets opened by splitting the two non-league games on their schedule, defeating Toledo Start, 49-8, then dropping a wild game to Norwalk High School, 56-36. They then went through their Senate schedule, winning seven in a row before dropping a 49-24 decision to Glenville. Finishing with an 8-2 record, the Hornets again qualified for the playoffs, this time in Division IV.

The Hornets' regional quarterfinal opponent was the Cardinals of Youngstown's Cardinal Mooney High School. John Hay put up an intense battle, but the Cardinals' defense was too strong and their offense too potent, and the Hornets fell 45-20.

The Hornets ended the season with 460 points or 41.8 points per game. They were led by running back Demarius Sanders, who scored 23 touchdowns and had a 3.66 GPA.

Under head coach Rodney Decipeda, the Hornets posted a record of 65-50 from 2009 to 2019 and qualified for the postseason twice. With the Hornets, Coach Decipeda showed that a team of talented kids in the classroom can also be winners on the gridiron.

TRACK

The two best years for John Hay's track came back-to-back in 1977 and 1978. Participating in the Class AAA state meet in 1977, the Hornets scored nine points to finish 18th. Leading the way was hurdler Anthony Hancock, who finished in a tie for fourth place in the 120 high hurdles and sixth in the 180 low hurdles. Also chipping in with some team points was shot putter Ravawn Harris, who finished in fourth place with a toss of 57'3½".

The following season, the Hornets had their best finish at the state meet. Scoring in four events, including three state championships, the Hornets amassed 36 points, completing the season in second place, just two points behind state champion Mansfield Senior High. Anthony Hancock won the 120 hurdles race in 13.6 seconds, while speedster Ricky Reynolds took home the gold in the 100-yard dash in 9.8 seconds. The team's third gold medal came from the 880-yard relay team; Sam McClain and Kevin Mondie joined Hancock and Reynolds on that team.

TRACK (GIRLS)

For the first time in John Hay's history, the 1988 Girls Track Team was State runner-up in the 4x200 meter relay race. The track team of 1988-1989 comprised girls with purpose, vision, and skill. This group was motivated and worked hard together, persevering to make something meaningful happen. uring those two seasons, the girls accomplished many accolades, ranging from City Outdoor Champions, City Indoor Champions, Cross Country Champions, Regional Champions, and State runners-up. The John Hay Girls 4x200 relay team was state runners-up for two consecutive years.

Returning the next track season with three seniors: Bostick, Carroll, and Gullett. The 4x200 meter relay team was without Angeliette. Natasha Townsend came and competed for the open spot. Natasha ran her race, and with her talents and ability to compete at the highest scholastic level, we MISSING TEXT!!

The girls track team captured its second State runner-up title in 1989 with team members Andrea Bostick, Tia Carroll, Wanda Coleman, Joyce Crosby, Angeliette Drake, Monique Gullett, Charlotte Hill, Sonja Ivey, Trennace Jones, Kim Kelly, Yvette Newby, Cija Russell, Iyonna Russell, and Natasha Townsend. Ending their senior year successfully, seniors Bostick, Carroll, and Gullett competed in the Midwest Meet of Champions at Butler University, placing second place in the 4x100, and Monique placed 6th place in the open 200.

In 2011, Chanitta Westbrooks, a freshman at John Hay, took sixth place in the 100m at OHSAA State Meet. As a senior at the OHSAA State Meet, she placed eighth in 200m and finished seventh in 100m. She was named the team's MVP three times and Cleveland Plain Dealer Athlete of the Week.

WRESTLING

John Hay High School played a key role in the earliest days of the state high school wrestling tournament. The tournament started in 1938, and the first tournament was held at John Hay High School. The first 17 tournaments were of the "invitational" variety, with 10 to 22 teams being asked to attend. Beginning in 1955, any school with a wrestling team could attend the tournament if it qualified through the preliminary rounds.

With Hall of Fame coach Harold Kester guiding the team, John Hay's wrestlers dominated the earliest days of the tournament. No official team champion was declared for the first tournament in 1938. Still, the Hay wrestlers did very well, led by star wrestler Joe Incorvaia, a 135-pound, three-time Cleveland high school wrestling champion who went undefeated from 1936 through 1938. Incorvaia continued winning at the state tournament by taking the state championship at 135. Joining him at the top of the podium was Bridar, who won at 95 pounds. Rounding out the team's point total was Labeck, who took third place at 106, and Chojnicki, who finished fourth at 165.

1939 would begin the heyday of John Hay wrestling under Coach Kester. Hay would win three state tournaments and four of the next five.

The 1939 state tournament found Harold Kester's John Hay grapplers win their first state championship with 23 points, ahead of four teams tied for second place with 14 points each. Frank Grankowitz won the team's lone gold medal at 145, but three boys came in second: Pete Brdar (115), Iggy Jarzinski (125), and Sam Ranaldo (135). Patrick Scrima added the team's final points with a third place at 165.

In 1940, the team scored only 21 points, but it was enough to bring home the school's second consecutive state title as the boys beat out Shadyside High School by just one point. This time, the Hay wrestlers took home the title with two firsts and two third-place finishes. Tom Davis won the state championship at 135, while Jerome Brentar took the gold at 165. Herbert Discont (140) and Tony Fatica (185) finished third.

In 1941, Kester's team made it three-in-a-row by again defeating Shadyside, this time by a score of 26-21. Phillipe (115) and Herbert Discont (135) finished first in their weight class, while Dominic Russo (104), Costro (155), and Jerome Brentor (165) all came in second.

The team scored its most points thus far, 29, at the 1942 state tournament, but that was only good enough for a third-place finish. Leading the way were first-place finishers Louis Russo at 122 and Art Hays at 145.

The 1943 state tournament would see John Hay set a team record for points scored and gold medals won, leading to the school's fourth state championship of the last five seasons. With 38 points, the Hay team easily out-distanced second-place West Tech with 24 points. Leading the way were three gold medalists: Gene Perchan (121), Louis Russo (128), and Frank Schmidt (155). Adding to the team's total were silver medalists Pete Catavolos (132) and Mahusky (139), plus a third-place finish and two fourth-place finishes. The team scored eight weight classes for a truly well-rounded state championship victory.

The following year, John Hay and West Tech again finished atop the state tournament podium, but their finishes were reversed this time. John Hay managed 28 points, which was good enough for only a second-place finish, while West Tech totaled 39 points to take the championship. Mike Stanik (134) and Louis Lekas (139) both won state titles for John Hay.

While the glory days of John Hay wrestling were now over, a couple of boys would still bring individual glory to the wrestling team. In 1947, Dick Walsh would win gold in the 186 lbs. category. Ian McEwen won the first of his two state championships the following year at 139. In 1948, McEwen would win his second state title, moving up a notch to 146.

In 2019, nationally renowned and Wrestling Hall of

Fame high school wrestling writer Pat Galbincea (John Marshall, 1965) was asked to name the best Senate League wrestlers ever. Two of those wrestlers came from John Hay High School:

Louis Russo – Two-time state champion, at 122 pounds in 1942 and 128 pounds in 1943.

Ian McEwan – Two-time state champion, in 1948 at 139 pounds and 1949 at 146 pounds.

TENNIS

Bob Binns Jr. was the Ohio High School Athletic Association's singles tennis champion 1968.

CHAPTER 15

John F. Kennedy High School

John F. Kennedy High School opened in 1965 in the Lee-Harvard area on Cleveland's southeast side. The current enrollment is slightly less than 700. The mascot is the Eagle, and the school colors are red, white, and blue.

BASKETBALL

The John F. Kennedy boys basketball team took a few years to establish itself in the East Senate. Still, the team finally broke through and won its first league championship in 1974, led by Lawrence Boston with teammates Wilber Lauderback, Daniel Smith, Johnny Bruce, and Daniel Walters. Unfortunately, a city title would have to wait, as the Eagles lost 61-51 to Saint Ignatius in that year's city championship game. Nine years later, in 1983, the Eagles again made it to the Senate championship game, dropping a close 57-55 decision to Glenville. It would be another 10 years before the Eagles played in another Senate title game, only to have their championship hopes dashed 69-46, this time by John Hay.

The Eagles fans had to wait another 15 years to see their team play for the Senate championship, but it was well worth the wait this time. JFK defeated Rhodes in a 2008 Senate League semifinal playoff game, raising its record to 13-4 and setting up a showdown with Senate power Glenville (16-1). The Eagles were coached by William Marrow Sr., who was in his seventh year coaching the Eagles — and in all of those years, not one of his teams had ever defeated the Tarblooders.

Unsurprisingly, Glenville grabbed the early lead and carried it into the halftime break; early in the third quarter, the Tarblooders had pushed their advantage to 11 points, 39-28. It was then that the Eagles started their comeback. Late in the fourth quarter, the Eagles pulled even with the Tarblooders but could never quite get over the hump. With just 14 seconds left on the game clock and the Eagles down by a point, 57-56, sophomore

William Marrow II swished a three-pointer from the baseline that gave Kennedy a thrilling 59-57 victory.

Coach Marrow's first win over Glenville was a thriller, and his son William had made it happen with his game-winning buzzer-beater. Senior guard Bryant Blair led the Eagles scorers with 16 points, while forward Fed Chatmon added 11 points and had eight blocked shots.

Postseason honors included Leonard Patterson being named the Northeast Lakes District Division II Co-Player of the Year. In contrast, head coach William Marrow was named Division II Co-Coach of the Year.

Four years later, Coach Marrow's team was at it again. This time, there was no doubt about who the king of the Senate Athletic League was. The Eagles came through their 2012 league schedule undefeated, then won their Senate playoff semifinal game to advance to the championship game against East Tech. The Eagles jumped out to a 15-5 lead by the end of the first quarter and never looked back. Their lead ballooned to 39-18 at the half, from where the Eagles cruised to a 67-55 victory and the team's second Senate League championship. Leading the team to victory was Saivon Jefferson, who scored 19 points and 20 rebounds. The coach's son, Jordon Marrow, was named the Senate League MVP.

FOOTBALL

No school is expected to have its sports teams at the top of its league standings from the first year, but the John F. Kennedy Eagles football team came close. For a team that had only played varsity football since 1966, the Eagles were already knocking on the door of East Senate dominance by the time the 1968 season rolled around.

As usual, the 1968 Senate divisional championships race would be very close and spirited, especially in the East Senate. There, Benedictine and John F. Kennedy High Schools would battle down to the last minutes of the season.

These two teams opened their seasons on Friday night, Sept. 6, with non-league games. Benedictine and St. Edward played to a 12-12 tie. The Eagles of John F. Kennedy were not as fortunate in their opener. Traveling to Steubenville to take on the Big Red, the Eagles fell behind early and dropped a 28-6 decision.

Just a few weeks into the season, Kennedy (2-0-0, 2-1-0) and Benedictine (1-0-0, 1-1-1) were still undefeated in league play, tied with Glenville (1-0-0, 3-0-0) atop the East Senate. Glenville had opened the season with three consecutive victories, but injuries would take their toll on a team without much depth, and they would eventually finish in third place.

Over the next several weeks, John F. Kennedy and Benedictine would feast on the division's second-tier teams, winning three league contests. This left the Eagles with a 5-0-0 record in the East Senate and tied them with Benedictine (4-0-0) for the divisional lead. The last three weeks of the season would indeed be interesting.

On Oct. 25, Kennedy played a non-league game, traveling to Barberton to take on the Magics. The Eagles took a 7-0 lead in the first quarter, then added a pair of touchdowns in the second half, giving Kennedy a 21-0 victory. The next day, Benedictine returned with a 30-0 East Senate victory over John Adams. That win left Benedictine and Kennedy dead-even atop the East Senate at 5-0-0, setting up their big showdown the following Friday – Halloween night!

It would be a crucial game for both teams, especially for Benedictine. The Bengals needed to win this game and had to defeat the resurgent Glenville Tarblooders the following week to win the East Senate title. The road to the stadium for the Charity Game was a little easier for Kennedy. Since a victory the following week against East Tech was all but a sure thing, the Eagles only needed a tie with Benedictine to win their first trip to the Charity Game. (If Benedictine and Kennedy ended the league season with identical records, the team that had not been to the Charity Game the longest would go. Since Kennedy had never played in the Charity Game, a tie would go to the Eagles.)

The game between the Eagles and the Bengals was incredible, one dominated by defense, where "the defenses were better than the offenses" (PD). Most of the game was spent somewhere on the Kennedy side of the midfield stripe. Benedictine reached the Eagle's 10-yard line in the first quarter, but the Eagle's defense rose to the challenge and denied them the end zone. In the second quarter, the Bengals reached the JFK 35 and 19-yard lines, while the Eagles made it to the Benedictine 43, but again the defenses prevailed. Kennedy would again make it to the

Bengals 43-yard line in the fourth quarter, but they would never get beyond that marker. Benedictine penetrated as far as the Kennedy 22 and 28-yard lines in the second half, but the Eagles defense kept them from the end zone again. On the game's last play, Benedictine's Gary Barnes stood in the end zone awaiting the pass from quarterback Frank Petruziello, but four Kennedy defenders leaped to bat the ball down. The game had incredibly ended in a 0-0 tie.

Following the game, Kennedy head coach Vic Hanchuk was carried off the field by his jubilant players. They knew that barring the upset of the century, they would be playing in Municipal Stadium on Thanksgiving morning – in only their third year in the Senate.

And there would be no upset the following week. Against East Tech, JFK's Robert Douglas took the opening kickoff on his 19-yard line and returned it 81 yards for a touchdown. The Eagles added another first-quarter touchdown, then exploded for 32 points in the second period en route to a 58-14 victory.

Benedictine held off a determined Glenville team, 7-0, but that victory was bittersweet for the Bengals. They had tied Kennedy for the East Senate title, but the Eagles would attend the Charity Game.

In the days leading up to the Charity Game, the local papers seemed to be making this a "classic battle" between the West Senate's Saint Ignatius (7-0-0, 9-0-0) defense and the John F. Kennedy (6-0-1, 7-1-1) offense. However, they could just as quickly have taken it the other way.

Being the new kids on the block without much of a reputation to fall back on, the John F. Kennedy Eagles did not get as much "ink" throughout the season as some of their more well-known adversaries, but they did have an excellent team. The defense of head coach Vic Hanchuk's Eagles was among the best in the area. They had allowed only 63 points for openers all season, and 28 of those were scored by Steubenville in the Eagles' first game. Since then the Eagles defense, especially the first-team defense, had been almost perfect; that unit had not allowed a touchdown since John Adams scored against it back on Sept. 21. the Eagles had registered four shutouts in their last six contests.

Leading the Kennedy defense was a trio of players who were among the best in the city at their respective positions. All-Scholastic Linebacker Larry Ford, a two-year starter, was the team's leading tackler, possessing exceptional speed, which made him especially effective whenever he was called upon to blitz. Another All-Scholastic selection, Malory "Mal" Stoudenmire, was the big man of the Eagles at 6'3" and 225 pounds. His name sounded like one you would find on one of Walter Camp's turn-of-the-century All-America teams, and he played like it. Stoudenmire was a two-way tackle with tremendous lateral movement and a remarkable ability to penetrate the opposing backfield. He also did all of the team's punting (41-yard average) and kickoffs and had booted eight placements in 10 attempts. Guard Charles Coats, also a two-way performer, was another key member of the Kennedy defense who, according to Coach Hanchuk, "does a majority of our trapping at long side guard."

Filling out the Eagles' first-team defensive unit were linemen Rennie Jones, Jack Adams, Joe Sharp, and Jerome Robinson and defensive backs Asbery Wilkerson, Larry Harris, and Bob Douglas.

Coach Vic Hanchuk's offensive unit scored 227 points during the season, but 158 came in only three games. Nonetheless, the Eagles had an offense that could not be taken lightly. Leading the offense was the team's third All-Scholastic selection, quarterback John Pighee. He was "a double threat with his ability to run or pass when he rolls out" (PD). Pighee was a left-handed thrower, described by his coach as a "take charge guy." Although the Eagles did not pass very often, Pighee threw seven touchdown aerials. When he decided to take off with the ball, Pighee was equally effective, scoring another eight touchdowns.

Joining Pighee in the backfield would be a few speedsters: Harry Banks, Bob Douglas, and Joe Sharp. Unfortunately, the Eagles would have to play the Charity Game without their best running back, Walter Davis. Davis had rushed for over 800 yards and led the team with 62 points scored; but, on Monday, Nov. 11, Davis was in the hospital for an emergency appendectomy, thus ending his football season. Coach Hanchuk tapped Bob Douglas to fill in for Davis, but as Hanchuk said, "Douglas will give us more speed, but we'll miss Davis' size, his power running and blocking."

Although the experts seemed to believe that the Saint Ignatius defense was its strong point, the Wildcats offense was nothing to sneeze at. The Wildcats scored 273 points during the season, extending their current winning streak to 17 games, and, unlike Kennedy, Saint Ignatius had been very consistent, scoring at least 21 points in all but their first game. The first-team Wildcats defense, like the Eagles, was hard to score on. Fully 75% of the points allowed by the Wildcats, and they had only allowed 84 all season, were scored in the fourth quarter when the game was usually well in hand and the reserves were seeing some action.

The 1968 Charity Game would be one of the best played. Unfortunately, it was played under perhaps the worst conditions in the 38-year history of that classic. The weather was terrible. It had rained several days before Thanksgiving Day, and a cold, steady downpour fell throughout the game (temperature in the low 40s). Although the playing surface had been covered with a tarpaulin until just before kickoff, the notoriously poor drainage at Municipal Stadium resulted in a cold quagmire, with at least an inch of standing water in most places. Scorecards were useless, and just minutes into the game, everyone on the field was caked with mud. To their credit, most of the 17,582 hearty fans who attended the game stayed until the end, and they were rewarded with a great game.

Saint Ignatius was on the receiving end of the opening kickoff. With the ball at the Wildcats 29-yard line and the field still, in relatively decent shape, halfback Chuck Kyle broke out of the Saint Ignatius backfield and went racing toward the Kennedy goal. Kennedy's Larry Harris finally caught up with Kyle and hauled him down at the Eagles 9-yard line after a 62-yard pickup. On first and goal from the 9, quarterback Don Pfeil again gave the ball to Kyle. Dashing through a huge hole, Kyle sped toward the goal line. Cutting at the one, Kyle smashed right into the Eagle's Bob Douglas. The collision jarred the ball loose and fell into the end zone. Kyle "recovered quickly to scramble forward and pounce on the ball" (PD) for a touchdown. Larry Berridge's placement sailed wide, leaving the Wildcats with a 6-0 lead.

Despite the terrible playing conditions, which only worsened by the minute in the steady rain, the Eagles returned. After the Saint Ignatius kickoff, the Eagles advanced the ball to the Wildcats' 44-yard line. Running a post pattern, end Asbery Wilkerson got behind the Wildcats' defense and caught quarterback John Pighee's pass at the 17-yard line. Wilkerson then outraced the Wildcats to the end zone for the game-tying touchdown. Mal Stoudenmire's placement also sailed wide, leaving the score deadlocked at 6-6.

Following the Kennedy kickoff, the Wildcats again went on a drive, marching from their 29-yard line to a first and goal at the Kennedy 5. The Eagles defense dug in, and on the first play of the second quarter, Chuck Kyle's fourth-down smash was stopped less than a yard from the end zone.

Late in the second quarter, the Eagles were again on the move. On second and three at the Saint Ignatius 41-yard line, Eagles assistant coach Mourad "Moose" Topalian sent in the play. Quarterback John Pighee "slipped a short screen pass to Harry Banks, who hugged the sideline before breaking loose and cutting down the middle and across the goal line" (PD) for the go-ahead touchdown.

Pighee then tossed a pass to Asbery Wilkerson for the two-pointer and a 14-6 Kennedy lead with just 1:08 left in the half.

During the halftime intermission, while the rain continued to fall on the field, the players in both locker rooms could do little more than wipe the mud off their hands and face in preparation for the second half.

With the field now in terrible shape, it was unsurprising that neither team threatened to score in the third quarter since the players could do little more than "slip about the field" (PD). If either team had an advantage, it probably went to Kennedy, as Mal Staudenmire's punts kept the Wildcats bottled up on their end of the field. The game progressed through the third quarter and into the fourth, and still, neither team could generate much in the way of offense.

With 7:50 left in the game, the Wildcats took over the ball at their 28-yard line. Quarterback Don Pfeil very patiently began to move the team. Since the "deplorable condition"(PD) of the playing field meant that long passes were out of the question, the Wildcats went to their two-minute offense, mixing runs with short passes; during this drive, Pfeil would complete six of 13. Finally, with a fourth and goal at the Kennedy 1-yard line, it was do-or-die time for the Wildcats. At the snap of the ball, the Wildcats offensive line, in the mud and muck, somehow got off a significant surge that pushed the Kennedy defenders backward. Following his line, Pfeil plunged over for the touchdown, completing an incredible 21-play drive that consumed better than five minutes. But even with the touchdown, the Wildcats still trailed by two points.

He sprinted to his right when the ball was snapped to Pfeil for the two-point attempt. Pfeil looked to his two primary receivers, then to receiver Roger Weir, standing before a Kennedy defender; Pfeil threw the pass to him. It was a low and very low throw, but Weir caught it just before it hit the mud. The official stood there and immediately lifted his arms, signaling that the conversion attempt was good. The Wildcats had tied the game at 14-14!

There were now just over two minutes left in the game.

Following the Wildcats kickoff, the Eagles could not move the ball, and with just 47 seconds left to play, Saint Ignatius regained the ball at its 46-yard line. The Wildcats went for the win, but Kennedy's Asbery Wilkerson intercepted Don Pfeil's pass at the Eagles 11-yard line with just 11 seconds remaining.

Kennedy also went for it all on their first-down play, trying a long pass that fell incomplete. With five seconds left in the game, it is time for one last play. Coach Vic Hanchuk explained his final play call: "With five seconds left, I told Pighee to run a quarterback sneak. I'd hate to lose the championship in the last five seconds." Pighee did as instructed, crashing for a yard or two as time ran out.

What a game! This incredible game played in the worst possible conditions, ended in a 14-14 tie.

Although the players on both teams were initially upset about settling for a tie, it seems fitting that they could both call themselves city champions—and no one would ever fault them for leaving off the "co-."

Six years later, in 1974, Kennedy would again be playing for the city championship, and again, it would be against the Saint Ignatius Wildcats. The game was played on a bitterly cold Saturday, Nov. 16, at John Adams Field. This was the third time that these two teams had met on the gridiron, Kennedy having defeated the Wildcats 14-8 in the final game of the 1971 season. The Eagles took advantage of an interception to take a 6-0 lead early in the first quarter, but by the halftime break, the Wildcats had moved ahead 19-6.

Saint Ignatius was on the receiving end of the second-half kickoff, but the Eagles fumbled and recovered the kick. Kennedy promptly scored a touchdown on its very first play. The Eagles missed the extra point try but cut the lead to only 19-12. The Eagles then added another touchdown by junior quarterback Clifford Varmall to make it a 19-18 game. Still, the Saint Ignatius defense batted down his pass attempt for the go-ahead two-point conversion. There would be no more scoring in the game, the Eagles falling by just a single point, 19-18.

The following season, 1975, the Eagles again won the East Senate title, this time clinching it with a win over East Tech on Nov. 7. This gave Kennedy a 6-0-0 Senate mark and 6-2-1 overall. The Eagles would now play West Tech for the Senate championship one week later at John Marshall Field.

During the first quarter of that championship game, miscues by the Eagles offense gave West Tech some early scoring opportunities. However, the Kennedy defense came to the rescue and held the Warriors to three field goal tries. Two of those were successful, giving West Tech an early 6-0 lead, but it could have been much worse.

After that shaky start, the Eagles settled down, while injuries began to take their toll on the Warriors.

Late in the first quarter, the Eagles finally dented the scoreboard on a 35-yard touchdown run by Ken Agee. Quarterback Keith Elam put his team ahead by running in the two-point conversion. Elam scored on a 1-yard run in the second quarter to expand the Kennedy lead to 14-6.

That was all the scoring for the game, and the Eagles came away with a 14-6 win. In large part, the Eagles can thank their defense for that victory, as the "D" unit held West Tech to just 96 total yards, only 20 yards through the air.

That season, head coach Roye Kidd, who would lead the Eagles for 39 years before retiring in 2007, was named the East Senate Coach of the Year.

For the third consecutive year, in 1976, the Eagles played for the Senate championship but again lost to the Saint Ignatius Wildcats, this time by a 23-8 score.

During the decade of the 1980s, the Eagles would play in the Senate championship game three more times. In 1981, they played Lincoln-West for the championship. That game was relatively close, 16-7 at halftime, but the Eagles exploded for 32 second-half points en route to a 48-13 win. The results were not as good in 1982 when Kennedy lost a close game to John Hay, 6-0. The story was similar in 1985, when the Eagles dropped a heartbreaker to Collinwood, 13-12.

Kennedy did not play in the Senate championship game again until 1998. That year, the Eagles had to overcome a furious South High comeback in the game's final 10 minutes to win the South Senate title, 20-18. The Eagles (7-1, 7-3) then faced Glenville (8-0, 9-1) for the Senate championship.

This was a hard-fought, defensive battle that was still 0-0 at halftime. Glenville managed a touchdown at 1:40 of the third quarter to take a 6-0 lead. Those would be the game's only points as Kennedy dropped the 6-0 decision.

In 2010, the Kennedy Eagles would achieve something few Senate teams have done: Led by head coach Scott Wodtly, the Eagles qualified for the OHSAA playoffs. Playing in Division II, Region 6, they finished with a record of 7-3, which was good enough to claim the sixth spot in the Region 6 computer standings. In a regional quarterfinal game, the Eagles played Olmsted Falls High School, also 7-3. The Eagles gave it their best shot but came short in a 41-12 loss.

2011, the Kennedy Eagles were moved up to Division I, Region 1. They improved to 9-1 and again qualified for the postseason. By finishing eighth in the Region 1 computer rankings, the Eagles would be playing the number-one seed in a regional quarterfinal game. In 2011, the Mentor Cardinals would be led by quarterback Mitch Trubisky. In this game, Kennedy quarterback Antonio Howard completed 12 of 21 passes for 162 yards and a pair of touchdowns to Marcus Martin. Unfortunately, those touchdown passes did not come until the fourth quarter, when the Eagles were already trailing by a large margin. The final score found Kennedy on the short end of a 48-16 score.

TRACK

For a new school, it did not take the John F. Kennedy Eagles long to make a mark for itself at the boys state track meet. In 1967, just two years after the school opened its doors, the Eagles finished fifth in the Class AA state meet. The team scored all of its points in just two events. In the 880-yard run, Jim Epps won the race with a state record time of 1:54.4, while his teammate, Bill Barrow, came in third. The team's other points came in the mile relay, which was won with a time of 3:18.9. Running on that team were Walter Davis, Asbury Wilkerson, Neverlin Fletcher, and Jim Epps.

The following year, the Eagles did even better at the state meet, scoring 13 points and finishing in third place. Leading the way was Kevon Blocke, who won the 880-yard run with a time of 1:54.5. The team's other points came from a second-place finish in the 880-yard relay and a third-place finish in the mile relay.

The high-water mark for the Eagles track came in 1969. Coached by Walt Killian, the team won every track meet it entered that year, topping it off by scoring 16 points and winning the state Class AA championship in only its third year of participation. Bob Douglas led the way by winning the 180-yard low hurdles with a time of 19.4 and finishing second in the 100-yard dash. The mile relay team scored the rest of the Eagles' points with a first-place finish in 3:19.8; Luther Sharp, Barry Alvis, James Lawrence, and Asbury Wilkerson were running on that championship relay team.

The following year, 1970, the Eagles again scored 16 points, but this time, it was only good enough for a fourth-place tie. Leading the way was the 880-yard relay team of Alan Tyler, Michael Brown, Bill Curry, and Joe Edmonds, who took the gold with a time of 1:27.8.

JFK boys track Coach Harold Kimball, with 35 years of coaching experience, guided more than 75 All-Ohio track athletes during his years at JFK. He finished his career with a team that became the Ohio Regional Runner-up in 2004, scoring a team-record 21 points; the Eagles finished in seventh place. His last team in 2005, a senior-led team, finished very high in the state scoring, led by new head coach Reggie Walker. Leading the way was Marcus Wilkerson, who won the long jump competition with a leap of 23'5¼". Wilkerson would also finish second in the long jump the following year and run in sixth place, finishing the 4x100m relay team.

The Eagles' last big "hurrah" at the state meet came in 2006. Without winning a single event but scoring points in five, the Eagles set a team record of 28 points and finished in fourth place. Tyrone Bolden finished second in the high jump (6'7") and third in the long jump (22'5¼"), as well as running the second leg on the 4x100m relay team. Also scoring multiple points for the Eagles was Anthony Thomas, who finished fourth in the 200m dash, sixth in the 100m dash, and running the anchor leg in the 4x100m relay.

The Eagles' last individual state track championship came in 2012 when Antwon Smith won the 400m dash with a time of 47.44.

TRACK (GIRLS')

When the first girls state track and field meet was held in 1975, the Lady Eagles were there to grab a bit of first-year glory. That year, Michele Stevens won the shot put competition with a heave of 18'2¼". Not only was that the first state championship for one of the Lady Eagles, but it remains today the only state title won by a Kennedy High School Lady Eagle.

It would be another 15 years before the Kennedy girls track team scored another point at the state meet, and it would all be the result of literally one outstanding athlete. In 1990, sophomore Donneika Kibble finished eighth place in the 200m run, scoring her team's only point. At the state meet the following year, Kibble finished third in the 100m dash and fourth in the 200m event. Her 10 points were again the total for the Kennedy team, good enough for a 15th-place finish.

In 1992, Donneika was at it again. She finished second in the 100m dash, fourth in the 200m dash, and ran the anchor leg on the 4x100m relay team, which finished in sixth place. The team scored 13 points, the most ever by a Kennedy girls track team at the state meet, and Donneika Kibble had a hand in all of them.

Easily the best athlete to ever compete for the Kennedy girls track team, Donneika Kibble earned All-Ohio recognition seven times, more than any other male or female athlete in the history of John F. Kennedy High School.

CHAPTER 16

John Marshall High School

The history of John Marshall High School stretches back to the late 1890s. When the area known as West Park (initially called Rockport) grew large enough, a high school was built at West 152nd Street and Lorain Avenue. The school was known as West Park High School until the West Park/Rockport area officially became a part of Cleveland when the school's name was changed to John Marshall High School. In late 1930, a new school site was found at the corner of Viola Avenue and West 140th Street, and the new John Marshall High School opened in 1932. The school was known for academic excellence and various extracurricular activities. 2013, the original 1932 building was torn down, and the new building opened in 2015.

John Marshall High School, formerly a member of the Greater Cleveland Conference, joined the Senate Athletic League during the league's significant expansion in 1937.

This chapter has been greatly aided by the book The History of John Marshall High School, Cleveland, Ohio, written by the late Ralph A. Pfingsten. This book can be purchased through the West Park Historical Society.

BASKETBALL

John Marshall High School had an excellent basketball team from the first time it began play in the old Greater Cleveland Conference in 1923. The Lawyers took the league championship that first year and won six titles over the 13 years, including three in a row in 1934-35-36. The last half-dozen of those years would be under the direction of head coach Alfred "Bud" Millsom, who would guide the John Marshall boys basketball team for a quarter of a century, from 1928 to 1952, winning numerous league championships in both the Greater Cleveland Conference and the Senate. Coach Millsom has been inducted into the John Marshall Hall of Fame.

The competition on the court got much stiffer when Marshall joined the Senate Athletic League in 1937 as a member of the West Senate, but the Lawyers did not give up their winning ways. Four years into the newly aligned West Senate, the 1940-41 season, the Lawyers showed the new league that John Marshall High School could play with the best of them. By the middle of February 1941, the Lawyers had moved into first place with a league record of 5-0 (10-1).

On Feb. 28, the Lawyers (6-0 in the West Senate) faced West Tech (5-1 in the West Senate) for the divisional title. The game was low-scoring, with the Lawyers trailing 15-13 at halftime, but the Lawyers came back to outscore West Tech 20-14 in the second half for a 33-29 win.

Next up for John Marshall was the city championship game at Public Hall in downtown Cleveland, its opponent to be the East Senate champions from Glenville High School. Glenville also had a clean record in league play, 8-0 (11-1), so an intense, close game was expected. But such was not to be the case. The Lawyers jumped out to a 13-4 lead, expanding that lead every quarter to bring home the city title with a 54-26 final. With that victory, John Marshall became the first West Senate team to win the Cleveland basketball championship since the Senate had expanded in 1937.

The Lawyers had another shot at a championship the very next season. On Feb. 20, 1942, the Lawyers got a scare from Lincoln but managed to keep their record clean with a 33-31 win — Marshall's 14th consecutive Senate victory. They lost their final West Senate game of the season, but their 6-1 league record was good enough to hold on to first place.

On March 16, the Lawyers (6-1, 10-1) would again meet Glenville (8-0, 12-0) for the city championship. Leading the Lawyers would be three returning starters from the 1940-1941 team: center Clarence Urbanek and guards Dan Deimling and Ed Kruger.

The game played at Cleveland's Public Hall before a near-capacity crowd of over 5,100, was a thriller from start to finish; more than three points never separated the two teams. Glenville led 7-6 after the first quarter, with Marshall gaining a point advantage at the half, 13-12. The game was deadlocked at 19-19 at the end of the third quarter. After a couple more ties, Marshall went ahead 25-23 on a Clarence Urbanek tip-in and never trailed again. When the final whistle sounded, Marshall had won the game 33-32. The Lawyers had played the entire game with only six players.

It would be seven years before the Lawyers again were in the hunt for West Senate and city honors. On Feb. 16, 1949, undefeated John Marshall clinched the West Senate championship with a 42-40 win over Lincoln. Five days later, the Lawyers took the court at the old Cleveland Arena before a crowd of 9,714 for the city championship against East Senate King, Central High. With time running out, Central took a 40-38 lead, but baskets by Marshall's Jerry Harriman and Ralph Burton gave the underdog Lawyers a 42-40 win and the Cleveland championship.

It would be several decades before the John Marshall Lawyers again wore a championship crown, but they did have some outstanding players, especially during the 1950s. Jim Gorsline broke the school scoring record on Feb. 6, 1954, with a 32-point effort against Norwalk High School. That remained the school record for about three seasons until the arrival of one of Marshall's all-time great basketball stars, Ralph Kistenmaker. On Dec. 14, 1957, Kistenmaker shattered Gorsline's record when he tossed in 39 points against West High. Known as "one of the first of the new generation of deadly jump shooters," Ralph averaged more than 21 points per game. At the end of the season, Ralph was named to the 1958 All-Scholastic First Team and an All-Ohio Honorable Mention.

Kistenmaker's record lasted just over a year, for in January 1959 the Lawyers' Bill Hoge eclipsed the record with a 40-point game against West High.

The 1980-1981 season produced what many consider Marshall's all-time best team, yet ironically, the Lawyers did not even win the South Senate championship that season. All season, they battled John Adams for the league lead. When the two teams met in January 1981, Adams returned with a 71-62 win to take sole possession of first place; the two teams remained 1-2 in the South Senate and the city rankings. They had their rematch on Feb. 13, Friday the 13th. John Adams poured in an incredible 32 points in the first quarter to jump to an early lead. Despite Dave Colbert's 36-point effort, the Lawyers could never catch the Rebels, and Adams came away with an 85-74 win that kept Marshall in second place. John Marshall's best team could not get by John Adams best team.

In that season's state playoffs, Marshall won sectional and district titles, advancing to regional play for the first time. The Lawyers were scheduled to play Lorain Southview in a regional semifinal game. Unfortunately for the Lawyers, they would have to go up against Southview without two of their players, one of whom was their top scorer (24 ppg), who had been suspended from school. Despite this handicap, the Lawyers played a tremendous game, leading 18-16 after the first quarter, pushing that to 33-26 at the intermission. The game was close throughout the second half, but with 3:11 to play, Southview took a 52-51 lead. Despite Dave Colbert's game-high 28 points, the Lawyers were never able to get back on top, dropping out of the tournament with a heartbreaking 59-57 defeat. (Ironically, John Adams would send Southview back to Lorain in the regional finals.)

Dave Colbert was named to the All-Ohio Second Team.

In 1985, Joe Barron, the Senate League MVP, would lead the Lawyers to the South Senate championship, but they would lose the overall league title to Glenville, 65-49. Marshall would end the season with an excellent 17-3 record.

Under the direction of head coach Andre Battle, the Lawyers won the 1989-90 South Senate championship. Led by South Senate MVP David Poe, they then defeated Collinwood, 91-39, for the overall Senate League championship. That 52-point margin of victory is a record for a Senate championship game. The Lawyers finished the season with a record of 17-6.

After winning the South Senate title again in the 1990-1991 season, the Lawyers defeated Lincoln-West, 68-57, for the overall Senate championship. They advanced to the district finals in the state tournament, only to drop a thriller in overtime to Saint Ignatius, 71-69. Dean Gavan was named All-Ohio Honorable Mention for the 19-4 Lawyers.

BASKETBALL (GIRLS)

During the 1922-1923 school year, when John Marshall High School was still known as West Park High, the girls basketball team finished 18-1 and went undefeated in the Cleveland girls basketball tournament to win the city championship. The girls would not be retaken to court for almost 50 years.

In 1993, John Marshall star April Mixon was the Most Valuable Player in the City Series. That season, she averaged 20.2 points and 4.6 steals, surpassing the 1,000-point mark for her career. Mixon earned Division I All-Ohio status as a Special Mention. Her outstanding play also earned her All-City and All-District honors for three years.

Two years later, the Lady Lawyers had another outstanding player in Vita Redding. Setting school records of 1,658 career points, 723 points in a season, and a single game high of 47 points, Redding was named the Senate League's MVP, the Plain Dealer's 1995 "Player of the Year," and the Division I All-Ohio First Team. Vita was also the runner-up in the voting for Ohio's Ms. Basketball, the first Senate League player to ever be considered for that honor.

Her coach, Dave Chollet, said about Redding, "What Vita has accomplished, both academically and athletically, can serve as a great example to the kids in the Cleveland Public Schools."

Upon graduation, Vita continued her education and basketball career at Brown University. There, her basketball was even more spectacular. In her four years at Brown, she was in the All-Ivy League four times and the Ivy MVP three times. With 1,962 points scored by graduation, she was the all-time high scorer for Brown, leading her team in scoring all four years and the fourth-highest scorer in Ivy League history.

The holder of nine Brown University and/or

Ivy League records, 2016 Vita Redding was inducted into the Brown University Hall of Fame. As the notice of her Hall of Fame induction stated, Vita Redding did much more than be a good student and play basketball: "Redding also made an impact off the court as a charismatic and relatable role model for students at Fox Point Elementary School. She made a particular bond with a young girl in a wheelchair, helping her open up to social situations and showing her classmates that they could include her in the classroom's activities."

CROSS-COUNTRY

John Marshall had its first cross-country team in the early 1930s, but it only lasted a few years. The team was re-established in 1942, and success came almost immediately. Under the direction of Coach John Neubauer, the Lawyers finished in second place in 1943 with a score of 79 points. Leading the way for the Lawyers were three boys who finished among the top 20: Stavole came in second, Steinmetz finished in 14th place, and right behind him in 16th was Hasari. Stavole's second- finish earned him All-Ohio recognition, which went to the first 10 tracers to cross the finish line.

There was little success for either the team or individual runners until the 1960 season. That year, Coach John T. Dietrich led the team to a state championship with a score of 58 points. Leading the way were four runners who finished among the top 20: Ross Maclachlan came in fourth, Richard Osicka finished ninth, Robert Zizak finished 11th, and in 15th place was Robert Osicka. Both Maclachlan and Osicka earned All-Ohio honors for their top-10 finishes.

Four years later, the Lawyers did it again, winning a second state championship. Coach Roger Ramseyer's team was led by Gary Gold, who beat all runners to the finish line at 9:38.8. Bob McElroy was right behind in third place, earning All-Ohio status. The Lawyers' last podium finished in 1965 when they finished in fourth place. Gary Gold again led the team, this time with a fourth-place finish. Dave Marshall was also named All-Ohio by finishing 10th.

In 1972, Marshall's runner, Larry Coy, won the State's cross-country individual title in 9:46.

FOOTBALL

John Marshall High School, then known as West Park High School, fielded its first football team in 1919. Playing as a member of the old Greater Cleveland Conference, the team had some success from 1924 to 1936, with a winning percentage of .646 and conference championships in 1929, 1930, 1931, and 1934. With the expansion of the Senate League in 1937, John Marshall became a member of the league's Western Division (West Senate). This did not bode well for the Lawyers, who won only 21 games over the next 16 seasons. The Lawyers, however, did have at least one outstanding player during these otherwise lean seasons; that player was Walt Schultz, who was named Third Team All-Ohio as a running back in 1945.

In the early 1950s, the team's performance started to improve, and by the end of the decade, the John Marshall Lawyers were at the top of their game.

In 1959, the Wildcats of Saint Ignatius High School attempted to win the West Senate title for a fifth consecutive season. On Saturday, Oct. 3, the Lawyers opened their West Senate campaign against the Wildcats in what would prove to be a pivotal game for both teams.

It was hot and muggy that Saturday afternoon, which made it all the hotter, perhaps because the game was a defensive struggle. Late in the fourth quarter, neither team had yet to score. The Lawyers had possession of the ball at the midfield stripe. On first down, quarterback Neil James fired a long pass to halfback Cliff Schmidt at the Saint Ignatius 14-yard line. The pass fell incomplete, but the Wildcats were flagged for pass interference, a costly penalty that gave John Marshall a first down at the Wildcats 14. On the very next play, James tossed a pass to end Pete Kalikin. Kalikin caught the ball "near the sidelines on the Ignatius 7-yard line, and the speedy end scampered the remaining distance" for a touchdown (PD). Halfback Tony Rizk ran in the conversion to give Marshall an

8-0 lead with only 1:57 left in the game.

The Lawyers defense then held the Wildcats in check to preserve their 8-0 victory. That win established the Lawyers "as a definite contender in the West Senate" race (PD).

On Saturday night, Oct. 10, the John Marshall Lawyers took on Holy Name's Green Wave at West Tech Field. The game was scoreless through three quarters, but in the fourth quarter, first Marshall and then Holy Name scored touchdowns, with the Green Wave taking an 8-6 lead. The Lawyers then scored on a 23-yard touchdown pass with just 51 seconds left to play, giving the Lawyers the lead and the win.

The Lawyers of Coach Bill Moritz were now 2-0-0 in West Senate play, the only undefeated team left in the division. Over the last 13 seasons, no team had been a more significant obstacle to the John Marshall Lawyers than the Warriors of West Tech. The Lawyers had managed a single victory and tie in their last 13 meetings with Tech. Another defensive struggle for the Lawyers, the game ended in a 6-6 tie.

The fact that Marshall had escaped its game with West Tech with a tie and not a loss would loom big as the season progressed. Marshall went on to win its remaining four Senate games, the final victory a 66-0 drubbing of a hapless Lincoln squad. After the game, the pandemonium broke out among the 2,500 Marshall fans. The Lawyers, 6-0-1 in league play, had just won their first West Senate title since joining the league 29 years before, and the celebration knew no bounds. It started when the team carried head coach Moritz and his two assistant coaches, Dave Richards and John Spezzaferro, off the field and into the showers for the traditional dunking.

Everyone at John Marshall — students, faculty, fans — was celebrating the school's most significant victory, which was especially sweet for Coach Moritz, himself a John Marshall grad. But Moritz knew they should not celebrate too much since there was still one crucial and even bigger game yet to be played. That game would come in under two weeks, the Charity Game on Thanksgiving morning against East Senate champion Benedictine, also 6-0-1 in league play.

The Lawyers featured a solid defense and a balanced offensive attack. The Marshall defense had been outstanding since giving up 28 points to McKinley in the first game, posting four shutouts, and allowing an average of only 4.25 points per game over their last eight games while going undefeated with a record of seven wins and a tie. It had also limited the opposition to only a 30% pass completion rate while intercepting 14 enemy aerials, with defensive backs Cliff Schmidt (the team's leading tackler) and Chuck Bronzi snaring four apiece. The Marshall defensive line was one of the biggest in the area, averaging 208 pounds. Leading the defensive charge were tackle Tom Wilhelm (246 pounds), middle guard Jim Szilagyi (230 pounds), tackle Tom Cholley (232 pounds), and linebacker Don Heller (202 pounds), who also played guard on offense. Quarterback Neil James was a standout on defense at safety.

Although tending toward the run, the Marshall offense was very effective, whether it stayed on the ground or went to the air. This was partly due to the job done by quarterback Neil James, one of the best signal callers in Northeastern Ohio, who accounted for almost one-third of the total Marshall offense. As a passer, he completed better than 51% of his throws, good for 778 yards and 10 touchdowns; his leading receivers were halfback Cliff Schmidt and end Dave Jones. James was also very effective in directing the attack when the Lawyers switched to the option from the split-T, deftly handing off to any one of several outstanding running backs or keeping the ball himself, which he did 72 times for 204 yards and three more touchdowns.

The main running back behind James was halfback Tony Rizk, one of "the best power runners in the district" (PD). Rizk, a starter on defense at right inside linebacker, averaged just under 7 yards per carry while gaining 701 yards, scoring seven touchdowns, and eight extra points. Rizk was known for his "excellent balance and coordination" (PD), and as Coach Moritz said of him, "... when we need that first down, he gets that yardage."

Rounding out the starting backfield for John Marshall was halfback Cliff Schmidt, who also had seven touchdowns, and Gary Jesser at fullback.

The newspapers were picking Benedictine to win the Charity Game based on the school's tougher schedule and a "faster and more aggressive" (PD) line, but the season's statistics told another story. Even though they had played one less game than the Bengals, John Marshall came out ahead of Benedictine in virtually every statistical category, and, more likely than not, it was not even close. The most glaring disparity came under "fumbles" and "fumbles lost." John Marshall had fumbled nine times, losing only four. On the other hand, Benedictine had coughed the ball up an incredible 41 times, losing it on 26 occasions. If the Bengals played giveaways like that against a team the caliber of the Lawyers, their chances of winning would not be good.

The pre-game estimate was for a crowd of around 30,000 for the 1959 Charity Game, but a somewhat disappointing 23,809 showed up on Thanksgiving morning. The attendance was undoubtedly hampered by the snow and sudden temperature drop that hit Cleveland the day before. Those who braved the weather would see another Turkey Day tradition—a great high school football game.

The first quarter ended in a scoreless deadlock as the teams probed for weaknesses. In the second quarter, starting on his 25-yard line, Neil James took to the air, and the Lawyers began to move the ball. Three times during the drive, James kept it going by completing passes for first downs. Finally, with the ball resting at the Benedictine 1-yard line, James kept the ball himself and went over the left side for a touchdown. Tony Rizk tried to run in the two-point conversion, but Benedictine's big defensive line stopped him.

The half ended with John Marshall still in front, 6 to 0.

As Marshall head coach Bill Moritz later described, the Bengals "came out for the second half all charged up, and we were sluggish." That aggressive play would lead to a game-tying touchdown by the Bengals in the third quarter, but the Lawyers defense prevented the Bengals from scoring the two-point conversion.

Early in the fourth quarter, with the game still tied at 6 to 6, disaster struck the Lawyers. With the ball on his 8-yard line, Neil James dropped back into the end zone to pass. The ball sailed downfield toward the intended receiver but was instead picked off by Benedictine's Dick Kestner, who returned it untouched 15 yards for a Benedictine touchdown. Benedictine's bid for the two-pointer failed.

James had little time to think about the interception because he was back on the field after the kickoff. Four plays after the kickoff, the Lawyers had the ball at the Benedictine 40-yard line. At the snap of the ball, Tony Rizk broke downfield. With his line giving him plenty of protection, James waited for Rizk to break into the open. When he did, the ball was right there; Rizk made the catch and ran into the end zone untouched. Again, the bid for the two-point conversion failed when James was spilled short of the goal line.

With about eight minutes left, the score was back to even at 12-12. The Bengals then put on a drive, moving from their 32-yard line to the Marshall 22. Four consecutive passes fell incomplete, and the ball went over to Marshall on downs.

That was the last real threat by either team, and the game ended in a 12-12 tie. It was the fifth time the Charity Game had ended in a stalemate. In their first trip to the city title game, the John Marshall Lawyers had returned as city champions, although they had to share that title with the Benedictine Bengals.

Neil James completed eight of 14 passes for 125 yards and the big touchdown, an effort that earned him the game's MVP award. It's not a bad way to celebrate your birthday.

A few weeks later, Neil James was named to the All-Ohio Defensive Second Team at safety.

In 1960, the West Senate would mostly be dominated by the defending champion John Marshall Lawyers; however, Bill Moritz's Lawyers had a rude awakening as they stumbled out of the gate in the first couple of weeks of the season. The Lawyers opened the campaign on Friday, Sept. 16, on the road, playing the Blue Streaks of Sandusky High School, a team that handed the Lawyers a 30-12 defeat. It was more of the same the following week in Berea, where the Lawyers suffered a 30-28 defeat.

After their humbling 0-2-0 start, the Lawyers began the defense of their West Senate championship on Friday, Sept. 30, against the Lincoln Presidents. The game started slowly for both teams but ended in an offensive flourish for the Lawyers. Leading by only 8-6 at the half, the Lawyers scored once in the third quarter and then piled on 22 points in the game's final six minutes to come away with a 36-6 victory.

The Lawyers then held on for a 14-12 victory over the Saint Ignatius Wildcats and used "a pulverizing ground attack and a deadly passing game" (PD), as well as some great defense, to hand the Green Wave of Holy Name a 42-8 thumping.

Having disposed of both Saint Ignatius and Holy Name, only one real obstacle remained for John Marshall to overcome: the Warriors of West Tech High School, whom the Lawyers had defeated only once in the previous 15 years. The Lawyers and the Warriors squared off at West Tech Field on Saturday, Oct. 23. The two teams played to a scoreless tie after two quarters, the lack of scoring no doubt aided by the six fumbles that were lost, three by each team. Also, "the Lawyers could have broken the game wide open . . . but Marshall receivers dropped three perfectly timed passes by Bill Maynard in the open" (PD).

Early in the third quarter, the Lawyers began to move the ball, using "old-fashioned power football" (PD). The drive started at the Marshall 36-yard line and ended 13 plays later when halfback Dave Asp crashed into the end zone on a 4-yard burst off tackle. Asp also added the two-pointer to give his team an 8-0 lead with the clock showing 6:54 left in the third quarter.

The Marshall defense shut down Tech's running game in the second half. West Tech would gain only 26 yards rushing for the entire game versus Marshall's 177 – and the Warriors would not complete a single pass. This great defensive play was all the Lawyers needed to make Dave Asp's eight points stand up as the Lawyers came away with their third key victory in as many weeks, 8-0.

Bill Moritz's team was now starting to pull away from the pack. On Friday night, Oct. 28, the Lawyers defeated the South High's Flyers, 16-0. The following Friday, the Lawyers faced Rhodes and demolished the Rams 42-8. Having now clinched the West Senate championship, the Lawyers "tuned up for their appearance in the Plain Dealer . . . [Charity Game] on Thanksgiving morning by routing West High, 34-0" (PD). It was Marshall's 17th consecutive West Senate game without a defeat.

John Marshall had now clinched the West Senate title and the right to play the East Senate champion in the Charity Game. However, the East Senate race ended with Benedictine, Cathedral Latin, and Collinwood tied atop the divisional standings with identical 5-1-0 records – the first three-way tie in the 56-year history of the Senate. The East Senate playoffs belonged to Benedictine's Bengals, who handed Collinwood a 24-14 defeat, then took the measure of Latin's Lions, 26-18. With John Marshall still to be played for the city championship, the Charity Game would be the Bengals' fourth football game in just 14 days, but nobody at Benedictine was complaining.

While Benedictine had been battling for its life since Nov. 11, Coach Bill Moritz's John Marshall Lawyers had been resting and getting ready for whichever East Senate team would emerge as the divisional champion. Since their last game on Nov. 11, the Lawyers had the luxury of taking a few days to let whatever bruises and ailments they may have sustained a chance to heal. By Wednesday, the 16th, they were back on the practice field getting ready for the Charity Game.

The Lawyers would try to be the first public school to win or share back-to-back Charity Game titles since Lincoln High School had done that in 1941 and 1942. If Marshall could win the game, it would mark only the sixth time in the 30-year history of the Charity Game that a West Senate school had won the city title outright. As Coach Bill Moritz said, "There is no need for pep talks, signs in the dressing room, or needling of players. This is the payoff, and the boys know it."

By their coach's admission, the 1960 John Marshall football team had been a bit of a "green team" when the season had started. But after opening losses to Sandusky and Berea, the Lawyers ran off seven consecutive West Senate victories. Coach Moritz attributed this success to defense and a versatile offense. It took a couple of games for the defense to finally jell, but under the tutelage of veteran assistant coach

John Spezzaferro, the Lawyers' defenders got better with each game. With a defensive line that averaged 205 pounds, the Lawyers had held five opponents to less than 100 yards from scrimmage and had given up only 16 points in their last five games, three being shutouts. Senior captain and defensive tackle Tom Wilhelm (233 pounds) led the defensive unit, which would be named All-Ohio Second Team. Other standouts included Ken Sokal and Bob Legan at the ends, tackles Dennis Whitticar and Ron Dalberg, and linebackers Jim Ludwig, Larry Supelak, and John Weidner.

The Marshall offense featured four running backs in halfbacks Dave Asp ("lightning fast," said the Plain Dealer) and Chuck Bronzi, fullback Gary Jesser, and quarterback Bill Maynard - who could "explode on any given play" (PD). Between them, they had accounted for 2,009 yards rushing. Jesser with 741 yards and Bronzi with 642 yards were the workhorses; Asp and Jesser were the team's leading scorers with 66 and 48 points respectively.

But the guy who brought it all together was quarterback Bill Maynard, Marshall's "play-caller deluxe" (PD). Maynard was perfect for Marshall's offense, which featured a lot of rollouts and wide sweeps. His "ball handling and faking . . . reflect experience and overall competence" (Press). Coach Bill Moritz felt that Maynard was the most dangerous runner out of the Marshall backfield. When he was not pitching the ball to one of the running backs, Bill could find the holes, averaging almost 5 yards per carry. When he went to the air, which Maynard did about nine times per game, he could throw with the best of them, completing 41 of 83 attempts for 529 yards. His favorite targets were his halfbacks, Dave Asp and Chuck Bronzi, who accounted for half his completions and passing yardage.

Although the Lawyers had been picked as slight favorites in the Charity Game, Benedictine was a sentimental favorite after clawing its way through two playoff games to finally reach the big game—playoff games, by the way, in which they were the underdog both times. Again, the underdog in the Charity Game, many were looking for the Bengals to confound the "experts once more" and win.

Although both teams were physically in good shape for the Charity Game, each would be without using one starter. Benedictine tackle Kevin Phile was out with a knee injury, while John Marshall end Greg Lashutka was sidelined while recovering from an emergency appendectomy.

Thanksgiving Day, November 24, 1960, was almost perfect for a football game. The 31,545 fans who made it down to Municipal Stadium watched the game with the temperature a delightful 47 degrees. Even at 11 a.m., some fortunate enough to sit in the sun took off their coats and jackets, while those seated in the shade were subjected to the slight chill coming in off Lake Erie.

John Marshall was on the receiving end of the opening kickoff and put the ball into play at its 25-yard line. The Lawyers moved the ball steadily down the field, with all four running backs getting in on the action. Most compelling was quarterback Bill Maynard, who would roll out to his left or right, fake the throw, and turn upfield for a healthy gain. Halfback Dave Asp climaxed the drive with a 2-yard dive into the end zone for a 6-0 Marshall lead. Bill Maynard's attempt to score the two-point conversion was stopped short of the goal line.

The Marshall defense kept the Bengals out of the end zone over the balance of the first half. A first-quarter Bengals drive was halted deep in Marshall territory by an interception by the Lawyers' Seth Halley, while a Bengals march down to the Marshall 13-yard line ran out of time as the first half expired.

The key to the second half would be "Marshall's aggressive [defensive] line and alert defensive backfield" (PD). "Aggressive" is hard-hitting, resulting in a nightmarish second half for Benedictine. The Bengals had the ball on offense nine times during the entire game and lost it six times on four fumbles and two interceptions. All four fumbles and one of the interceptions came in the second half. Three fumbles came "as a result of good hard tackles by Marshall's linemen" (PD).

The Lawyers had scored on the game's first possession and had used tough, aggressive defense and some timely ball-control offense to make those six points hold up for the entire game. Bill Maynard had done an excellent job mixing up his plays, as was evident by the fact that all four Marshall running backs had almost identical totals rushing the ball. Maynard's five punts, for nearly 39 yards per kick, also helped keep the Bengals bottled up at their end of the field.

Marshall's second consecutive city championship was all its own. Coach Bill Moritz was now a perfect four for four city title games with two West Senate schools. He had been an assistant coach with Rhodes when the Rams won their city titles in 1951 and 1953, and now he had done it in back-to-back seasons with the Lawyers.

The Lawyers would not see any real Senate gridiron success again until more than 25 years later. However, from 1986 to 1993, under head coach Al Valenzisi, they dominated South Senate play and were in the thick of the Senate championship picture every season.

In 1986, the Lawyers won the South Senate title with a 4-1 league record but lost the Senate championship to Collinwood, 21-0. After missing out on the South Senate championship the following year, the Lawyers were back in the championship hunt in 1988. That season, they defeated John Adams, 39-6, to clinch the South Senate championship with a perfect record of 5-0. On Nov. 11, they met West Tech (5-0) for the overall Senate title. It was a closely contested, low-scoring game, but when the final whistle sounded, the John Marshall Lawyers won the Senate championship, 7-6.

In 1989, the South Senate title race ended in a three-way tie between John Marshall, South, and John Adams, with John Adams selected to play in the Senate championship game. The Rebels went on to defeat Glenville, 42-20.

In 1990, the Lawyers were again atop the South Senate with a perfect 5-0 record. The team's overall record for the season was 8-2, tying the team record for most victories. The Lawyers were led by senior tailback Michael Edwards, who had already rushed for 1,257 yards (60% of the team total) and six touchdowns.

The 1990 Senate championship game would feature a couple of the league's most successful teams over the last few seasons. John Marshall, representing the South Senate, had a 22-3 record over the previous five seasons. Collinwood (5-0, 7-3), representing the North Senate, had won 31 Senate games while losing just four over the previous seven campaigns.

John Marshall got a couple of early breaks when Collinwood lost a fumble on the opening kickoff, and then the Lawyers blocked a Railroaders punt deep in the Collinwood end of the field on the Railroaders' next possession. Unfortunately, despite these significant breaks, the Lawyers could only manage a field goal for an early 3-0 lead. Those would prove to be the Lawyers only points of the game as the Collinwood defense held Marshall to just 63 yards of total offense. Meanwhile, the Railroaders' offense settled down and scored three touchdowns for a 20-3 win.

The Lawyers were back at it again in 1991, winning the South Senate title with another perfect 5-0 (6-4) mark. Meeting the Lawyers in the Senate championship game would be the Glenville Tarblooders, 5-0 (7-3). Surprisingly, this would be the first time these two teams met in a football game.

The game was a thriller played on a snow-covered John Marshall Field on Nov. 8, one in which the Lawyers trailed, or were tied, throughout. With just 19 seconds left on the game clock and the score tied, 20-20, the Lawyers regained possession of the football at the Glenville 30-yard line. On first down, WR Jonathan Burrell gained 8 yards on a reverse. With just seven seconds left to play, the Lawyers had time for one last snap of the ball. Quarterback Eric Younkin took the snap from the center and fired a pass at WR Andre Burkholder near the goal line. Burkholder made the catch, twisted around a defender, and fell into the end zone for the game-winning touchdown with no time left on the clock. By a score of 26-20, the John Marshall Lawyers had won the 1991 Senate League championship with one of the most thrilling finishes ever.

In 1992, the John Marshall Lawyers completed their South Senate schedule unscathed for the third consecutive season, finishing with a league record of 5-0, 7-3 overall. This had been a remarkable season for head coach Al Valenzisi. The team's seven victories gave Valenzisi 66 wins as the John Marshall head coach, making him the team's all-time winningest football coach.

For the second consecutive season, they faced Glenville (4-1, 6-4) in the Senate championship game. This time, however, the Tarblooders took home overall Senate honors, winning the game 18-12.

In 1993, John Marshall (5-0, 7-3) won outright or shared the South Senate championship for the sixth consecutive season. No team had ever won that many consecutive Senate divisional titles. The Lawyers had won those divisional titles in grand style by winning 29 30 South Senate games, the last 24 in a row.

Playing the Lawyers in the Senate championship game on Nov. 12 were the East High Blue Bombers, who had won the North Senate title with a 4-1 record. With the score tied at 14-14, the Lawyers took a 20-14 lead early in the fourth quarter on an 8-yard run by Steve Owens. The Marshall defense then preserved the lead and the victory by shutting out East High over the entire second half. Marshall's 20-14 win gave the Lawyers their third Senate championship of the past six seasons.

SOFTBALL

For unknown reasons, information, such as Senate Athletic League sports records, was thrown out after the court-ordered busing in the late 1960s. This did a great disservice, particularly to many of the so-called lesser sports, among them girls softball. The league again resumed collecting records in the mid-1990s. However, from records compiled by John Marshall High School historian Ralph Pfingsten, the Lady Lawyers finished the 1977 season with a record of 12-5 and won the Senate championship.

From 1998 to 2005, the Lady Lawyers won six city championships, including four in a row from 2002-2005. In 1998, when the league was still playing slowpitch softball, the Lady Lawyers, coached by Ed "Buzzy" Haller, won a thriller from Lincoln-West, 11-10, to clinch the city title. Pitcher Kathy Bragg was the league MVP that season.

In 1999, Marshall played Lincoln-West for the Senate championship for the third consecutive year. This time, the Lady Lawyers lost to the Wolverines, 7-6. The Marshall team ended its season with a record of 17-3, and all three losses had been to Lincoln-West.

The following season, under the direction of Coach Lori Hein, John Marshall followed the statewide trend and switched from slowpitch to fastpitch softball. Nonetheless, not only did the Lady Lawyers play for the Senate championship, but they again did so against Lincoln-West. This time, there would be little drama in the title game as Marshall pounded out a 14-7 victory over the Wolverines. Freshman Sarah Shikner, aided by four double plays, went six innings for the championship game win, raising her record to 8-0.

Marshall did not figure in the league championship in 2001. Still, in 2002, they started an incredible run in Senate League play – and it was mainly due to the extraordinary pitching of Betsy Aviles. That season, the Lady Lawyers again played Lincoln-West for the championship, winning easily by a 12-2 score. On the mound was freshman Aviles, whose victory in that game gave her a 14-0 record against Senate League opponents, 14-1 overall. Betsy ended the season with a sparkling 0.875 era.

In 2003, now playing for head coach Dave Roesch, the Lady Lawyers and Betsy Aviles took up right where they had left off the previous season. They blew through Senate League play like a hot knife through butter, posting another undefeated league season after defeating Rhodes in the championship game, 10-3. Aviles pitched a three-hitter in that game, raising her record for the season to 15-1 and giving her 28 consecutive Senate League victories.

It was more similar in 2004 for the John Marshall team and Aviles. The Lady Lawyers again swept through their Senate League schedule undefeated, with Betsy Aviles finishing the season with an overall 13-1 record and stretching her record to 41-0 against Senate opponents. The Lady Lawyers humbled East High, 18-3, in the league championship game. In that game, Betsy allowed just three unearned runs in six innings while striking out 10; she also aided her cause with a double, a triple, and six RBI.

Aviles finished the season with an overall record of 13-1, an incredible 0.095 era, 85 strikeouts, and a no-hitter — and she had a .529 batting average. It is little wonder that she was named the Senate MVP.

Although again successful, the Lady Lawyers found their 2005 season to be a bit bittersweet. They did win their fourth consecutive city championship, but on May 19, they suffered their first Senate defeat since late 2002 when Rhodes thumped them by a score of 11-3. Betsy Aviles was on the mound for John Marshall that day, who saw her Senate record "drop" to 52-1 — with an impressive 52 consecutive victories.

In 2010, while still being led by Coach Dave Roesch, the Lady Lawyers won their last Senate League championship by defeating Rhodes in the title game, 15-6. In that game, John Marshall was led by Senate Co-MVP, junior shortstop Alysha Ellis, who went four for four with a pair of triples, a double, a single, and seven RBI.

TRACK

One of the oldest sports at John Marshall High School, the track was organized in 1925. The first team's initial success at the state meet came about a dozen years later when Al Kurnat won the school's first state championship with a state record time of 14.9 seconds in the 120-yard high hurdles. Two years later the Lawyers finished in fifth place at the state meet. Leading the way for Marshall that year was Bob Stroemple, who won the 440-yard dash (48.7) and finished second in the 100-yard dash. The mile relay team, which finished fourth, added to the team's point total.

In 1943, the Lawyers, led by head coach John Neubauer, scored eight times in six different events to finish second at the state meet with 23½ points. Leading the way was Tom Hasari, who won the 440yd dash with a time of 50.1 seconds. Adding to the team's total were four second-place finishes, a third-place finish, and two fourth-place finishes.

It would be almost 50 years before John Marshall would enjoy what could arguably be called its golden era of track success at the state meet, but there were a few highlights along the way. In 1944 and 1945, the school made a name for itself in the pole vault event. In 1944, Foster won a state championship in that event with a vault of 11'8½", while his teammate Bill Hillyard finished in a tie for third place. In 1945, Foster again succeeded in the pole vault by coming in tied for second while finishing second in the high jump. In 1946, Bill Weitzel won the state championship in the 440yd dash with a time of 50.3 seconds. In 1964, the mile relay team of Don Sabo, Hugh Ruffing, Mike Bird, and Tony Paci won gold with a time of 3:21.6.

Like one or two other Senate schools, John Marshall had a unique indoor practice track in what amounted to a sub-basement of the school. A track team member, Gerard Hudak, Class of 1972, described that track this way: "The indoor track at Marshall was under the school with tight curves and quite dusty. Distance runners found it hard to breathe. The ceiling was low, and I remember our hurdler, Bruce Holloway, who was about 6'3", was always afraid of hitting his head on the pipes over the track. The track's infield [was littered with] animal skeleton heads like you would see in the desert."

In 1980, the John Marshall Lawyers' 880-yard relay team tied for the fastest time in Ohio, 1:29.2, and placed third in the Dayton Invitational. Team members were Michael Cunningham, Kyle Jackson, Spencer Johnson, and future Olympian Thomas Jefferson.

John Marshall High School's most significant era of success in track came in 1991, 1992, and 1993, under the direction of head coach Tom Elkins. Led by sprinter Jonathan Burrell, the Lawyers won the state tournament in 1991 with a total of 42 points. Burrell won the 100m dash with a state tournament record time of 10.51 seconds and the 200m race of 21.30. Burrell was also a member of the 4x100m relay team that finished second and the 4x400m relay team that came in fourth. Also making a significant contribution to the team's victory that year was Gerald Jones; Jones was fifth in the 300m high hurdles and a member of the two already mentioned relay teams.

The Lawyers returned and won the state championship in 1992 with 36 points, just edging out Solon High School and its 34 points.

The Lawyers were again led by two outstanding athletes: Jonathan Burrell and Dorian Green. With a time of 10.64 seconds, Burrell repeated as the winner of the 100m dash. Dorian Green won the 400m race with 47.57 seconds and finished third in the 200m. Both boys were members of the state champion 4x100m relay team, along with Archie White and Elige Longino.

In 1992, John Marshall track coach Tom Elkins was named the OATCCC Coach of the Year and was inducted into the OATCCC Hall of Fame in 1995.

In 1993, the Lawyers' last great year at the state track meet, they finished in fourth place with 30 points. Now a senior, Jonathan Burrell again led the team; he had a hand in every point the Lawyers scored. Burrell won the 100m dash (10.75) and the 200m dash (21.41). He was also on the 4x100m relay team that came in fifth and the 4x400m relay team that finished eighth. For his three-year career at the state meet, Jonathan Burrell won six gold medals and was named All-Ohio no less than 10 times.

In 1995, Jeffrey Limpert won Marshall's last gold medal with a winning time of 1:52.44 in the 800m run.

TRACK (GIRLS)

The OHSAA girls state track meet was first run in 1975. That year, Lorrie Oldham finished fourth in the 440yd race to score the first state tournament points for the John Marshall girls. The first star of the Marshall girls track team was Charlene Stemm, who qualified for the state tournament in 1976 and 1977. In 1976, Charlene finished sixth in the shot put, but the following year, she won the state championship with a state meet record toss of 41'1¼".

The Lawyers would have another two-time state meet participant a few years later. In both 1979 and 1980, Michelle Stoyka finished in second place in the high jump, posting a jump of 5'6" both years. At the 1980 meet, Michelle's jump of 5'6" actually tied the winning height, but the tie-breaker gave the other girl first place.

Fifteen years later, in 1995, John Marshall would have its most successful state meet, and one girl scored all the points. Rochel Russell won the 400m race in a meet record time of 54.17 seconds; she then finished third in the 200m dash — accounting for all 16 of John Marshall's points.

VOLLEYBALL (GIRLS)

1976 was the second year of the OHSAA girls volleyball state tournament. It also marked the most incredible season for John Marshall girls volleyball.

Led by head coach Linda J. Beebe, the Lady Lawyers had a perfect season that saw them lose only two matches. The Lady Lawyers then advanced through the playoffs, reaching the Class AAA Final Four held in Westerville, Ohio. In its semifinal match, Marshall played the team from Stow High School (17-1). Stow won the first set, 15-6, but behind eight points by Grace Czarny and five from Dawn Scheuerman, the Lady Lawyers pulled even with a 15-11 second set win. The Lady Lawyers relied on balanced scoring to carry the day in the third and deciding set. Beth Scebbi led the way with four points, while Mary Beth Casale, Grace Czarny, and Karen Todd scored three points each to give Marshall a 15-6 win.

In the state championship match, John Marshall went up against undefeated Kettering Fairmont West (19-0). The Lady Lawyers gave it their all, but Fairmont West was too good, winning the championship in straight sets, 15-5, 15-4.

The girls of the 1976 John Marshall volleyball team (18-3) can be justly proud of their remarkable season. They are still the only Senate girls volleyball team to make it to the state Final Four and the state championship match. According to Ms. Beebe, it was a team effort!

WRESTLING

From its days as a member of the Greater Cleveland Conference, John Marshall High School enjoyed wrestling success for almost 50 years, from the team's first match in 1924 until the mid-1970s. At the very beginning, as a member of the Greater Cleveland Conference, the John Marshall wrestling team won the Cleveland city championship four consecutive years: 1928, 1929, 1930, and 1931.

Al Carroll was one of the pioneers of Ohio high school wrestling and one of the earliest champions at John Marshall High School. According to wrestling writer extraordinaire Pat Galbincea, also a John Marshall grad (See Pat's story in Chapter 2), "Carroll was an undefeated, three-time city wrestling champ at John Marshall High School in 1931-1933, but his accomplishments went unrecognized." That was because there was little or no newspaper coverage of high school wrestling in those days. Because of that, Al took it upon himself to keep the records and give the information to all three Cleveland newspapers as an unofficial stringer. Al once told Galbincea, "The first news stories I sent were by telegraph."

In 1936, just three years after graduating from John Marshall, Al officiated at high school and college matches, eventually earning a well-deserved reputation as the finest wrestling official in Ohio. Al Carroll was one of a trio of men who took leading roles in co-founding the Ohio State Wrestling Tournament, which debuted in 1938 and for which he served as the official scorer for its first 60 years.

Al Carroll was inducted into the Ohio Wrestling Hall of Fame in 1972, named Ohio's "Man of the Year" by Wrestling USA Magazine in 1993, and is an inductee into the Greater Cleveland Sports Hall of Fame. Carroll died at the age of 85 in January 1999.

The first state wrestling tournament, held in 1938, took place at John Hay High School. Twenty schools participated, including John Marshall. However, the Lawyers failed to score a point in this tournament, and no team champion was named that first year.

John Marshall's first successful year at the state tournament came in 1943 when the team finished in a tie for third place with Shaker Heights. Paul Varga won the state championship at 139 pounds, the school's first wrestling gold medal. The Lawyers also had three second-place finishes and a fourth-place finish.

Over the next 30 years, the Lawyers were one of the state's most competitive and successful high school wrestling teams, finishing among the tournament's top seven teams 18 times. In 1946, the Lawyers finished in fourth place, with Walter Schultz taking the state championship at 146 pounds. In 1947 and 1948, they came in fifth; Gilbert Dubray won the state title at 155 pounds 1947. In 1948, the Lawyers earned their fifth-place finish in true team style by scoring in six different events, with three boys placing third and three more coming in fourth.

In 1949 and 1950, the Lawyers were led by one of Cleveland's all-time best grapplers, Alan Peterson. In 1949, Peterson took the state championship at 134 pounds and returned the following year to take the championship at 139 pounds. In 1951, the Lawyers finished in third place, led by Richard Goodwin and his state championship at 104 pounds; the Lawyers added to their point total with a third place and two fourth-place finishes. Goodwin would return to the state tournament in 1953 and finish second at 128 pounds.

The years 1952-1955 saw the emergence of two other outstanding John Marshall wrestlers. In 1953 and 1954, Ray Rieder earned two fourth-place finishes, the first at 166 pounds and the second at 155 pounds. In 1955, Rieder moved to the 175-pound weight class and won the state championship.

However, the outstanding wrestler at this time, not only in the Senate but in the entire state of Ohio, was James Dregalla. Dregalla dominated the heavyweight wrestlers by winning three consecutive state championships at 186 pounds. At that time, James was only the fourth wrestler in Ohio to achieve that outstanding accomplishment.

John Marshal had at least one state champion wrestler every year from 1946 through 1955. After not having a state championship in 1956 or 1957, the Lawyers started another run of team and individual success in 1958.

After finishing second at 112 pounds at the 1957 state meet, Russell Di Santo returned to take the state championship in 1958. 1958 was the first of three consecutive seasons in which the Lawyers placed third at the state tournament. James Morrill, second at 133 pounds in 1958, led the team to their third-place finish in 1959 by winning the state championship at 133. Also adding to the team's success, John Tobin, who was third at 138 pounds in 1958, improved to second at 145 pounds in 1959. Despite the graduation of these fine grapplers, the Marshall team came back in 1960 to claim their third consecutive third-place finish, led by Tony Rizk's state championship at 175 pounds.

In 1961, the John Marshall team, coached by Eugene Gibbons, had a somewhat unusual finish at the state tournament. The team did not have any state champions that year, but John Sabo finished second at 103 pounds (up from fourth the year before), John Henderson finished fourth at 133 pounds, Larry Supelak was fourth at 175, and Tom Wilhelm finished fourth in the heavyweight division. When their points were added up, the boys had scored 32 points, which was enough to win the state championship by three points over second-place Euclid High School.

The Lawyers next big splash at the state tournament came in 1964. That year, the team finished in third place, led by Bill Burke at 112 pounds and Cecil Sallee at 133, both of whom won state championships. The Lawyers would enjoy their last excellent finish at the state wrestling tournament two years later. With Robert Buddie winning the state championship at 120 pounds and Jim Eiben finishing second at 154, the Lawyers scored 25 points and finished second behind Maple Heights and its 33 points.

In 1972, the Lawyers would have their last individual state champion. Dave Kenney, who finished second at 98 pounds in 1971, returned to take the state championship in 1972.

According to wrestling writer Pat Galbincea, Hollis Frierson was the last outstanding wrestler from John Marshall and the Senate. Frierson, who was once described as "being in a class by himself," was a lightweight who placed at state three times. In 1973, he was third at 98 lbs.; in 1974, he finished fourth at 112 pounds; in 1975, he was fifth at 119 pounds.

When asked to name the Senate League's greatest wrestlers, Pat Galbincea had two John Marshall Lawyers on his list. At #3 was Jim Dregalla, a three-time state champion at 186 pounds from 1952 through 1954, and at #15 was two-time state champion Alan Peterson, winning gold at 134 pounds in 1949 and 139 pounds in 1950.

The golden era of John Marshall High School wrestling came during the 24 years from 1953 to 1976, coinciding with the high school coaching career at Hall of Fame coach Eugene Gibbons. Not much is known about Gibbons' high school wrestling career, but in 1948, he was a national AAU junior champion and finished as a national runner-up in 1949 and 1950. At Michigan State University, he was a Big Ten and a national champion in 1951, earning Division I All-America honors in 1950 and 1951.

As the head coach at John Marshall, Eugene Gibbons coached 11 individual state champions. During his time at Marshall Gibbons, his teams dominated West Senate and city championship wrestling, posting 14 undefeated regular seasons. One measure of Coach Gibbons' influence on his sport is that, as of 2004, some 67 of his former wrestlers have become wrestling coaches themselves.

After years as the head coach of John Marshall, Eugene Gibbons was the head coach at Padua Franciscan High School and then an assistant coach at Saint Ignatius before retiring from coaching in 2004. Amateur Wrestling News named him the Coach of the Year in 1969. One of his many honors was being chosen as a charter member of the Ohio High School Wrestling Hall of Fame and a member of the Greater Cleveland Sports Hall of Fame.

CHAPTER 17

James Ford Rhodes High School

James Ford Rhodes High School is in the Westside neighborhood known as Old Brooklyn. The school is commonly referred to as "Rhodes High School" and is named after the American historian and industrialist of the same name. The school opened as a six-year high school (Grades 6-12) in February 1932, but it was changed to a four-year high school within a year. The school's combined football and athletic field was dedicated in September 1933. Rhodes High School, formerly a member of the Greater Cleveland Conference, joined the Senate Athletic League during the 1937 expansion.

BASEBALL

The number "13" proved lucky for Coach Tim Hogan and his Rhodes Rams in 2001. That year was Hogan's 13th as the Rams baseball coach. Thirteen was also the number of runs the Rams scored in the Senate championship baseball game on June 5, more than enough to defeat Glenville by a score of 13-3 to give Rhodes its first Senate baseball crown.

Senior centerfielder and league MVP Miguel Ulloa led the way for Rhodes (19-5, 18-1), who put the Rams ahead to stay with an RBI double in the fifth inning. Entering that final game with a .512 batting average, 26 RBI, 35 runs scored, 18 stolen bases, and only three errors, Miguel was also named to the All-Ohio baseball team, the first Rhodes player so honored.

It would be five years before the Rams had another shot at the league championship, but the championship game in 2006 almost did not get played. That game, between Rhodes and Collinwood, was initially scheduled for May 26 at Jacobs Field, the home of the Cleveland Indians, but it was rained out. The game was rescheduled for May 31, but the game was halted after three innings due to heavy rain and lightning; the Rams were leading 1-0. Finally, on June 5, the game was resumed and played to its conclusion at Gordon Park. It was worth the wait, as the Rams' (15-0, 15-6) 4-3 victory gave them their second Senate League championship. Winning pitcher David Keeton finished the season 7-0 and was named the Senate MVP.

The Rams would win eight Senate baseball championships over the next 16 years, including a league record four from 2015 to 2018.

BASKETBALL

Rhodes High had been a member of the Senate Athletic League's Western Division, aka the West Senate, since the league expanded in 1937. For almost 30 years, the Rams basketball team had never captured a West Senate championship, much less the city title. All of that would change in 1964.

Led by Second Team All-Ohio star Bill Hann (Hann would earn First Team honors in 1965), the Rams head coach Andy Moran, who took the court that season, was the most exciting basketball team ever to represent Rhodes High School and one of the all-time best in Senate history. Hann was a 6'1" guard who led the team in scoring 18.1 points per game and in assists with almost eight per game. But Hann was not the only sharpshooter on the team, as all five starters averaged in double figures, including forwards Claude Cooney and Steve Christafaris, center Jim Basista, and guard Frank Baumholtz, who at 5'9" was the only starter under 6'1". The team would set nine Rams basketball records that season and, for a little extra excitement, did their pre-game warm-up to an instrumental version of "Sweet Georgia Brown."

On Jan. 31, 1964, the Rams handed Lincoln a 103-70 defeat – one of four times during that season that the Rams broke the century mark with their scoring. It was the Rams' 12th consecutive league win, 14th overall, and clinched for them their first West Senate basketball title with two league games yet to play. In that game, the Rams set one of those nine team records by pulling down a whopping 78 rebounds. According to The Plain Dealer's story of the game, Bill Hann poured in 39 points and handed out many assists "with dazzling passing."

The Rams closed the season with equally convincing wins over West High, 95-74, and Holy Name, 90-48. With that win over Holy Name, the Rams completed their first undefeated season, 14-0, 16-0.

In the city championship game, played at the Cleveland Arena before 10,614 fans, Rhodes would be taking the court against the East Senate champions from East High. Those who came looking to see a close game were sorely disappointed. Coming out of the gate as hot as a pistol, the Rams shot 66% from the field in the first quarter, building a 20-6 lead that was never in jeopardy. As The Plain Dealer aptly noted, the Rams "completely outclassed the befuddled Blue Bombers ... with their ball-handling, faking and aggressive defense." East scored 25 field goals to 21 for Rhodes, but Rhodes scored 25 of 28 from the charity stripe to win the game, 67-57.

Rhodes' offense and defense won the game. This was most evident when the Rams held All-Ohio star Manny Leaks to just 10 points, his lowest total in two years.

In the final Class AA AP state poll, Rhodes was ranked fourth; the Rams and #5 Athens High School were the only undefeated teams in the top 10.

Having just won their first Cleveland championship, the Rams took to the tournament trail hoping to capture an even bigger title. They were assigned to the Berea sectional, where the Rams were the #1 seed. Rhodes defeated West Tech in a first-round game, 70-49. They beat St. Edward High School 70-54 in the sectional semifinal.

In the sectional final, the Rams had to overcome a tactic they had not encountered before. Berea High School slowed the game to keep the Rams' high-scoring attack in check. That tactic succeeded, but as the saying goes, two can play in that game. After grabbing an early lead, the Rams resorted to their defense and ball control to keep Berea in check; at one point, Berea went scoreless for 15 consecutive minutes, or the equivalent of almost two complete quarters. The Rams were held to their lowest point total of the season but still came away with a 40-22 victory. It was the team's first sectional championship.

Moving on to Berea district play, the Rams took the court in a district semifinal game against West Senate foe John Marshall. Despite jumping out to a 16-4 lead after the first quarter, this would be the Rams' most brutal game thus far. The Lawyers crept closer by halftime, then staged a furious comeback during the second half. The Rams, however, could hang on to come away with a 55-49 win.

The district final had the Rams taking on Elyria High School. This one went back and forth throughout, with neither team able to maintain a substantial lead. With the score tied, 42-42, and just two seconds left on the clock, Elyria canned a free throw. A desperation shot by the Rams after inbounding the ball was off the mark.

After a team-record 21 consecutive wins, the Rams best season had ended.

While he did not earn All-Ohio recognition, Dave Kyle was an outstanding basketball player for the Rams in the early 1970s. After graduation, he played basketball at Cleveland State University, where he became the first basketball player in Vikings history to earn All-America recognition. The Boston Celtics then drafted him.

After their incredible 1964 season, the Rams would have to wait 40 years for another shot at a Senate League championship. In 2004, the Rams, coached by Keith Schofield, entered the Senate playoffs with an overall record of 10-5 and ranked eighth in the city. In a Senate semifinal game, they defeated South High, 70-53, to advance to the Senate championship game. Their opponent would be Collinwood, which entered the game at 13-2 and ranked right behind the Rams in The Plain Dealer Top 25.

It would be a close game, but the Rams would rely on their defense and foul shooting to hold off the Railroaders. Rhodes made almost half its 59 points from the free-throw line, connecting on 28 of 34, including 17 of 22 in the crucial fourth quarter. The Rams also controlled the boards, outrebounding Collinwood by 32 to 20. Led by All-Ohio senior Joe Roberts, the league's "Player of the Year," and his game-high 21 points, the Rams were able to hang on for a 59-55 win and their second league championship.

The Rams' fine season earned them the top seed at the Baldwin-Wallace sectional in the Division I state tournament. Their first-round game was with Benedictine. It was a fierce struggle that would go into double overtime, but at the final buzzer, the Rams were on the short end of the 77-71 final score. Their season ended with a 12-6 record.

CROSS-COUNTRY

The Rhodes Rams regularly participated in the state cross-country meet from 1936 until the mid-1960s. After finishing sixth and fifth in 1943 and 1944, respectively, the Rams of Coach Ellsworth Holden had their all-time best finish in 1945. That year, led by three boys who placed among the top 20 runners, the Rams scored 119 points and finished second place. The boys that led the Rams to that excellent finish were Lawrence Long (12th), Walter Cates (16th) and Neil Richardson (18th).

The Rams enjoyed another good run at the state meet during the years 1955-1957, and it was mainly due to the excellent running of one boy. The Rams' Steve Tekesky finished in second place all three years. Although the Rhodes team did not qualify for the state meet in 1956, Tekesky's efforts helped the Rams finish in fourth place in 1955, and in 1957, he led the Rams to a fifth-place finish.

Led by Steve Korinchak (sixth place) and James Emery (seventh place), the Rhodes team enjoyed its last good season at state in 1964, finishing in third place.

While the Rams' days of team success at the state meet were over, the 1970s produced two individual cross-country state champions from Rhodes High School. In 1970, running as an individual entrant, Ron Addison earned All-Ohio honors with a 16th-place finish. He returned the next year and set a state record, winning the race at 9:26.9.

In 1977, Rhodes had two individual entrants at the state meet who earned All-Ohio honors. Craig Stadler finished in 20th place to earn his All-Ohio status. With a winning time 12:10.7, Gerald Vilt won his All-Ohio recognition as the state champion.

FOOTBALL

The first football game held at the new Rhodes Field was on Sept. 23, 1933, when the Rams took on Lincoln High. Played before some 4,000 fans, the Rhodes team came up just a few points short, dropping a 7-3 decision.

Rhodes joined the Greater Cleveland League that same year, winning the league championship in 1936 with a record of 3-0-2, 5-0-3. That championship season started the Rams on the longest undefeated streak in school history. After finishing 5-0-3 in 1936, the Rams went 5-0-4 in 1937 (now playing in the West Senate). In 1938, the Rams won their first eight games, extending their undefeated streak to 25 in a row, only to lose the last game of the season to a powerful West Tech team, 20-0.

That loss to West Tech cost the Rams a West Senate championship and a chance to play in the Charity Game that season, which would have been an excellent showcase for Rhodes' all-time most outstanding player, Les Horvath. Horvath transferred to Rhodes from Parma

High School for the 1938-39 school year and quarterbacked the Rams to victories in their first eight games. Les went on to play at Ohio State and won the Heisman Trophy in 1944, the first player from Ohio State to be so honored.

After those first two seasons of 1937 and 1938, Rhodes did not enjoy much luck in the West Senate until 1947. That season, the West Senate race was a wide-open, upset-filled affair that would not be settled until the final whistle blew.

Rhodes and West Tech met in the league opener for both squads on Sept. 26, a game that would help to keep the West Senate close all season. Rhodes, at the time not seriously considered a West Senate contender, had already played two non-league games, defeating Newark (Ohio) High School, 20-0, and playing Lakewood High to a 6-6 tie. In its only game of the season thus far, West Tech had dropped a 27-0 decision to East Tech.

In this West Senate opener, Rhodes halfback Art Martin scored touchdowns for the Rams in the first and third quarters, but in between those scores, West Tech quarterback Ralph Mlady would lead the Warriors to three touchdowns and a 19-14 victory. Rhodes had a very legitimate chance at winning this game, but fumbles — eight of them, all recovered by West Tech — put a huge crimp in the Rams' effort.

Rhodes and West Tech continued putting marks in the win column for the next several weeks. West Tech and Holy Name were now tied atop the West Senate with 3-0-0 league records, with Rhodes right behind at 2-1-0. Each of the three contenders now had four games remaining, all West Senate contests. It would be an exciting final four weeks of the season.

With just two weeks remaining in the season, Rhodes, West Tech, and Holy Name were tied atop the West Senate with identical 4-1-0 league marks. Holy Name would have the most significant say in the West Senate's outcome in those two weeks, as the Green Wave would first play West Tech and then finish the season against Rhodes the following week.

Holy Name's 6-0 victory over West Tech on Nov. 8 and Rhodes' 19-6 triumph over South High that same day meant that the Rhodes-Holy Name match-up on the season's final day, Nov. 14, would decide the West Senate title.

Coach Andy Moran's Rams showed how badly they wanted their first West Senate championship as soon as the game with Holy Name was underway. Rhodes fullback Chuck Lucas returned the opening kickoff 27 yards to give the Rams excellent field position at their 45-yard line. They then marched 55 yards in only seven plays, with quarterback Bill Putich sneaking the last few inches for the game's first touchdown. The extra point kick failed, leaving Rhodes with an early 6-0 lead.

Despite that quick start by the Rams, the score remained 6-0 until the third quarter, when the Green Wave scored a touchdown on its second possession of the quarter but failed to make the extra point. The action stayed hot and heavy as the Rams wasted no time getting those points back. After the ensuing kickoff, a Rhodes drive ended the third quarter and opened the fourth. Five plays into the final period, fullback Chuck Lucas attempted to score from the one. Lucas fumbled the ball as he was hit going across the goal line, but Rhodes center Joel Bohner fell on the loose ball in the end zone for the touchdown and a 12-6 Rams lead.

Late in that final quarter, Holy Name came storming back in an attempt to tie the game or take the lead. With fewer than two minutes remaining to play, the Green Wave was at the Rams 9-yard line, and "even the most ardent Rhodes rooter would not have given much for the Rams 12-6 lead then" (PD). With the overflow crowd of 8,000 on its feet at John Adams Field and cheering wildly, Holy Name's Tony Ferrante "took the pass from center, faded back, and ran a few steps to his right before jumping into the air and firing a short pass out to the right" (PD). From out of nowhere, Rhodes' Chuck Lucas intercepted the ball on the dead run and was gone down the sideline, outracing his desperate pursuers 91 yards for the clinching touchdown.

"When the final gun sounded a few seconds later, the joyful Rhodes players carried Coach Moran across the field and into their dressing room, where they let go"(PD). With its 18-6 victory, Rhodes had finally won its first West Senate championship and, with it, a trip to its first Charity Game.

Coach Moran had the aid of a former Rhodes player to help inspire his team during the season. Les Horvath, Rhodes 1939, had become an All-American and Heisman Trophy winner at Ohio State in 1944. An enlarged photo of Horvath hung in the Rhodes locker room. Moran told his kids Horvath had no more natural ability than they did, but he could attain fantastic success through dedication and challenging practice. Moran's charges took this message to heart, with many of them staying after the regular practice sessions to get in some extra work. That additional work had paid off in a trip to the Charity Game.

One of the key players leading the Rhodes attack was Chuck Lucas, "a pile-driving fullback and bone-crushing tackler" (PD). Lucas did not score many touchdowns, but his forays into the line kept opposing defenses honest and helped set up quarterback Bill Putich's passing attack. Lucas was also an excellent blocking back and pass defender.

Halfback Art Martin also ran out of the Rhodes backfield. Martin, the team's leading scorer with six touchdowns, was known for "his speed, keen sense of timing, and shrewd ability to pick a hole in the enemy's line" (PD).

Directing the Rhodes attack on the ground, primarily through the air, was quarterback Bill Putich. Putich was a brilliant young man, and Coach Moran had such confidence in him that he let Putich direct the offense when he was on the field. Putich was also "known and feared throughout the Senate for his passing, which has become the Rams' principal offensive threat" (PD). Putich's favorite targets were ends Ralph Armstrong and Dick Velotta, as well as halfback Art Martin.

While not spectacular, Rhodes' defense was very steady. Except for West Tech, no team had scored more than six points on the Rams, and three opponents were whitewashed.

Charity Game Day, Saturday, November 22, dawned dark and dreary, and a steady drizzle started falling just before the day's festivities began. Although the drizzle had stopped by game time, the weather remained slightly nippy, with the sky dark and threatening. It is estimated that the weather probably cut attendance by about 10,000. However, a massive crowd of 57,329 fans, the second largest total in Charity Game history, still made it to Municipal Stadium. These hardy fans witnessed a fine pre-game show, including 36 high school bands staffed by almost 2,000 student musicians.

If the Rhodes Rams were nervous or intimidated by playing the nationally reputed Cathedral Latin Lions for the city championship before almost 58,000 people, they certainly did not show it. Rhodes, a relatively young school, had been waiting since 1932 for this very opportunity, and they planned to make the most of it. They very nearly did.

The Rhodes defense played an excellent game. With the Lions' personnel, everyone knew that Latin could move the ball on the ground, but the Rhodes defenders held them to only 140 yards. The Lions' aerial game was stopped cold, with only three completions for eight net yards.

The Rams' running backs were not expected to accumulate much yardage on offense, and the Latin defense held them to just 44 yards. But Rhodes' offense revolved around Bill Putich's passing. Latin's Coach, Augie Bossu, knew this and prepared his defense accordingly.

The Lions capitalized on a first-quarter interception, marching 56 yards for the game's first touchdown and a 6-0 lead. With both defenses playing tough, the score remained 6-0 through the intermission and into the early minutes of the third quarter. At that time, another Bill Putich pass was intercepted by the Lions, who then went 23 yards to score the second touchdown of the game, upping their lead to 12-0.

Neither team could muster much of an offensive attack after that, and the game ended with Latin still clinging to a 12-0 lead.

Rhodes had waited 15 years to play in its first Charity Game; it would not be that long a wait for its next shot at the title. Rams end Ralph Armstrong was named to the UPI All-Ohio Second Team that season.

Four years later, the Rams opened the 1951 season with wins over Findlay and Ashtabula High Schools. It was an impressive start for the Rams, but it was now time for the games that counted in the race for the league championship and a chance to go to the Charity Game. The Rams' next seven games would all be against West Senate opponents.

Their first Senate assignment would be difficult: the two-time defending city champions from Saint Ignatius High School. In the third quarter of a scoreless game, the Rams scored on an 18-yard pass, then added the extra point. Those would be the game's only points as Rhodes upped its early season mark to 3-0-0.

Wins over South, Holy Name, and John Marshall quickly followed, leaving the Rams with a league mark of 4-0-0. In the following two weeks, Rhodes played its two closest West Senate rivals in two games to decide the league championship.

First up were the Warriors of West Tech, a game played at West Tech Field on Saturday, Oct. 27. Tech was in second place in the West Senate, right behind Rhodes, with a record of 3-1-0. A crowd of 3,500 showed up "at soggy West Tech Field" for this one, and they witnessed a fascinating game. The Rams wasted little time getting on the scoreboard, grabbing a 7-0 lead just minutes into the game. Early in the second quarter, the Rams added to their lead, completing a 54-yard drive in just six plays to go up 13-0.

West Tech stormed back with a pair of fourth-quarter touchdowns, but both times, they missed the extra point, allowing the Rams to hold on for a 13-12 win.

On Saturday afternoon, Nov. 3, the Rams faced the Lincoln High Presidents at a snow-covered Rhodes Field with below-freezing temperatures. The Rams scored early and often en route to a 46 to 0 win.

Rhodes' victory, behind a school record 46 points, clinched Andy Moran's Rams the West Senate championship and a trip to the Charity

Game, to be played on Nov. 24. However, the Rams still had one more game to play, a league battle with West High, which the Rams won easily, 25-0.

The Rams were now ready for the Charity Game, but they would have to wait another eight days to learn the outcome of one of the tightest East Senate races in history to find out who their stadium opponent would be. Benedictine and Collinwood ended the season tied for the East Senate championship, 6-0-0 in league play. Since they had not played each other during the season, the two teams met on Saturday, Nov. 17, in a playoff game that would finally decide the East Senate's representative in the 1951 Charity Game. That playoff game ended in a 12-12 tie. By prearrangement, the team that had gained the most net yardage would be declared the East Senate champion. You could have heard a pin drop at John Adams Field as everyone waited for the two official scorers to total up the yardage for both teams. Finally, after what must have seemed forever, Lloyd Griffith, the West Tech athletic director, made the long-awaited announcement: "Ladies and gentlemen, the Senate eastern division champion and representative in Saturday's Plain Dealer Charity Game is Collinwood." (PD). By a margin of 162 yards to 128 yards, a difference of only 34 yards, the Railroaders had made it to their fifth Charity Game to take on the West Senate's Rhodes High.

The 1951 Plain Dealer Charity Game would see "two of the finest teams ever produced in the state" (PD) squaring off against each other. Collinwood had gone 12 straight games without a loss, while Rhodes was enjoying an 11-game win streak. Both teams were well-placed in the state's high school football polls, with one poll placing Collinwood as high as #7 and the Rams at #10. The Plain Dealer, calling it "by all odds the biggest and most important high school football game in the state," was even predicting that the winner of the Charity Game might legitimately claim the state championship, too. Collinwood had defeated Warren Harding High School earlier in the season, and Warren was the only team to beat the #1-ranked Massillon Tigers. (Clevelanders, no doubt, looked upon the polls with a jaundiced eye, as five of the six teams ranked ahead of undefeated Collinwood had suffered at least one loss — including the Warren team that the Railroaders had defeated.)

Quarterback Don Kasner led coach Andy Moran's undefeated and untied Rhodes Rams and end Frank Guzik. Kasner, "one of the most feared passers in the district" (PD), had already thrown for well over 1,100 yards and had completed 16 passes for touchdowns. Kasner's advantage as a passer lay in the fine corps of players on the receiving end of his aerials. These included halfbacks Tony Rocco, Chuck Galmarini, Bob Kurtz, and end John Tekesky.

But by far, the best receiver at Rhodes and in Cleveland was Frank Guzik. Labeled by his coach as "the best all-around football player and athlete I've seen in my 14 years" at Rhodes, Guzik could do it all. As Coach Moran said, "He has missed only one pass thrown to him all season. He kicks off, punts, runs, and passes. In addition to all this, he provided the type of leadership that has made the team the most confident and versatile in the school's records." Guzik had six touchdown receptions to his credit and was also a stalwart on the Rhodes defensive unit. With Guzik and his teammate, end John Tekesky (three touchdown receptions), both standing 6'3" and weighing 195 pounds, it was easy for Don Kasner to pick them out downfield.

Although the Rams were known mainly for their passing on offense, running backs Tony Rocco, Chuck Galmarini, Bob Kurtz, and quarterback Don Kasner (five rushing touchdowns) were adept at picking up yardage on the ground. This versatile offense had thus far, in 1951, set school records for the most points in a game (46), most points in a season (242), and most wins in a season (9). The Rhodes offense was backed up by an equally capable defense that allowed only 45 points while shutting out four opponents.

Saturday, Nov. 24, was a cold, damp day. The tarp that had covered the stadium's gridiron had kept the field dry from the previous night's rain, with only a few puddles where the water had seeped under the covering. The raw weather, however, undoubtedly contributed to the low turnout of only 18,759 hardy fans, the third-lowest attendance in Charity Game history. Nonetheless, those who plunked down 50 cents for a student seat, 75 cents for general admission, or up to 3 bucks for the "expensive" reserved seats got to see the usual great show of high school band entertainment and an outstanding football game.

Rhodes won the coin toss and opted to receive. The Rams' Tony Rocco took the kickoff in his end zone and ran it out but only advanced to the 14-yard line, where he fumbled the ball; fortunately for the Rams, a teammate recovered it. When the Rams could not move the ball, Frank Guzik punted it away, with Collinwood putting it into play at its 45-yard line. It only took a half-dozen plays before Joe Trivisonno crashed into the end zone for the game's first score; the extra point kick gave Collinwood a 7-0 lead just a few minutes into the game.

The slightly favored Railroaders were off to a good start, but that early lead would be short-lived. Rhodes halfback Bob Kurtz took the ensuing kickoff, but instead of starting upfield with the ball, he went across the field and handed it off to John Budko, who usually played only on defense, on a reverse. Budko picked up some excellent blocking from his teammates, "broke into the clear on the Collinwood 40," and just had enough speed to stay ahead in the race for the score. Rocco's place kick tied the score, 7-7 (PD). Rhodes had dipped into its bag of tricks and came up with a 74-yard touchdown.

Late in the second quarter, the Rams went on offense at the Collinwood 40-yard line following a Rairoaders punt. On first down, the Rams' Don Kasner dropped back to pass. Frank Guzik raced downfield and cut to the left sideline, getting behind the defenders. He caught Kasner's pass at the 10-yard line and ran into the end zone with Rhodes' second touchdown. Tony Rocco's placement was again good, giving Rhodes a 14-7 lead with less than four minutes left in the half.

Neither team was able to score in the third quarter. As the fourth quarter opened, the Railroaders again coughed up the ball (one of seven fumbles by Collinwood), which the Rams recovered at the 5-yard line. On first down, Tony Rocco went up the middle for the touchdown, then kicked the extra point to give the Rams a 21-7 lead. Later in the final frame, Collinwood added a second touchdown but could get no closer. When the final gun ended the game, Rhodes had won its first city championship, 21-14, completing the season with a perfect 10-0-0 record.

Rhodes' Andy Moran, whose team had now gone to the Charity Game twice in his four years as head coach, had nothing but praise for his team. "That was typical of my gang's play all season. They have poise and came right back after that quick Collinwood touchdown, and with a play, we never used before.... I knew this was a good team, and I said so before we played our first game.... Collinwood has a great team, and we knew they would score, but we knew we could score some points, too."

It was the best football season in the 20-year history of Rhodes High School. Although the team failed to finish on the AP Top Ten, defensive end Frank Guzik was named All-Scholastic for the second straight year, First Team All-Ohio, and First Team All-America.

In 1952, Coach Andy Moran's Rhodes Rams slipped a little, finishing the season at 4-2-1 in the West Senate and 5-3-1 overall. However, they were determined to get back on top.

"Loaded with veteran material and pegged as one of the powers in Cleveland football this season" (PD), the Rams got the 1953 season off to a flying start on Friday, Sept. 18, when they traveled to Sandusky to take on the Sandusky High Blue Streaks. Playing opportunistic defense, the Rams turned three Sandusky fumbles into first-half touchdowns as they raced to a 35-0 lead at the intermission. The Rams added another touchdown in the third quarter in burying the Blue Streaks, 41-0.

The Rams were off and running on what would be one of their greatest seasons ever. Their next three games were against West Senate foes, games the Rams easily put away by a combined score of 101-0.

The high-flying Rams were now 3-0-0 in the West Senate and 4-0-0 overall. They then played a non-league game against the Steelmen of Lorain High School. The game went back and forth, with the Steelmen proving almost too much for the Rams to handle, ending in a 12-12 tie.

The following week, Rhodes played its biggest game of the season when it met the defending West Senate champion Saint Ignatius Wildcats in a night game on Friday, Oct. 23, at West Tech Field. Billed as "the game that should settle the West Senate championship" (PD), the Wildcats were tied with Rhodes for the league lead. Although the teams were pretty evenly matched, the Rams were given a slight edge on defense, especially against the pass, having intercepted 19 passes in just five games.

It would be that defense that would be the difference in the game. Rhodes would force seven Ignatius turnovers on five fumbles and a couple of interceptions while holding the Wildcats offense to only 121 net yards. The Rhodes defense would score one touchdown and set up another, while the Rams offense would have its one sustained drive late in the game when it was most needed. The result would be a massive 21-7 victory for the Rhodes Rams.

Although they still had three West Senate games to play, barring a major upset, the Rams had pretty much wrapped up another West Senate title with their win over Saint Ignatius - and there would be no surprises this year. On Halloween night, the Rams humbled the orange-and-black South High Flyers 48-6 and took the measure of Holy Name the next week, 38-0.

The victory over Holy Name clinched Andy Moran's team's second West Senate title in three years. On November 14, the Rams made it official by closing the season on a winning note, defeating West Tech 32-7.

Next up for the Rams would be The Plain Dealer Charity Game on Friday night, Nov. 20, against the East Senate champion and defending city champion, Benedictine Bengals, 8-1-0, of head coach Joe Rufus.

Rhodes was looking to take the city title away from Benedictine, and so far, the team had done everything right to put itself in a position to accomplish that goal. Although the Rams and the Bengals were a fairly even match on defense, the Rams had a slight edge in versatility on the offensive side of the ball. The leading runner for Rhodes was halfback Adam Robertson. Described by his coach as a "slippery runner," Robertson was the man they called on when the Rams needed the big yardage, especially when the team was inside the 20-yard line, as his 13 touchdowns would attest. Joining Robertson in the Rhodes backfield were halfbacks Jerry Ihnat and Don Thrall, as well as fullbacks Joe Mirka and Ray Hartman.

However, the undisputed leader of the Rhodes offense was Brian Burke, "one of the city's most talented quarterbacks" (PD). Burke was an excellent field leader who could handle the ball well. His 41 pass completions in 101 tries included nine for touchdowns. Burke's primary target was 6'4" end Al Reinke, who played every minute on offense and had four touchdown receptions.

The Rhodes defense was also excellent, having yielded only 32 points all season while posting five shutouts. The Rams' pass defense was efficient and had 19 interceptions in the first five games alone. Mainstays of that defense were ends Glen Preising and Dick Swasey, tackles Adam Robertson and Bob Turchanik, guards Bob Kovacs and Bill Saunders, nose tackle Ron Chochola, and defensive backs Eldon Oberacker, John Gerdel, Joe Mirka, and Brian Burke.

The weather at Municipal Stadium on Friday night, Nov. 20, was almost perfect for football, with the temperature in the 60s and just "a minor few drops of rain until the game's end" (PD). The excellent conditions and a match-up of two of the state's best teams no doubt contributed to another great Charity Game turnout since 38,058 high school football fans were on hand for what most felt would be a close, exciting game.

The game got underway promptly at 8:15 p.m., with Rhodes kicking off. The Rams got an early break as John Gerdel recovered a fumble at the Bengals' 37-yard line just 30 seconds into the game. The Bengals held, and Rhodes punted the ball away, failing to cash in on a great early opportunity. Later in the period, Benedictine put the ball into play at its 30-yard line and marched 70 yards in seven plays to take a 7-0 lead.

The Rams came right back, as Adam Robertson returned the ensuing kickoff 60 yards to give Rhodes excellent field position. However, the Bengals defense would not yield, as the Rams came up short on a fourth-down attempt and had to give up the ball on downs at the Bengals 20-yard line.

As the second quarter opened, the Bengals attempted to move the ball downfield, but the Rams defense would not budge. Forced to punt from deep in their end of the field, the Bengals went back on defense with the ball, and the Rams, at the Benedictine 41-yard line. This time, Andy Moran's boys were able to make some headway. Brian Burke went to the air and connected with end Al Karp for gains of 8 and 9 yards. Rhodes then went to its running game, and halfback Ray Hartman picked up 6 yards and Adam Robertson five more, leaving Rhodes with a first and 10 at the Bengals 13-yard line. "From there, Rhodes lined up in a spread formation, and Hartman ran up the middle for 12 yards to the one" (PD). Quarterback Brian Burke closed out the drive, plunging over for the touchdown. Tackle John Jacobson's extra point kick tied the score at 7 to 7.

A few plays after the kickoff, Rhodes got the ball back when the Bengals fumbled a handoff attempt, and the Rams' Rick Swasey recovered the loose ball at the Benedictine 41-yard line. Rhodes then took the lead with a bit of razzle-dazzle. As The Plain Dealer said, "Swasey, who had been sparkling as a defensive end all season, moved into the Rhodes backfield. The Rams lined up in a double-wing offense, with Swasey as the left wingback. The pass from center went to fullback [Ray] Hartman, who spun and handed off to Swasey. Swasey then drifted back and sailed a long pass to [end Al] Karp, who eluded the Benedictine secondary to make the catch on the 6-yard line and trot over" for the touchdown.

The Bengals continued to have problems hanging onto the ball when, on the third down following the Rhodes kickoff, they again coughed up the ball. An alert Glen Preising caught the ball "in midair and rambled 34 yards to the touchdown" (PD). John Jacobson added the extra point, and Rhodes scored 20 quick points to take a 20-7 halftime lead.

Beginning play on their 23-yard line following the second-half kickoff, the Rams gradually worked the ball to midfield with a series of short-yardage runs. Quarterback Brian Burke then faked a short jump pass and instead "dropped out of his pocket and sent a long aerial to (Adam) Robertson on the 20" (PD). Robertson made the catch and raced into the end zone for another Rhodes touchdown. The extra point try failed.

Now trailing 26-7, the Bengals began an 80-yard march that ended on the second play of the fourth quarter with a touchdown, the extra point cutting the Rhodes lead to 26-14. It was not long before disaster again struck Benedictine, this time in the form of another fumble that Rhodes recovered at the Benedictine 9-yard line. On the next play, Brian Burke connected with Al Karp on a hook pass for the touchdown, John Jacobson's extra point pushing the Rhodes lead to

33-14. Later in the quarter, the Rams started a drive at their 38-yard line. At the Benedictine 38, Adam Robertson took a pitchout from Brian Burke, "cut through the tackle, and was away for the touchdown" (PD). John Jacobson connected on his third extra point try of the game as the Rams put the finishing touches on an incredible 40-14 Charity Game victory.

It was supposed to have been a close contest. Still, five lost fumbles by the Benedictine Bengals had given the Rhodes Rams plenty of extra scoring opportunities. Andy Moran's team turned three of those miscues into touchdowns en route to their second Cleveland football championship in three years. Rhodes also had a pass interception for a total of six Benedictine turnovers. The Rams did not commit a single turnover.

When the final AP Ohio poll came out, the Rhodes Rams, with a record of 9-0-1, had finished as the #9-ranked team in Ohio. Defensive end Al Karl was named First Team All-Ohio.

Four days later, Rhodes head coach Andy Moran, who had guided the Rams to some of their greatest seasons, retired as head football coach, but he would stay on as the Rams' basketball mentor. Andy Moran started his coaching career at Rhodes in 1938 as an assistant coach for football and basketball. After 31 months of active duty with the U.S. Navy during World War II, Moran returned to Rhodes in 1945 as the head football coach. He led the Rams to a record of 45-21-7 in that time, including 2-1-0 in the city championship Charity Game.

The Rams would not win another West Senate or Cleveland championship, but in 1955, offensive tackle Bob Schmidt was named to the All-Ohio Second Team.

SOFTBALL

As it has been for the Rams baseball team, the 21st century has proven very good for the Rhodes softball teams. The Lady Rams came close to winning the Senate championship four times from 2001-2005, but they always got beat out in the title game. Finally 2007, the girls put it all together, defeating Glenville, 9-0, in the title game to bring home their first Senate League championship. That victory got the Lady Rams started on a run in which they won 11 Senate League championships from 2007-2022, including a record six in a row from 2014 to 2019.

TRACK

The Rhodes Rams have been sending participants to the state track meet since 1935. While the results have been spotty, the school has produced some very talented athletes, including 11 individual state champions; the Rams also have one state championship team trophy in their trophy case.

The Rams' first state track champion was Lowell Shirley, who won the 120yd high hurdles in 1944 with a time of 15.1 seconds. He was also second in the 220yd low hurdles to account for all of Rhodes' points that year.

Two years later, in a very close race for the team championship, the Rams finished with 16 points to place third behind champion Toledo DeVilbis (18 points) and runner-up East Tech (17 points). Scoring all of the Rams' points was hurdler Dick Sistek. Sistek won the 120yd high hurdles with a time of 14.6 seconds, tying the state meet record. He then won the 220yd low hurdles with a tie of 24.4. Sistek is among only two Rhodes athletes to win multiple state championships in individual track competitions.

Rhodes' next competitive trip to the state came in 1956. Although the team did not have a single state champion, it scored points in six different events, enough to finish in fifth place.

In 1965, Steve Korinchak set an All-Time Ohio record in the mile with 4:15.4 at the 1965 State Regionals with a previous mark of 4:18.0.

The team's next top-10 finish came in 1972, and it was all the result of the efforts of one runner. Distance runner Ron Addison had finished second in the mile run the previous year at the state meet. In 1972, he won the state championship in that event with a time of 4:13.5, giving the school its first state champion in track in 26 years. Ron also finished third in the 880yd race, scoring all of the team's points, which was good enough for a sixth-place finish.

1993 and 1994 would be huge for the Rams' track team, especially for one young man on that team – sprinter Antoine Lundy. In 1993, the Rams finished 10th at the state meet in no small part due to the efforts of Lundy. That year, he won the state championship in the 400m race with a time of 48.43, then returned and finished fifth in the 100m event. Delonte Perkins added to the team's point total with a sixth-place finish in the 110m hurdles, giving the Rams 13 points and a 10th-place finish.

Under the direction of head coach Tim Franzinger, the 1994 state meet would prove to be the high-water mark in the history of Rhodes track. Star sprinter Antoine Lundy would play a massive role in the team's success that year. Lundy would win both the 100m (10.99) and 200m (22.18) races and be a member of the school's state championship 4x400m team (3:23.81); other members of that relay team were Wayne Wren, Mike Shoals, and Delonte Perkins. In addition to those gold medals, Lundy took silver in the 400m race. For his two-year career at Rhodes, Antoine Lundy was a six-time All-Ohio performer with four state championships.

Another significant contributor to that year's Rhodes point total was Mike Shoals, a sprinter. Shoals won the 400m race (48.90) and, as mentioned, was also on the winning 4x400m relay team. He also added big points to the team total with a second-place finish in the 100m race and a third-place finish in the 200m race.

The team's final points came when the 4x100m relay team of Leshaunte Edwards, Wayne Wren, Ernest Ponder, and Delonte Perkins won the event with a time of 42.98. After all their points were totaled, the Rams of head coach Tim Franzinger scored 72, easily winning the Division II state championship over second-place Bay Village and its 30 points.

Despite not winning any event at the 2000 state tournament, sprinter Muhammad Saafir earned All-Ohio recognition four times with his consistently fine performances in the 100m (fifth place) and 200m (fourth place) and on the 4x100m and 4x400m relay teams, both of which finished in the points.

TRACK (GIRLS)

The Rhodes' girls track team had scored points almost every year in the OHSAA Track and Field Championship since 1979 when Cindy Nolan placed 4th in the 800-meter run. They have produced outstanding track athletes who have won multiple All-Ohio honors. The next great athlete was Cindy Anzalone, who earned All-Ohio honors four times in her career, placing 4th in the 800 meters in 1980, scoring in the 1600 meter run in 6th place in 1981, and finishing in 3rd place in 1982. For the first time in Rhodes Rams' history in girls' track & field, coached by Tyrone Owens, in 1988, they could qualify in multiple events. Carol Sims placed 4th in the 400-meter dash. Carol was also a member of the 4 x 200 relay, and along with members Teresa Crews, Carmella Marshall, and Ester McMillon, she placed 4th in that event. That team continued to score, with Cynthia Davis placing 4th in the shot put. Another great sprinter was Carmella Marshall, a four-time All-Ohio sprinter from 1989-1991. Katonya Harding was All-Ohio in 1990-1994. In 1993 and 1994, hurdler/ sprinter Keneitha Smith earned four times. Sprinter Nylisha Guy was another four-time All-Ohio winner in 1999 and 2000. The 2000 4 x 400 relay team at the state meet consisted of Alisha Brown, Sommer Saddler, Chanel Hill, and Nylisha Guy. They ran down the last three teams and placed sixth in the state meet. Historically, Rhodes also had five outstanding field event competitors. Amanda Perkins was one of them, winning All-Ohio honors in 1997 and 1998 in the discus throw. At the state meet in 2001 and 2002, Tiffany Colvin, another outstanding field event athlete, was the only qualifier from the Rhodes girls' track team. At that event, she earned all of the teams' points and made All-Ohio in the 100m high hurdles and the high Jump both seasons. Both years, she earned High School All-American honors at the indoor and outdoor national championships. The 2005 team set a goal to compete for a state title, led by senior co-captains and hurdlers Francine Jennings and Cierra Robinson. The Rams won the OATCCC State Indoor Runner-ups championship, finishing behind cross town rivals Collinwood High School.

The Senate schools are generally not known for having outstanding long-distance runners, but Rhodes has produced two great distance runners. They are Cindy Anzalone from 1979-1982 and Sediah Erskine from 2003-2006. Cindy ran the two-mile course and became the first Senate Athletic League distance runner to qualify for the OHSAA Cross Country Championships. Cindy was awarded a track scholarship to the University of Houston, where she earned All-American honors. Sediah Erskine was another outstanding long-distance runner. She broke all of the long-distance records previously held at Rhodes. As a sophomore, Sediah Erskine earned All-Ohio status with a seventh-place finish in the 3200m race. As a junior, she earned All-Ohio honors with a second-place finish in the same event, completing the race in 10:54.96. As a senior in 2006, Sediah closed out her high school career with a third-place finish in the 1600m run, earning her third All-Ohio honor.

From 2005-2007, twin sister sprinters Shelli and Shannon Rimmer earned All-Ohio recognition seven times. Shelli won the honor four times, and Shannon won the honor three times.

As a team, the Lady Rams' two best years were 2006 and 2009. In 2006, the team scored 22 points, earning sixth place and its highest finish ever at the state meet. The 4 x 200 relay team of Ryan Harris, Shelli Rimmer, Tenisha Taylor, and Bonita Pace led the way. This team finished second with a time of 1:41.42. Adding to the team's point total were a pair of third-place finishes: Sediah Erskine in the 1600m (4 57.96) and the 4 x 100m team of Ryan Harris,

Tenisha Taylor, Shellie Rimmer, and Shannon Rimmer (48.20). Closing out the scoring was Jennifer Roman, who finished seventh in the 800-meter race at 2:16.25.

The 2009 team scored 20 points to finish in seventh place. One of the most outstanding athletes to ever attend Rhodes High School scored all the points: sprinter Mahagony Jones. Jones finished second in the 100m dash (12.17), third in the 200m dash (24.69), and third in the 400m (55.61). Not only did Mahagony score all the teams' points in 2009, but she also did so in 2007, earning fourth in the 200m, and 2008, earning fourth in the 100m and third in the 200m.

Running indoors her senior year, Jones was the state champion in the 60m, 200m, and 400m dashes. She also won the 100m and 400m races at the 2009 Mid-West of Champions, where she ran against top runners from Ohio, Michigan, and Indiana. Jones earned All-American honors twice at the Nike National Championship that same year, finishing sixth in the 100m and 400m races.

Jones continued her track career by earning a track scholarship at Penn State University, where she was named Second Team All-American in 2013 and First Team All-American in 2014.

WRESTLING

Rhodes' best success came during the earliest years of the state wrestling tournament. The tournament's first year was in 1938, held at John Hay High School. Although there were no team rankings that first year, had there been, Rhodes would probably have finished in second place behind Garfield Heights High School.

1938 would also prove to be the Rams' best year at the state tournament, with the team placing four wrestlers in the points, including three state champions. Those champion wrestlers were Bob Ingram (105), Stanley Kakosky (155), and Fred Schleicher (185), while Mike Slepicky came in third at 125.

The following year, 1939, team scores were kept. Under the direction of Coach George Seedhouse, the Rams finished in a tie for second place. They did this by scoring two more state championships, one by Joe Malanowski (105) and one by Fred Schleicher (185). With that second state championship, Fred Schleicher became the first wrestler in Ohio to win two state championships. He was rated by nationally renowned high school wrestling writer Pat Galbencia, a Senate product from John Marshall High School, as one of the all-time top Senate League wrestlers.

After a two-year hiatus, the Rams' wrestling success would continue for three more years, 1942-1944. In 1942, with 11 points, the Rams finished sixth place in the state tournament. John Juhas led the way, winning a state championship at 105 pounds, while Casimir Pavlak finished fourth at 135. In 1943, the Rams improved one place at the state tournament with a fifth-place finish. Ruttolph won a state championship at 134, while Levandowsky (113), Chuck Kuehn (128), and Norman Metzgar (166) all finished in third place in their respective weight class.

In 1944, the Rams had their last significant team finish at the state tournament by again finishing in sixth place. Barney Brunson won the state championship at 104 pounds, while Chuck Kuehn improved on his 1943 placing at 134 pounds by finishing in second place.

Although the Rams have not finished among the top 10 teams at the state tournament since 1944, nor had another state champion, they have had a couple of wrestlers earn multi-year success at the state tournament. In 1950, at 121 pounds, Clyde Simpson finished in second place. He returned to the state tournament the following year and earned All-Ohio honors with a third-place finish.

It would take 60 years before Rhodes had another wrestler earn All-Ohio honors, and he would do it two consecutive years, like Clyde Simpson. That wrestler was Irayel Williams, who finished eighth at 189 pounds in 2010 and then returned to finish fourth in 2011.

CHAPTER 18

Lincoln-West High School

Lincoln-West High School emerged due to the merger of the old Lincoln and West high schools in 1970. Carrying on a tradition from the original two schools, Lincoln-West has a large multicultural and multilingual population representing more than 41 nationalities and 25 languages. Initially, the Lincoln-West sports teams played in the West Senate. In the late 1970s, after the CMSD reorganized the conferences into the North and South Senate Conferences, Lincoln-West teams played in the North Senate. The Lincoln-West nickname is the Wolverines, and the school colors are red, white, and blue.

BASEBALL

The Lincoln-West Wolverines have had their most notable athletic success when competing in Senate League baseball. In 1974 and 1975, Lincoln-West won its first two Senate championships in any sport when the Dave Ford-led Wolverines won the city championship yearly. (See "Two Outstanding Athletes" below.) Beginning in 2000 and running through the 2023 season, the Wolverines have won 10 more league championships (2000, 2004, 2005, 2008, 2009, 2012-2014, 2021, 2022, 2023).

TRACK

Lincoln-West's best year at the state track meet was in 1984, when the team scored 10 points and finished in 15th place. Terry Sullivan finished fifth in the 400m race with a time of 49.24. In the 1600m relay (4x400m), the Wolverines came within 1.02 seconds of a state championship. The team of Amin Muhammad, Terry Sullivan, Tim Goler, and Ron Smith finished at 3:14.59, good for second place. John Adams was the only team to finish ahead of the runners, and the Rebels had to set a meet record 3:13.57 to do it.

In 1988 and 1990, the Wolverines featured a three-time All-Ohio sprinter named Alonzo Wilson. At the 1988 state meet, Wilson finished fifth in the 200m dash at 21.64. He did not compete at the 1989 state meet but was back on the track in Columbus in 1990. That year, Wilson finished third in the 100m dash with a time of 10.70, then came in sixth in the 400m with a time of 48.88. In both 1988 and 1990, Wilson accounted for all of his team's points at the state meet.

TWO OUTSTANDING ATHLETES

Lincoln-West High School has produced only a few outstanding athletes in its short history. One of these, wrestler Dartanyon Crockett, was profiled in the first chapter of this book (Olympians). Here, we will tell you about two other exceptional athletes.

The first is Dave Ford, Class of 1975. Dave earned All-Ohio basketball honors his senior year, but his actual sport was baseball, where he was an all-around player of outstanding ability.

In 1974, Ford led Lincoln-West to its first West Senate and/or city championship in any sport since the school had been formed five years earlier. Although he was known to be an outstanding batsman, his pitching was superb. Over the last 10 days of May, Ford hurled three consecutive three-hitters, the previous two being shutouts, 1-0 over Holy Name and 4-0 over Saint Ignatius.

Having won the West Senate title on June 6, the Wolverines squared off against East Tech for the city championship. Saving one of his best performances for last, through seven innings, Ford had allowed just two hits while striking out 12, but as the Wolverines came to bat at the bottom of the seventh, the score was still deadlocked at 0-0. With one out, third baseman Dave Kalas doubled and was promptly replaced by pinch runner Pete Herbst. Dave Ford was then intentionally walked. Herbst moved to third base on a wild pitch and scored the winning run on a grounder to second base, giving Lincoln-West a 1-0 victory and the Cleveland city championship.

Dave Ford finished the 1974 season with a record of 11-1, an earned run average of 0.35, and 130 strikeouts in 81-1/3 innings. He was designated the West Senate MVP and named to the All-Scholastic first team, the only junior on either the first or second team.

It was more of the same for Dave Ford and the Wolverines in 1975. Led by Ford's pitching and hitting, the Wolverines, with a record of 14-3, again won the West Senate championship. Lincoln-West and East Tech squared off for the city championship for the second consecutive season. It would be a battle of star pitcher Dave Ford against Tech's James Evans. Once again, though, Dave Ford would dominate. Pitching a three-hitter and allowing just one unearned run, Ford led the Wolverines to a 4-1 championship game victory. Dave Ford kept the Scarabs in check by striking out 14 while relinquishing just one walk.

Once again, Ford was named the West Senate's MVP and All-Scholastic with a record of 10-1 (21-2 over the last two seasons) and an ERA of 0.42 with 124 strikeouts and only five walks. But Dave did not have much time to bask in those laurels. The very next day after the city championship game, Dave Ford was the 23rd player drafted in the annual Major League Baseball amateur draft. He was picked by the Baltimore Orioles, who had him listed as OF – an outfielder. This was undoubtedly due to his .482 batting average and to the fact that some of his home runs had been described as "prodigious" by The Plain Dealer.

But Dave was a pitcher. He wanted to pitch in the big leagues – and it did not take long for the Orioles organization to figure out that Ford was a pitcher. In 1976, while pitching for the

Orioles farm team in Charlotte, Ford had a record of 17-7 with an ERA of 2.50, earning him the Southern League's "Pitcher of the Year" award. Dave pitched for the Orioles from 1978-1981, posting a record of 5-6.

The second incredible athlete, one of the finest all-around female athletes Cleveland has ever produced, is Sue Koziol, Class of 1980. She earned nine varsity letters while at Lincoln-West, three each in basketball, volleyball, and softball, but her main sports were basketball and softball.

When Sue Koziol's final basketball season ended in 1980, she finished among the top six in the city in scoring average (24.6), free throw percentage (.727), and rebounds (13.9 per game).

She was named to the All-Scholastic First Team and All-Ohio Class AAA First Team. When Sue Koziol's basketball playing days with the Wolverines were over, she held every team record except for single-game rebounds.

If it was possible to top her performance on the basketball court, Sue just might have done so on the softball diamond. Playing three years as the Wolverines' starting shortstop (her sister Sandy was the other half of the team's keystone combo at second base), Sue put up almost unbelievable numbers. For her senior year in 1980 (the team still played slowpitch softball back then), Sue hit an incredible .720 with 10 home runs. On defense, she committed only four errors in 99 chances. Sue was named First Team All-Scholastic and the Slowpitch "Player of the Year." There was no softball All-Ohio team then, but if there had been, Sue Koziol would undoubtedly have been a First Team selection. Sue finished her three-year career at Lincoln-West with a 40-game hitting streak, having gotten a hit in all 40 games the team had played. Her career batting average was .650 and included more than 20 home runs.

Sue Koziol's athletic achievements continued in college and beyond. She started her college career at the University of Pittsburgh but soon transferred to Cleveland State University. In high school, Sue starred in basketball and softball at CSU. She set many school records on the basketball court, and her strong right arm even enabled her to set a school record in the javelin toss. However, it was in softball that Sue made her most significant achievements, as the following notes: "Already a recognized star in the sport when she began playing for Cleveland State, she led the Vikings to the OAISW Regional Championships and a spot in the national tournament, earning first-team All-American honors in 1982 while also garnering the first of her four awards as the team's Most Outstanding Player."

In 2004, when Sue Koziol was inducted into the Greater Cleveland Sports Hall of Fame, her bio included this additional information about her extraordinary softball accomplishments: "After her graduation [from Cleveland State] in 1986 [and continuing] through 2001 she would win a total of 13 Women's Class 'A' All-World All-American awards while competing in the U.S. Slow-pitch Softball Association and ASA (nine-time USSSA All-World, four-time ASA All-America), and playing on six USSSA national championship teams. She was selected as the MVP of the USSSA World Series in 1987, 1989, and 1992, and the MVP of the National Triple Crown Championship Tournament in 1992. Capping her career, she was chosen in 1993 for the USSSA's All-Time All-World Team, one of just 12 players to be so honored."

EPILOGUE

THE JOURNEY CONTINUES

by

Nicole Antoinette Smith
(Founder of the Sports Legends of Cleveland)

*Stories by Vita (Redding) Shields, Bill Hann,
Ron Addison, and Luke Owens.*

The journey of the Sports Legends of Cleveland continues. This book, a testament to the unwavering spirit and remarkable achievements of Cleveland athletes, is just the beginning. As we turn the page on this chapter, we embark on a new adventure that delves deeper into the heart of athletic inspiration: the profound impact of coaches.

Our next project, a documentary film, will illuminate the enduring influence coaches have on their athletes, extending far beyond the playing field and into the arena of life. Through intimate stories and personal reflections, we will explore the transformative power of mentorship, guidance, and unwavering belief.

This epilogue offers a glimpse into the stories that await you. In the voices of our athletes, you'll discover the profound ways in which their coaches shaped not only their athletic careers but also their character, resilience, and paths to success. These are stories of dedication, perseverance, and the enduring bonds forged through shared passion and unwavering support.

Come journey with us once more as we explore the profound impact of those who inspire greatness on and off the court, field, or track. For in the world of sports, as in life, true legends are not just born – they are bred.

Stay with us as we continue to document and celebrate Cleveland's rich history of sports legends and look forward to new projects that honor our community's legacy and future. Together, we will ensure that the spirit of Cleveland's athletic excellence lives on for generations.

In the following pages, you will find stories from some of our athletes, offering a glimpse into what's coming next. These narratives will showcase the enduring bonds between coaches and athletes and illustrate how the lessons learned in sports extend far beyond the game.

VITA (REDDING) SHIELDS

"You could average 30 points a game if you wanted to!" In my junior year, my head coach of varsity stated those words. It was something I'd later be reminded of before graduation.

I was "that" tomboy. You know, the girl who grew up climbing trees, has bruised knees, plays nearly every sport she can find, and wrestles with the neighborhood boys. I have always loved sports, and had it not been for it being a faux pas, I would have likely tried to play football. I found my first love for spots in volleyball and basketball. And although I was a 4x league selection in Volleyball, my first sports love was basketball.

The first year, I lettered as a Varsity in three sports (Volleyball, Basketball, and Track). In volleyball, I was a decent hitter, setter, and back row (playing all positions at some point In between seasons, I played pick-up, did basketball drills at the playground or local gym, and played a ton of 1 on 1 or 33 with the neighborhood guys. I attended a basketball camp and AAUs during the summer after my first year. I ran track as a sprinter and threw the shot put in my first year. I was strong in the shot put. Sprinting, I learned the hard way (by seeing the backs of everyone in front of me) that I would never be the fastest person on the track. I tried another activity with the long jump. I fractured my foot at the end of my sophomore year and missed basketball camp and AAUs that summer, so I decided to quit track permanently and focus on my two best sports instead, but basketball was my love.

Backtracking a little to my Freshman year of high school, I was extremely excited to try out for the varsity team at John Marshall High School. I never assumed I would play JV. I had looked up to the varsity team, who used to practice occasionally at Carl F. Shuler Junior High. The varsity team the year before was among the winningest teams in JMH Lawyer history. The team had a fantastic front/backcourt with Janetta Graham, JoJo Grattan, Andrea Linear, and April Mixon…all great players in their own right. I had determined I would make varsity, having stood out at Shuler and playing with guys only in the off-season. I achieved the goal when I saw my name listed in the lineup of varsity players for the 1991-1992 season as a Guard/Forward.

Most of my memories of being on varsity were hilarious. The typical teen girl was fitting in, making jokes, singing songs in the locker room, and looking up to the upper-level students. When our first preseason game came around, the team committed to purchasing black and white Adidas shoes. Our uniforms ran small, so the night before a game, I would wash my jersey and shorts and strengthen them out across two chairs so they wouldn't fit as snugly during the game. I already had my socks, wristbands, and shoes in my backpack the night before. My selected locker before our first game was open when I prepared to leave that day. The gym lockers didn't have padlocks. When I pulled out my shoes that day, I realized someone had taken a straight razor to the side of my brand-new shoes. A feeling of horror and then embarrassment ran through my mind. My mom had paid for the shoes; I couldn't ask her for a new pair. I mentioned it briefly to my teammates, who were quiet or didn't know who slashed them.

That night, I went to work, putting my home economics skills to the test. I placed a large, double-wide shoelace across the gash and began sewing with a large needle used for upholstery. I was so excited to play the game I loved; nothing would stop me from lacing up those same shoes for our first home game. "My Adidas" had a makeshift patch across them, but from a distance, no one could tell anything was wrong with my shoes. I played the entire freshmen season with those shoes, starting all games and gaining Plain Dealer Player of the Week honors as a freshman at one point. I was a Forward for most of the year, being a defensive stopper and averaging low double-digits in scoring. Our team finished with a winning record of 13+ wins and, at one point, was ranked as one of the top teams in our Region (again, Cleveland Plain Dealer). We lost our Sectional appearance by 1 point to the Westlake Demons. That is all I can recall from that year.

Sophomore year was more of the same. Coach Jim Wasowski was great at bringing the team together in a way that made it feel good. He had a mentoring style, a fatherly approach, and a book complete with coaching schemes that he hoped we'd practice. He was our varsity coach in the first and second years. And while I don't remember many games, I remember us having a lot of laughter, bus rides, and upper-level students who were exceptional at the guard positions (i.e., April Mixon). We weren't expected to be a solid team, but we finished with 15+ wins and were a team that could surprise any great team on a good day. We would be having a rebuilding year in my junior year of high school.

Junior year, we were a young, scrappy team. We had no seniors and were experiencing a rebuilding year. Coach Wasowski decided to participate in an exchange program with a Japanese school, so we had a new coach for junior year, Dave Chollet. Coach Chollet often commented that I needed to tone down my foul language (I'd cuss when I missed a shot or upset at a play that could've been made). I would laugh when he said he imagined the portrait of the Mona Lisa having mud thrown on it every time I cussed. I learned to control my language more but was still fiery on the court.

Our team had two powerful forwards (Rachel Overton and Erma Robinson) and a speedy point guard who could defend (Quanza Currie), a great core to build upon. We played a series of ranked teams on the strength of the prior year's schedule, including Magnificat H.S., who, at the time, was a powerhouse in girls basketball. We didn't play well in that competition, which was not a strong game for me. I had committed at that point never to have that poor a showing again. I blossomed as a 2-guard who also played point during that season. I moved quickly into scoring low 20 points per game and was averaging six steals again in a fast-breaking style of play.

Entering Sectionals that year, we weren't favored to make much rumbling, but with a few standout performances from myself, Overton, and Robinson, we ended the season on a high note. We defeated our first two teams in the Sectional and would face the 15th ranked team in the region, Westlake High School, to whom we lost 1 point two years prior. The game was an amazingly close game with back-and-forth buckets. I had a great tournament, averaging more than 30 points per game. My coach's words were manifesting! The Westlake divisional game came down to the wire as we were down two points with less than 30 seconds. I recall getting an outlet pass, speeding up the court with one defender in the chase, pulling up at the 3-point line, and draining it! We were UP by 1 point with less than 10 seconds to go in the game. The team was cheering and running on the court as if we had won already. It was a surreal moment. Westlake called timeout. When we stepped back on the court, I could tell we would defend our lives. Westlake's best player, post-Julie Anthony, took a shot that hit the back rim, circled the hoop....and rolled out. John Marshall Lawyers had become like David, who had slayed the giant! No one would have expected us to win that game, but it is one of my fondest memories of high school basketball.

Senior year was a blur. Rachel had a season-ending knee injury, and Erma transferred to another school, so we had a new starting five. We weren't strong at any position other than point and shooting guard, of which Quanza and I would swap roles often. That year, I took on a large bulk of scoring as a challenge from Coach Chollet, who noted we lost our #2 and #3 scorers on the team. That is when he said, "You could score 30…". It was never a goal of mine; I wanted to win.

That year, I would finish the season with a state record 36.5 point per game scoring average and a slew of accolades, including MVP of the Senate, Runner-Up Ms. Basketball, USA-Today All-American honorable mention, First team All-Ohio and Academic All-Ohio. After several recruiting visits, I went to Brown University to gain experience playing NCAA Division I in the best academic environment I could find, which was offered in the Ivy League. John Marshall inducted me into the school's Sports Hall of Fame in 2018.

At Brown University, I learned more about the game, worked harder, and found the Ivy League to be the proper challenge for me personally and athletically. After being a four-year starter, I left College Hill a decorated athlete with 2 First Team All-Ivy League selections, 1 All-Rookie Team, and 2nd Team All-Ivy (junior season, through injury). I left as the all-time leading scorer in school history. I was later inducted into the Brown Sports Hall of Fame and honored by the Ivy League as a "Legend of the Ivy League," an honor given to select athletes annually at the Ivy League tournament.

Through it all, I remember attending CMSD, seeing my peers graduate, and enjoying what it meant to be a student-athlete. The lessons and friendships I've gained through sports have been one of the biggest blessings of my life. If there is anything I could share with student-athletes today, I would want them to know to maximize their moments: work hard, work in the offseason, and maintain their academic standing. It will be one of the best things you ever do in life. Your athletic career is short, so enjoy it and let it take you as far as possible!

Vita (Redding) Shields
All-Senate Basketball Player from John Marshall H.S. 1995, JMH HOF 2018 4-Year All-Ivy League Selection Brown University's All-time leading scorer (women's basketball), Brown HOF 2016 Legend of the Ivy League (2019)

BILL HANN

My sports journey started by playing Class "F" baseball at Brookside Park as a pitcher; I moved on to Brooklyn Little League All-Stars as a shortstop and then on to the Excelsior Post American Legion Team as a shortstop. I was blessed with great coaches, including Mike Carrick, who had played for the Pittsburgh Pirates. Highlight was starting for the best West Side Little League Team and Best West Side American Legion Team (which recruited from Rhodes High School, St. Ignatius, and St Edwards). We won the West Side Championship and competed against the Euclid Admirals for the city championship yearly. Thanks to this start in athletics, I developed a foundation of dedication, teamwork, and discipline that played an important role that was further developed in my basketball career.

My Dad took me to the Greater Cleveland Basketball League games at Navy Park. He was superintendent for Bruscino Construction, which had one of the best teams in the league. My Dad introduced me to Cleveland's "best of the best" players and became the team's ball boy.

I began my basketball career at age five thanks to having an older brother, Walt, who also played basketball, and the opening of Estabrook Recreation Center within walking distance from my home. My first coach was Andy Okulovich, who played quarterback at the Ohio State University and managed the recreation center. Although I was not old enough to play in the league, he allowed me to play and taught me much about the game and competition. From that day on, basketball became my favorite game, and I played against older, stronger, and more experienced players.

I started on each of my school teams in 1959-60 at Harper Junior High and 1961-65 at Rhodes High School. I had another great basketball coach, Andy Moran, who was called the "dean of high school coaches" at the time. He coached a state championship football team and our city championship basketball team at Rhodes High School. I played against many great high school players like Phil Argento (West), Charles Parnell (East Tech), Manny Leaks (East High), and John Petch (Lincoln/West). I was fortunate to play against the city's best players weekly by competing at Estabrook Recreation, Fairfax Recreation, Central Recreation, Clark Recreation, Lakewood Park, Brooklyn Park, and Parma Heights Park. I joined a few friends from East Tech and traveled to Akron, where we competed against many great players, including Gus Johnson (N.B.A. All-Star of the Baltimore Bullets).

Following are some highlights of my basketball career at Rhodes High School:

- Set a Rhodes High school scoring record of 44 points in 1963 as a sophomore and 55 points in 1965 as a senior
- After winning the West Senate in 1964 with a perfect 18-0 record, we beat East High School in the City Championship Game before 10,000 people at the Cleveland Arena and finished the year at 21-1 with the #4 ranking in the State of Ohio
- Chosen as the Most Valuable Player in the City Championship Game in 1964
- Chosen First Team All Senate and All-Scholastic as a junior and senior
- Chosen All Sectional and District Tournament as a junior and senior
- Chosen All Ohio 1st Team as a senior in 1965 and All-Ohio 2nd Team as a junior in 1964
- Chosen All-American as a senior in 1965
- Averaged 18.5 points as a junior and 23 points as a senior
- Chosen as the top Northeastern Ohio Player and played in the Ohio All-Star Game in 1965

After graduating high school in January 1965, I played on great amateur teams in Cleveland before starting college in September. This experience of playing against ex-college players helped prepare me for playing central college basketball. I played on the city championship Cleveland Jets in the Greater Cleveland Basketball League under coach Joe Wise (Lincoln Univ.), who was an outstanding college player and elected into the Greater Cleveland Sports Hall of Fame. I played with great players like Ron Hamilton (Tennessee State), Jim Stone (Providence), Skeeter Wallace (Kent State), Jim Robertson (Kentucky State), and Wavey Junior (Bowling Green). Ironically, we beat Bruscino Construction, where my Dad worked in the league and tournament championships. They were also loaded with incredible talents like Clark Kellogg Sr. (East High and father of Cleveland's great basketball player), Jerry Cummings (Central State), Jim Betts (Ohio University), and Dick Furry (Ohio State). We advanced to win outside Cleveland in the Amateur Athletic Union (A.A.U.) of the United States. We made it to the United States Regional Championship Game (Ohio-Kentucky-Michigan) in 1965, where Jones Brother Morticians of Dayton, Ohio, finally beat us. Members of that team included the great Roger Brown (Dayton), Al Jackson (Wilberforce), Willie Davis (DePaw), Ron McKnight (Kentucky State), and Henry Burlong (Dayton).

Also, in 1965, I was chosen to play with the Clevelanders in the Midwest Industrial League, the nation's premier amateur basketball league with teams like Akron Goodyear Wingfoots and Oklahoma Phillip 66ers. Coach John Broski, another Greater Cleveland Hall of Fame Member, was my coach. Our team included greats Jim Stone (Providence College), Jerry Cummings (Central State & league M.V.P.), Bobby Green (Univ Akron), Wavery Junior (Bowling Green), Jerry McGinty (Kent State) and Chuck Hall (Central State). In my first game, I guarded Larry Brown (North Carolina & Basketball Hall of Famer), who later played professional basketball, coached the N.C.A.A. Champions at Kansas, and professionally with the Philadelphia 76ers and New York Knicks in the N.B.A.

During the summers of 1964-65, while in high school, I was fortunate to work at Navy Park for Cleveland's Recreation Department along with Phil Argento, where we continued to develop a friendship and rivalry. John Nagy, Head of the City of Cleveland's Recreation Department, wanted us to attend and play for the Ohio State University. He even had Governor Jim Rhodes come to Cleveland to recruit us. Phil went on to play for Kentucky, and I did the same for Tennessee, both in the S.E.C. from 1965 to 1969. I was fortunate to play for Coach Ray Mears, who previously coached the College National Champions Wittenberg Tigers before moving on to Tennessee. Although I considered Ohio State, Duke, Michigan, and Cincinnati, I chose Tennessee due to Coach Mears' style and success. He was the #2 winning N.C.A.A. basketball coach when he retired, behind Coach John Wooten of U.C.L.A.

Following are some highlights of my college career at the University of Tennessee from 1965-1969:

- As required at the time, I played on the first-year team and then became the starting point guard for three years.
- Won the S.E.C. Championship with a 21-7 record and #4 national rank as a sophomore - 1967.
- Played in the N.C.A.A. Tournament in 24-team field as Champions of the S.E.C - 1967.
- Achieved second place in the S.E.C. with a 20-6 record as a junior in 1968.
- Achieved second place with a 21-7 record as a senior - 1969.
- All S.E.C. – 1968-69
- Led the S.E.C. in assists -1968-69. Set the single-game S.E.C. assist record of 19 vs Alabama in January 1968. I am honored that this record still stands some 52 years later.
- All N.I.T. (National Invitational Tournament) -1969. We were the first S.E.C. team to play in the tournament at Madison Square Garden in almost 50 years. We won 3 of 4 games and the Consolation Championship by beating Army (Coach Bobby Knight and player Mike Krzyzewski – both Hall of Fame Coaches at Indiana and Duke).
- Honorable Mention All-American - 1969
- Voted Best Team Player for two years, 1968-69
- All Volunteer Classic Tournament -1969.
- Held nation's leading scorer Pistol Pete Maravich (44+ point average) to 21, 21, 20, and 17 points – 1968-69.
- Invited to the Olympic Games - 1968.
- Played in the Kentucky All-Star Game - 1969.

Although I had to retire from competitive basketball due to back issues and multiple surgeries, the following are some highlights after college:

- Drafted #3 by the Atlanta Hawks - 1969
- Played two exhibition games with the Atlanta Hawks before returning to Tennessee to complete my education and coach the first-year team as a graduate assistant.
- Offered a job on Akron Goodyear's training program and position for their Wingfoots basketball team - 1970.
- Chosen to try out for the first Cleveland Cavaliers team along with fellow Clevelander Al Jackson (Wilberforce) - 1970.
- Chosen on the first team as an All-time Cleveland Press basketball player - 1979.
- Inducted into the Greater Cleveland Sports Hall of Fame in 1989 as the first basketball player of my era.
- Inducted into Rhodes High School Sports Hall of Fame.

I am grateful for the gifts God has given me, for being raised in Cleveland, my loving and nurturing parents and family, the coaches and teachers who poured into my life, and the team members and competitors who made me a better athlete. The lessons learned from athletics contributed to my 35-year career at KeyBank in the Midwest. They allowed me to serve at Seacoast Church and Water Mission International in Charleston, SC. Basketball allowed me to use God's gifts and contribute to something bigger than myself. I am thankful that I grew up in Cleveland, "The best location in the nation."

RON ADDISON

I have always been proud to be born and raised in Cleveland. When people ask me where I am from, I always say Cleveland, the city, not the suburbs.

When I was growing up, the big names in Cleveland Sports were Jim Brown and Louis Tiant. I lived 6 miles from Cleveland Stadium, where I would watch the Indians play with 2,000 people in the stands.

My friends and I spent all fall playing football, all winter playing basketball outside, and all spring and summer playing baseball.

I was naturally drawn to running. I just always loved it. My mom would give me a quarter and tell me to run down to the corner store to purchase a loaf of bread, and I would run there and back. Sometimes, I would ask her to time me.

As I was preparing to enter 10th grade at Rhodes High School, I planned to try out for football, as skinny and scrawny as I was. But I missed the first day of tryouts due to a needed medical procedure, and if you missed the first day, you were out.

Just before school started, I attended an orientation event where all the coaches of the various sports gave a short talk. A coach named Jim Zickes began to talk about Cross Country. As I learned Cross Country was running, I started paying attention. I had never imagined that running could be a real sport. Right then and there, I decided to try Cross Country.

I attended the first practice, which was held at Brooklyn Park on a Saturday morning. Brooklyn Park was several miles away, so I rode my bike there. Even though I had run a lot as a kid, I had never been on an extended training run. The coach sent us on a five-mile easy run on this first day of practice. I did not know anyone at the practice but was smart enough to realize that winning the workout would not make me any new friends.

I just positioned myself in the middle of the group and started running. No one was pushing the pace, but people started dropping quickly. I kept at the back of the lead group, doing whatever they did. Soon, there were only a handful of us, and I could see guys, juniors, and seniors looking at me funny. Soon enough, we had finished the five-mile run. Then I biked home.

Over the next week or so, we started light intervals, hills, etc., and I stayed with the leaders, never pushing anything.

Soon enough, we had our first dual meet against Lincoln. I was pleased I could run as hard as I wanted and placed 7th and 4th on the team. After the race, the assistant coach, Steve Korinchak, said, "Not bad for a junior with no background in running. And by the way, you should buy some spikes and not race in those Keds." I said, "I am a sophomore, and Yeah, I will get some spikes."

I enjoyed getting to know the guys on the team and learning the running history of Rhodes. Volunteer assistants Steve Korinchak and Jim Emory had graduated from Rhodes 4 years earlier, and both had gone on to run college cross country and track at Miami University, Ohio. Recent graduate Kent Newman was now a freshman cross-country runner at Ohio State. Head coach Jim Zickes had been a pole vaulter at Bowling Green and coached track and football but had never coached Cross Country before. He and I would learn much from each other over the next few years.

I don't remember any details about the next meet except to know that that day, I was the team's second man behind Terry Davidson and maintained that position until the Senate meet when I moved up to number 1.

Our team ran the sectionals and qualified for districts. At districts, neither I nor the team qualified for the state meet. But there was one more race to run: the Cleveland Senate meet, which was a big deal to us. I wanted to do well as an individual, learning that the top 10 individuals would receive a trophy. I had never received a trophy for anything, and my goal was to win one.

We were successful at the Senate meet, taking second place, and I placed third as an individual, beating Terry for the first time. I remember being so excited about placing third and winning that trophy. Over the years, I have disposed of most of my running awards, keeping only those special to me, and I still have that first trophy.

Indoor track season started in January, and fortunately, Rhodes had an indoor track. The Rhodes indoor track was infamous, and if you never had the opportunity to see it, I am not sure you will appreciate the description. Students in the 1930s dug it out, literally with picks and shovels. It was ten laps to the mile. The sprints and hurdles were run on the straight. The stairs up to the school were placed so that taller sprinters and hurdlers had to run the inside lanes to keep from hitting their heads. For the longer races, there was a first tight hairpin turn, then a short straight, a quick turn to the right, and then you circled back to the left and ended up at the top of the straight. And, of course, the track was dirt. There was a set of bleachers for spectators. The space was small, with tight turns, a low ceiling, and posts all around supporting the school. But we had some exciting meets there, and the atmosphere was electric. Most importantly, it was a place to train in the winter.

After the indoor season, the Cleveland City Championships were held downtown on a 10-lap-to-the-mile banked board track. I was entered in the mile and the 880 and had never run on boards before. No one gave me any tactical advice, and I was unsure what to do, but I found myself in the early lead. Then I started sprinting the straights and slowing down on the turns. This frustrated the other entrants but seemed to work for me as I won the city meet mile as a sophomore. I figured it worked in the mile, so I decided to try it in the 880, and it worked again; I won that race, also.

Our first outdoor event of the 1970 track season was the Mansfield Relays, a massive event with participants from several states and Canada. We were entered in the Distance Medley relay. I don't remember anything about that race except that we won, which is the most crucial part. Willy Kaulfersch, Marc Kolanz, and Kirk Muir were my teammates.

The next day, I entered the open mile, and I must admit my coach fudged my time to get me in the fast section.

I remember being in the middle of the pack next to a tall guy with a green singlet. He and another guy pull away from the pack briefly, making it a two-person race. I was still racing but also watching these two. They finished in a photo finish, and I could not tell who won. I finished 7th in 4:30, my first-ever outdoor mile race. I saw the guy with the green singlet and asked who had won, and he said the other guy. The other guy was Ohio legend Les Nagy. The guy in the green singlet was named Doug Brown, from Notre Dame High School in Harper Woods, Michigan. I would not see Doug again until the fall of 1972 when I arrived at the University of Tennessee for cross-country camp. Doug, the Tennessee cross country team captain, was late for camp, busy participating in the 1972 Munich Olympics.

As the 1970 outdoor season progressed, I got my mile time down to 4:22 and ran 9:43 for the two miles.

At the end of the season came the outdoor city championships held at my home track at Rhodes. And I remember taking the lead down the backstretch and into the final turn. Then, for some inexplicable reason, I slowed in the turn. And I got passed. Since the finish was in the middle of the straight, I did not have enough time to recover. That may be the stupidest thing I have ever done in a race. I have no idea what I was thinking, and it was a hard lesson, but it was one I learned from.

My sophomore year was over. I had some success and a lot of fun. I did everything my coach told me to do, no less and no more. And I was thrilled I had missed the football tryouts. It was time now for summer vacation. And vacation I did, running very little.

My junior year of cross country came, and I won most events, dual meets, and the Senate Championships. But my fundamental objective was to do well at the state meet. I won sectionals and districts. I remember being very happy at winning districts and qualifying for the state meet, which was to be held at the Ohio State University Golf Course. I qualified as an individual, but my coach told me I could invite a teammate to travel with us and share my hotel room. I chose Alan Kofsky, a senior who had recognized my abilities very early and wanted to see me succeed. Another reason I liked and respected Alan was because when I was a sophomore cross-country runner, he gave me specific and direct advice on managing my early success personally. One of his better advice was, "Don't be a jerk."

The state meet came on a bright and sunny Saturday morning. The field was vast, and the race was only 2 miles long, so I knew I had to get out quickly, which I did, probably being in the top 5 at the half-mile mark. And it was all downhill from there. No, it was the race course, but my performance. I felt horrible and kept getting past it until the finish finally arrived. I had placed a very disappointing 16th. I had never participated in such a large and prestigious event before and felt unprepared. I had not run during the previous summer. My workouts were the same as everyone else on my team and not excessively strenuous. I was placed 16th, highlighting that there are many talented people worldwide and true success comes from hard physical work and mental focus. I took this as a learning experience and vowed to do better.

I ran daily—usually 10 miles for the rest of that fall and winter. Even when the indoor season started and we had regular meets, I ensured I ran 10 miles on my distance and weekend days. I was building a base even though, at that time, I had never heard or used that phrase. I became a contender during these lonely, long runs in the winter snows. And my coach, who had never coached a distance runner until my sophomore year, started to come into his own as a distance coach.

I was very fortunate that I had a great high school coach. Jim Zickes was a military veteran who played and coached football and participated in Division 1 Track and Field as a Bowling Green State University pole vaulter. First of all, he was a great guy who was sincerely interested in the betterment of his students and athletes. He wanted to nurture my talent long-term, not abuse it for short-term gain. And he studied and learned how to coach distance runners. And he became very good at it.

My goal for my junior track season was to win the state meet mile. And I won race after race. I won the sectional meet, and a senior from Berea named Mike Burley was a distant second. I won the district meet, and Burley was a close second. I started to look into this guy and discovered he had won the Cross Country State Meet in the race where I was 16th. And during the winter, he was a swimmer, not a runner. So when the outdoor season started, he was fit but not sharp. And each week, he was getting sharper.

Burley was competent and experienced, and I was still relatively inexperienced. I usually win by a lot, but I am not good at tactical racing yet. At the state meet, I took the lead as usual. When Burley came up to my shoulder with one lap to go, I did not show any patience or smartness. I just reacted and started sprinting, which was a big mistake. Burley followed me around the track, drafting off of me and waiting. He timed his kick perfectly and beat me by two-tenths a second to claim the state championship. 4:14.7 to 4:14.9. Mike went on to participate in some college track events so that I would see him on occasion in college. But he was using those meets as training as he parleyed his abilities at running and swimming into a spot on the US Olympic Team participating in the Modern Pentathlon.

Defeated but not discouraged, I ran a lot through the summer. My new goal was to win the state Cross-Country meet.

During a dual meet with Padua at the Rhodes Cinder track the previous spring, I was racing Peter Hadtisch in a driving rainstorm. I replied that Pete told me about the weather during the two-mile race. He then said he spoke to competitors frequently during competition, but no one had ever replied before. After the race, we cooled down and became friends. From that time on, we ran and socialized a lot together.

We were friends: Pete, Joe Hurd, Don Jerningan, Larry Coy, and others.

I have fond memories of all of these competitors. Even though we were fierce competitors, we were truly friends.

Another example of sportsmanship occurred in the spring of 1972 at a meet I did not attend, but the story circulated quickly. Ohio had a sensible rule: you could not run another race if you ran the 2 mile. Pete Hadtisch and Don Jerningan were the principals of the story. Everyone knew the rule, but for some reason, Peter ran the 880 miles and 2 miles and won all 3. Don was second in two of the races. After the awards were handed out at the end of the meet, the management realized what had happened. They took the first-place medals from Pete and gave two of them to Don. Don promptly found Pete and gave him the medals back, saying, well, you did beat me.

A cross-country meet called the Bowling Green Cross Country Relay was held that fall. And it was a relay of sorts. There were seven races run on flights. All of the team's 7th men ran a race. Then, the 6th men, etc., until all seven races had been completed. They scored it on total team time. But it allowed many other deserving athletes to cross the finish line first. That was an enjoyable event.

After the sectional cross country meet in the fall of 1972, Larry Coy of John Marshall and I had qualified to move on as individuals. Larry's coach, Dick Emory, and coach Zickes were excellent friends. So, the 4 of us got together for some training sessions in anticipation of the state meet. Larry, who was a junior, and I became friends. The 4 of us even traveled together to the state meet, where Larry and I shared a room.

I had been training and racing hard the entire summer and cross-country season. My coach tapered me just before the state meet, the first time I had tapered. On Friday before the meet, I ran two easy miles on the course and a few strides. My energy level and excitement were off the charts, and I felt great.

Race day arrived, and I still felt excited and energetic. There were 200 of us on the line, ready to go, and I false-started.

Fortunately, before the rule of one false start, you are out.

I went out hard but controlled, and, at the one-half mile, I was in the top ten but probably 20 yards off of the leaders. I was in 4th and 10 yards off the leader at the mile mark, with one-half mile to go. Jerningan and I shared the lead with Joe Hurd behind us and solidly in 3rd. I started to push hard with a quarter to go, but Don was hanging with me, and I was worrying. Finally, to my great relief, Don fell back, and I crossed the finish line as the Ohio State Cross Country Champion. Joe Hurd passed Don for second, and Don ended up 3rd.

My friend and roommate Larry Coy finished ?? in that race and won it the following year.

My next goal was to win the state mile meet and break Reggie McAfee's Ohio State mile record of 4:08.5. Reggie became the first African American to break 4:00.

Fortunately, Rhodes had some other talented distance runners. Their talent and coach Zickes' growing skill as a distance coach allowed us to enjoy running various relays during the outdoor season. My teammates in these relays were Willie Kaulfersch, Marc Kolanz, and Rick Furman. Rhodes won the Distance Medley Relay at Mansfield for the third straight year.

The next big relay meet was the Berea Relays, and we were competing in the four-by-one-mile relay. One of the most formidable competitors I continually faced was Glen Wilburn from Amherst Steele High School. He and I ran anchor on our four-by-one team that day. Amherst also had a solid cross-country team and was historically an excellent distance school.

When I received the stick, I was a little bummed out as Glen was a total of 110 yards ahead of me. I took off as hard as I have ever in a one-mile race. At the end of the first lap, I was still 110 behind. I was still a complete 110 behind at the halfway point. I had not heard any split times and would not tell the entire race. At the start of the final lap, I still had to be 75 yards behind. Then, as I came off the turn into the back straight, I could tell the gap was closing quickly. Encouraged, I gave it everything I had. But the time I was halfway down the back straight, I could tell I would catch him. The gap was closing dramatically into the final turn, off the turn, and down the home straight. It would be close, but again, I knew Rhodes would win. I finally passed Glen's steps before the tape.

It turns out that Glen had gone out at 2:02, as did I.

I had no idea we were going that fast. I don't know the three-quarter split. But Glen paid the price for trying to put the race away early. His time was in the mid-4:20s, and I was clocked at 4:10. It was an enjoyable and exciting race.

The next big event on our schedule was the West Tech Relays. Our coach planned on entering us in the DMR and the four 1-mile relays, and we would be heavy favorites in both. But for a change of pace, Willy, Marc, and Rick asked our coach to enter us in the four-by-one and the four-by-880. Winning the four by 880 would be a challenge.

As expected, we won the four by 1. We were lined up for the four by 880 a short time later. Rhodes and East Tech fought for the lead as the third leg ended. Chris Ayers of East Tech got the stick for the final. Let one step ahead of Chris. I was pleased to get the stick one step behind rather than one step ahead.

I dropped in right behind him and made no effort to go around. We ran hard and in single file for the first 660 yards. Going down the backstretch, I looked down and said his calves were quivering like Jello. I had never seen calves so loose. I had no idea if that was good or bad, but I decided if he were that loose, it would probably be wrong for me as he would have a lot of speed left. I still did not make an effort to pass him. The race was so close I could not afford to run even an extra yard trying to pass him into or on the final turn. After we came out of the final turn into the home stretch, I moved slightly to the right, kept my head up, and continued pumping my arms. I was gaining on him inch by inch, right next to him, and then we hit the finish line in a photo finish. It took several minutes for the officials to review the pictures, but in the end, Rhodes was declared the winner.

By then, I had a reputation for exciting relay finishes, and as I came off of the last turn, the stands were chanting my name: ADDISON, ADDISON, ADDISON. I was so focused on the race that I did not hear this, but I was told about it later.

The following week, we traveled to Toledo for the Toledo Blade meet, where I would run the open mile and open 880. However, for some reason, there was a mix-up in the entries, and I was not entered in the mile. My coach tried to get me in, but to no avail. So, I ran the 880 Fresh for the first time and won the race with a personal best of 1:55.00.

At the district meet, I ran the mile and the 880. I also won the mile in 4:11 flat and qualified for state in the 880, running 1:56 flat. I habitually added my mile and 880 times at each competition to see the total. This total of 6:07 was my best combination time ever. I was ready for state.

The Ohio State University track was inside the football stadium. The meet day was scorching and humid, and the artificial turf on the football field magnified the heat. I won the mile in 4:13 and returned to place 5th in the 880. I had accomplished my goal of winning the 1972 state meet but had not broken Reggie's State High School Record.

There was no internet, e-mail, or cell phones in high school. If someone wanted to call you, they had to dial your number on a rotary telephone connected by wires to the wall. The phone in my home hung on the wall in the kitchen. Our home phone rang often as college coaches called me about attending their schools. By the end of my senior year in high school, I had received letters or phone calls from over 200 colleges and universities asking me to attend their schools.

One day in October 1971, I received a call from recruiting coordinator Mike Tomasello of the University of Tennessee. I did not know anything about UT at the time and had no particular interest in them. But Mike told me they were hosting the NCAA Cross Country Championships that November, and he suggested I visit that weekend. Not only could I check out UT, but I could also see the meet. That got my attention; I agreed to fly to Knoxville that weekend.

Two UT track athletes, Dennis Flood and Danny Zoeller, met me at the airport. Danny was from the Cincinnati area and had run his high school track in Ohio. I was 5 foot 9 inches tall, weighed 125 pounds, had no upper body strength, and wore glasses and braces. When they asked me my goals for the upcoming 1972 track season, I told them I wanted to break Reggie's state record of 4:08.5. After I started school at UT and they became my teammates, they said to me about the good laugh they had about that one.

Fortunately, I still had an opportunity to get that record I wanted so badly. I had been invited to the All-American High School Championships, which were to be held in Baton Rouge, Louisiana, at Louisiana State University. I was also invited to the Golden West meet in Sacramento, California, and my coach entered me in the National Junior Championships, which were to be held in Denver, Colorado.

I will be forever grateful to the Rhodes Senior class, my friends Larry Coy, and others from John Marshall High School. Between them, they raised the money needed to pay expenses for Coach Zickes and me to attend these prestigious events. Raising this money for me was a fantastic act.

Coach Zickes and I arrived in Baton Rouge on a hot, humid afternoon in June. Stepping off of the plane was like stepping into an oven. LSU is a lovely college campus, and we stayed in one of the dorms. We explored the campus and the city and generally waited for race day. The race was in the evening, still hot and humid but with no sun beating down on us. Before the race, I met some competitors in the mile run and saw their PRs. Of the 12 athletes in the field, I think my open best of 4:11 was about the 8th fastest time. I would have my work cut out for me.

When the gun went off, I went out with the group and tried not to get boxed in. We were 62 and 2:04. I took the lead Sometime during the 3rd quarter. We passed the three-quarter mark in 3:08, so we had run 62 62 64. With precisely one lap to go, a few people passed me, but I was in control and let them. I did not panic like I had at the state meet my junior year. The pace started to pick up. I felt great and was in the lead group. But going into the final turn, I allowed myself to get boxed in. I wanted to start my kick but was boxed on the inside. I had never been in this situation before. Looking back on it and having the experience I do now, I should have been patient, as things usually open up down the home stretch, or I could have just pushed my way through. Instead, I slowed, let a few people pass me, and then moved to the outside. Coming off the turn, I was free but behind. Reed Fisher of Dallas, Texas, was a step ahead of the field in lane one. I was at the back of a group of 6 or so guys and in lane 3. I took off and quickly passed the field except for Reed, who was pulling away. But I kept sprinting and started to close rapidly on Reed. I thought I would win, but the line came up too quickly, and I finished second in a very close race. Reed ran 4:05.7, and I ran 4:05.9, breaking the Ohio State record.

A week later, I found myself in Sacramento for the Golden West. I had run a solo 9:06 two miles earlier in the season and wanted to break 9 minutes. I figured the Golden West would be a perfect opportunity for that. It was another hot day, but not as humid. But the meet was run in the afternoon, and the sun blazed down on the clay track. Again, most other guys in the race had better PRs than I did. But I was hoping to hang on and run under 9. I am unsure what happened that day as I had never had a bad race before. I had made my share of tactical mistakes, or maybe I did not run as fast as I wanted, but I had never before run poorly, which is what I did that day. I felt horrible, my legs were tired, and I finished well off the pace.

We left Sacramento and traveled directly to Denver for the National Junior Championships, where I was entered in the mile and the 3000-meter steeplechase. At a summer fun meet, I had seen steeple barriers for the first time the previous summer and asked about the race. After I understood it, I decided to try it that day. I put a hurdle on the infield and did a stride over it. I did not fall, so I went to the start line for the steeplechase. I ran very slowly but did not hurt myself and won the race.

Coach Zicked entered me in the steeplechase in case I did not make the mile final or had another bad race. Entering the steeplechase was a backup plan I hoped I did not need.

There were prelims for the mile run competition, a new concept for me. I went to the line knowing I had to finish in the top 6 to make the final. Many of the guys I had raced in Baton Rouge were in the race, but this was also open to first-year college students. These guys were older and more experienced than us high school guys. All I remember about the preliminary round was coming off the final turn, slowing down as others did, and making sure I was in the top 6. Several guys slowed down more than me, and I " won" the prelim. That was not my goal; it just happened. But none of the qualifiers were working too hard at the finish line.

The finals were the next day. I don't remember much about the race, except I fell asleep on the final lap and let Chuck Forys of Syracuse University get away from me. I was in the pack on the final lap, feeling good, making sure I did not get boxed, and then I made my move. I again passed the field but fell short of winning, placing second to Chuck. I felt good that I did not have another bad race, that I beat all of the high school guys, including Reed Fisher, and that I made the national junior team, but I was disappointed to finish 2nd when victory was so close.

A couple of hours later, the steeple chase was, and I decided to run it—not as a desperate hail Mary due to a poor mile performance, but because I felt excellent and figured, why not?

Denver is at altitude, the mile-high city. That slowed us a bit in the mile, but altitude would affect the steeplechasers. I did not think I could do well; I ran for training and fun. sBecause of that, I went out slowly, careful not to extend myself or hurt myself over the barriers. This worked to my benefit as most of the field went out pretty hard. Because of this and the altitude, they went into oxygen debt much sooner than they would have at sea level. Because I went out slower, I ran within myself and felt good. All of a sudden, I started picking people off. So, I started running harder and continued to pick people off. Before I knew it, I was in third place, and the race was almost over. Granted, 1 and 2 were a long way ahead of me. They were both college freshmen and had been running this race for the entire season, and this was only my second one ever. And to the surprise of many people, including me, I placed third.

My second-place finish at the National Junior Championships in the mile run earned me a place on the United States National Junior Team. A couple of weeks later, I returned to Sacramento for a dual meet, a USA vs. Russia meet. This was the same track that had hosted the Golden West earlier in the summer. I was so excited to receive a USA singlet and warmup suit. I could not believe I would represent the United States in an international competition. The US and Russian teams stayed in the dorms where we had stayed for the Golden West meet. The other miler, Chuck, and I were roommates. It was fun and exciting to meet and interact with the Russian athletes. They were very friendly and excited to be in the United States. Unfortunately for Chuck, he had a bad cold the day before the competition. I felt terrible for him but also felt additional pressure to do well.

There were only 4 in the field to start with, and with Chuck being ill, the field shrunk to 3 quickly. The Russians ran as a team, and I kept trying to get around them. I would make a move, and one of the Russians would block me. I did this several times. Later, I realized I should have just relaxed behind them and made one big move when the opportunity presented itself. Especially with such a small field, there was no danger of getting truly boxed. I know I made a big move down the backstretch that put me into second place for the first time. Off the final turn, it was a wild, mad dash for the finish line with me between the Russians. I ended up a disappointing 3rd, but we were all within ½ of a second of each other, so at least I was competitive. And I again learned some lessons about tactics. And I ran 3:49.5 in my first 1500 ever, equivalent to a 4:06 mile.

My parents and three sisters had driven to California to watch the race. We drove south to Santa Barbara the next day to visit an uncle. While en route, we stopped at a pizza place for lunch. And by chance, the TV in the pizza restaurant was on, and the track meet was being shown, and there I was, running the 1500 on national TV. What struck me was listening to the commentary. As I moved, the announcers said I would never last like that and should relax until the time was right. They were right; again, I learned this lesson for future reference. However, I was more than pleased when I finished the hunt, and they gave me credit for running a gutsy race and almost winning.

LUKE OWENS SR.

Luke Owens Sr. was born in Roe, Arkansas, the eldest son of Albert and Esther Owens and the second of five children. The family migrated to Cleveland, Ohio, in 1936. His parents wanted their children to have a better education and opportunities to excel.

Luke Owens Sr.'s sports career began at Moses Cleveland Junior High School. He excelled in track and field and football. Later, he attended John Adams High School in Cleveland, Ohio. 1953, he led the Rebels to its first Ohio Boys Track and Field Championship. He placed first in the discus and second in the shot put. Later, he was recruited by Kent State University for a football scholarship. At Kent State University, he was a two-way star and an ALL-American First Team selection for the Golden Flashes.

Luke Sr. was part of a defense that posted six shutout victories. The Green Bay, Cleveland Browns, and Baltimore Colts were scouting him. They all wanted to see him work out. He was selected as the 32nd overall pick in the third round of the 1957 NFL Draft, which included names of soon-to-be great players such as Paul Horning and Jim Brown. He was selected by the Baltimore Colts in 1957 and played his rookie year. Later, he was traded to the Chicago Cards team, which later became the St. Louis Cardinals. He played first as a defensive end and later as a defensive tackle. In 1963, he was the Most Valuable Player (MVP) for the St. Louis Cardinals after making 10.5 quarterback sacks. His tenure in the NFL was from 1957 to 1965.

Luke returned to Cleveland after his tenure with the NFL. He used the business degree he acquired and later owned a couple of Mexican restaurants called Taco Luke. He later worked for the city of Cleveland as director of consumer affairs and finally for the state of Ohio as director of Cleveland East Unemployment Services, from which he retired.

APPENDIX

The Appendix provides additional details, records, and resources that further illuminate the rich history of the Senate Athletic League and its legendary athletes. This section serves as a comprehensive reference for readers who wish to delve deeper into the topics explored in the main chapters. This appendix is designed to be a valuable resource for historians, researchers, alumni, and sports enthusiasts who wish to honor and preserve the legacy of Cleveland's remarkable athletic tradition.

APPENDIX I

OLYMPIANS

MEDAL WINNERS

JOHN ADAMS

Nathan E. "Nate" Brooks: 1952 Helsinki – Boxing (Flyweight) – Gold

COLLINWOOD

Carmen Barth (Carmine R. Di Bartholomeo): 1932 Los Angeles – Boxing (Middleweight) – Gold

EAST TECH

David Albritton: 1936 Berlin – Track (High Jump) – Silver

Harrison Dillard: 1948 London – Track: 100m – Gold; 4x100m Relay – Gold, 1952 Helsinki – Track: 100m Hurdles – Gold; 4x100m Relay – Gold

Paul Fina: 1940 – Gymnastics (Olympics canceled due to World War II)

Louis Laurie: 1936 Berlin – Boxing – Bronze

Jesse Owens (James Cleveland Owens): 1936 Berlin – Track: 100m – Gold, Long Jump – Gold, 200m – Gold, 4x100m Relay – Gold

George G. "Jackie" Wilson: 1936 Berlin – Boxing (Bantamweight) – Silver

JOHN HAY

Madeline Manning-Jackson: 1968 Mexico City – Track (800m) – Gold, 1972 Munich – Track (4x400m Relay) - Silver, 1976 Montreal – Track – No Medal, 1980 Moscow – Track – USA Boycott

LINCOLN-WEST

Dartanyon Crocket: 2012 London Paralympics – Judo – Bronze, 2016. Rio de Janiero – Judo – Bronze

JOHN MARSHALL

Thomas Jefferson: 1984 Los Angeles – Track: 200m Dash – Bronze, 4x100m Relay – Bronze

SOUTH HIGH

Stella Walsh (Stanislawa Walasiewicz): 1930 Prague Women's Olympics – Track: 60m Dash – Gold; 100m Dash – Gold; 200m Dash – Gold, 1932 Los Angeles Olympics – Track: 100m Dash - Gold, 1934 London Women's Olympics – Track: 60m Dash – Gold, 1936 Berlin Olympics – Track: 100m Dash – Silver

NON-MEDAL OLYMPIANS

LINCOLN

Ida Jean Hopkins: 1972, Winte Olympics, Sapporo, Japan, Luge

JOHN ADAMS

Eleanor Montgomery: 1964 Tokyo – Track (High Jump), 1968 Mexico City – Track

Cynthia Bernice Robinson-Holland (Bernice Holland): 1948 London – Track (80m Hurdles)

EAST TECH

Vivian Brown (Brown-Reed): 1964 Tokyo – Track (200m)

Paul Fina: Honorary USA Olympic Team – Gymnastics 1940, 1944 (No Olympics held these years due to World War II.)

Ted Kara: 1936 Berlin – Boxing – USA Team Captain

Toccara Montgomery: 2004 Athens – Women's Wrestling

GLENVILLE

Terrell Gausha: 2012 London – Boxing

Morelle McCane: 2024 Paris – Boxing

SOUTH HIGH

Frances Kaszubski (Sobczak): 1948 London – Track (Discus, Shot Put, 1960 Rome – Manager of USA Women's Team

APPENDIX II

COLLEGE AND PROFESSIONAL HALLS OF FAME

Many honorees listed below have been inducted into more than one Hall of Fame. This listing includes only inductees into national collegiate (NCAA) and professional sports Halls of Fame. It does not include individual college and high school Halls of Fame. Inductees in the Greater Cleveland Sports Hall of Fame can be found in Appendix III.

CENTRAL

Edward Delahanty – Major League Baseball Hall of Fame

COLLINWOOD

Joe Maxim (Giuseppe Antonio Berardinelli) – International Boxing HOF, National Italian-American Sports Hall of Fame

EAST HIGH

William Earl "Bill" Sprackling – College Football HOF

EAST TECH

David Albritton – U.S. Track and Field HOF

Gordon Cobbledick – National Baseball HOF (Sportswriter)

Harrison Dillard – U.S. Track and Field HOF, U.S. Olympic HOF

James Richard "Jim" Martin – College Football HOF

Jesse Owens (James Cleveland Owens) – U.S Track and Field HOF, U.S. Olympic HOF

Joseph "Joe" Giallombardo – U.S. Gymnastics HOF, Helms Foundation HOF

Robert Stanford "Bob" Brown – College Football HOF, Pro Football HOF

Toccara Montgomery, National Wrestling Hall of Fame

William T. (Wee Willie) Smith – Naismith Basketball HOF

GLENVILLE

Benjamin "Benny" Friedman – College Football HOF, Pro Football HOF

Hal Lebovitz – National Baseball HOF (Sportswriter)

JOHN ADAMS

Eleanor Montgomery – U.S. Track and Field HOF

JOHN HAY

John Charles Hicks, Jr. – College Football HOF

Madeline Manning Mims – U.S. Track and Field HOF

JOHN MARSHALL

Eugene Gibbons – National Wrestling Hall of Fame (Coach)

Patrick "Pat" Galbincea – National Wrestling HOF (Writer)

Vita Reddiing, Brown University HOF

LINCOLN

Willie Avery, Baldwin Wallace University Athletic Hall of Fame

Marty Hunt, Kenyon College Hall of Fame

Walt Yowarsky, Kentucky Pro Football Hall of Fame

RHODES

Chris Parks, Ashland University HOF

Dave Kyle - Cleveland State University HOF

Leslie "Les" Horvath – College Football HOF

Toure Carter – Ashland University HOF

SOUTH HIGH

Gomer Jones – College Football HOF

Stella Walsh (Stanislawa Walasiewicz) – U.S. Track and Field HOF

WEST HIGH

Dick Bonacci, Toledo University Hall of Fame

Elmer Gedeon, Michigan Collegiate Athletic Hall of Fame

Gene "Sonny" Degyansky, Baldwin Wallace Alumni Athletic Association Hall of Fame

John Matteucci, National Wrestling Hall of Fame

Richard Bonacci, National Wrestling Hall of Fame

Vincent R. "Vince" Matteucci, National Wrestling Hall of Fame

WEST TECH

August Michael "Mike" Michalske – Pro Football Hall of Fame

APPENDIX III

GREATER CLEVELAND SPORTS HALL OF FAME

CENTRAL

Philip Goldstein - Boxing

Ralph Tyler – Class of 1939, Track

COLLINWOOD

Carmen Barth (Carmine R. Di Bartholomeo) – Early 1930s, Boxing

Joey Maxim (Giuseppe Antonio Berardinelli) – Class of 1940, Boxing

Sam Palumbo – Class of 1952, Football

Tony Adamle – Class of 1941, Football

EAST HIGH

Emanuel "Manny" Leaks – Class of 1965, Basketball

John Olszewski – 1930s, Basketball

Roger Peckingpaugh – Class of 1909, Baseball

Theodore "Ted" Abrams – Class of 1923, Swimming/Diving

EAST TECH

David Albritton – Class of 1933, Track

Estus Newberry – Class of 1954, Track

George G. "Jackie" Wilson – Class of 1936, Boxing

Gordon Cobbledick – Class of 1918, Sportswriter

Harrison Dillard – Class of 1941, Track

James Cleveland "Jesse" Owens – Class of 1933, Track

Jim Martin – Class of 18944, Football

Jim Stone – Class of 1959, Basketball

Joe Gilliambardo – Class of 1935, Gymnastics

Joe Vosmik – Class of 1926, Baseball

John Behm – Class of 1922, Football Player, Coach

John Broski – Basketball Coach, 1956-60

Louis Fina – Class of 1937, Gymnastics

Louis Laurie – Early 1930s, Boxing

Paul Fina – Class of 1939, Gymnastics

Peter Amico – Class of 1929, Football/Basketball

Robert "Bob" Brown – Class of 1959, Football

Sherlie Herford Rainey – Class of 1953, Track

Ted Theodore – Class of 1947, Track

Vivian Reed Brown – Class of 1960, Track

Wally Edwards – Class of 1978, Basketball

Willie Smith – Class of 1930, Basketball

GLENVILLE

Benny Friedman – Class of 1923, Football

Hal Lebovitz – Class of 1934, Sportswriter

Harry Weltman – Class of 1950, Basketball Management

Merle Levin – Class of 1946, College Sports Information Director

267

Ted Ginn Sr. – Class of 1976, Football and Track

JOHN ADAMS

Bernice Holland Robinson – Track Coach, 1980s-1990s

Eddie Finnigan – Class of 1928, Football and Basketball

Eleanor Montgomery – Class of 1964, Track

Luke Owens – Class of 1953, Football

Nate Brooks – Class of 1976, Boxing

Nick Mileti – Class of 1949, Pro Sports Entrepreneur

Ray Mack (Raymond J. Mikovsky) – Class of 1938, Baseball

William Fleishman – Class of 1931, Basketball

JOHN HAY

Harold Kester – Wrestling Coaching, 1934-1943 (West High 1944-1951)

John Hicks – Class of 1969, Football

Madeline Manning Jackson – Class of 1965, Track

Tim McGee – Class of 1981, Football

JOHN MARSHALL

Al Carroll – Class of 1933, Wrestling

Gene Gibbons – Class of 1948, Wrestling

Howard Ferguson – Class of 1959, Wrestling

LINCOLN

Ida Jean Hopkins – Class of 1957, Softball

RHODES HIGH SCHOOL

Bill Hann – Class 1965, Basketball

Don McCafferty – Class 1938, Football

George Seedhouse – Athletic Director and Sports Administration

Les Horvath – Class 1939, Football

SOUTH

Anthony "Tony" Pianowski – Class of 1928, Official (Basketball, Baseball, Football)

Chet Adams – Class of 1933, Football

Frances Sobczak Kaszubski – Class of 1934, Track and Basketball

Gomer Jones – Class of 1976, Football

John Broski, Class of 1986, Basketball

Stella Walsh – Class of 1932, Basketball and Track

WEST HIGH

Dick Bonacci – Class of 1952, Wrestling

Elmer Gedeon – Class of 1935, Football and Track

Jim Theiling – Class of 1948, Football and Track

Ken McBride – Class of 1953, Baseball

Phil Argento – Class of 1965, Basketball

Phil Bova – Class of 1964, Basketball Official

WEST TECH

Art "Dynie" Mansfield – Class of 1924, Football

Barclay Sanders – Class of 1923, Football

George Kozak – Football Coach and Administration

John Sforzo – Class of 1953, Wrestling

Marty Karow – Class of 1922, Football and Baseball

Ray Gura – Class of 1968, Gymnastics

Russ Schneider – Class of 1946, Sportswriter

Steve Rudo – Class of 1957, Wrestling

APPENDIX IV

COLLEGE ALL-AMERICA

COLLINWOOD

Cecil Shorts – Track; Mount Union College, 2009

Eppie Barney – Football; Iowa State University, 1966 – 2nd Team

EAST HIGH

April Wonzo – Track; Notre Dame College, 2006

Carl Taseff – Football: John Carroll University, 1947

Earl Sprackling – Football; Brown University, 1909-1910-1911 – 1st Team

Exodus Lett – Track; Ashland University, 1971

Larry Jenkins – Basketball; U. of Akron, 1972

Stanley Cofall – Football; Notre Dame, 1916 – 1st Team

EAST TECH

Aki Bradley – Track; Mississippi State University, 1994

Barry King – Track; Ashland University; 1974

David Albritton – Track; Ohio State University, 1936

Estus Newberry – Track; Baldwin-Wallace College, 1957

Harrison Dillard – Track; Baldwin-Wallace College, 1948

James Martin – Football; Notre Dame, 1949 – 1st Team

Jesse Owens – Track; Ohio State University, 1935

Joe Giallombardo – Gymnastics; U. of Illinois, 1940

Leroy Powell Carter – Track; Central State University, 1991

Michael Kosmetos – Swimming; Purdue, 1951 – Honorable Mention

Paul Fina – Gymnastics; U. of Illinois, 1940

Rickey Pittman – Track; U. of Tennessee, 1985

Robert Stanford "Bob" Brown – Football; U. of Nebraska, 1963 – 1st Team

Vivian Reed Brown – Track; Tennessee State University, 1964

Wanda Ford – Basketball; Drake University, 1987

Willie Hibbler – Track; U. of Nebraska, 1996

GLENVILLE

Benjamin "Benny" Friedman – Football; U. of Michigan, 1925-1926 – 1st Team

Derick Harbour – Track; Villanova University, 1979

Louis Defreeze – Track; Western Kentucky University, 1974

Quincy Downing – Track; Louisiana State University, 2012

Richard Bishop – Football; Marshalltown Community College, 1970

Richard Ware – Track; Western Kentucky University, 1974

Raleigh Clemons – Wrestling; Ashland University, 1974

Ted Ginn, Jr. – Football; Oho State University, 2006 – 2nd Team

Troy Smith – Football; Ohio State University, 2006 – 1st Team

JOHN ADAMS

Bob Reynolds – Football; Bowling Green State University, 1963

Charita Johnson-Stubbs – Volleyball; U. of Arizona, 1985

Clinton Smith – Basketball; Cleveland State University, 1986

Demetrius Jackson – Track; Akron University, 2020

Derek McKinley – Track; Baldwin-Wallace College, 1980

Ed Casalicchio – Wrestling; Michigan State, 1953

Edward L. "Eddie" Finnigan – Basketball; Western Reserve University, 1933

Eleanor Montgomery – Track; Tennessee State University, 1964

Gene Slewaski – Football; Purdue University, 1958

Harold Kimball – Track; Southern University, 1971

Harold Madox – Track; Odessa Community College, 1985

Jonte Baker – Track; Tiffin University, 2020

Kelley Jones – Track, Findlay University, 1994

Kevin McKinley – Track; Prairie View A & M, 1986

Luke Owens – Football; Kent State University, 1956 – 1st Team.

Marie Lassiter – Track; Findlay University, 1994

William Fleishman – Basketball; Western Reserve University, 1936 – 3rd Team

Willie Brown – Track; U. of Akron, 2011

JOHN HAY

Anthony Hancock – Track; U. of Tennessee, 1980

Charles Oakley – Basketball; Virginia Union University, 1985 – 1st Team

Crystal Neal – Track; Cuyahoga Community College, 1989

George Sample - Track; John Carroll, 2002

John Hicks – Football; Ohio State University, 1972-1973 – 1st Team

Leonard Paul – Basketball; Akron University, 1971

Madeline Manning-Mims – Track; Tennessee State University, 1968

Robert Dudley – Track; Western Kentucky University, 1974

Ruben Patterson – Basketball; U. of Cincinnati, 1998 – 3rd Team

Tim McGee – Football; U. of Tennessee, 1985 – 1st Team

JOHN F. KENNEDY

Anthony Murphy – Track; South Alabama State University, 2004

Greg Morrow – Track; Wilmington College, 2002

Ken Agee – Football; Findlay University, 1981

Lawrence Lenin – Track; Central State University, 1993

JOHN MARSHALL

Cadeau Kelley – Track; Akron University, 2008

Dorian Green – Track; U. of Illinois, 1995

Jonathan Burrell – Track; Ohio State University, 1993

Larry Coy – Track and Cross Country; Baldwin-Wallace College, 1977

Pam Floyd Macer – Track; Baldwin-Wallace College, 1982

Spencer Johnson – Track; Baldwin-Wallace College, 1982

Thomas Jefferson – Track; Kent State University, 1984, 1985

LINCOLN HIGH

Marty Hunt – Basketball; Kenyon College, 1968

LINCOLN-WEST

Sue Koziol – Softball; Cleveland State University, 1982 – 1st Team

RHODES

Bill Hann – Basketball; U. of Tennessee, 1969

Carol Simms – Track; Cuyahoga Community College, 1989

Chris Parks – Track; Ashland University, 1987

Cynthia Anzalone-Fox – Track; U. of Houston, 1985

David Liam Kyle – Basketball; Cleveland State University

Don McCafferty – Football; Ohio State University, 1942

Katonya Harding – Track; Findlay University, 1993, 1994

Les Horvath – Football; Ohio State University, 1944

LeShaunte Edwards – Track; U. of Akron, 2000-2001

Mahagony Jones – Track; Penn State, 2013 (2nd Team 3times)-2014 (1st Team)

Ron Addison – Track; U. of Tennessee, 1976

Toure Carter – Football; Ashland University, 2003

SOUTH

Art Massey – Soccer, Ohio State University, 1963

Fred Sawyer – Basketball, University of Louisville, 3rd Team, 1961

Gomer Jones – Football, Ohio State University, 1935

Gonna Holmes – Track; Southwest Michigan Community College, 1987

Markeya Jones – Track, Kansas State University, 1991

WEST HIGH

Dick Bonacci – Wrestling; U. of Toledo, 1953, 1954

Elmer Gedeon – Track; U. of Michigan, 1938

Gene Gibbons – Wrestling; Michigan State University, 1951

WEST TECH

August "Mike" Michalske – Football; Penn State University, 1925

Donnie Hughley – Football; Vermillion Community College, 1991

Jay Miranda – Track; U. of Notre Dame, 1979

Pat Semary – Wrestling; Kent State University, 1960

Ray Gura – Gymnastics; U. of Michigan, 1972, 1973

Raymond Novotny – Football; Ashland University, 1929

Steve Rudo, Jr. – Wrestling; Ohio University, 1957

Terrence Isaacs – Football; Vermillion Community College, 1997

DIRECTOR OF ATHLETICS

Floyd A. Rowe – Track; U. of Michigan, 1908

APPENDIX V

ALL-OHIO

(HM – Honorable Mention, SM – Special Mention, SC – State Champion)

Under each school, the All-Ohio honorees are listed by year. First and last names are used when available; every effort has been made to identify an athlete's first and last name.

All-Ohio recognition can vary by sport. For instance, in Track and Wrestling, all athletes who make the podium (first eight finishers) in the state finals are recognized as having earned All-Ohio recognition; unfortunately, in many years, only the first two, first four, or first six finishers are listed, so there are probably All-Ohio athletes who are missing from this list. In Cross Country, the first 20 finishers in the state meet and earn All-Ohio honors, plus the first 20 individuals running without a school team. In other sports, the All-Ohio honorees are often named by a panel of sports writers, etc

For Wrestlers, the number after "Wrestling," for example, "Wrestling (122)," indicates the weight class; "Hvy" means heavyweight. In some instances, such as the Track and Swim relay teams, the names of the participants on that relay team are not available. In those cases, the team's name (880yd Relay Team) will be given.

CENTRAL HIGH

1925	Kelly	Track-100yd Dash	5th
1925	Kelly	Ttrack-220yd Dash	4th
1933	Taylor	Track-120yd Hurdles	3rd
1933	Burke	Track-High Jump	2nd
1934	Burke	Track-High Jump	SC
1934	Caesar	Track-880yd Run	SC
1934	Williams	Track-Discus	2nd
1937	Withers	Track-440yd Dash	5th
1937	Roberson	Track-440yd Dash	3rd
1937	Rufus Allison	Track-Broad Jump	SC
1938	Rufus Allison	Track-Broad Jump	SC
1938	Smith	Track-440yd Dash	2nd
1938	Withers	Track-440yd Dash	3rd
1938	Shaw	Track-Mile Relay	SC
1938	Smith	Track-Mile Relay	SC

Year	Name	Event	Place
1938	S. Thompson	Track-Mile Relay	SC
1938	Withers	Track-Miler Relay	SC
1945	Carter	Track-120yd Hurdles	4th
1946	Perrine	Track-440yd Dash	5th
1946	Wilkes	Track-High Jump	2nd
1947	Jarvis	Track-High Jump	SC (tie)
1947	Louderdale	Track-High Jump	SC (tie)
1947	Robinson	Track-440yd Dash	3rd
1947	Wilkes	Track-220yd Low Hurdles	SC
1947	Wilkes	Track-120yd-high Hurdles	2nd
1947		Track-Mile Relay Team	3rd
1948	Lenny Blair	Track-220yd Dash	5th
1948	Jarvis	Track-High Jump	SC
1948		Track-Mile Relay Team	2nd
1948		Track-880yd Relay Team	4th
1949	Lenny Blair	Track-100yd. Dash	SC
1949	Lenny Blair	Track-220yd Dash	3rd
1949	Lenny Blair	Track-880yd Relay	SC
1949	Walter DeVaughn	Track-880yd Relay	SC
1949	Nate Moore	Track-880yd Relay	SC
1949	Ed Sweeney	Track-880yd Relay	SC
1949	Jarvis	Track-High Jump	2nd
1949	Ken Mischal	Track-120yd High Hurdles	2nd
1949	Ken Mischal	Track-220yd Low Hurdles	2nd
1950	Ken Mischal	Track-120yd High Hurdles	2nd
1950	Ken Mischal	Track-220yd Low Hurdles	5th
1950	Clarence Smith	Track-220yd Low Hurdles	4th
1950	Reggie Victor	Track-880yd Run	SC
1950		Track-Mile Relay Team	3rd
1951	Clarence Smith	Track-120yd High Hurdles	3rd
1951	Clarence Smith	Track-180yd Low Hurdles	2nd
1951		Track-880yd Relay Team	3rd
1952	Bernard Brison	Track-180yd Low Hurdles	3rd
1952	Ray Clark	Track-Broad Jump	2nd
1952		Track-880yd Relay Team	3rd

| 1952 | | Track-Mile Relay Team | 5th |

COLLINWOOD

1929	Zich	Track-220yd Low Hurdles	5th
1930	Finsell	Gymnastics-Indian Clubs	3rd
1930	Trino	Gymnastics-Side horse	5th
1930	Zorman	Gymnastics-Tumbling	4th
1930	Spehek	Gymnastics-Parallel Bars	4th
1930	Jordan	Gymnastics-High Bar	4th
1931	Frey	Gymnastics-Horizontal Bars	SC
1931	Zorman	Gymnastics-Horizontal Bars	4th
1931	Mericle	Gymnastics-Indian Clubs	3rd
1931	Mericle	Gymnastics-Flying Rings	3rd
1931	Zorman	Gymnastics-Flying Rings	4th
1931	Frey	Gymnastics-Parallel Bars	5th
1933	Ed Fair	Track-880yd Run	SC
1934	Dalton	Track-880yd Relay	SC
1934	Paul Lundblad	Track-120yd High Hurdles	3rd
1934	Charles Nance	Track-100yd Dash	3rd
1934	Charles Nance	Track-880 Relay	SC
1934	Ralph Ohlsen	Track-880 Relay	SC
1934	Ralph Ohlsen	Track-220yd Dash	3rd
1934	Adolph Worthy	Track-880 Relay	SC
1935	Nick Cannarozzi	Football	1st Team
1935	Paul Lundblad	Football	3rd Team
1935	Dalton	Track-880 Relay	SC
1935	Charles Nance	Track-880 Relay	SC
1935	Ralph Ohlsen	Track-880 Relay	SC
1935	Adolph Worthy	Track-880 Relay	SC
1935	Adolph Worthy	Track-100yd Dash	3rd
1935	Adolph Worthy	Track-220yd Dash	2nd
1935	Paul Lundblad	Track-220yd Low Hurdles	4th
1935	McKee	Track-880yd Run	5th
1936	Adolph Worthy	Track-100yd Dash	2nd
1936	Adolph Worthy	Track-220yd Dash	2nd

Year	Name	Sport/Event	Place
1936	McKee	Track-880yd Run	5th
1936		Track-880yd Relay Team	SC
1937	Carmony	Track-100yd Dash	3rd
1937	Carmony	Track-220yd Dash	3rd
1937	Pierce	Track-120yd High Hurdles	2nd
1937	Pierce	Track-220yd Low Hurdles	2nd
1937		Track-880yd Relay Team	4th
1938	Carmony	Track-100yd Dash	2nd
1938	Carmony	Track-220yd Dash	2nd
1939	H. Stassfurth	Wrestling (156)	3rd
1941	Tony Adamle	Football	2nd Team
1941	Parrott	Football	HM
1941	Oliver Bailey	Track-880yd Relay	SC
1941	Sam Dawson	Track-880yd Relay	SC
1941	Fred Nance	Track-880yd Relay	SC
1941	Wilbur Schweitzer	Track-880yd Relay	SC
1941	Oliver Bailey	Track-220yd Dash	2nd
1941	Wilbur Schweitzer	Track-Broad Jump	4th
1943	Mazzocco	Cross Country	4th
1944	Mike Cannavine	Football	HM
1946	Walter Draxler	Cross Country	8th
1946	John Minnick	Cross Country	6th
1947	Frank Ulle	Cross Country	13th
1947	Joe Gotarello	Wrestling (134)	4th
1950	Tom Skerl	Track-880yd Run	5th
1950	Sam Palumbo	Football	1st Team
1951	Joe Trivisonno	Football	2nd Team
1951	Al Demell	Football	HM
1952	Calvin Hurd	Cross Country	3rd
1952	Joe Trivisonno	Football	HM
1954	Joe Cannavino	Football	HM
1955	Zalokar	Football	HM
1959	Morgan Powell	Basketball	HM
1960	Joe Zanello	Wrestling (133)	4th
1961	John Zanella	Wrestling (175)	3rd

Year	Name	Sport	Place
1962	Mike Cavotta	Track-Shot Put	SC
1962	Wally Hale	Wrestling (138)	4th
1962	Theo Marrow	Track-100yd Dash	SC
1962	Theo Morrow	Track-120yd. Hurdles	2nd
1962	Theo Morrow	Track-Long Jump	3rd
1965	Francis Zanello	Wrestling (133)	4th
1967	Dan Karchenko	Wrestling (112)	2nd
1967	Bruce Kordic	Football	1st Team
1968	Glenn Knific	Wrestling (138)	5th
1969	Glen Knific	Wrestling (138)	5th
1971	Ralph Hale	Track-440yd Dash	2nd
1972	Steve Graves	Football	2nd Team
1973	Steve Graves	Track-Discus	2nd
1973	Steve Graves	Track-Shot Put	3rd
1973	Robert Hennings	Track-100yd Dash	SC
1973	Robert Hennings	Track-220yd Dash	SC
1974	Bill Calabrase	Wrestling (138)	2nd
1974	Robert Hennings	Track-180yd Low Hurdles	SC
1974	Robert Hennings	Track-100yd Dash	2nd
1974	Robert Hennings	Track-220yd Dash	2nd
1975	Gloria Winston	Track-80yd Hurdles	5th
1976	Debra Shealy	Track-440yd Relay	6th
1976	Blanche Jackson	Track-440yd Relay	6th
1976	Julie Rufus	Track-440yd Relay	6th
1976	Sandra Benson	Track-440yd Relay	6th
1976	Osman Walker	Track-Mile Relay	3rd
1976	Paul Suber	Track-Mile Relay	3rd
1976	Michael McQueen	Track-Mile Relay	3rd
1976	Bruce Sibert	Track-Mile Relay	3rd
1976	Chuck Bradford	Basketball	3rd Team
1977	Vincent Brookins	Basketball	1st Team
1977	Gerald Kates	Basketball	HM
1977	Barbara Washington	Basketball	HM
1977	Bruce Sibert	Track-440yd Dash	5th
1977	Paul Suber	Track-880yd Relay	5th

1977	Alfonso Williams	Track-880yd Relay	5th
1977	Donametric Murray	Track-880yd Relay	5th
1977	Osman Walker	Track-880yd Relay	5th
1978	Robert Williams	Track-880yd Relay	5th
1978	Eurall Graham	Track-880yd Relay	5th
1978	Denton Tapp	Track-880yd Relay	5th
1978	Louis Cobble	Track-880yd Relay	5th
1979	Robert Williams	Track-300m Hurdles	3rd
1979	Eurall Graham	Track-220yd Dash	6th
1979	Louis Cobble	Track-Mile Relay	6th
1979	Tony Patrick	Track-Mile Relay	6th
1979	Robert Williams	Track-Mile Relay	6th
1979	Eurall Graham	Track-Mile Relay	6th
1980	David Griffin	Basketball	SM
1980	Eurall Graham	Track-100m Dash	4th
1980	Eurall Graham	Track-200m Dash	4th
1980	Tony Patrick	Track-300m Low Hurdles	3rd
1980	Ramon Davis	Track-400m Relay	4th
1980	Tony Patrick	Track-400m Relay	4th
1980	Theodis Windham	Track-400m Relay	4th
1980	Eurall Graham	Track-400m Relay	4th
1982	Preston Bright	Wrestling (155)	4th
1984	Dennis Driggens	Track-Shot Put	6th
1984	Benny Bright	Wrestling (126)	2nd
1984	Latonya Johnson	Track-400m Dash	SC
1984	Latonya Jackson	Track-400m Relay	SC
1984	Betty Brooks	Track-300m Hurdles	4th
1984	Betty Brooks	Track-400m Relay	SC
1984	Shawn Booker	Track-400m Relay	SC
1984	Angeleque Strong	Track-400m Relay	SC
1985	Benny Bright	Wrestling (132)	2nd
1985	Dennis Driggins	Track-Discus	SC
1985	Dennis Driggens	Track-Shot Put	6th
1986	Desmond Maddox	Wrestling (126)	2nd
1986	Liz Wilcox	Track-400m Relay	6th

Year	Name	Sport/Event	Placement
1986	Shawn Booker	Track-400m Relay	6th
1986	Yvonne Bullock	Track-400m Relay	6th
1986	Blanche Jackson	Track-400m Relay	6th
1987	LeRon Jones	Track-400m Dash	6th
1988	Vince Brookings	Football	HM
1989	Camille Cain	Track-High Jump	5th
1989	Sam Thomas	Track-400m Relay	3rd
1989	Greg Carley	Track-400m Relay	3rd
1989	LaRon Jones	Track-400m Relay	3rd
1989	Phil Wright	Track-400m Relay	3rd
1990	Freddie Smith	Football	HM
1990	Camille Cain	Track-Long Jump	5th
1990	Greg Carley	Track-800m Run	5th
1994	Lakisha Zanders	Track-100m Relay	SC
1994	Erica Evans	Track-100m Relay	SC
1994	Talisha Rogers	Track-100m Relay	SC
1994	Aneesah Wooten	Track-100m Relay	SC
1995	Keomi Johnson	Track-Long Jump	SC
1995	Lakisha Zanders	Track-100m Relay	SC
1995	Dede Owens	Track-100m Relay	SC
1995	Talisha Rogers	Track-100m Relay	SC
1995	Shonda Robinson	Track-100m Relay	SC
1995	Shonda Robison	Track-100m Dash	8th
1995	Shonda Robison	Track-200m Dash	5th
1995	Rah Sheen Clay	Track-400m Dash	SC
1995	Rah Sheen Clay	Track-200m Dash	5th
1996	Melvin Scott	Basketball	2nd Team
1996	Shonda Robinson	Track-100m Dash	2nd
1996	Shonda Robinson	Track-200m Dash	3rd
1996	Cherre'e Jones	Track-100m Relay	2nd
1996	Deda Owens	Track-100m Relay	2nd
1996	Keomi Johnson	Track-100m Relay	2nd
1996	Shonda Robinson	Track-100m Relay	2nd
1996	Rhondalynn Crawford	Track-400m Relay	SC
1996	Donita Scott	Track-400m Relay	SC

1996	Shonda Robinson	Track-400m Relay	SC
1996	Rashida Cameron	Track-400mRelay	SC
1996	Keomi Johnson	Track-Long Jump	2nd
1996	Keomi Johnson	Basketball 1st Team	
1997	Richard Mason	Baseball	
1997	Christina Estrict	Track – High Jump	2nd
1997	Rhondalynn Crawford	Track-400m Dash	4th
1997	Shonda Robinson	Track-100m Dash	SC
1997	Shonda Robinson	Track-200m Dash	SC
1997	Deda Owens	Track-100m Relay	4th
1997	Donita Scott	Track-100m Relay	4th
1997	Cherre'e Jones	Track-100m Relay	4th
1997	Ocie Lassiter	Track-100m Relay	4th
1997	Donita Scott	Track-200m Relay	SC
1997	Rhondalynn Crawford	Track-200m Relay	SC
1997	Rashida Cameron	Track-200m Relay	SC
1997	Shonda Robinson	Track-200m Relay	SC
1997	Donita Scott	Track-400m Relay	SC
1997	Rhondalynn Crawford	Track-400m Relay	SC
1997	Rashida Cameron	Track-400m Relay	SC
1997	Shonda Robinson	Track-400m Relay	SC
1997	Ken Battle	Track-400m Relay	5th
1997	Cyrus Starr	Track-400m Relay	5th
1997	Tyron McNeal	Track-400m Relay	5th
1997	Caleb Dyer	Track-400m Relay	5th
1997	Ken Battle	Track-800m Relay	6th
1997	Cyrus Starr	Track-800m Relay	6th
1997	Tyron McNeal	Track-800m Relay	6th
1997	Keith McNeal	Track-800m Relay	6th
1998	Christina Estrict	Track-High Jump	SC
1998	Kandace Stone	Track-100m Hurdles	SC
1998	Christina Estrict	Track-100m Hurdles	3rd
1998	Kandace Stone	Track-300m Hurdles	SC
1998	Kandace Stone	Track-100m Relay	3rd
1998	Christina Christian	Track-100m Relay	3rd

1998	Christina Estrict	Track-100m Relay	3rd
1998	Donita Scott	Track-100m Relay	3rd
1998	Rhondalynn Crawford	Track-400m Relay	SC
1998	Kim Jordan	Track-400m Relay	SC
1998	Donita Scott	Track-400m Relay	SC
1998	Kandace Stone	Track-400m Relay	SC
1998	Rhondalynn Crawford	Track-400m Dash	4th
1998	Kim Jordan	Track-800m Run	5th
1999	Christina Estrict	Track-100m Dash	8th
1999	Christina Estrict	Track-100m Hurdles	4th
1999	Christina Estrict	Track -High Jump	SC
1999	Christina Estrict	Track-Long Jump	SC
1999	Kimberly Jordan	Track-800m Run	SC
1999	Kandace Stone	Track-100m Hurdles	2nd
1999	Kandace Stone	Track-200m Hurdles	4th
1999	Kimberly Jordan	Track-100m Relay	SC
1999	Christal Christian	Track-100m Relay	SC
1999	Kandace Stone	Track-100m Relay	SC
1999	Christina Christian	Track-100m Relay	SC
2000	Christina Estrict	Track-High Jump	SC
2000	Kandace Stone	Track-200m Dash	2nd
2000	Kandace Stone	Track-100m Hurdles	2nd
2000	Kandace Stone	Track-100m Relay	SC
2000	Christina Christian	Track-100m Relay	SC
2000	Christal Christian	Track-100m Relay	SC
2000	Shamika Jones	Track-100m Relay	SC
2000	Kandace Stone	Track-200m Relay	SC
2000	Christina Christian	Track-200m Relay	SC
2000	Christal Christian	Track-200m Relay	SC
2000	Shamika Jones	Track-200m Relay	SC
2001	Kandace Stone	Track-300m Hurdles	SC
2001	Mignon Banks	Track-100m Relay	SC
2001	Christine Christian	Track-100m Relay	SC
2001	Christal Christian	Track-100m Relay	SC
2001	Kandace Stone	Track-100m Relay	SC

2001	Mignon Banks	Track-200m Relay	SC
2001	Christine Christian	Track-200m Relay	SC
2001	Christal Christian	Track-200m Relay	SC
2001	Kandace Stone	Track-200m Relay	SC
2001	George Blade	Track-Long Jump	4th
2002	Swaney Cooper	Basketball	HM
2003	Myron Howard	Track-100m Relay	3rd
2003	Curtis Terry	Track-100m Relay	3rd
2003	Jermaine Harris	Track-100m Relay	3rd
2003	Andre Evans	Track-100m Relay	3rd
2003	Swaney Cooper	Basketball	SM
2004	Jay Hunt	Wrestling (119)	3rd
2004	Daniel Palmer	Track-400m Relay	3rd
2004	Rico Edwards	Track-400m Relay	3rd
2004	Jason Johnson	Track-400m Relay	3rd
2004	Montel Spencer	Track-400m Relay	3rd
2004	Janice Williams	Track-200m Relay	SC
2004	Charnee Lumbus	Track-200m Relay	SC
2004	Shantell Lewis	Track-200m Relay	SC
2004	Christy Horn	Track-200m Relay	SC
2004	Courtney Jones	Track-100m Relay	SC
2004	Charnee Lumbus	Track-100m Relay	SC
2004	Jenice Williams	Track-100m Relay	SC
2004	Shantell Lewis	Track-100m Relay	SC
2004	Sabrina Parr	Track-800m Relay	3rd
2004	Joi Smith	Track-800m Relay	3rd
2004	Brandi Taylor	Track-800m Relay	3rd
2004	Dorothy Dye	Track-800m Relay	3rd
2004	Sabrina Parr	Track-400m Relay	SC
2004	Joi Smith	Track-400m Relay	SC
2004	Brandi Taylor	Track-400m Relay	SC
2004	Regina Adams	Track-400m Relay	SC
2005	Charnee Lumbus	Track-100m Hurdles	3rd
2005	Elizabeth Yates	Track-800m Relay	2nd
2005	Brandi Taylor	Track-800m Relay	2nd

Year	Name	Event	Place
2005	Joi Smith	Track-800m Relay	2nd
2005	Sabrina Parr	Track-800m Relay	2nd
2005	Charnee Lumbus	Track-200m Relay	SC
2005	Shantell Lewis	Track-200m Relay	SC
2005	Christy Horn	Track-200m Relay	SC
2005	Jenice Williams	Track-200m Relay	SC
2005	Courtney Jones	Track-100m Relay	SC
2005	Jenice Williams	Track-100m Relay	SC
2005	Shantel Lewis	Track-100m Relay	SC
2005	Christy Horn	Track-100m Relay	SC
2006	Myron Andrews	Wrestling (189)	6th
2006	Cecil Shorts	Track-800m Relay	8th
2006	Terrance Byrd	Track-800m Relay	8th
2006	Trevor Eason	Track-800m Relay	8th
2006	Ernest Kerr	Track-800m Relay	8th
2006	Cecil Shorts	Track-800m Run	7th
2006	Charnee Lumbus	Track-100m Hurdles	SC
2006	Charnee Lumbus	Track-300m Hurdles	SC
2006	Whitney Miller	Track-300m Hurdles	6th
2006	Brandi Taylor	Track-400m Dash	3rd
2006	Laurin Slayton	Track-100m Relay	SC
2006	Courtney Jones	Track-100m Relay	SC
2006	Charnee Lumbus	Track-100m Relay	SC
2006	Christy Horn	Track-100m Relay	SC
2006	Wonderful Jennings	Track-400m Relay	SC
2006	Whitney Miller	Track-400m Relay	SC
2006	Charnee Lumbus	Track-400m Relay	SC
2006	Brandi Taylor	Track-400m Relay	SC
2007	Erin Busbee	Track-200m Relay	SC
2007	Shannon Willis	Track-200m Relay	SC
2007	Whitney Mller	Track-200m Relay	SC
2007	Christy Horn	Track-200m Relay	SC
2007	Shannon Willis	Track-400m Relay	2nd
2007	Erin Busbee	Track-400m Relay	2nd
2007	Laurin Slayton	Track-400m Relay	2nd

2007	Christy Horn	Track-400m Relay	2nd
2008	Tiera Royal	Track-400m Relay	5th
2008	Shannon Willis	Track-400m Relay	5th
2008	Wonderful Jennings	Track-400m Relay	5th
2008	Amber Smith	Track-400m Relay	5th
2008	Shannon Willis	Track-200m Relay	8th
2008	Erin Busbee	Track-200m Relay	8th
2008	Chanae Gainer	Track-200m Relay	8th
2008	Wonderful Jennings	Track-200m Relay	8th
2008	Amber Smith	Track-100m Hurdles	3rd
2008	Amber Smith	Track-300m Hurdles	SC
2008	Tiera Royal	Track-300m Hurdles	7th
2009	Chanae Gainer	Track-200m Relay	3rd
2009	Shannon Willis	Track-200m Relay	3rd
2009	Erin Busbee	Track-200m Relay	3rd
2009	Amirah Harbour	Track-200m Relay	3rd
2009	Amber Smith	Track-100m Hurdles	3rd
2009	Amber Smith	Track-300m Hurdles	2nd
2009	Shannon Willis	Track-400m Relay	3rd
2009	Tiera Royal	Track-400m Relay	3rd
2009	Chanae Gainer	Track-400m Relay	3rd
2009	Amber Smith	Track-400m Relay	3rd
2009	Erin Busbee	Track-Long Jump	3rd
2010	Amber Smith	Track-100m Hurdles	SC
2010	Amber Smith	Track-300m Hurdles	SC
2010	Amber Smith	Track-200m Relay	SC
2010	Brittney Brown	Track-200m Relay	SC
2010	Jasmine Lett	Track- 200m Relay	SC
2010	Amirah Harbour	Track-200m Relay	SC
2010	Erica Sawyer	Track-100m Relay	2nd
2010	Jasmine Lett	Track-100m Relay	2nd
2010	Amirah Harbour	Track-100m Relay	2nd
2010	Brittini Brown	Track-100m Relay	2nd
2010	Erica Sawyer	Track-400m Relay	2nd
2010	Jasmine Lett	Track-400m Relay	2nd

2010	Amirah Harbour	Track-400m Relay	2nd
2010	Brittini Brown	Track-400m Relay	2nd
2017	Jayshon Bester	Football	2nd Team
2018	Jayshon Bester	Football	3rd Team

EAST HIGH

1924	Ed Carlson	Basketball	
1928	Nate Granger	Tennis – Doubles	2nd
1928	Ed Funk	Tennis – Doubles	2nd
1929	Nate Granger	Tennis – Singles	SC
1929	Nate Granger	Tennis – Doubles	SC
1929	Ed Funk	Tennis – Doubles	SC
1931	Dabrowski	Gymnastics-Side Horse	5th
1933	Robert Politzer	Track-100yd Dash	4th
1933	Robert Politzer	Track-220yd Dash	3rd
1933	Robert Politzer	Track-Long Jump	2nd
1933	Sabath	Football	HM
1935	Sabath	Football	3rd Team
1937	Bibbs	Track-880yd Relay	SC
1937	Reitenbach	Track-880yd Relay	SC
1937	Rish	Track-880yd Relay	SC
1937	Thomas	rack-880yd Relay	SC
1937	Rish	Track-880yd Run	2nd
1938	Thompson	Track-High Jump	3rd
1938	Bibbs	Track-880yd Relay	SC
1938	Jackson	Track-880yd Relay	SC
1938	Thompson	Track-880yd Relay	SC
1938	Thomas	Track-880yd Relay	SC
1938	Bibbs	Track-100yd Dash	5th
1938	Rish	Track-Mile Run	3rd
1938	E. Thomas	Track-220yd. Dash	3rd
1938	Rish	Track-880yd Run	SC
1938		Track-880yd Relay Team	SC
1938	Thompson	Track-High Jump	3rd
1939	Rish	Track-880yd Run	SC
1939	Rish	Track-Mile Run	SC

Year	Name	Event	Place
1939	Bibbs	Track-High Jump	5th (Tie)
1939	Thompson	Track-High Jump	5th (Tie)
1939	Keagan	Track-Pole Vault	4th (Tie)
1939	Feisler	Track-Pole Vault	4th (Tie)
1939	Furpahs	Cross Country	9th
1940	Maxwell	Track-120yd Hurdles	3rd
1940		Track-Mile Relay Team	SC
1941	Gibson	Track-440yd Dash	4th
1941	Carrillo	Track-Shot Put	3rd
1941	Witham	Track-Broad Jump	5th
1941		Track-Mile Relay Team	2nd
1941	Clark	Swimming-50yd Freestyle	6th
1942	Acheson	Swimming-50yd Freestyle	5th
1942	Balfour	Swimming-100yd Breast Stroke	3rd
1942	Hassel	Swimming-Diving	4th
1943	Mertz	Cross Country	9th
1944	Barton	Swimming-100yd Freestyle	4th
1944	Izant	Swimming-100yd Freestyle	6th
1944	Richie	Swimming-Diving	6th
1950	Allan Lubino	Cross Country	11th
1951	Poe	Track-880yd Run	3rd
1952	Okulovich	Football	HM
1952	Prelock	Football	HM
1954	Shelby Kellogg	Track-Shot Put	3rd
1956	Randell Jefferson	Cross Country	12th
1957	Clark Kellogg	Football	3rd Team
1957	Slacas	Football	HM
1957	Clark Kellogg	Track-Discus	2nd
1957	Clark Kellogg	Track-Shot Put	3rd
1958	Ray Palmer	Cross Country	11th
1959	Gene Kellogg	Football	HM
1959	Davis Jones	Football	2nd Team
1960		Track-Mile Relay Team	3rd
1960	Gene Smith	Track-Shot Put	3rd
1961		Track-Mile Relay Team	3rd

Year	Name	Sport/Event	Place
1962	Ken Robinson	Track-180yd Hurdles	3rd
1962	Ed Shilling	Track-High Jump	SC
1964	Manny Leaks	Basketball	HM
1965	Dorsey Lampley	Cross Country	15th
1965	Exodus Lett	Track-440yd Dash	2nd
1965		Track-Mile Relay Team	2nd
1965	Gregory Morton	Tennis-Singles	HM
1966	Gregory Morton	Tennis-Singles	HM
1966	Don Foggio	Track-180yd Hurdles	2nd
1967	Gregory Morton	Tennis-Singles	HM
1967	Don Foggio	Track-180yd Hurdles	SC
1969	Bob Tate	Track-100yd Dash	5th
1969		Track-880yd Relay Team	3rd
1971	Casimier Moss	Basketball	HM
1971	Marvin Jones	Track-100yd Dash	3rd
1972	Marvin Jones	Track-440yd Dash	SC
1979	Terry Jefferies	Track-Mile Run	6th
1980	Stephon Moore	Football	HM
1980	Jerome Evans	Track-400m Dash	4th
1980	Anthony Holmes	Track-400m Relay	5th
1980	James Thomas	Track-400m Relay	5th
1980	Dewayne Calloway	Track-400m Relay	5th
1980	Kenneth West	Track-400m Relay	5th
1980	Otealua Jones	Track-100m Dash	6th
1981	Anthony Holmes	Track-200m Dash	6th
1981	Anthony Holmes	Track-100m Relay	SC
1981	Keith Galloway	Track-100m Relay	SC
1981	Ron Brown	Track-100m Relay	SC
1981	Kenneth West	Track-100m Relay	SC
1983	Robert Martin	Track-1600m Run	5th
1985	Brian Parker	Basketball	HM
1986	Charles Jenkins	Basketball	3rd Team
1987	Alisha Hill	Basketball	HM
1987	Merrill Tilley	Track-Long Jump	5th
1988	Merrell Tilley	Track-Long Jump	2nd

1991	DaJuan Banks	Track-400m Run	5th
1999	Mike Graves	Track-100m Relay	4th
1999	Kevin Dukes	Track-100m Relay	4th
1999	Tony Black	Track-4x100m Relay	4th
1999	Jerry Jones	Track-4x100m Relay	4th
2000	Steve Sanders	Track-300m Hurdles	2nd

EAST TECH

1919	Finn	Basketball	1st Team
1919	Harry Neeley	Basketball	1st Team
1919	Mose Lefkowitz	Basketball	2nd Team
1919	Fussner	Track-120yd High Hurdles	2nd
1919	Fussner	Track-High Jump	2nd
1919	Fussner	Track-220yd Low Hurdles	4th
1919	Smith	Tack-Javelin	3rd
1919	Smith	Track-Broad Jump	2nd
1919	Clenthorne	Track-440yd Run	3rd
1919	Clenthorne	Track-Broad jump	3rd
1920		Track-Mile Relay Team	SC
1920	Beale	Track-880yd Run	SC
1920	Beale	Track-Mile Run	3rd
1920	"Swede" Carlson	Track-Discus	SC
1920	"Swede" Carlson	Track-Shot Put	SC
1921	Clemons	Track-100yd Dash	2nd
1921	Clemons	Track-220yd Dash	SC
1921		Track-Mile Relay Team	SC
1921	Norton Behm	Track-High Jump	4th
1921	Sturney	Track-120yd High Hurdles	3rd
1921	Fussner	Track-120yd High Hurdles	4th
1921	"Swede" Carlson	Track-Javelin	3rd
1921	Don Willaman	Track-Javelin	4th
1921	Norton Behm	Track-Broad Jump	SC
1921	Don Willaman	Track-Broad jump	2nd
1921	John Behm	Track-Pole Vault	2nd
1921	Jack Trice	Track-Shot Put	SC
1921	Jack Trice	Track-Discus	2nd

1921	"Swede" Carlson	Track-Discus	3rd
1922	Norton Behm	Track-Broad Jump	SC
1922	Norton Behm	Trasck-100yd Dash	2nd
1922		Track-Mile Relay Team	2nd
1922	Don Willaman	Track-Javelin	3rd
1922	Brickner	Track-440yd Dash	2nd
1922	Bechtold	Track-440yd Dash	4th
1922	Douglas	Track-440yd Dash	5th
1922	Larrick	Track-Pole Vault	rd (Tie)
1922	John Behm	Basketball	SM
1923	Griswold	Track-High Jump	SC
1923	Mann	Track-220yd Dash	5th
1923		Track-Mile Relay Team	2nd
1923	Havel	Track-440yd Dash	4th
1923	Hurlebus	Track-880yd Run	5th
1923	Lariche	Track-Broad Jump	4th
1924	Dixon	Track-220yd Low Hurdles	SC
1924	Carrington	Track-Pole Vault	2nd (Tie)
1925	Bright	Track-220yd Low Hurdles	5th
1926	Dunlap	Track-880yd Run	4th
1926	Kelley	Track-Pole Vault	3rd (Tie)
1928	Hanferd	Track-Broad Jump	SC
1928	Davis	Track-Shot Put	4th
1928	Hooper	Track-High Jump	3rd (Tie)
1929	Kelly	Track-120yd High Hurdles	3rd
1929	Wyrostek	Track-High Jump	4th (Tie)
1930	Davis	Track-Shot Put	SC
1930	Watson	Track-120yd High Hurdles	4th
1930	Carter	Gymnastics-Tumbling	SC
1930	Sloan	Gymnastics-High Bar	5th
1930	Box	Gymnastics-Indian Clubs	5th
1930	Liptak	Gymnastics-Flying Rings	4th
1931	Jesse Owens	Track-Broad Jump	SC
1931	Jesse Owens	Track-100yd Dash	4th
1931	Jesse Owens	Track-220yd Dash	2nd

1931	David Albritton	Track-High Jump	2nd (Tie)
1931	Volk	Swimming-100yd Backstroke	3rd
1931	Lad Andrahazy	Gymnastics-Horizontal Bars	2nd
1931	Lad Andrahazy	Gymnastics-Side Horse	4th
1931	Carter	Gymnastics-Tumbling	SC
1932	Jesse Owens	Track-100yd Dash	SC
1932	Jesse Owens	Track-220yd Dash	SC
1932	Jesse Owens	Track-Broad Jump	SC
1932	Jesse Owens	Track-880yd Relay	SC
1932	Schraufl	Track-880yd Relay	SC
1932	Surtzs	Track-880yd Relay	SC
1932	Copeland	Track-880yd Relay	SC
1932	David Albritton	Track-High Jump	SC
1932	Wrobbel	Track-Shot Put	SC
1932	Erker	Gymnastics-Horizontal Bars	2nd
1932	Sadowsky	Gymnastics-Side horse	3rd
1933	Erker	Gymnastics-Horizontal Bars	SC
1933	Erker	Gymnastics-Flying Rings	SC
1933	Kentor	Gymnastics-Side Horse	SC
1933	Goldstein	Gymnastics-Side Horse	2nd
1933	Joe Giallombardo	Gymnastics-Tumbling	SC
1933	Lad Andrahazy	Gymnastics-Tumbling	4th
1933	Lad Andrahazy	Gymnastics-Parallel Bars	SC
1933	Gershon	Gymnastics-Parallel Bars	2nd
1933	Klosinski	Gymnastics-Indian Clubs	4th
1933	Jesse Owens	Track-100yd Dash	SC
1933	Jesse Owens	Track-220yd Dash	SC
1933	Jesse Owens	Track-Broad Jump	SC
1933	Jesse Owens	Track-880yd Relay	SC
1933	Tiff	Track-880yd Relay	SC
1933	Williams	Track-880-yard Relay	SC
1933	Story	Track-880yd Relay	SC
1933	Dave Albritton	Track-High Jump	SC
1933	Carter	Swimming-Fancy Divin	4th
1934	Marcus	Track-Broad Jump	SC

Year	Name	Event	Place
1934		Track-880yd Relay	3rd
1934	Brown	Track-Shot Put	5th
1934	Erker	Gymnastics-Horizontal Bars	SC
1934	Kiacz	Gymnastics-Horizontal Bars	3rd
1934	Erker	Gymnastics-Flying Rings	3rd
1934	Joe Giallombardo	Gymnastics-Tumbling	SC
1934	Goldstein	Gymnastics-Tumbling	2nd
1934	Bogden	Gymnastics-Indian Clubs	2nd
1934	Edwards	Gymnastics-Parallel Bars	SC
1934	Zupancic	Gymnastics-Parallel Bars	2nd
1934	Joe Giallombardo	Gymnastics-Long Horse	SC
1934	Stepnicka	Gymnastics-Long Horse	3rd
1935	Joe Giallombardo	Gymnatstics-Tumbling	SC
1935	Janu	Gymnastics-Tumbling	3rd
1935	W. Cameron	Gymnastics-Side Horse	SC
1935	Metzdorf	Gymnastics-Side Horse	2nd
1935	Paul Fina	Gymnastics-Flying Rings	SC
1935	Paul Fina	Gymnastics-Horizontal Bars	3rd
1935	Zupancic	Gymnastics-Parallel Bars	SC
1935	Joe Giallombardo	Gymnastics-Parallel Bars	2nd
1935	Joe Giallombardo	Gymnastics-Long Horse	2nd
1935	Walko	Gymnastics-Long Horse	3rd
1935	Haven Robinson	Track-100yd Dash	SC
1935	Haven Robinson	Track-220yd Dash	SC
1935	Saniuk	Track-120yd High Hurdles	2nd
1935	Saniuk	Track-220yd Low Hurdles	3rd
1935		880yd Relay Team	2nd
1935	Brown	Track-Shot Put	5th
1936	Markowski	Gymnastics-Long Horse	2nd
1936	Paul Fina	Gymnastics-Long Horse	3rd
1936	Yakovochuck	Gymnastics-Side Horse	SC
1936	W. Cameron	Gymnastics-Side Horse	2nd
1936	Musil	Gymnastics-Tumbling	SC
1936	Faun	Gymnastics-Tumbling	2nd
1936	Paul Fina	Gymnastics-Horizontal Bars	SC

Year	Name	Event	Place
1936	Neitze	Gymnastics-Horizontal Bars	2nd
1936	Paul Fina	Gymnastics-Flying Rings	SC
1936	Hruska	Gymnastics-Flying Rings	2nd
1936	T. Cameron	Gymnastics-Parallel Bars	SC
1936	Haven Robinson	Track-100yd Dash	SC
1936	Haven Robinson	Track-220yd Dash	2nd
1936	Lee	Track-100yd Dash	3rd
1936	Lee	Track-220yd Dash	4th
1936	Leahy	Track-Mile Run	3rd
1936	Daugherty	Track-Javelin	2nd
1936	Slowinski	Track-Pole Vault	3rd (Tie)
1937	Freeman Leigh	Track-100yd Dash	4th
1937	Freeman Leigh	Track-220yd Dash	4th
1937	Leahy	Track-Mile Run	SC
1937		Track-880yd Relay Team	3rd
1937	Paul Fina	Gymnastics-Horizontal Bar	SC
1937	Leahy	Cross Country	2nd
1937	Zollnick	Gymnastics-Horizontal Bar	2nd
1937	Tollis	Gymnastics-Side Horse	SC
1937	Hruska	Gymnastics-Side Horse	4th
1937	Janu	Gymnastics-Long Horse	2nd
1937	Tollis	Gymnastics-Long Horse	5th
1937	Paul Fina	Gymnastics-Flying Rings	SC
1937	Hruska	Gymnastics-Flying Rings	2nd
1937	Janu	Gymnastics-Tumbling	2nd
1937	T. Cameron	Gymnastics-Parallel Bars	2nd
1938	Chester Thomas	Track-220yd Dash	SC
1938	Chester Thomas	Track-100yd Dash	3rd
1938	Leahy	Track-Mile Run	SC
1938	Crable	Track-High Jump	3rd (Tie)
1939	Chester Thomas	Track-100yd Dash	SC
1939	Chester Thomas	Track-220yd Dash	SC
1939	Harold Lane	Track-220yd Low Hurdles	SC
1939	Harold Lane	Track-120yd High Hurdles	4th
1939	Bill Clayton	Track-880yd Relay	SC

1939	Stanley Kuly	Track-880yd Relay	SC
1939	Lloyd Crabbe	Track-880yd Relay	SC
1939	Chester Thomas	Track-880yd Relay	SC
1939	Chester Thomas	Track-Broad Jump	2nd
1939	Clark	Track-Broad Jump	3rd
1939	Crable	Track-High Jump	5th (Tie)
1939	Polger	Swimming-200yd Freestyle	SC
1939	Halas	Swimming-100yd Freestyle	SC
1940	Nicely	Swimming-50yd Freestyle	6th
1940	Chester Thomas	Track-220yd Dash	SC
1940	Chester Thomas	Track-100yd Dash	2nd
1940	Harold Lane	Track-120yd High Hurdles	SC
1940	Harold Lane	Track-220yd Low Hurdles	SC
1940	Harrison Dillard	Track-120yd High Hurdles	2nd
1940	Harrison Dillard	Track-220yd Low Hurdles	3rd
1940	Chester Thomas	Track-880yd Relay	SC
1940	Stanley Kuly	Track-880yd Relay	SC
1940	Bill Clayton	Track-880yd Relay	SC
1940	Harold Lane	Track-880yd Relay	SC
1940	Chester Thomas	Track-Broad Jump	SC
1940	Crable	Track-High Jump	2nd
1941	Jim Martin	Football	HM
1941	Harrison Dillard	Track-120yd High Hurdles	SC
1941	Harrison Dillard	Track-220yd Low Hurdles	SC
1941	George Clark	Track-Broad Jump	SC
1941		Track-880yd Relay Team	2nd
1942	Gassoway	Track-220yd Dash	SC
1942	Jackson	Track-120yd High Hurdles	SC
1942	Jackson	Track-220yd Low Hurdles	SC
1942		Track-Miler Relay Team	SC
1942		Track-880yd Relay Team	SC
1942	Few	Track-Broad Jump	SC
1942	Boddie	Track-Broad Jump	2nd
1943	Dubani	Tennis-Doubles	HM
1943	Ensler	Tennis-Doubles	HM

Year	Name	Event	Place
1943		Track-Mile Relay Team	SC
1943		Track-880yd Relay Team	SC
1943	Boddie	Track-Broad Jump	SC
1943	Carter	Track-100yd Dash	2nd
1943	Afzal	Track-100yd Dash	5th
1943	Carter	Track-220yd Dash	2nd
1943	Afzal	Track-220yd Dash	5th
1943	Tolliver	Track-440yd Dash	3rd
1943	Jones	Track-220yd Low Hurdles	4th
1944	Henderson	Swimming-50yd Freestyle	5th
1944	Putring	Swimming-100yd Breaststroke	SC
1944	Johnson	Track-Broad Jump	SC
1944	White	Track-Broad Jump	2nd
1944	Afzal	Track-220yd Dash	SC
1944	Johnson	Track-220yd Low Hurdles	SC
1944	Jones	Track-220yd Low Hurdles	3rd
1944		Mile Relay Team	2nd
1944	Jones	Track-100yd Dash	2nd
1944		880yd Relay Team	4th
1944	Tolliver	Track-440yd Dash	2nd
1944	Dick Rutti	Football	3rd Team
1945	Afzal	Track-100yd Dash	3rd
1945	Afzal	Track-220yd Dash	4th
1945	White	Tack-Broad Jump	4th
1946	Ralph Ciprianni	Tennis-Single	2nd
1946		Swimming-150yd Medley Relay Team	4th
1946	Student	Swimming-100yd Breaststroke	SC
1946		Swimming-200yd Freestyle Relay Team	4th
1946		Track-880yd Relay Team	SC
1946	Ward	Track-High Jump	SC
1946	Hughley	Track-120yd High Hurdles	4th
1946		Track-Mile Relay Team	3rd
1947	Bob Evans	Tennis-Doubles	HM
1947	John Callahan	Tennis-Doubles	HM
1947	Scott	Track-Broad Jump	SC

1947	Crump	Track-Broad Jump	4th
1947	Hughley	Track-220yd Dash	4th
1948	Ted Stevens	Swmming-200yd-Freestyle	SC
1948	Mucha	Swimming-50yd Freestyle	5th
1948	Mucha	Swimming-100yd Freestyle	5th
1948	Foley	Swimming-100yd Backstroke	2nd
1948	Peters	Swimming-100yd Backstroke	5th
1948	Ted Stevens	Swimming-150yd Medley Relay	SC
1948	Foley	Swimming-150yd Medley Relay	SC
1948	Student	Swimming-150yd Medley Relay	SC
1948	Elkanich	Swimming-Fancy Diving	SC
1948	Nick Vodanoff	Tennis-Singles	HM
1948	Kipis	Tennis-Doubles	HM
1948	Nunn	Tennis-Doubles	HM
1948	McCadden	Track-220 Low Hurdles	4th
1948		Track-880yd Relay Team	5th
1948	Wintle	Track-880yd Run	3rd
1949	Bob Center	Football	3rd Team
1949	Ed Bilinovich	Football	HM
1949	Chuck McMillan	Football	HM
1949	Kolach	Football	HM
1949	Cliff Prosek	Football	HM
1949	Nick Vodanoff	Tennis-Singles	4th
1949	Al Skodis	Tennis-Doubles	HM
1949	Bob Kover	Tennis-Doubles	HM
1949	Sirpan	Swimming-100yd Breaststroke	4th
1949	Flemings	Swimming-100yd Breaststroke	6th
1949	Peters	Swimming-100yd Backstroke	2nd
1949	Sirpan	Swimming-150yd Individual Medley	3rd
1949		Swimming-150yd Medley Relay Team	5th
1949	McCadden	Track-120yd High Hurdles	5th (Tie)
1949		Track-Mile Relay Team	5th
1949		Track-880yd Relay Team	4th
1949	Sammons	Track-High Jump	4th
1949	Ed Wardlow	Track-880yd Run	5th

Year	Name	Event	Place
1950	Harry Harasymchuk	Swimming-Fancy Diving	4th
1950	Bishop Harkess	Track-100yd Relay	SC
1950	Norman Jackson	Track-100yd Relay	SC
1950	Fred Jackson	Track-100yd Relay	SC
1950	Emanuel Gleason	Track-100yd Relay	SC
1950	Ed Wardlow	Track-880yd Run	2nd
1951	Herb Burns	Football	HM
1951	Wenson	Track-100yd Dash	2nd
1951	Gleason	Track-220yd Dash	4th
1951	Bill Whitman	Track-120yd High Hurdles	4th
1951	Bill Whitman	Track-180yd Low Hurdles	5th
1951	Bill Whitman	Track-Broad Jump	SC
1951		Track-Mile Relay Team	4th
1951		Track-880yd Relay Team	SC
1951	Hill	Track-Shot Put	SC
1951	Sirpan	Swimming-100yd Breaststroke	2nd
1951		Swimming-150yd Medley Relay	6th
1952	Louis Connel	Swimming-100yd Backstroke	4th
1952		Swimming-150yd Medley Relay Team	6th
1952	Bill Whitman	Track-120yd High Hurdles	SC
1952	Bill Whitman	Track-180yd Low Hurdles	SC
1952	Bill Whitman	Track-Broad Jump	SC
1952	Bill Whitman	Track-880yd Relay	SC
1952	Chuck Cofield	Track-880yd Relay	SC
1952	Maury Sykes	Track-880yd Relay	SC
1952	Ben Suber	Track-880yd Relay	SC
1952	Jordan Landon	Track-High Jump	3rd (Tie)
1953	Steve Gwin	Basketball	2nd Team
1953	Louis Connell	Swimming-100yd Breaststroke	2nd
1953	Charles Cofield	Track-880yd Relay	SC
1953	Charles Bibb	Track-880yd Relay	SC
1953	Jake Tatum	Track-880yd Relay	SC
1953	Ben Suber	Track-880yd Relay	SC
1953	Ben Suber	Track-220yd Dash	5th
1953	Estes Newberry	Track-120yd High Hurdles	3rd

1953	Wilbur Mays	Track-180yd Low Hurdles	5th
1953		Track-Mile Relay Team	2nd
1954	Louis Connel	Swimming-200yd Freestyle	3rd
1954		Swimming-200yd Freestyle Relay Team	6th
1954	Joe Byrd	Track 120yd High Hurdles	5th
1954	Joe Byrd	Track-180yd Low Hurdles	4th
1954		Track-880yd Relay Team	2nd
1954		Track-Mile Relay Team	3rd
1955	Charles Nance	Track-440yd Dash	SC
1955	Fred Acoff	Track-Mile Relay	SC
1955	James Jackson	Track-Mile Relay	SC
1955	Robert Carter	Track-Mile Relay	SC
1955	Charles Nance	Track-Mile Relay	SC
1955	Walter Killian	Track-880yd Relay	SC
1955	Don Jackson	Track-880yd Relay	SC
1955	Louis Laisure	Track-880yd Relay	SC
1955	Joe Byrd	Track-880yd Relay	SC
1955	Joe Byrd	Track-120yd High Hurdles	SC
1955	Joe Byrd	Track-180yd Low Hurdles	SC
1956	Joe DeLoach	Basketball	2nd Team
1956	Don Jackson	Track-Mile Relay	SC
1956	Tony Wilcox	Track-Mile Relay	SC
1956	Roosevelt Love	Track-Mile Relay	SC
1956	Fred Tatum	Track-Mile Relay	SC
1956	Roosevelt Love	Track-880yd Relay	SC
1956	Tony Wilcox	Track-880yd Relay	SC
1956	Fred Boker	Track-880yd Relay	SC
1956	Louis Laisure	Track-880yd Relay	SC
1957		Track-880yd Relay Team	2nd
1958	Jim Stone	Basketball	2nd Team
1958	Ken Glenn	Basketball	HM
1958	David Paige	Track-Pole Vault	2nd (Tie)
1958	Lemoyne Porter	Track-High Jump	SC
1959	Ken Glenn	Basketball	1st Team
1959	Jim Stone	Basketball	3rd Team

Year	Name	Sport	Result
1959	Lemoyne Porter	Basketball	HM
1959	Ed Ferguson	Basketball	HM
1959	Henry Windborn	Track-Mile Relay	SC
1959	Dave Paige	Track-Mile Relay	SC
1959	Willie Love	Track-Mile Relay	SC
1959	Bob Copeland	Track-Mile Relay	SC
1959	Lemoyne Porter	Track-High Jump	2nd
1959	David Paige	Track-Pole Vault	2nd
1959	Willie Love	Track-Broad Jump	2nd
1959	James Gay	Track-120yd High Hurdles	5th
1959	Bob Copeland	Track-440yd Dash	2nd
1959		Track-880yd Relay Team	2nd
1960	Gene Lane	Basketball	1st Team
1960	Wilson Graham	Basketball	HM
1960	Lawrence Smith	Cross Country	4th
1961	Lawrence Smith	Cross Country	4th
1961	Wilson Graham	Basketball	3rd team
1961	Melvin Orr	Track-220yd Dash	SC
1961	Melvin Orr	Track-10yd Dash	2nd
1961	Sullivan Hunter	Track-880yd Relay	SC
1961	Gil Pace	Track-880yd Relay	SC
1961	Bob Warmack	Track-880yd Relay	SC
1961	Mel Orr	Track-880yd Relay	SC
1961	Sullivan Hunter	Track-Mile Relay	SC
1961	Don Burkes	Track-Mile Relay	SC
1961	Bob Warmack	Track-Mile Relay	SC
1961	Charles Mitchell	Track-Mile Relay	SC
1962	James Robertson	Basketball	HM
1962	Wilson Graham	Basketball	1st Team
1962	Bob Warmack	Basketball	HM
1962	Bob Warmack	Track-220yd Dash	3rd
1962	Bob Warmack	Track-440yd Dash	2nd
1962		Track-880yd Relay Team	3rd
1963	Marvin Henderson	Track-220yd Dash	4th (Tie)
1963		Track-880yd Relay Team	4th

1963	James Robertson	Basketball	HM
1964	Arthur Nixon	Track-High Jump	3rd (Tie)
1965	Arthur Nixon	Track-High Jump	3rd (Tie)
1965	Dwight Johnson	Track-440yd Dash	4th
1965	Reuben Thompkins	Track-880yd Relay	SC
1965	Ron Barnes	Track-880yd Relay	SC
1965	Dan Crawl	Track-880yd Relay	SC
1965	Dwight Johnson	Track-880yd Relay	SC
1966	Dwight Johnson	Track-440yd Dash	SC
1966	Dwight Johnson	Track-220yd Dash	3rd
1966	Marvin Raine	Track-220yd Dash	4th
1966	John Goens	Track-High Jump	3rd
1966	John Goens	Track-120yd High Hurdles	5th
1966	Dwight Johnson	Track-Mile Relay	SC
1966	Jones	Track-Mile Relay	SC
1966	Cargile	Track-Mile Relay	SC
1966	Ron Barnes	Track-Mile Relay	SC
1966	Larry Mitchell	Basketball	HM
1967	Sam Thomas	Basketball	HM
1967	Ron Barnes	Track-880yd Run	5th
1968	Larry Johnson	Baseball	2nd Team
1969	Don Perry	Track-180yd Low Hurdles	5th
1971	Chris Ayers	Track-Mile Run	3rd
1971	Fred Beamon	Basketball	1st Team
1972	Larry Welch	Tennis-Singles	HM
1972	Monroe Larkin	Track220yd Dash	3rd
1972		Track-Mile Relay Team	3rd
1972	James Abrams	Basketball	2nd Team
1972	Lawrence Bolden	Basketball	HM
1973	Lawrence Bolden	Basketball	1st Team
1973	Barry King	Track-440yd Dash	2nd
1973	James Humphrey	Track-440yd Dash	4th
1974	Warrick Jones	Tennis-Singles	4th
1975	Keith Oglesby	Basketball	3rd Team
1976	Keith Oglesby	Basketball	2nd Team

Year	Name	Sport	Place
1977	James Smith	Basketball	1st Team
1977	James "Bo" Green	Basketball	HM
1977	Ray Marks	Track-440yd Dash	4th
1978	James "Bo" Green	Basketball	HM
1978	Rickey Pittman	Cross Country	5th
1978	Ray Marks	Track-440yd Dash	3rd
1979	Ray Marks	Track-880yd Run	3rd
1979	Rickey Pittman	Cross Country	2nd
1979	Rickey Pittman	Track-Mile Run	5th
1980	Rickey Pittman	Track-3200m Run	2nd
1980	Rickey Pittman	Track-1600m Run	3rd
1982	Wanda Ford	Basketball	1st Team
1983	Linda Wilson	Basketball	HM
1986	Jerome Gambrel	Basketball	2nd Team
1987	Aki Bradley	Track-100m Dash	4th
1987	Reggie Reid	Cross Country	13th
1988	Reggie Reid	Track-800m Run	2nd
1988	Darwin Henderson	Track-3200m Relay	5th
1988	Raymond Howard	Track-3200m Relay	5th
1988	Leroy Powell	Track-3200m Relay	5th
1988	Reggie Reid	Track-3200m Relay	5th
1989	Aki Bradley	Track-200m Dash	3rd
1989	Aki Bradley	Track-100m Dash	5th
1989	Regina Webb	Track-200m Dash	3rd
1990	Aki Bradley	Track-200m Dash	6th
1990	Aki Bradley	Track-100m Dash	5th
1990	Aki Bradley	Track-100m Relay	4th
1990	Connor Torian	Track-100m Relay	4th
1990	Craig Fields	Track-100m Relay	4th
1990	Eric Lee	Track-100m Relay	4th
1991	Willie Hibler	Track-300m Low Hurdles	6th
1992	Willie Hibler	Track-100m High Hurdles	SC
1992	Willie Hibler	Track-300m Low Hurdles	SC
1994	Larry Walker	Track-300m Low Hurdles	7th
1999	Merelenea Dozier	Basketball	3rd Team

2000	Barbara Turner	Basketball	1st Team
2000	Deandre Chandler	Basketball	HM
2001	Marcus Moore	Track-100m Dash	5th
2001	Barbara Turner	Basketball	1st Team
2002	Barbara Turner	Basketball	1st Team
2003	Marcus Moore	Track-100m Dash	4th
2004	Miguel Snyder	Track-200m Dash	5th
2006	Christine Pendleton	Track-100m	7th
2006	Christine Pendleton	Track-200m Relay	4th
2006	Jasmine Prunty	Track-200m Relay	4th
2006	Christle Pendleton	Track-200m Relay	4th
2006	Ashley Minor	Track-200m Relay	4th
2007	Christine Pendleton	Track-100m Dash	4th
2007	Christine Pendleton	Track-200m Dash	6th
2007	Christle Pendleton	Track-100m Dash	6th
2007	Christine Pendleton	Track-100m Relay	4th
2007	Christle Pendleton	Track-100m Relay	4th
2007	Jasmine Prunty	Track-100m Relay	4th
2007	Alice Legg	Track-100m Relay	4th
2008	Jasmine Prunty	Track-100m Relay	3rd
2008	Christle Pendleton	Track-100m Relay	3rd
2008	Takila Robinson	Track-100m Relay	3rd
2008	Christine Pendleton	Track-100m Relay	3rd
2014	Kyauta Taylor	Basketball	HM
2015	Markell Johnson	Basketball	3rd Team
2015	Anthony Carmon	Basketball	HM
2017	Isaiah Washington	Basketball	HM

GLENVILLE

1926	Chaffin	Track-Mile Run	SC
1933	Revard	Track-440yd Dash	3rd
1933	Goode	Track-High Jump	3rd (Tie)
1934	Mills	Track-100yd Dash	2nd
1934	Allen	Track-High Jump	2nd (Tie)
1934	Goode	Track-High Jump	4th (Tie)
1934		Track-880yd Relay Team	5th

1935	Allen	Track-High Jump	SC
1935	Allen	Track-Broad Jump	2nd
1936	Allen	Track-High Jump	SC
1937	Forman	Gymnastics-Long Horse	4th
1937	Forman	Gymnastics-Flying Rings	4th
1940	Assun	Track-880yd Run	5th
1941	Norman Sadofsky	Track-220yd Dash	SC
1941	Norman Sadofsky	Track-100yd Dash	2nd
1941	Bob Miller	Tennis-Doubles	HM
1941	Jim Shank	Tennis-Doubles	HM
1942	White	Track-100yd Dash	3rd
1942	White	Track-220yd Dash	5th
1943	Cutter	Tennis-Doubles	HM
1943	Simon	Tennis-Doubles	HM
1943	Jack Harsh	Tennis-Singles	2nd
1945	Cowan	Tennis-Doubles	HM
1945	Fine	Tennis-Doubles	HM
1945	Wade	Track-Broad Jump	SC
1945	Wade	Track-100yd Dash	5th
1946	Wade	Track-Broad Jump	2nd
1949	Al Rappaport	Tennis-Doubles	HM
1949	Larry Weimer	Tennis-Doubles	HM
1950	Al Rappaport	Tennis-Doubles	HM
1950	Larry Weimer	Tennis-Doubles	HM
1950	John Tucker	Track-100yd Dash	5th
1950		Track-800yd Relay Team	4th
1951	Dick Fryman	Tennis-Doubles	HM
1951	Dave James	Tennis-Doubles	HM
1951	Cornell Hawkins	Track-100yd Dash	5th
1951	Cornell Hawkins	Track-220yd Dash	5th
1951		Track-Mile Relay Team	5th
1952	Cornell Hawkins	Track-100yd Dash	3rd
1952	Cornell Hawkins	Track-220yd Dash	4th
1955	Leroy Cowan	Football	2nd Team
1955	Crawford White	Track-Broad Jump	SC

Year	Name	Event	Place
1956	Walt Williams	Track-Broad Jump	3rd
1957	Walt Williams	Track-Broad Jump	SC
1957	Rod Crayton	Track-High Jump	2nd
1957	Rod Crayton	Track-120yd High Hurdles	4th
1958	Tom Perez	Track-Broad Jump	4th
1958		Track-880yd Relay Team	2nd
1958		Track-Mile Relay Team	4th
1959	Nate Adams	Track-100yd Dash	SC
1959	Nate Adams	Track-100yd Dash	SC
1959	Nate Adams	Track-220yd Dash	SC
1959	Victor Reed	Track-220yd Dash	3rd
1959	Bill Boyd	Track-440yd Dash	3rd
1959	Al Woodall	Track-880yd Relay	SC
1959	Doug Williams	Track-880yd Relay	SC
1959	Victor Reed	Track-880yd Relay	SC
1959	Nate Adams	Track-880yd Relay	SC
1959	Ed Braden	Track-Broad Jump	4th
1959		Track-Mile Relay Team	3rd
1960	Nate Adams	Track-100yd Dash	SC
1960	Victor Reed	Track-100yd Dash	3rd
1960	Nate Adams	Track-220yd Dash	SC
1960	Victor Reed	Track-220yd Dash	2nd
1960	Al Woodall	Track-880yd Relay	SC
1960	Frank Perez	Track-880yd Relay	SC
1960	Victor Reed	Track-880yd Relay	SC
1960	Nate Adams	Track-880yd Relay	SC
1960	Cal Jeter	Track-Mile Relay	SC
1960	Frank Perez	Track-Mile Relay	SC
1960	Frank Gordon	Track-Mile Relay	SC
1960	Owen Patterson	Track-Mile Relay	SC
1961		Track-880yd Relay Team	4th
1961	James Gilber	Cross Country	2nd
1962	James Gilbert	Cross Country	SC
1962	Curtis Sharp	Track-220yd Dash	4th
1962	Theo Morrow	Track-180yd Low Hurdles	2nd

1962	Jim Malone	Tennis-Singles	3rd
1963	Bob Bailey	Track-100yd Dash	SC (Tie)
1963	Bob Bailey	Track-220yd Dash	SC
1963	Warren Adam	Track-880yd Relay	SC
1963	Theron Sumpter	Track-880yd Relay	SC
1963	Louis Evans	Track-880yd Relay	SC
1963	Bob Bailey	Track-880yd Relay	SC
1963	Jim Gilbert	Track-Mile Run	2nd
1963		Track-Mile Relay Team	2nd
1963	William Burt	Track-120yd High Hurdles	3rd
1963	William Burt	Track-180yd Low Hurdles	4th
1964	William Burt	Track-120yd High Hurdles	4th
1964	William Burt	Track-180yd Low Hurdles	SC
1964	Henry Harris	Track-880yd Relay	SC
1964	Mike Alexander	Track-880yd Relay	SC
1964	Stan Robbins	Track-880yd Relay	SC
1964	Stan Gay	Track-880yd Relay	SC
1964		Track-Mile Relay Team	4th
1964	Ron Bolden	Track-Broad Jump	2nd
1964	Jim Sanders	Cross Country	9th
1965	Ron Bolden	Track-Long Jump	SC
1965	Stanley Albright	Track-Long Jump	2nd
1965	Stanley Albright	Track-High Jump	SC
1965	Stan Gay	Track-100yd Dash	5th
1965	Jim Sanders	Cross Country	12th
1966	Don Price	Track-220yd Dash	SC
1966	Marvin Landingham	Track-180yd Low Hurdles	SC
1966	Marvin Landingham	Track-1250yd High Hurdles	2nd
1966	Robert Ware	Track-880yd Relay	SC
1966	Willie Smith	Track-880yd Relay	SC
1966	Kerry Anderson	Track-880yd Relay	SC
1966	Don Price	Track-880yd Relay	SC
1966	Kerry Anderson	Track-Long Jump	4th
1966	James Saunders	Track-2 Mile Run	4th
1967	Robert Ware	Track-100yd Dash	SC

1967	Don Price	Track-100yd Dash	2nd
1967	Don Price	Track-220yd Dash	SC
1967	Robert Ware	Track-220yd Dash	2nd
1967	James Biggom	Track-880yd Relay	SC
1967	William Clair	Track-880yd Relay	SC
1967	Robert Ware	Track-880yd Relay	SC
1967	Don Price	Track-880yd Relay	SC
1968	Robert Ware	Track-100yd Dash	2nd
1968	Robert Ware	Track-220yd Dash	SC
1968	Claude Reeves	Track-220yd Dash	5th
1968	Ken Kuhn	Track-880yd Relay	SC
1968	Claude Reeves	Track-880yd Relay	SC
1968	James Biggom	Track-880yd Relay	SC
1968	Robert Ware	Track-880yd Relay	SC
1969	Vincent Pope	Baseball	2nd Team
1970	Don Williams	Track-100yd Dash	6th
1970	Louis Defreeze	Track-880yd Run	SC
1970	Steve Gruber	Track-880yd Run	3rd
1970	Fred Lane	Track-120yd High Hurdles	SC
1970		Track-880yd Relay Team	2nd
1970		Track-Mile Relay Team	2nd
1971	Louis Defreeze	Track-880yd Run	SC
1971		Track-Mile Relay Team	2nd
1971	Bernard Derricoate	Track-Long Jump	2nd
1972	Larry Jackson	Track-100yd Dash	5th
1972	Eric Jones	Track-120yd High Hurdles	2nd (Tie)
1972	David White	Track-880yd Relay	SC
1972	Bobby Bridget	Track-880yd Relay	SC
1972	Floyd Ware	Track-880yd Relay	SC
1972	Calvin Johnson	Track-880yd Relay	SC
1972		Track-Mile Relay Team	4th
1973	Floyd Ware	Track-100yd Dash	3rd (Tie)
1973	Calvin Johnson	Track-100yd Dash	3rd (Tie)
1973	Calvin Johnson	Track-220yd Dash	2nd
1973	Floyd Ware	Track-100yd Dash	3rd

1973	Charles Byrd	Track-440yd Dash	3rd (Tie)
1973	David White	Track-Mile Relay	SC
1973	Kermit Woolfolk	Track-Mile Relay	SC
1973	Frank Lewis	Track-Mile Relay	SC
1973	Charles Byrd	Track-Mile Relay	SC
1973	David White	Track-880yd Relay	SC
1973	Robert Martin	Track-880yd Relay	SC
1973	Floyd Ware	Track-880yd Relay	SC
1973	Calvin Johnson	Track-880yd Relay	SC
1974	Derrick Harbour	Track-880yd Relay	SC
1974	Ron Page	Track-880yd Relay	SC
1974	Floyd Ware	Track-880yd Relay	SC
1974	David White	Track-880yd Relay	SC
1974	Derrick Harbour	Track-Mile Relay	SC
1974	Ron Page	Track-Mile Relay	SC
1974	David White	Track-Mile Relay	SC
1974	Frank Lewis	Track-Mile Relay	SC
1974	Frank Lewis	Track-440yd Dash	3rd
1974	Floyd Ware	Track-100yd Dash	2nd (Tie)
1974	Floyd Ware	Track-100yd Dash	4th (Tie)
1975	Derrick Harbour	Track-220yd Dash	SC (Tie)
1975	Derrick Harbour	Track-440yd Dash	SC
1975	Danny Baldwin	Track-Mile Relay	4th
1975	Stanley Hamblin	Track-Mile Relay	4th
1975	Kevin Hambrick	Track-Mile Relay	4th
1975	Derrick Harbour	Track-Mile Relay	4th
1975	Derrick Harbour	Track-Long Jump	2nd
1976	Donald Wright	Track-Mile Relay	2nd
1976	Stanley Hamblin	Track-Mile Relay	2nd
1976	Billy Allen	Track-Mile Relay	2nd
1976	Derrick Harbour	Track-Mile Relay	2nd
1977	Michael Cook	Track-880yd Relay	2nd
1977	Robert Crawford	Track-880yd Relay	2nd
1977	Delbert Fowler	Track-880yd Relay	2nd
1977	Donald Wright	Track-880yd Relay	2nd

Year	Name	Sport	Honor
1977	Thomas Grant	Track-Mile Relay	SC
1977	Robert Crawford	Track-Mile Relay	SC
1977	Donald Wright	Track-Mile Relay	SC
1977	Calvin Thomas	Track-Mile Relay	SC
1978	Calvin Thomas	Track-440yd Dash	2nd
1978	Calvin Thomas	Track-220yd Dash	6th
1978	Barbara Jones	Track-880yd Relay	5th
1978	Renee Wright	Track-880yd Relay	5th
1978	Lytonia Echols	Track-880yd Relay	5th
1978	Darlene Embry	Track-880yd Relay	5th
1979	Charlene Malone	Basketball	2nd Team
1979	Bernard Johnson	Basketball	3rd Team
1979	Leonard Scruggs	Track-440yd Dash	SC
1979	Hussain Baseer	Track-100yd Dash	5th
1980	Dwayne Shields	Football	1st Team
1981	Clarence Kelley	Track-300m Low Hurdle	2nd
1981	Brian Scruggs	Track-400m Dash	5th
1981	Brian Scruggs	Track-1600m Relay	5th
1981	Arthur Swaney	Track-1600m Relay	5th
1981	Sam Hamilton	Track-1600m Relay	5th
1981	Clarence Kelley	Track-1600m Relay	5th
1981	Cindy Anzalone	Track-1600m Run	6th
1982	Karen Parker	Basketball	HM
1983	Marcia Brentson	Basketball	HM
1984	Dwayne Shields	Football	1st Team
1985	Lorraine Lofton	Basketball	2nd Team
1985	William Stanley	Basketball	1st Team
1985	Ray Foster	Basketball	HM
1988	Adolph Barr	Baseball	1st Team
1989	Bryan Pope	Baseball	
1989	Vance Benton	Football	2nd Team
1990	Sonya Swopes	Basketball	1st Team
1991	Darnell Bolden	Football	2nd Team
1993	Eric Nix	Track-100m Relay	8th
1993	Jarmain Owens	Track-100m Relay	8th

Year	Name	Sport/Event	Result
1993	Anthony Wallace	Track-100m Relay	8th
1993	Omar Dhyll	Track-100m Relay	8th
1993	Jarmain Owens	Track-400m Relay	6th
1993	Eric Nix	Track-400m Relay	6th
1993	Elliott Gates	Track-400m Relay	6th
1993	Omar Dhyll	Track-400m Relay	6th
1993	Omar Dhyll	Track-400m Dash	6th
1994	Omar Dhyll	Track-400m Dash	SC
1994	Jarmain Owens	Track-400m Relay	SC
1994	Eric Nix	Track-400m Relay	SC
1994	Christopher Chambers	Track-400m Relay	SC
1994	Omar Dhyll	Track-400m Relay	SC
1994	Ebony Kinney	Track-100m Dash	8th
1995	Timothy Overton	Football	2nd Team
1995	Anthony Gilmore	Basketball	HM
1995	Darren Spates	Track-400m Relay	2nd
1995	Kirk Gibbs	Track-400m Relay	2nd
1995	Chris Chambers	Track-400m Relay	2nd
1995	Omar Dhyll	Track-400m Relay	2nd
1995	Omar Dhyll	Track-400m Dash	5th
1996	Tavares Bolden	Football	2nd Team
1996	Simeon Boddie	Football	2nd Team
1996	Kelli Turner	Track-400m Dash	SC
1997	Adrienne King	Track-200m Relay	6th
1997	Tiffany Ginn	Track-200m Relay	6th
1997	Deana Franklin	Track-200m Relay	6th
1997	Kelli Turner	Track-200m Relay	6th
1997	Kelli Turner	Track-400m Dash	5th
1997	Adrienne King	Track-400m Relay	3rd
1997	Erica Gaines	Track-400m Relay	3rd
1997	Deana Franklin	Track-400m Relay	3rd
1997	Kelli Turner	Track-400m Relay	3rd
1998	Latonia Berry	Track-400m Relay	5th
1998	Aalliyah Gillespie	Track-400m Relay	5th
1998	Joynelle Franklin	Track-400m Relay	5th

Year	Name	Sport	Place
1998	Kelli Turner	Track-400m Relay	5th
1999	Terrance Hudson Jr.	Football	2nd Team
1999	Terrance Hudson Jr	Track-300m Hurdles	7th
1999	Latonia Berry	Track-200m Relay	7th
1999	Kelli Turner	Track-200m Relay	7th
1999	Bridget Hatchett	Track-200m Relay	7th
1999	Joynelle Franklin	Track-200m Relay	7th
2000	Erica Carstaphen	Track-400m Relay	4th
2000	June Stamper	Track-400m Relay	4th
2000	Sherilynn Fantroy	Track-400 Relay	4th
2000	Joynelle Franklin	Track-400m Relay	4th
2000	Terrance Hudson Jr	Track-300m Hurdles	2nd
2000	Terrance Hudson Jr	Track-110m Hurdles	2nd
2000	Pierre Woods	Football	st Team
2000	Cedrick Baker	Football	2nd Team
2000	Aaron Nichols	Football	3rd Team
2000	Eric Smith	Football	HM
2001	Donte Whitner	Track-100m Relay	6th
2001	Darnell Grady	Track-100m Relay	6th
2001	Mark Lewis	Track-100m Relay	6th
2001	Pierre Woods	Track-100m Relay	6th
2001	Darius Hiley	Football	2nd Team
2001	Eseck Bryant	Football	HM
2001	Erica Carstaphen	Track-400m Relay	2nd
2001	Shaylann White	Track-400m Relay	2nd
2001	June Stanper	Track-400m Relay	2nd
2001	Cassandra Smith	Track-400m Relay	2nd
2002	James "Woo" Griffin	Football	HM
2002	Ted Ginn Jr.	Track-110m Hurdles	2nd
2002	Ted Ginn Jr.	Track-300m Intermediate Hurdles	2nd
2002	Freddie Lenix	Track-100m Relay	2nd
2002	Ted Ginn Jr.	Track-100m Relay	2nd
2002	Roland Sweet	Track-100m Relay	2nd
2002	Donte Whitner	Track-100m Relay	2nd
2002	Freddie Lenix	Track-400m Relay	SC

Year	Name	Sport	Honor
2002	Ted Ginn Jr.	Track-400m Relay	SC
2002	Roland Sweet	Track-400m Relay	SC
2002	Donte Whitner	Track-400m Relay	SC
2003	James "Woo" Griffin	Basketball	SM
2003	Ted Ginn Jr.	Football	1st Team
2003	Ted Ginn Jr.	Track-100m Hurdles	SC
2003	Ted Ginn Jr.	Track-300m Hurdles	SC
2003	Roland Sweet.	Track-300m Hurdles	3rd
2003	Ted Ginn Jr.	Track-200m Dash	2nd
2003	Raheem Armstrong	Track-100m Relay	SC
2003	Daven Jones	Track-100m Relay	SC
2003	Stephon Fuqua	Track-100m Relay	SC
2003	Freddie Lenix	Track-100m Relay	SC
2003	Antwan Molden	Track-400m Relay	SC
2003	Troy Cloud	Track-400m Relay	SC
2003	Ted Ginn Jr.	Track-400m Relay	SC
2003	Roland Sweet	Track-400m Relay	SC
2003	Freddie Lenix	Track-100m Dash	7th
2004	Tim Conner	Football	1st Team
2004	Michael Russell	Football	1st Team
2004	Freddie Lenix	Football	1st Team
2004	Jamario O'Neal	Football	1st Team
2004	Curtis Smith	Football	2nd Team
2004	Freddie Lenix	Track-100m Dash	3rd
2004	Jamario O'Neal	Track-100m Dash	4th (Tie)
2004	Freddie Lenix	Track-200m Relay	SC
2004	Stephon Fuqua	Track-200m Relay	SC
2004	Andre Evans	Track-200m Relay	SC
2004	Jamario O' Neal	Track-200m Relay	SC
2004	Daven Jones	Track-100m Relay	SC
2004	Myron Howard	Track-100m Relay	SC
2004	Freddie Lenix	Track-100m Relay	SC
2004	Stephon Fuqua	Track-100m Relay	SC
2004	Dante Cloud	Track-400m Relay	SC
2004	Freddie Lenix	Track-400m Relay	SC

2004	Stephon Fuqua	Track-400m Relay	SC
2004	Ted Ginn Jr.	Track-400m Relay	SC
2004	Ted Ginn Jr.	Track-200m Dash	SC
2004	Stephon Fuqua	Track-200m Dash	2nd (Tie)
2004	Ted Ginn Jr.	Track-400m Dash	2nd
2004	Ted Ginn Jr.	Track-110m Hurdles	SC
2004	Curtis Smith	Track-Shot Put	5th
2005	Denise Tate	Basketball	2nd Team
2005	Ray Small	Football	1st Team
2005	Robert Rose	Football	1st Team
2005	Bryant Browning	Football	2nd Team
2005	Arvell Nelson	Football	2nd Team
2005	Bruce Frieson	Football	2nd Team
2005	Freddie Lenix	Track-200m Relay	SC
2005	Andre Evans	Track-200m Relay	SC
2005	Derek McBryde	Track-200m Relay	SC
2005	Ray Fisher	Track-200m Relay	SC
2005	Clemson Caffey	Track-100m Relay	SC
2005	Daven Jones	Track-100m Relay	SC
2005	Jamario O'Neal	Track-100m Relay	SC
2005	Derek McBryde	Track-100m Relay	SC
2005	Eddie Masson	Track-400m Relay	SC
2005	Freddie Lenix	Track-400m Relay	SC
2005	Andre Evans	Track-400m Relay	SC
2005	Jamario O'Neal	Track400m Relay	SC
2005	Curtis Smith	Track-Shot Put	SC
2005	Michael Russell	Track-Shot Put	8th
2005	Curtis Smith	Track-Discus	4th
2005	Andre Evans	Track-110m Hurdles	3rd
2005	Freddie Lenix	Track-200m Dash	2nd
2005	Freddie Lenix	Track-100m Dash	4th
2005	Kyle Jefferson	Track-400m Dash	4th (Tie)
2006	Bruce Davis	Football	1st Team
2006	Jermale Hines	Football	1st Team
2006	Allen Boyd	Basketball	HM

2006	Raina Spencer	Track-High Jump	2nd
2006	Clenson Caffey	Track-100m Relay	SC
2006	Daven Jones	Track-100m Relay	SC
2006	Otis Merrill	Track-100m Relay	SC
2006	De' Erick Barber	Track-100m Relay	SC
2006	Raymond Fisher	Track-200m Relay	SC
2006	De' Erick Barber	Track-200m Relay	SC
2006	Xavier Clements	Track-200m Relay	SC
2006	Kyle Jefferson	Track-200m Relay	SC
2006	Eddie Mason	Track-400m Relay	SC
2006	Kyle Jefferson	Track-400m Relay	SC
2006	Xavier Clements	Track-400m Relay	SC
2006	Daven Jones	Track-400m Relay	SC
2006	Kyle Jefferson	Track-400m Dash	2nd
2006	Xavier Clements	Track-400m Dash	5th
2006	Raymond Fisher	Track-300m Hurdles	3rd
2006	Robert Rose	Track-Shot Put	6th
2007	Toriel Gibson	Football	1st Team
2007	Shawntel Rowell	Football	1st Team
2007	Jermol Martin	Football	1st Team
2007	Cordale Scott	Football	1st Team
2007	Dawawn Whitner	Football	2nd Team
2007	Donnie Fletcher	Football	2nd Team
2007	Kendall Hol	Basketball	HM
2007	Tyshaun Peoples	Track-110m Hurdles	SC
2007	Otis Merrill	Track-110m Hurdles	2nd
2007	Kyle Jefferson	Track-400m Dash	SC
2007	Tyshaun Peoples	Track-100m Relay	SC
2007	Branden Goodall	Track-100m Relay	SC
2007	Otis Merrill	Track-100m Relay	SC
2007	Xavier Clements	Track-100m Relay	SC
2007	Ernest Downing	Track-200m Relay	SC
2007	Xavier Clements	Track-200m Relay	SC
2007	Cardale Scott	Track-200m Relay	SC
2007	Kyle Jefferson	Track-200m Relay	SC

Year	Name	Sport/Event	Result
2007	Ernest Downing	300m Hurdles	2nd
2007	Kyle Jefferson	Track-200m Dash	3rd
2007	Shelton Lundy	Track-400m Relay	5th
2007	Xavier Clements	Track-400m Relay	5th
2007	Dontez Copes	Track-400m Relay	5th
2007	Kyle Jefferson	Track-400m Relay	5th
2007	Raina Spencer	Basketball	3rd Team
2008	Michael Edwards	Football	1st Team
2008	Marcul Hall	Football	2nd Team
2008	Jonathan Newsome	Football	SM
2008	Travis Freeman	Football	SM
2008	Mike Edwards	Football	SM
2008	Travis Freeman	Football	HM
2008	Kendall Holt	Basketball	HM
2008	Rayshawn Goins	Basketball	HM
2008	Tyshaun Peoples	Track-Long Jump	SC
2008	Tyshaun Peoples	Track-110m Hurdles	3rd
2008	Cordale Scott	Track-200m Dash	6th
2008	Ronald Griffin	Track-200m Relay	2nd
2008	Shane Wynn	Track-200m Relay	2nd
2008	Cordale Scott	Track-200m Relay	2nd
2008	Tyshaun Peoples	Track-200m Relay	2nd
2008	Marcus Brooks	Track-400m Relay	4th
2008	Cordale Scott	Track-400m Relay	4th
2008	Marvel Brooks	Track-400m Relay	4th
2008	Quincy Downing	Track-400m Relay	4th
2008	Raina Spencer	Track-High Jump	SC
2009	Randall Holt	Basketball	SM
2009	Christian Bryant	Football	1st Team
2009	Latwan Anderson	Football	2nd Team
2009	Jayrone Elliott	Football	3rd Team
2009	Shane Wynn	Track-200m Relay	SC
2009	Latwan Anderson	Track-200m Relay	SC
2009	Marvel Brooks	Track-200m Relay	SC
2009	Marcus Brooks	Track-200m Relay	SC

2009	Marcus Brooks	Track-800m Relay	SC
2009	Lamar Thomas	Track-800m Relay	SC
2009	Quincy Downing	Track-800m Relay	SC
2009	Marvel Brooks	Track-800m Relay	SC
2009	Latwan Anderson	Track-200m Dash	2nd
2009	Marcus Brooks	Track-300m Hurdles	2nd
2009	Stefone Black	Track-100m Relay	5th
2009	Quincy Downing	Track-100m Relay	5th
2009	Shane Wynn	Track-100m Relay	5th
2009	Latwan Anderson	Track-100m Relay	5th
2009	Quincy Downing	Track-800m Run	8th
2010	Aundrey Walker	Football	1st Team
2010	Andre Sturdivant	Football	1st Team
2010	Cardale Jones	Football	3rd Team
2010	Shane Wynn	Football	3rd Team
2010	Devon Board	Football	SM
2010	Justin Hardee	Track-200m Relay	SC
2010	Quincy Downing	Track-200m Relay	SC
2010	Shane Wynn	Track-200m Relay	SC
2010	Latwan Anderson	Track-200m Relay	SC
2010	Jacquez Riggs	Track-400m Relay	2nd
2010	Shane Wynn	Track-400m Relay	2nd
2010	Latwan Anderson	Track-400m Relay	2nd
2010	Quincy Downing	Track-400m Relay	2nd
2010	Latwan Anderson	Track-100m Relay	3rd
2010	Quincy Downing	Track-100m Relay	3rd
2010	Shane Wynn	Track-100m Relay	3rd
2010	V. Angelo Bentley	Track-100m Relay	3rd
2010	Quincy Downing	Track-800m Run	4th
2010	Shane Wynn	Track-100m Dash	5th (Tie)
2011	Lady Walker	Basketball	HM
2011	De'Van Bogart	Football	1st Team
2011	Quincy Downing	Track-400m Dash	SC
2011	Jacquez Riggs	Track-400m Relay	SC
2011	Justin Hardee	Track-400m Relay	SC

2011	Shane Wynn	Track-400m Relay	SC
2011	Quincy Downing	Track-400m Relay	SC
2012	Herbert Walker Jr.	Football	3rd Team
2012	Christopher Worley	Football	SM
2012	DeAnthony Riggs	Track-400m Relay	3rd
2012	Justin Hardee	Track-400m Relay	3rd
2012	Farakahan Ameen	Track-400m Relay	3rd
2012	Jacquez Riggs	Track-400m Relay	3rd
2012	Jacquez Riggs	Track-400m Dash	8th
2013	Marshon Lattimore	Football	1st Team
2013	Marcelys Jones	Football	1st Team
2013	Davon Anderson	Football	SM
2013	Keesha Henderson	Basketball	HM
2013	Jacquez Riggs	Track-400m Dash	3rd
2013	Willian Robinson	Track-400m Relay	4th
2013	Omar Dhyll Jr.	Track-400m Relay	4th
2013	Darren Hickman	Track-400m Relay	4th
2013	Jacquez Riggs	Track-400m Relay	4th
2014	Latrice Legion	Basketball	SM
2014	Jimond Ivey	Basketball	HM
2014	Sam McKnight	Football	2nd Team
2014	Trevon Story	Football	SM
2014	Davon Anderson	Track-110m Hurdles	SC
2014	Davon Anderson	Track-300m Hurdles	2nd
2014	Falonte Jackson	Track-100m Relay	SC
2014	Darrien Hickman	Track-100m Relay	SC
2014	Demarius Goodwin	Track-100m Relay	SC
2014	Davon Anderson	Track-100m Relay	SC
2014	Adam Lett	Track-400m Relay	SC
2014	Falonte Jackson	Track-400m Relay	SC
2014	Darrien Hickman	Track-400m Relay	SC
2014	Davon Anderson	Track-400m Relay	SC
2014	Adam Lett	Track-200m Relay	7th
2014	Kelvin Spates	Track-200m Relay	7th
2014	Falonte Jackson	Track-200m Relay	7th

Year	Name	Sport	Honor
2014	Darrien Hickman	Track-200m Relay	7th
2015	Aaron Pope	Football	SM
2015	Ralph Davis	Football	SM
2015	Roy Hatchett	Basketball	HM
2015	Brandon Haynes	Track-100m Relay	2nd
2015	Desmond West	Track-100m Relay	2nd
2015	Demerius Goodwin	Track-100m Relay	2nd
2015	Brian West	Track-100m Relay	2nd
2016	Christian Guess	Basketball	HM
2018	Aaron Loines	Basketball	3rd Team
2019	Bryon Ottrix Jr.	Basketball	HM
2019	Gamari Peterson	Football	2nd Team
2019	Willie Anglen	Football	3rd Team
2019	Cornelius McClain	Football	3rd Team
2021	Malik Davis	Football	1st Team
2021	Bryce West	Football	2nd Team
2021	Damarion Witten	Football	3rd Team
2021	Fred Johnson Jr.	Football	3rd Team
2021	Sir'Sean Ingram	Football	3rd Team
2021	Da'Shaun Whatley	Football	HM
2021	Deasean Evans	Track-400m Relay	SC
2021	Jeremiah Powell	Track-400m Relay	SC
2021	Malik Davis	Track-400m Relay	SC
2021	Eric Richards	Track-400m Relay	SC
2021	Jeremiah Powell	Track-110m Hurdles	2nd
2021	Jeremiah Powell	Track-200m Relay	2nd
2021	Deasean Evans	Track-200m Relay	2nd
2021	Joe Larkin	Track-200m Relay	2nd
2021	Dashaun Whatley	Track-200m Relay	2nd
2021	Deasean Evans	Track-200m Dash	3rd
2021	Deasean Evans	Track-400m Dash	3rd
2021	Jeremiah Powell	Track-300m Hurdles	6th
2022	Arvell Reese	Football	1st Team
2022	D'Shawntae Jones	Football	1st Team
2022	Fred Johnson Jr.	Football	1st Team

2022	Bryce West	Football	1st Team
2202	Braylon Smith	Football	2nd Team
2022	Braylon West	Football	2nd Team
2022	Milique Herron	Football	3rd Team
2022	Malik Davis	Football	3rd Team
2022	Milique Herron	Track-200m Relay	SC
2022	Jamari Townsend	Track-200m Relay	SC
2022	Joe Larkins	Track-200m Relay	SC
2022	Bryce West	Track-200m Relay	SC
2022	Malik Davis	Track-400m Relay	2nd
2022	Joe Larkins	Track-400m Relay	2nd
2022	Gregory Howard	Track-400m Relay	2nd
2022	Jayson Williams	Track-400m Relay	2nd
2022	Jayson Williams	Track-300m Hurdles	2nd
2022	Milique Herron	Track-200m Dash	3rd
2022	Dashaun Whatley	Track-100m Relay	3rd
2022	Micquan Gravely	Track-100m Relay	3rd
2022	Milique Herron	Track-100m Relay	3rd
2022	Marquise Davis	Track-100m Relay	3rd
2022	Jermaine Foster	Track-High Jump	3rd
2022	Micquan Gravely	Track-100m Dash	8th
2023	Domareyon Oliver	Basketball	SM
2023	D'Shawntae Jones	Football	1st Team
2023	Damarion Witten	Football	1st Team
2023	Fred Johnson Jr.	Football	1st Team
2023	Jamiel Hill	Football	1st Team
2023	Kareem Jennings	Football	1st Team
2023	Bryce West	Football	1st Team
2023	Matthew Cray	Football	2nd Team
2023	Micquan Gravely	Football	2nd Team
2023	Micquan Gravely	Track-200m Relay	SC
2023	Jamari Townsend	Track-200m Relay	SC
2023	Milique Herron	Track-200m Relay	SC
2023	Bryce West	Track-200m Relay	SC
2023	Isaiah McCallum	Track-400m Relay	SC

2023	Jamari Townsend	Track-400m Relay	SC
2023	Jacob Rice	Track-400m Relay	SC
2023	Malik Davis	Track-400m Relay	SC
2023	Jordin Johnson	Track-100m Relay	2nd
2023	Micquan Gravely	Track-100m Relay	2nd
2023	Milique Herron	Track-100m Relay	2nd
2023	Bryce West	Track-100m Relay	2nd
2023	Jermaine Foster	Track-High Jump	2nd
2023	Bryce West	Track-200m Dash	3rd
2023	Malik Davis	Track-400m Dash	5th

JOHN ADAMS

1929	Milligan	Track-Mile Run	3rd
1929	Jusak	Track-High Jump	SC (Tie)
1929	Prybe	Track-High Jump	3rd
1930		Track-Mile Relay Team	2nd
1930	Trybyszewski	Track-High Jump	3rd (Tie)
1930	Ozmac	Track-440yd Dash	5th
1931		Track-880yd Relay Team	5th
1932	Andrezejiwski	Track-220yd Dash	5th
1932	Jones	Track-Shot Put	4th
1934	Preble	Track-Broad jump	2nd
1934	Kymanko	Track-High Jump	3rd (Tie)
1936	Sam Goldman	Track-Shot Put	SC
1936	Armstrong	Trak-Discus	3rd
1936	Brahtin	Track-High Jump	4th
1936	Brahtin	Track-Broad Jump	5th
1937	Nick Barile	Football	2nd Team
1937	Logan	Track-Broad jump	5th
1937	Bailey	Gymnastics-Parallel Bars	SC
1937	Bailey	Gymnastics-Long Horse	SC
1937	Adkins	Gymnastics-Tumbling	SC
1939	John Saccutto	Football	3rd Team
1940	Hunt	Cross Country	5th
1940	Steve Homolak	Wrestling (105)	2nd
1940	Ignatius Jarzynski	Wrestling (122)	SC

Year	Name	Event	Place
1941	Aroito	Wrestling (165)	4th
1941	Ben Payne	Track-100yd Dash	SC
1941	Johnson	Track-100yd Dash	4th
1942	Sal Helflore	Wrestling (140)	4th
1942	Ben Payne	Track-100yd Dash	2nd
1945	Mihaleje	Wrestling (128)	2nd
1945	Burman	Wrestling (146)	SC
1946	Dick Stack	Wrestling (128)	2nd
1946	Ed Ferris	Wrestling (Hvy)	2nd
1946	Tom Grepher	Wrestling (166)	2nd
1947	Santo Barbarbotta	Wrestling (104)	4th
1947	Charles Arcoria	Wrestling (113)	3rd
1947	Patsy Santoli	Wrestling (156)	4th
1948	Johnson	Track-High Jump	2nd (Tie)
1948	Sciria	Wrestling (113)	SC
1948	Fazio	Wrestling (128)	SC
1948	Giampetro	Wrestling (134)	4th
1949	Ed Casalicchio	Wrestling (128)	SC
1949	Joe Barotta	Wrestling (134)	4th
1949	Attillo Russo	Wrestling (104)	3rd
1949	Hy Eisenberg	Wrestling (155)	2nd
1950		Track-880yd Relay Team	3rd
1950	Ed Casalicchio	Wrestling (128)	SC
1950	Atillo Russo	Wrestling (104)	SC
1950	Julius Competto	Wrestling (113)	3rd
1950	Karl Zahtilla	Wrestling (166)	3rd
1951	Gus Delrosa	Football	2nd Team
1951	Leon Pryor	Track-180yd Low Hurdles	SC
1951	Leon Pryor	Track-Mile Relay	SC
1951	John Pazdzierski	Track-Mile Relay	SC
1951	Frank Leath	Track-Mile Relay	SC
1951	Burl Owens	Track-Mile Relay	SC
1951	Leon Pryor	Track-120yd High Hurdles	2nd
1951	Julius Competto	Wrestling (112)	SC
1951	Jerry Silver	Wrestling (104)	4th

Year	Name	Event	Place
1951	Charles Pagan	Wrestling (146)	3rd
1952	Jerry Silver	Wrestling (104)	2nd
1952	Burl Owens	Track-440yd Dash	2nd
1953	Burl Owens	Track-440yd Dash	2nd
1953	Marshall Laney	Track 440yd Dash	4th
1953	Richard Danko	Track-880yd Run	SC
1953	Richard Danko	Track-Mile Run	3rd
1953	Luke Owens	Track-Discus	SC
1953	Luke Owens	Track-Shot Put	2nd
1953		Track-Mile Relay Team	4th
1953	Angelo Incorvaia	Wrestling (134)	SC
1953	Angelo Bonina	Wrestling (104)	2nd
1953	Joe Monielo	Wrestling (121)	2nd
1953	Buddy Ardito	Wrestling (139)	2nd
1953	Lester Nader	Wrestling (185)	4th
1953	Luke Owens	Football	HM
1953	Leonard Sims	Cross Country	4th
1954	Leonard Sims	Track-880yd Run	5th
1954	Marshall Laney	Track-440yd Dash	3rd
1954	Leonard Sims	Track-Mile Relay	SC
1954	Swann	Track-Mile Relay	SC
1954	Howell	Track-Mile Relay	SC
1954	Marshall Laney	Track-Mile Relay	SC
1954	Leonard Sims	Cross Country	9th
1954	James Bahleda	Cross Country	14th
1954	Sam Algeri	Cross Country	16th
1954	Ed Simpson	Cross Country	17th
1954	Anthony Sinito	Wrestling (104)	3rd
1954	Howard Reminick	Wrestling (134)	4th
1954	Carmen Baratta	Wrestling (155)	3rd
1954	Lester Nader	Wrestling (185)	2nd
1955	Dick Shawn	Track-180yd-Low Hurdles	3rd
1955		Track-Mile Relay Team	2nd
1955		Track-880yd Relay Team	4th
1955	Ed Butler	Cross Country	14th

1955	Tyrone Smith	Cross Country	20th
1955	Bob McConnell	Wrestling (Hvy)	3rd
1955	Howard Reminick	Wrestling (155)	3rd
1956	Ed Butler	Track-Mile Run	SC
1956	Tyrone Smith	Track-880yd Run	2nd
1956		Track-880yd Relay	2nd
1956	Carl Sanford	Track-100yd Dash	3rd
1956		Track-Mile Relay Team	4th
1956	Ed Butler	Cross Country	SC
1956	Tyrone Smith	Cross Country	10th
1956	Joe Martines	Wrestling (165)	2nd
1956	David Hall	Wrestling (175)	2nd
1957	Carl Sanford	Track-180yd Low Hurdles	2nd
1957	Jim Murphy	Track-440yd Dash	2nd
1957		Track-880yd Relay Team	4th
1957		Track-Mile Relay Team	5th
1957	David Hall	Wrestling (175)	3rd
1957	Ludie Grady	Wrestling (145)	2nd
1957	Thomas Kilroy	Wrestling (165)	4th
1958	Choice Phillips	Cross Country	18th
1958	Ludie Grady	Wrestling (145)	SC
1958	Thomas Kilroy	Wrestling (165)	SC
1958	Bill Worthington	Track-120yd High Hurdles	5th
1959	Choice Phillips	Track-Mile Run	SC
1959	Darnell Mitchell	Track-Mile Run	2nd
1959	Darnell Mitchell	Track-880yd Run	4th
1959	Choice Phillips	Cross Country	SC
1959	Darnell Mitchell	Cross Country	6th
1960	Darnell Mitchell	Track-Mile Run	SC
1960	Charles Dawson	Track-120yd High Hurdles	SC
1960	Charles Dawson	Track-180yd Low Hurdles	4th
1960	Darnell Mitchell	Track-880yd Run	2nd
1962		Track-880yd Relay Team	4th
1962	Bill Morton	Tennis-Singles	HM
1962	George Phillips	Basketball	HM

Year	Name	Sport	Place
1962	Ron Farris	Cross Country	10th
1962	George Leaks	Cross Country	15th
1963	Don Farris	Track-880yd Run	3rd
1963	Ben Brown	Cross Country	5th
1963	George Aloshen	Cross Country	7th
1964	Ben Brown	Cross Country	5th
1965	Jim Barry	Baseball	1st Team
1965	Harold Kimball	Track-440yd Dash	SC
1965	Ben Brown	Cross Country	3rd
1966	Marvin Scott	Track-100yd Dash	2nd
1966	Dial Hewlett	Track-440yd Dash	2nd
1966		Track-Mile Relay Team	4th
1966	Garland Stallworth	Basketball	1st Team
1966	Willie Primm	Wrestling 175 lbs	4th
1967		Track-880yd Relay Team	3rd
1968	Murcelle Leeth	Track-Mile Relay	SC
1968	Sidney DeLooch	Track-Mile Relay	SC
1968	Larry Ramsey	Track-Mile Relay	SC
1968	Bryan Jones	Track-Mile Relay	SC
1968	Bryan Jones	Track-440yd Dash	rd
1969	Cleophas McNeal	Basketball	HM
1972	Duane Childs	Track-220yd Dash	6th
1972		Track-Mile Relay Team	5th
1973	Larry Blakely	Track-Mile Relay	3rd
1973	Arthur Brown	Track-Mile Relay	3rd
1973	Claude Holland	Track-Mile Relay	3rd
1973	Travis Kimbrough	Track-Mile Relay	3rd
1974	Arthur Brown	Track-880yd Relay	4th (Tie)
1974	Stephen Davis	Track-880yd Relay	4th (Tie)
1974	Cleo Sapp	Track-880yd Relay	4th (Tie)
1974	Norman Warren	Track-880yd Relay	4th (Tie)
1974	Curtis Morgan	Track-Mile Relay	5th (Tie)
1974	Stephen Davis	Track-Mile Relay	5th (Tie)
1974	Claude Holland	Track-Mile Relay	5th (Tie)
1974	Arthur Brown	Track-Mile Relay	5th (Tie)

1975	Norman Warren	Track-Mile Relay	2nd
1975	Karl Kimbrough	Track-Mile Relay	2nd
1975	Curtis Morgan	Track-Mile Relay	2nd
1975	Stephen Davis	Track-Mile Relay	2nd
1975	Norman Warren	Track-100yd Dash	2nd (Tie)
1975	Michael Murray	Track-880yd Relay	3rd (Tie)
1975	Roy Hairston	Track-880yd Relay	3rd (Tie)
1975	Stephen Davis	Track-880yd Relay	3rd (Tie)
1975	Norman Warren	Track-880yd Relay	3rd (Tie)
1976	Michael Murray	Track-Mile Relay	SC
1976	Roy Hairston	Track-Mile Relay	SC
1976	Jeffrey Craft	Track-Mile Relay	SC
1976	Stephen Davis	Track-Mile Relay	SC
1976	Anthony Thompson	Track-880yd Relay	SC
1976	Michael Murray	Track-880yd Relay	SC
1976	Gary Simpson	Track-880yd Relay	SC
1976	Roy Hairston	Track-880yd Relay	SC
1976	Stephen Davis	Track 440yd dash	2nd
1977	Marvin Adams	Basketball	HM
1977	Darryl Anderson	Track-Mile Relay	3rd
1977	Derek McKinley	Track-Mile Relay	3rd
1977	Gary Simpson	Track-Mile Relay	3rd
1977	Michael Murray	Track-Mile Relay	3rd
1977	Derek McKinley	Track-Long Jump	6th
1978	Cevera Jeffries	Football	HM
1978	Tyrone Evans	Basketball	3rd Team
1978	Carl Jacobs	Basketball	HM
1978	Twyla Sealy	Track-880yd Medley Relay	SC
1978	Karen Kirtley	Track-880yd Medley Relay	SC
1978	Emma Edmonds	Track-880yd Medley Relay	SC
1978	Rochelle Nelson	Track-880yd Medley Relay	SC
1978	Querica Jackson	Track-440yd Relay	SC
1978	Twyla Sealy	Track-440yd Relay	SC
1978	Emma Edmonds	Track-440yd Relay	SC
1978	Rochelle Nelson	Track-440yd Relay	SC

1978	Peola Jefferson	Track-220yd Relay	2nd
1978	Karen Kirtley	Track-220yd Relay	2nd
1978	Twyla Sealy	Track-220yd Relay	2nd
1978	Emma Edmonds	Track-220yd Relay	2nd
1978	Deborah McMillon	Track-110yd Relay	4th
1978	Emma Edmonds	Track-110yd Relay	4th
1978	Twila Sealy	Track-110yd Relay	4th
1978	Karen Kirtley	Track-110yd Relay	4th
1978	Rochelle Nelson	Track-440yd Dash	2nd
1979	Marty Freeman	Track-440yd Relay	SC
1979	Bryan Cleamons	Track-440yd Relay	SC
1979	Bryan McKinley	Track-440yd Relay	SC
1979	Eric Anderson	Track-440yd Relay	SC
1979	Rochelle McKenzie	Basketball	HM
1979	Querica Jackson	Track-440yd Dash	SC
1979	Brenda Butts	Track-440yd Dash	SC
1979	Peola Jefferson	Track-440yd Dash	SC
1979	Rochelle Nelson	Track-440yd Dash	SC
1979	Deborah McMillon	Track-880yd Medley Relay	SC
1979	Karen Kirtley	Track-880yd Medley Relay	SC
1979	Emma Edmonds	Track-880yd Medley Relay	SC
1979	Rochelle Nelson	Track-880yd Medley Relay	SC
1979	Peola Jefferson	Track-220yd Dash	3rd
1979	Deborah McMillon	Track-220yd Relay	4th
1979	Karen Kirtley	Track-220yd Relay	4th
1979	Emma Edmonds	Track-220yd Relay	4th
1979	Peola Jefferson	Track-220yd Relay	4th
1980	Danny Miller	Basketball	HM
1980	Carl Durham	Track-400m Relay	2nd
1980	Bryan Cleamons	Track-400m Relay	2nd
1980	Marty Freeman	Track-400m Relay	2nd
1980	Eric Anderson	Track-400m Relay	2nd
1980	Eric Anderson	Track-200m Dash	5th
1980	Noel Leard	Track-800m Run	4th
1980	Querica Jackson	Track-100m Relay	3rd (Tie)

Year	Name	Event	Place
1980	Karen Kirtley	Track-100m Relay	3rd (Tie)
1980	Marlene Flanagan	Track-100m Relay	3rd (Tie)
1980	Peola Jefferson	Track-100m Relay	3rd (Tie)
1980	Rochelle Nelson	Track-400m Dash	2nd (Tie)
1980	Querica Jackson	Track-400m Relay	2nd
1980	Karen Kirtley	Track-400m Relay	2nd
1980	Peola Jefferson	Track-400m Relay	2nd
1980	Rochelle Nelson	Track-400m Relay	2nd
1980	Peola Jefferson	Track-200m Relay	4th
1980	Marlene Flannagan	Track-200m Relay	4th
1980	Rochelle Nelson	Track-200m Relay	4th
1980	Karen Kirtley	Track-200m Relay	4th
1980	Greg Jefferies	Football	2nd Team
1981	Greg Brown	Basketball	2nd Team
1981	Robert Hall	Basketball	SM
1981	Marlene Flanagan	Track-400m Relay	2nd
1981	Karen Brooks	Track-400m Relay	2nd
1981	Brenda Butts	Track-400m Relay	2nd
1981	Corretta Pittman	Track-400m Relay	2nd
1981	Craig Parker	Track-400m Relay	5th
1981	Mike Oliver	Track-400m Relay	5th
1981	Ken McNair	Track-400m Relay	5th
1981	Kevin McKinley	Track-400m Relay	5th
1981	Kevin McKinley	Track-110 High Hurdles	6th
1982	Clinton Smith	Basketball	1st Team
1982	Marlene Flanagan	Track-100m Hurdles	SC
1982	Gail Counts	Track-200M Dash	3rd
1982	Toni Tell	Track-400m Relay	3rd
1982	Angela Small	Track-400m Relay	3rd
1982	Marlene Flanagan	Track-400m Relay	3rd
1982	Lorretta Pittman	Track-400m Relay	3rd
1982	Kevin McKinley	Track-110m High Hurdles	SC
1982	Bernard Strong	Track-800m Relay	SC
1982	Henry McKnight	Track-800m Relay	SC
1982	William Jones	Track-800m Relay	SC

Year	Name	Event	Place
1982	Kevin McKinley	Track-800m Relay	SC
1982	Kevin McKinley	Track-300m Low Hurdles	2nd
1982	William Jones	Track-800m Run	4th
1983	William Jones	Track-800m Run	3rd
1984	Harold Madox	Track-400m Dash	SC
1984	Melran Leach	Track-1600m Relay	SC
1984	Harold Madox	Track-1600m Relay	SC
1984	Paul Thomas	Track-1600m Relay	SC
1984	Donald Taylor	Track-1600m Relay	SC
1984	Harold Madox	Track-200m Dash	4th
1984	Melran Leach	Track-100m Dash	5th
1985	Donald Taylor	Track-1600m Relay	2nd
1985	Sanchez Madox	Track-1600m Relay	2nd
1985	Anthony Morgan	Track-1600m Relay	2nd
1985	Paul Thomas	Track-1600m Relay	2nd
1985	Paul Thomas	Track-400m Dash	3rd
1985	Donald Taylor	Track-400m Dash	4th
1985	Sanchez Madox	Track 110m High Hurdles	5th
1985	Geneva Bivins	Track-100m Relay	2nd
1985	Benita Hobbs	Track-100m Relay	2nd
1985	Sonya Cheatwood	Track-100m Relay	2nd
1985	Sheilah Smiley	Track-100m Relay	2nd
1985	Geneva Bivins	Track-200m Relay	3rd
1985	Benita Hobbs	Track-200m Relay	3rd
1985	Sheila Smiley	Track-200m Relay	3rd
1985	Cynthia Miller	Track-200m Relay	3rd
1986	Anthony Morgan	Football	2nd Team
1986	Anthony Morgan	Track-400m Relay	SC
1986	Ken Rucker	Track-400m Relay	SC
1986	Shelby Redding	Track-400m Relay	SC
1986	Jeff Mason	Track-400m Relay	SC
1986	Anthony Morgan	Track-300m Low Hurdles	2nd
1986	Anthony Morgan	Track-100m Dash	2nd
1986	Jeff Mason	Track-400m Dash	3rd
1986	Geneva Bivins	Track-200m Dash	2nd

1986	Geneva Bivins	Track-100m Dash	6th
1987	Ken Rucker	Track-800m Relay	2nd
1987	Shelby Redding	Track-800m Relay	2nd
1987	Lorenzo Thomas	Track-800m Relay	2nd
1987	Kevin Chambers	Track-800m Relay	2nd
1987	Leonard Cooper	Basketball	SM
1987	Lorenzo Thomas	Cross Country	19th
1987	Cleo Anderson	Track-Discus	2nd
1987	Benita Hobbs	Track-100m Relay	2nd
1987	Debra Malone	Track-100m Relay	2nd
1987	Sheilah Smiley	Track-100m Relay	2nd
1987	Geneva Bivins	Track-100m Relay	2nd
1987	Benita Hobbs	Track-400m Relay	2nd
1987	Tonja Workman	Track-400m Relay	2nd
1987	Sheilah Smiley	Track-400m Relay	2nd
1987	Marie Lassiter	Track-400m Relay	2nd
1987	Geneva Bivins	Track-100m Dash	4th
1987	Geneva Bivins	Track-200m Dash	3rd
1988	Lorenzo Thomas	Track-800m Relay	SC
1988	Kevin Chambers	Track-800m Relay	SC
1988	Kenneth Rucker	Track-800m Relay	SC
1988	Shelby Redding	Track-800m Relay	SC
1988	Lorenzo Thomas	Track-1600m Run	3rd
1988	Shelby Redding	Track-800m Run	4th
1988	Tangetta Miller	Track-400m Relay	SC
1988	Tonya Workman	Track-400m Relay	SC
1988	Marie Lassiter	Track-400m Relay	SC
1988	Debra Malone	Track 4-400m Relay	SC
1988	Tonja Workman	Track-200m Relay	5th
1988	Marie Lassiter	Track-200m Relay	5th
1988	Tangetta Miller	Track-200m Relay	5th
1988	Debra Malone	Track-200m Relay	5th
1988	Debra Malone	Track-300m High Hurdles	4rh
1989	Troy Miller	Basketball	HM
1989	Marcus Bennett	Track-400m Relay	2nd

Year	Name	Event	Result
1989	Kevin Chambers	Track-400m Relay	2nd
1989	Robert Golden	Track-400m Relay	2nd
1989	Jeff Gooch	Track-400m Relay	2nd
1989	Kelley Jones	Track-400m Relay	SC
1989	Selena Murray	Track-400m Relay	SC
1989	Tangetta Miller	Track-400m Relay	SC
1989	Marie Lassiter	Track-400m Relay	SC
1989	Marie Lassiter	Track-400m Dash	3rd
1989	Tangetta Miller	Track-800m Run	3rd
1991	Melvin Stewart	Football	HM
1991	Antonio Cook	Track-100m Relay	SC
1991	Joe Harmon	Track-100m Relay	SC
1991	Damione Williams	Track-100m Relay	SC
1991	Senghor Hobbs	Track-100m Relay	SC
1991	Thurman Tyus	Track-800m Relay	SC
1991	Westley Edrington	Track-800m Relay	SC
1991	Charles Weaver	Track-800m Relay	SC
1991	Donte Johnson	Track-800m Relay	SC
1991	Damione Williams	Track-400m Relay	2nd
1991	Frank Clark	Track-400m Relay	2nd
1991	Donte Johnson	Track-400m Relay	2nd
1991	Clarence Howard	Track-400m Relay	2nd
1991	Tangetta Miller	Track-800m Run	2nd
1991	Kelley Jones	Track-800m Run	4th
1992	Carmen Banks	Track-200m Dash	SC
1992	Carmen Banks	Track-100m High Hurdles	SC
1992	Carmen Banks	Track-300m Low Hurdles	SC
1992	Senghor Hobbs	Track-400m Relay	2nd
1992	Damion Williams	Track-400m Relay	2nd
1992	Clarence Howard	Track-400m Relay	2nd
1992	Donte Johnson	Track-400m Relay	2nd
1993	Mike Grove	Track-400m Relay	4th
1993	Henry Thompson	Track-400m Relay	4th
1993	Michael Shoals	Track-400m Relay	4th
1993	Clarence Howard	Track-400m Relay	4th

Year	Name	Event	Place
1993	Clarence Howard	Track-400m Dash	5th
1993	Carmen Banks	Track-100m High Hurdles	SC
1993	Carmen Banks	Track-300m Low Hurdles	SC
1993	Carmen Banks	Track-200m Dash	5th
1993	Candace Nicholson	Track-400m Relay	8th
1993	Mariette Lassiter	Track-400m Relay	8th
1993	Kimyatta Carver	Track-400m Relay	8th
1993	Carmen Banks	Track-400m Relay	8th
1994	Terry Smith	Basketball	SM
1994	Carmen Banks	Track-100m High Hurdles	SC
1994	Carmen Banks	Track-300m Low Hurdles	SC
1994	Carmen Banks	Track-200m Dash	2nd
1994	Candace Nicholson	Track-400m Dash	2nd
1994	Candace Nicholson	Track-200m Relay	3rd
1994	Rashida Cameron	Track-200m Relay	3rd
1994	Carmen Banks	Track-200m Relay	3rd
1994	Mariette Lassiter	Track-200m Relay	3rd
1994	Mariette Lassiter	Track-400m Relay	3rd
1994	Rashida Cameron	Track-400m Relay	3rd
1994	Kallica Cole	Track-400m Relay	3rd
1994	Candace Nicholson	Track-400m Relay	3rd
1995	Candace Nicholson	Track-800m Run	SC
1995	Candace Nicholson	Track-200m Relay	4th
1995	Obie Lassiter	Track-200m Relay	4th
1995	Kallica Cole	Track-200m Relay	4th
1995	Rashida Cameron	Track-200m Relay	4th
1995	Kallica Cole	Track-400m Relay	4th
1995	Obie Lassiter	Track-400m Relay	4th
1995	Rashida Cameron	Track-400m Relay	4th
1995	Candace Nicholson	Track-400m Relay	4th
2008	Willie Brown	Track-400m Dash	7th
2009	John James	Track-400m Relay	2nd
2009	Jermol Martin	Track-400m Relay	2nd
2009	Willie Brown	Track-400m Relay	2nd
2009	Timothy Griffin	Track-400m Relay	2nd

Year	Name	Event	Place
2009	Willie Brown	Track-800m Run	3rd
2009	Darryl Wilson	Track-100m Relay	7th
2009	Jermol Martin	Track-100m Relay	7th
2009	John James	Track-100m Relay	7th
2009	Bart Evans	Track-100m Relay	7th
2014	Reggie Thomas	Track-100m Dash	4th

JOHN HAY HIGH

Year	Name	Event	Place
1933		Track-Mile Relay Team	2nd
1933		Track-880yd Relay Team	3rd
1938	Pete Bridar	Wrestling (96)	SC
1938	Joe Incorvia	Wrestling (135)	SC
1938	Labeck	Wrestling (106)	3rd
1938	Chojnzicki	Wrestling (165)	4th
1939	Frank Grankowitz	Wrestling (145)	SC
1939	Ed Tripp	Wrestling (155)	SC
1939	Pete Bridar	Wrestling (115)	2nd
1939	Iggy Jarzinsky	Wrestling (125)	2nd
1939	Sam Ranaldo	Wrestling (135)	2nd
1939	Patrick Scrima	Wrestling (165)	3rd
1940	Tom Davis	Wrestling (135)	SC
1940	Jerome Brentar	Wrestling (165)	SC
1940	Herbert Discont	Wrestling (140)	3rd
1940	Tony Fatica	Wrestling (185)	3rd
1941	Phillipe	Wrestling (115	SC
1941	Herbert Discont	Wrestling (135)	SC
1941	Dominic Russo	Wrestling (104)	2nd
1941	Castro	Wrestling (155)	2nd
1941	Jerome Brentor	Wrestling (165)	2nd
1942	Louis Russo	Wrestling (122)	SC
1942	Art Hays	Wrestling (145)	SC
1942	Dominic Russo	Wrestling (105)	2nd
1942	Gene Perchan	Wrestling (115)	3rd
1942	Sam Wiedershorn	Wrestling (130)	4th
1942	Frank Schmidt	Wrestling (155)	4th

1943	Louis Russo	Wrestling (128)	SC
1943	Gene Perchan	Wrestling (121)	SC
1943	Frank Schmidt	Wrestling (155)	SC
1943	Catavalas	Wrestling (134)	2nd
1943	Mahusky	Wrestling (139)	2nd
1943	Montague	Wrestling (104)	3rd
1943	Stanik	Wrestling (166)	4th
1943	Kelly	Wrestling (186)	4th
1944	Mike Stanik	Wrestling (134)	SC
1944	Louis Lekas	Wrestling (139)	SC
1944	Fred Montague	Wrestling (113)	2nd
1944	Xavier Hzapis	Wrestling (121)	2nd
1947	Dick Walsh	Wrestling (186)	SC
1947	Anthony Rini	Wrestling (134)	2nd
1947	Hank Laconti	Wrestling (139)	3rd
1948	Ian McEwan	Wrestling (139)	SC
1948	Poland	Wrestling (186)	3rd
1948	Hank Laconti	Wrestling (155)	4th
1949	Ian McEwan	Wrestling (146)	SC
1950	Guy Crain	Wrestling (146)	3rd
1950	William Blynn	Wrestling (166)	4th
1951	Ronald Wendz	Wrestling (113)	3rd
1951	Richard Frate	Wrestling (134)	3rd
1952	Robert Kallay	Wrestling (121)	3rd
1952	Vincent D'Amico	Wrestling (146)	3rd
1953	Vincent D'Amico	Wrestling (146)	3rd
1953	Ed Strong	Wrestling (166)	3rd
1964		Track-880yd Relay Team	5th
1965	Brenton Wright	Track-180yd Low Hurdles	SC
1968	Robert Dudley	Track-100yd Dash	4th
1968	Bobby Binns	Tennis-Singles	SC
1969	Bobby Binns	Tennis-Singles	2nd
1973	James Sheppard	Track-180yd Low Hurdles	4th
1973	Walter Hawkins	Track-Mile Relay	4th
1973	Steve Banks	Track-Mile Relay	4th

1973	John Wesley	Track-Mile Relay	4th
1973	Ronald Butler	Track-Mile Relay	4th
1977	Ravawn Harris	Track-Shot Put	4th
1977	Anthony Hancock	Track-120yd-High Hurdles	4th
1977	Anthony Hancock	Track-180yd-Low Hurdles	6th
1978	Rich Reynolds	Track-100yd Dash	SC
1978	Rich Reynolds	Track-880yd Relay	SC
1978	Anthony Hancock	Track-880yd Relay	SC
1978	Sam McClain	Track-880yd Relay	SC
1978	Kevin Mondie	Track-880yd Relay	SC
1978	Anthony Hancock	Track-120yd High Hurdles	SC
1978	Anthony Hancock	Track-300m Low Hurdles	5th
1978	Kevin Mondie	Track-220yd Dash	4th
1981	Tim Hatchett	Football	2nd Team
1981	Charles Oakley	Basketball	HM
1984	Diana Thomas	Track-1600m Relay	6th
1984	Crystal Neal	Track-1600m Relay	6th
1984	Shirley Wallace	Track-1600m Relay	6th
1984	Sonia Mitchell	Track-1600m Relay	6th
1985	Jonathan Walker	Basketball	HM
1985	Crystal Neal	Track-400m Relay	2nd
1985	Linda Irons	Track-400m Relay	2nd
1985	Sonia Mitchell	Track-400m Relay	2nd
1985	Sonya Smiley	Track-400m Relay	2nd
1985	Crystal Neal	Track-100m Relay	6th
1985	Linda Irons	Track-100m Relay	6th
1985	Sonia Mitchell	Track-100m Relay	6th
1985	Sonya Smiley	Track-100m Relay	6th
1985	Crystal Neal	Track-200m Relay	6th
1985	Linda Irons	Track-200m Relay	6th
1985	Sonia Mitchell	Track-200m Relay	6th
1985	Sonya Smiley	Track-200m Relay	6th
1986	Aaron Thompkins	Track-400m Relay	3rd
1986	Cedric Stevenson	Track-400m Relay	3rd
1986	Maurice Kellogg	Track-400m Relay	3rd

Year	Name	Sport/Event	Result
1986	Ronnie Coleman	Track-400m Relay	3rd
1986	Aaron Thompkins	Track-100m Relay	6th
1986	Cedric Stevenson	Track-100m Relay	6th
1986	Maurice Kellogg	Track-100m Relay	6th
1986	Ronnie Coleman	Track-100m Relay	6th
1986	Crystal Neal	Track-400m Relay	2nd
1986	Monica Coley	Track-400m Relay	2nd
1986	Linda Irons	Track-400m Relay	2nd
1986	Sonya Smiley	Track-400m Relay	2nd
1988	Monique Jones	Track-200m Relay	2nd
1988	Angeliette Drake	Track-200m Relay	2nd
1988	Tia Carroll	Track-200m Relay	2nd
1988	Andrea Bostick	Track-200m Relay	2nd
1988	Kim Kelly	Track-400m Relay	4th
1988	Angeliette Drake	Track-400m Relay	4th
1988	Tia Carroll	Track-400m Relay	4th
1988	Andrea Bostick	Track-400m Relay	4th
1989	Monique Jones	Track-200m Relay	2nd
1989	Andrea Bostic	Track-200m Relay	2nd
1989	Tasha Townsend	Track-200m Relay	2nd
1989	Tia Carroll	Track-200m Relay	2nd
1989	Kim Kelly	Track-400m Relay	5th
1989	Tia Carroll	Track-400m Relay	5th
1989	Tasha Townsend	Track-400m Relay	5th
1989	Andrea Bostick	Track-400m Relay	5th
1991	Dorian Green	Track-400m Dash	4th
1993	Ruben Patterson	Basketball	SM
1994	Ruben Patterson	Basketball	3rd Team
1995	Tiffany Engle	Basketball	SM
1996	Nicole Lavan	Basketball	3rd Team
2009	Chanitta Westbrook	Track-100m Dash	6th
2011	Chanitta Westbrook	Track-100m Dash	7th
2011	Chanitta Westbrook	Track-200m Dash	8th
2019	Laurene Tere	Basketball	HM
2020	Amaya Maxie	Basketball	SM

| 2023 | Zhaniah Ervin | Basketball | HM |

JOHN F. KENNEDY

1966	James Epps	Cross Country	8th
1967	James Epps	Track-880yd Run	SC
1967	Walter Davis	Track-Mile Relay	SC
1967	Asbury Wilkerson	Track-Mile Relay	SC
1967	Neverlin Fletcher	Track-Mile Relay	SC
1967	James Epps	Track-Mile Relay	SC
1967	Kevin Blake	Cross Country	3rd
1968	Mal Stoudenmire	Football	2nd Team
1968	Kevin Blocke	Track-880yd Run	SC
1968		Track-880yd Relay Team	2nd
1968		Track-Mile Relay Team	3rd
1969	Bob Douglass	Track-180yd Low Hurdles	SC
1969	Luther Sharp	Track-Mile Relay	SC
1969	Barry Alvis	Track-Mile Relay	SC
1969	James Lawrence	Track-Mile Relay	SC
1969	Asbury Wilkerson	Track-Mile Relay	SC
1969	Bob Douglass	Track-100yd Dash	2nd
1970	Alan Tyler	Track-880yd Relay	SC
1970	Michael Brown	Track-880yd Relay	SC
1970	Bill Curry	Track-880yd Relay	SC
1970	Joe Edmunds	Track-880yd Relay	SC
1970		Track-Mile Relay Team	4th
1970	Alan Tyler	Track-100yd Dash	5th
1972		Track-880yd Relay Team	5th
1973	Prentiss Wenson	Track-440yd Dash	2nd (Tie)
1974	Lawrence Boston	Basketball	1st Team
1974	Charles Bibb	Track-Mile Relay	3rd
1974	Morris Jordan	Track-Mile Relay	3rd
1974	Kenneth Johnson	Track-Mile Relay	3rd
1974	Wenners Ballard Jr.	Track-Mile Relay	3rd
1974	Wenners Ballard Jr.	Track-440yd Dash	5th
1975	Tony Brown	Wrestling	5th

Year	Name	Sport/Event	Place
1975	Ronnie Mitchell	Track-880yd Relay	6th
1975	Larry Sinclair	Track-880yd Relay	6th
1975	Nate Smith	Track-880yd Relay	6th
1975	Larry Garth	Track-880yd Relay	6th
1975	Michele Stevens	Track-Shot Put	SC
1976	Linda Washington	Track-440yd Relay	5th
1976	Earlene Berry	Track-440yd Relay	5th
1976	Toi Steele	Track-440yd Relay	5th
1976	Norma Washington	Track-440yd Relay	5th
1976	Darrell Sharp	Track-Mile Relay	5th
1976	Ronnie Mitchell	Track-Mile Relay	5th
1976	Marc Aden	Track-Mile Relay	5th
1976	Nathan Smith	Track-Mile Relay	5th
1977	Larry Sinclair	Track-880yd Relay	4th
1977	Mark Maple	Track-880yd Relay	4th
1977	Ronnie Mitchell	Track-880yd Relay	4th
1977	Nathan Smith	Track-880yd Relay	4th
1977	Fred McKenney	Basketball	SM
1978	Aparicio Curry	Basketball	3rd Team
1980	Charles Morgan	Track-400m Relay	5th (Tie)
1980	Reggie Triggs	Track-400m Relay	5th (Tie)
1980	Curtis Hardley	Track-400m Relay	5th (Tie)
1980	Andre Carr	Track-400m Relay	5th (Tie)
1983	Al Carpenter	Basketball	3rd Team
1984	Lloyd Strafford	Track-3200m Relay	3rd
1984	Ronald Strafford	Track-3200m Relay	3rd
1984	Chris Ceasor	Track-3200m Relay	3rd
1984	Norman Lynch	Track-3200m Relay	3rd
1987	Lawrence Lenin	Track-800m Run	2nd
1989	Michael Golliday	Track-800m Run	6th
1990	Bonnie Dove	Basketball	2nd Team
1990	Donneika Kibble	Track-200m Dash	8th
1991	Donneika Kibble	Track-100m Dash	3rd
1991	Donneika Kibble	Track-200m Dash	4th
1992	Donneika Kibble	Track-100m Dash	2nd

1992	Donneika Kibble	Track-200m Dash	4th
1992	Donneika Kibble	Track-100m Relay	6th
1992	Donetta Taylor	Track-100m Relay	6th
1992	Tiffany Powers	Track-100m Relay	6th
1992	Odessa Fields	Track-100m Relay	6th
1996	Darnell Kimmie	Track-200m Dash	4th
2002	Jayrl Hunt	Wrestling (103)	6th
2002	Anthony Murphy	Track-400m Dash	2nd
2002	Marcus Wilkerson	Track-100m Relay	7th
2002	Marlon Galbreath	Track-100m Relay	7th
2002	Antonio Kellom	Track-100m Relay	7th
2002	Marcus McIntosh	Track-100m Relay	7th
2003	Anthonio Kellom	Track-200m Dash	5th
2003	Marcus Wilkerson	Track-Long Jump	8th
2004	Brittney Walker	Basketball	SM
2004	Marcus Wilkerson	Track-Long Jump	SC
2004	Antonio Kellom	Track-200m Relay	3rd
2004	Gilbert Evans	Track-200m Relay	3rd
2004	Brandon Boston	Track-200m Relay	3rd
2004	Marcus Wilkerson	Track-200m Relay	3rd
2004	Antonio Kellom	Track-200m Dash	4th
2005	Marcus Wilkerson	Track-100m Relay	6th
2005	Jamall Smith	Track-100m Relay	6th
2005	Anthony Thomas	Track-100m Relay	6th
2005	Darnell Davis	Track-100m Relay	6th
2005	Marcus Wilkerson	Track-Long Jump	2nd
2005	Tyrone Bolden	Track-Long Jump	4th
2006	Tyrone Bolden	Track-High Jump	2nd
2006	Tyrone Bolden	Track-Long Jump	3rd
2006	Demonte Clements	Track-100m Relay	3rd
2006	Suave Harris	Track-100m Relay	3rd
2006	Anthony Thomas	Track-100m Relay	3rd
2006	Tyrone Bolden	Track-100m Relay	3rd
2006	Anthony Thomas	Track-200m Dash	4th
2006	Anthony Thomas	Track-100m Dash	6th

2006	Tyrone Bolden	Basketball	SM
2006	Anita Malone	Basketball	SM
2007	Arnez Hardnick	Track-100m Relay	6th
2007	Antione Wooten	Track-100m Relay	6th
2007	Deonta Robinson	Track-100m Relay	6th
2007	Deonte Toler	Track-100m Relay	6th
2007	Chris Roberts	Basketball	SM
2009	Rachael Walker	Basketball	HM
2010	D'Wanda Ford	Track-Long Jump	3rd
2012	Antwon Smith	Track-400m Dash	SC
2012	Antwon Smith	Track-200m Relay	7th
2012	D'Juan Ross	Track-200m Relay	7th
2012	Desmond Waden	Track-200m Relay	7th
2012	Malcolm Martin	Track-200m Relay	7th
2012	Jordan Marrow	Basketball	SM
2012	Anthony Howard	Basketball	HM
2013	Antwon Smith	Track-400m Dash	2nd
2013	Antwon Smith	Track-Long Jump	3rd
2014	David Williams	Track-Long jump	7th
2014	Sierra Williams	Track-200m Dash	4th
2015	Diamond Cummings	Track-100m Dash	3rd
2015	Diamond Cummings	Track-100m Relay	5th
2015	Ayanna Medley	Track-100m Relay	5th
2015	Asia Lee	Track-100m Relay	5th
2015	Briauna Murray	Track-100m Relay	5th
2017	Kershawn Goodwin	Football	2nd Team

JOHN MARSHALL

1927	Moore	Track-220yd Hurdles	4th
1934	Henderson	Track-880yd Run	3rd
1935	Johnson	Cross Country	11th
1936	Pagel	Track-440yd Dash	2nd
1937	Al Kurnat	Track-120yd High Hurdles	SC
1938		Track-880yd Relay Team	3rd
1939	Bob Stroemple	Track-440yd Dash	SC
1939	Bob Stroemple	Track-10yd Dash	2nd

Year	Name	Event	Place
1939		Track-Mile Relay Team	4th
1940	Uschelbec	Track-880yd Run	4th
1941		Track-Mile Relay Team	4th
1941	Solarz	Track-440yd Dash	5th
1941		Track-880yd Relay Team	5th
1941	Ed Sustersic	Wrestling (185)	4th
1942	Donnelly	Track-Mile Run	3rd
1942		Track-880yd Relay Team	4th
1942		Track-Mile Relay Team	5th
1942	Ed Maro	Wrestling (165)	2nd
1942	Paul Varga	Wrestling (145)	4th
1943	Tom Hasari	Track-440yd Dash	SC
1943	Tom Donnelly	Track-Mile Run	2nd
1943		Track-Mile Relay Team	2nd
1943	Winters	Track-High Jump	2nd (Tie)
1943	Conda	Track-High Jump	2nd (Tie)
1943	Stroemple	Track-880yd Run	3rd
1943	Tom Donnelly	Track-880yd Run	4th
1943	Ester	Track-pole Vault	4th (Tie)
1943	Paul Varga	Wrestling (139)	SC
1943	Nichols	Wrestling (128)	2nd
1943	Varga	Wrestling (155)	2nd
1943	Blumenstein	Wrestling (186)	2nd
1943	Phillips	Wrestling (121)	4th
1943	John Stavole	Cross Country	2nd
1943	Steinmetz	Cross Country	14th
1943	Tom Hasari	Cross Country	16th
1944	Bruce	Cross Country	8th
1944	Foster	Track-Pole Vault	S C
1944	Bill Hillyard	Track-Pole Vault	3rd (Tie)
1944	Katzman	Track-Broad Jump	3rd
1945	Foster	Track-High Jump	2nd
1945	Foster	Track-Pole Vault	2nd (Tie)
1945		Track-880yd Relay Team	5th
1945	Walter Schultz	Football	3rd Team

Year	Name	Event	Place
1945	Straslicka	Wrestling (113)	2nd
1945	Yohoscik	Wrestling (121)	2nd
1946	Bill Weitzel	Track-440yd Dash	S C
1946	Richard Martin	Cross Country	16th
1947	Dick Kucera	Cross Country	20th
1947	Gilbert Dubray	Wrestling (156)	SC
1947	Tom Hanson	Wrestling (121)	2nd
1947	Jim Vastleff	Wrestling (104)	3rd
1948	Straslicka	Wrestling (113)	3rd
1948	Alan Peterson	Wrestling (124)	3rd
1948	Dragall	Wrestling (146)	3rd
1948	Vassiloff	Wrestling (121)	4th
1948	Beckert	Wrestling (139)	4th
1948	Sasaler	Wrestling (186)	4th
1949	Grombol	Football	HM
1949		Track-Mile Relay Team	3rd
1949	Weber	Track-440yd Dash	5th
1949	Alan Peterson	Wrestling (139)	SC
1949	Gary Shade	Wrestling (146)	4th
1950	Dick Skurko	Track-220yd Dash	3rd
1950	Jim Zickes	Track-Pole Vault	3rd (Tie)
1950	Alan Peterson	Wrestling (139)	SC
1950	Bruce Holland	Wrestling (128)	3rd
1950	Clayton Brummer	Wrestling (134)	4th
1951	Dick Skurko	Track-220yd Dash	2nd
1951	Dick Skurko	Track-100yd Dash	4th
1951	Richard Goodwin	Wrestling (104)	SC
1951	Mladen Zuppan	Wrestling (156)	3rd
1951	Paul Ferrell	Wrestling (134)	4th
1951	Robert Zwolenick	Wrestling (148)	4th
1951	Don Yager	Tennis-Doubles	HM
1951	Ron Bucholz	Tennis-Doubles	HM
1952	James Dregalla	Wrestling (186)	SC
1952	Ralph Ezzo	Wrestling (121)	4th
1952	Don Wood	Wrestling (128)	4th

Year	Name	Sport	Place
1952	Ron Bucholz	Tennis-Singles	HM
1953	James Drugalla	Wrestling (186)	SC
1953	Richard Goodwin	Wrestling (128)	2nd
1953	Ray Rieder	Wrestling (166)	4th
1953	Andy Hellian	Cross Country	12th
1954	James Drugalla	Wrestling (186)	SC
1954	Robert Morrill	Wrestling (166)	3rd
1954	Phil Bednar	Wrestling (128)	3rd
1954	Bill Harnett	Wrestling (104)	4th
1954	Ray Rieder	Wrestling (155)	4th
1955	Bob Ramlow	Track-Pole Vault	2nd (Tie)
1955	Dave Emery	Track-Mile Run	3rd
1955	Ray Rieder	Wrestling (175)	SC
1956	Dave Emery	Track-Mile Run	3rd
1956	Robert Zukie	Wrestling (103)	4th
1956	Dave Emery	Cross Country	3rd
1957	Russell DiSanto	Wrestling (112)	2nd
1957	Fred Loeffler	Wrestling (154)	2nd
1958	Russell Di Santo	Wrestling (112)	SC
1958	James Morrill	Wrestling (133)	2nd
1958	Jeffrey Kasler	Wrestling (127)	3rd
1958	John Tobin	Wrestling (138)	3rd
1959	Neil James	Football	2nd Team
1959	James Morrill	Wrestling (133)	SC
1959	John Tobin	Wrestling (145)	2nd
1959	John Joeright	Wrestling (112)	3rd
1959	Jack Leonti	Wrestling (120)	4th
1960	Tom Wilhelm	Football	2nd Team
1960	Tony Rizk	Wrestling (175)	SC
1960	ohn Sabo	Wrestling (103)	4th
1960	Jack Leonti	Wrestling (120)	4th
1960	Ross Maclachlan	Cross Country	4th
1960	Richard Osicka	Cross Country	9th
1960	Robert Zizak	Cross Country	11th
1960	Robert Osicka	Cross Country	15th

1961	John Sabo	Wrestling (103)	2nd
1961	John Henderson	Wrestling (133)	4th
1961	Larry Supelak	Wrestling (175)	4th
1961	Tom Wilhelm	Wrestling (Hvy)	4th
1963	Bill Burkle	Wrestling (103)	3rd
1963	Bob McElroy	Cross Country	15th
1964	Gary Gold	Cross Country	SC
1964	Bob McElroy	Cross Country	3rd
1964	Bill Burkle	Wrestling (103)	SC
1964	Cecil Sallee	Wrestling (133)	SC
1964	Tony Paci	Track-Mile Relay	SC
1964	Hugh Ruffing	Track-Mile Relay	SC
1964	Don Sabo	Track-Mile Relay	SC
1964	Mike Bird	Track-Mile Relay	SC
1964		Track-880yd Relay Team	7th
1965	Gary Gold	Cross Country	4th
1965	Dave Marxhall	Cross Country	10th
1965	Alan Gerboc	Wrestling (120)	2nd
1965	S. Croycraft	Wrestling (133)	2nd
1966	Robert Buddie	Wrestling (120)	SC
1966	Jim Eiben	Wrestling (154	2nd
1968		Track-Mile Relay Team	2nd
1968	Dave Mayher	Track-440yd Dash	4th
1968	Dave Shupe	Swimming-1m Diving	6th
1971	Dave Kenney	Wrestling (98)	2nd
1971	Larry Coy	Cross Country	17th
1972	Larry Coy	Cross Country	SC
1972	Dave Kenney	Wrestling (98)	SC
1972	Jim Kurtz	Wrestling (155)	3rd
1973	Pete Deluca	Wrestling (132)	2nd
1973	Hollis Frierson	Wrestling (98)	3rd
1974	Hollis Frierson	Wrestling (112)	4th
1975	Hollis Frierson	Wrestling (119)	5th
1975	Lorrie Oldham	Track-440yd Dash	4th
1975	Mark Chapin	Cross Country	15th

Year	Name	Sport	Place
1976	Charlene Stemm	Track (Shot Put)	6th
1977	Charlene Stemm	Track-Shot Put	SC
1977	Modesto Ruggierio	Tennis-Doubles	HM
1977	Mike Roman	Tennis-Doubles	HM
1978	Modesto Ruggierio	Tennis-Doubles	HM
1978	Mike Roman	Tennis-Doubles	HM
1978	Ricardo Ragland	Basketball	HM
1979	Michelle Stoyko	Track (High Jump)	2nd
1979	Modesto Ruggierio	Tennis-Doubles	4th
1979	Mike Roman	Tennis-Doubles	4th
1980	Michelle Stoyko	Track (High Jump)	2nd
1980	Jim Kerr	Wrestling (105)	3rd
1981	Dave Colbert	Basketball	2nd Team
1982	Belfred Clark	Track-110yd High Hurdles	2nd
1982	Belfred Clark	Track-300yd Lpw Hurdles	5th
1983	John Ginley	Basketball	HM
1985	Joe Baron	Basketball	HM
1990	Mike Penn	Baseball	
1991	Janetta Graham	Basketball	3rd team
1991	Jonathan Burrell	Track-100m Dash	SC
1991	Jonathan Burrell	Track-200m Dash	SC
1991	Larry King	Track-1600m Run	2nd
199	Elige Longino	Track-100m Relay	2nd
1991	Jonathan Burrell	Track-100m Relay	2nd
1991	Gerald Jones	Track-100m Relay	2nd
1991	Archie White	Track-100m Relay	2nd
1991	Jonathan Burrell	Track-400m Relay	4th
1991	Larry King	Track-400m Relay	4th
1991	Elige Longino	Track-400m Relay	4th
1991	Gerald Jones	Track-400m Relay	4th
1991	Gerald Jones	Track-300m Low Hurdles	5th
1992	Jonathan Burrell	Track-100m Dash	SC
1992	Dorian Green	Track-400m Dash	SC
1992	Dorian Green	Track-100m Relay	SC
1992	Archie White	Track-100m Relay	SC

1992	Elige Longno	Track-100m Relay	SC
1992	Jonathan Burrell	Track-100m Relay	SC
1992	Dorian Green	Track-200m Dash	3rd
1993	Johnathan Burrell	Track-100m Dash	SC
1993	Johnathan Burrell	Track-200m Dash	SC
1993	Dorian Green	Track-100m Relay	5th
1993	Keith Golphin	Track-100m Relay	5th
1993	Archie White	Track-100m Relay	5th
1993	Jonathan Burrell	Track-100m Relay	5th
1993	Jeff Limpert	Track-400m Relay	8th
1993	Jonathan Burrell	Track-400m Relay	8th
1993	Keith Golphin	Track-400m Relay	8th
1993	Archie White	Track-400m Relay	8th
1993	April Mixon	Basketball	SM
1995	Jeffrey Limpert	Track-800m Run	SC
1995	Vita Redding	Basketball	1st Team
1995	Rochel Russell	Track-400m Dash	SC
1995	Rochel Russell	Track-200m Dash	3rd
2010	DeAndre Brown	Football	SM
2023	Carson Diolio	Football	HM

LINCOLN HIGH

1931	Dianiska	Gymnastics-Parallel Bars	2nd
1932	Matulus	Cross Country	4th
1932	White	Cross Country	16th
1932	Westfall	Cross Country	19th
1933	White	Track-440yd Dash	SC
1933	White	Cross Country	12th
1933	Westfall	Cross Country	15th
1933	Matulus	Cross Country	18th
1934	Harold Vacha	Track-100yd Dash	SC
1934	Harold Vacha	Track- 220yd Dash	SC
1934	East	Track-High jump	2nd (Tie)
1935	Bean	Cross Country	4th
1935	Scuba	Cross Country	16th
1936	Dochtor	Track-Shot Put	4th

1936	Petlowany	Cross Country	17th
1936	Kolzynski	Cross Country	20th
1937	Petlowany	Cross Country	4th
1937	Kolzynski	Cross Country	14th
1937	Gubanich	Cross Country	16th
1937		Track-Mile Relay Team	4th
1937	Dochtor	Track-Shot Put	5th
1938	Stasuk	Cross Country	13th
1939	Lytle	Cross Country	5th
1939	Langer	Cross Country	15th
1940	Langer	Track-Mile Run	5th
1941	Walt Poremba	Football	2nd Team
1941	Markovic	Football	HM
1942	Danellshen	Football	HM
1943	Don Bania	Football	2nd Team
1943	Dodzinski	Track-Long Jump	3rd
1944	Paul Maximuk	Track-Shot Put	3rd
1944	Stuart Wilkens	Football	HM
1945	Paul Maximuk	Track-Shot Put	2nd
1946	Walt Yowarsky	Football	HM
1947	Walt Yowarsky	Football	HM
1970	Tim Casey	Wrestling	2nd

LINCOLN-WEST

1970	Vance Pate	Football	1st Team
1975	Dave Ford	Basketball	3rd Team
1976	Joe Williams	Basketball	HM
1978	Laurie Collins	Basketball	HM
1979	Sue Koziol	Basketball	HM
1980	Sue Koziol	Basketball	1st Team
1982	Michael Carter	Basketball	HM
1984	Terry Sullivan	Track-400m Dash	5th
1984	Terry Sullivan	Track 400m Relay	2nd
1984	Amin Muhammad	Track-400m Relay	2nd
1984	Tim Goler	Track-400m Relay	2nd

1984	Ron Smith	Track-400m Relay	2nd
1988	Alonzo Wilson	Track-200m Relay	5th
1990	Alonzo Wilson	Track-100m Dash	3rd
1990	Alonzo Wilson	Track-400m Dash	6th
1996	James Carter	Basketball	3rd Team

MARTIN L. KING

1980	Willie Dawson	Track-300m Hurdles	SC
1980	Bobbie Dotson	Track-400m Relay	2nd
1980	James Lang	Track-400 Relay	2nd
1980	Willie Wise	Track-400 Relay	2nd
1980	Willie Dawson	Track-400 Relay	2nd
2019	Dion Hardy	Basketball	HM

MAX HAYES

| 1967 | Bob Ward | Track-120m High Hurdles | 5th |
| 1975 | Michael Ward | Basketball | HM |

RHODES

1935		Track-Mile Relay Team	5th
1936		Track-Medley Relay Team	5th (Tie)
1938	Bob Ingram	Wrestling (105)	SC
1938	Stanley Kakowsy	Wrestling (155)	SC
1938	Fred Schleicher	Wrestling (185)	SC
1938	Mike Slepicky	Wrestling (125)	3rd
1938	Hagadus	Cross Country	6th
1938	Kenneth Hall	Track-880yd Run	3rd
1938	Donald Bailey	Track-220yd Low Hurdles	3rd
1938	Donald Bailey	Track-120yd High Hurdles	4th
1939	Fred Schleicher	Wrestling (185)	SC
1939	Joe Malanowski	Wrestling (105)	SC
1940		Track-Mile Relay Team	2nd
1942	John Juhas	Wrestling (106)	SC
1942	Casimir Pavlak	Wrestling (135)	4th
1943	Contofalsky	Track-100yd Dash	3rd
1943	Contofalsky	Track-220yd Dash	3rd

Year	Name	Event	Place
1943		Track-880yd Relay Team	4th
1943	Roth	Track-Shot Put	4th
1943	Ruttolph	Wrestling (134)	SC
1943	Chuck Kuehn	Wrestling (128)	3rd
1943	Norman Metzgar	Wrestling (166)	3rd
1943	Levandowsky	Wrestling (113)	3rd
1943	Fred Briedigan	Cross Country	10th
1943	Gordon Cox	Cross Country	12th
1944	Barney Brunson	Wrestling (104)	SC
1944	Chuck Kuehn	Wrestling (134)	2nd
1944	Neil Richardson	Cross Country	19th
1944	Lowell Shirey	Track-120yd High Hurdles	SC
1944	Lowell Shirey	Track-220yd Low Hurdles	2nd
1945		Track-Mile Relay Team	5th
1945	Lawrence Lange	Cross Country	12th
1945	Walter Cates	Cross Country	16th
1945	Neil Richardson	Cross Country	18th
1946	Dick Sistek	Track-120yd High Hurdles	SC
1946	Dick Sistek	Track-220yd Low Hurdles	SC
1947	Ralph Armstrong	Football	2nd Team
1948	George Kruichuk	Wrestling (121)	3rd
1948	Fox	Wrestling (155)	3rd
1949	Joe Rocco	Wrestling (121)	2nd
1949	Richard Musall	Wrestling (186)	3rd
1949	Gregory DeCesare	Wrestling (113)	4th
1950	Clyde Simpson	Wrestling (121)	2nd
1950	Dale Bussman	Cross Country	9th
1950	Ray Dobskey	Track-440yd Dash	3rd
1951	Frank Guzik	Football	1st Team
1951	Cliff Callaghan	Track-120y. High Hurdles	5th
1951	Clyde Simpson	Wrestling (121)	3rd
1952	Robert Mackulin	Cross Country	5th
1952	Dale Block	Track-220yd Dash	2nd
1952		Track-880yd Relay Team	4th
1953	Al Karp	Football	2nd Team

1953	Jacobson	Football	HM
1953	Bob Mackulin	Track-Mile Run	5th
1954	Edwin Herman	Track-Mile Run	5th
1955	Joe Mirka	Track-Shot Put	3rd
1955	Dick Safran	Track-180yd Low Hurdles	5th
1955	Bob Schmidt	Football	2nd Team
1955	Steve Tekesky	Cross Country	2nd
1956	Steve Tekesky	Cross Country	2nd
1956	Al Dewerth	Track-880yd Run	3rd
1956	George Mirka	Track-Shot Put	3rd
1956	George Mirka	Track-Discus	3rd
1956	Dick Safran	Track-180yd Low Hurdles	4th
1956	Dick Safran	Track-120yd High Hurdles	5th
1956	Dave Nabinger	Track-440yd Dash	5th
1957	Steve Tekesky	Cross Country	2nd
1957	Dan Burton	Cross Country	17th
1958	Carl Swanson	Cross Country	15th
1960	Thomas Work	Cross Country	13th
1963	Frank Lewis	Track-Pole Vault	5th (Tie)
1964	Steve Korinchak	Cross Country	6th
1964	Jim Emery	Cross Country	7th
1964	Bill Hann	Basketball	2nd Team
1965	James Emery	Cross Country	6th
1965	Bill Hann	Basketball	1st Team
1969	Dale Kosyk	Track-440 Dash	5th
1970	Ron Addison	Cross Country	16th
1971	Ron Addison	Cross Country	SC
1971	Ron Addison	Track-Mile Run	2nd
1971	Dave Stachowski	Track-220yd Dash	4th
1972	Ron Addison	Track-Mile Run	SC
1972	Ron Addison	Track-880yd Run	3rd
1977	Gerald Vilt	Cross Country	SC
1977	Craig Stalder	Cross Country	20th
1977	Gerald Vilt	Track-Mile Run	5th
1979	Terri Nolan	Track-880yd Run	4th

1980	Cindy Anzalone-Fox	Track-800m Run	4th
1981	Cindy Anzalone-Fox	Cross Country	14th-T
1982	Cindy Anzalone-Fox	Track-1600m Run	3rd
1985	Greg Sims	Track-300m Low Hurdles	5th
1988	Carol Sims	Track-200m Relay	4th
1988	Ester McMillon	Track-200m Relay	4th
1988	Teresa Crews	Track-200m Relay	4th
1988	Carmella Marshall	Track-200m Relay	4th
1989	Cynthia Davis	Track-Shot Put	4th
1989	Carmella Marshall	Track-200m Dash	6th
1990	Carmella Marshall	Track-200m Dash	4th
1990	Carmella Marshall	Track-200m Relay	4th
1990	Jarice Washington	Track-200m Relay	4th
1990	Kathy Kimbrough	Track-200m Relay	4th
1990	Katonya Harding	Track-200m Relay	4th
1990	William Jewell	Track-400m Relay	2nd
1990	Jermel Wilkerson	Track-400m Relay	2nd
1990	Terrence McMillon	Track-400m Relay	2nd
1990	Willie Hall	Track-400m Relay	2nd
1992	Katonya Harding	Track-400m Dash	6th
1993	Antoine Lundy	Track-400m Dash	SC
1993	Antoine Lundy	Track-100m Dash	5th
1993	Delonte Perkins	Track-110m High Hurdles	6th
1993	Kenitha Smith	Track-200m Relay	4th
1993	Katonya Harding	Track-200m Relay	4th
1993	Tameka Randle	Track-200m Relay	4th
1993	Lateeshia Jennings	Track-200m Relay	4th
1993	Katonya Harding	Track-100m Dash	5th
1993	Keneithia Smith	Track-100m Hurdles	6th
1994	Keneitha Smith	Track-100m Hurdles	5th
1994	Zanette Bussey	Track-200m Relay	5th
1994	Lewanda Hall	Track-200m Relay	5th
1994	Tameka Randle	Track-200m Relay	5th
1994	Keneithia Smith	Track-200m Relay	5th
1994	Lashaunte Edwards	Track-100m Relay	SC

1994	Wayne Wren	Track-100m Relay	SC
1994	Ernest Ponder	Track-100m Relay	SC
1994	Delonte Perkins	Track-100m Relay	SC
1994	Wayne Wren	Track-400m Relay	SC
1994	Mike Shoals	Track-400m Relay	SC
1994	Antoine Lundy	Track-400m Relay	SC
1994	Delonte Perkins	Track-400m Relay	SC
1994	Antoine Lundy	Track-100m Dash	SC
1994	Mike Shoals	Track-100m Dash	2nd
1994	Antoine Lundy	Track-200m Dash	SC
1994	Mike Shoals	Track-200m Dash	3rd
1994	Antoine Lundy	Track-400m Dash	2nd
1994	Dana Hall	4 x 200 Relay	5th
1996	Leshante Edwards	Track-200m Dash	SC
1996	Leshante Edwards	Track-100m Dash	2nd
1997	Amanda Perkins	Track-Discus	3rd
1998	Amanda Perkins	Track-Discus	5th
1999	Chester Gantt	Track-100m Relay	6th
1999	Toure Carter	Track-100m Relay	6th
1999	Thomas Dobson	Track-100m Relay	6th
1999	Muhammad Saafir	Track-100m Relay	6th
1999	Chester Gantt	Track-110m Hurdles	7th
1999	Nylisha Guy	Track-200m Dash	3rd
1999	Wiltosha Allen	Track-200m Relay	3rd
1999	Mignon Banks	Track-200m Relay	3rd
1999	Chanel Hill	Track-200mm Relay	3rd
1999	Nylisha Guy	Track-200m Relay	3rd
1999	Chanel Hill	Track-400m Relay	6th
1999	Nylisha Guy	Track-400m Relay	6th
1999	Sommer Saddler	Track-400m Relay	6th
1999	Akisha Brown	Track-400m Relay	6th
2000	Muhammad Saafir	Track-200m Dash	4th
2000	Muhammad Saafir	Track-100m Dash	5th
2000	Thomas Dobson	Track-100m Relay	7th
2000	Victor Miller	Track-100m Relay	7th

Year	Name	Event	Place
2000	Roland Sweet	Track-100m Relay	7th
2000	Muhammad Saafir	Track-100m Relay	7th
2000	Muhammad Saafir	Track-400m Relay	8th
2000	Roland Sweet	Track-400m Relay	8th
2000	Tristen Gilliam	Track-400m Relay	8th
2000	Keith Aghee	Track-400m Relay	8th
2000	Wiltosha Allen	Track-200m Relay	8th
2000	Jasmaine Johnson	Track-200m Relay	8th
2000	Nylisha Guy	Track-200m Relay	8th
2000	Mignon Banks	Track-200m Relay	8th
2001	Magdiel Ulloa	Baseball	
2001	Tiffany Colvin	Track-100m High Hurdles	3rd
2001	Tiffany Colvin	Track-High Jump	5th
2002	Tiffany Colvin	Track-High Jump	5th
2002	Tiffany Colvin	Track-100 m High Hurdles	6th
2003	Juan Goodwin	Basketball	HM
2004	Cierra Robinson	Track-200m Relay	4th
2004	Joe Roberts	Basketball	3rd Team
2004	Francine Jennings	Track-300m Low Hurdles	4th
2004	Darcel Formby	Track-200m Relay	6th
2004	Joyce Kennedy	Track-200m Relay	6th
2004	Ryan Harris	Track-200m Relay	6th
2004	Francine Jennings	Track-200m Relay	6th
2004	Darcel Formby	Track-200m Dash	7th
2004	Sediah Erskine	Track-3200m Run	7th
2004	Joyce Kennedy	Track-400m Relay	8th
2004	Jennifer Roman	Track-400m Relay	8th
2004	Francine Jennings	Track-400m Relay	8th
2004	Ernestine Jones	Track-400m Relay	8th
2004	Francine Jennings	Track-1200m High Hurdles	8th
2005	Sediah Erskine	Track-3200m Run	2nd
2005	Darcelle Formby	Track-200m Relay	8th
2005	Ryan Harris	Track-200m Relay	8th
2005	Shelli Rimmer	Track-200m Relay	8th
2005	Joyce Kennedy	Track-200m Relay	8th

2006	Rayshawn Goins	Basketball	HM
2006	Shellie Rimmer	Track-200m Relay	2nd
2006	Bonita Pace	Track-200m Relay	2nd
2006	Ryan Harris	Track-200m Relay	2nd
2006	Tenisha Taylor	Track-200m Relay	2nd
2006	Shannon Rimmer	Track-100m Relay	3rd
2006	Ryan Harris	Track-100m Relay	3rd
2006	Shellie Rimmer	Track-100m Relay	3rd
2006	Tenisha Taylor	Track-100m Relay	3rd
2006	Sediah Erskine	Track-1600m Run	3rd
2006	Jennifer Roman	Track-800m Run	7th
2006	Roneisha Campbell	Basketball	HM
2007	Anthony Goodwin	Football	1st Team
2007	Matt Crossland	Baseball	1st Team
2007	Mahagony Jones	Track-200m Dash	4th
2008	Mahagony Jones	Track-200m Dash	3rd
2008	Mahagony Jones	Track-100m Dash	4th
2009	Mahagony Jones	Track-100m Dash	2nd
2009	Mahagony Jones	Track-200m Dash	3rd
2009	Mahagony Jones	Track-400m Dash	3rd
2010	Irayel Williams	Wrestling (189)	8th
2011	Irayel Williams	Wrestling (189)	4th
2021	Jamal Sumlin	Football	1st Team
2021	Jumernous Hope	Football	HM
2022	Jamal Sumlin	Basketball	2nd Team

SOUTH HIGH

1937	Arvine Laughlin	Gymnastics-Horizontal Bars	3rd
1949	John Turk	Football	2nd Team
1949	Lou Sawchik	Football	HM
1949	John Turk	Baseball	
1956	Robert Mantarro	Wrestling (165)	SC
1957	Ralph Wisnlewski	Baseball	HM
1957	Robert Mantarro	Wrestling (165)	SC
1957	Ted Arslanian	Wrestling (175)	2nd

Year	Name	Sport	Place
1958	Henry Arslanian	Wrestling (175)	SC
1958	Angelo Rodriguez	Baseball	
1959	Michael Craycraft	Wrestling (127)	2nd
1959	Darrall Popovitch	Wrestling (Hwt)	3rd
1959	Frank Reyes	Baseball	
1961	Tom Fisher	Baseball	1st Team
1962	Jan Maynard	Wrestling (103)	SC
1962	James Williams	Wrestling (112)	2nd
1963	Jan Maynard	Wrestling (103)	SC
1967	Don Lamka	Football	2nd Team
1968	John Katona	Baseball	
1968	Don Lamka	Wrestling (175)	3rd
1969	Dale Tolar	Baseball	
1973	John Czarniakowski	Wrestling (175)	2nd
1973	Michael Kotowski	Wrestling (Unlimited)	4th
1974	Ralph Carnes	Basketball	HM
1977	Len Burris	Basketball	HM
1978	Kevin Howard	Track-Discus	5th
1985	Ghana Kennedy	Track-200m Dash	3rd
1986	Markeya Jones	Track-200m Relay	6th
1986	Sherry Wilson	Track-200m Relay	6th
1986	Konswella Wilkerson	Track-200m Relay	6th
1986	Traci Washington	Track-200m Relay	6th
1987	Markeya Jones	Track-200m Dash	2nd
1988	Markeya Jones	Track-200m Dash	SC
1988	Markeya Jones	Track-100m Dash	2nd
1988	Angie Johnson	Track-400m Relay	5th
1988	Elizabeth Beasley	Track-400m Relay	5th
1988	Markeya Jones	Track-400m Rely	5th
1988	Konswella Wilkerson	Track-400m Relay	5th
1990	Aloha Spy	Track-200m Relay	6th
1990	Angie Quinn	Track-200m Relay	6th
1990	Kimberly Mund	Track-200m Relay	6th
1990	Nicole Freeman	Track-200m Relay	6th
1990	Aloha Spy	Track-400m Relay	6th

1990	Angie Quinn	Track-400m Relay	6th
1990	Kimberly Mund	Track-400m Relay	6th
1990	Nicole Freeman	Track-400m Relay	6th
1991	Carmen Banks	Track-100m High Hurdles	2nd
1991	Aloha Spy	Track-200 Relay	2nd
1991	Carmen Banks	Track-200m Relay	2nd
1991	Kimberly Mund	Track-200m Relay	2nd
1991	Angela Quinn	Track-200m Relay	2nd
1991	Nicole Freeman	Track-100m Relay	4th
1991	Carmen Banks	Track-100m Relay	4th
1991	Kimberly Mund	Track-100m Relay	4th
1991	Angela Quinn	Track-100m Relay	4th
1991	Aloha Spy	Track-400 Relay	5th
1991	Carmen Banks	Track-400m Relay	5th
1991	Kimberly Mund	Track-400m Relay	5th
1991	Angela Quinn	Track-400m Relay	5th
1995	Marcus Turman	Track-800m Run	5th
1996	Marcus Turman	Track-800m Run	3rd
1996	Lee Parks	Track-200m Dash	6th
1999	Jonathan Burge	Basketball	1st Team
2000	Chet Mason	Basketball	1st Team
2000	Ed Farmer	Basketball	HM
2008	Patrick Nicely	Football	2nd Team

WEST HIGH

1923	Clinger	Track-Shot Put	2nd
1926	Duke	Gymnastics-Flying Rings	2nd
1926	Stropp	Gymnastics-Indian Clubs	3rd
1927	Burnett	Track-Mile Run	2nd
1927	Mitchell	Track-880yd Run	3rd
1927		Track-Mile Relay Team	5th
1930	Szabo	Track-Broad Jump	5th
1931	Helfer	Gymnastics-Indian Clubs	4th
1933	Kundtz	Ttrack-220yd Dash	5th
1934	Elmer Gedeon	Track-120yd High Hurdles	SC
1934	Elmer Gedeon	Track-220yd Low Hurdles	5th

1935	Elmer Gedeon	Track-120yd High Hurdles	SC
1935	Elmer Gedeon	Track-220yd Low Hurdles	SC
1941	Dick Hall	Cross Country	20th
1942	Dick Hall	Track-880yd Run	SC
1944	Harry Bostwick	Wrestling (113)	SC
1944	Bob Julius	Wrestling (Hvy)	2nd
1944	Edwards	Cross Country	7th
1944	Grevin	Cross Country	10th
1945	Harry Bostwick	Wrestling (113)	SC
1945	Frank Giammarino	Wrestling (121)	SC
1945	Gene Gibbons	Wrestling (155)	2nd
1945	John Minnick	Cross Country	17th
1946	Bill Buckingham	Wrestling (103)	SC
1946	John Matteucci	Wrestling (114)	SC
1946	John Saunders	Wrestling (121)	SC
1946	Gene Gibbons	Wrestling (155)	2nd
1947	Ardelean	Track-Pole Vault	3rd (Tie)
1947	Bill Buckingham	Wrestling (103)	SC
1947	Joe DiBello	Wrestling (113)	SC
1947	John Matteucci	Wrestling (121)	SC
1947	Bob Santillo	Wrestling (146)	2nd
1947	Gene Gibbons	Wrestling (155)	2nd
1947	Frank Giammarino	Wrestling (134)	3rd
1948	Jim Theiling	Track-220yd Low Hurdles	SC
1948	John Matteucci	Wrestling (121)	SC
1948	Joe Cassarino	Wrestling (104)	2nd
1948	Ralph Giammarino	Wrestling (113)	2nd
1948	Al Prioletti	Wrestling (139)	3rd
1949	Joe Cassarino	Wrestling (104)	SC
1949	Ralph Giammarino	Wrestling (121)	SC
1949	Richard Bonacci	Wrestling (139)	SC
1949	John Morabito	Wrestling (128)	3rd
1950	Stapleton	Tennis -Singles	HM
1950	Ralph Giammarino	Wrestling (121)	SC
1950	Fred Darienzo	Wrestling (134)	SC

Year	Name	Sport	Place
1950	Richard Bonacci	Wrestling (155)	SC
1950	James Shiller	Wrestling (104)	2nd
1950	Robert Pogue	Wrestling (113)	2nd
1950	Peter Rossi	Wrestling (146)	2nd
1950	John Morabito	Wrestling (139)	3rd
1950	Anthony Stavole	Wrestling (128)	4th
1950	Robert Fenston	Cross Country	2nd
1950	Dick Benz	Cross Country	7th
1950	Meade Burnette	Track-440yd Dash	SC
1951	Clarence Smith	Cross Country	13th
1951	Bill Clark	Track-Mile Run	SC
1951	Meade Burnette	Track-440yd Dash	SC
1951	Kaze	Track-Pole Vault	2nd (Tie)
1951		Track-Mile Relay Team	2nd
1951	Bob Pogue	Wrestling (121)	SC
1951	Vince Matteucci	Wrestling (128)	SC
1951	Fred Darienzo	Wrestling (134)	SC
1951	Emil Palmieri	Wrestling (139)	SC
1951	Pete Rossi	Wrestling (155)	SC
1951	Dick Bonacci	Wrestling (166)	SC
1951	John Morabito	Wrestling (146)	2nd
1951	Sandy Colosimo	Wrestling (186)	4th
1952	Ken McBride	Basketball	HM
1952	Don Bennett	Cross Country	13th
1952	Dominic Constanzo	Cross Country	20th
1952	Dan Vacca	Wrestling (113)	3rd
1952	Vince Matteucci	Wrestling (139)	3rd
1952	Joe Richardson	Wrestling (155)	3rd
1952	Joe Tuccione	Wrestling (104)	4th
1953	Ken McBride	Basketball	HM
1953	Robert Stoessner	Cross Country	9th
1953	Dominic Constanzo	Cross Country	20th
1953	Stan Lyons	Track-Pole Vault	3rd (Tie)
1953	Sandy Colosimo	Wrestling (166)	2nd
1954	Dominic Constanzo	Cross Country	9th

1954	Stan Lyons	Track-Pole Vault	SC (Tie)
1955	Charles Ferrari	Wrestling (104)	SC
1955	Dan Mason	Football	HM
1956	Charles Ferrari	Wrestling (104)	2nd
1956	Don Foldesy	Wrestling (120)	2nd
1956	Tony Natale	Wrestling (127)	2nd
1957	Charles Ferrari	Wrestling (120)	SC
1957	Tony Natale	Wrestling (127)	SC
1959	Al Drews	Baseball	1st Team
1960	Art Pappas	Wrestling (Hvy)	3rd
1961	Louis Natale	Wrestling (103)	SC
1962	Bill Deutcher	Baseball	2nd Team
1962	Rick Shirok	Cross Country	5th
1962	Dennis Morgan	Cross Country	9th
1962	John Ostrowski	Basketball	HM
1963	Dennis Morgan	Cross Country	4th
1963	Richard Shirok	Cross Country	6th
1964	Paul Zink	Cross Country	5th
1964	Phil Bova	Baseball	1st Team
1964	Phil Argento	Basketball	HM
1965	Phil Argento	Basketball	HM
1965	Paul Zink	Cross Country	SC
1966	John Petch	Basketball	HM
1967	Ken Kovac	Baseball	1st Team

WEST TECH

1929	Eckhart	Swimming-200yd Freestyle	2nd
1929	Krohn	Swimming-200yd Freestyle	3rd
1932	Seitz	Track-220yd Low Hurdles	SC
1932	Seitz	Track-120yd High Hurdles	2nd
1933	Seitz	Track-120yd High Hurdles	2nd
1933	Seitz	Track-220yd Low Hurdles	2nd
1933	Wightman	Tennis-Doubles	3rd (Tie)
1933	Marchard	Tennis-Doubles	3rd (Tie)
1933	Kreuger	Cross Country	8th

1934	Mayer	Track-120yd High Hurdles	5th
1934	Arnold	Track-440yd Dash	2nd
1934	Kreuger	Cross Country	8th
1935	Connant	Track-880yd Run	3rd
1935	Webber	Track-High Jump	2nd (Tie)
1935	Sterba	Gymnastics-Horizontal Bars	SC
1935	Stechmeyer	Gymnastics-Parallel Bars	3rd
1935	Stechmeyer	Gymnastics-Side Horse	5th
1935	Stechmeyer	Gymnastics-Long Horse	5th
1937	Schmidt	Track-440yd Dash	4th
1937	Zelazo	Track-Broad Jump	4th
1937	Arro Alapoti	Track-Mile Run	5th
1937	Rosenberger	Gymnastics-Side Horse	2nd
1937	Bruckner	Gymnastics-Side Horse	3rd
1937	Lakosky	Gymnastics-Long Horse	3rd
1937	Lakosky	Gymnastics-Horizontal Bars	4th
1937	Lakosky	Gymnastics-Parallel Bars	4th
1937	Rosenberger	Gymnastics-Horizontal Bars	5th
1938	Stamatis	Wrestling (125)	2nd
1938	Mike Kurash	Wrestling (145)	3rd
1938	Spencer	Wresting (Hwt)	3rd
1938	Oris Hicks	Wrestling (185)	4th
1938	Ruhrkraut	Track-Shot Put	2nd
1938	Grumney	Track-High Jump	2nd (Tie)
1938	Robbins	Track-Pole Vault	3rd
1939	Ruhrkraut	Track-Shot Put	SC
1939	Grumney	Track-High Jump	2nd
1939	Henderson	Track-Mile Run	5th
1939	Henderson	Cross Country	11th
1939	Joe DeCesare	Wrestling (125)	SC
1939	Oris Hicks	Wrestling (Hvy)	SC
1939	George Span	Wrestling (145)	3rd
1940	Joe Ruggiero	Wrestling (145)	SC
1940	Joe DeCesare	Wrestling (130)	2nd
1940	Joe Stelbasky	Wrestling (185)	2nd

1941	Crook	Track-Shot Put	2nd
1941	Joe DeCesare	Wrestling (130)	SC
1941	Roy Rossman	Wrestling (115)	2nd
1941	James Trammel	Wrestling (140)	3rd
1941	James Schultz	Wrestling (145)	4th
1941	Al Kulka	Wrestling (155)	4th
1942	Ray Puzzitielo	Wrestling (122)	2nd
1942	Al Hospodar	Wrestling (185)	2nd
1942	Al Kukla	Wrestling (165)	3rd
1943	Steve Skogan	Wrestling (104)	SC
1943	Joe Naso	Wrestling (113)	SC
1943	Bassett	Wrestling (146)	2nd
1943	Carl Hicks	Wrestling (155)	3rd
1944	Sewell	Cross Country	2nd
1944	Edward Dunn	Cross Country	11th
1944	Henry DeCesare	Wrestling (121)	SC
1944	Joe Naso	Wrestling (128)	SC
1944	Gus Taber	Wrestling (155)	SC
1944	Tony Vransky	Wrestling (146)	2nd
1944	Julius Parsnick	Wrestling (166)	2nd
1945	Robert Sewell	Track-Mile Run	5th
1945	Walt Culkowski	Cross Country	4th
1945	Bob Gedeon	Cross Country	15th
1945	Bill Williamson	Wrestling (103)	SC
1945	Bill Bassett	Wrestling (128)	SC
1945	Don Tighe	Wrestling (134)	SC
1945	Julius Parsnick	Wrestling (165)	2nd
1945	Joe Prchlik	Wrestling (Hvy)	2nd
1946	George Gross	Cross Country	3rd
1946	Bob Gedeon	Cross Country	10th
1946	Williamson	Wrestling (103)	SC
1946	Tom Dubin	Wrestling (128)	SC
1946	Dick Prchlik	Wrestling (Hvy)	SC
1946	Bob Jacupka	Wrestling (131)	SC
1947	George Gross	Cross Country	2nd

Year	Name	Event	Place
1947	George Gross	Track-Mile Run	3rd
1947	Tom Dubin	Wrestling (128)	SC
1947	Ray Martinez	Wrestling (139)	SC
1947	Gene Kraczonek	Wrestling (166)	2nd
1947	Joe Soza	Wrestling (113)	4th
1947	Ed Jakupca	Wrestling (121)	4th
1948	Jim Bennett	Cross Country	10th
1948	John Prokop	Cross Country	16th
1948	Ronald Grabnegger	Track-100yd Dash	4th
1948	Edward Jakupca	Wrestling (134)	SC
1948	Gordon Steiner	Wrestling (121)	2nd
1948	Arthur Massa	Wrestling (155)	2nd
1948	Arthur Prchlik	Wrestling (166)	2nd
1948	George Lazar	Wrestling (104)	3rd
1948	Victor Mio	Wrestling (146)	4th
1949	Francis Johnson	Track-440yd Dash	4th
1949	Eddie Lee	Wrestling (113)	2nd
1949	Arthur Prchlik	Wrestling (186)	4th
1950	Chuck Biabolil	Track-Shot Put	3rd
1950	Donald Petro	Wrestling (104)	3rd
1950	Donald Hardy	Wrestling (134)	3rd
1950	John Rudo	Wrestling (139)	4th
1950	James Sasena	Wrestling (146)	4th
1951	George Leith	Cross Country	SC
1951	Milo Bivjak	Cross Country	12th
1951	Andy Klobousnik	Cross Country	17th
1951	Herbert Frantz	Wrestling (166)	4th
1952	Gene Hendrickson	Track-440yd Dash	3rd
1952	Milo Bivjak	Cross Country	7th
1952	John Sforzo	Wrestling (139)	SC
1952	Tom Nevits	Wrestling (104)	2nd
1952	Steve Rudo	Wrestling (134)	3rd
1952	Robert Karban	Wrestling (146)	4th
1952	Thomas Ehlert	Wrestling (155)	4th
1953	Tom Nevits	Wrestling (121)	SC

Year	Name	Event	Place
1953	John Sforzo	Wrestling (139)	SC
1953	Lino Deanna	Wrestling (155)	SC
1953	John Ornowski	Wrestling (104)	3rd
1953	Joe Harbuck	Wrestling (128)	3rd
1953	James Krupa	Wrestling (134)	4th
1954	Dick Mendicino	Wrestling (128)	SC
1954	Joe Harbuck	Wrestling (134)	SC
1954	Edward Yurovich	Wrestling (113)	2nd
1954	Alfred Sforzo	Wrestling (139)	3rd
1955	Art Soles	Cross Country	9th
1955	Russ Ciphers	Track-Broad Jump	5th
1955	Joe Ornowski	Wrestling (121)	SC
1955	Alfred Sforzo	Wrestling (139)	SC
1955	Dick White	Wrestling (113)	3rd
1956	Don Tukosh	Cross Country	6th
1956	James Planicka	Cross Country	16th
1957	Angelo Privitera	Track-200yd Dash	5th
1957	James Planicka	Cross Country	9th
1957	Arnold Ebert	Cross Country	17th
1958	Arnold Ebert	Cross Country	3rd
1958	Richard Rios	Cross Country	8th
1958	Joe Basko	Cross Country	17th
1958	Ken Gailey	Cross Country	21st
1959	Richard Rios	Cross Country	4th
1960	Richard Basko	Cross Country	7th
1961	Lester Moss	Wrestling (Hwt)	3rd
1961	ohn Udris	Basketball	HM
1965	Fred Corpuz	Cross Country	8th
1965	Jim Redima	Baseball	HM
1967	Vic Solodlow	Basketball	HM
1968	Dave Freeman	Track-180yd Low Hurdles	3rd
1968	Ray Gura	Gymnastics-Long Horse	SC (Tie)
1968	Ray Gura	Gymnastics-Side Horse	2nd
1968	Ray Gura	Gymnastics-Horizontal Bars	2nd (Tie)
1968	Ray Gura	Gymnastics-All-Around	2nd

1968	Ray Gura	Gymnastics-Free Exercise	3rd
1968	Ray Gura	Gymnastics-parallel Bars	3rd (Tie)
1968	Ray Gura	Gymnastics-Still Rings	5th
1969	Don Cooper	Basketball	HM
1969	Benansio Camargo	Wrestling (103)	6th
1972	Charles Schill	Wrestling (185)	6th
1973	Jay Miranda	Cross Country	18th
1973	Patrick Kelly	Soccer	
1974	Jay Miranda	Track – 880yd Run	2nd
1975	John McCafferty	Football	1st Team
1975	Henry Jontony	Football	2nd Team
1975	Jay Miranda	Track-880yd Run	SC
1976	John McCafferty	Wrestling (175)	6th
1976	Mark Stasek	Track-Mile Run	3rd
1976	William Gawn	Cross Country	8th
1977	Chris Semary	Wrestling (155)	2nd
1979	Tony Copassa	Basketball	SM
1979	Brian Seguin	Cross Country	7th
1979	Matt Semary	Wrestling (185)	2nd
1980	Brian Seguin	Cross Country	3rd
1981	Mike Massie	Tennis – Singles	SC
1982	Mike Massie	Tennis – Singles	SC
1982	Arthur Goode III	Track-Mile Relay	6th
1982	Marcus Jagers	Track-Mile Relay	6th
1982	Sherman Agnew	Track-Mile Relay	6th
1982	Larry Overton	Track-Mile Relay	6th
1989	Eric Brown	Track-300m Low Hurdles	4th
1989	Eric Brown	Track-110m High Hurdles	5th
1990	Eric Brown	Track-300m Low Hurdles	2nd
1990	Eric Brown	Track-110m High Hurdles	6th
1994	Michael Parks	Basketball	SM

APPENDIX VI

HIGH SCHOOL ALL-AMERICA

COLLINWOOD

Bruce Kordic – 1967 – Football

Theo Morrow – 1962 – Track

EAST HIGH

Emanuel "Manny" Leaks – 1964 – Basketball

EAST TECH

Barbara Turner – 2002 – Basketball

Wilson Graham – 1962 - Basketball

GLENVILLE

Erick Smith – 2013 – Football

Jamario O'Neal – 2004 – Football

Latwan Anderson – 2009 – Football

Marcelys Jones – 2013 – Football

Marcus Hall – 2008 – Football

Marshon Lattimore – 2013 – Football

Pierre Woods – 2000 – Football

Ted Ginn Jr. – 2004 – Football

RHODES

Frank Guzik – 1951 – Football

Mahagony Jones – 2009 – Track

Ron Addison – 1972 – Track

Tiffany Colvin – 2001-2002 – Track

William "Bill" Hann – 1965 – Basketball

APPENDIX VII

PROFESSIONAL ATHLETES

(AAFC – All-American Football Conference, ABA – American Basketball Association, AFL – American Football League, APFA – American Professional Football Association, BAA – Basketball Association of America, CFL – Canadian Football League, MLB – Major League Baseball, NASL – North American Soccer League, NFL – National Football League, USA – United Soccer Association)

CENTRAL

Frank Civiletto: Football – NFL, 1923: Cleveland Indians

Ed Delahanty: Baseball – MLB, 1888-1903: Philadelphia, Cleveland, Washington

Jim Delahanty: Baseball – MLB & Federal League, 1901-1902, 1904-1912, 1914-1915: Chicago Orphans, New York Giants, Boston Beaneaters, Cincinnati Reds, St. Louis Browns, Washington Senators, Detroit Tigers, Brooklyn Tip-Tops

Joe Delahanty: Baseball – MLB, 1907-1909: St. Louis Cardinals

Tom Delahanty: Baseball – MIB, 1894, 1896-1897: Philadelphia Phillies, Cleveland Spiders, Pittsburgh Pirates, Louisville Colonels

Jimmy Bivins: Boxing, Light Heavyweight and Heavyweight, 1940-1955

Johnny Kilbane: Boxing, Featherweight, 1912-1923

Ted Rosequist: Football – NFL, 1934-37: Chicago Bears, Cleveland Rams

COLLINWOOD

Tony Adamle: Football – AAFC & NFL, 1947-1951, 1954: Cleveland Browns

Eppie Barney: Football – NFL, 1967-1968: Cleveland Browns

Joe Cannavino: Football – AFL, 1960-1962: Oakland Raiders, Buffalo Bills

Jerome "Jerry" Dybzinski: Baseball – MLB, 1980-1985: Cleveland Indians, Chicago White Sox, Pittsburgh Pirates

Omari Jordan: Football – NFL, 2004: Carolina Panthers

Joey Maxim (born Giuseppe Antonio Berardinelli): Boxing, Light Heavyweight, 1940-1958

Dick Nardi: Football – NFL, 1938-1939: Detroit Lions, Pittsburgh Steelers, Brooklyn Dodgers

Sam Palumbo: Football – NFL, 1955-1957: Cleveland Browns, Green Bay Packers

Mike Perrotti: Football AAFC, 1948-1949: Los Angeles Rams

Cecil Shorts: Football – NFL, 2011-16: Jacksonville Jaguars, Houston Texans, Tampa Bay Buccaneers

EAST HIGH

Stanley Cofall: Football – APFA, 1920: Cleveland Tigers

Emanuel "Manny" Leaks: Basketball – ABA & NBA, 1968-1974: Dallas Chaparrals, Kentucky Colonels, New York Nets, Utah Stars, Floridians, Philadelphia 76ers, Washington Bullets

Arthur Matsu: Football – NFL, 1928: Dayton Triangles

Roger Peckinpaugh: Baseball – MLB, 1910, 1912-1927: Cleveland Indians, New York Yankees, Washington Senators, Chicago White Sox

Steve Sanders: Football – NFL, 2008: Cleveland Browns

Carl Tasseff: Football – NFL, 1951, 1953-1962: Cleveland Browns, Baltimore Colts, Philadelphia Eagles, Buffalo Bills

J. C. Wilson: Football – NFL, 1979-1983: Houston Oilers

EAST TECH

Robert Stanford "Bob" Brown: Football – NFL, 1964-1973: Philadelphia Eagles, Los Angeles Rams, Oakland Raiders

Larry Doby Johnson: Baseball – MLB, 1972-1978: Cleveland Indians, Montreal Expos, Chicago White Sox

Andrew Jones: Football – NFL, 1975-1976: New Orleans Saints

Walter Kreinheder: Football – NFL, 1922, 1923, 1925: Akron Pros, St. Louis All-Stars, Cleveland Bulldogs

Pete Lalich: Basketball – NBA & BAA, 1942-1946: Sheboygan Redskins, Cleveland Brass, Pittsburgh Raiders, Youngstown Bears, Cleveland Rebels

James Richard "Jim" Martin: Football – NFL, 1950-1964: Cleveland Browns, Detroit Lions, Baltimore Colts, Washington Redskins

Chuck McMillian: Football – NFL, 1954: Baltimore Colts

Nate Schenker: Football – NFL, 1939: Cleveland Rams

Burrell Shields: Football – NFL, 1954-1955: Pittsburgh Steelers, Baltimore Colts

Jim Smith: Basketball – NBA, 1981-1982: Detroit Pistons, San Diego Clippers

Mike St. Clair: Football – NFL, 1976-1982: Cleveland Browns, Cincinnati Bengals

GLENVILLE

Richard Bishop: Football – NFL, 1976-1983: New England Patriots, Miami Dolphins, Los Angeles Rams

Bryant Browning: Football – NFL, 2011-2012: Carolina Panthers, Cleveland Browns

Christian Bryant: Football – NFL, 2014-2016: St. Louis/Los Angeles Rams, Arizona Cardinals

Frank Clark: Football – NFL, 2015-2023: Seattle Seahawks, Kansas City Chiefs, Denver Broncos, Kansas City Chiefs

Davon Coleman: Football – NFL & CFL, 2014-2015, 2017-2022: Dallas Cowboys, Hamilton Tiger-Cats, BC Lions, Toronto Argonauts, Ottawa Redblacks

Jayrone Elliott: Football – NFL, 2014-2017, 2019-2020: Green Bay Packers, Dallas Cowboys, Pittsburgh Steelers

Donnie Fletcher: Football – NFL, 2012: New York Jets

Benjamin "Benny" Friedman: Football – NFL, 1927-1934: Cleveland Bulldogs, Detroit Wolverines, New York Giants, Brooklyn Dodgers

Ted Ginn, Jr.: Football – NFL, 2007-2020: Miami Dolphins, San Francisco 49ers, Carolina Panthers, Arizona Cardinals, New Orleans Saints, Chicago Bears

Donn Greenshields: Football – NFL, 1932-1933: Brooklyn Dodgers

Mark Gunn: Football – NFL, 1991-1996: New York Jets, Philadelphia Eagles

Justin Hardee: Football – NFL, 2017-2023: New Orleans Saints, New York Jets

Will Henry: Football – NFL, 2016-2018, 2020: Baltimore Ravens, San Francisco 49ers

Jermale Hines: Football – NFL, 2012: Indianapolis Colts

Cardale Jones: Football – NFL, 2016-2018: Buffalo Bills, Los Angeles Chargers

Marshon Lattimore: Football – NFL, 2017-2023: New Orleans Saints

Franklin Lewis: Football – NFL, 1931: Cleveland Indians

Antwan Molden: Football – NFL & CFL, 2008-2012, 2014: Houston Texans, New England Patriots, Jacksonville Jaguars, Toronto Argonauts

Jonathan Newsome: Football – NFL & CFL, 2014-2020: Indianapolis Colts, Saskatchewan Roughriders, Ottawa Redblacks, BC Lions

Mike Robinson: Football – NFL, 1981-1982: Cleveland Browns

Troy Smith: Football – NFL & CFL, 2007-2010, 2013-2014: Baltimore Ravens, San Francisco 49ers, Montreal Alouettes

Donte Whitner: Football – NFL, 2006-2016: Buffalo Bills, San Francisco 49ers, Cleveland Browns, Washington Redskins

Pierre Woods: Football – NFL, 2006-2010: New England Patriots, Buffalo Bills

Chris Worley: Football – NFL, 2018: Cincinnati Bengals

Curtis Young: Football – NFL, 2011: Green Bay Packers

JOHN ADAMS

Rashaun Allen: Football – NFL, 2014: Seattle Seahawks

Sam Goldman: Football – NFL, 1944-1949: Boston Yanks, Chicago Cardinals, Detroit Lions

Bob Hein: Football – AAFC, 1947: Brooklyn Dodgers

Tom Jackson: Football – NFL, 1973-1986: Denver Broncos

Bob Kolesar: Football – AAFC, 1946: Cleveland Browns

Lorenzo "Rimp" Lanier: Baseball – MLB, 1971: Pittsburgh Pirates

Ray Mack (Raymond Mickovsky): Baseball – MLB, 1938-1944, 1946-1947: Cleveland Indians, New York Yankees

Anthony Morgan: Football – NFL, 1991-1996: Chicago Bears, Green Bay Packers

Luke Owens: Football – NFL, 1957-1965: Baltimore Colts, Chicago/St. Louis Cardinals

Bob Reynolds: Football – NFL, 1963-1973: St. Louis Cardinals, New England Patriots

Gene Selawski: Football – NFL & AFL, 1959-1961: Los Angeles Rams, Cleveland Browns, San Diego Chargers

Chuck Smith: Baseball – MLB, 2000-2001: Florida Marlins

Sam Tidmore: Football – NFL, 1962-1963: Cleveland Browns

JOHN HAY

Wesley Carroll: Football – NFL, 1991-1993: New Orleans Saints, Cincinnati Bengals

Earl Douthitt: Football – NFL, 1973: Chicago Bears

Anthony Hancock: Football – NFL, 1982-1986: Kansas City Chiefs

John Hicks: Football – NFL, 1974-1977: New York Giants

Tim McGee: Football – NFL, 1986-1994: Cincinnati Bengals, Washington Redskins

Charles Oakley: Basketball – NBA, 1985-2004: Chicago Bulls, N.Y. Knicks, Toronto Raptors, Washington Wizards, Houston Rockets

Ruben Patterson: Basketball – NBA, 1998-2007: Los Angeles Lakers, Seattle Supersonics, Portland Trail Blazers, Denver Nuggets, Milwaukee Bucks, Los Angeles Clippers

JOHN F. KENNEDY

Lawrence Boston: Basketball – NBA, 1979: Washington Bullets

Tony Harris: Football – NFL, 1971: San Francisco 49ers

Walt Love: Football – NFL, 1973: New York Giants

Anthony Montgomery: Football – NFL, 2006-2009: Washington Redskins

JOHN MARSHALL

Norm Greeney: Football – NFL, 1933-1935: Green Bay Packers, Pittsburgh Pirates

Thomas Stincic: Football – NFL, 1969-1972: Dallas Cowboys, New Orleans Saints

Ed Susteric: Football – AAFC, 1949: Cleveland Browns Lincoln High School

LINCOLN

Richard Skora: Soccer – USA & NASL, 1967-1968: Cleveland Stokers, Boston Beacons

Walt Yowarsky: Football – NFL, 1951, 1954-1958: Washington Redskins, N.Y. Giants, Detroit Lions, San Francisco 49ers

LINCOLN-WEST

Dave Ford: Baseball – MLB, 1978-1981: Baltimore Orioles

RHODES

Ron Addison: Track – 1978-1984: Athletes West

Sue Hlavacek: Basketball – Women's Basketball League, 1976: Philadelphia Fox

Les Horvath: Football – NFL & AAFC, 1947-1949: Los Angeles Rams, Cleveland Browns

Mahogany Jones: Track – European Diamond League, 2006-2008: New Balance

Ronald Kinney: Basketball – European Pro League, 2012-2016: Angri, Olavarria

Don McCafferty: Football – NFL, 1946, New York Giants

Woodie Pippens: Football – NFL, 1987: Kansas City Chiefs

SOUTH HIGH

Chester Adams (Chester Frank Adamczyk): Football – NFL & AAFC, 1939-1943, 1946-1950: Cleveland Rams, Green Bay Packers, Cleveland Browns, Buffalo Bills, New York Yanks

Tom Fisher: Baseball – MLB, 1967: Baltimore Orioles

Len Janiak: Football – NFL, 1939-1942: Brooklyn Dodgers, Cleveland Rams

Chester "Chet" Mason: Basketball – European Pro Leagues, 2005, 2007-2014

Henry "Hank" Ruszkowski: Baseball – MLB, 1944-45, 1947: Cleveland Indians

Lou Sawchik: Football – NFL, 1954: Chicago Cardinals

Fred Sawyer: Basketball – ABL, 1961: Hawaii Chiefs

WEST HIGH

Elmer Gedeon: Baseball – MLB, 1935: Washington Senators

Ken McBride: Baseball – MLB, 1959-1965: Chicago White Sox, Los Angeles/California Angels

WEST TECH

Albert Aber: Baseball – MLB, 1950, 1953-1957: Cleveland Indians, Detroit Tigers, Kansas City Athletics

George L. Catavolos: Football – NFL Coach, 1984-2011: Indianapolis Colts, Washington Redskins, Detroit Lions, Buffalo Bills

Gene Cook: Football – NFL, 1959: Detroit Lions

Mike Hubach: Football – NFL, 1980-1981: New England Patriots

Rudy Kutler: Football – NFL, 1925: Cleveland Bulldogs

Raymond Novotny: Football – NFL, 1930-1932: Portsmouth Spartans, Cleveland Indians, Brooklyn Dodgers

Paul O'Dea: Baseball – MLB, 1944-1945: Cleveland Indians

John Prchlik: Football – NFL, 1949-1953: Detroit Lions

August M. "Mike" Michalske: Football – NFL & AFL, 1926-1935, 1937: New York Yankees, Green Bay Packers

APPENDIX VIII

TEAM STATE CHAMPION AND RUNNER-UP

CENTRAL

Basketball: 1905

Football: 1895, 1900

Track (Boys): 1947, 1949

COLLINWOOD

Track (Boys): 1962

Track (Girls): 1997, 1998, 1999, 2000, 2001, 2004, 2005, 2006, 2010. Runner-up: 2007

Indoor Track: 2005, 2006, 2007, 2009, 2010. Runner-up: 2008

EAST HIGH

Basketball (Boys): Runner-up 1964

Football: 1907

Tennis (Boys): Singles 1929; Doubles 1929. Runner-up: Doubles 1928.

Track (Boys): Runner-up 1938

EAST TECH

Basketball (Boys): 1958, 1959, 1972. Runner-up: 1960, 1962, 1967

Basketball (Girls): 2002

Football: 1920

Gymnastics: 1933, 1934, 1935, 1936, 1937. Runner-up: 1932

Swimming: 1947, 1948

Tennis (Boys): Runner-up: Singles 1946

Track (Boys): 1920, 1921, 1932, 1933, 1936, 1939, 1940, 1941, 1942, 1943, 1944, 1952, 1955. Runner-up: 1922, 1935, 1946, 1951, 1959, 1961, 1966.

GLENVILLE

Football: AP Poll Champion: 2010. Playoff Champion 2022, 2023. Runner-up: 2009, 2013.

Track (Boys): 1959, 1960, 1965, 1966, 1967, 1968, 1970, 1973, 1974, 1975, 2003, 2004, 2005, 2006, 2007, 2014, 2022, 2023 Runner-up: 1963, 1964, 2009, 2021

Indoor Track: 2005, 2006, 2009, 2010. Runner-up: 2008

JOHN ADAMS

Cross Country (Boys): 1954, 1959, 1963

Gymnastics (Boys): Runner-up 1937

Track (Boys): 1953, 1956, 1976, 1982. Runner-up: 1986, 1991

Track (Girls): 1978, 1979, 1994. Runner-up: 1987, 1992

Wrestling: Runner-up 1950

JOHN HAY

Tennis (Boys): Singles 1968. Singles Runner up 1969

Track (Boys): Runner-up 1978

Wrestling: 1938, 1939, 1940, 1941, 1943. Runner-up: 1944

JOHN F. KENNEDY

Track (Boys): 1969

JOHN MARSHALL

Cross Country (Boys): 1960, 1964. Runner-up 1943

Track (Boys): 1991, 1992. Runner-up 1943

Track (Girls): 2005 Indoor Runner-up

Volleyball (Girls): Runner-up 1976

Wrestling: 1961. Runner-up 1966

LINCOLN

Baseball: 1946

Cross Country (Boys): Runner-up 1932, 1933

RHODES

Cross Country (Boys): Runner-up 1945

Track (Boys): 1994

Track (Girls): Indoor Runner-up 2005

Wrestling: Runner-up 1939

SOUTH

Baseball: 1961

WEST

Basketball (Boys): 1906, 1908

Cross Country (Boys): 1950. Runner-up 1944

Wrestling: 1947, 1951, 1950. Runner-up 1946, 1949

WEST TECH

Cross Country (Boys): 1945, 1948, 1951. Runner-up 1946, 1958

Tennis (Boys): Singles 1981, 1982

Wrestling: 1944, 1945, 1946, 1948, 1953. Runner-up 1939, 1943, 1952

APPENDIX IX

TITLE IX AND SENATE LEAGUE ATHLETICS

Signed into law by President Richard Nixon, the Education Amendments Act of 1972 contained a key provision known as Title IX, which prohibits schools that receive federal funds from discriminating based on sex. The exact wording of Title IX is as follows: "No person in the United States shall, based on sex, be excluded from participation in, be denied the benefits of, or be subjected to discrimination under any education program or activity receiving Federal financial assistance."

Whether or not it was the purpose of this amendment, once passed, it had an incredible effect on sports participation by girls at the high school and college levels. By 1978, when compliance with Title IX became mandatory, the law had already significantly impacted. According to a story in a June 1978 issue of Time Magazine, six times as many girls participated in high school athletics in 1978 than in 1970. That number continued to rise almost yearly until, by 2012, more than 3,000,000 girls across the country were active in high school athletics.

So, how did Title IX affect high school athletics in Ohio, specifically in Cleveland and the Senate Athletic League? There had not been a lot of opportunities for girls to participate in sports before the passing of Title IX, not just in Ohio but in virtually every state. However, girls played some sports as little as the 1920s. In many cases, it was felt that girls' participating in sports was not ladylike. While that attitude changed over the years, it did so slowly.

By 1972, when Title IX was passed, Ohio had only one state championship tournament for girls' sports. That was in gymnastics, and that championship had only gone into effect the year before. As has been mentioned, with the enactment of Title IX, there was a veritable explosion across the country of participation in girls' athletics at the high school level, and Ohio was no exception. At that time, to have a state championship tournament for a sport, at least 150 schools had to be playing that sport. From 1972 to 1979, eight more girls' sports qualified for a state championship tournament; since then, three more girls' sports have been added to a state championship tournament.

As for the girls playing in the Senate Athletic League in the pre-Title IX days, opportunities to excel were limited, but a few achieved greatness. The best in those earliest days was track star Stella Walsh from South High, who won five gold medals at three different Olympics beginning with Berlin in 1936; Stella is a member of the U.S. Track and Field Hall of Fame. Another successful young lady was track star Eleanor Montgomery from John Adams High School. Eleanor earned All-America honors at Tennessee State University in 1964; she was also a member of the 1964 and 1968 United States Olympic teams and the U.S. Track and Field Hall of Fame.

Gretchum Taylor coached Glenville girls' basketball for 23 years with a record of 337-117. Her teams qualified for the OHSAA girls' basketball tournaments for the regional semi-final in 1978 and 1979. She won two District Championships and eight city titles and coached three outstanding basketball players. The first player, Charlene Malone, was voted 1979 second team All-Ohio; the next was Loraine Lofton, earning second-team All Ohio 1984, and the following year, 1985, first team All-Ohio. Sonja Swoope was the best player in Glenville history, who made the first team All-Ohio and was voted Ohio co-player of the year in 1990.

Before Title IX, only two percent of overall college athletic budgets benefited female athletes, and athletic scholarships for women were virtually nonexistent. However, the expanded opportunities that Title IX provided for girls playing in the Senate Athletic League, along with better equipment and better coaching, have led to many notable achievements that might not have been possible had these girls not been given the opportunity that Title IX provided. Most notable is the awarding of college athletic scholarships. The following is a partial list of Senate Athletic League female athletes who have been able to participate in college athletics since the passing of Title IX in 1972 as a result of receiving athletic scholarships:

Year	Name	High School	College	Sport
1975	Michelle Stevens	John F. Kennedy	Leave Blank	Track
1976	Sue Halavecak	James F. Rhodes	Cleveland State U.	Basketball
1977	Charlene Stemn	John Marshall	Leave Blank	Track
1979	Rochelle Nelson	John Adams	Prairie View AM	Basketball
1979	Terri Nolan	James F. Rhodes	Bowling Green U.	Track
1980	Michelle Stoyk	John Marshall	Kent State U.	Track
1982	Gail Counts	John Adams	U. of Pittsburg	Track
1982	Pam Floyd	John Marshall	Baldwin-Wallace	Track
1982	Cindy Anzalone	James F. Rhodes	U. of Houston	Track
1982	Sue Koziol	Lincoln West	Cleveland State U.	Basketball
1983	Wanda Ford	East Tech	Drake U.	Basketball
1984	Lorain Lofton	Glenville	Leave Blank	Basketball
1984	Marie Flanaghan	John Adams	Niagara U.	Basketball
1985	Gonna Kennedy	South High	SW Michigan	Track
1985	Rita Baker	James F. Rhodes	U. of Toledo	Track
1985	Latonya Johnson	Collinwood	U. of Toledo	Track
1986	Sonja Smiley	John Hay	U. of Akron	Track
1987	Cleo Anderson	John Adams	SW Michigan	Track
1987	Camille Cain	Collinwood	Case Western U.	Track
1988	Nicole Antoinette Smith	James F. Rhodes	Ohio U.	Basketball
1988	Ester McMillion	James F. Rhodes	U. of Cincinnati	Basketball
1988	Carol Simms	James F. Rhodes	U. of Akron	Track
1988	Debra Malone	John Adams	Kansas State U.	Track
1988	Markeya Jones Owens	South High	Kansas State U.	Track
1989	Cynthia Davis	James F. Rhodes	Ohio State U.	Track
1989	Crystal Neal	John Hay	Tri-C	Track
1989	Charita Johnson-Stubbs	John Adams	U. of Arizona	Volleyball
1989	Regina Webb	East Tech	Ohio State U.	Track
1989	Kenomi Johnson	Collinwood	Wichita State U.	Basketball/Track
1989	Cherrell Reese	John F. Kennedy	Virginia Union U.	Basketball
1989	Lakeisha Golphin	John F. Kennedy	Virginia Union U.	Basketball
1990	April Davis	John F. Kennedy	Shaw U.	Basketball
1990	Carmella Marshall	James F. Rhodes	Ohio State U.	Track
1990	Sonja Swoop	Glenville	Purdue/Stephen F. Austin U.	Basketball
1990	Bonnie Dove	John F. Kennedy	U. of Arizona	Basketball

Year	Name	School	College	Sport
1990	Charlotte Powel	East High	Salem U.	Basketball
1990	Shay Moore	East Tech	U. North Carolina	Basketball
1992	Donneka Kibble	John F. Kennedy	Southern Illinois	Track
1992	Candance Nicholson	John Adams	Notre Dame U./Findlay	Track
1992	Tangetta Miller	John Adams	Purdue U.	Track
1993	Kim Jordan	Collinwood	Purdue U.	Track
1993	Shonda Robinson	Collinwood	Purdue U.	Track
1993	Monique Jennings	James F. Rhodes	Findlay U.	Track
1993	Katonya Harding	James F. Rhodes	Findlay U.	Track
1994	Carmen Banks	John Adams	U. of Texas	Track
1994	Marie Lassiter	John Adams	Findlay U.	Track
1994	Kelley Jones	John Adams	Findlay U.	Track
1994	Tamika Randle	James F. Rhodes	Eastern Michigan U.	Basketball
1994	Lawanda Hall	James F. Rhodes	Eastern Michigan U.	Track
1994	Kenitha Smith	James F. Rhodes	Youngstown State U.	Track
1995	Rochelle Russell	John Marshall	U. of Kentucky	Track
1996	Aaliyah Gillespie	Glenville	Youngstown State U.	Track
1996	Latonia Berry	Glenville	Youngstown State U.	Track
1997	Kellie Turner	Glenville	Texas Christian U.	Track
1999	Channel Hill	James F. Rhodes	Eastern Kentucky U.	Track
2001	Kandance Stone	Collinwood	Indiana U.	Track
2001	Rondalyn Crawford	Collinwood	Ohio State U.	Track
2001	Jawanna Rivers	East Tech	Washburn U.	Basketball
2002	Tiffany Colvin	James F. Rhodes	U. of Colorado/Purdue U.	Track
2002	Lauren Billingsley	East Tech	Gannon U.	Basketball
2003	Barbara Turner	East Tech	U. Conn.	Basketball
2003	Chanara Wilson	East Tech	Cleveland State U.	Basketball
2003	Cierra Malone	East Tech	Notre Dame College	Basketball
2004	Francine Jennings	James F. Rhodes	U. of Toledo	Track
2004	Cierra Robinson	James F. Rhodes	Independence CC	Track
2004	Toccara Montgomery	East Tech	Olympics	Wrestling
2005	Rhoniesha Kinney	James F. Rhodes	Elon U.	Basketball
2005	Joyce Kennedy	James F. Rhodes	U. of Toledo	Track
2005	Denise Tate	Glenville	Florida A&M	Basketball
2005	Darcel Formby	James F. Rhodes	Youngstown State	Track

2005	Shantell Lewis	Collingwood	Bowling Green U.	Track
2005	Sabrina Parr	Collinwood	Cal Poly U.	Track
2005	Joi Smith	Collinwood	U. Michigan	Track
2006	Ryan Harris	James F. Rhodes	Findlay U.	Track
2006	Sediaha Erskins	James F. Rhodes	U. of Akron	Track
2006	Jennifer Roman	James F. Rhodes	Youngstown State U.	Track
2006	Tanisha Taylor	James F. Rhodes	U. of Akron	Track
2006	Special Jennings	East Tech	Xavier U.	Basketball
2006	Tenisha Taylor	James F. Rhodes	U. of Akron	Track
2006	Bonita Pace	James F. Rhodes	Liberty U.	Track
2006	Charnae Lumbus	Collinwood	U. of Michigan	Track
2006	Brandi Taylor	Collinwood	U. of Washington	Track
2006	Terria Royal	Collinwood	Cornell U.	Track
2006	April Wonzo	East High	Notre Dame College	Track
2007	Ashley Minor	East Tech	Eastern Michigan U.	Track
2007	Shannon Rimmer	James F. Rhodes	Eastern Michigan U.	Track
2007	Shellie Rimmer	James F. Rhodes	Eastern Michigan U.	Track
2007	Annette Torres	James F. Rhodes	Notre Dame College	Track
2007	Rainer Spencer	Glenville	Fordham U.	Basketball
2007	Kyla Rollins	East Tech	Ohio U.	Basketball
2008	Monique McMillian	James F. Rhodes	Notre Dame College	Track
2008	Chevy DeJesus	James F. Rhodes	Notre Dame College	Track
2009	Amirah Harbour	Collinwood	U. of Akron	Track
2009	Mahogany Jones	James F. Rhodes	Penn State U.	Track
2010	Fon' Taine	James F. Rhodes	Ursuline College	Track
2010	Amber Smith	Collinwood	U. of Michigan	Track
2010	Erin Busby	Collinwood	U. of Michigan	Track
2011	Chanita Westbrook	John Hay	Kent State U.	Track
2016	Corrine Cardwell	East Tech	Eastern Michigan U.	Basketball
2016	Chantel Bostick	East Tech	North Carolina A&T	Basketball
2016	Morgan Daniels	East Tech	Virginia Union U.	Basketball

With the continued assistance that Title IX provides, local sports fans can look forward to many more great accomplishments by the young lady athletes from the Senate schools.

APPENDIX X

SPORTS LEGENDS OF CLEVELAND

"Legend" means a highly famous or notorious person, especially in a particular field. In the context of the Sports LEGENDS of Cleveland, the Founder (Nicole Antoinette Smith) purposely used the word LEGEND to give it meaning to celebrate ALL the athletes who competed under the Senate athletic leagues banner, meeting specific criteria. To qualify as a Sports Legend, the person must have an affiliation as a high school athlete, coach, staff, athletic director, or administrator from the Cleveland Metropolitan School District (CMSD), and one or more of the following criteria have been established to be documented in the Sports Legends of Cleveland History Book:

Sports Team or Individual (City/Senate Champion)	Sports Team or Individual (Regional Runner-up)
Sports Team or Individual (City/Senate Runner-up)	Sports Team or Individual (State Champion)
Sports Team or Individual (District Champion)	Sports Team or Individual (State Runner-up)
Sports Team or Individual (District Runner-up)	Collegiate Athlete
Sports Team or Individual (Regional Champion)	Professional Athlete
	International Athlete

ATHLETES

BARD

Harris, Tania	Hullett, Cameron	Murry, Jeremy
Parker, Tylia	Wimberly, Giovanni	

CENTRAL

Bernard, Lewis	Bevins, Jimmy	Blair, Leonard
Carter, Donald	Civiletto, Frank	Clark, Ray
Corso, Martin	Delahanty, Ed	Delahanty, Frank
Delahanty, Jim	Delahanty, Joe	Delahanty, Tom
Edmonds, Calvin	Goggins, Thomas	Goldstein, Phil
Gwin, Steve	Lauderdale, Charles	Mahomes, Grover
Mischal, Ken	Patti, Tony	Rose, Paul
Rosequist, Ted	Safford, Earl	Smith, Clarence

Smith, Walker · Sweeney, Eddie · Terry, James
Victor, Reggie · Wilkes, Bill · Williams, Phil

COLLINWOOD

Adamle, Tony · Adams, Regina · Anderson, Denzel
Anderson, Raymod · Armstrong, David · Bailey, Oliver
Ball, Jexie · Bandy, Devin · Banks, Mignon
Barney, Eppie · Barth, Carmen · Bates, Jeremiah
Battle, Ken · Baxter, Dainerah · Benson, Sandra
Bester, Jayshon · Bester, Kevin · Bishop, Curtis
Booker, Shawn · Bookins, Vincent · Bowens, Henry
Bowman, Tayvonne · Brantley, Donte · Braxton, James
Bright, Benny · Brookings, Vince · Brooks, Betty
Brown, Brittini · Brown, Claudia · Brown, Devonte
Busbee, Erin · Byrd, Terence · Calabrase, Bill
Cannarozzi, Nick · Cannavino, Joseph · Cannavino, Michael
Canreski, N. · Carter, Rodney · Casey, Dennis
Cavotta, Mike · Christian, Christal · Christian, Christina
Clay, Rahsheen · Cobble, Louis · Colombo, Anthony
Conkle, Thomas · Contorno, Dom · Cooper, Devin
Cornachione, Silvio · Cotton, Sean · Cowan, Tokeshia
Crawford, Rhondalyn · Dawson, Dyrek · Daye, Darin
Dent, Conrad · Dent, Eric · Drexler, Walter
Driggins, Dennis · Dybzinski, Jerry · Dye, Dorothy
Eason, Trevor · Easton, Dewayne · Edwards, Rico
Estrict, Christina · Evans, Andre · Evans, Chris
Evans, Erica · Fisher, Robert · Fisher, Stephen
Flonnory, Derrick · Fourtner, James · Fussell, Avundre
Garner, Chanae · Gary, Taylor · Gibson, Marlon
Goodgame, Jimmy · Gotarello, Joe · Graham, Eurall
Graves, Steve · Greathouse, Kenny · Green, Ashley
Guenther, Wallace · Gunn, Nigel · Hale, Ralph
Hale, Wally · Hall, Darian · Hall, Emethius
Hall, John · Halley, Ty · Harbour, Amirah
Harper, Darnnell · Harris, David · Harris, Jermaine
Hartson, Charles · Hemmingway, Vashonne · Hennings, Robert

Hill, Melvin	Holmes, Britany	Holmes, Jahmyl
Horn, Christy	Howard, Myron	Hubb, William
Hunt, Jay	Hunt, Kareem	Hurd, Calvin
Hython, Patrick	Iammararion, Domenick	Jackson, Blanche
Jennings, Wonderful	Johnson, Doriann	Johnson, Jasmine
Johnson, Jason	Johnson, Keomi	Johnson, LaTanya
Jones, Brittney	Jones, Cherr'e	Jones, Courtney
Jones, LaRon	Jones, Mignon	Jones, Shaika
Jordan, Kim	Jordan, Omari	Kerr, Ernest
Kinton, John	Kinton, Tracy	Kuhel, Jerry
Lainer, John	Lanier, Jeff	Lavan, Nicole
Lett, Jasmine	Lewis, Courtney	Lewis-Webb, Shantell
Lumbus, Charnea	Mack, Chimara	Mack, Jaichaunah
Maddox, Desmond	Mapango, Emanuel	Marrow, Theo
Marshall, Laron	Martin, Roshaud	Mason, Richard
Mason, Rod	Matthews, James	McClain, De'andre
McCoy, D' Maris	McDaniels, Vince	McIntosh, Soyna
McNeal, Keith	McNeal, Tyron	McNeil, James
McQueen, Michael	Merencky, Steve	Miller, Whitney
Mines, Jameica	Minnick, John	Mitchell, Raymond
Mitchell, Sam	Montgomery, Damarcus	Moore, Bryant
Morgan, David	Morrow, Theo	Morson, Daniel
Murphy, Chris	Murray, Donametric	Nance, Charles
Nance, Fred	Nash, Jamal	Owens, Dede
Palmer, Daniel	Palumbo, Sam	Pannitto, Domenic
Parr, Sabrina	Patrick, Tony	Patrizzi, Joe
Paul, Lavelle	Paul, Velonte	Philipash, Robert
Pitts, Granvel	Ponder, Eldridge	Reddish, Eddie
Robinson, Mike	Robinson, Shonda	Rogers, Talisha
Royal, Tiera	Rufus, Julie	Russ, Bernard
Sanders, Loreatha	Sas, Joseph	Sawyer, Ericka
Schady, Ciarra	Schweitzer, Wilbur	Scott, Donita
Scott, Maurice	Sharif, Rashid	Shealy, Debra
Sheldon, William	Shorts III, Cecil	Shorts Jr., Cecil
Shorts, Danny	Sibert, Bruce	Simmons, Oudisy

Simon, Jason	Simpson, Shanice	Sims, Anton
Sims, Rob	Skerl, Tom	Slapnick, Lou
Slater, James	Slayton, Laurin	Smiley, Regina
Smith, Amber	Smith, Brittany	Smith, Joi Renee
Solomon, DeAngelo	Sorrell, Stacy	Spencer, Montel
Starr, Cyrus	Stassfurth, H.	Stepp, Ja'Shaun
Stone, Kandance	Strong, Angelique	Suber, Paul
Tapp, Denton	Taylor, Brandy	Taylor, Geno
Taylor, Lashawn	Terry, Curtis	Thatcher, Charles
Thomas, Cerenity	Thomas, Sam	Thompson, Michael
Townsend, Henry	Trivisonno, Joseph	Ulle, Frank
Utenham, Aliyah	Vaccariello, Donald	Verba, Robert
Walker, Osman	Ware, Thomas	Washington, Barbara
Weaver, Jeremy	Wells, Shannon	Williams, Jenice
Williams, Robert	Williams, Roger	Williams, Terrance
Willis, Shannon	Wilson, DaSharee	Winston, Gloria
Woods, Chazmine	Wooten, Aneesah	Worthy, Adolph
Yates, Elizabeth	Zackarchenko, Dan	Zanders, Lakisha
Zanella, Francis	Zanella, John	Zust, Robert

EAST HIGH

Abernathy, Marlon	Abernathy, Monolito	Abrams, James
Adams, Clara	Agee, Michael	Avery, Jameil
Baker, London	Bane, Ken	Banks, Dajuan
Bates, Vernetta	Bessick, Don	Black, Tony
Blankenship, Brian	Brooks, Alex	Brown, Deaundra
Brown, Kevin	Brown, Patricia	Brown, Ron
Burns, Arion	Burns, Jermaine	Callaway, Keith
Calloway, Dewayne	Cook, Calvin	Cook, Kenneth
Cook, Sharonda	Cotton, Adell	Cranity, Leslie
Davis, Allen	Davis, Jerome	Davison, Jeremy
Dial, Teasha	Doctor, Quinn	Dorsey, Charles
DosReis, Marshall	Doss, Richard	Dukes, Kevin
Dunn, Jason	Elkins, Ben "Chip"	Etheridge, Shantaka
Evans, Jerome	Foggio, Don	Frazier, Marian
Funk, Edward	Furlick, Mike	Galloway, Keith

Ganger, Nate	Geter, Brian	Goodwin, Makeba
Graves, Mike	Griffin, Ricardo	Harrison, Edward
Harrison, Fred	Higgins, Markeeta	Hill, Alice
Hill, Anita	Holmes, Anthony	House, Demond
Howell, Jerry	Huddleston, ThaVain	Jackson, Tammy
Jefferies, Terry	Jefferson, Randell	Jenkins, Larry
Johnson, Kim	Johnson, William	Jones, Davis
Jones, Jerry	Jones, Marvin	Jones-Thomas, Teresita
Kellogg Sr., Clark	Kellogg, Gene	Kellogg, Shelby
Killings, Leonard	Laird, John	Lampley, Dorsey
Lane, Paul	Leaks, Manny	Ledwell, Tracie
Lett, Exodus	Linder, Ronnie	Lubino, Allan
Martin, Robert	Martin, Ron	Maver, Bob
McBryde, Derek	McMillian, Kalina	McWhorter, James
Menefee, Demetrius	Monroe, Yvonne	Moss, Lejuan
Moss, Reggie	Owes, Terry	Palmer, Ray
Parker, Brian	Parker, Jerry	Parks, Tracy
Pavlik, John	Payne, Reggie	Perry, Don
Powell, Charlotte	Robinson, Gary	Roskowski, Leo
Ross, Rogrell	Sallach, Fred	Sanders, Steve
Santos, Yariel	Scott, Arthur	Shilling, Ed
Smith, Donald	Smith, Gene	Steele, Edward
Stenson, Greg	Stricharczuk, Paul	Strozier, Aaron
Taseff, Carl	Taylor, Mark	Thomas, C.
Thomas, Eric	Thomas, James	Thomas, Lonnie
Tolbert, Jermaine	Townsend, Anna	Trammer, Rory
Vidal, Juan	Walker, Reggie	Walker, Sharmela
Washington, Daniel	West, Ken	West, Kenney
Whiter, Shawn	Williams, Lynn	Wilson, JC
Wonzo, April	Wren, Bob	Wynn, Lamont

EAST TECH

Adams, John	Adams, Rawnai	Adams, Tamalia
Agee, Sharren	Albritton, Dave	Alford, Clarence
Allen, Dae'Juandre	Allen, David	Allen, Jame
Allen, Tierra	Anderson, Eric	Arrington, Charnita

Austin, Raymon	Austin, Willie	Ayers, Chris
Bailey, Lawrence	Banks, Samuel	Barclay, Yvonne
Barnes, Ronald	Barns, Roy	Beddell, Eric
Behm, John	Bennett, Malike	Bessick, Art
Biggins, James	Biggins, Sheridine	Bigsby, Johnny
Bolden, Antonio	Bolden, Bobby	Bolden, Lawrence
Bolden, Tyrone	Bostick, Shantell	Bradford, George
Bradley, Aki	Bradley, Helen	Brenner, Ernie
Brookings, Troy	Brooks, Shantell	Brown Reed, Vivian
Brown, Bob	Brown, Derrin	Brown, Edmond
Brown, Fred	Brown, Nelson	Brown, Ulysses
Bryant, Diashon	Bryant, Rawn	Bryd, Phillip
Byers, Donna	Byrd, Andrew	Byrd, Joe
Byrd, Phillip	Cain, Greg	Cardwell, Corrione
Carley, Greg	Carter, Earl	Carter, Leroy
Carver, Famous	Carver, Larry	Carver, Ramus
Childress, David	Ciprianni, Ralph	Clark, Charles
Clark, George	Clark, Lawrence	Clark-Beachum, Cynthia
Collins, Sam	Cooper, Alicia	Cooper, Ben
Copeland, Bob	Cranfield, Kamalita	Crawl, Danny
Cullum, Dylon	Daniel, Morgan	Davenport, Chris
David, Eugene	Davis, Tina	De Forrest, Vincent
Deal, Antonio	Dillard, Harrison	Dozier, Merelenea
Dozier, Vernon	Drake, Yasmeen	Drane Jr., Tyric
Dubose, Victor	Dunklin, Ken	Eanes, Al
Evans, James	Ferguson, Bob	Ferguson, Ed
Fields, Craig	Fina, Paul	Flemming, Terry
Ford, Chris	Ford, Wanda	Fort, Raleigh
Franklin, Sam	Frazier, Kristopher	Free, Johnell
Gaines, Arthur	Gambrell, Jerome	Garner, Elizelz
Gay, James	Glenn, Ken	Glover, Ronald
Goens, John	Gordon, Robert	Graham, Wilson
Greene, Devonta	Griffin, Keith	Griffin, Rondell
Grisby, Gene	Grisby, Murvis	Guyton, Ta'Naejah
Hale, Barbara	Hardy, Alfred	Harper, D'Anthony

Harrell, Deval	Harrell, DJ	Harris, Clarence
Harris, Nikia	Harris, Rick	Harris, Ronald
Harris, William (Sonny)	Hemphill, Rose	Henderson, Darwin
Henderson, Marvin	Hendon, Lovie	Henry, William
Hibbit, John	Hilbbler, Willie	Hill, Chardai
Hodges, Marianne	Holmes, Branity	Howard, Leroy
Howard, Marvin	Howard, Raymond	Howard, Tyshaun
Howell, Shaunita	Huff, Jordan	Huff, Julian
Humphrey, James	Hutti, Dick	Isler, Luke
Isom, DeVonte	Jackson, Anthony	Jackson, Howard
Jackson, Willie	Jackson, Wilmer	James, David
James, Janice	Jenkins, Edward	Jenkins, Luna
Jenkins, William	Jennings, Jeremy	Jennings, Special
Johnson, Dwight	Johnson, Larry	Johnson, Markell
Johnson, Rahjanae	Jolly, Emitt	Jones, Andrew
Jones, Jasmine E.	Jones, Shaun	Jones, Thomas
Kara, Ted	Killian, Walt	King, Barry
Lacy, Homer	Laisure, Louis	Landon, Jaford
Lane, Eugene	Larkin, Monroe	Larkin, Richard
Lauria, Louis	Laurie, Lou	Lawson, Peter
Lee, Bernard	Lee, Eric	Letman, Samilah
Little, Howard	Lockett, Reggie	Love, Willie
Lowe, J T	Malone, Jaida	Manning, Shelby
Marks, Ray	Marsh, Mike	Martin, Jim
Mason, Celeste	Matthews, Tiffany	Mays, Wilbur
McCullum, Annie	McNeal, Kendall	McPhearson, Santay
Meadows, Lawrence	Merritt, Brinase	Mills, Will
Minor, Ashley	Mitchell, Charles	Mitchell, Randy
Montgomery, Quinn	Montgomery, Toccara	Moore, Marcus
Moore, Norbert	Morgan, Mike	Morton, Jimmy
Mosley, Ervin	Murray, Charles	Murray, Vernon
Mutsu, Arthur	Nance, Charles	Neal, Van
Newberry, Estus	Nlxon, Arthur	Orr, Mel
Osborne, Dennis	Owens, Jesse	Paige, David
Pangburn, Don	Parnell, Charles	Patterson, Tanya

Peckinpaugh, Roger	Pendleton, Christine	Pendleton, Christle
Peraza, Jose	Pittman, Rickey	Poage, Reginald
Poindexter, Charles	Pope, Rhonda	Porter, Lamoyne
Poston, Brialand	Powell, Leroy	Preston Jr., Alfred
Pritchard, Bill	Prunity, Jasmine	Raine, Melvin
Reid, James	Reid, Reggie	Rekowski, Steven
Repress-Davis, Cordell	Reynolds, Forrest	Reynolds, Ray
Richardson, Hal	Rivers, Juwanna	Robertson, Elvonte
Robertson, James	Robinson, Haven	Robinson, Takila
Rodriguez, Jim	Rollins, Kyla	Rozier, Robert
Ruffin, Myron	Russell, Pete	Rutti, Dick
Salamin, Shakorie	Sample, Stephanie	Samuels, Raymond
Sangster, Brandon	Schenker, Nate	Scott, Isaac
Sellers, Cory	Sellers, Henry	Sellers, LaRon
Shakir, Mahommed	Sheffield Jr., Ramon	Shelton, David
Shields, Burrell	Shields, Celina	Shropshire, Michael
Shropshire, Shalita	Shropshire, Shella	Sigler, T'Andre
Simmons, Jack	Simmons, Thomas	Sims, Destiny
Smith, Alex	Smith, Craig	Smith, Issac
Smith, James	Smith, Joe	Smith, Lawrence
Smith, Willie	Snyder, Marquel	Soeder, Len
Solomon, Darrylreona	Spivey, Luther	Stadford, Quintin
Starks, Jerrell	Starr, Richard	St. Clair, Mike
Steele, Tanisia	Stewart, Dontrell	Stone, Jim
Stoval, Densil	Stryker, Harry	Suber, Ben
Summers, George	Tate, Denise	Taylor, Abrielle
Taylor, Janice	Taylor, Kyauta	Tell Sr, William
Terry, Gerald	Theodore, Ted	Thomas, Richard
Thomas, Sam	Thurman, Antonio	Tisbye, Alex
Tolliver, Stanley	Torian, Conner	Trice, Jack
Trundle, Geno	Turner, Barbara	Upton, Jazmin
Vaden, Lawrence	Vance, Larnae	Vaughn, James
Veasley, Charles	Vidal, Juan	Vosmik, Joe
Walker, Lady	Walker, Larry	Walker, Virgil
Ward, Jada	Wardlow, Ed	Warfield, Gerald

Warmack, Robert
Washington, Isaiah
Washington, Nate
Webb, Regina
Webb, Steve
Welch, Drew
Wells, Johnny
Whitman, Bill
Wilcox, Tony
Wiley, Christine
Willaman, Sam
Williams, Jerry
Williams, Keith
Williams, Lisa
Williams, Nathaniel
Williams, Paul
Williams, Roosevelt
Willis, Delonte
Wilson, Chenara
Wilson, Graham
Wilson, Jack
Wilson, Jackie
Wilson, Linda
Wilson, Richard
Winborn, Keith
Woodard, Albert
Wooley, Albert
Wynn, Michael
Zeigler, Grady

GARRETT MORGAN

Daniels, Datwon

GLENVILLE

Abernathy, Kira
Adams, Martece
Adams, Nate
Adamson, Ronald
Agee, Jessie
Albright, Stanley
Allen, Billy
Ameen, Farakahan
Anderson, Devon
Anderson, Kerry
Anderson, Latwan
Andrews, Frank
Andrews, Glen
Armstrong, Raheem
Bailey, Bob
Baldwin, Danny
Ballard, Freddie
Banton, Vance
Barfield, Reggie
Basseer, Hussain
Bell, Demeris
Bello, Leroy
Benjamin, Jemall
Bentley, Angelo
Benton, Vance
Berger, Wilbert
Berry, Shawn
Bishop, Richard
Black, Stefone
Boddie, Simeon
Bolden, Anthony
Bolden, Darrell
Bolden, Ron
Bolden, Tarvares
Bonda, Ted
Bowie, Jermaine
Boyd, Bill
Boykins, J.
Braden, Ed
Bradley, Whitney
Brenston, Marcia
Brooks, Marcus
Brooks, Marvel
Brown, Patricia
Browning, Bryant
Bryant, Christian
Bryant, Coby
Bryant, Homer
Burt, William
Bush, Dashon
Byrd, Charles
Caffey, Clenson
Calabrese, Kiana
Carson, Antwan
Carter, Dante
Cecil, Sonja
Cecil, Sonya
Chambers, Chris
Clark, Christian
Clark, Frank
Clements, Xavier
Clemons, Raleigh
Cleveland, Jeremiah
Cloud, Donte
Coleman, Davon
Collins, Chanel

Colston, Javon	Conners, Tim	Cook, Jacques
Cook, Michael	Copes, Dontez	Cousett, John
Crawford, Robert	Crayton, Rod	Crayvins, Dalvon
Curry, Arjhanee	Daniel, Lebron	Davis Jr., Carl
Davis, Bruce	Davis, Demetrius	Davis, Derrick
Davis, Kevin	Davis, N.	Davis, Phillip
Davis, Shavontae	Dawson, Janon	DeFreeze, Louis
Derricoate, Bernard	Dhyll, Omar	Dimmings, Treyvon
Downing, Ernest	Downing, Quincy	Driscoe, Lorenzo
Drish, Denise	Drish, Devon	Drish, Marcus
Dunn, Evonte	Echols, Lytonia	Elliott, Jayrone
Elson, Leotis	Elston, Leotis	Embry, Deriene
Eubanks, Craig	Evans, Andre	Farmer, Taliesin
Fisher, Raymond	Fletcher, Donnie	Floyd, Jason
Ford, Antione	Foster, Ray	Fowler, Delbert
Frazier, Chris	Friedman, Benny	Frier, Sharonica
Frieson, Bruce	Fullerton, Tre'Ron	Fuqua, Stephon
Gaddis, Robert	Gates, Elliott	Gausha, Terry
George, Cassandra	Germany, Larry	Gibbs, Kirk
Gibson, Gandhi	Gibson, Kelvon	Gilbert, James
Gilbert, Jim	Ginn Jr., Ted	Ginn Sr., Ted
Ginn, Tiffany	Goings, Rashod	Goins, Tyrell
Goins, Tyron	Goldsby, Beverly	Goodall, Brandon
Goodwin, Demarius	Grady, Darnell	Grant, Adrian
Grant, Thomas	Graves, David	Gray, Stanley
Greenshields, Donn	Griffin, Ronald	Guess, Christian
Gunn, Mark	Hall, Derek	Hall, Duray
Hamblin, Stanley	Hamilton, Sam	Harbour, Derrek
Hardee, Justin	Harris, Sylvester	Harrison, Harold
Hawkins, Cornell	Hawkins, Mia	Haynes, Brandon
Hearns, Mike	Hembrick, Kevin	Henderson, Akie
Henderson, Keisha	Henry, Will	Hickman, Darrien
Hicks, Andre	Hicks, Byron	Higgins, Robert
Hiley, Darius	Hill, Thurlon	Hines, Jermaine
Holmes, Reggie	Holt, Kendall	Holt, Mariah

Hooks, L.
Howard, Greg
Ingram, Sir'Sean
Jackson, Falonte
Jackson, Marlina
Jefferson, Kyle
Johnson, Teonna
Jones, Alaura
Jones, Dave
Jones, Kevin
Jones, T.
Kinney, Ebony
Lane, Fred
Legion, Wyanna
Lewis, Frank
Little, Brionna
Lopez, Dayna
Mannigham, Joshua
Mathews, Deiter
McCornell, Kenny
McQueen, Robert (Rob J)
Molden, Antwaun
Nelson, Arvell
Newsome, Jonathan
Ottrix, Bryon
Owens, Brian
Page, James
Paul, Tomio
Pope, Aaron
Price, Don
Reed Willie
Riggs, DeAnthony
Robinson, Burton
Robinson, Jemal
Ross, John

House, Tiyana
Hubbard, Craig
Ivy, Reagan
Jackson, Larry
Jackson, Nikita
Jenkins, Jimmie
Johnson, Trevion
Jones, Barbra
Jones, Eric
Jones, N.
Kelley, Clarence
Ladiner, Lorenzo
Lattimore, Marshone
Lenix, Freddie
Lewis, Mark
Lofton, Lorraine
Lundy, Shelton
Martin, Nathaniel
Mays, Debra
McGlothan, Leslie
Merrill, Otis
Morris, A. J.
Nelson, Lawren
Nix, Eric
Overton, Kreg
Owens, Jamain
Page, Ron
People, Tyshaun
Posey, Tyon
Redding, Devine
Reeves, Claude
Riggs, Jacquez
Robinson, Greg
Robinson, LeeShawn
Rowell, Shawntell

Houston, Devonate
Hudson, Terrance
Jackson, Charles "Red"
Jackson, Lee
Jefferson, Ken
Johnson, Calvin
Johnson, Warren
Jones, Cardale
Jones, G.
Jones, Robert
Kimbrough, Debra
Landingham, Marvin
Legion, Latrice
Lett, Adam
Lewis, Marquise
Loines, Aaron
Malone, Charlene
Mason, Eddie
McBride, Derrick
McKnight, Sam
Mielziner, Saul
Morris, Brandon
Newman, John
O'Neal, Jarmario
Overton, Tim
Owens, William
Parker, Karen
Perez, Tom
Powell, Quinton
Reed, Vic
Richmond, Lamont
Robinson Jr., Johnny
Robinson, Janae
Rose, Robert
Russell, B.

Russell, Mike	Sadofsky, Norman	Sanders, B.
Sanders, Jim	Sanders, Tavareon	Saunders, James
Scott, Cordale	Scruggs, Leonard	Seals, Ageel
Sharp, Charles	Sheffield, Ra'iana	Shields, Dwayne
Shorts, Kevin	Shoulders, Chanell	Shoulders, Desiree
Simmmons, Trayvon	Sims, Ariez	Sims, LaSalle
Small, Ray	Smith, Curtis	Smith, Eric
Smith, Evelyn	Smith, Jeff	Smith, Mike
Smith, Troy	Smith, William	Solomon, Garnett
Spates, Darren	Spates, Kevin	Spencer, Raina
Stanley, William	Stephens, Michelle	Stone, James
Story, Tre'von	Sturdivant, Andre	Sumpter, Frank
Swaney, Arthur	Swoopes, Sonya	Sykes, Harry
Tate, Deneen	Tate, Denise	Taylor, Lavelle
Taylor, Terry	Terry, Curtis	Thomas, Calvin
Thomas, Danita	Thomas, Eric	Thomas, Kevin
Thomas, Lamar	Thomas, Nicole	Thomas, Rex
Thomas, Shyaira	Tucker, John	Turner, Kelli
Turpin, Teeshawn	Wainwright, Aswan	Walker, Aundrey
Walker, Lady	Wallace, Christiana	Walton, Robert
Ware, Floyd	Ware, Robert	Warner, Willie
Warren, Deavion	Washington, Lamonte	Watson, Ariel
West Jr., Bryan	West, Desmond	Whatley, Da' Shaun
Wheatley, Nelson	Whichard, Taliyah	White, Briana
White, Crawford	White, David	Whitley, Sabrina
Whitner, Dawawn	Whitner, Donte	Williams, Brandon
Williams, Courdale	Williams, Daymon	Williams, Don
Williams, Glen	Williams, Ralpheal	Williams, W.
Williams, Walt	Witten, Lindsey	Woods, Lejon
Woods, Pierre	Worley, Chris	Wright, Donald
Wright, Jerome	Wright, Latrice	Write, Renee
Wynn, Michael	Wynn, Sabrina	Wynn, Shane
Young, Curtis		

JAMES FORD RHODES

Addison, Ron	Agee, Keith	Anzalone-Fox, Cindy

Armstrong, Ralph
Bates, Michael
Berkley, Michael
Block, Dale
Boykins, Moniquea
Brunson, Barney
Bussey, Zanetta
Byrd, Antwione
Campbell, Roneisha
Carter, A.C.
Cavillo, John
Clancy, Erin
Clow, Marcus
Colon, Keisha
Courey, Ron
Davis, Chance
Decessare, Gregory
Dewerth, Al
Doskey, Ray
Duncan, Tasha
Eck, Diamond
Edwards, LeShaunte
Emery, Jim
Floyd, Dion
Fwamba, Didier
Gates, Water
Givens, Anaiyah
Goodwin, Juan
Guthrie, Destiny
Hall, Lawanda
Hanning, Derrick
Harris, Alex
Harris, John
Harris, Ryan
Hayes, Gaston

Baker, Rita
Bell, Deondra
Biascochea, Kiwi
Bost-Floyd, Jordan
Brown, Autumn
Burkholder, Jayda
Bussman, Dale
Byrd, Terrence
Campiri-Thamann, Debra
Carter, Aaron
Chestnut, Adrian
Clark, Brandon
Clow, Mikayla
Colvin, Cy
Croskey, Jevonte
Davis, Cynthia
DeJesus, Chevy
Dickerson, Amarion
Dotson, Thomas
Duncan, Thomas
Edeh, Chiamaka
Egan, David
Erskine, Sediah
Forte, Donovan
Gant, Chester
Giles, Kenyon
Godbott, Darrick
Gore, Calvin
Guy, Nylisha
Hall, Shania
Harding, Katonya
Harris, Fred
Harris, LaDaryle
Harris, Victor

Barnett, Erin
Benton, Jayvon
Blade, Karl
Boykin, Naila
Bruce, Brian
Burton, Dan
Byrd, Antoine
Caminero, Brittany
Cartagena, Ariel
Carter, Toure
Christley, Elijah
Clinghan, Jeff
Collins, Daniel
Colvin, Tiffany
Cummings, Steven
Davis, Eric
Demcho, Dennis
Dixon, Tahli
Douglas, James
Durda, Benji
Edeh, Mmesoma
Ellis, Cathy
Farmer, Paul
Franks, Miranda
Garner, Sevanneh
Gilliam, Tristen
Golson, Edward
Griffin, Eric
Haggins, Celeste
Hann, Billy
Harold, Henry
Harris, Hubert
Nick, Harris
Hatcher, Damien

Hayes, Shyianne
Hill, Channel
Hope, Jumerious
Howard, Eusavius
Jackson, Anthony
Jennings, Francine
Jimenez, A. J.
Jones, Brenna
Juhas, John
Kelly, Evelyn
Keuhn, Chuck
Kinney, Roneisha
Kosyk, Dale
Lane, Tyshawn
Lave, Josh
Lewis, Frank
Lockhart, Warren
Lucas, Chuck
Mackilin, Robert
Marshall, Carlos
Martin, Ray
Maul, Charles
McCafferty, Don
McCoy, William
McMillon, Terrence
Miles, Dimitri
Miller, Victor
Monday, Richard
Moore, Phil
Morris, Jeff
Moss, Najee
Neman, Edward
Novak, Jessica
Panza, Frank
Patterson, Sha'Tayah

Hernandez, Luis
Hlavacek, Sue
Hopkins, Harry
Howze, Aaliyah
Jackson, Kenneth
Jennings, Monique
Johnson, Joseph
Jones, Demetrius
Kalish, Dan
Kennedy, Joyce
Kimbrough, Kathy
Kirkman, Nijon
Kyle, David
Lange, Lawrence
Lee, Tasheania
Libran, Sara
Loftis, Messiah
Lugo, Stephanie
Malanoski, Joe
Marshall, Carmella
Matos, Zuleika
Maxwell, Cedrick
McCaully, Dakota
McMichael, Chase
McMillon-Hall, Ester
Miles, Furman
Mirka, George
Montanez, Ansel
Morales, Erika
Morris, Phillip
Musall, Richard
Newman, Ed
Noyola, Abel
Parks, Chris

Hickman, Miranda
Hoagan, Tyrell
Horvath, Les
Hughey, Hierram
Jacome, Rasool
Jewell, William
Jones, Ashley
Jones, Mahagony
Kay, Philip
Kennedy, Kordell
Kinney, Ronald
Korinchak, Steve
Landingham, Marlon
Laster, Anita
Levert, Ernest
Lockhart, Tia
Long, Lashone
Lundy, Antoine
Malone, Lou
Martin, Art
Matthews, Deshawn
Mays, Derrick
McCaully, Fontaine
McMillon, Darryl
Metro, Annalyse
Miller, Maurice
Mirka, Joe
Moore, George
Morlan, Veronica
Mosley, Victor
Naringer, Dave
Nolan, Cindy
Pace, Bonita
Patterson, Reuben

Pavlak, Casmir
Perkins, Anthony
Pettigrew, Patricia
Pollock, Joseph
Prince, Stephanie
Putich, Bill
Randle, Tameka
Rengifo, Kiara
Rimmer, Shannon
Rivera, Pablo
Roberts, Joe
Robinson, Cierra
Rodriguez, Arielis
Rodriguez, Pamela
Rosado, Norverto
Ruble, Adrianna
Sanders, Simon
Sangster, Justin
Shirey, Lowell
Simms, Greg
Sistek, Dick
Smith, Kenitha
Spoko, Wendy
Stewart, Jazzmyn
Sullen, Rich
Summerville, Derekia
Sweet, Roland
Tekesky, Steven
Thomas, Daniel
Tobin, Breane
Tompkins, Nashea
Tucker, Melvin
Valdez, Tiffany
Vazques, Briana
Velotta, Dick

Pena, Kendrick
Perkins, Delonte
Pippens, Woody
Ponder, Earnest
Pringle, Chris
Radovanic, Andrew
Randle, Tim
Richardson, Neil
Rimmer, Shelly
Rivera, Savannah
Roberts, Troy
Robinson, Eddie
Rodriguez, Dlynn
Roggenburk-Kyle, Judy
Rosado, Tony
Rucker, Lazaria
Safir, Muhammad
Schleicher, Fred
Shoals, Mike
Simms, Ronnie
Sistek, Frank
Smith, Nicole Antoinette
Spraggins, Angela
Stiegelmeyer, Nicole
Sumlin, Jamal
Swanson, Carl
Tables, Tekeli
Telischak, Ronald
Thomas, Duane
Todd, James
Torres, Annette
Turner, David
Valencia, Miya
Vega, Alexis
Verhosek, Tammy

Perkins, Amanda
Perkrul, Kathleen
Platt, Victor
Porter, Vanessa
Prock, Robby
Ramos, Thalia
Rengifo, Ashley
Riggins, Michelle
Rivera, Angely
Riveria, Cristina
Robi, Asmaa
Rocco, Joseph
Rodriguez, Luis
Roman, Jennifer
Rouse, Maurice
Sabater, Stephanie
Safran, Dick
Sealey, Thelma
Simms, Carol
Simpson, Clyde
Smith, Avery
Soto, Joanchelys
Stachowski, Dave
Stone, Jocelyn
Summers, Dave
Swasey, Dick
Taylor, Tenisha
Tetreault, Nick
Thomas, Ed
Tomlinson, Lloyd
Tucker, Kevin
Ulloa, Miguel
Vasquez, Carlos
Vega, Gianette
Vilt, Ed

Vilt, Gerald	Vlach, Tiffany	Walls, Lakeith
Washington, Isaiah	Washington, Jerice	Weems, Syhee
Wells, Rayshawn	Wells, Rodney	Wilkerson, Jermel
Williams, Antuan	Williams, Charles	Williams, Irayel
Woods, Marquis	Work, Thomas	Wren, Wayne
Young, Nick	Zeleny, Ray	Zidek, Dave

JANE ADDAMS

Campbell, Jada

JOHN ADAMS

Abernathy, Jovon	Adams, Erinna	Akram, Rasool
Algeri, Sam	Allen, Jasper	Allen, Jonathan
Allen, Rashaun	Aloshen, George	Anderson, Cleo
Anderson, Darryl	Anderson, Eric	Anderson, Stoker
Arcoria, Charles	Ardito, Buddy	Bailey, Lavell
Banks-Priester, Carmen	Baratta, Carmen	Barbarotta, Santo
Barille, Angelo	Barille, Nick	Barleda, Joe
Barotta, Joe	Bishop, Opal	Bivins, Geneva
Black Sr., Chardon	Blackmon, Lela	Blount, Gil
Bonina, Angelo	Boyer, Jerome	Bridges, Dwayne
Brooks, Nathan	Brown, Arthur	Brown, Ben
Brown, Greg	Brown, Querica	Brown, Willie
Bryson, Raheem	Butler, Ed	Butler, Tyrone
Cameron, Rashida	Carver, Kerontae	Casalicchio, Ed
Caver, Kimyatta	Chambers, Kevin	Chambers, Tonya
Chapman, Sam	Childs, Duane	Clark, Frank
Claudio, Ed	Cleamons, Bryan	Coker, Kiauna
Cole, Kallica	Collier, Cheri	Collins, Johnny
Collins, Jonta	Competto, Julius	Counts, Gail
Craft, Jeffrey	Crawford, Rhondalynn	Cross, Delontae
Danko, Richard	Davis, Alan	Davis, James
Davis, LaVon	Davis, Stephen	Davis, Talasia
Dawson, Charles	Dudley, Isaiah	Durham, Carl
Eaton, Gina	Edmonds, Emma	Edrington, Westley
Edwards, Ema	Ellington, Richard	Eskut, Joe
Evans, Tyrone	Farris, Don	Farris, Ed

Farris, Ron	Finch, Selena	Finnigan, Eddie
Flanagan-Byrd, Marlene	Flucker, Angie	Foster, Husian
Freeman, Marty	French, Regan	Gillom, Pamela
Goings Kamfolt, Crystal	Golden, Robert	Goldman, Sam
Gooch, Jeff	Grady, Ludie	Green, Bo
Greer, Tanner	Greer, Tristian	Grepher, Tom
Griffin, Timothy	Grove, Mike	Hairston, Roy
Hall, David	Hall, Robert	Hardin, Ju'Ruan
Harmon, Joe	Harmon, Terry	Harper, Keith
Harris, Benita	Harris, Brittanie	Harrison, Bob
Harriston, Roy	Haymon, Al	Helfiore, Sal
Hewlett, Dial	Hill, John	Hobbs, Benita
Hobbs, Senghor	Holland, Claude	Homolak, Steve
Houze, Jessica	Hubbard, Blanche	Hughley, Kiena
Hughley, Nathaniel	Hull, Dave	Hundley, Jojaun
Incorvaia, Angelo	Ivy, Keith	Jackson, Querica
Jackson, Reggie	Jackson, Tom	James, John
Jarrett, Sherman	Jarzynski, Ignatius	Jefferson, Peola
Jeffries, Greg	Johnson, Charita	Johnson, Donte
Johnson, Joey	Johnson, Laquan	Johnson, Starett
Johnson-Stubbs, Charita	Jones, Bill	Jones, Brian
Jones, Bryan	Jones, Kelly	Jones, Willie
Kilroy, Thomas	Kimball, Harold	Kimbrough, Abrionna
Kimbrough, Karl	King, Don	Kirtley, Karen
Laney, Marshall	Lanier, Lorenzo Rimp	Lankford, Lavelle
Lassiter, Marie	Lassiter, Obie	Leach, Melran
Leaks, George	Leard, Noel	Lee, Justlee
Lester, Janan	Leverette, Jordan	Lipscomb, Jamel
Love, Erianna	Luke, Semaj	Luke, Tremond
Madison, Tre'von	Madox, Harold	Madox, Sanchez
Malone-Jones, Debra	Manning, Madeline	Martemus, Ken
Martin, Jamal	Martinez, Kameron	Mason, Jeff
McCafferty, Valarie	McConnell, Bob	McCowns, Alex
McGee, Darrin	Mcgraw, Keyon	McKenzie, Rochelle
McKinley, Bryan	McKinley, Derek	McKinley, Kevin

McKinley, Michael	McKnight, Henry	McMillan, Deborah
McMillian, Debra	McMullen, Carmella	McNair, Kenneth
McPherson, Pamela	Merriweather, D.	Mileo, Leonard
Mileti, Nick	Miller, Cynthia	Miller, Donte
Miller, Tangetta	Mitchell, Darnell	Mondello, Joe
Montgomery, Charles	Montgomery, Eleanor	Morgan, Anthony
Morgan, Curtis	Morman, Lajanae	Morton, Stephanie
Murphy, Jim	Murray, Michael	Murray, Selena
Nader, Lester	Nelson, Marvin	Nelson, Rochelle
Oliver, Mike	Owens, Burl	Owens, Luke
Pagan, Charles	Parker, Craig	Patrick, Archie
Patterson, Meaghen	Payne, Ben	Penn, Shaune
Philips, Choice	Pittman-Scott, Loretta	Poward, Donna
Powell, John	Ramsey, Robert	Redding, Shelby
Reminick, Howard	Reynolds, Bob	Roberson, Jeffrey
Robinson, Devin	Robinson, Devon	Robinson, Jamie
Robinson, Kaylah	Robinson, Micah	Rucker, Ken
Russo, Attilio	Sains, Paul	Sanford, Carl
Santoli, Patsy	Sapp, Cleo	Scacutto, John
Scott, Erick	Scott, Marvin	Scott, Ti'yonna
Sealy, Twyla	Selawski, Gene	Shaw, Brian
Shawn, Dick	Shirak, Richard	Silver, Jerry
Simms, Leonard	Simon, Donnell	Simpson, Ed
Simpson, Gary	Sinito, Anthony	Sisenberg, Hy
Small, Angela	Small, Mia	Smiley, Sheliah
Smith, Chuck	Smith, Clinton	Smith, Ed
Smith, Marcia	Smith, Myron	Smith, Rasheen
Smith, Tyrone	Sorrell, Erika	Springer, Mike
Stack, Dick	Stallworth, Garland	Stanford, Carl
Stevenson, Ralonda	Stevenson, Tyrez	Stirtmire, Kavione
Strong, Angela	Strong, Bernard	Taylor, Donald
Tell, Toni	Thomas, Lorenzo	Thomas, Paul
Thomas, Reggie	Thompson, Anthony	Thompson, Henry
Thompson, Rochelle	Thompson, Tray'von	Tidmore, Sam
Townsend, Raheem	Turner, David	Turner, LeAndra

Turner, Ronnie	Tyus, Thurman	Upshaw, Lonnell
Walker, Holly	Warren, Mac	Warren, Norman
Warren, Tommie	Washington, Bill	Weaver, Charles
West, Eric	Williams, Domione	Williams, Isaiah
Williams, Jamon	Wilson, Darryl	Woodard, Henry
Woodruff, Jada	Workman, Tonja	Wright, Delica
Wright, Gwyn	Zantila, Karl	Zeigler, Bourbon

JOHN F. KENNEDY

Adams, Darnell	Aden, Marc	Adigwe, Nnena
Alexander, Jessica	Atkins-Smith, Ray	Averheart, Aaron
Bailey, Javain	Bailey, Kesi	Baily, Charles
Ballard, Wenners	Banks, David	Barron, Jarett
Baston, Brandon	Bell, JahMire	Bell, Ra'mond
Berry, Earlene	Blair, Chania	Blake, Kevin
Blue, Tim	Bolden, Tyrone	Boston, Lawrence
Bouldin, Markieo	Brown, David	Brown, Mike
Brown, Shacila	Brown, Tony	Brown, Tracianna
Burks, Kendall	Burns, Andre	Byrd, Terry
Carnegie, Wayne	Carr, Andre	Carswell, Kevon
Carter, Chris	Ceasor, Chris	Chambers, Corella
Chapman, Marilyn	Chatmon, Fred	Cistrunk, Patrica
Clark, Brian	Clements, Thomas	Clemons, Jamar
Cook, Evette	Cummings, Denzel	Dalton, Kareema
Davis, April	Davis, Darnell	Davis, Everett
Davis, Pong	Day, Montez	Dickson, Endia
Dotson, Dexter	Douglas, Robert	Dove, Bonnie
Drakeford, Ronnie	Edgerson, Marcellius	Edwards, Otis
Elams, Da-Lia	Epps, James	Evans, Gilbert
Fields, Odessa	Fisher, Janiyah	Flonnory, Gabbrielle
Francis, Deshaud	French, Marcus	Fulton, Jazmine
Galbreath, Marlin	Gardner, James	Garner, Nevach
Garth, Larry	Gates, Leslie	Gedson, Matthew
Gholston, Denise	Golliday, Michael	Golphin, Lakeitha
Goodson, Keyshawn	Grant, Shawn	Hackney, Nordine
Hagwood, Norman	Hall, Tuanisha	Hard, Tiffany

Hardley, Curtis	Hardnick, Arnez	Harris, Amber
Harris, Jason	Harris, Sonja	Haywood, Omar
Henderson, Eric	Henderson, Josh	Hill, Ahmad
Hollowell, Marcedes	Hooks, Esau	Howard, Anthony
Howard, Antonio	Hutchins, Renaldo	Jackson, Destiny
Jacobs, Jeremiah	Jefferson, Saivon	Jenkins, Keyuana
Johnson, Fred	Johnson, Trevon	Jones, Divard
Kellen, Antonie	Kelley, Reginald	Kellom, Antonio
Kibble, Donita	Kibble, Donneika	Kimmie, Darnell
King, Jamat	King, Toma	Kirk, Curtis
Kirkland, Clevon	Knight, Randy	Lawrence, Paul
Lee, Eric	Lee, Steward	Lenin, Lawrence
Lindsay, Andre	Lindsay, Donte'	Lockhart, Kennedy
Lykes, Bobby	Lynch, Norman	Madison, Leon
Malone, Jeffery	Maple, Mark	Marrow, Greg
Marrow, Jordan	Martin, Ebony	Martin, Laddree
Martin, Malcolm	Martin, Marcus	McCain, Robert
McCloud, Chris	McCrary, Mychale	McIntosh, Marcus
Minter, Austin	Mitchell, Furb	Mitchell, Ronnie
Montgomery, Anthony	Moore, Bruce	Moore, Mike
Morgan, Charles	Morris, Paul	Murphy, Anthony
Nelson, Dale	Nowden, Kyle	Parker, Anthony
Parson, Jackie	Patrick, DeVelvet	Patterson Jr., Leonard
Perkins, Claude	Pitts, Eric	Powers, Tiffany
Price, Jarred	Ramsey, Bruce	Reese, Shurrell
Reynolds, Ahmad	Roach, Shawana	Roberts, Christopher
Roberts, Damien	Roberts, Myguel	Robinson, Deonta
Rogers, Danndray	Rome, Lawrence	Ross, D'Juan
Ruffin, Ray	Salters, Ronald	Seals, Reginald
Shabazz, Javezz	Sharp, Darrell	Shaw, Shanell
Sheffield, Dejah	Shoulders, Dexter	Shuttlesworth, Ed
Sims, Michael	Sinclair, Larry	Smart, Marcus
Smith, Allen	Smith, Andre	Smith, Antonio
Smith, Antwon	Smith, Donece	Smith, Jamall
Smith, Nathan	Stafford, Lloyd	Stafford, Ronald

Steele, Toi
Stephens, Frank
Stephens-Porter, Lauryn
Stevens, Michael
Stevens, Michelle
Stone, Donta
Stoudenmire, Mel
Stribling, Maurice
Sumbay, Larry
Tatum, Sterling
Taylor, Joe
Thomas, Anthony
Thomas, Kayla
Thomas, Shander
Toler, Deonte
Tomlinson, Kenyon
Triggs, Reggie
Trone, Evander
Truett, Daijha
Tucker, Anthony
Turner, Arlene
Tyler, Alan
Waden, Desmond
Walker, Britney
Walker, Robert
Ward, Tiffany
Ware, Julie
Ware, Marqueshia
Warren, Julius
Warren, Tim
Washington, Linda
Washington, Norma
Watkins, Thurston
Wenson, Prentis
Wilkerson, Marcus
Williams, Dana
Williams, David
Williams, Vera
Willis, Calvin
Wilson, Christen
Young, Jason
Young, Keshijetta
Zebbs, Phillip

JOHN HAY

Abed, Asya
Akins, Treyvon
Austin, Anthony
Banks, Ella
Banks, Rayshawn
Beard, George
Beck, Dominique
Bell, Airelle
Bell, Jeremy
Bell, Marcus
Bennett, Mike
Berry Sr., Carlos
Berry, Keith
Binns, Bob
Black, Marvin
Blackwell, James
Blynn, William
Bolden, Angel
Bolden, Devan
Bostick, Andrea
Boyd, Jalen
Bradford, Michael
Brentar, Jerome
Brown, Jason
Cain, Marshall
Cannon, Angel
Capeles, Enrique
Capeles, Joshua
Carroll, Tia
Carroll, Wesley
Carter, Devon
Catavolos, Archie
Catavolos, Pete
Chambers, RauShiya
Clayton, Leone
Cline, Pual
Cofield, Donald
Coleman, Randy
Coleman, Ronnie
Conner, Khadazia
Cooper, Dan
Cooper, Shondale
Cooper, Thomas
Crain, Guy
Crawford, Ken
Cuthberison, George
D'Amico, Vincent
D'Mico, Vince
Darden, Anthony
Davis, Ki'Anthony
Davis, Maurice
Davis, Tom
Davis-Hereford, Raequan
Deloney, Brenda
Discont, Herbert
Douglas, Talasia
Dowdell, John

Drake, Angliette L.	Drake, Karlos	Dudley, Bob
Dulaney, Nicole	Easterling, Arthur	Elliot, Jimmy
Ellis, Justin	Engle, Tiffany	Erdar, Pete
Fatica, Tony	Ferchron, Gene	Fields, Herman
Franklin, Marcus	Frigic, Kevin	Gaffney, Aldolphus
Galloway, Quavon	Grankowitz, Frank	Grayer, Marcus
Griffin, Rajon	Hagler, Averett	Hairston, Jada
Hancock, Anthony	Harris, Anthony	Harris, Ravawn
Hart, Amara	Hatchett- McGee, Tim	Hays, Art
Hicks, John	Hill, Johnny	Horn, Greg
Horton, Jamar	Huston, Jamir	Ihema, Emeka
Jackson, Aryana	Jarziwski, Iggy	Jeffries, Keith
Jeffries, Makayla	Johnson, Derek	Johnson, Destiny
Johnson, Fernandez	Jones, Charee	Jones, Dorinda
Jones, Monique	Jordan, William	Kallay, Robert
Kaye, Johny	Kelley, Brandon	Kellogg, Maurice
Kurns, Dyna	Laconti, Hank	Latham, Romel
Lawson, Willie	Lekas, Louis	Lewis, Shakira
Lumbus, Josh	Lurns, Dyna	Lynch, Michelle
Malave, Yarimar	Manning-Mims, Madeline	Marshall, Dennis
Martin, Nigel	Matlock, William	Maxie, Amaya
May, Janira	McCewan, Ian	McClain, Sam
Melton, Love	Meltzer, Isabel	Mitchell, Mylik
Mondie, Kevin	Montague, Fred	Morgan, Deeshawn
Muhammed, Tynetta	Murray, Tommie	O'Field, Maurice
Oakley, Charles	Owens, Lamiah	Owens, Thomas
Patterson, Bailey	Patterson, Reuben	Paul, Leonard
Phillips, John	Phillips, Sharia	Phillips, Tamara
Pollard, Camryn	Porch, Donelle	Priester, Ernest
Pruitt, Tevin	Ragland, Kevin	Ranaldo, Sam
Reed, Ka'ierra	Reed, Symone	Reese, Paul
Reynolds, Rich	Reynolds, Rick	Ricks, Michael
Rini, Anthony	Riveria, Danny	Ross, Steve
Rush, Michael	Russo, Dominic	Russo, Louis
Sample, George	Sanders, Chauncy	Schmidt, Frank

Scrima, Patrick
Shearer, Jasmine
Smith, Marquis
Stevenson, Cedric
Strong, Ed
Tere, Lauren
Thompkins, Aaron
Townsend, Tasha
Turpin, Stanley
Walker-Wright, Renee
Wells, Deonte
White, Deonna
Williams, Keaja
Wood, Kendall
Woolard, Michael

Sebring, Michael
Sheppard, James
Smith, Rickey
Stith, Antione
Sweeney, Jakada
Tere, Welline
Thompson, Maurice
Tripp, Ed
Walker, Jonathan
Walsh, Dick
Wendz, Ronald
Wiederhorn, Sam
Williams, Malcolm
Woodson, Cherie
Wright, Brenton

Shaw, Nicola
Sipp, Brandon
Stanik, Mike
Stokes, Joe
Sweeney, Jalyn
Thomas, Amber
Tolliver, Robert
Tucker, Darnell
Walker, Malik
Warren, Raymone
Westbrooks, Chanitta
Williams, Javaughn
Wilson, Kyle
Woolard, Greg

JOHN MARSHALL

Adams, Jonaz
Aviles, Besty
Bailey, Jacob
Barnett, Ashley
Bednar, Phil
Bennett, Angel
Boyd, Moreland
Brooks, Steven
Brown, Nate
Brummer, Clayton
Burkle, Bill
Chambers, Guy
Clark, Belford
Cook, Jaylin
Craycrafth, S.
Cunningham, Marcettes
Dancy, Terry
Davis, Larry
Dickerson, Dominique

Asberry, Rodney
Aviles, Jaritza
Banks, Ron
Barron, Joe
Bell, Allentha
Blade, Marcellus
Bradberry, Ralph
Brown, DeAndre
Brown, Reggie
Buddie, Robert
Burrell, Jonathan
Chaplin, Mark
Coles, Taeyvn
Cooper, Thomas
Crist, Jeremiah
Cunningham, Michael
Davis, Jelisa
Degraffenreid, S.
Disanto, Russell

Aufmuth, Ken
Bagwell, Keisha
Barkley, Kevin
Beasley, Shamareo
Bellian, Andy
Boyd, Amber
Bradley, Rochell
Brown, Desmond
Brown, Virgil
Burgess, Fred
Busha, Adelbert
Chappell, Tamaine
Collins, Ronald
Coy, Larry
Crosky, Regina
D'Aurello, Ed
Davis, Juanita
Deluca, Pete
Dolan, Michelle

Donahue, Marty	Drayton, Stanley	Dregalla, James
Dubay, Gilbert	Edwards, Mike	Elben, Jim
Elkins, Tom	Ellison, Glenn	Emery, Dave
Erby, Sam	Evans, Brandon	Ezzo, Ralph
Farrell, Paul	Fernandez, Salina	Finley, Tonya
Finney, Lashawn	Floyd, Pam	Flynn, Eric
Frierson, Hollis	Gandy, Kurt	Garcia, Daniella
Gates, Jasmine	Gates, Terri	Gentry, Ben
Gerboc, Alan	Giles, Damond	Gold, Gary
Golphin, Keith	Goodwin, Richard	Goss, Alexus
Graham, James	Graham, Janetta	Gratten, Jomoree
Green, Dorian	Gregg, Robert	Gunn, Cha'nice
Hale, Ken	Hall, Mandrell	Haller, Ed
Hanson, Tom	Harriman, Howard	Hartnett, Bill
Henderson, John	Hernandez, Tanisha	Holland, Bruce
Horvath, Ray	Howard, Lynae	Hudson, Theo
Hughes, Ayeesa	Humphrey, Lorenzo	Jackson, Ayana
Jackson, John	Jackson, Kyle	Jackson, Tavion
James, Neil	Jefferson, Louis	Jefferson, Thomas
Jiminez, Vincent	Joeright, John	Johnson, Spencer
Jones, Gerald	Jones, Mike	Justice, Olivea
Kasler, Jeffery	Kennedy, Mike	Kenny, Dave
Kerr, Jim	King, Larry	King, Melvin
Kinney, Matt	Kirkman, Deneen	Knight, Alonzo
Kucera, Dick	Kurtz, Jim	Lee, Mike
Lennox, Cary	Lennox, Kelly	Leonti, Jack
Lett, Andrea	Limpert, Crystal	Limpert, Jeff
Line, Nate	Loeffler, Fred	Longino, Elige
Maclachlan, Ross	Maguth, Brad	Mahon, Dan
Markworth, Kirk	Maro, Ed	Martin, Andre
Martin, Richard	Marxhall, Dave	Mayher, Dave
McBride, Michael	McCray, Jeremy	McDermott, Ryan
McElroy, Bob	McElwee, Matthew	McKee, Marita
McKinney, Keith	McNeal, Patrick	Medina, Alan
Millson, Bud	Miners, Mark	Mitchell, Nick

Mixon, April
Morrill, Robert
Nieves, Kevin
Oliver, Michael
Paci, Antwuan
Perez, Remi
Plummer, James
Pope, Jamaree
Ramlow, Bob
Respress, Terrell
Ritter, Billy
Ross, Matt
Russell, Rochelle
Sanford, Ronshida
Schultz, Walter
Sims, Dainium
Smith, Jim
Stanley, Terell
Stemm, Charlene
Stofan, Maria
Stubblefield, Theresa
Supelak, Larry
Tell Jr., William
Thomsen, Jeremiah
Truax, Joe
Venotzy, Ted
Vinci, Sam
Watts, Daymon
Whitsitt, Re'ianna
Williams, Quentin
Wood, Don
Yun, Charlie
Zizak, Robert
Zwolenik, Robert

Moreno, Jerimiah
Moxley, Jermaine
Oates, Ramier
Osicka, Richard
Paschal, Jeff
Peterson, Alan
Pogue, Kim
Prince, Ryan
Redding-Shields, Vita
Revay, Mike
Rivera, Yami
Rountree, Rasheed
Sabo, John
Sanka, James
Scott, Brandon
Skeens, Christopher
Smith, Victor
Starks, Andre
Stephens, Michael
Straky, John
Studdard, Nicolas
Sustersic, Ed
Thomas, Jim
Thornton, Saeed
Varga, Paul
Vickerstaff, Lawrence
Walton, Eugene
White, Archie
Wilhelm, Tom
Wilson, Dey'jon
Woodridge, Chris
Zacharias, Kris
Zunie, Robert

Morrill, James
Negron, Shakiesha
Oldham, Lorrie
Osicka, Robert
Peck, Dylan
Pierce, Eric
Pollard, Kermit
Raines, Randle
Reindi, Amy
Rieder, Ray
Rizk, Tom
Ruiz, Giovanni
Sallea, Cecil
Santana, Magdiel
Shade, Gary
Skurko, Dick
Spear, Jeffrey
Starks, Andrew
Stincic, Tom
Stoyka, Michelle
Summerville, Lashaina
Tate, Elijan
Thomas, Patryce
Tobin, John
Vastleff, Jim
Victor, Joe
Ward, Harry
White, Cervante
Wilkins, Mike
Wiltshire, Alison
Wright, Wanda
Zickes, James
Zuppan, Mladen

LINCOLN

Adkins, Lloyd	Almasi, John	Anderson, Karl
Avery, Willie	Anderson, Karl A.	Babicz, Teb
Bania, Don	Barna, Michael	Baron, Ronald
Berdysz, Walter	Boczulak, Steve	Boulton, Frank
Buckner, Bernie	Budzik, Ted	Casey, Richard
Casey, Tim	Charchenko, Andy	Cugini, Joe
Dianiska	Dillon, Quinton	Durda, Ray
Economy, Diamond	Feliciano, Gilbert	Frey, Carl
Gaba, Rudy	Gainer, Bill	Gratewski, Richard
Graziolli, Herman	Grivess, Mike	Grupe, Raymond
Gus, Bill	Gus, Nick	Hakenberg, Isaac
Haregsin, Larry	Haschak, John	Hilow, Fred
Hoffman, Danny	Hopkins, Ida Jean	Hotz, Andy
Hotz, John	Hunt, Marty	Hyduke, Bob
Iley, Frank	Jubak, Bill	Jung, Ken
Karabinos, Mike	Kasel, Rich	Kaznoch, Jerry
Kingery, Leslie	Klypchak, Walter	Knavel, Stan
Knowalczyk, Al	Konchan, Ken	Kopin, Chris
Kormos, John	Koscianski, Ray	Kowza, Jeff
Lewandowski, Rich	Loede, Russ	Lung, Bob
Lunter, John	Maciag, Jerry	Majerczak, Roman
Maximuk, Paul	Messuri, Joe	Mezuch, Rich
Molina, Dave	Nigro, William "Bill"	Olbrys, John
Pacak, Andy	Pacak, Wally	Pate, Vance
Perciado, Michael	Petch, John	Petryshyn, Michael
Pieciak, Mark	Piorkowski, Larry	Piotrowski, Stan
Polevacik, Jeff	Polevacik, Jeff	Poremba, Walt
Porma, Walt	Pual, Harold	Pyrtko, Mike
Quinnones, Victor	Ramirez, Adolph	Ramirez, Gil
Rini, Guy	Rocha, Richard	Romankowski, Len
Ruff, Al	Sabat, Mike	Sadie, George
Siedlecki, Tim	Simich, Walter	Sivik, Nicholas
Skora, John	Skora, Richard	Slezak, Arnold
Slusarski, Gene	Solary, Jim	Stacey, Bill

Starzak, Ed
Tkacz, Frank
Trzebuckowski, Frank
Tytko, Gary
Vacha, Harold
Whitecer, Don
Zachartschulk, John
Zandes, Nick

Sutton, Gene
Torres, Mario
Turchyin, Walter
Tytko, Rick
Vargo, Joe
Wilkens, Stuart
Zak, John
Zylowski, Stan

Timateo, Frank
Trzebuckowski, Bob
Turchyn, William
Urbanowiccz, Ted
Vivolo, Joseph
Yowarsky, Walt
Zaleski, Ken

LINCOLN-WEST

Abdul-Karim, Linda
Barberan, Brenda
Beverly, Robert
Bozeman, Christie
Burgos, Terra Burgos
Cancel, Jessica
Chavers, James
Clark, Robbie
Crawford, Mike
Delvalle, Adalis
Felton, Dennis
Ford, Dave
Garcia, Manny
Goss, Alexus
Hicks, Darnell
Johnson, Alexis
Kievicz, Kusia
Koziol, Maryann
Lebron, Alma
Lozado, Hector
McClarin, Melvin
Mitchell, Cameron
Moore, Otis
Navarro, David
Ortiz, Carlos
Pate, Vance

Alvarado, Jose
Barnes, Zack
Bey, Vincent
Broner, Marlin
Camacho, Adaliz
Caradine, Andwan
Cherry, Adam
Collins, Laurie
Crockett, Dartanyon
Echoles, Ali
Fletcher, Alan
Fugua, Rodney
Goler, Tim
Guerra, Nick
Hill, Elijah
Johnson, Michael
Kindell, Tierra
Koziol, Sue
Lewis Jr., Donald
Major, Morgan
McIlwaine, Shawn
Mitchell, Ricardo
Muhammand, Amin
Negron, Devin
Ortiz, Jessica
Perez, Yarianna

Alverez, Walter
Barnett, Ashley
Blade, Marcellus
Brown, Tifaun
Campbell, Leelan
Chavers, Alexis
Christburg, Joe
Conner, Carol
Dawson, Pam
Feliciano, Bobby
Flores, Humberto
Garcia, Jessica
Gonzales, Alicia
Harris, Elijah
Jackson, Clarence
Jones, Tamika
King, Antonio
Lane, Andy
Littlejohn, Robert
Mammett, Mike
McMichael, Chase
Moore, Anthony
Murphy, Stephen
Norton, Javon
Pacheco, Charles
Piowell, Matthew

Pique, Rashon	Pitts, Greg	Powell, Mathew
Purifoy, Mike	Ramirez, Jose	Ramirez, Juan
Ramos, Genesis	Ramos, Josue	Rembert, Kevin
Roberson, Sherry	Robinson, Cortez	Robinson, Cynthia
Rodriquez, Abmieal	Rodriquez, Manny	Roldan, Nemesis
Ruiz, Brian	Russell, Damien	Sales, John
Sanders, Forrest	Santiago, Anthony	Santiago, Rinaldi
Singleton, Ben	Smith, Andre	Smith, Ronald
Smith, Williams	Stalla, Mark	Studmire, Roger
Suhm, Samantha	Sullivan, Terry	Tabb, Marvin
Talley, Maurice	Tandy, George	Thomas, Masrkisha
Thorpes, Barbara	Thorton, Mya	Torres, Eddie
Torres, Josue	Velez, Mariangely	Veras, Katherine
Ward, Audre	Whitfield, La'Mia	Wiley, Rodney
Williams, Calvin	Williams, Evie	Williams, Trevon
Wilson, Alonzo	Wilson, Jahrod	Young, James

MARTIN LUTHER KING

Atterberry, Daniel	Carr, Robert	Carter, Denzell
Collins, Javon	Dawson, Willie	Floyd, Brandon
Ford, N'Dia	General, Deveda	Glass, Michael
Green, Nia	Hardy, Dion	Harris, Vonda
Harshaw, Vonetta	Hicks, Thomas	Johnson, Dierra
Johnson, Jermani	Jones, Anthony	Jones, Michael
Kyle, Sherman	Mason, Preshus	McCargo, Darnell
McGowin, Rhianna	Sales, Sasha	Sanford, Vonetta
Stabler, Danielle	Vann, Ronald	Wright, Shaniya

MAX S. HAYES

Abed, Sara	Bermudez, Guadalupe	Brown, Ariyanna
Bulux, Gilbert	Carter, Tre'von	Charette, Punit
Crosby, Alonzo	Crosby, Anthony	Devaile, Brenda
Duncan, Michael	Farrah, Ezzah	Fletcher, Angel
Gonzales, Joshua	Green, William	Harshaw, Sharonda
Jackson, Keysha	Kules, Nick	Lewis, Breanna
Long, Delvin	Martinez, Carliany	Mercado, Nautica
Meredith, Shannon	Morales, Abimelech	Moye, Tariq

Muhammed, Habeeb
Ortiz, Jose
Pope, Antonio
Spraggins, Angwlique
Ware, Bob

Ortiz, Ariana
Perez, Yuleidys
Ransaw, Mandell
Torres, Carolainee

Ortiz, Eric
Pinkston, Willie
Rodrigues, Elizabeth
Torres, Samy

SOUTH

Abella, Michael
Allen, Greg
Arslanian, Hank
Atkinson, Bob
Beasley, Elizabeth
Bireo, Al
Bowman, Sherry
Bray, Mathew
Brown, Bob
Burge, Jonathan
Calamante, Mike
Casini, Norm
Ciricola, Jim
Collins, Larry
Coulter, Crystal
Czarniakowski, John
Demopoulos, Bill
DiBaggio, Harry
Dortich, Dennis
Dumas, Greg
Eggleston, Ron
Faircloth, Joe
Fay, Jim
Ferjo, Bob
Fiori, Mike
Freeman, Nicole
Garcia, Andrew
Gibson, Jarvis
Greathouse, Edna

Adams, Chet
Anderson, Chantelle
Arslanian, Ted
Atwood, Theresa
Berzansky, Frank
Bixel, Edward
Boyd, Brandon
Broski, Charles
Brown, Gary
Butler, Ben
Canterbury, Dennis
Chojnowkski, Dave
Clark, Shannell
Cook, Debbie
Craig, Dick
Cytlak, Frank
DePompei, Greg
Dickson, Anthony
Draus, Lou
Dutka, Jim
Evans, Artez
Faircloth, Mathew
Ferricci, Cathy
Fetchik, Andy
Fisher, Tom
Friston, Ramiri
Garcia, Kevin
Glinka, Ervin
Greene, Kernia

Alford, Darryl
Arslanian, Armen
Aschenbrenner, Brian
Barrett, Joe
Bialowas, Ted
Bornino, Len
Boyd, Moreland
Broski, John
Brown, James
Calloway, Terry
Caruso, Stan
Ciesia, Jim
Coleman, Lawrence
Cook, Jack
Craycraft, Mike
Davis, Phillip
Deptowicz, Dave
Dluzynski, Edward
Drozdowski, Stan
Edwards, Yvonne
Exline, Kevin
Farrow, Lutul
Ferricci, Tracy
Fields, Isaac
Fitzgerald, Dennis
Gallegos, Mickey
Gear, Bob
Golembieski, John
Gretta, Jim

Gromelski, Ralph	Gronski, Darlene	Gross, John
Grzybowski, Ed	Hall, Rhonda	Hamm, Michael
Harmocz, Rich	Hearn, Olando	Helton, Brian
Henderson, Marilyn	Herron, LaShonda	Hlatky, Dick
Holmes, Gonna	Hood, Bryce	Horton, Alex
Howard Jr., Ben	Howard, Craig	Howard, Kevin
Hrivnak, George	Hunt, Edward	Isom, Malika
Jackson, Brian	James, Jerome	Janik, George
Janik, Len	Jarosz, Clarence	Jiminez, Danita
Iwucz, Stanley	Johnson, Andrew	Johnson, Angie
Johnson, Michelle	Jones, Gomer	Jones, Markeya
Jone, Ta'Shay	Joziuk, Enrique	Kappel, Mike
Katona, John	Kawczyski, Lisa	Kawolski, David
Kennedy, Ghana	Keely, Demetrius	Kelley, Janese
Kinney, Vance	Klicman, Chuck	Klicman, Roger
Koprowski, Kim	Kotowski, Michael	Kowalczyk, Chris
Kowalcyk, Ken	Krakowiak, Eugene	Ksiezyk, Tom
Kuhar, Theresa	Kulwicki, Stanley	Kuska, John
LaBuda, Paul	Lamka, Don	Latarski, Ronald
Lee, Maurice	Lee, Patrick	Leggett, Dery
Liedtke, Herbl	Lenix, Fred	Lesiak, Ted
Lewis, Kevin	Libertini, Rudy	Lippian, Dennis
Love, Arthur	Love, Chris	Mack, Richard
Majewski, William	Mancini, Dan	Mantarro, Bob
Marcum, Bill	Marick, Paul	Martin, Bob
Mason, Chester	Massey, Art	Maynard, Jan
Maynard, John	McClain, Dustin	McGovern, John
McIntosh, Brian	McKay, Kenyatta	McPherson, Eric
Meczka, Mike	Meczka, Nick	Meklemburg, Melissa
Merrick, Mike	Miller, Charles	Mitchell, Robert
Molasky, Bob	Morino, Mario	Mudd, Kimberly
Musiel, Dave	Musiel, Gerald	Muetzel, Dennis
Nalepa, Dave	Nelson, Dale	Nemec, Art
Nieves, Carmen	Noack, Eric	Olsheski, Ed
Olszak, Ron	Olszewski, Walter	Ortega, Kathy

Orzech, Stan	Jones, Markeya	Owens, Debbie
Pavlasek, Bob	Papushak, John	Papushak, Vic
Parks, Lee	Pawlak, Al	Payne, Devontae
Pendleton, Rose	Penn, Michaela	Pescaru, Mike
Peterson, Dezmond	Pflug, Ken	Pisczak, John
Pitts, Durrell	Pniewski, Donald	Polcyn, Wally
Popovitch, Darrall	Posendek, Henry	Prochaska, Jack
Quidatano, Tony	Quinn, Angie	Racinowkski, Ray
Rameriz, Juan	Ramicone, Al	Ramicone, Jim
Ramicone, John	Reed, Rayneira	Richardson, Wallace
Robinson, Matthew	Rodriguez, Angelo	Rojalski, Ed
Ronell, Edarius	Rosolowski, Ben	Rubaszweski, John
Ruszkowski, Hank	Samuels, Richard	Sautchouk, Russell
Sawchik, Lou	Sawyer, Fred	Schiel, Ron
Schrosniak, Dan	Scott, DeAndre	Scott, Jeovante
Shields, Ken	Simmons, Brenda	Sitars, Ralph
Slesinger, John	Smejkal, Marlene	Smilanich, Mike
Smith, Grady	Smith Larry	Sofranac, Rodo
Spy, Aloha	Starling, Kevin	Stokes, Stoney
Stoner, Donnell	Stuble, Al	Szczepaniak, Mike
Szweda, Bob	Szweda, Dale	Tatum, Tim
Thomas, Jeff	Turk, Frank	Turk, John
Turowski, Andy	Tyminski, Jim	Uridel, Tom
Vene, Sabrin	Viera, Amanda	Walczak, Paul
Walker, David	Walsh, Stella	Ware, Armeka
Washington, Tracy	Waskiewicz, Tony	Weatherspoon, Vic
Webb, Reggie	Werstock, Leo	Westfall, Keith
Whitlow, Greg	Wilkerson, Konswella	Williams, Jim
Williams, Rickey	Willis, Renee	Wilson, Angela
Wilson, Asia	Wilson, Sherry	Winston, Martez
Wisniewski, Ralph	Wolanski, Eugene	Woods, Dennis
Woods, James	Woods, Marcus	Young, Keyundra
Zajac, Nic	Zalack, Ron	Zaremba, Lou
Zarembski, Kelly	Zebrowski, Matt	Zehnal, Jim
Zerucha, John	Zieleniewski, Christy	Zusy, Jack

WEST HIGH

Argento, Phil	Auzenburgs, Ed	Bennett, Don
Benz, Dick	Bonacci, Dick	Bostwick, Harry
Boswell, Ron	Bova, Frank	Bova, Phil
Buckingham, Bill	Burnette, Meade	Cassarino, Joe
Chambers, Pat	Clark, Bill	Clinger, Mike
Colosimo, Sandy	Comella, Tony	Cook, Gene
Coreno, Ron	Costanzo, Dominic	Coup, Ronnie
D'Amore, Dan	Dargaj, Ed	Darienzo, Fritz
De Vito, Dan	Degyansky, Gene "Sonny"	Del Vecchio, Jim
DePolo, Ron	DeVito, Dan	DeWitt, Tom
Dibello, Joe	DiBiasio, Sparky	DiBiasio, Tony
Drews, Al	Edwards, Tom	Fackelman, Marty
Farland, Jim	Fenton, Robert	Ferrari, Charles
Fink, Jim	Foldesy, Don	Friedberg, Tom
Galvin, Ralph	Gedeon, Elmer	Gervin, George
Giamarino, Frank	Giamarino, Ralph	Gibbons, Gene
Harboldt, O.J.	Heinz, Jim	Herman, Fred
Herman, Funsie	Hoban, Rick	Holl, Bruce
Julius, Bob	Kane, Mike	Kaze, Ron
Keese, Jim	Koski, Bob	Kovac, Ken
Kundtz, Jim	Lyons, Stan	Mason, Dan
Matteucci, John	Matteucci, Vince	McBride, Ken
McMillan, Doug	Minnick, John	Mitchell, Larry
Morabito, John	Morgan, Dennis	Moulton, Chuck
Mueller, Fritz	Naskoviak, Ed	Natale, Anthony
Natale, Louis	Nesky, Bob	Ostrowsky, John
Palmieri, Emil	Pappas, Art	Parsons, Ron
Paul, Dave	Petch, John	Pogue, Bob
Prioletti, Al	Rains, Rich	Richardson, Joe
Rocco, Peppy	Rodriguez, Al	Rossi, Pete
Rudo, John	Rudolph, John	Rutledge, John
Santillo, Bob	Sauer, George	Saunders, John
Shirak, Rich	Smith, Bob	Smith, Clarence
Smith, Ernie	Snyder, Bill	Sprague, Ed

Starkey, Charles
Szabo, George
Vacca, Dan
Willoughby, Ron

Stavole, Anthony
Theiling, Jim
Veltre, Ed
Wise, John

Stroessner, Bob
Tucciaone, Joe
Williford, Lloyd
Zink, Paul

WEST TECH

Abdullah, Hassan
Adkins, Kenneth
Alberty, Eric
Anguilano, Gary
Bahhur, Jamal
Basko, Richard
Biabolil, Chuck
Blanton, Dante
Broadnax, Kim
Brown, Keith
Bussey, Reggie
Cameron, Darryl
Caruso, Joe
Christian, Andre
Clark, James
Clemons, Fred
Colon, Carmelo
Couper, James
Cunningham, Richee
Deanna, Lino
Delaney, Percy
Dickerson, Glenn
Dubin, Tom
Ebert, Arnold
Emerson, James
Evans, Australia
Fletcher, Michael
Frantz, Herbert
Fritz, Nigel
Gardner, Andre

Abdussatar, Haneef
Agnew, Sherman
Ali, Muhammad
Anthony, Thomas
Baker, Frank
Beard, Richard
Bivjak, Milo
Bonds, Roy
Brooks, Jerrod
Brown, Terrel
Callahan, Karsen
Capasso, Mike
Catavolos, George L.
Christian, Dawn
Clark, Vince
Coleman, Antonio
Colton, Javier
Crider, Debbie
Cunningham, Tathlyn
DeCesare, Henry
Demsey, James
Dirksen, Paul
Dunn, Edward
Ehlert, Tom
Emerson, Willam
Fairbanks, Mike
Flowers, Kara
Freeman, Dave
Gailey, Ken
Gawne, William

Abedlijaber, Feras
Alapoti, Arro
Alikic, Emil
Apger, Chris
Basko, Joe
Bennett, Jim
Blake, Allen
Brister, Douglas
Brown, Eric
Bush, Robert
Callahan, Karlisle
Capasso, Tony
Catavolos, George P.
Clark, Bernard
Clayton, Ronzell
Collins, Nicole
Corpuz, Fred
Culkowski, Walter
Davis, Elton
DeCesare, Joe
Dianiska, Jerry
Divjak, Milo
Dunn, James
Ellis, Greg
English, Timothy
Felton, Mike
Foley, Jim
Frimel, Kim
Gambrell, Jamie
Gedron, Bob

Genco, Vincent	Gerber, Chip	Gibson, Dean
Gibson, Yvonne	Goins, George	Gomez, Ruben
Goode III, Arthur	Grabnegger, Ronald	Graf, Jim
Grant, Donald	Grant, Michael	Gray, Dink
Green, Reggie	Green, Richard	Greene, Henry
Gross, George	Hajewky, Nick	Hall, Tom
Hammad, Mohammad	Hamp, Sandra	Harbuck, Joseph
Hardy, Donald	Harris, Michael	Hartman, Lance
Hasan, Mazen	Hazan, Nader	Hendrickson, Gene
Hicks, Carl	Hicks, Orris	Hollis, James
Hospudar, Al	Hubach, Mike	Hubbard, Danny
Hughley, Donnie	Humphreys, Robert	Hunter, Xavier
Hurt, Duane	Hurt, Shelley	Irizarry, Jaime
Issac, Terrence	Jacupkas, Bob	Jackson, Penton
Jackson, Rayshawn	Jackson, Rayshon	Jagers, Marcus
Jakupca, Edward	James, Mark	Jancura, Charles
Janke, Al	Johnson, Francis	Johnson, John Henry
Johntony, Henry	Jones, Michele	Kaiser, Bill
Kajatroka, Chan	Kamenos, William	Karban, Robert
Kash, Jacob	Katona, Skip	Kebl, Alberc
Kendig, Craig	Kerl, Albert	Kirks, Andrea
Kitzerow, Bob	Klobusnik, Andy	Koepke, Robert
Kosakoski, Dave	Kotlan, Don	Kranczonek, Gene
Krupa, James	Kula, Al	Lackey, Bernard
Lam, Nguyen	Lassiter, James	Lazar, George
Lee, Hasan	Lee, James	Lee, John
Leith, George	Leone, Bob	Levison, Antonio
Lewis, Dennis	Lewis, Fred	Lilly, Chuck
Locke, Calvin	Lunt, Thomas	Marrero, Marixa
Martinez, Gary	Martinez, Oscar	Martinez, Ray
Massa, Arthur	Massie, Mike	Mattern, Tracy
McAlpine, Reginald	McCafferty, John	McClure, Helen
McCord, David	McDaniels, Tony	McKibben, Leroy
Mendicino, Dick	Michalski, Mike	Mio, Victor
Miranda, Jay	Moes, Lester	Moore, Brett

Morris, Samuel	Morrow, Julian	Moton, Sheryl
Murphy, Jason	Nabring, Richard	Nackley, Greg
Naso, Joe	Navits, Thomas	Neal, Ronnie
Nevits, Tom	Nichols, Bryan	Oday, Pat
Onysko, Dave	Orenich, Larry	Ornowski, Joe
Ott, George	Overton, Larry	Paranick, Julius
Parks, Michael	Patterson, Alfonzo	Patterson, Latif
Patton, Thomas F.	Petro, Donald	Pettis, Reginald
Pillows, Rasul	Planicka, James	Polacek, James
Powell, Mark	Prchlik, Arthur	Prchlik, John
Privitera, Angelo	Privitera, Sam	Prokop, John
Puzzitello, Ray	Quill, George	Raimondo, Don
Ranzey, Tara	Raufman, Charles	Ray, Eric
Reaves, Alicia	Reid, Eric	Rios, Richard
Rivera, Alfonso	Rivera, Eddie	Rivera, Robert
Robinson, Billy	Rodriguez, Jorge	Rodriguez, Oscar
Rodriguez, Thomas	Rolen, James	Rose, Rashi
Roseberry, Olympia	Rossman, Roy	Rudo, John
Rudo, Steve	Ruggiero, Joe	Ruiz, Elliot
Ruper, John	Russell, David	Russell, Louis
Russell, Sandra	Saksa, Ed	Saksa, George
Salters, Norrenza	Sargent, William	Sasena, James
Savage, Juan	Schill, Charles	Schultz, James
Scott, Anthony	Seguin, Brian	Seguin, Tony
Semary, Chris	Semary, Matt	Serda, Meeca
Setta, Mike	Settles, Chuck	Settles, George
Sewell, Robert	Sharp, Billy	Simovic, Danny
Singh, Gurvinder	Skogan, Steve	Smiley, George
Smith, Andrew	Smith, Wayne	Sneed, Tim
Soles, Art	Soloweigo, Victor	Solowiow, Vic
Soza, John	Spain, George	Sparks, Byron
Sporzo, Alfred	Sporzo, John	Stasek, Mark
Steiner, Gorden	Stelbasky, Joe	Stepp, Leonard
Story, Jayna	Story, John	Story, Pam
Sturgis, Gamalier	Sunyak, Rick	Taber, Gus

Tailon, Ron	Tam, Mike	Taylor, Dawain
Taylor, Eric	Taylor, Joe	Taylor, Kamil
Taylor, Linda	Taylor, Mathis	Thomas, Bob
Thomas, Creshawn	Thomas, Daniel	Thomas, Shelander
Tillman, Gentry	Torres, Angel	Torres, Germaine
Townsend, Clifford	Trammell, James	Tuckosh, Don
Url, Eddie	Vance, Engene	Vasquez, Pedro
Vichex, Robert	Volosin, Richard	Vransky, Tony
Walker, Eddie	Walker, Ronney	Walker, Ronnie
Watts, Jamal	Webb, Danny	Webb, Robert
White, Dick	Whitehead, Dan	Wilcox, Richard
Williams, James	Williams, Kareem	Williams, Michael
Willis, Eddie	Winbush, Antonio	Wright, Dana
Yuronvich, Edward	Zeda, Moises	

WHITNEY M. YOUNG

Brown, Alexius	Butler, Michael	Dumetz, Davon
Hardaway, Virgil	Harris, Anthony	Harris, Eric
Johnson, Joy	Jordan, Anthony	Jordan, Elvert
Knight, Kristen	Lake, DeAngelo	Lewis, Amyr
Lewis, Leeajah	Pryor, Darohn	Putman, Braxton
Sapp, Alicia	Tucker, Quinton	Westmoreland, Thomas
Williamson, Lyric	Young, Darohn	

COACHES

BARD

Fair, Derrick	Shah, Sweer	

CAMPUS INT.

Phillips, Carmen	Sarantopoulos, Athan	

CENTRAL

Alexander, Russ	Barden, Marril	Civiletto, Frank
Rose, Paul		

COLLINWOOD

Anderson, Sgt. Gregory	Beacham, Cynthia	Calhoun, Cornell
Carter, Livesteen	Fisher, Bob	Fuller, Varick

Gary, Phil
Jordan, R.
Priah, J.
Slapnik, Louis
Trivisonno, Joe
Vana, Ken

Hofelich, Charles
Lauterbur, Francis
Reed, Raymond
Stacey, Corbin
Vaccariello, Donald
Wheeler Jr., Greg

Hudson, Clarence
Littlejohn, Kevin Vincent
Shorts Jr., Cecil
Spurrier, James
Vaccariello, Urban
Yost, Paul

EAST HIGH

Arnold, George
Krakowiak, Gene
Randle, Vernon
Stephens, Mike
Wilcox, Tony

Dawson, Robert
Lett, Exodus
Register, Allen
Suarve, Bob

Fogg, Joe
Midoagh, J.E.
Simmons, Bernard
Thorpe, Jim

EAST TECH

Amico, Pete
Behm, John
Burke, Melvin
Emery, Jim
Hall, Bertha
Moore, Brett
Pope, Rhonda
Smith, Isaac "Ike"
Stoval, William
Willaman, Sam
Garrett Morgan

Anderson, Paul
Binford, Shantel
Chavers, John
Forrest, Daryl
Howell, Joe
Neil, Edward
Priah, Jeffrey
Smith, Joe
Stueber, Gerry
Williams, Charles
Schroth Jr. Ronald

Bailey, Eleanor
Broski, John
Delong, Maddie
Greene, Ivan
Lennox, Floyd
Newberry, Estus
Schemer, Paul
Steuber, Gerry
Thompson, G.P.
Williamson, Carl
Veg, Alexis

GLENVILLE

Demaske, Devin
Ginn Sr, Ted
Johnson, James
Moss, Gerald
Smith, Kimberly
Winston, Ladonna
Zubovich, Frank

Demo, James
Griggs, Teresa
Johnson, LaDonna Winston
Perez, Frank
Taylor, Gretchen
Woods, Dennis T.

Fronczak, Ernie
Hubbard, James
Moor, Louie
Ranta, Jacob
Taylor, Robert (Bump)
Wright, Renee

JAMES FORD RHODES

Andrews, Robert

Anzalone-Fox, Cindy Anne

Cunningham, Michael

Franzinger, Tim
Greenwood, Jimmy
Joines, Jim
Marrero-Gonzalez, Marixa
Meisinger, William
Renk, Dennis
Schofield, Keith
Spencer, Shawn
Tropole, Babe
Whipkey, John

Gargiulo, Courtney
Hogan, Tim
Laderer, Mark
McCullough, Greg
Moran, Andy
Richardson, Taylor
Seedhouse, George
Templeton, Jim
Tuma, Mary
Zickes, Jim

Gary, Phil
Holden, Ellsworth
Major, Bernice
McHolland, Brian
Owens, Tyrone B.
Riddley, Allan
Sims, Robert
Thomas, Sargent Gunning
Vannorsdall, Gail

JOHN ADAMS

Alexander, Mark
Brodt, Mel
Chapman, Sedrina
Gary, Monica
Holland-Robinson, Bernice
Kronik, Bill
Mitchell, Earvetta
Ramicone, John
Young, Gene

Bianchi, John
Bush, Ed
Collins, Canning
Harrison, Bob
Jackson, Gary
Lloyd, Terry
Partee, David
Tribble, Janet

Blount, G.
Caldwell, Ed
Emery, Dick
Holland, Claude
Kozak, George
McGroarty, Bernard
Patterson, James
Unguvary, Joe

JOHN F. KENNEDY

Camp Lewis
Collins, Carlwin
Kidd, Roye
Marrow, William
Reed, Lionel
Wodtly, Scott

Chambers, Jim
Dove, Bonnie
Killian, Walt
Murawsky, Mike
Vallery, Helene

Cianciolo, Matt
Hanchuk, Vic
Kimball, Harold D.
Patterson, Leonard
Walker, Reggie

JOHN HAY

Bailey, Michael
Harris, William (Sonny)
Johnson, Ishmael
Lett, Chris
Newsome, Mr.
Scharf, Rhonda

Banks-Priester, Carmen
Hawkins, Brandon
Kerr, Ernest
Miller, Keith
Olson, Loren
Sims, Roger

Crider Vynetta
Howery, Fred
Kester, Harold
Mueller, Joseph
Sanders, Christopher
Sims, George

Thomas, Mykal
Wilson, Jerry
Toles, Steve
Wright-Walker, Renee
Wilcox, Tony

JOHN MARSHALL

Alpine, Ron
Crawford, McHenry
Emery, Richard
Gibbons, Gene
Neubauer, John
Shalay, David
Valenszi, Al
Austin, Richard
Dieterich, John
Ferguson, Howard
Hein, Lorie
Ramseyer, Roger
Tramontana, Katelyn
Wasowski, Jim
Cleggett, Terrance
Elkins, Thomas
Frei, Eric
Marrero, Marixa
Reinke, Al
Vadini, Joe

LINCOLN

Coreno, Ron
Fraser, Glen
Emery, Don
Reppa, Bill
Filiere, Howard
Sawchik, Lou

LINCOLN-WEST

Casselberry, Tom
Sovchik, Doug
Williams, Omar
Conner, Anitza
Suarez, Vicente
Potter, Ronn
Williams Jr., Carlton

MARTIN LUTHER KING

Bailey, Michael
Priah, Jeffrey

MAX S. HAYES

Ali, Shaun
Gorius, Todd
Lee, Ivan
Dallas, Joe
Huckaby, Kim
Galaszewski, Gary
Lammermeier, Russ

SOUTH

Abel, Al
Alpine, Ron
Bell, Rodrick
Bozickovick, Milan
Caruso, Stan
Deutsch, Robert
Everhart, Willie
Harrison, Kenndra
Jencik, Georgia
Krakowiak, Gene
Accordino, Joe
Averyhart, Willie
Bolden, Byron
Brubaker, Carl
Curl, Miguel
Dickson, Sam
Gentile, John
Hickey, Michael
Jisa, Jack
Kraft, Ray
Allen, Frank
Aukerman, Ron
Bowers, Roger
Cartwright, C.
Dallas, Joe
Dillon, Frank
Gibson, Jarvis
Jancura, Charles
Kosta, Noel
Lasko, Bob

Ledger, Mark	Lee, Robert	Mader, Joel
Martin, Sherian-Poole	Mason, Dan	Maver, Bob
McCollough, Cedric	McGroarty, Bernie	McKenzie, Nicole
Oblak, Fed	Partee, David	Patterson, James
Rasper, Charles	Reeves, Wendell	Rodriguez, Angelo
Rotsky, Jeff	Sanders, Brian	Shallcross, John
Shorts, Cecil	Sims, Tomasina	Smith, Jennifer
Snee, Patrick	Story, John	Tyus, Cedric
Ungers, Ed	Warren, Norman	Whitt, Akai
Wolanski, Gene	Wooten, John	

WEST HIGH

Bilardo, Chuck	Blickle, Charlie	Degyansky, Gene
Del Vecchio, Jim	Drews, Al	Faranda, Tom
George, Fred	Kalbrunner, Russ	Kester, Harold
Leibold, Bob	Metzler, Jerry	Mussilin, Dan
Pluto, Tom	Quayle, Bill	Reinke, Al
Schupp, Walter	Topole, Babe	Torgler, Jim
Waffen, Cy	Wolfe, Harmon	

WEST TECH

Bailey, Michael	Bauer, Karl	Blickle, Charley
Chernauskas, Larry	George, Fred	Griffith, Lloyd
Hall, Thad	Hicks, William	Jackson, Early
Jancura, Frank	Kazmar, Jacob	Kirk, Don
Kolach, Eugene	Kosak, George	Lazzaro, Robert (Bob)
Lucas, Paul	Madison, Bob	Maric, Nick
Montain, Gary	Prchlik, Art	Ralston, Lou
Schupp, Walter	Semary, Matt	Whitney M. Young
Hunt, Vincen		

ATHLETIC DIRECTORS

COLLINWOOD

Anderson, Sidney	Kronik, Bill	Reddix, Terrell
Richmond, Sherman		

EAST HIGH

Hoehn, Kenneth	Kinschner, T. L.	Lett, Exodus
Trotter, Paul		

EAST TECH

Carter, Leroy	Flenoury, Thomas	Greene, Ivan
Marcus, Oscar	Stueber, Gerry	Taylor, Temujin
White, Al	Yeck, Ray	

GLENVILLE

Benedict, James	Haynes, Andre	Taylor, Gretchen
Woods, Dennis		

JAMES FORD RHODES

Anderson, Sandra	Dzuro, Cheryl	Kresse, John
Scott, Bill	Sovey, Bob	Seedhouse, George
Templeton, Jim	Winters, Paul	

JOHN ADAMS

Caldwell, Ed	Kane, Spencer D.	Vogel, Eric

JOHN F. KENNEDY

Chambers, James	Chappell, Cameille	Gambrel, William
Knox, Deirdra	Pettigrew, Velma	Taylor, Stuart
Urb, Robert		

JOHN HAY

Gnabah-Mortenson, Karen	Morrow, Diauntae	Newsome, Richard
Spronz, George	Wilson, Jerry	

JOHN MARSHALL

Beebe, Linda	Gilbert, Joe	Jacobson, John
Vineyard, Robert		

LINCOLN-WEST

Rice, Mack	Simeone, Anthony	

MAX S. HAYES

Huckaby, Kim		

SOUTH

Abel, Al	Jancura, Charles	Lambert, George

Mader, Joe	Poole-Martin, Sherian	Ralston, Lou

WEST HIGH

DelVecchio, James	Torgler, Jim	

WEST TECH

DelVecchio, James	Griffith, Lloyd	Kinschner, T. L.
Panigutti, Carol		

DIRECTOR OF ATHLETICS

Barringer, Dan	Hicks, William	Kane, Spencer
Long, Calvin	Marquard Jr., Vincent	Seedhouse, George
West, Maralyn H.		

ATHLETIC COMMISSIONERS

Jackson, Leonard B.	Kosak, George	Powell, Desiree
Reppa, William (Bill)	Rowe, Floyd A.	

APPENDIX XI

SPORTS LEGENDS OF CLEVELAND HALL OF FAME

GUIDELINES

NUMBER OF NOMINATIONS PER ALUMNI ASSOCIATION.
Each alumni association can nominate a maximum of three Sports Legends.

NOMINATION GUIDELINES

1. Eligibility: The nominee must be directly affiliated with the Cleveland Metropolitan School District (CMSD) as a high school graduate or have served in a coaching, staff, athletic director, or administrative capacity.

2. Selection Criteria: Individuals may be nominated based on their exceptional sports achievements, community contributions, sportsmanship, and other relevant factors, including academic success and commitment to the district. Emphasis may be placed on recognizing student-athletes excelling in both sports and academics. Nominees should have made a lasting impact on Cleveland sports. Consider nominees who have significantly impacted the District's legacy and historical context.

3. Documentation: Each alumni association must provide detailed documentation for each nominee, including a biography, a list of accomplishments, photos (if available), and any other supporting materials that highlight the nominee's contributions.

4. Diversity and Inclusion: Encourage alumni associations to consider diversity and inclusion when making nominations, ensuring that nominees come from diverse backgrounds, genders, and abilities.

NOMINATION REVIEW PROCESS BY SCHOOL:

1. Nomination Submission: Alumni associations submit their nominations, along with supporting documentation, by the specified deadline.

2. Initial Review: The Sports Legends of Cleveland Committee conducts an initial review to ensure that all nominations meet the eligibility and documentation requirements.

3. Discussion: The Sports Legends of Cleveland Committee discusses the nominations and shares insights.

4. Final Selection List: The Sports Legends of Cleveland Committee confirms Hall of Fame recipients.

5. Transparency: Ensure transparency by documenting the selection process and criteria, and communicating the selected Sports Legends to the alumni associations, CMSD Athletics and Administration, and the public.

2019 HALL OF FAME INDUCTEES

HIGH SCHOOL	INDUCTEE	GENDER	SPORT
Central	Paul Rose*	Male	Football
Central	Tony Patti*	Male	Football
Central	Ted Rosequist*	Male	Football
Collinwood	Lou Slapnick	Male	Track & Field
Collinwood	Theo Morrow	Male	Track & Field
Collinwood	Mike Cavotta*	Male	Track & Field
East High	Manny Leaks	Male	Basketball
East High	Clark Kellogg Sr.*	Male	Basketball
East High	Bob Wren*	Male	Baseball
East Tech	Jesse Owens*	Male	Track & Field
East Tech	Harrison Dillard*	Male	Track & Field
East Tech	Vivian Brown (Reed)*	Female	Track & Field
Glenville	Benny Friedman*	Male	Football
Glenville	Ted Ginn Sr.	Male	Football
Glenville	Don Price	Male	Track & Field
James Ford Rhodes	Les Horvath*	Male	Football
James Ford Rhodes	Don McCafferty*	Male	Football
James Ford Rhodes	Bill Putich*	Male	Football
John Adams	Carmen Banks (Priester)	Female	Track & Field
John Adams	Harold Madox	Male	Track & Field
John Adams	Anthony Morgan	Male	Football
John F. Kennedy	Walt Killian*	Male	Track & Field
John F. Kennedy	Harold Kimball	Male	Track & Field

HIGH SCHOOL	INDUCTEE	GENDER	SPORT
John F. Kennedy	Roye Kidd*	Male	Football
John Hay	Madeline Manning	Female	Track & Field
John Hay	Anthony Hancock	Male	Track & Field
John Hay	John Hicks*	Male	Football
John Marshall	Janetta Graham	Female	Basketball
John Marshall	Eugene "Gene" Gibbons*	Male	Wrestling
John Marshall	Thomas Jefferson	Male	Track & Field
Lincoln High	Paul Maximuk*	Male	Football
Lincoln High	Walt Yowarsky*	Male	Football
Lincoln High	Marty Hunt*	Male	Basketball
Lincoln-West	Dave Ford	Male	Baseball
Lincoln-West	Dartanyon Crockett	Male	Wrestling
Martin Luther King	Willie Dawson	Male	Track & Field
South High	Stella Walsh*	Female	Track & Field
South High	Gene Wolanski*	Male	Basketball
South High	Jan Maynard*	Male	Wrestling
West High	Ken Mcbride	Male	Baseball
West High	Phil Argento	Male	Basketball
West High	Dick Bonacci*	Male	Wrestling
West Tech	George L. Catavolos	Male	Football
West Tech	Mike Hubach	Male	Football
West Tech	John Henry Johnson	Male	Track & Field

*Posthumously

JESSE OWENS LIFETIME ACHIEVEMENT AWARD: Bill Putich, Harrison Dillard, Ted Theodore

2022 HALL OF FAME INDUCTEES

HIGH SCHOOL	INDUCTEE	GENDER	SPORT
Central	James Terry*	Male	Football/Track & Field
Central	Phil Goldstein*	Male	Boxing
Central	Steve Gwin*	Male	Basketball
Collinwood	Carmen Barth*	Male	Boxer
Collinwood	Cecil Shorts III	Male	Football
Collinwood	Joi Renee Smith*	Female	Track & Field
East High	Carl Taseff*	Male	Football
East High	Brian Parker	Male	Basketball
East High	Exodus Lett*	Male	Track & Field
East Tech	Wanda Ford	Female	Basketball
East Tech	Bob Brown*	Male	Football
East Tech	Mike St. Clair	Male	Football
Glenville	Robert Ware	Male	Track & Field
Glenville	Terry Jones*	Male	Basketball/Baseball/Football
Glenville	Louis Defreeze	Male	Track & Field
James Ford Rhodes	Mahagony Jones	Female	Track & Field
James Ford Rhodes	Dave Kyle	Male	Basketball
James Ford Rhodes	Ron Addison	Male	Track & Field
John Adams	Luke Owens*	Male	Football
John Adams	Nate Brooks*	Male	Boxer
John Adams	Eleanor Montgomery*	Female	Track & Field
John F. Kennedy	Lawrence Boston	Male	Basketball

HIGH SCHOOL	INDUCTEE	GENDER	SPORT
John F. Kennedy	James Epps	Male	Track & Field
John F. Kennedy	Bonnie Dove	Female	Basketball
John Hay	Charles Oakley	Male	Basketball
John Hay	William Sonny Harris*	Male	Football/Tennis Coach
John Hay	Yvonne Renee Walker-Wright	Female	Volleyball/Basketball
John Marshall	Michelle Stoyka	Female	Track & Field
John Marshall	Linda J. Beebe	Female	Volleyball
John Marshall	Jonathan Burrell	Male	Track & Field
Lincoln	Richard Skora*	Male	Soccer
Lincoln	Willie Avery	Male	Football/Baseball
Lincoln	Karl A. Anderson*	Male	Football
Lincoln-West	Sue Koziol	Female	Softball/Basketball
South High	Marlene Smejkal Jess	Female	Volleyball/Basketball/Softball
South High	Gomer Jones*	Male	Basketball/Football
South High	Angelo Rodriguez	Male	Football/Basketball/Baseball
West High	Elmer Gedeon*	Male	Baseball/Football/Track & Field
West High	Dan Mason*	Male	Baseball/Football/Basketball
West High	Gene "Sonny" Degyansky*	Male	Basketball Coach
West Tech	August Michael "Mike" Michalske*	Male	Football
West Tech	Art Prichlik*	Male	Football/Wrestling
West Tech	Jesus Jay Miranda	Male	Track & Field

*Posthumously

JESSE OWENS LIFETIME ACHIEVEMENT AWARD: Dr. Madeline Manning Mims, George Seedhouse

2024 HALL OF FAME INDUCTEES

HIGH SCHOOL	INDUCTEE	GENDER	SPORT
Central	James "Jimmy" Louis Bivins*	Male	Boxing
Central	Ed Delahanty*	Male	Baseball
Collinwood	Charnee Lumbus	Female	Track & Field
Collinwood	Joey Maxim*	Male	Boxing
East High	Ted Abrams*	Male	Swimming & Diving
East High	Arthur Matsu*	Male	Football
East Tech	Barbara Turner	Female	Basketball
East Tech	Jack Trice*	Male	Football
East Tech	William "Wee Willie" Smith*	Male	Basketball
Glenville	Ted Ginn Jr.	Male	Football/Track & Field
Glenville	Troy Smith	Male	Football
Glenville	Kelli Turner	Female	Track & Field
John Adams	Monica Gary	Female	Track & Field
John Adams	Claude Holland	Male	Track & Field
John Adams	Leonard Simms*	Male	Track & Field/Cross-Country
John F. Kennedy	Leonard Patterson	Male	Basketball
John F. Kennedy	Bobby Franklin	Male	Basketball
John F. Kennedy	Prentis Wenson III	Male	Track & Field
John Hay	Chanitta Westbrooks	Female	Track & Field
John Hay	Wesley Carroll	Male	Football
John Hay	Timothy Hatchett Mcgee	Male	Football

HIGH SCHOOL	INDUCTEE	GENDER	SPORT
John Marshall	Larry "Splash" Coy	Male	Track & Field/Cross-Country
John Marshall	Thomas Stincic*	Male	Football
John Marshall	Al Carroll*	Male	Wrestling
Lincoln	Theodore "Ted" Budzik*	Male	Basketball Baseball
Lincoln	Ida Jean "Hoppy" Hopkins*	Female	Winter Olympics Luge
Lincoln	Harold Vacha*	Male	Track & Field
James Ford Rhodes	Cindy Anzalone-Fox	Female	Track & Field
James Ford Rhodes	Bill Hann, Jr.	Male	Basketball
James Ford Rhodes	Jim Emery*	Male	Track & Field
South High	Chester Mason	Male	Basketball
South High	Markeya Jones-Owens	Female	Track & Field
South High	Dennis Woods	Male	Baseball
West High	Phil Bova	Male	Basketball/Baseball
West High	Al Drews	Male	Baseball/Handball
West High	John Matteucci*	Male	Wrestling
West Tech	Eric Sean Brown	Male	Track & Field
West Tech	Mike Massie	Male	Tennis
West Tech	Larry Chernauskas*	Male	Basketball

Posthumously

2024 TEAM INDUCTION:
John Adams Boys, 1953 AA OHSAA State Track Champion, 1954 AA OHSAA Cross-Country Champion

JESSE OWENS LIFETIME ACHIEVEMENT AWARD: Eleanor Montgomery, Harold Kester

HOPE FUND INC. LIFETIME ACHIEVEMENT AWARD: Donald "Don" King

THANK YOU TO OUR SPONSORS

We extend our heartfelt gratitude to our generous sponsors, whose support made this history book possible. Your commitment to preserving and celebrating our shared heritage has helped bring these important stories to life. Thank you for believing in the power of history to inspire future generations.

Carmella Marshall
City of Cleveland Department of Public Utilities
Cleveland Browns
Cleveland Cavaliers
Cleveland Guardians
Cleveland Metropolitan School District (CMSD) Athletics
Coach Tyrone & Rosalyn Owens
Forest City Tree Protection Company
Hassan Ayoub
Hope Fund Inc.
James Ford Rhodes Alumni Association
Mario Morino
Nicole Antoinette Consulting
Pro Football Hall of Fame
Timothy Piai & Dara Krueger

THANK YOU TO OUR COMMITTEE MEMBERS

A sincere thank you to our dedicated committee members for your time, insight, and unwavering commitment throughout the creation of this history book. Your thoughtful guidance and collaboration have been essential in shaping a meaningful and lasting tribute to our shared past. We couldn't have done it without you.

Al Drews	Lawrence Boston
Alicia Moore	Leroy Carter
Anthony Longino Thomas	Michael Bailey
Bonnie Dove	Michael Cunningham
Cheryl Dzuro	Nicole Antoinette Smith
Cindy Anzalone-Fox	NiQuita Baker
Claude Holland	Noreen Roderick
Darnell Simmon	Paula Buckhaulter
Dennis Harris	Prentis Wenson III
Desiree Powell	Ralph Gromelski
Don Price	Robert Zellers
Dr. Wanda Shoulders	Steve Korinchak
Fred Tischler	Tangetta Cox
George Catavolos	Tim Isaac
Joe Gilbert	Timothy L. Hudak
John Lunter	Tyrone Owens
John Ramicone	Wayne Moss
Joyce Murphy	Willie Beaman (Brown)
Kathy Quintiliano	Willie Jones

www.ingramcontent.com/pod-product-compliance
Lightning Source LLC
Chambersburg PA
CBHW041238240426
43661CB00070B/2913